SECURED CREDIT

ASPEN SELECT SERIES

SECURED CREDIT
LOUISIANA AND AMERICAN PERSPECTIVES

L. DAVID CROMWELL
Member, Louisiana State Bar
Reporter, Louisiana State Law Institute Security Devices Committee

DIAN TOOLEY-KNOBLETT
Jones Walker Distinguished Professor of Law
Loyola University College of Law

JOHN RANDALL TRAHAN
Louis B. Porterie Professor of Law and
Saul Litvinoff Distinguished Professor of Law
Louisiana State University Paul M. Hebert Law Center

CHRISTOPHER K. ODINET
Horatio C. Thompson Endowed Assistant Professor of Law
Southern University Law Center

Published by Wolters Kluwer in New York.

Wolters Kluwer Legal & Regulatory U.S. serves customers worldwide with CCH, Aspen Publishers, and Kluwer Law International products. (www.WKLegaledu.com)

To contact Customer Service, e-mail customer.service@wolterskluwer.com, call 1-800-234-1660, fax 1-800-901-9075, or mail correspondence to:

Wolters Kluwer
Attn: Order Department
PO Box 990
Frederick, MD 21705

Printed in the United States of America.

1 2 3 4 5 6 7 8 9 0

ISBN 978-1-4548-8754-6

About Wolters Kluwer Legal & Regulatory U.S.

Wolters Kluwer Legal & Regulatory U.S. delivers expert content and solutions in the areas of law, corporate compliance, health compliance, reimbursement, and legal education. Its practical solutions help customers successfully navigate the demands of a changing environment to drive their daily activities, enhance decision quality and inspire confident outcomes.

Serving customers worldwide, its legal and regulatory solutions portfolio includes products under the Aspen Publishers, CCH Incorporated, Kluwer Law International, ftwilliam.com and MediRegs names. They are regarded as exceptional and trusted resources for general legal and practice-specific knowledge, compliance and risk management, dynamic workflow solutions, and expert commentary.

For my children, David Ford Cromwell and Stephanie Claire Cromwell

- L.D.C.

For Mike Rubin and Jason Kilborn, who taught me everything I know about security devices

- J.R.T.

For my four sons, James, Alexander, Michael, and Christopher

- D.T.K.

For Randy P. Roussel and Erik C. Piazza, who taught me how to be a lawyer

- C.K.O.

Summary of Contents

CONTENTS

PREFACE

The law of secured credit is both very important and very complex. Perhaps because of this, law students, lawyers, judges, and lawmakers struggle to master its many nuances. Secured credit law may not have the initial appeal that criminal or constitutional law hold in the minds of many, but it forms the backbone of everything from day-to-day consumer transactions to large-scale commercial financing, both around the corner and across the world.

In Louisiana the law of secured credit is often referred to as the law of "security devices." It is comprised of constructs imported from common law and uniform law sources, as well as concepts and institutions that remain, to this day, distinctly civilian in nature. In writing this book, we attempt to show how the law of security devices in Louisiana has come to form an intricate but beautiful system that, although composed of many disparate parts, works to turn the wheels of our state's economy on a daily basis.

A new casebook on secured credit has been long in coming in Louisiana, but we would be remiss if we did not recognize that we are forever indebted to those on whose shoulders we now stand. We specifically acknowledge that this text would not have been possible without the important and insightful work of Professors Joseph Dainow, Harriet Daggett, and Thomas Harrell, all of whom were giants in the field and are responsible for the development of the law in this area. We also commend the more recent but equally important work of Michael Rubin, Max Nathan, and Jason Kilborn, who together taught many of the lawyers in this state the law of security devices (including the authors of this book).

In working on this project we received support from our law schools, law firms, and families, whom we duly thank and acknowledge, particularly Yolunda Righteous (SULC) for her research assistance and editing. We hope that this casebook will be helpful to the many future generations of lawyers doing the important work of commercial and consumer transactions in this state.

L. David Cromwell
Dian Tooley-Knoblett
John Randall Trahan
Christopher K. Odinet

November 2016

ACKNOWLEDGMENTS

We wish to thank the following who graciously granted permission to reprint excerpts of the following materials:

The Tulane Law Review for permission to reprint portions of Ralph Slovenko, *Suretyship,* 39 Tulane Law Review 427, 427-28 (1965).

The Louisiana State Law Institute for permission to reprint portions of the Report to the Legislature in Response to in Response to SR No. 158 Of 2012: Louisiana Lien Laws (Private Works Act) (Feb. 15, 2013) and the *Exposé des Motifs: Suretyship,* Elimination of Division and Discussion (Louisiana State Law Institute).

The Loyola Law Review for permission to reprint portions of Nadia E. Nedzel, *Comment, Please Release Me: A Comparative Study of Louisiana Suretyship Law,* 40 Loyola Law Review 955, 961-970 (1995) and Henry Deeb Gabriel, *Louisiana Chapter 9 (Part One): Creating and Perfecting the Security Interest,* 35 Loyola Law Review 311, 312–16 (1989).

The Tulane European and Civil Law Forum for permission to reprint portions of Richard D. Moreno, Scott v. Corkern: *Of Precedent, Jurisprudence Constante, and the Relationship Between Louisiana Commercial Laws and Louisiana Pledge Jurisprudence,* 10 Tulane European & Civil Law Forum 31, 40–41 (1995).

The Rutgers Law Review for permission to reprint portions of Roger A. Cunningham & Saul Tischler, *Disguised Real Estate Security Transactions as Mortgages in Substance,* 26 Rutgers L. Rev. 1 (1972).

The Louisiana Law Review for permission to reprint portions of Michael H. Rubin, *Ruminations on Suretyship,* 57 Louisiana Law Review 565, 567-571 (1997), Michael H. Rubin & Stephen P. Strohchein, *Developments In The Law 1993-1994: A Faculty Symposium: Security Devices,* 55 Louisiana Law Review 611 (1995), James A. Stuckey, *Louisiana's Non-Uniform Variations in U.C.C. Chapter 9,* 62 Louisiana Law Review 793 (2002), Michael H. Rubin, *Ruminations on the Louisiana Law of Pledge,* 75 Louisiana Law Review 697 (2015), David S. Willensek, *Louisiana Future Advance Mortgages—A 20-Year Retrospective*, 75 Louisiana Law Review 613 (2015), A. N. Yiannopoulos, *Real Rights in Louisiana and Comparative Law: Part 1,* 23 Louisiana Law Review 161, 222 (1963), Joseph

Dainow, *Ranking Problems of Chattel Mortgages and Civil Code Privileges in Louisiana Law,* 13 Louisiana Law Review 537 (1953), Joseph Dainow, *Civil Code and Related Subjects: Security Devices,* 22 Louisiana Law Review 322 (1962), Joseph Dainow, *Art. 3267 and the Ranking of Privileges,* 9 Louisiana Law Review 370 (1949), Joseph Dainow, *Vicious Circles in the Louisiana Law of Privileges,* 25 Louisiana State Law Review 1 (1964).

Thomson Reuters/West Publishing for permission to reprint portions of Peter S. Title, *Louisiana Real Estate Transactions* (West 2000), A. N. Yiannopoulos, 2 La. Civ. L. Treatise Series: *Property* § 237 (4th Ed. 2014), and Marcel Planiol & Georges Ripert, 2 *Traité Élémentaire de Droit Civil,* pt. 2 (La. State Law Inst. trans., 1959) (12th ed. 1939) (Fr.).

Secured Credit

Chapter 1
Introduction

It is virtually undisputed that the availability of credit is the cornerstone of any economy. Indeed, the United States has long recognized how important credit is to the health of the nation. "As Senator Daniel Webster suggested over 170 years ago, the urgency for the country to keep afloat its credit system was as much of a concern for national security as it was for the economic health of the nation."[1]

A robust credit system turns the wheels of the market, specifically by allowing businesses to provide a variety of goods and services and by allowing consumers to avail themselves of such items. Lenders, in turn, who provide credit are allowed under the law to take a form of property interest (called security) in assets of the debtor (called collateral) in order to entice the lender to extend credit. In doing so, creditors are given a mechanism whereby they can reduce the risk of being unpaid in the event of a default and, as a result, will ostensibly agree to extend a larger amount of credit across the economy. For instance, in the case of automobile credit markets, lenders are routinely advancing credit to less than creditworthy borrowers, based merely on the lender's ability to take a security interest in the vehicle being purchased.[2]

That is not to say that all creditors require collateral in making a loan to a debtor. Large and established companies—particularly those that are publicly traded with a wide range of financial information available to the public—with significant assets, cash, and healthy credit histories are often advanced funds even without the provision of collateral. While even these debtors can take a financial turn for the worse, creditors generally take the position that routine

---

[1] Costantino Panayides, *The Federal Response to the Credit Crisis*, 28 Rev. Banking & Fin. L. 13 (2008).

[2] Jim Hawkins, *Credit on Wheels: The Law and Business of Auto Title Lending*, 69 Wash. & Lee L. Rev. 535 (2012).

monitoring and reporting requirements are sufficient to guard against undue credit risk. Moreover, many types of loans made to everyday consumers also lack collateral. Consider that credit card loans, student loans, and loans made between families and friends are all made without requiring any security.

But without a doubt, in a significantly large number of transactions across this country (mortgage loans, car loans, commercial loans, etc.) borrowers must post some form of collateral to secure their obligation to repay the funds advanced. Usually this comes in the form of equipment; real estate; inventory, accounts receivable; or forms of investment property, such as stocks and bonds. Of these, perhaps the most prominent are real estate-backed loans, whereby the credit obligation is secured by a mortgage or related security instrument over the real estate of the debtor. In the event the borrower fails to make payment or otherwise defaults on his obligations, the creditor may have the property seized and sold pursuant to a public or private sale. In the realm of personal property, inventory financing is prominent. Here, Walmart, Best Buy, car dealerships, and other retail-related companies will typically use the proceeds from a loan to acquire a significant amount of inventory for sale to their customers. In exchange, the companies will grant a security interest in the acquired inventory in favor of their creditors to secure the obligation to repay.

Louisiana law is no different in recognizing the tremendous power and importance of credit—particularly secured credit. The same policy goals and business objectives that animate national credit markets are equally applicable in the Bayou State. However, like many aspects of Louisiana's private law, there are a number of ways in which the law diverges from the national or more common law-based approach. As you work your way through the material, you will find a number of places where comparative information is included. Sometimes you will notice that the law in Louisiana and the law in other states on a particular matter is fairly uniform (such as with Article 9 of the Uniform Commercial Code). However, in other cases you will find a number of places where the law is particular to Louisiana (such as the prohibition on creditor self-help or the unique collateral mortgage concept). Appreciating the similarities and the differences are integral to understanding what we call the law of "security devices."

A. The Importance of Being Secured

Before diving into the substantive material, it is important to spend a few moments considering in a more concrete fashion why a creditor would care to use a security device. In other words, why be *secured*? There are a number of reasons that support going through the trouble of hiring a lawyer or otherwise drawing up the documents necessary to confect security. The following sections explain the main reasons why doing so is worthwhile.

1. Preference Over Other Creditors

One of the most importance reasons to obtain security is to be preferred over other creditors. An example may help. Under Louisiana Civil Code article 3133, a debtor is bound to fulfill his obligations to his creditors "out of all of his property, movable and immovable, present and future." These creditors share the debtor's property on a pro rata basis, determined by how much of the debt each is owed as it bears to the whole. *See* La. Civ. Code art. 3134. Let's assume Debtor owes Creditor A $25,000, Creditor B $25,000, Creditor C $25,000, and Creditor D $25,000. Although the total debt is $100,000, when Debtor defaults he has only $60,000 worth of assets. That means there is not enough money for each of the creditors to be satisfied in full. The Civil Code states that they share in the assets ratably. Under these facts, each creditor has a 25 percent share in the overall debt. That means that each will receive $15,000 of the total $60,000, which also means that each of them will have to absorb a loss of $10,000.

But there's one very important thing to note about our hypothetical above: All of the creditors were *unsecured*. A creditor who anticipates that his debtor might have multiple creditors and might not, in the end, have enough assets to satisfy all of the obligations to each of them has the ability to become "secured" in his claim against the debtor by taking a property interest (a security right) in some of the debtor's property or else by acquiring the right to sue a third party and go after his assets in the event the debtor fails to pay. Once again, an example is helpful here. Let's assume the same facts as above, but that the $60,000 worth of assets that Debtor has is comprised solely of a piece of immovable property—Blackacre. Also, at the time the obligation arose between Creditor A and Debtor, Debtor granted a mortgage over Blackacre in favor of Creditor A to secure Debtor's obligation to pay him. Now when Debtor defaults, Creditor A will have the first "bite at the apple" to receive payment by seeking recourse against Debtor's asset—Blackacre. Rather than having to share with the other creditors, Creditor A can enforce his mortgage through a process called "foreclosure" and have the property seized from Debtor and sold by the sheriff at a public auction.

Let's assume, for simplicity's sake, that at the public auction someone makes a bid to purchase Blackacre for the full $60,000. That person is now the owner of Blackacre (no longer Debtor) and he gets to walk away with the property. Meanwhile, the $60,000 he paid goes first to Creditor A to pay him what he is owed. Therefore, he will take a full $25,000 from the bid amount and be made whole. The remaining money ($35,000) will be ratably distributed among the remaining creditors. Since they each have a claim to one-third of that amount, they will only receive $11,666.67 each. Notice how much better off Creditor A is under our modified fact pattern. Why, you may ask?—because he is a *secured* creditor. The major right that security conveys to a creditor is the ability to have a preference over other creditors when it comes to the assets of the debtor.

Conversely, the unsecured creditors did not fare as well. Their losses increased. Furthermore, there are many scenarios where the unsecured creditors might not have gotten anything at all. Consider what would have happened if Blackacre sold at the auction for only $20,000. Creditor A's secured claim for $25,000 would have eaten up the entire pot of money. Although he would have taken a loss in the amount of $5,000, the unsecured creditors would have gotten nothing at all.

2. A Right of Pursuit

Yet another significant right that comes along with security (specifically, with real security) is the right of pursuit. The right of pursuit has to do with the fact that security over property constitutes a real right—a right that is good against the world and that follows the property into whoever's hands it may come. To understand the concept, think about a predial servitude. It does not matter whether the current owner of the servient estate is the person who initially granted the servitude or if it is some third party that acquired the property from that original owner. In either case the burden of the servitude "runs with the land." Security is no different—it remains with the property even if the grantor of the security right is no longer the owner of the collateral.

Consider the following: Debtor owns Blackacre and also owes Creditor $50,000. However, Creditor is unsecured. Over the course of the term of the loan, Debtor sells Blackacre to Purchaser. Debtor then spends all the money he received from the sale. When it comes time to repay Creditor, Debtor defaults. If Debtor still had Blackacre, then Creditor, as an ordinary unsecured creditor, could proceed to get a judgment against him and then seek to have the property seized and sold. However, Debtor no longer has Blackacre—indeed, he lacks any assets of significance from which Creditor can seek recourse. Here again is one of the weaknesses of being unsecured—a debtor may, in the ordinary course, divest himself of valuable assets that a creditor might otherwise rely upon in the event of a default (in addition to the problem discussed above of having to share pro rata with other unsecured creditors).

Under these facts, Creditor could certainly avail himself of the revocatory action under Civil Code article 2036[3] and seek to have the sale undone, but that can be a cumbersome process and expensive. Instead, Creditor should have taken a security right in Blackacre in the form of a conventional mortgage. By having done so (and properly filed), the mortgage would remain with the property even after the sale to Purchaser. Then, once Debtor defaulted, Creditor could seek to have Blackacre seized from Purchaser and sold at a sheriff's sale in satisfaction of the debt that was owed. The mortgage—like all real security—runs with the property itself. It does not matter how many times the property is sold from one person to another, the security interest remains such that the Creditor has a right to "pursue" the collateral whenever it may be. The right of pursuit is an essential feature of security devices law.

3. Expedited Means of Enforcing Payment

The next major benefit of being a secured creditor has to do with the means by which one can get paid. In a typical unsecured scenario, a creditor must go through a long process to be paid. Let's consider a situation where Debtor owes Creditor $60,000, and Creditor is unsecured. Creditor must first get a judgment against Debtor utilizing ordinary process. This can be both time-consuming and costly (perhaps so costly that Creditor decides it just isn't worth it if the amount due is too small). After Creditor obtains his judgment he must

---

[3] *See* La. Civ. Code art. 2036 ("An obligee has a right to annul an act of the obligor, or the result of a failure to act of the obligor, made or effected after the right of the obligee arose, that causes or increases the obligor's insolvency.").

then go through a series of steps to enforce it. Perhaps Creditor wants to use the judgment to garnish the Debtor's wages or seize various assets of the Debtor. That means Creditor has to go back to court and get a special order from the judge known as a "writ of *fieri facias*" (or as it is more commonly called, a "writ of *fifa*"). This writ is necessary for the sheriff to seize any of the Debtor's property in satisfaction of the judgment. It should be noted that even with a judgment and a writ of *fifa*, there are some assets of a debtor that the law exempts from seizure (such as tools of the trade, basic household furnishing, and the debtor's vehicle). *See generally* La. Rev. Stat. § 13:3881. These exemptions further limit what the unsecured creditor can go after to recoup his loss.

Notably, Creditor cannot go after any of Debtor's property without the help of the sheriff. And, as you might imagine, the sheriff does not do all this for free. Rather, when the sheriff seizes property of Debtor and then conducts an auction of that property, he will first take a percentage of the price fetched at auction as his fee. What's left after that will go to Creditor (further reducing his chances of being made whole). If the auction does not bring in a good price, the further reduction of that amount by the sheriff's fee can be a real drag to the creditor.

A final downside to being unsecured when it comes to enforcement deals with identifying the property a creditor wants to seize. The writ of *fifa* must identify exactly what property of the debtor is to be executed upon. That means a creditor must actually know what assets the debtor has and where they are located. Certainly the creditor can haul the debtor into court and force him to disclose his assets, but the debtor can hide his assets or lie. In any case, the creditor is not in a good position—he has to go through a long and expensive process that can be easily frustrated by the debtor and ultimately result in a lot of effort for little reward.

Being secured helps solve this problem. If Creditor had gotten security in particular assets of Debtor (i.e., land, vehicles, equipment, etc.) then Creditor could seek recourse directly against those items. Moreover, the law provides a relatively quick, expedited process for seizing these assets, without first getting a judgment and going through ordinary process. As you will learn in later chapters, a creditor can utilize a procedure known as "executory process" in the context of foreclosing on a mortgage that alleviates a great deal of the waiting periods and expense involved in going through ordinary process. Moreover, various types of movable property under Article 9 of the Uniform Commercial Code (known as Chapter 9 of Title 10 here in Louisiana) can be executed upon without the need to involve the sheriff or even a judge (such as with accounts receivable, deposit accounts, and sometimes automobiles). Again, being secured can save the creditor both time and money.

4. Favored Treatment in Bankruptcy

In the realm of bankruptcy, secured creditors are accorded significant rights over unsecured claimants. Without having taken a class in bankruptcy (and we surely do not try to cover such material here in any depth), you probably already know that when a debtor gets into serious financial trouble he can seek protection under the federal Bankruptcy Code. This can involve causing the debtor to sell (liquidate) all of his assets, keeping certain essential items needed for survival, and then using the money from the liquidation to pay his creditors. If creditors are not paid the entirety of what they are owed, the remainder is discharged (extinguished). The debtor gets a fresh start. In other instances, bankruptcy law allows for a restructuring of the debt. The debtor and the creditors come up with a plan whereby the debtor will, over time, pay the creditors, but the creditors agree to take less than what was originally owed and/or allow for more time to pay.

Bankruptcy law, however, treats secured creditors and unsecured creditors very differently—and in major ways. For instance, although a debt can be discharged in bankruptcy (meaning the creditor cannot go after the debtor individually on that debt anymore), if that debt is secured, then even after the discharge the creditor can go after the asset over which he has security. The unsecured creditor, having no security, is without any remedy and walks away with nothing.

Also, in bankruptcy the various creditors of the debtor have "claims" as to the amounts that they are owed. The creditors might have provisions in their agreements with the debtor that, in the event the debtor defaults, entitle the creditors to penalties, fees, and attorney's fees and court costs accrued in connection with collection procedures. Here the Bankruptcy Code treats unsecured and secured creditors differently. Once the bankruptcy petition is filed by the debtor, unsecured creditors may no longer include fees, interest, attorney's fees, etc., in the total amount of their "claim" against the debtor. *See*

11 U.S.C. § 502(b)(1). Those amounts that accrued prior to filing the petition remain part of the claim, but those that arose after filing are excluded. This means, in some sense, the unsecured creditor's claim is frozen, even if the real amount of the debt is still growing. And, in the bankruptcy context, generally the only thing that matters is the "claim." Secured creditors, on the other hand, can have late fees, interest, attorney's fees, etc., included in their claim if certain requirements are met. *See* 11 U.S.C. § 506(b). This means that the total amount that the secured creditor can get paid from the debtor can grow, even after the petition is filed (not good news for unsecured creditors).

There are a number of other important rights that the Bankruptcy Code affords to secured creditors in the way of the sale of assets, retention of lien rights after debt modification or substitution, and valuing future payments made by the debtor. While a discussion of these rights goes beyond the scope of this book, it is important to know that they exist and why it is a good idea to seek security on the front end before financing a transaction, lest one's debtor lands in bankruptcy court.

5. Seeking Payment Beyond Debtor's Patrimony

Last but not least, security offers a way for the creditor to seek recourse as a result of the debtor's nonperformance from a source wholly separate and apart from the pool of assets of the debtor himself. This is accomplished through the use of personal security—or, more specifically, the law of suretyship. As you will learn further in this text, sometimes the creditor obtains security, not in property, but in another person. In other words, a third party, separate from the debtor, agrees that if the debtor fails to pay, then the creditor can demand such payment from the third party. This third party is known in Louisiana law as a surety, or in common law parlance: a guarantor.

For instance, Debtor owes Creditor $30,000 and, to secure payment of this debt, Surety agrees to guarantee the loan. Therefore, if Debtor fails to pay Creditor, Creditor can turn around and go directly after Surety for payment. Indeed, Creditor does not even need to exhaust his remedies against Debtor before suing Surety. Security like this essentially gives another person for Creditor to sue if Debtor fails to pay. If Surety is asset rich, then it is very likely that Creditor will get paid, even if Debtor is insolvent. And, like Debtor, Surety is obligated to satisfy the obligation to Creditor from all his present and future movable and immovable property. Now Creditor has two (or even more, depending upon how many sureties he procures) sources from which to seek payment.

B. The Taxonomy of Security in Louisiana

Like all areas of Louisiana law steeped in the civil law tradition, classification and taxonomy play a hugely important role in the law of security devices. The following section sets forth the major categories of and involving security. As you move through the material throughout the course of the semester you will often come back to these major categories in seeking to understanding both the rules that govern each security device, as well as the policies behind them.

1. Principal v. Accessory Rights

The first distinction is one not between different security devices, but between security devices and everything else. In the realm of juridical relations, it is important to understand one very fundamental thing about all security devices—they are accessory rights. That means that they must be attached to a principal obligation or right in order to exist at all. In other words, one cannot grant a mortgage over one's immovable property unless that mortgage is securing the right of some creditor to a performance. Without the obligation, there can be no mortgage. Similarly, one cannot grant a security interest in one's car without that security interest being attached to some obligation. Sometimes laypersons conflate the terms of security and principal obligations, which adds to some of the confusion in this distinction. Consider, for example, that many people speak of "paying their mortgage." While it is true that the vast majority of homeowners have a mortgage on their home, it is not true that the monthly check they send to the bank goes toward paying down "the mortgage." Rather, it is the loan that they are paying back, and that loan happens to be secured by a mortgage on immovable property. While this is a fine way to speak in a more informal setting or for shorthand, it is not legally correct. The mortgage is just a legal mechanism that a creditor can use to recover from the non-performance of the obligor—it cannot exist alone.

Because of the secondary nature of security, if anything happens to the principal obligation that makes it cease to exist (i.e., it is extinguished through prescription, confusion, compensation, or performance), then the security right goes away as well. Generally speaking, security rights cannot exist without a principal obligation on which to attach. You will see later in this book, however, that there are certain instances where the accessory nature of certain security devices is set aside in order to facilitate certain desires of the parties (i.e., in the case of the multiple indebtedness mortgage).

2. Personal v. Real Rights

Moving on to exclusively the realm of accessory real rights (i.e., security), there is a major threshold distinction: personal security versus real security. Personal security is security in the form of a person. Suretyship, discussed above, is an example and, in fact, is the only example. The most prominent and widely used type of personal security in Louisiana law is suretyship. It is the ability to seek recourse against someone other than the debtor in the event the debtor does not perform. Sometimes the surety is a natural person, but it is often a juridical person with many assets, such as a trust or limited liability company (LLC).

The other category—real security—is where everything else falls. All other types of security devices form the basis of real security, meaning security in a thing. Mortgage, pledge, UCC article 9, and all the privileges are types of real security.

Within the realm of real security, some types of security devices are more versatile than others. Sometimes the security is in a moveable thing, sometimes an immovable, and sometimes both. For instance, generally mortgages can only encumber immovable property and generally UCC article 9 interests can only encumber movable property. But, there are a number of times when the law makes an exception. As you will learn below, the Civil Code allows a mortgage to be granted over the rights that a lessee has in the lease of immovable property (called a "leasehold mortgage"). A contract right is, under our law, an incorporeal movable. Therefore, one would assume that it could not be mortgaged. Nevertheless, the law allows for it. Similarly, standing timber, which is always immovable under Louisiana law, can in certain instances be subject to a UCC article 9 interest. Be sure to pay attention to these distinctions, as they can ultimately create confusion if you try to paint with too broad a brush in dealing with these rules.

3. Consensual v. Nonconsensual

Another major category, and perhaps one of the most important ones, is the difference between security that is granted by agreement of the parties and security that is granted by law. Consensual security occurs when the owner of the property agrees to grant a security interest in that property in favor of someone else. When a person purchases a home and gets a loan from the bank, that person agrees to grant a mortgage over the home in favor of the bank in exchange for having received the money to purchase it. A conventional mortgage is a type of consensual security. The same can be said of conventional suretyship. Son wants to purchase a car on credit, and the dealership agrees to sell it to him on credit, but only on the condition that he gets his mother or father to guarantee the loan. Father's or Mother's agreement to serve as surety is consensual security. Consensual security serves as the backbone of commercial financing transactions.

Nonconsensual security is the opposite. In these instances, the owner of the encumbered property never agrees to give it as security. Rather, the law grants the security right to the creditor by operation of law. For instance, still using the concept of mortgage, if a creditor obtains a judgment against a debtor and then files that judgment into the mortgage records of the parish where the debtor owns immovable property, then automatically and without the debtor's consent the creditor acquires a judicial mortgage over all the immovable property that the debtor may now or in the future own in that parish. Notice how, unlike in the home-buying scenario above, the debtor never agrees to grant a mortgage. Similarly, if a property owner hires a builder to construct a home and that builder fails to pay his subcontractors (like the electrician, the plumber, or the carpenter), then those subcontractors can obtain a security right the owner's immovable property where the work was done. Here again, the property owner never agreed to give these claimants a security interest—rather, it arose by operation of law without his consent. Nonconsensual security (often called legal security) is granted as a matter of policy—usually because the legislature believes that these individuals serve such an important function, but have such little bargaining power, that it is in the best interest of society to give them a security right to ensure that they get paid. You will learn more about this when you get to the section on privileges.

4. Possessory v. Nonpossessory

A final distinction involves who retains the collateral during the course of the existence of the security right. For some types of property, a creditor can have a security interest in the thing only if the creditor actually has possession (or sometimes, if it's intangible, has "control") of it. For other types though, the creditor can have a security interest even if the debtor still has possession. And for some types of property, the creditor and debtor have the option of choosing which they desire (and there are consequences to selecting one over the other). Consider the conventional mortgage. Although the bank has a mortgage on the property, the homeowner still has possession of it—he lives in the house and the bank (through its agent) generally never physically sets foot on the property. The lack of possession on the part of the bank, however, does not impair its security right.

On the other hand, other types of security require possession. For instance, the law grants to a person who repairs a thing a security right over it called the "artisan's privilege" that secures the owner's obligation to pay him for the work. As long as the repairman has possession of the thing, the privilege persists. However, once the repairman hands the thing back over to the owner, his privilege is lost—he becomes just another unsecured creditor of that debtor.

You will learn more about the distinction between possessory and nonpossessory security rights in later chapters. Over time possessory security interests have become less and less prevalent because of the obvious reason that often the debtor needs to have possession and use of the collateral in order to undertake his trade or business and thereby to have the resources necessary to repay the loan. Requiring that the creditor have possession at all times greatly undercuts this notion, and because of this it is rare to see requirements for possessory security.

With that introduction to the importance of secured credit and the major categories of security in Louisiana, this casebook proceeds to explore the various devices under state law. You will learn about suretyship, Article 9 of the Uniform Commercial Code, pledges, mortgages, privileges, and then the special class of privileges known as the Private Works Act. We hope that this material will serve not only as a useful tool for you in understanding the many complexities of the law of security devices, but will also help prepare you to contribute in practice to the important work of consumer, commercial, and business lawyers across Louisiana.

Chapter 2
The Law of Suretyship

A. In General

Suretyship is first and foremost a contract of security. As a contract it must meet all the basic requirements of a contract under the law of conventional obligations (capacity, cause, consent, and object). As a contract of personal security, suretyship is different from traditional asset-based security (i.e., real security) because the collateral is, in fact, not a thing at all. Rather, it is a person, or, to be more specific, it is a surety promising that in the event the obligor does not perform, then the surety will do so in his place. At common law, and even in Louisiana, suretyship contracts are often called guaranty agreements and the surety is often known as the guarantor.

In every other state, the law of suretyship can generally be found in that state's version of the Uniform Commercial Code. Louisiana's provisions on suretyship, however, are found in Title XVI of Book III of the Civil Code, consisting of articles 3035 through 3070. This title was revised effective January 1, 1988. *See* 1987 La. Acts, No. 409, § 1, eff. Jan. 1, 1988.

See La. Civ. Code arts. 1913; 3035-3036

* * * * * *

SURETYSHIP

RALPH SLOVENKO

39 TULANE LAW REVIEW 427, 427-28 (1965)

Suretyship is a contract which allows a creditor to look for payment from several persons instead of one, and he thereby diminishes considerably the risks of nonperformance or insolvency of the debtor. This protective device has a history of over 4,500 years. In early times, the family and clan members and other social groups were collectively responsible for the wrongs of their individual members. The Code of Hammurabi (2250 B.C.) placed responsibility upon a city and its governor for failure to capture a brigand. The Greek historian Herodotus tells of the important role that the surety played in the Babylonian marriage; whatever his reports may be worth, he states that every year the maidens of marriageable age were assembled in the market place to be sold at auction into marriage by a crier, and whether the maiden was beautiful or ugly, "no man could take away the woman he purchased without first producing a surety that he would make her his wife."

In the history of Roman law, personal security was, at first, preferred to real security. At the beginning of the Empire (27 B.C.), real security was employed as an alternative when a surety could not be found. Earlier, because of the strong ties between the members of social groups, it was difficult for one asked to serve as surety to refuse support to a parent or neighbor, but even when the ties later weakened, suretyship remained in usage. The political mores of the Republic (527-509 B.C.) caused influential men to act as sureties for the debts of their electors. However, under the Empire this factor disappeared, and it became more and more difficult to find a surety. To encourage suretyship, legislation was passed to make the service less perilous, but the result was to remove the efficacy of the security. Pomponius, who is frequently quoted by classical writers, is credited with saying in the middle of the second century A.D. that "real security offers more protection than personal security." By the end of the classical period (235 A.D.), the hypotheca became the more desirable instrument of credit.

Pronouncements on the dangerous position of the surety have been numerous. Solomon in 950 B.C. warned that "he that is surety for a stranger shall smart for it." In Shakespeare's "The Merchant of Venice," Bassanio risked a pound of his flesh to guarantee a loan made to his closest friend by Shylock, the moneylender, who insisted, "I crave the law, the penalty and forfeit of my bond."

* * * * * *

RUMINATIONS ON SURETYSHIP

MICHAEL H. RUBIN

57 LOUISIANA LAW REVIEW 565, 567-571 (1997)

Louisiana law divides "rights" into two main areas: "real rights" and "personal rights."

Unlike the common law, where the phrase "real rights" refers to rights in immovable property, Louisiana law uses the phrase "real rights" to refer to rights related, on the one hand, to ownership of any item (be it movable or immovable), and, on the other, to a right to seize and sell property (of any kind) and obtain a privilege on the proceeds of the sale. Personal rights, on the other hand, are claims against another individual or entity; it is roughly equivalent to a cause of action in the context of a lawsuit. Suretyship is a personal right under Louisiana law. It gives the creditor the right to sue someone or some entity in addition to the one who is principally obligated on the debt.

The distinguished French commentator of the last century, Planiol, enumerated five distinct characteristics of suretyship; this listing is a useful checklist even today. The five characteristics that Planiol uses (accessory contract, unilateral contract, gratuitous contract, consensual relationship, and express contract) are incorporated in the Civil Code's introductory articles on suretyship, Articles 3035 through 3040.

A. SURETYSHIP IS AN ACCESSORY OBLIGATION

Article 3035 explicitly defines suretyship as an "accessory contract." Suretyship by nature is not primary; it is secondary to the obligation of another. The principal obligation may be any lawful obligation, and although suretyship may be co-extensive with the principal obligation, it can be less broad than the principal obligation if the parties so agree in writing.

B. SURETYSHIP IS UNILATERAL

A suretyship contract is unilateral; it obligates the surety to the creditor and imposes a contractual obligation on the surety to the creditor; there is no necessary contractual obligation running from the creditor to the surety, although the parties contractually may create such an obligation. Civil Code article 3035 defines the unilateral nature of suretyship when it states that suretyship is an accessory "contract by which a person binds himself to a creditor. . . ."

It is useful to remember that there are at least three separate relationships involved in any suretyship arrangement; each is treated separately by the Civil Code. There is a relationship between the creditor and the debtor, a relationship between the creditor and the surety, and a relationship between the surety and the debtor. . . . When there is more than one surety, additional relationships are added.

C. SURETYSHIP MAY BE GRATUITOUS

Planiol notes that suretyship is "gratuitous" because "the surety alone obligates himself toward the creditor who furnishes nothing in exchange." There is nothing in the Civil Code that requires "consideration" for a contract of suretyship. "Consideration" is a common law concept, not a civilian one. The spirit of liberality that supports any donative act is a sufficient cause for a contract of suretyship. This is not to say that suretyship is always gratuitous; there are many instances in which there is direct or indirect compensation given by the debtor to induce a surety to sign a contract of suretyship.

D. SURETYSHIP IS CONSENSUAL

There are areas in which the Civil Code imposes obligations on parties regardless of their actual or even implied consent. Suretyship, in contrast to obligations that arise by law, requires an express consent in a contractual form. Louisiana courts frequently have referred to the "contract of suretyship" or "contract of guaranty." Because suretyship is a consensual contract, the general rules involving contractual obligations are applicable in addition to the special rules relating to suretyship contracts, which require a writing and do not require a formal acceptance.

E. EXPRESS CONTRACT OF SURETYSHIP

As Planiol writes that suretyship is not "presumed" and Civil Code article 3038 states succinctly, in its entirety: "Suretyship must be express and in writing." The requirement that suretyship be a written agreement is re-emphasized by Civil Code article 1847, which provides that "parol evidence is inadmissible to establish . . . a promise to pay the debt of a third person." Suretyship, by definition, is a promise to pay the debt of a third person because it is a contract by which the surety is bound "to fulfill the obligation of another upon the failure of the latter to do so."

* * * * * *

B. Requirements

***See* La. Civ. Code arts. 1833; 1836-1837; 2993; 2996-2997; 3038-3040**

1. Written Promise to Pay

Suretyship deviates from the general rule of contract in that there is a solemnity requirement. In other words, the contract of suretyship must be in writing. As with other contracts in Louisiana, the law often requires a writing (whether as simple as an act under private signature or as intricate as an authentic act) in order to serve two functions. The first is a proof (i.e., evidentiary) function. Clearly contracts that are reduced to writing make it easier to prove their contents, since memories fade and recollections may differ as to the terms of the deal. Second, writing requirements serve a cautionary function. This is perhaps particularly important in the context of suretyship. The act of agreeing to serve as surety for the obligations of another is significant and carries great consequences. In the event the obligor fails to perform then the obligee may call upon the surety to do so at once, with there being a very real chance that the surety may never be able to recover from the obligor himself in the event he, for instance, is insolvent. Therefore, by requiring the suretyship contract to be in writing the law imposes a level of ceremony and formality in hopes of impressing upon the surety the weight of the agreement he is about to enter. Importantly, however, as with any time that the law requires a contract to be merely "in writing" the only form of writing that is required is an act under private signature. While a greater level of formality (like an authentic act) will certainly be sufficient, it is not necessary.

Consider the following case that explores the contours of the writing requirement for suretyship.

* * * * * *

QUEEN INS. CO. OF AMERICA v. BLOOMENSTIEL
168 So. 302 (La. 1936)

FOURNET, Justice.

This is an action instituted by the Queen Insurance Company of America on a surety bond furnished by one of its agents, United Agencies, Inc., against Charest Thibaut and M. F. Bloomenstiel, the sureties in said bond, to recover the sum of $114.06, alleged to be owing the plaintiff on account of a shortage in the accounts of the agent while in plaintiff's employ. The defendants filed exceptions of no right or cause of action, which were sustained by the lower court, and the judgment was affirmed on appeal to the Court of Appeal, First Circuit. 165 So. 22. The matter is now before us for review on writs granted by this court.

The exceptions of no right or cause of action are based on the failure of the principal to sign the bond. The bond in effect recites that the United Agencies, Inc. (which had been appointed agent for the Queen Insurance Company of New York), as principal, and Charest Thibaut and M. F. Bloomenstiel, as sureties, are bound jointly and severally unto the Queen Insurance Company of America in the sum of $1,000. The condition of the bond is "that in the event of any default by the principal specified in this bond, . . . the Sureties agreeing to pay the amount defaulted (not exceeding the sum specified herein) as may be proved to be due. . . ." [C]ounsel for defendants contend that the bond in question is a surety bond and not an indemnity bond and, therefore, requires the signature of the principal to render it valid and binding upon the sureties and rely upon the case of *Selby et al. v. City of New Orleans, et al.*, 119 La. 900, 44 So. 722. . . .

In the case of *Selby v. New Orleans,* supra, the court said:

> The instrument signed by them, like the work which plaintiffs bound themselves to do for defendant, bears on its face the evidence of its incompleteness. It was never signed by the principal.
>
> We infer that there was an intended principal who never bound himself. There cannot be a guarantor in a contract in which it is expressed that both guarantor and principal should be bound if both do not sign in accordance with the condition of the contract.

Unlike the case of *Selby v. New Orleans,* supra, in this case the principal is primarily liable, and in the bond it is recited that the sureties are bound jointly and severally, and that case, therefore, is not an authority to support defendant's contention. We have repeatedly held that it is not necessary for the principal or appellant to sign the appeal bond for the reason that the principal or appellant is primarily liable without reference to the bond. [Citations omitted. . . .

We are of the opinion that the failure of the principal to sign the bond in the instant case does not invalidate the same as to the sureties who, under the terms of the bond, are jointly and severally liable to plaintiff for such amount as plaintiff's agent, who was primarily liable, may have defaulted. The exceptions of no cause or right of action must, therefore, be overruled. For the reasons assigned the judgments of the lower court and the Court of Appeal are set aside and annulled, the exceptions of no right or cause of action are overruled, and the case is hereby remanded to the district court to be proceeded with according to law and consistent with the views herein expressed; costs of appeal to be paid by the defendants and appellees, all other costs to await the final outcome of this suit.

2. Language Sufficient for Suretyship

Keeping with the idea of caution, the contract of suretyship must contain language that clearly evidences that the person intends to be a surety. Thus, the law states that a contract of suretyship must be "express" so that it leaves little doubt as to whether the person really intends to guarantee the obligations of another. This particular requirement, however, has not always been easily understood and courts have variously struggled with exactly what language places the contract within the ambit of suretyship, and what comes up short.

The following two cases exemplify this difficulty, as well as point out how important it is to advise clients to be careful in the words they use when discussing the creditworthiness of others.

* * * * * *

BALL MARKETING ENTERPRISE v. RAINBOW TOMATO CO.

340 So. 2d 700 (La. App. 3d Cir. 1976).

CULPEPPER, Judge.

This is a suit on an open account. Defendants are the debtor, Rainbow Tomato Company (Rainbow) and its alleged surety, Plant Industries, Inc. (Plant). The trial court rendered a judgment by default against both Rainbow and Plant declaring them liable to plaintiff "jointly and solidarily" for $11,069.78 due on the open account. Only the defendant Plant appealed.

The principal issue on appeal is whether a certain letter constitutes a continuing guarantee that Plant will pay the open account owed by Rainbow. The letter, dated January 22, 1976, from Hyman Katz, Chairman of the Board of Plant Industries, Inc., addressed to Charles Goss of Ball Marketing Enterprises, states:

> Gentlemen:
>
> You have advised us that Rainbow Tomato Company, Inc. ("Rainbow") is indebted to you in the amount of $8,408.40 for deliveries of fuel oil made from "December 19, 1975 through January 7, 1976. This will confirm our understanding with you that Plant Industries, Inc. will take such steps as are necessary to assure payment to you by Rainbow of amounts due for past and future deliveries of fuel oil to Rainbow, to the extent necessary for heating its greenhouses.
>
> /s/ Hyman Katz
> Chairman of the Board

Plaintiff describes this letter as a "continuing guaranty" obligating Plant to pay plaintiff amounts due for past and future deliveries of fuel oil to Rainbow. In Louisiana, a contract of guaranty is equivalent to a contract of suretyship. The two terms are used interchangeably. *American Bank & Trust Company v. Bluebird Restaurant & Lounge*, 279 So. 2d 720 (La. App. 1st Cir. 1973), *affirmed* 290 So. 2d 302 (La. 1974). Therefore, we will look to the provisions of our Civil

Code governing the contract of suretyship to test plaintiff's assertion that the letter is a continuing guaranty. . . .

A general rule which emerges from the substantial body of jurisprudence interpreting these provisions is that the surety's contract need not observe technical formalities but must contain an absolute expression of intent to be bound. *See* Hubert, *The Nature and Essentials of Conventional Suretyship*, 13 Tul. L. Rev. 519, 525 to 526 (1939) and cases discussed therein. The letter from Plant to plaintiff does not contain an absolute expression of intent to pay Rainbow's open account. It provides, instead, that Plant, "will take such steps as are necessary to assure payment . . . by Rainbow. . . ." The letter clearly contemplates payment by Rainbow, not Plant. If we were to presume otherwise, we would violate the express instructions of Article 3039 (current art. 3038; *cf.* art. 3044): "Suretyship can not be presumed." Therefore, we hold that the letter did not bind Plant as a surety or guarantor.

Our holding is consistent with the bulk of the jurisprudence interpreting Article 3039 (current art. 3038) and is supported particularly by the decision of our Supreme Court in *Exchange National Bank v. Waldron*, 177 La. 1015, 150 So. 3 (1933). In *Waldron*, the alleged surety wrote a letter to the creditor stating "we are behind Mr. Waldron [the debtor] and are financing him and we feel that you are perfectly safe on this sort of a contract. . . ." The court held that this vague statement of support fell short of the stringent requirements set by Article 3039 (current art. 3038). Likewise, Plant's promise to "take such steps as are necessary to assure payment" by Rainbow is insufficient to bind Plant as a surety or guarantor.

Plaintiff argues that the language of the letter is ambiguous and should, therefore, be construed against Plant, the party who drafted it. LSA-C.C. Articles 1957 and 1958 (current art. 2057). We do not agree. The critical part of the artfully drafted letter is unambiguous, in that it assures payment by Rainbow rather than Plant. Even if we were to agree that the letter is ambiguous, we could not presume that it creates a contract of suretyship. Articles 1957 and 1958 (current art. 2057) embody rules of general application which would yield in the present case to the special rule of construction laid down in Article 3039 (current art. 3038). The controlling rule is that a contract of suretyship cannot be presumed. . . . For the reasons assigned, the judgment appealed is reversed and set aside insofar as it holds Plant Industries, Inc. to be liable to the plaintiff. All costs of this appeal are assessed against the plaintiff.

* * * * * *

BLAIR RUBBER CO. v. ALTRA COATINGS TECHNOLOGY, INC.
575 So. 2d 504 (La. App. 5th Cir.), *cert. denied,* 577 So. 2d 37 (La. 1991)

GAUDIN, Judge.

The primary issue involved in this case is whether a letter sent by appellant Whitney J. Poirrier to appellee Blair Rubber Company, Inc. bound Mr. Poirrier personally for goods purchased from Blair by a third party, Altra Coatings Technology, Inc. The appealed-from judgment of the 24th Judicial District Court found Mr. Poirrier responsible for the amount specified in the letter. We affirm.

The letter, from Mr. Poirrier to Blair dated October 6, 1988, contained this wording:

> It is my understanding that Altra Coatings Tech., Inc. will be purchasing rubber from you in the near future. I am willing to personally guarantee the account of Altra Coatings Technology, Inc. up to the amount of $50,000.00. If in the future we need to extend the account we will work on a job basis. Enclosed you will find a copy of my personal financial statement. Along with a check for the old balance of this account.

Appellant argues that he had not made a precise and explicit promise to pay if Altra did not. At best, Mr. Poirrier contends, the letter's wording was an invitation to negotiate a guarantee. The trial judge was not impressed by these assertions nor are we. The trial judge found paragraph two of Mr. Poirrier's letter "to be very clear and unequivocal and I find an intent on Mr. Poirrier to be personally bound for the purchases that the corporation may make after that date of October 6, 1988. . . ."

Mr. Poirrier's suretyship was in writing and was for a debt arising in the near future. Acceptance by Blair is presumed, no formal notice of acceptance being required. Further, the letter does not suggest any reservation, condition or limit except for the $50,000.00 amount.

In *Guaranty Bank & Trust Co. v. Jones*, 489 So. 2d 368 (La. App. 5 Cir. 1986), this Court said at pages 370 and 371:

> A contract of guaranty is equivalent to a contract of suretyship, and the two terms may be used interchangeably. A contract of guaranty (or suretyship) is subject to the same rules of interpretation as contracts in general, *Keller Industries v. Deauville Consultants*, 459 So. 2d 636 (La. App. 5th Cir.1984). An agreement legally entered into have the effect of laws for those who formed them and must be performed in good faith, LSA-C.C. art. 1901 (current art. 1953). Our courts are bound to give legal effect to all such contracts according to the true intent of the parties and this intent is to be determined by the words of the contract when these are clear and explicit and lead to no absurd consequences, LSA C.C. art. 1945 (current art. 2046). All clauses of an agreement are interpreted one by the other, giving to each the sense that results from the entire act, LSA-C.C. art. 1955 (current art. 2050).
>
> A continuing guaranty agreement (surety contract) need not observe technical formalities, but must embody an absolute expression of an intent to be bound, *Keller*, supra. "It is an accessory promise by which one binds himself for another already bound and agrees with the creditor to satisfy the obligation if the principal debtor does not do so," *Keller*, supra. Furthermore, the continuing guaranty must be in writing, explicit and parol evidence must not be used to establish either its existence or a promise to pay the debt of another, *Keller,* supra.

Considering these *Guaranty Bank* principles and the wording of Mr. Poirrier's letter, we cannot say the trial court erred. Appellant is to bear costs. Affirmed.

* * * * * *

AMERICAN BANK & TRUST CO. OF COUSHATTA v. BOGGS & THOMPSON
821 So. 2d 585 (La. App. 2d Cir.), *cert. denied,* 827 So. 2d 1175 (La. 2002)

KOSTELKA, Judge.

American Bank and Trust Company of Coushatta ("AB&T") appeals the summary judgment granted by the Twenty-Sixth Judicial District Court, Bossier Parish, in favor of Boggs and Thompson, A Professional Law Corporation and A. Michael Boggs ("Boggs"). For the following reasons, we affirm.

FACTS

Boggs represented Thomas and Denise Washburn (the "Washburns") who were indebted to AB&T for approximately $45,000. In connection with that indebtedness, AB&T had instituted foreclosure proceedings against the Washburns upon their default. In response to the foreclosure lawsuit, Boggs wrote AB&T a letter ("the letter") dated November 21, 1997 on behalf of the Washburns, which stated as follows:

> Please accept this letter as notice of my representation of Washburn, Inc. in relation to a claim regarding a construction project in the United States Virgin Islands [the "Virgin Islands litigation"]. On the referenced project, Washburn, Inc. incurred substantial losses due to circumstances caused by other contractors. At the present time, I am in the process of initiating a lawsuit against the contractors and the bonding company regarding the project.
>
> Please allow this letter to serve as confirmation that in the event any funds are obtained regarding this litigation in the form of settlement and/or judgment, that your institution will be satisfied regarding any outstanding loans with Denise and/or Tommy Washburn. . . .

The letter was directed to Leslie Gray ("Gray") and Randall Harrison of AB&T. After Gray received the letter, he met with the Washburns informing them that he would not forebear on the bank's foreclosure suit and would proceed to judgment; however, he agreed that AB&T would not execute any judgment obtained pending the outcome of the Virgin Islands litigation. In return, the Washburns agreed to make interim payments, which they initially did, but which stopped in mid-1998. AB&T then proceeded with its foreclosure against the Washburns. Subsequently, the Virgin Islands litigation settled, from which the Washburns received proceeds—none of which were paid to AB&T in satisfaction of the Washburns' debt. In September, 1999, AB&T filed a breach of contract lawsuit against Boggs, claiming that Boggs defaulted and/or breached an obligation created in the letter. Boggs filed a Motion for Summary Judgment which was granted by the trial court. This appeal by AB&T ensued.

DISCUSSION

. . . In this case, the trial court determined that there were no genuine issues of material fact, and the record supports such a finding. At issue is the letter of November 21, 1997. Although there are issues of law in dispute, clearly none of the pertinent facts of the case are at issue, i.e., neither party disputes the statements made in the letter or even Boggs' intent under the letter.

Boggs contends that the intent of the letter was to have AB&T forebear on its foreclosure action against the Washburns pending the outcome of the Virgin Islands litigation. The record reflects that this fact was known by AB&T and was, therefore, undisputed. In deposition, Gray agreed that the purpose of the letter was to "stop" the foreclosure litigation. Specifically, when questioned regarding the letter, Gray acknowledged that AB&T knew it was going to get a letter for forbearance on its foreclosure with the promise of payment from the proceeds of the Virgin Islands litigation. In fact, Gray did not believe that Boggs intended to pay the Washburns' indebtedness in the event they did not. Thus, the pertinent facts of this litigation regarding the letter are not in dispute.

Additionally, summary judgment in favor of Boggs was proper as a matter of law. Under various legal theories, we reject the notion, as did the trial court, that Boggs was personally obligated as a result of the language in the letter.

First, we note that pursuant to the law of mandate, Boggs would not be personally obligated for the Washburns' indebtedness with AB&T. A mandatary who contracts in the name of the principal within the limits of his authority does not bind himself personally for the performance of the contract. La. C.C. art. 3016; *Wirthman-Tag Const. Co., L.L.C. v. Hotard,* 2000-2298 (La. App. 4th Cir. 12/19/01), 804 So. 2d 856. On the other hand, a mandatary who contracts in his own name without disclosing his status as a mandatary does bind himself personally for the performance of the contract. La. C.C. art. 3017. Generally, an agent will be held to have bound himself personally when he enters into an agreement without disclosing the identity of his principal. *Frank's Door & Bldg. Supply, Inc. v. Double H. Const. Co., Inc.*, 459 So. 2d 1273 (La. App. 1st Cir. 11/20/84). The agent has the burden of proving that he disclosed his agency status and the identity of his principal if he wishes to avoid personal liability. Id. However, express notice of the agent's status and the principal's identity is not required to escape personal liability if the agent proves that sufficient evidence of the agency relationship was known by the third party so as to put him on notice of the principal-agent relationship. Id.

Here, Boggs expressly notified AB&T in the letter that he represented the Washburns as their attorney. Additionally, the record shows that before the letter was ever sent by Boggs and received by AB&T, a representative of AB&T had participated in a telephone conference with Boggs regarding the Washburns' loan status with the bank. Thus, AB&T obviously had knowledge other than that expressed in the letter that Boggs represented the Washburns as their attorney.

Second, Boggs was not the surety of the Washburns' debt. Suretyship is an accessory contract where a person binds himself to a creditor to fulfill the obligation of another upon the failure of the latter to do so. La. C.C. art. 3035. Such an agreement must be express and in writing. La. C.C. art. 3038. Revision Comment (b) to Article 3038 states [in pertinent part]:

> It is sometimes doubtful whether an individual has guaranteed payment of another's debt or has merely given an opinion as to the person's ability and willingness to perform. In such cases doubts are resolved against holding the individual as a surety on the theory that suretyship is a burden that one does not lightly undertake. *See Ball Marketing Enterprise v. Rainbow Tomato,* 340 So. 2d 700 (La. App. 3rd Cir. 1976); *Exchange Nat. Bank v. Waldron Lumber Co.*, [177 La. 1015,] 150 So. 3 (La. 1933).

An overriding rule regarding the principle of suretyship is that a contract of suretyship cannot be presumed or created by inference. *Williams v. Williams*, 95-13 (La. App. 5th Cir. 04/25/95), 655 So. 2d 405; *Jimco, Inc. v. Gentilly Terrace Apartments, Inc.*, 230 So. 2d 281 (La. App. 4th Cir. 1970).

Here, there is nothing in the letter which indicates Boggs' express intent to be personally bound in the event the Washburns failed to pay AB&T out of the Virgin Islands litigation proceeds. We cannot presume Boggs' intent to be bound from the language of the letter. Therefore, the letter clearly did not create a suretyship agreement by Boggs in favor of AB&T.

Finally, we cannot say that Boggs is obligated to AB&T under the general principles of contract law. Even if we consider the statements in the letter as an offer by Boggs to be personally obligated to AB&T, said offer was never accepted by AB&T; thus, no contract existed between Boggs and AB&T. A basic principle of contract formation is that a contract is formed by the consent of the parties established through offer and acceptance. La. C.C. art. 1927.

Under the facts of this case, AB&T never accepted the "offer" it insists Boggs made in the letter. Instead, after receiving the letter, Gray contacted the Washburns and the parties met in Coushatta to discuss the pending foreclosure against the Washburns. Notably, Boggs did not attend the meeting between Gray and the Washburns. At that meeting, Gray declined to stop the foreclosure proceeding, stating he would proceed with the litigation and obtain a judgment against the Washburns; however, he agreed not to execute the judgment in exchange for the Washburns' promise to make interim payments. Gray's subsequent offer to the Washburns constituted a counteroffer, which had the effect of negating any offer that might have been made by Boggs in his letter. An acceptance not in accordance with the terms of the offer is deemed to be a counteroffer. La. C.C. art.1943. This subsequent agreement made in Coushatta constituted the contract between the parties, AB&T and the Washburns. When the Washburns failed to make the agreed-upon payments, AB&T commenced executing its judgment against the Washburns. See, *Morehouse Parish Hosp. Service Dist. v. Pettit*, 25,396 (La. App. 2d Cir.01/19/94), 630 So. 2d 1338, writ denied, 94-0449 (La. 04/07/94), 635 So. 2d 1135.

Moreover, for these same reasons, it is evident that AB&T did not rely to its detriment on the statements made by Boggs in the letter. Obviously, AB&T chose not to take the course of action suggested in the letter, i.e., stopping the foreclosure proceeding in anticipation of being satisfied from the proceeds of the Virgin Islands litigation. AB&T did not rely on the representations made by Boggs, but rather negotiated another contract with the Washburns regarding the repayment of their loans. Because there was no reliance by AB&T on the letter, Boggs could not be liable to AB&T under the theory of detrimental reliance. . . . For the foregoing reasons, the trial court's judgment granting the Motion for Summary Judgment filed by Boggs is hereby affirmed.

* * * * * *

GULF COAST BANK AND TRUST CO. v. MONTOLI & PITRE, LLC
138 So. 3d 57 (La. App. 5th Cir. 2014)

FREDERICKA HOMBERG WICKER, Judge.

At issue in this appeal is whether the power of attorney executed by defendants, Mr. Jerry H. Muhs and Ms. Wanda C. Muhs, expressly authorized Mr. Muhs to bind Ms. Muhs personally as a surety on a loan to Montoli & Pitre, LLC, a company they owned together. We conclude that the power of attorney at issue here did expressly authorize this act and therefore affirm the trial court's grant of summary judgment in favor of plaintiff, Gulf Coast Bank and Trust Company.

FACTS AND PROCEDURAL HISTORY

Together, Mr. Jerry H. Muhs and Ms. Wanda C. Muhs owned, as members, Montoli & Pitre, LLC (hereinafter "the L.L.C."). On September 30, 2009, the L.L.C. secured a Small Business Administration loan from Gulf Coast Bank and Trust (hereinafter "the Bank") for the principal amount of $132,000.00. This loan was executed by the L.L.C. through Mr. Muhs' signatures on at least three documents. First, Mr. Muhs signed the promissory note on the loan both as a member of the L.L.C. himself, and as the agent of Ms. Muhs. This promissory note alleges Mr. Muhs' status as agent for Ms. Muhs was created "by virtue of a power of attorney dated September 28, 2009." Second, Mr. Muhs signed a "commercial guaranty" in which he obligated himself to be personally liable as a surety to the L.L.C.'s loan. Finally, Mr. Muhs signed a separate "commercial guaranty," as the agent of Ms. Muhs, which obligated Ms. Muhs to be personally liable as a surety to the L.L.C.'s loan. Ms. Muhs' commercial guaranty stated that Mr. Muhs signed on behalf of Ms. Muhs "by virtue of a power of attorney dated September 28, 2009."

By his signatures, Mr. Muhs bound the L.L.C. to make regular payments on this loan starting on October 30, 2009. There is no indication in the record that the L.L.C. failed to abide by the loan's terms during the first two years of its effect. However, from October 31, 2011 onwards, the L.L.C. failed to make payments on the loan and the Bank placed the L.L.C. in default.

On May 29, 2012, the Bank filed suit against the L.L.C., Mr. Muhs, and Ms. Muhs. In this suit, the Bank alleged that these defendants were liable to it for: the principal amount of the loan; accrued interest on the loan; late fees; and attorney's fees with legal interest.

On January 22, 2013, the Bank moved for summary judgment against defendants. The parties argued this motion through memoranda with attached exhibits and at a hearing on March 27, 2013. In opposition to summary judgment, defendants argued that Ms. Muhs was not personally liable for the L.L.C.'s loan because she had not validly authorized Mr. Muhs to bind her as a personal surety on the loan.

On April 18, 2013, the trial court granted summary judgment in favor of the Bank. The court found defendants liable for: the loan's principal amount of \$130,502.95; accrued interest of \$10,527.20 as of January 14, 2013; a per diem of \$22.35 for each day thereafter; attorney fees in the amount of 5% of the loan's principal balance; and the costs of these proceedings.

Thereafter, Ms. Muhs moved for a devolutive appeal. The trial court granted Ms. Muhs' appeal on June 24, 2013. Neither the L.L.C. nor Mr. Muhs appealed the trial court's April 18, 2013, judgment against them.

DISCUSSION

In her sole assignment of error, Ms. Muhs argues the trial court erred in finding her personally liable for the L.L.C.'s debt to the Bank and in granting summary judgment in the Bank's favor. Ms. Muhs contends that she is free from this liability because she did not authorize Mr. Muhs to execute the "commercial guaranty" on her behalf. While Ms. Muhs does not deny that she and Mr. Muhs signed the above referenced power of attorney document, she asserts that the power of attorney document gave Mr. Muhs authority to act as her agent in her capacity as a member of the L.L.C., but not in her personal and individual capacity. We disagree. . . .

In the above referenced "power of attorney dated in September 28, 2009," Mr. and Ms. Muhs described themselves as residents "of the full age of majority of . . . North Carolina." Ms. Muhs then appointed Mr. Muhs to be her "agent and attorney-in-fact" and gave Mr. Muhs the following powers to act:

> [Mr. Muhs may] act for [Ms. Muhs] in connection with a loan transaction with Gulf Coast Bank & Trust Company and to execute any and all documents necessary to consummate said loan transaction.
>
> [Ms. Muhs] . . . does hereby authorize [Mr. Muhs] to incorporate in said instruments such terms, conditions and agreements as said agent shall deem necessary and proper in his own sole discretion, to sign all papers, documents and acts necessary in order to complete the herein above described transaction, and to do any and all things [Mr. Muhs], in her [sic] sole discretion, deems necessary and proper in connection therewith.
>
> [Ms. Muhs] does further . . . give and grant [Mr. Muhs] complete power to perform any and all acts necessary and proper in the premises as fully as [Ms. Muhs] could do if she were personally present and acting for herself.

This power of attorney did not reference the L.L.C.

To resolve Ms. Muhs' assignment of error, we must determine whether the power of attorney executed by the Muhses validly gave Mr. Muhs authority to bind Ms. Muhs, in her personal capacity, as a guarantor of the L.L.C.'s loan. To answer this question, we first look to the relevant Civil Code articles governing mandate.

The power of attorney at issue is a contract of mandate governed by the provisions of the Louisiana Civil Code, articles 2989 *et seq*. Under our Civil Code, a general mandate may confer authority to do whatever is appropriate under the circumstances. Acts that are incidental or necessary for the performance of the general mandate need not be specified. La. C.C. art. 2995. However, in articles 2996 and 2997, the Civil Code sets forth those instances in which authority of an agent to act on behalf of the principal must be specifically described or "express." Under Article 2997, authority to "(3) Contract a loan, acknowledge or make remission of a debt, or become a surety" must be given expressly.

Furthermore, while a contract of mandate is not generally required to be in any particular form, when the law prescribes a certain form for an act, a mandate authorizing the act must be in that form. La. C.C. art. 2993. Here, the act in question is a suretyship agreement and the law prescribes that a "suretyship must be express and in writing." La. C.C. art. 3038. Therefore, in order to be valid, Mr. Muhs' mandate contract must be in writing and expressly give him authority to bind Ms. Muhs as a surety to the L.L.C.'s loan. We find that both requirements are met in this case.

The power of attorney at issue here was written, witnessed, and signed by both the principal, Ms. Muhs, and the mandatary, Mr. Muhs. Furthermore, the power of attorney expressly gives Mr. Muhs authority to act as her agent in connection with "a loan transaction" with the Bank "and to execute any and all documents necessary to consummate said loan transaction." Ms. Muhs gave Mr. Muhs this authority to act "as fully" as she could "if she were personally present and acting for herself." Importantly, this power of attorney did not limit Mr. Muhs to acting for Ms. Muhs in her capacity as a member of the L.L.C. Instead, the power of attorney authorizes Mr. Muhs to perform any "any and all acts necessary and proper . . . as fully as [Ms. Muhs] could do if she were personally present and acting for herself." Most particularly, the words "for herself" authorize Mr. Muhs to bind Ms. Muhs personally, not merely in her capacity as a member of the L.L.C.

Ms. Muhs argues that under persuasive authority of the case *In re Succession of Aucoin*, 99–2171 (La. App. 1 Cir. 11/8/00), 771 So. 2d 286, this Court should find that the power of attorney contract at issue in this case did not meet the requirement that authority to bind a person as a surety must be expressly given. We again disagree. In *Aucoin*, the First Circuit was faced with the question of whether a wife, by a power of attorney, gave her husband the legal authority to donate her immovable property. Id. at 287. The Court correctly recognized that this is another situation where a contract of mandate must expressly give the mandatary authority to donate immovable property in order for the mandatary to have that authority. Id. at 288 (citing La. C.C. arts. 2996 and 2997). The court then went on to analyze the contract of mandate in question. It determined that, while the contract did provide the husband-mandatary with "general authority" over the principal-wife's affairs, it did not expressly give the husband-mandatary the authority to donate the wife-principal's immovable property. Id. The court therefore concluded that the husband-mandatary did not have the legal authority to donate the wife-principal's immovable property. Id.

After studying *Aucoin*, we find that it is distinguishable from this case. The power of attorney at issue in *Aucoin* was a general grant of authority executed over four years before the transaction in question. In contrast, in the present case, the power of attorney is a limited grant of authority to Mr. Muhs to act "in connection with a loan transaction" with the Bank executed only two days before Mr. Muhs bound Ms. Muhs as a surety on the loan to the L.L.C.

Furthermore, we recognize that under Civil Code article 3021, "[o]ne who causes a third person to believe that another person is his mandatary is bound to the third person who in good faith contracts with the putative mandatary." In the circumstances of this case, even if we were to find that the mandate contract did not expressly give Mr. Muhs the authority to bind Ms. Muhs as a surety for this loan, we would find that Ms. Muhs' act of executing this particular power of attorney caused the Bank to believe that Mr. Muhs was her mandatary for this purpose and contract with him as such. Therefore, even if we were to find that Ms. Muhs did not give the express authority in question here, we would still find that the trial court's judgment finding her liable in the stated amounts was correct.

Considering the above, we find that the particular power of attorney executed by Mr. and Ms. Muhs expressly gave Mr. Muhs the power to bind Ms. Muhs as a surety to the LLC's loan. The trial court correctly granted the Bank's motion for summary judgment and ordered the defendants to pay amounts in accordance with the terms of the loan.

CONCLUSION

Based on the foregoing, the judgment appealed from is affirmed. All costs of this appeal are assessed to appellants. Affirmed.

* * * * * *

C. Interpretation—Surety Acting as an Ostensible Principal

***See* La. Civ. Code art. 3037**

What often makes suretyship difficult to discern are those instances where all parties around the closing table understand and appreciate that one of them is entering the transaction as merely a surety, even though the way in which the transaction is put down on paper makes it appear as though such person is acting as a co-obligor. The question that likely immediately comes to mind is why anyone would do such a thing, rather than just making it clear that this person is a surety and not signing the documents as, for instance, a co-borrower. The reason for this is often convenience. In many small-value transactions it is not economically feasible to redraft documents or hire a lawyer each time. Therefore, a form or template contract may be used whereby there are two lines for the "borrower." The true borrower signs on one, and then the person everyone appreciates to be acting as surety signs on the other. The law, rather than treating the second co-borrower as a true borrower, treats the party as what he really is (substance over form) and deems him to be a surety as against a creditor who "clearly knows" the true relationship of the surety and his principal obligor. This concept is called ostensible suretyship. It is rare that such situations come up in commercial deals, but they are quite common in consumer transactions.

Consider the following hypothetical to better understand how such transactions occur in everyday life.

HYPOTHETICAL

(from La. Civ. Code art. 3037 revision comment (c))

A and B purchase an automobile from C, agreeing to be solidarily bound for the price. The car is obtained exclusively for A, with B joining in the transaction only to lend his credit to it. C, in ignorance of their relationship accepts half of the price from A and gives him a release. He may still hold B for one-half of the debt. If, however, A initially approaches C to purchase the vehicle and C requires him to obtain B as a "co-maker" because of A's weak credit rating, C is entitled to treat A as a principal and B as a surety, even though A and B sign the contract of sale as "co-purchasers" solidarily bound for the price.

D. Parol Evidence Implications

***See* La. Civ. Code arts. 1848-1849**

Few things confuse law students enrolled in this course more than the strange rules and nuances that govern the interaction between the requirements of suretyship on the one hand and the parol evidence rule on the other. The question essentially comes down to this: To what extent can parol evidence (i.e., extrinsic evidence) be used either to prove that a valid suretyship contract exists or to contradict the contents of a suretyship agreement that is otherwise foundationally valid?

1. To Vary the Scope of the Surety's Liability

The interaction between parol evidence and suretyship arises in a host of situations and in a number of important cases. Consider the following facts taken from *First Acadiana Bank v. Bollich*, 532 So. 2d 248 (La. App. 3d Cir. 1988):

First Acadiana Bank (hereinafter plaintiff) filed suit against Donald J. Bollich (hereinafter defendant) to recover $20,000.00 allegedly owed to plaintiff as a result of defendant's continuing guaranty agreement given on behalf of his son, David Bollich (hereinafter David). Defendant's son, David, sought a loan from plaintiff and was advised that, because he was extended financially, a cosigner would be necessary to secure the requested $20,000.00 loan. Defendant signed what he thought was a document that made him a cosigner for his son's $20,000.00 loan, when in fact the document he signed was a continuing guaranty agreement for up to $20,000.00 for any of his son's obligations to plaintiff. David borrowed $20,000.00 and repaid it, but later defaulted on other loans totaling in excess of $20,000.00 and was adjudicated bankrupt. After the son's default, plaintiff contacted defendant and demanded that he make good on his continuing guaranty agreement on behalf of David. Defendant denied liability claiming that he was in error in signing the continuing guaranty agreement. Plaintiff filed suit against defendant on his continuing guaranty agreement. Defendant filed a general denial and an affirmative defense of error in signing the continuing guaranty agreement document. After a trial on the merits the trial judge rendered judgment dismissing plaintiff's suit.

* * * * * *

NOTES AND QUESTIONS

The third circuit affirmed the trial court's judgment. Do you believe the court of appeal's affirmance was correct? Does it violate La. Civ. Code art. 3038? Does it violate La. Civ. Code arts. 1848-1849? Consider the arguments made by Mr. Rubin in the following excerpt from "Ruminations on Suretyship."

* * * * * *

Ruminations on Suretyship

Michael H. Rubin

57 LOUISIANA LAW REVIEW 565, 573-590 (1997)

A. THE CREDITOR-SURETY RELATIONSHIP—NO PAROL EVIDENCE SHOULD BE ADMISSIBLE

There are three instances in which parties may wish to use oral testimony in connection with a suretyship agreement. The first is where the creditor wishes to delineate the surety's responsibility. The second is where the surety wishes to limit liability. The third is where one surety seeks to clarify his or her rights as against another surety. The Civil Code is clear; parol evidence is inadmissible in a creditor-surety relationship, but is admissible in a surety-surety relationship. Laws enacted for public order and the public interest may not be altered by a contract; any attempted alterations are "an absolute nullity." Unambiguous laws must be applied as written. There is no ambiguity in the Civil Code concerning the requirements of a written contract between the creditor and the surety in order to enforce a suretyship obligation.

The requirement that the relationship between the creditor and the surety be in writing is a rule of a public order that should not be susceptible of variance.

The rationale that underlies the mandate of a written, express agreement is, in the words of Planiol, "because of the seriousness of the surety's engagements." Because suretyship is unilateral and because the acceptance of the surety's offer to be bound is presumed without further action by the creditor, the Civil Code provides no exception for the writing requirement; likewise, there is no rule in the Civil Code that allows parol evidence to "explain" the extent of the surety's engagement, whether the explanation is offered by the creditor or the debtor.

Prior to the 1987 revisions to the Civil Code articles on suretyship, some cases had made a distinction between "gratuitous" sureties and "compensated" sureties; the former received more lenient treatment by the courts and were more likely to have the suretyship contract read in their favor while the latter were subjected to a reading of the contract in favor of the creditor. Now, however, the Code's requirements are unequivocal; sureties are bound solely by virtue of the language of their written contract.

The Civil Code does allow the parties to limit a suretyship agreement. Civil Code article 3040 allows suretyship to be "qualified, conditioned, or limited in any lawful manner." Therefore, the parties may make the suretyship contract less broad than the principal obligation, but the limitations of the surety's obligation must be express. The Official Law Institute Revision Comments describe this as an "imperative requirement" in other words, a Civil Code requirement that may not be altered by the parties.

One of the "imperative requirements" that the Law Institute lists in its Revision Comments is the express, written suretyship agreement rule. Civil Code article 1848 provides: "testimonial or other evidence may not be admitted to negate any vary the contents of . . . an act under private signature." The only exception is to prove error, fraud, or duress. Modification of a suretyship contract cannot be proven through oral testimony because a contract of suretyship only exists in writing and therefore any modification must be in writing.

Under the Civil Code, a creditor is prohibited from using parol evidence to alter what the written contract describes as the surety's obligation. Likewise, it follows that a surety is prohibited from using parol evidence to alter what the written contract describes as the surety's obligation to the creditor.

Lower Louisiana courts that have looked at the issue and that have allowed some form of oral testimony on the scope of the surety-creditor relationship have not squarely addressed the public policy that underlies the requirement of a written agreement between surety and creditor. In the absence of a vice of consent sufficient to vitiate a contract,[1] parol evidence should be inadmissible by either a creditor or the surety to "explain" what the suretyship contract means. Because the Civil Code requires that the suretyship be "express," if the contract is so ambiguous that it cannot be determined what obligation the surety is agreeing to pay or the extent of the obligation, there should be no suretyship at all. Although the Louisiana Supreme Court has yet to directly examine the issue, it can be anticipated that the Court will hold that a suretyship contract which is clear on its face must be enforced as written and that parol evidence is inadmissible by either the creditor or the surety to explain any aspect of the contract.[2]

---

[1] If a purported surety thought that he or she was signing a receipt rather than a contract of suretyship, this error goes to the cause of the agreement, could be found to vitiate the consent, and would render the purported suretyship unenforceable. *See* La. Civ. Code arts. 1949, 1950. If fraud is involved in misrepresenting to the signer of a document what is being executed, the signer could allege a vice of consent. *See* La. Civ. Code arts. 1953-1958. Fraud may be difficult to prove in many instances where the surety is capable of reading and understanding the written agreement and signs it knowing it is a contract of suretyship. A surety who merely misconstrues the wording of the contract as opposed to being misled as to the type of contract being entered into should not be able to claim a vice of consent, because fraud may not be claimed when the person could have ascertained the truth of the document "without difficulty, inconvenience, or special skills." La. Civ. Code art. 1954.

[2] It is submitted that the correct result is reached in *Pat S. Todd Oil Co., Inc. v. Wall,* 581 So. 2d 333 (La. App. 3d Cir.), *writ denied,* 585 So. 2d 569 (1991). There, guarantors argued that a continuing guaranty which, on its face, was unlimited should in fact be restricted to secure only one debt through the use of parol evidence. The Court held the parol evidence was not admissible to vary the terms of the contract. Id. at 336. Compare the holding in *Wall* with *First Acadiana Bank v. Bollich,* 532 So. 2d 248 (La. App. 3d Cir. 1988), which held that a surety could limit his liability under a suretyship agreement through the use of parol evidence. It is questionable whether the holding in *Bollich* is an accurate depiction of the Code requirements and, in addition, it is unclear from the appellate opinion whether counsel objected to the parol

B. THE CREDITOR-DEBTOR RELATIONSHIP—USE OF PAROL EVIDENCE

While oral testimony should be inadmissible between creditor and surety to either expand or limit the surety's obligation beyond that which is express in the written suretyship contract, parol evidence is permitted in the three other instances: in the creditor-debtor relationship, in the surety-surety relationship; and in the surety-debtor relationship.

The creditor-debtor relationship need not be in writing. The Civil Code rules of suretyship concern an express written obligation only between the surety and the creditor. Because suretyship may secure any lawful obligation, the general Civil Code obligation articles control the enforceability of the principal relationship between the creditor and the debtor.

Although the burden of proof of an obligation is upon the party seeking to enforce it, only those contracts required by law to be in written form must be in writing; all other contracts may be oral and proved by parol and other evidence. Louisiana courts have had no problem in finding that although a suretyship must be in writing, the principal obligation need not be.

C. THE SURETY-SURETY RELATIONSHIP—USE OF PAROL EVIDENCE

A surety's relationship with other sureties, particularly in the areas of virile share allocation and contribution rights, may be shown through oral testimony. While the surety's contract with the creditor must be in writing and the surety's obligation to the creditor is controlled by the writing, as among the sureties they are only "presumed to share the burden of the principal obligation in proportion to their number unless the parties agreed otherwise." Although co-sureties no longer may use the plea of "division" to limit their liability to the creditor, they may use parol evidence among themselves to demonstrate the extent of virile share liability. The Law Institute Comments to Civil Code article 3055 are clear on this point.

---

evidence at the trial court level. For a critique of *Bollich*, *see* Michael H. Rubin, *Ruminations on Security Devices*, 56 La. L. Rev. 641, 653-54 (1996).

D. THE DEBTOR-SURETY RELATIONSHIP—USE OF PAROL EVIDENCE

When the surety is a commercial bonding company, the surety not only enters into a written agreement with the creditor, but also usually enters into a written agreement with the debtor covering such matters as repayment and additional security for the surety. Many times, however, those who sign "continuing guarantee" agreements with a creditor seldom have a written agreement with the debtor.

There is nothing in the Civil Code that requires the debtor-suretyship relationship to be evidenced by a written instrument, and thus there is nothing that prohibits a debtor and surety from using parol evidence against each other to prove the nature of their relationship, the scope of their relationship, or the terms of their relationship.

E. SUMMARY ON PAROL EVIDENCE AND SURETYSHIP

When the debtor is a closely held business entity, with only one or a few owners, negotiations were ongoing between a creditor and one already bound as a surety, a creditor or surety may later seek to offer parol evidence to vary the terms of the written agreement. [I]t is often tempting for the creditor to attempt to use oral testimony to make the owner pay for the business entity's debt. Likewise, when cases that might be cited in support of these temptations, it is submitted that such cases should not be followed. It is suggested that the confusion in the lower courts' jurisprudence results from a failure to adequately analyze the four differing relationships that are involved in any suretyship agreement: creditor-debtor, creditor-surety, surety-debtor, and surety-surety. In creditor-surety relationships, parol evidence is inadmissible in any form, because, as noted above, the Civil Code expressly mandates, as an "imperative requirement," that the creditor-suretyship agreement must in writing, must be express, and no variation is permitted except in writing. On the other hand, all of the other three relationships (creditor-debtor, debtor-surety, and surety-surety) are susceptible of proof and modification through oral testimony.

* * * * * *

2. To Resolve Ambiguity as to the Signatory's Personal Liability

***See* La. Civ. Code arts. 2989; 2993; 2996-2997**

As noted above, lawyers are not intimately involved in most legal transactions, even when the parties are somewhat sophisticated and the amount involved in the transaction is significant. As a result, parties often end up entering deals that are not well "papered" (meaning the contract is not clear or not necessarily indicative of what was agreed to). Consequently, parties to the transaction may find themselves in court at a later date arguing over what exactly they agreed to do. When suretyship is involved, as in the case that follows, the issue of parol evidence often comes up.

* * * * * *

VETERANS COMMERCIAL PROPERTIES, LLC v. BARRY'S FLOORING, INC.
67 So. 3d 627 (La. App. 5th Cir. 2011)

FACTS

Barry's Flooring signed a lease with Veterans. The lease had a guarantee provision that Barry's owner, Barry W. Wilbert, signed, but he had written "Barry's Flooring" near his signature in the guarantee section. The lease was signed by Ray Peacock representing the lessor, 3848 Veterans BLVD, LLC, and by Barry M. Wilbert representing the lessee, Barry's Flooring, Inc. Mr. Wilbert also signed the following continuing guaranty:

> For value received and to induce the granting of the above lease, the undersigned make themselves party to this lease and bind themselves in solido with Tenant for the faithful execution of and compliance with all of the obligations, conditions and stipulations assumed or agreed to by Tenant, guaranteeing to Lessor, its successors and assigns, the payment of the rent and all other sums provided for in the above lease and the performance by Tenant of the covenants therein contained without requiring any notice of non-payment, demand, dishonor or non-performance.
>
> This 23 day of October, 2007
> /s/Barry's Flooring

/s/Barry M. Wilbert
Barry's Flooring

. . .

FREDERICKA HOMBERG WICKER, Judge.

In its sole assignment of error, Veteran's contends that the trial court erred in finding that Mr. Wilbert did not act in his personal capacity as a surety for Barry's Flooring when he signed the lease agreement.

A contract of guaranty is equivalent to a contract of suretyship, and the two terms may be used interchangeably. *Keller Indus., Inc. v. Deauville Consultants, Inc.*, 459 So. 2d 636, 638 (La. App. 5 Cir. 1984). Although a surety's contract need not observe technical formalities, it must contain an absolute expression of an intent to be bound. Id. citing *Ball Mktg. Enter. v. Rainbow Tomato Co.*, 340 So. 2d 700 (La. App. 3 Cir. 1976). It is an accessory promise by which one binds himself for another already bound and agrees with the creditor to satisfy the obligation if the principal debtor does not do so. Id. (citation omitted). An agreement of suretyship must be express and in writing and must be explicit. Id. (citation omitted).

excellent rule statement

Contracts of guaranty are subject to the same rules of interpretation as contracts in general. *Custom–Bilt Cabinet & Supply, Inc. v. Quality Built Cabinets, Inc.*, 32–441, p. 4 (La. App. 2 Cir. 12/8/99), 748 So. 2d 594, 598. "The courts are bound to give legal effect to all written contracts according to the true intent of the parties and this intent is to be determined by the words of the contract when these are clear, explicit and lead to no absurd consequences." Id. The meaning and intent of the parties to the written contract in such cases must be sought within the four corners of the instrument and cannot be explained or contradicted by parol evidence. Id. The determination of whether a contract is clear or ambiguous is a question of law. Id. at 599. (citation omitted). . . .

In this case, the first set of signatures by Ray Peacock and Barry's Flooring consummate the lease agreement that existed between 3848 Veterans BLVD, LLC and Barry's Flooring. Immediately following those signatures, however, is a provision which states, in pertinent part, that the undersigned "bind themselves in solido with Tenant for the faithful execution of and compliance with all of the obligations, conditions and stipulations assumed or agreed to by Tenant, guaranteeing to Lessor, its successors and assigns, the payment of the rent and all other sums. . . ."

In *Pelican Plumbing Supply, Inc. v. J.O.H. Construction Co., Inc.*, 94–991 (La. App. 5 Cir. 3/28/95), 653 So. 2d 699, we held that the defendant who signed a credit application in a similar manner as was done in the present case was not a surety. In that case, the credit application contained the following language:

> In consideration of an open account privilege, I hereby understand and agree to the above terms. Should it become necessary to place this account for collection, I shall personally obligate myself and my corporation, if any, to pay the entire amount due including service charges (as outlined above terms) thirty-three and one third (33 1/3%) attorney's fees, and all costs of collection, including court costs.
>
> SIGNED Harold H. Heidingsfelder
> COMPANY J.O.H. Const. Co., Inc.

Although the above language more expressly depicts the creation of a suretyship than the language in the present case, the defendant in *Pelican Plumbing*, signed the credit application just as Mr. Wilbert did here with both his name and the name of the company he represented. In *Pelican Plumbing*, however, we deferred to the trial court's credibility determination and found that the defendant did not intend to sign in his personal capacity. In that case, the trial court used parol evidence—Mr. Heidingsfelder's testimony—to ascertain his true intent. And we found that the trial court was not manifestly erroneous in doing so. In this case, however, there are no Reasons for Judgment or a transcript from the trial on the merits that would indicate parol evidence was considered in the trial court's determination.

In *American Bank & Trust Company of Houma v. Wetland Workover, Inc.* 523 So.2d 942, 945 (La. App. 4 Cir. 1988), however, the fourth circuit held that to construe that the guarantors executed the guarantees in a representative capacity would render the documents meaningless. In that case, the defendant signed a continuing guaranty in favor of American Bank & Trust. The defendant argued, however, that his signature was affixed to the document in a representative capacity for Wetland Workover because his signature was accompanied by his title—vice-president. The fourth circuit found that under the terms of the mortgage, "Wetland was already bound to pay back the loan proceeds. If the guarantors had signed guarantees in a representative capacity for Wetland, the corporation would be guaranteeing an obligation for which it was already bound, rendering the guarantees worthless." Id. at 945 (citation omitted). (See also, *McKesson Chemical Co., Inc. v. Tideland Chemical Co., Inc.*, 471 So. 2d 812 (La. App. 3 Cir. 1985); *American Cas. Co. v. Howard*, 175 So. 2d 355 (La. App. 4 Cir. 1965)).

We find that the present case is more in line with *American Bank & Trust*, supra. This finding, however, does not overrule our decision in *Pelican Plumbing*, supra, as that case turned on a different issue.

The clear and unambiguous language in this case states that the undersigned guarantees payment of the tenant's obligation to the lessor. This language is immediately followed by the signatures of Barry's Flooring and Barry M. Wilbert. However, the capacity in which a party executes a document is largely a matter of that party's intention as determined from the circumstances surrounding the transaction. *American Bank & Trust*, supra, at 945. Considering the entirety of the lease agreement, the fact that Mr. Wilbert made a handwritten notation of Barry's Flooring above his signature does not obviate the fact that the clear and unambiguous language created a suretyship agreement in which Mr. Wilbert personally guaranteed Barry's Flooring's obligation to the lessor. The notation of a corporate position, or in this case, the notation of the company's name, "is merely a title identification instead of a signature in a representative capacity." Id. To construe otherwise would render the guaranty worthless as Barry's Flooring was already obligated to abide by the terms of the agreement.

In sum, we find that the trial judge erred in finding that Mr. Wilbert did not act as surety in his personal capacity to the agreement that existed between 3848 Veterans BLVD, LLC and Barry's Flooring. Accordingly, that portion of the judgment is reversed. Reversed.

* * * * * *

NOTES AND QUESTIONS

An interesting question that often arises in the context of suretyship is whether parol evidence can be used to show representative capacity. The fifth circuit's 2011 *Veterans* decision distinguishes its 1995 decision in *Pelican Plumbing Supply, Inc. v. J.O.H. Construction Co., Inc.,* 653 So. 2d 699 (La. App. 5th Cir. 1995). In *Pelican Plumbing,* the fifth circuit affirmed the trial court's ruling that the vice president of the principal obligor did not intend to sign the credit agreement in his personal capacity. In the fifth circuit's most recent decision on this issue, *Dror International, LP v. Thundervision LLC,* 84 So. 3d 560 (La. App. 5th Cir. 2011). the president of the principal obligor, a limited liability company, signed an "Individual and Personal Guaranty" without any reference that he was signing it in his representative capacity. Although the fifth circuit in *Dror* did not cite *Veterans,* the *Dror* decision reached an identical result. In his "2012 Current Developments in Security Rights" materials, Mr. Rubin poses the following question:

> Was *Pelican Plumbing* correctly decided initially? C.C. art. 1847 states that parol evidence is "inadmissible to . . . a promise to pay the debt of a third person." While C.C. art. 1848 allows parol evidence in certain circumstances, is it really applicable to change C.C. art. 1847's absolute "no parol" rule? The Supreme Court has not yet spoken on this issue in the context of continuing guarantees.

Consider also the following excerpt from Professors Morris and Holmes's treatise on Business Organizations:

> Undisclosed agency theory, properly understood, poses risks of liability only for those shareholders who involve themselves personally in negotiating contracts on behalf of their corporation, and only with respect to those particular transactions in which disclosure or notice about the agency has not been adequate. . . . "Undisclosed" agency may be something of a misnomer, for while express disclosure is certainly sufficient to preclude this sort of liability, actual disclosure by the agent is probably not necessary. If, under the circumstances, a third party already knows, or should know, the things that disclosure would tell him, then the pre-1998 jurisprudence held that actual, express disclosure was not required. It is not clear whether this

jurisprudential rule is still good law, for the current Civil Code provision on the subject say nothing about it. Current art. 3017 says simply that "a mandatary who contracts in his own name without disclosing his status as a mandatary binds himself personally for the performance of the contract."

It seems unlikely that the legislature really meant to change the law on this subject, however. No reason would exist to grant a third party a windfall claim against an agent whom the third party knew was contracting as agent on behalf of someone else, merely because the third party's knowledge on the subject came from some source other than the agent himself. The point of the disclosure rule is to allocate the risk of a misunderstanding between the parties about the identity of the persons bound by the contract. An agent who fails to disclose takes the risk that he may be held personally liable if the other party believes reasonably that the agent is contracting for himself personally. The agent should not be held liable if no misunderstanding occurs.

Now more than ever, express disclosure of agency is the best policy from a planning standpoint. It is the agent who bears the burden of proof on the disclosure issue, and purely circumstantial notice to the third party is difficult to prove. When defendants are forced to fall back on an argument that "I didn't tell him but he must have known," their positions are usually weak; sometimes they do win, but more frequently they lose.

See Glenn G. Morris & Wendell H. Holmes, *Business Organizations* § 33.8 in 4 La. Civil Law Treatise Series (2012 ed.).

E. Effects

The contract of suretyship creates a number of relationships and therefore produces a number of effects. At a minimum there are three parties involved in every suretyship: the surety, the principal obligor, and the obligee. Every suretyship thus involves at least three legal relationships. First there is the relationship between the principal obligor and the obligee. This relationship forms the basis of the suretyship transaction because it is through the dealings of the principal obligor and the obligee that the principal obligation arises, without which no security right can exist. Then there is the relationship between the surety and the obligee that is created by the suretyship agreement. Finally there is the relationship between the surety and the principal obligor.

This tri-party state of affairs has a number of implications. As for the relationship between the principal obligor and the obligee, the rights and duties created by this relationship are governed by the law of obligations and are not implicated by security devices principles. Accordingly, the relationship between the principal obligor and the obligee will not be discussed in this chapter.

The rights and duties created by the relationships between the surety and the obligee and between the surety and the principal obligor are governed both by the law of obligations and by suretyship law. Finally, if there are two or more sureties for the same principal obligation, legal relationships exist among the sureties. These relationships are also governed by obligations law and by suretyship law. The following sections discuss all of these relationships (except the relationship between the principal obligor and the obligee) and explore the contours of the rights and duties that the law imposes on each of the parties.

1. Surety–Obligee Relationship

***See* La. Civ. Code arts. 3045-3046**

The first relationship to be considered is that between the surety and the person to whom he owes performance—the obligee. The surety's duty is to perform in the event the obligor does not, but it would be wrong to say that the law furnishes the surety no rights to go along with this duty. Consider the following provisions from the Louisiana State Law Institute's *Exposé des Motifs* explaining some of the rationales behind various changes to the law of suretyship that the institute recommended to the legislature during its revision of this area of the law in 1987.

* * * * * *

Exposé des Motifs: Suretyship
Elimination of Division and Discussion
Louisiana State Law Institute

Because of the supposed harshness of suretyship the Romans gave the surety a right of discussion, permitting him to demand that the creditor first pursue the principal debtor if the latter had property from which the debt could be satisfied. For similar reasons several sureties were given the right of division which required the creditor to divide the liability for the debt among those sureties who were solvent at the time they were sued and claimed the right.

Discussion and division proved to be thoroughly unsatisfactory to surety and creditor alike and almost from the beginning they have been routinely waived in contracts of suretyship. This revision eliminates both as suppletive provisions of the contract for reasons that are amplified below.

1. The Right of Discussion

Creditors who require sureties for their debtor generally do so to avoid the uncertainties of default and litigation. A creditor ordinarily wants payment, not problems, and expects the surety to perform the obligation he has guaranteed at the time and in the manner agreed to by the debtor, if the latter does not. Furthermore, the right can easily become an instrument of delay, rather than one of assurance. Discussion requires the surety to point out unencumbered property of the debtor that may be seized in an amount adequate to satisfy the debt and to advance the funds necessary to pursue that property. It is unlikely that a debtor will actually possess such assets after a default. If he does have any assets, the surety may delay his performance without having to deny his liability, by requiring the creditor to litigate whether the assets are in fact unencumbered or whether their value is sufficient to satisfy the debt. Since the law gives the surety an independent right to sue the principal debtor for protection the moment the debt becomes due and since the right of discussion requires him to bear the cost of his creditor's action against the debtor, there is little social utility in requiring the parties to litigate who will pursue the debtor. The creditor may always give the surety time to perform if he so desires. He is, however, unlikely to commit himself to the kind of indefinite extension implicit in the plea of discussion at the time the parties are negotiating the terms of the credit. In cases where the creditor will agree to pursue the debtor before calling upon the surety for payment, the parties usually agree upon terms more reasonable and liberal to the surety than those provided by the right of discussion. Consequently, the right has never served a useful purpose.

2. Division

The right of division has proven to be as unsatisfactory to both parties as the right of discussion. Division permits a surety who is sued by the creditor to require the creditor to divide his claim equally among all sureties who are solvent and bound upon their contracts when the surety claims the right. Under existing law, however, the creditor may release one or more ordinary sureties before the right of division is claimed without affecting the liability of those who remain. Furthermore, if a surety becomes insolvent before the right is claimed his share must be borne by the others.

Creditors ordinarily expect each surety to stand for the entire debt. If a creditor is willing to accept joint or limited liability from several sureties, the sureties, rather than relying upon the plea of division, ordinarily will limit their guarantees to a fraction or portion of the debt. This effectively frees the surety from the possibility that the other sureties will be released or become insolvent and thereby impose additional responsibility upon him, as is the case if the right of division alone is relied upon.

In last analysis, unless particular suppletive provisions are intended to advance some substantial public policy, they should reflect the customary or prevailing expectations of the majority of the parties to the contract they regulate. The persistent and universal waiver of the rights of discussion and division over the last one hundred seventy-five years provides reason enough for their suppression as presumptive, albeit optional, provisions of suretyships.

* * * * * *

2. Surety–Principal Obligor Relationship

***See* La. Civ. Code arts. 3047-3054**

The next relationship, and one that is particularly important to the surety, is that between the surety and the principal obligor. It is the surety who is agreeing to perform in favor of the obligee in the event the obligor does not.

But make no mistake: It is always contemplated that the person on whom the law imposes ultimate liability is the principal obligor. Therefore, the surety has a number of rights (and duties) when it comes to the person on whose behalf he promises to perform. The following excerpt from Michael Rubin's seminal law review article on suretyship illuminates this relationship.

* * * * * *

Ruminations on Suretyship

Michael H. Rubin

57 Louisiana Law Review 565, 587-590 (1997).

A. THE RIGHT OF SUBROGATION

The Civil Code grants a surety who pays the principal obligation two separate sets of claims against the debtor: legal subrogation and the right of reimbursement. The Civil Code also gives the surety an additional claim that is not necessarily dependent upon payment—the right to obtain security from the obligor.

The right of legal subrogation exists under Civil Code article 1829 when a person pays a debt "he owes . . . for others"; this aptly describes a surety's obligation. The surety obtains through legal subrogation the creditor's rights against the debtor on the principal obligation. Because subrogation occurs by operation of law, no special language is needed to grant subrogation and no contractual act of subrogation is required. Indeed, the Civil Code prohibits one who benefits from legal subrogation from obtaining an additional benefit through conventional subrogation. Because a surety is entitled to legal subrogation and cannot get more through conventional subrogation, a surety can only collect the amounts that the surety has paid to the creditor. A surety cannot attempt to "purchase" the principal obligation at a discount or have it "assigned" to him for a partial payment and then seek to collect the full amount of the principal obligation from the debtor. The Civil Code obligation articles and suretyship articles prevail and prevent the surety from bettering his position. This rule is just because the surety's contract is accessory to the principal obligation, and the surety should not be able to achieve a windfall through clever bargaining with the creditor.

An exception to the rule that a surety may not collect more than a surety has paid involves attorney's fees. If the principal obligation provides for attorney's fees and interest, then the surety may collect "such attorney's fees and interest as are owed with respect to the principal obligation" although the surety has paid less for the full amount of the principal obligation.

If a debtor had a valid defense against the creditor, the debtor may assert that defense against the surety who is suing through subrogation.

B. THE RIGHT OF REIMBURSEMENT

A surety who pays the creditor without asking the debtor about the legal enforceability of the debt proceeds at his peril in subrogation, because the surety may find that when it comes time to sue the debtor, the debtor has a valid defense to the debt. The Civil Code addresses this situation and allows the surety the right to collect from the debtor, despite the existence of a defense to the principal obligation, if the debtor knew of the forthcoming payment and did not advise the surety of the defense. Practically, the surety should notify the debtor prior to payment to preserve this claim, and cautious sureties' counsel should contact the debtor, usually in writing prior to payment, to inquire whether there is a defense, and to state that payment will be made within a certain period of time if the surety is not notified of a legal defense. When such actions are taken and the debtor does not act to notify the surety of a valid defense to the principal obligation, the surety who pays may collect from the debtor although the debtor might have had a valid defense against the creditor.

The right of the surety to collect from the debtor if the debtor had prior notice of payment and did not object is through an action for reimbursement, not through subrogation. Subrogation is the substitution "of one person to the rights of another." Reimbursement is not dependent upon the creditor's rights against the surety but, rather, upon the surety's relationship with the debtor. Thus, the right of reimbursement is a separate claim against the debtor.

In some instances, the surety-debtor relationship is evidenced by a written act, as in the case of legal bonds where the debtor enters into an agreement with the surety and pays a premium. In the absence of a written contract, the surety-debtor relationship is controlled by operation of law. Whether the surety-debtor relationship is written or merely legal, the surety always has the right of reimbursement; however, the right of reimbursement is limited to those instances where the surety has paid the creditor after notification to the debtor and the debtor did not prevent the surety from paying by apprising the surety of a defense.

If the surety pays the creditor without notifying the debtor, and if the debtor has a defense, then the surety may not obtain payment from the debtor, but the surety is not without recourse. "In these circumstances, the surety may recover from the creditor." The concept that underlies the surety's right to collect from the creditor is the actio de in rem verso, the right to collect for payment of a thing not due.

C. THE RIGHT TO REQUIRE SECURITY

In addition to subrogation and reimbursement, the third effect of the relationship between surety and debtor is the surety's right to require security. The security that the surety obtains is to secure the surety's right of reimbursement (the surety-debtor relationship) not to secure the creditor; therefore the right to obtain security has nothing to do with subrogation.

Civil Code article 3053 states that a surety may obtain security from a debtor (before making payment) in four separate instances. The four instances in which a surety may obtain security even prior to payment include: when a suit is brought by the creditor against the surety; when the principal obligor is insolvent (such as filing bankruptcy proceedings); when the principal obligor "fails to perform an act promised in return for the suretyship"; or when the principal obligation is due according to its terms and the surety has not consented to an extension of time.

The right to require security, unfortunately, may have little practical impact if the surety has not required security from the debtor at the inception of the suretyship. Articles 3053-3054 only grant the surety a right to file a lawsuit against the debtor to put up the security. The suit may be filed ten (10) days after delivery of a written demand upon the debtor. In the real world, it is unlikely that the surety who is being sued by the creditor has not already third-partied the debtor into the lawsuit. Likewise, it is a remote possibility that the debtor who has not paid the creditor, thereby necessitating some action by the surety, is in a position to give real security to the surety.

* * * * * *

3. Multiple Sureties Relationship

***See* La. Civ. Code arts. 1794; 1802-1803; 1806; 1892; 3045; 3055-3057**

So far the effects of suretyship have been presented in the context of merely three parties—a single suretyship contract and accompanying principal obligation. However, there are many times when the principal obligation is secured not by one, but by many sureties. Therefore, the law must take into account the increased complexity that is presented by there being many more parties that may be called upon to perform on behalf of the obligor, particularly when one surety completes all, some, or none of the performance required. Again, consider the following doctrinal writings on the topic.

* * * * * *

Developments In The Law 1993-1994: A Faculty Symposium: Security Devices

Michael H. Rubin & Stephen P. Strohchein

55 Louisiana Law Review 611, 653-655 (1995)

Litigation involving guarantees and suretyship has been greatly diminished since the 1988 revisions to the Louisiana Civil Code articles on suretyship. This is true partly because the confusion caused by some of the earlier jurisprudence has been abolished by Article 3037, which provides that if a creditor knows the true relationship of the parties, the creditor cannot treat someone who is "ostensibly" bound as a principal as anything other than a surety. Therefore, "solidarity" language in a continuing guaranty will not allow the creditor to treat the guarantor as a solidary obligor; rather, the rules of suretyship apply. Even among solidary obligors, rules of suretyship can apply "if the circumstances giving rise to the solidary obligation concern only one of the obligors."

Normally, the release of a surety has no impact on the principal debtor but does release the co-sureties for the right of contribution to the extent the right of contribution has been impaired. The general rules are contained in Article 1892. Remission of the debt of the principal obligor releases the surety because the principal obligation has been extinguished. On the other hand, remission of the debt to the surety does not release the principal obligor because the principal obligor at all times remains bound. Finally, remission of a debt granted to one surety "releases the other sureties only to the extent of contribution the other sureties might have recovered from the surety to whom the remission was granted." This right, however, may be waived by express language in the contract. That was the holding in *First National Bank v. Green Garden Processing Co.*, which was relied upon recently in *FDIC v. Gilbert*. If there is language in the contract in which the surety agrees to be bound, notwithstanding the release of other sureties, then a lender can settle with one surety without losing rights against another.

It is important to note the "extent of contribution" referred to in Article 1892 is not necessarily easily ascertainable. For example, assume a situation in which Debtor is the maker of a note for $120,000. There are three sureties who all signed the same continuing guaranty, S1, S2, and S3. Assume that the creditor has released S1 for $10,000. In this situation, the $10,000 would be attributed to the principal obligation ($120,000) and Debtor would still be liable for the remaining $110,000.

On the other hand, the release granted to S1 would release S2 and S3 "only to the extent of the contribution the other sureties might have recovered from the surety to whom the remission was granted." Assuming the sureties were liable for one-third each, then the release of S1 would release S1's virile share (one-third), thereby reducing the right of contribution (since the original debt was for $120,000) by that $40,000. Therefore, of the $110,000 that is outstanding now on the principal obligation ($120,000 minus the $10,000 payment), sureties S2 and S3 should be liable only for the principal obligation minus the virile share of S1, for a total of $80,000 (principal obligation of $120,000 minus the $40,000 virile share of S1). Therefore, the lender could collect $110,000 from Debtor, or $80,000 from S2, or $80,000 from S3.

On the other hand, it may be the virile share is not one-third. Under Article 3055, it is possible parol evidence could be used to show the parties were to be bound in a different fashion. Article 3055 provides:

> Co-sureties are those who are sureties for the same obligation of the same obligor. They are presumed to share the burden of the principal obligation in proportion to their number unless the parties agreed otherwise or contemplated that he who bound himself first would bear the entire burden of the obligation regardless of others who thereafter bind themselves independently of and in reliance upon the obligation of the former.

If S1 had signed the continuing guaranty at a time when he was 100% owner of Debtor and later sold a one (1%) percent stock interest to S2 and one (1%) percent stock interest to S3, both of whom were then required to sign the continuing guaranty, it might be argued S1's virile share is 98%. In such an instance, it may well be that the release of S1 for $10,000, although it has no impact on Debtor's liability (Debtor would remain liable for $110,000) would have released 98% of the obligation as to S2 and S3 because that would have been the extent of the impairment of contribution rights. This makes it important that a creditor at least get a representation from the surety being released of that surety's virile share. Even more preferable from a creditor's standpoint is to have language stating that the release of a surety or the impairment of subrogation rights does not release co-sureties at all.

* * * * * *

Comment, Please Release Me: A Comparative Study of Louisiana Suretyship Law

Nadia Nedzel

40 Loyola Law Review 955, 961-970 (1995).

A. THE EFFECTS OF REMISSION, TRANSACTION, AND COMPROMISE

The revision of Civil Code articles 3035-3070 updated Louisiana suretyship law and resolved some long standing problems. Nevertheless, article 1892 on remission of sureties and article 3076 [no current article] on transaction with a surety were not revised at that time. Although located in different sections of the Civil Code, these two articles are drafted in a parallel manner. Article 1892 provides that a creditor's grant of a remission of debt to the sureties does not release the principal obligor; however, if the remission is granted to the principal obligor, then the sureties are released. Article 3076 [no current article] states that while the creditor's transaction with the surety need not discharge the principal obligor, if the transaction is with the principal obligor himself, then "the surety will likewise have the benefit of the transaction." Because both articles have the same effect—they extinguish either the suretyship, the principal obligation, or both—they will be considered simultaneously.

The remission of a debt by an obligee extinguishes the obligation. A transaction or compromise of a debt is an agreement between two or more persons putting an end to a lawsuit arising out of that debt, and thus by definition, it also extinguishes that debt. According to articles 1892 and 3076 [no current article], the remission or transaction of a debt granted to the principal obligor releases the sureties. But prior to the 1988 revision, the Louisiana Civil Code made a distinction between those sureties who had waived discussion and were known as "solidary" sureties, and those who had not and were known as "simple" sureties. The nature of a "solidary" suretyship was problematic because former article 3045 provided that a solidary surety is "regulated by the same principles which have been established for debtors in solido." This created difficulties where the rules regulating the liability of solidary obligors conflicted with those regulating suretyship. Remission of the principal debtor posed a special problem in this regard.

This difficulty was made apparent in *Louisiana Bank & Trust v. Boutte,* a pre-revision case, in which the Louisiana Supreme Court strictly applied article 1803 to a "solidary" suretyship. Article 1803 provides that the remission or transaction of a debt by the obligee in favor of one obligor benefits the other solidary obligors in the amount of the portion of that obligor. The anomalous result of the *Boutte* holding was that while remission of the principal debtor fully released his "simple" surety, if that same surety had waived discussion and division, then he was released only to the extent of the principal debtor's virile portion. Moreover, as a second consequence of *Boutte*, the "solidary" surety of a released principal debtor also lost his right of subrogation and could not recoup the whole of the amount he paid from the principal obligor.

The surety's loss of his subrogation rights made the *Boutte* holding inconsistent with fundamental suretyship principles. After a great deal of criticism, this decision was legislatively overruled by the 1988 revision of the Louisiana suretyship articles which abolished the rights of discussion, thus making each surety liable to the creditor for the principal obligor's full performance, "even in the absence of an express agreement of solidarity." Although "[t]he nature of the surety's promise is to satisfy the entire obligation if the debtor fails to do so," since the revision, one matter of concern has been whether all Louisiana suretyships are now "solidary."

Because the suretyship contract is accessory to the principal contract and the suretyship relationship is still governed by the detailed provisions of Title XVI of the Civil Code, the solidarity between the principle debtor and his surety, if it exists, is imperfect. Solidarity is imperfect when each obligor is liable for the whole, but some of the secondary effects normally associated with perfect solidarity are lacking. Thus, a paying surety is entitled to be fully repaid by the principal obligor, whereas a paying solidary obligor is indemnified only to the extent that he has paid more than his virile share. The paying surety maintains his rights to subrogation, reimbursement, and the right to require security from the principal obligor.

Whatever the exact nature of solidary suretyship in Louisiana, the combined effect of the revision of former article 3045, along with the 1984 revision of article 1804, was to make suretyship and solidarity work together in the Louisiana Civil Code. Article 1803 provides that the remission, transaction, or compromise of a debt by the obligee in favor of one solidary obligor benefits the other solidary obligors in the amount of the portion of that obligor. The third paragraph of article 1804 now states that "[i]f the circumstances giving rise to the solidary obligation concern only one of the obligors, that obligor is liable for the whole to the other obligors who are then considered only as his sureties." Therefore, when an obligor lends his credit to another to secure an obligation in which he has no direct interest, he is in fact a surety, and his article 1803 "part" of the debt is essentially nothing; his release by the creditor does not effect the principal obligor. Conversely, the principal debtor's "part" of the debt is the entire amount so that if he is released, the surety is also released, because the surety's accessory obligation is no part of the debt. The same result is reached under article 1892, and the comments indicate not only that the *Boutte* anomaly was undone, but also that Louisiana suretyship law was again in accord with fundamental suretyship principles.

According to French commentators, even though the parties may stipulate that the suretyship is "solidary," such suretyship may approach true solidarity, but the one does not equate with the other. To equate them (as in *Boutte*) is to go against the intentions of the contracting parties. "Certainly, a solidary surety had no intention of renouncing in advance the advantages of subrogation or his right of recourse." Moreover, there are subtle substantive differences, such as the effects of confusion between suretyship and solidarity. If a solidary co-obligor becomes an obligee, then the obligation due is reduced to the extent of his virile portion, but if the principal obligor becomes the creditor, then the surety is released—because the underlying obligation is extinct. A similar difference between solidarity and suretyship exists with the interruption of prescription. . . .

B. REMISSION COUPLED WITH A RESERVATION OF RIGHTS

Another ambiguity of the revised Louisiana Civil Code is the effect that a remission, transaction, or compromise of the principal obligor has on the surety where the release is coupled with a reservation of rights against that surety. The second paragraph of article 1803 states that surrender of the instrument evidencing the obligation to the released solidary obligor gives rise to a rebuttable presumption that the release is intended to benefit the other solidary obligors. Comment (e) of that article states that this presumption can be rebutted either by a showing that the obligor did not intend to release the co-obligor or by an express reservation of rights against that co-obligor. Thus, article 1803 implies that a remission of the principal obligor coupled with an express reservation of rights against the surety would effectively preserve the existence of the surety's obligation.

According to the traditional reservation of rights doctrine, two consequences follow from the mere act of informing the principal obligor that the obligee is reserving rights against the surety. First, the surety's rights are preserved as though the conduct had never occurred, and second, the surety himself is held liable according to a presumption that this merely preserves an obligation to which he had already agreed.

Respected French commentators Cabrillac and Mouly mention a controversy in France regarding whether such a reservation of rights should be allowed because it deceives the principal obligor into believing that he is no longer responsible for the underlying obligation. In fact, unless the surety has personally agreed to release the principal obligor, the surety can demand subrogation. Cabrillac and Mouly thus conclude that because of this unfairness, such reservation of rights clauses must be regarded as nullities, unless the remission is merely a procedural exercise brought on by the bankruptcy or insolvency of the principal debtor. . . .

While the release, transaction, or compromise of the principal obligor will release the surety, if a surety himself is remitted or transacts or compromises with the creditor, this release of an accessory obligation does not affect the principal obligation—in the same way that a tail cannot wag a dog.

C. REMISSION AND MULTIPLE SURETIES

If a cosurety or subsurety is involved, the effect of a remission, transaction, or compromise can seem complicated, but the same basic suretyship principles still apply. The accord between the Louisiana Civil Code's suretyship and solidarity articles extends to cosureties, as indicated by article 1804's use of the plural "sureties." As regards each other, cosureties are presumed to share the burden of the principal obligation in proportion to their number, and a cosurety who pays the creditor may proceed to recover either the entire amount from the principal obligor or virile shares from his cosureties. If one of the cosureties becomes insolvent, then the others must bear his share because the purpose of suretyship is to protect the creditor against the risk of the principal debtor's insolvency. By extension, the purpose of cosuretyship is to reduce that risk still further so that the creditor is protected against the insolvency of both the principal debtor and one or more cosureties.

In order to understand how a remission, transaction, or compromise affects a complex suretyship relationship, the interrelationship is easily visualized as an inverted pyramid, with the principal obligor on the bottom, the cosureties in the middle, and the subsureties on top. Removal or release of the top level affects no one below, but removal of a middle or bottom support causes the upper levels to come crashing down. Thus, the release of a subsurety releases neither the principal suretyship nor the principal obligation, and the release of a cosurety does not effect the principal obligation. But the release of a principal surety would release a subsurety, and the release of the principal obligor would release all cosureties and subsureties.

The pyramid analogy fails, however, with members of the same level: because a cosurety who pays the entire debt can only expect virile-share contribution from his cosureties, as opposed to full indemnification from the principal debtor, he can only expect a virile-share remission when his cosurety is released. Louisiana Civil Code article 1892 states: "Remission of debt granted to one surety releases the other sureties only to the extent of the contribution the other sureties might have recovered from the surety to whom the remission was granted."

Although the French Civil Code does not specifically provide for deduction of the released cosurety's portion of the debt from the amount the other cosureties must pay, this result is indicated by annotators and is confirmed by jurisprudence. While the creditor may want to favor a cosurety by liberating him, if that liberation does not diminish the debt, then the unreleased cosureties would bear a greater portion of the debt. Thus, the liberation would be at the expense of the other cosureties. While the nature of suretyship requires that cosureties bear the risk that one of them will become insolvent, they should not bear the risk that the creditor will release one cosurety to the detriment of the rest.

* * * * * *

NOTES AND QUESTIONS

1. In thinking about solidarity in the multiple suretyship relationship, consider the following hypothetical: Ann, Burt, Cal, and Dick, eager to help Edwin obtain a loan, met with a loan officer for Bank of Boutte ("BB"), and each of them signed the following document:

> July 6, 2007
>
> I, we, and all of us in solido now unconditionally guarantee any and all loans that Edwin has borrowed in the past, borrows currently, or may borrow in the future from BB up to the amount of $12,000.
>
> /s/ Ann
> /s/ Burt
> /s/ Cal
> /s/ Dick

When Ann, Burt, Cal, and Dick signed the above agreement, Edwin already owed BB $5,000. On July 7, 2007, Edwin borrowed an additional $7,000 from BB. On February 9, 2008, Edwin paid BB the entire $12,000. On November 1, 2010, BB loaned Edwin $20,000. In the written loan agreement Edwin agreed to repay the $20,000 by November 1, 2012. In 2011 Burt became insolvent and was granted a discharge in bankruptcy. On July 18, 2012, BB entered into a written agreement with Cal, pursuant to which BB released Cal from any further liability in consideration of Cal's payment of $1,000 to BB. As of today (December 10, 2012), Edwin has not repaid any of the $20,000 owed to BB, and his loan is in default. Answer the following questions based on the above facts. Any additional fact assumed within a question applies only to that question.

1.1 How much can BB recover from Edwin?

1.2 Assume that BB sues Edwin, who pays BB the amount for which he is liable. What recourse (if any) does Edwin have against Ann, Burt, Cal, and Dick? How much can Edwin recover from each person against whom he has recourse?

1.3 Assume alternatively that BB does not sue Edwin, but only Dick. How much can BB recover from Dick?

1.4 Assume that BB sues Dick, who pays BB the amount for which he is liable. What recourse (if any) does Dick have against Ann, Burt, Cal, and Edwin? How much can Dick recover from each person against whom he has recourse?

2. Work the following short hypotheticals to help you understand the nuances and permutations of the rules governing multiple sureties.

2.1: Four sureties for PO (principal obligor): A, B, C, and D. They owe $24,000 to E. B goes bankrupt. How much can E collect from A, C, or D?

2.1A: Four sureties for PO (principal obligor): A, B, C, and D. They owe $24,000 to E. B goes bankrupt. How much can E collect from PO?

2.2: Four sureties for PO (principal obligor): A, B, C, and D. They owe $24,000 to E. B goes bankrupt. E renounces solidarity in favor of C. How much can E collect from A or D?

2.2A: Four sureties for PO (principal obligor): A, B, C, and D. They owe $24,000 to E. B goes bankrupt. E renounces solidarity in favor of C. How much can E collect from C?

2.2B: Four sureties for PO (principal obligor): A, B, C, and D. They owe $24,000 to E. B goes bankrupt. E renounces solidarity in favor of C. How much can E collect from PO?

2.3: Four sureties for PO (principal obligor): A, B, C, and D. They owe $24,000 to E. E gratuitously remits the debt in favor of C. How much can E collect from A, B, or D?

2.3A: Four sureties for PO (principal obligor): A, B, C, and D. They owe $24,000 to E. E gratuitously remits the debt in favor of C. How much can E collect from PO?

2.4: Four sureties for PO (principal obligor): A, B, C, and D. They owe $24,000 to E. B goes bankrupt. E renounces solidarity in favor of C. A thereafter goes bankrupt. How much can E collect from C?

2.4A: Four sureties for PO (principal obligor): A, B, C, and D. They owe $24,000 to E. B goes bankrupt. E renounces solidarity in favor of C. A thereafter goes bankrupt. How much can E collect from D?

2.4B: Four sureties for PO (principal obligor): A, B, C, and D. They owe $24,000 to E. B goes bankrupt. E renounces solidarity in favor of C. A thereafter goes bankrupt. How much can E collect from PO?

2.5: Four sureties for PO (principal obligor): A, B, C, and D. They owe $24,000 to E. E enters into a compromise with C, who pays E $4,000 pursuant to their agreement. How much can E collect from A, B, or D?

2.5A: Four sureties for PO (principal obligor): A, B, C, and D. They owe $24,000 to E. E enters into a compromise with C, who pays E $4,000 pursuant to their agreement. How much can E collect from PO?

2.6: Four sureties for PO (principal obligor): A, B, C, and D. They owe $24,000 to E. B goes bankrupt, then E remits the debt in favor of C. How much can E collect from A or D?

2.6A: Four sureties for PO (principal obligor): A, B, C, and D. They owe $24,000 to E. B goes bankrupt, then E remits the debt in favor of C. How much can E collect from PO?

2.7: Four sureties for PO (principal obligor): A, B, C, and D. They owe $24,000 to E. E renounces solidarity in favor of C who then pays E $6,000. A makes an $18,000 partial payment to E. B thereafter goes bankrupt. What recourse (if any) does A have against C?

2.7A: Four sureties for PO (principal obligor): A, B, C, and D. They owe $24,000 to E. E renounces solidarity in favor of C, who then pays E $6,000. A makes an $18,000 partial payment to E. B thereafter goes bankrupt. What recourse (if any) does A have against PO?

2.8: Four sureties for PO (principal obligor): A, B, C, and D. They owe $24,000 to E. A makes a $4,000 partial payment to E. B then goes bankrupt. How much can E recover from A, C, or D?

2.8A: Four sureties for PO (principal obligor): A, B, C, and D. They owe $24,000 to E. A makes a $4,000 partial payment to E. B then goes bankrupt. How much can E recover from PO?

2.9: Four sureties for PO (principal obligor): A, B, C, and D. They owe $24,000 to E. C enters into a compromise with E according to which C pays $20,000 to E as full payment of the debt. What can C collect from A, B, or D?

2.9A: Four sureties for PO (principal obligor): A, B, C, and D. They owe $24,000 to E. C enters into a compromise with E according to which C pays $20,000 to E as full payment of the debt. What can E collect from PO?

2.10: Four sureties for PO (principal obligor): A, B, C, and D. They owe $24,000 to E. C and PO go bankrupt: C's debt to E is discharged as is PO's debt. How much can E collect from A, B, or D?

2.11: Four sureties for PO (principal obligor): A, B, C, and D. They owe $24,000 to E. B goes bankrupt, then E gratuitously remits the debt in favor of PO. How much can E collect from A, C, or D?

F. Termination of Suretyship

As with most all contracts, there is a beginning and an end. Suretyship is no different. The following sections explore the ways in which suretyship can be terminated and thereby relieve the surety from any additional liability.

1. Extinction of the Principal Obligation

***See* La. Civ. Code arts. 1894; 1897; 1903-1904; 3058-3059**

As with all security devices, once the principal obligation is extinguished, the contract of suretyship terminates as well. This is fundamental to the nature of all security devices—they are accessory rights that depend upon the principal obligation in order to exist. If there no longer exists a principal obligation, then nothing can serve as security for it.

The law of obligations provides a variety of ways in which obligations are extinguished. *See generally* La. Civ. Code arts. 1854-1905. The most obvious (and most common) method of extinguishing the principal obligation is by performance. La. Civ. Code art. 1854. Also included among the ways in which obligations are extinguished are compensation and confusion. Regarding compensation, also called set-off, Civil Code article 1894 states: "Compensation takes place by operation of law when two persons owe to each other sums of money or quantities of fungible things identical in kind, and these sums or quantities are liquidated and presently due." As applied to suretyship, compensation between the obligee and the principal obligor extinguishes the surety's obligation. By contrast, compensation between the obligee and the surety does not extinguish the principal obligor's obligation. La. Civ. Code art. 1897.

Another way in which obligations are extinguished is through confusion, also called merger, which takes place "[w]hen the qualities of obligee and obligor are united in the same person." La. Civ. Code art. 1903. In the context of suretyship, the obligation of the surety is extinguished when "confusion of the qualities of the obligee and the obligor in the person of the principal obligor" occurs, but not when the qualities of obligee and obligor in the person of the surety takes place. La. Civ. Code art. 1904.

2. Modification of the Principal Obligation

***See* La. Civ. Code arts. 3041-3044; 3062**

It is not unusual for the obligor and the obligee to get together and agree to a change in the terms that govern their transaction. For instance, if the obligation is for the repayment of a loan, an obligor who is cash strapped might request that the obligee give him additional time to pay (i.e., an extension or a forbearance). This obviously benefits the obligor because it allows him to still perform and not cause a default (and whatever ills might result therefrom). It also benefits the surety because, by allowing the obligor an opportunity to be timely on his payments, it avoids a situation where the obligee is looking to the surety for payment.

But obligees rarely give such concessions lightly. Indeed, they often require something additional from the obligor in exchange for the accommodation, and this often takes the form of a penalty fee or perhaps an increase in the interest rate on the loan. This does not necessarily benefit the obligor because he will have to pay more on the loan than he would otherwise, but it is in his interest to avoid an outright default. The surety, however, suffers a loss because now the amount he may be called upon to pay has increased. In other words, he must pay the loan (as he originally anticipated) as well as additional amounts resulting from the increased interest rate or the penalty fee. What should the consequences be if the principal obligation has been modified without the surety's permission and if, as a result, the surety has suffered a loss?

The Civil Code provides rules governing the effects of "[t]he modification or amendment of the principal obligation, or the impairment of real security held for it, by the creditor, in any material manner and without the consent of the surety." La. Civ. Code art. 3062. The rules provided in article 3062 vary depending upon whether the suretyship at issue is commercial or ordinary.

It is stated in article 3042 that a suretyship is commercial in each of the following scenarios:

(1) The surety is engaged in a surety business;

(2) The principal obligor or the surety is a business corporation, partnership, or other business entity;

(3) The principal obligation arises out of a commercial transaction of the principal obligor; or

(4) The suretyship arises out of a commercial transaction of the surety.

If the suretyship is not a legal suretyship, and if none of these scenarios is applicable, the suretyship is ordinary. Article 3062 provides that any material modification of the principal obligation without the surety's consent extinguishes an ordinary suretyship. By contrast, material modification of the principal obligation without the surety's consent causes a commercial suretyship to be "extinguished to the extent the surety is prejudiced by the action of the creditor, unless the principal obligation is one other than for the payment of money, and the surety should have contemplated that the creditor might take such action in the ordinary course of performance of the obligation. The creditor has the burden of proving that the surety has not been prejudiced or that the extent of the prejudice is less than the full amount of the surety's obligation." La. Civ. Code art. 3062. Consider the following cases on the effects (if any) that modification of the principal obligation has upon the surety.

* * * * * *

ROBBINS TIRE & RUBBER COMPANY, INC. v. WINNFIELD RETREAD, INC.
577 So. 2d 1189 (La. App. 2d Cir. 1991)

HIGHTOWER, Judge.

From a trial court decision applying the doctrine of equitable estoppel as a bar to enforcement of a suretyship agreement, the creditor, Robbins Tire & Rubber Co., Inc. ("Robbins"), appeals. We reverse the previous determination, uphold the validity of the suretyship agreement, and render judgment accordingly.

FACTS

In 1980, Straughan, Inc., through its president Thomas Straughan, executed a "Guaranty Agreement" in favor of appellant to assist the principal debtor, Winnfield Retread, Inc. ("Winnfield"), in obtaining credit. At that time, Mr.

Straughan was the primary stockholder of both Winnfield and Straughan, Inc., the latter concern operating a tire store. The subject document contained the following pertinent language:

> [W]e the undersigned, absolutely and unconditionally, guarantee the full and prompt payment to Robbins of all debts and obligations which said Purchaser [referring to Winnfield] is now, or may hereafter be, in any manner liable to the said Robbins; and we do further, absolutely and unconditionally, guarantee to pay to Robbins any sum or sums of money as may now be due or which may at any time or times hereafter become due to Robbins from said Purchaser, and Robbins is at liberty, without notice to the undersigned, to give the Purchaser at any time, and from time to time, renewals or extensions of credit on time of payment on any obligations of the Purchaser as Robbins may deem proper.
>
> This guarantee shall be a continuing guarantee and shall remain in full force and effect until it has been revoked by the undersigned in writing and a copy of such revocation delivered to Robbins.

Some three years later, Straughan transferred his interest in Winnfield to another individual, a Mr. Stroud. Shortly before the change in ownership, Winnfield apparently remitted a check paying Robbins for all outstanding amounts due. Additionally, Mr. Straughan notified Robbins of the transfer, but said nothing about the suretyship agreement. Thereafter, Robbins continued to extend credit and sell goods to Winnfield; Straughan, Inc., as before, did business with Winnfield.

In March 1986, Winnfield executed a collateral chattel mortgage, a general assignment of accounts receivable, and a real estate mortgage to secure its line of credit with Robbins. Subsequently, in order to facilitate Stroud's request for a Small Business Association (SBA) loan, Robbins cancelled the real estate mortgage. The surety received notice of neither the acquisition nor release of the security.

In 1987, the creditor called upon the surety to fulfill the terms of its agreement, after the principal debtor failed to pay a $23,828.78 outstanding debt. Robbins later instituted the present suit, obtained a default judgment against Winnfield, and proceeded to trial against Straughan, Inc. The surety's answer to the original petition denied the continued validity of the 1980 agreement and additionally pleaded the defense of equitable estoppel.

After trial, the district judge decided in favor of Straughan, Inc. A written opinion concluded that the suretyship agreement clearly specified continued validity until written revocation, and that appellee would have been responsible for the indebtedness absent proof of equitable estoppel. The decision then proceeded to reason that:

> [T]he actions of the petitioner in failing to notify STRAUGHAN'S, INC., of its continuing liability after the transfer in 1983, the payment in full of any indebtedness prior to the transfer, the actions of the petitioner in securing numerous documents from the defendant, WINNFIELD RETREAD, INC., in 1986, and the failure of petitioner to communicate with STRAUGHAN'S, INC., in any way until July, 1987, clearly present a case where the doctrine of equitable estoppel should apply.

This appeal ensued.

DISCUSSION

Equitable Estoppel

[In this portion of the opinion, the court of appeal reversed the trial court's application of the doctrine of equitable estoppel, holding that "equitable considerations and estoppel cannot prevail in conflict with the positive written law. Thus, issues such as here presented are in most instances governed by the Civil Code articles on suretyship, LSA-C.C. Art. 3035, *et seq.*, rather than equitable estoppel."]

Validity of the Suretyship Obligation

Save for the suretyship agreement, Robbins originally held no security for payment of the principal obligation. It later received the three additional devices of security as stated; then subsequently released one of those, the real estate mortgage. Based on that action, the cancellation of the mortgage, appellee argues that its obligation as surety is extinguished due to impairment of subrogation rights. Although its brief does not succinctly address the matter, appellant orally maintained no prejudice resulted, that indeed appellee's potential exposure actually decreased as a result of the additional security taken.

Of course, a contract of guaranty and one of suretyship are synonymous. The contract of suretyship is an accessory promise by which one party binds himself to fulfill the obligation of another if the latter fails to do so. LSA-C.C. Art. 3035 (1870, Rev. 1987). And, the surety promises to satisfy the entire obligation, unless his agreement is otherwise limited. *Bossier Medical Properties*, supra. *See* Comments to LSA-C.C. Art. 3045 (Rev. 1987).

Under the present facts and 1987 codal revisions, Straughan would be classified as a commercial surety, LSA-C.C. Art. 3042 (Rev. 1987), and the impairment of real security for the principal obligation would result in a discharge correlative to the prejudice caused, LSA-C.C. Art. 3062 (Rev. 1987). Former provisions failed to differentiate between types of sureties, and granted complete extinguishment if prejudice occurred. See former LSA-C.C. Art. 3061 (current art. 3062). Jurisprudentially, however, the surety who collected a fee for his services did not receive the same rigid protection. *See* Expose des Motifs to Act 409 of 1987.

Prior to January 1, 1988, the effective date of the 1987 revisions, a surety invoking extinguishment as a defense faced the burden of preponderately proving his claim. LSA-C.C.P. Art. 1005. Presently, however, LSA-C.C. Art. 3062 (Rev. 1987) requires that the creditor show a lack of prejudice once the issue arises. Hence, to that extent, the extent of such procedural changes, arguably the changes to Article 3062 necessitate retroactive application.

Yet, irrespective of positioning of the burden of proof, no prejudice occurred in the present case. In point of fact, with reference to the subrogation opportunities afforded, the surety's status improved. Upon payment of the principal obligation, Straughan will be vested, by operation of law, with the ability to enforce at least two items of security unavailable to it at the time of execution of the suretyship agreement. Standing more secure than when it became a surety, appellee cannot now claim prejudice. Consequently, the defense of extinguishment fails. . . . For the above reasons, the trial court's decision is reversed, and, pursuant to the suretyship agreement, judgment is rendered in favor of appellant. Appellee is taxed with costs, here and below. . . .

IT IS HEREBY ORDERED, ADJUDGED AND DECREED, that there be judgment in favor of plaintiff, ROBBINS TIRE & RUBBER COMPANY, INC., and against defendant, STRAUGHAN, INC., as surety, in the sum of $23,828.78, plus legal interest from date of judicial demand until paid, and for attorney's fees of $2,500, as provided in the judgment against the principal debtor, Winnfield Retread, Inc., and for all costs of this proceeding here and below.

* * * * * *

ABADI v. MARKEY
710 So. 2d 327 (La. App. 5th Cir. 1998)

CANNELLA, Judge.

Plaintiff, Helen Abadie, appeals from a judgment dismissing her suit for delinquent rental payments, taxes and attorney fees against the sureties to a lease, defendants, Daniel J. Markey, Jr. (Markey), G. Patrick Hand, Jr. (Hand), and Charles Augustine, Sr. (Augustine). We affirm in part, reverse in part and render an award. We affirm the dismissal of the third-party actions.

Plaintiff owned a piece of property in New Orleans, Louisiana which was used as a gas station and convenience store. Three leases were executed in relation to this property in 1984, 1986 and 1989 with U–Cut Corners, Inc. (U–Cut). The company was owned and managed by Augustine. The three defendants signed the leases as sureties. The last lease, for five years, was executed in June of 1989, along with a promissory note for $5,000. The note was executed because U–Cut was delinquent in the rent. Under the note, the company was obligated to pay $1,000 monthly, until the $5,000 was paid.

In December of 1989, pursuant to an Authorization to Sub–Lease given by plaintiff, a sub-lease was executed by U–Cut Corners, Inc. and Equipco, incorporating the terms and conditions of the original lease. . . . Subsequently, Equipco became delinquent in rental payments and taxes. Thus, in February of 1993, plaintiff filed a Rule to Evict Equipco in First City Court in New Orleans. . . . On May 3, 1993, plaintiff also filed an ordinary suit on the contract of lease and the promissory note against defendants as sureties, for unpaid rentals, for taxes owed by the lessee but paid by plaintiff, for principal and interest on the

promissory note and for attorney's fees. The petition claimed breach of lease and default of the promissory note. . . .

Defendants, Markey and Hand, filed answers to plaintiff's petition asserting . . . modification of the lease, as [an] affirmative defense to plaintiff's claims. They next filed a third-party demand against Augustine, alleging a hold harmless and indemnity agreement. Augustine filed an answer to plaintiff's petition, generally denying the allegations and asserting extinguishment of the debt. . . .

A trial was held on September 11, November 21, 1995, and September 12, 1996. The trial judge rendered a judgment on January 31, 1997, dismissing all the claims. He found that plaintiff failed to prove her case by a preponderance of the evidence.

On appeal, plaintiff asserts that the trial judge erred in finding that she failed to prove her case by a preponderance of the evidence and that . . . the sureties were not released by modification, failure of consideration or agreement.

PREPONDERANCE OF THE EVIDENCE

Plaintiff first claims that she clearly proved by testimony and documentary evidence that the lease was breached by Equipco's failure to pay rentals and taxes owed under the lease. She contends that defendants did not contest the amounts of her claim for either the lease rentals or the amount due on the promissory note. Thus, she asserts, she is entitled to the rentals, taxes and amounts due on the promissory note. We agree. . . .

In her second argument, plaintiff contends that the sureties were not released from their obligations through . . . modification of the lease.

The trial judge determined that plaintiff failed to prove her case for the debts, which we have already determined was error. He did not make a finding on the extinguishment question, which was pled by defendants. It is their burden to prove their defenses. Since this was not addressed by the trial judge, we must address the extinguishment issue de novo.

A contract is an agreement by two or more parties whereby obligations are created, modified or extinguished. La. C.C. art.1906. It is the law between the parties and is full proof of the agreement. C.C. art. 1835; *McCarroll v. McCarroll*, 95–1972 (La. App. 1 Cir. 6/28/96); 680 So. 2d 681, 685.

Courts are bound to give legal effect to written contracts according to the true intent of the parties. La. C.C. art. 2045. This intent is to be determined by the words of the contract when they are clear, explicit and lead to no absurd consequences. *Ochsner Clinic v. Maxicare Louisiana, Inc.*, 95–959 (La. App. 5 Cir. 3/26/96); 672 So. 2d 979, 981. "The meaning and intent of the parties to a written contract must be sought within the four corners of the instrument and cannot be explained or contradicted by parol evidence." *McCarroll v. McCarroll*, 680 So. 2d at 685; *Ochsner Clinic v. Maxicare Louisiana, Inc.*, 672 So. 2d at 982; C.C. art. 1848. However, when the terms of a contract are susceptible to more than one meaning, or there is uncertainty or ambiguity as to its provisions, or the intent of the parties cannot be ascertained from the language, parol evidence is admissible to clarify the ambiguity or show the intention of the parties. *McCarroll v. McCarroll*, 680 So. 2d at 685.

Suretyship is an accessory contract by which a person binds himself to a creditor to fulfill the obligation of another upon the failure of the latter to do so. La. C.C. art. 3035. The surety may assert against the creditor any defense to the principal obligation that the principal obligor could assert, except lack of capacity or discharge in bankruptcy of the principal obligor. C.C. art. 3046. The obligations of a surety are extinguished by the different ways in which conventional obligations are extinguished and, further, by extinguishment of the principal obligation, prescription and termination of the suretyship. C.C. art. 3058, 3059. Modification of the principal obligation without the consent of the surety also extinguishes the surety's obligation. C.C. art. 3062.

EXTINGUISHMENT BY MODIFICATION

Plaintiff argues that the sureties were not released due to modification because the sub-lease was not a modification of the lease and/or because, in the suretyship agreement, the sureties waived their right to release due to modification. Plaintiff argues that the sureties waived release due to modification of the lease specifically in the suretyship agreement. Alternatively, she contends that the sub-lease was not a modification because paragraph 11 of the lease permits the lessee, U–Cut, to sublet with the written permission of the lessor. She contends that all defendants consented by initialing this page, which does not stipulate that the sureties' consent must be obtained.

The suretyship agreement states:

> SURETY: And now comes Charles L. Augustine, Daniel J. Markey, Jr. and G. Patrick Hand, Jr., WHO ARE MADE A PARTY to this contract of lease and is bound with Lessee IN SOLIDO for the faithful execution of all the obligations to be performed on the part of the Lessee, and furthermore waives all rights to release from this obligation due to . . . any modification of this lease. . . .

Under this provision of the lease, the sureties waived their rights to release due to modification. The waiver language is clear and unambiguous. In addition, the lease provides in paragraph 11 that the lessee may sub-let the premises with the consent of lessor. It does not require the consent of the sureties. The sureties initialed this page and, thus, agreed to this provision. For these reasons, we find that the sureties were not released by modification of the lease. . . .

[W]e reverse the judgment of the trial court as to defendants' liability as sureties under the lease agreement for overdue rental payments, unpaid taxes, expenses and attorney's fees. Judgment is hereby rendered in favor of plaintiff and against Hand, Markey and Augustine, in solido, in the sum of $35,889.951, plus attorney's fees in the amount of $5,000, with legal interest from date of judicial demand. The judgment of the trial court is affirmed in all other respects. Costs of the trial and appeal are to be paid by defendants. AFFIRMED IN PART; REVERSED IN PART; AWARD RENDERED.

* * * * * *

3. Liberative Prescription

***See* La. Civ. Code art. 3060**

If the principal obligation is extinguished due to liberative prescription, then the security device is extinguished as well. So, for instance, a loan is made by Creditor to Debtor and is secured by the suretyship of G. If Debtor fails to repay the loan, and three years pass (which is the prescriptive period for loans,

La. Civ. Code art. 3494, as opposed to those that are evidenced by a promissory note, which is five years, La. Civ. Code art. 3498), then not only may Creditor not seek performance from Debtor but Creditor is also precluded from seeking performance from G. Without the ability to enforce the principal obligation there can be no enforcement of the accessory obligation.

Questions concerning liberative prescription have also been raised in the context of a continuing guaranty, in which the suretyship is not limited to a single transaction but contemplates a future course of dealing that may encompass a series of transactions, often for an indefinite period of time. Does liberative prescription apply to a continuing guaranty that is for an indefinite period of time? The cases that follow examine these issues.

* * * * * *

COTTONPORT BANK v. REASON
801 So. 2d 1236 (La. App. 3d Cir. 2001)

DOUCET, Chief Judge.

The Defendants, Alfred and Rose Reason, appeal the judgment of the trial court finding them liable for payment under consumer guaranty agreements and ordering them to pay $5,000.00 each to the Plaintiff, The Cottonport Bank (the Bank).

In March 1990, the Reasons each signed a "Consumer Guaranty" agreement in the amount of $5,000.00, for the benefit of their son, Brent Reason.

In April 2000, the Bank filed this suit to collect on the continuing guaranties, alleging that it was entitled to collect on the guaranties because of Brent Reason's failure to pay as required by a promissory note he executed in October 1999. The court denied the Defendants' exception of prescription.

After a trial on the merits, the court granted judgment in favor of the Bank and against the Reasons in the amount of $5,000.00 each plus attorney's fees of $700.00 each and court costs. The Reasons appeal.

PRESCRIPTION

The Defendants first assert that the trial court erred in denying their exception of prescription. Noting that a suretyship depends on the principal obligation for its validity, they assert that the principal obligation secured by the guaranties was the loan taken by their son to buy his trailer and lot, which was extinguished in May 1991. Since that obligation was extinguished more than five years before this suit was filed, they argue that the guaranties have prescribed pursuant to La. Civ. Code art. 3498.

"A contract of guaranty is a contract of suretyship. The terms are interchangeable." *Pat S. Todd Oil Co., Inc. v. Wall*, 581 So. 2d 333, 335 (La. App. 3 Cir.), writ denied, 585 So. 2d 569 (La. 1991). Principal obligation for purposes of suretyship is defined in La. Civ. Code art. 3036, as follows: "Suretyship may be established for any lawful obligation, which, with respect to the suretyship, is the principal obligation."

Had the Defendants' contracts of guaranty been tied to a particular obligation, this argument might be meritorious. However, the contracts entered by the Defendants contained the following language.

> CONTINUING GUARANTY: I UNDERSTAND AND AGREE THAT THIS IS A "CONTINUING GUARANTY" UNDER WHICH I AM GUARANTEEING THE PROMPT AND PUNCTUAL PAYMENT AND SATISFACTION OF BORROWER'S PRESENT AND FUTURE INDEBTEDNESS IN FAVOR OF LENDER. I FURTHER UNDERSTAND AND AGREE THAT THE CONTINUING NATURE OF MY OBLIGATIONS AND LIABILITY UNDER THIS AGREEMENT WILL REMAIN IN FULL FORCE AND EFFECT UNTIL SUCH TIME AS LENDER AGREES TO CANCEL THIS AGREEMENT AS PROVIDED BELOW.
>
> DEFINITIONS: The following words have the following meaning when used in this agreement:
>
> Indebtedness. The word "indebtedness" means individually, collectively and interchangeably any and all present and future loans, extensions of credit, and other obligations and liabilities of every nature and kind that borrower may now and in the future owe to or

> incur in favor of Lender, whether direct or indirect or by way of assignment, and whether absolute or contingent, voluntary or involuntary, determined or undetermined, liquidated or unliquidated, due or to become due, secured or unsecured, whether alone or with others on a "solidary" or "joint and several" basis, or otherwise, all up to a maximum amount outstanding from time to time, at any more or more times, not to exceed U.S. $5,000.00, in principal, interest, costs, expenses, attorneys' fees and other fees and charges, whether or not any such indebtedness may be barred under any statute of limitations or prescriptive period or may be otherwise unenforceable or voidable for any reason.
>
> GUARANTEE OF BORROWERS INDEBTEDNESS. I hereby absolutely and unconditionally agree to guarantee the prompt and punctual payment and satisfaction of any and all Borrower's present and future indebtedness in favor of Lender. I agree that my obligations and liabilities under this Agreement and otherwise with respect to Borrower's Indebtedness, shall be on a "solidary" or "joint and several" basis along with Borrower and any or all additional guarantors, endorsers or sureties of Borrower's indebtedness.

Finally, directly after the guarantors' signatures, the agreements contain, in pertinent part, the following statement:

> NOTICE TO COSIGNER
>
> You are being asked to guarantee this debt, as well as all other present and future debts of Borrower to the creditor of up to Five Thousand & 00/100 Dollars ($5,000.00). Think carefully before you do. If Borrower doesn't pay the debt, you will have to. Be sure you can afford to pay if you have to, and that you want to accept this responsibility.

These guaranties are not tied to a specific debt but to all "present and future indebtedness," which debts comprise the principal obligation with regard to these agreements.

The Defendants also attempted to present evidence that they did not intend to enter continuing guaranty agreements and that it was not explained to them that this was what they were agreeing to do. An alleged oral agreement may not be allowed to vary the clear and unambiguous terms of a written guaranty agreement. *Whitney Nat'l Bank of New Orleans v. Badalamenti*, 499 So. 2d 1267 (La. App. 4 Cir. 1986). Additionally, failure to read a document before signing it will bar relief for the error. *First Financial Bank, FSB v. Austin*, 514 So. 2d 281 (La. App. 5 Cir.), *writ denied*, 515 So. 2d 1112 (La. 1987), citing *Guaranty Bank and Trust v. Jones*, 489 So. 2d 368 (La. App. 5 Cir. 1986).

Under the clear language of the agreements, the obligations of Brent Reason to the Cottonport Bank which existed at the time the guaranties were entered, as well as those undertaken afterwards, constitute the principal obligations to the contracts. Since the obligation sought to be enforced under the continuing guaranties did not become due until April 13, 2000, it had not prescribed at the time this suit was filed. Therefore, the action on the guaranties has not prescribed. . . .

In the case currently before the court, the Bank proved a prima facie case by producing the note sued upon. At that point, the burden shifted to the Defendants to show that the note had been paid. The trial court found no evidence of payment of this note. After carefully examining the record, we find no error in this finding. . . . For these reasons, we find no error in the trial court's judgment finding the Defendants obligated to pay $5,000.00 each to the Bank under the guaranty agreements. Accordingly, the judgment of the trial court is affirmed. Costs of this appeal are to be paid by the Defendants. AFFIRMED.

* * * * * *

BONURA v. CHRISTIANA BROS. POULTRY CO. OF GRETNA, INC.
336 So. 2d 881 (La. App. 4th Cir. 1976).

BOUTALL, Judge.

This appeal involves the liability of a guarantor for an amount due on open account based on a continuing guaranty.

In 1961, Nicholas (Nick) Christiana, Jr., Anthony Christiana and Joseph Christiana executed a continuing guaranty for the account of Christiana Bros. Poultry Co. of Gretna, Inc. (Christiana Bros.) and/or Christiana Bros. Poultry Co. of Baton Rouge, Inc. in favor of Felix Bonura Company, Inc. (Bonura Co.). For at least the next ten years, except for Joseph Christiana leaving New Orleans in 1967 and taking over the operation of the Baton Rouge Corporation, business was conducted without much incident. In November of 1972, however, in the face of a mounting open account indebtedness to Bonura Co., Anthony Christiana executed a personal note to Felix Bonura in the amount of $12,486.00, the proceeds of which were to be applied to the balance of the open account.

On August 7, 1973, Christiana Bros.' account had a balance of $67,809.73. On August 23, 1973, Anthony Christiana, President of Christiana Bros. assigned all the accounts receivable of the corporation to Bonura Co. . . . On September 13, 1973, plaintiffs Felix Bonura and Bonura Co., filed suit against defendants, Christiana Bros., Anthony, Nick and Joseph Christiana, seeking recovery of $67,809.73 under the continuing guaranty agreement. Also included in the suit was a claim for the remaining balance of the note personally executed by Anthony. . . .

Defendant contends the trial court erred in failing to find that the continuing guaranty was no longer enforceable. . . . Defendant asserts that a continuing guaranty is a personal action which prescribes in ten years under LSA-R.C.C. 3544 (current art. 3499). We do not agree. It is recognized by all parties that a contract of continuing guaranty is equivalent to a contract of suretyship. *See Brock v. First State Bank & Trust Co.*, 187 La. 766, 175 So. 569, 570 (1937). As such, rights and obligations arising from it are accessory to the principal obligation. LSA-R.C.C. Art. 3035. In *Louisiana Bank and Trust Co. v. Bouttee*, 298 So. 2d 884, 887 (La. App. 3 Cir. 1974), in determining the prescriptive period on a similar continuing guaranty agreement the court stated:

> Under our law, the suretyship undertaking is vitiated by prescription of the principal obligation. Therefore, normally the suretyship obligation depends for its vitality upon the prescriptive period applicable to the primary obligation involved. La. C.C. Art. 3060 [now art. 3046].

Although the Supreme Court subsequently amended the holding at 309 So. 2d 274, 279 (1975), the opinion recognized that prescription on a guaranty does not begin to run until the principal indebtedness sued on arises. Hence, for the purposes of prescription, the date the agreement was signed is of no moment.

In the case at bar, the debts sought to be enforced under the continuing guaranty were incurred during the period November 1972 through August 1973. As these debtors were on open account, they prescribe three years after they become due. LSA-R.C.C. Art. 3538 [now art. 3494]. Suit was filed on September 13, 1973. Accordingly, since suit was filed clearly before the principal indebtedness had prescribed, the continuing guaranty remains enforceable.

Defendant argues that in the event we do not find the prescriptive period of LSA-R.C.C. Art. 3544 [now art. 3499] to be applicable, plaintiffs are nevertheless barred from enforcing the continuing guaranty because of estoppel or laches. He asserts that a 12 year delay in enforcement is unreasonable and that his rights were prejudiced thereby.

While delay in enforcing a right is an element of laches, it is not a sole consideration. Laches will only apply where the enforcement of the right asserted would work injustice. *Labarre v. Rateau*, 210 La. 34, 26 So. 2d 279 (1946). We do not believe the circumstances of this case warrant a utilization of this doctrine. We point out that there were continuous sales from the time of confection of the continuing guaranty through August, 1973. The account was paid up into 1972. There was no need for the creditor to have called upon the guaranty until that time. Additionally, we note that during the entire period Anthony and Nicholas Christiana were bound for sales made to the Baton Rouge corporation.

We find nothing in the record to sufficiently demonstrate how the delay prejudiced appellant's rights to justify sustaining a plea of laches or estoppel. To the contrary the facts show that the intent of the parties was to provide a security device to Bonura to induce that company to sell chickens for an indeterminate period on credit to the Christiana companies: That the sales began immediately causing the continuing guaranty to become effective; that the sales continued within the knowledge of Joseph Christiana, keeping the continuing guarantee in effect. See, for example, *Hibernia Bank & Trust Co. v. Succession of Cancienne,* 140 La. 969, 74 So. 267 (1917); *Interstate Trust & Banking Co. v. Sabatier,* 189 La. 199, 179 So. 80 (1937); *Magnolia Petroleum Co. v. Harley*, 13 So. 2d 84 (La. App. 1943).

The law is well settled that a continuing guaranty remains in force until revoked by the guarantor, expressly or impliedly; or its effectiveness is extinguished in some other mode recognized by law. *Magnolia Petroleum Co. v. Harley,* supra.

The guaranty agreement provides for termination on the part of the guarantors as follows:

> This guaranty shall continue in full force and effect until such time as you shall receive from us, Written notice of revocation, and such revocation shall not in any way relieve us from liability for any indebtedness incurred prior to the actual receipt by you in hand of said notice.

Defendant concedes that written notice of revocation was not given until August 7, 1973. He asserts, however, that a verbal notice of revocation, which he testified he gave to a now deceased ex-owner and officer of Bonura Co., given when defendant moved to Baton Rouge, was sufficient to terminate his liability under the continuing guaranty. Specifically, he argues that if the parties meant that the agreement could be revoked only by written notice, the phrase "written notice only" should have been used in the agreement.

We see no merit to this contention. The wording of the contract is clear and unambiguous. Revocation is to be carried out solely through the process of written notification. To hold otherwise would be in derogation of the true intent of the parties. . . .

* * * * * *

4. Revocation of Suretyship

***See* La. Civ. Code art. 3061 ¶ 1.**

Revocation of suretyship is similar to, although different from, the methods of termination previously considered. The concept of revocation of suretyship is important for any suretyship that is not limited to a single transaction, but which encompasses multiple transactions, perhaps for an indefinite period of time. It may very well be that the principal obligor might owe additional performances to the obligee in the future. And it may also be that, at least initially, the surety agreed to guarantee the obligations of the principal obligor on an on-going basis. However, things may change and the surety may decide that he no longer wishes to continue the current state of affairs and that he now desires to relieve himself of any potential liability that would result from obligations that the principal obligor may incur in future. In such cases the law allows the surety to revoke his contract of suretyship, albeit under limited circumstances and provided he gives notice.

Importantly, the Civil Code requires only notice, not written notice. Consider the following case disussing the subject of revocation of suretyship and the issue of proper notice.

* * * * * *

SHERWIN–WILLIAMS CO. v. CULOTTA
2012 WL 1550589 (La. App. 1st Cir. 2012)

KUHN, Judge.

The defendant-appellant, Frank. J. Culotta, Jr. (Culotta), appeals a summary judgment holding him liable to plaintiff-appellee, The Sherwin–Williams Company (Sherwin–Williams), under a written guaranty for goods and services supplied by Sherwin–Williams to Frank Culotta Contractor, Inc. (FCC). For the following reasons, we affirm.

FACTS AND PROCEDURAL BACKGROUND

In June 2004, Culotta executed and signed a commercial credit application with Sherwin–Williams on behalf of FCC, of which he was a shareholder. The document signed by Culotta included a guaranty that he would individually pay for all goods, wares and merchandise supplied to him or FCC by Sherwin–Williams. Subsequently, in 2005, Culotta retired and transferred his entire interest in FCC to his son through the sale of his shares therein. He contends that he has had no affiliation with FCC since that time.

In November 2007, FCC and Sherwin–Williams executed two "Purchase Order/Subcontract" agreements, pursuant to which Sherwin-Williams supplied floor covering and carpet to FCC for a construction project on which it was the general contractor. Culotta was not a party or signatory to these purchase orders.

. . . [T]he trial court granted summary judgment in favor of Sherwin–Williams ordering Culotta to pay the principal amount of $50,375.73, plus attorney fees of $3,500.00, interest, and court costs. The summary judgment specified that the award against Culotta was in solido with the award previously rendered against FCC. Culotta now appeals the summary judgment, arguing that the trial court erred in granting summary judgment for Sherwin–Williams when its employees knew that Culotta no longer had an ownership interest in, or was affiliated with, FCC.

SUMMARY JUDGMENT

Culotta contends the trial court erred in granting Sherwin–Williams' motion for summary judgment, because Culotta was not a signatory to the purchase orders and employees of Sherwin–Williams were aware at the time that the purchase orders were executed that Culotta had sold his interest in FCC and had not been affiliated with that business for several years. He argues that, since La. C.C. art. 3061 allows termination of a suretyship by notice to a creditor, the actual knowledge possessed by Sherwin–Williams' employees was sufficient to terminate the guaranty he signed, even though the agreement specifically required written notice of termination. Culotta asserts that, at the very least, there are genuine issues of material fact regarding the actual knowledge possessed by Sherwin–Williams employees that precluded summary judgment.

The motion for summary judgment at issue herein arose in the context of a suit on a continuing guaranty. A contract of guaranty is equivalent to a contract of suretyship; the terms are interchangeable. *First National Bank of Crowley v. Green Garden Processing Company, Inc.*, 387 So. 2d 1070, 1073 (La. 1980). The law is well-settled that a continuing suretyship remains in force until revoked. Moreover, it is the responsibility of the surety to cancel the suretyship agreement, and further, to prove the cancellation. *Wooley v. Lucksinger*, 06–1140 (La. App. 1st Cir. 12/30/08), 7 So. 3d 660, 667. A continuing guaranty is not revoked merely by notice to the creditor that a guarantor has sold his interest in a business entity on whose behalf he executed the guaranty. See *Wooley*, 7 So. 3d at 667; *Custom–Bilt Cabinet & Supply, Inc. v. Quality Built Cabinets, Inc.*, 32,441 (La. App. 2d Cir. 12/8/99), 748 So. 2d 594, 601; *W.H. Ward Lumber*

Company, Inc. v. Merit Homes, Inc., 522 So. 2d 648, 651 (La. App. 5th Cir. 1988). It is necessary that the creditor be given notice that the suretyship is being terminated. La. C.C. art. 3061; *Custom–Bilt Cabinet & Supply, Inc.*, 748 So. 2d at 600.

In the instant case, the continuing guaranty signed by Culotta provides that:

> In consideration of Sherwin–Williams extending credit to the above business [FCC], I/We do hereby agree jointly and individually, to pay for all goods, wares and merchandise supplied to me or to any of us or the above business. In the event that the account is placed with a third party for collection, I/We agree to pay all costs including reasonable attorney fees, court costs and finance charges.
>
> . . . I/We agree to: (i) immediately notify Sherwin–Williams in writing, delivered in person or by certified mail return receipt requested, of any change in ownership, form of business, or address, or the termination of a person's authority to incur charges under the account on behalf of the applicant [FCC], and (ii) indemnify Sherwin–Williams for any loss incurred thereby as a result of our failure to provide said written notice. *This agreement shall remain in full force and effect until written notice of revocation is received by Sherwin–Williams*. [Emphasis added.]

Culotta alleges that this guaranty was implicitly revoked when Sherwin–Williams employees learned that he had retired, had sold his interest in FCC, and was no longer affiliated with that company. In opposition to the motion for summary judgment, he presented the affidavits of two individuals who declared that they knew of their own personal knowledge that certain Sherwin–Williams employees were aware since 2007 that Culotta had sold his interest in FCC to his son and was no longer affiliated with that company. They further declared that these facts had been well known in the Baton Rouge construction business community since 2005.

Regardless, for the following reasons, these affidavits do not raise any genuine issues of disputed fact. First, Sherwin–Williams does not dispute, for purposes of the motion for summary judgment, that Sherwin–Williams employees knew that Culotta had sold FCC to his son. Second, whether or not

Sherwin–Williams knew that Culotta had sold his interest in FCC and was no longer affiliated with that business is immaterial to the issue of Culotta's liability under the guaranty agreement. As previously noted, a continuing guaranty is not revoked merely by notice to the creditor that a guarantor has sold his interest in a business; the pertinent inquiry is whether the creditor was given notice that the guaranty is being *terminated. See Wooley,* 7 So. 3d at 667; *Custom–Bilt Cabinet & Supply, Inc.,* 748 So. 2d at 600–01; *W.H. Ward Lumber Company, Inc.*, 522 So. 2d at 651.

Louisiana Civil Code article 3058 states that: "The obligations of a surety are extinguished by the different manners in which conventional obligations are extinguished. . . ." Pursuant to La. C.C. art. 1983, "[c]ontracts have the effect of law for the parties and can be dissolved only through the consent of the parties or on grounds provided by law." The guaranty agreement between Culotta and Sherwin–Williams does not permit revocation of the contract by any means other than written notice. It specifically provides that the continuing guaranty will remain in full force and effect until written notice of its revocation is received by Sherwin–Williams. Therefore, the fact that Sherwin–Williams may have had actual notice of the sale of Culotta's interest in FCC cannot constitute a revocation of the guaranty agreement, as such would not comply with the terms of the contract requiring written notice of revocation. *See W.H. Ward Lumber Company, Inc.*, 522 So. 2d at 651.

Finally, Culotta argues that Sherwin–Williams' failure to file a lien pursuant to La. R.S. 9:4802 asserting a privilege against the owner of the property where the floor coverings that it sold to FCC were installed released him from liability. He maintains that Sherwin–Williams' failure to do so impaired a security interest available to pay the debt, thereby extinguishing his suretyship obligation under La. C.C. art. 3062. However, we note that Culotta did not raise this defense in his answer to this suit. In fact, it appears that he may be raising this defense for the first time on appeal. In any event, as the defense urged, if sustained, would constitute an extinguishment of the obligation to the extent of any prejudice suffered by Culotta, it constitutes an affirmative defense. See La. C.C.P. art. 1005; *Pioneer Bank & Trust Company v. Foggin*, 177 So. 2d 131, 134 (La. App. 2d Cir.), *writ denied*, 248 La. 423, 179 So. 2d 18 (1965). A defendant is required to affirmatively set forth in his answer any matter constituting an affirmative defense on which he will rely. *Hanks v. Wilson*, 93–0554 (La. App. 1st Cir.

3/11/94), 633 So. 2d 1345, 1348. Thus, since Culotta did not specially plead or raise this affirmative defense in the trial court, he cannot do so for the first time on appeal.

CONCLUSION

For the reasons assigned, the judgment of the trial court granting summary judgment in favor of The Sherwin–Williams Company and against Frank J. Culotta, Jr., in the principal amount of $50,375.73, plus $3,500.00 attorney fees, interest, and court costs is hereby affirmed. Culotta is to pay all costs of this appeal. Affirmed.

* * * * * *

NOTES AND QUESTIONS

If notice effectuates a revocation of suretyship, then the obvious question that arises is what constitutes sufficient notice. The court in *Sherwin-Williams* cited a number of Louisiana decisions, including *Custom–Bilt Cabinet & Supply, Inc. v. Quality Built Cabinets, Inc.,* 748 So. 2d 594, 601 (La. App. 2d Cir. 1999), for the following principle: "It is necessary that the creditor be given notice that the suretyship is being terminated." Unlike the continuing guaranty signed at issue in *Sherwin-Williams*, which expressly required written notice of termination, the guaranty at issue in *Custom-Bilt* did not require written notice. Here are the facts as recited by the second circuit opinion in *Custom-Bilt*:

> In 1994, David Peters and Larry Wayne Hattaway opened a business known as Quality Built Cabinets, Inc. (Quality Built). They frequently purchased supplies and materials from Custom-Bilt Cabinet and Supply Company, Inc. (Custom-Bilt) on open account. Peters and Hattaway executed a continuing guaranty to Custom-Bilt to secure payment for the purchases. In 1996, Peters thought his family would be required to relocate out of state due to his wife's employment. Hattaway purchased Peters' interest in Quality Built. However, Peters did not leave the state and opened his own personal account at Custom-Bilt to purchase materials. He did not resume his co-owner relationship with Hattaway at Quality Built. Later, Quality Built fell into arrears in payment of its debt to Custom-Bilt.

On May 28, 1998, Custom-Bilt filed suit on open account against Quality Built, Hattaway, and Peters, contending that Quality Built purchased $8,766.40 in materials from December 3, 1997, to February 23, 1998, and failed to pay. Custom-Bilt sought to recover against Peters and Hattaway personally by virtue of the continuing guaranty. Peters and Hattaway answered the petition, but Quality Built did not. On July 13, 1998, a default judgment was taken against the corporation, ordering it to pay Custom-Bilt $8,766.40, with legal interest and attorney's fees in the amount of $1,250.

Peters argued that he was not liable on the continuing guaranty. In his answer to the petition, Peters contended that in May 1996, Hattaway purchased his share of Quality Built. The sale was memorialized in a document executed August 9, 1996. Peters also alleged that after the sale of his interest in the corporation, he worked on his own and not with Hattaway. According to Peters, at the time he sold his interest in Quality Built to Hattaway, he contacted Custom-Bilt and learned that the credit balance for Quality Built was zero. He also alleged that he told those working in the financial department of Custom-Bilt that he was no longer responsible for any debts owed by Quality Built. Peters claimed that his responsibility on the continuing guaranty was canceled by the sale of his interest in Quality Built to Hattaway.

Here is the court's explanation as to why the continuing guaranty had not been revoked:

It is the responsibility of the guarantor to cancel the guaranty agreement, and further, to prove the cancellation. *Security First National Bank v. Richards*, 584 So. 2d 1174 (La. App. 3d Cir. 1991).

Walter W. McCook, secretary-treasurer of Custom-Bilt and the person who handles credit for the business, testified that Peters gave him a copy of the sale of his interest in Quality Built only after the corporation's account became delinquent in 1998. McCook denied discussing the sale with Peters prior to that time.

Kenneth Lee Frizzel, the salesman with Custom-Bilt who handled the Quality Built account, testified that Peters told him several times that he was no longer involved in Quality Built. However, Frizzel was aware that Peters occasionally performed work for Quality Built after Hattaway purchased Peters' interest in the company. Frizzel also testified that Peters never asked him to tell McCook that Peters was not responsible for Quality Built's debts.

Peters testified that he saw McCook at Custom-Bilt on several occasions and told him that Hattaway had purchased his interest in the business. Peters also claims to have had several discussions with Frizzel in the summer of 1996 regarding the sale of his interest in Quality Built to Hattaway. However, Peters admitted that he never directly told anyone at Custom-Bilt that he did not expect to be responsible for the debts of Quality Built. He also stated that after Hattaway purchased his interest in Quality Built, he occasionally performed work for the company and was paid on an hourly basis.

The question is whether Peters notified Custom-Bilt of the cancellation of the guaranty and whether he carried his burden of proof at trial that he provided sufficient notification to cancel the suretyship. The testimony set forth above shows only that Peters notified a Custom-Bilt salesman, Frizzel, that he was no longer in business with Quality Built. We find that, under the jurisprudence, Peters' action in merely informing a salesman that he was no longer involved with Quality Built was not sufficient to revoke the continuing guaranty.

* * * * * *

5. Death of Surety

See La. Civ. Code art. 3061 ¶ 2

All obligations are either heritable or strictly personal. In other words, they are either able to be passed on to others (either voluntarily or involuntarily) or they are not. The general rule is that all obligations are heritable and thus are freely assignable and transferable from one person to another (whether through a sale or donation or through intestacy).

The Civil Code establishes a special rule when it comes to the nature of the rights of a surety. Review paragraph 2 of article 3061 and consider the policy implications of the way the law addresses this issue. What interests is the law trying to protect?

Chapter 3
UCC Article 9 and the Law of Pledge

This chapter begins the discussion of the different types of real security—security in property. The first is security in movable property. But before going any further, it is important to note that at most law schools this topic is covered in its own course—called Secured Transactions. There are innumerable national casebooks and commercial materials available on the topic and all its various nuances. This book does not attempt to duplicate those efforts. The reason for this is simple—for the most part Louisiana's law governing security in movable property and that of other states is virtually the same. Whether in Louisiana or elsewhere the law in this area is fairly uniform. Nevertheless, there are a number of ways (some small, others significant) in which Louisiana's rules for governing security in movable property differs. This chapter concerns itself with pointing out those essential differences.

A. The History of Movable Security in Louisiana

The law of movable security has been quite dynamic of late. Although the original framework governing consensual security in movable property was very much tied to the civil law tradition, it gradually changed over time, resulting in a major overhaul in 1990 and a revision again in 2001. As you read the following material and the chapters that follow, consider why it is that the law governing movable property has been the subject of such wide-scale (and successful) harmonization across states and jurisdictions, while other areas of security devices law remain so Louisiana-specific.

1. Pre-1990 Law—Pledge, Chattel Mortgages, and Others

For much of this state's history, the ancient civil law of pledge governed the granting of a security interest in movable property. One of the main features of pledge was that the creditor had to take possession of the property in order for the security interest to be effective. So, for instance, if a debtor wished to borrow money from a creditor who required collateral, the debtor had to furnish movable property to him (often very valuable movable property) and could not have it returned until the loan was repaid.

* * * * * *

Scott v. Corkern: *Of Precedent, Jurisprudence Constante, and the Relationship Between Louisiana Commercial Laws and Louisiana Pledge Jurisprudence*
Richard D. Moreno
10 TULANE EUROPEAN & CIVIL LAW FORUM 31, 40–41 (1995)

Pledge is one of the oldest security devices known to any system of law. Although a person's patrimony is the common pledge of all creditors, a pledge of a movable and perfection of that pledge by delivery of the thing gave the pledgee a superior right over all other creditors to the pledged thing if the debtor defaulted on the primary obligation. Under Roman law, the creditor's fist held above the pledged thing symbolized the contract of pledge. The fist over pledged object symbolically underscored and emphasized the reality of the pledgee-creditor's undisputed dominion and control over the pledged object by virtue of physical possession. Physical possession of the pledged thing gave unmistakable notice to the world of the pledgee's interest. Conversely, it also demonstrated the pledgor-debtor's complete dispossession of the pledged thing. Reflecting the fist-over-pledge ideal, civil-law and common-law courts have continually recognized the inviolate rule of pledge: the pledgee-creditor must retain possession of the pledged thing to avail himself of the privilege arising from possession.

* * * * * *

The pledge arrangement was, of course, problematic. There were often times when the movable property held by the creditor was actually important (if not essential) to the debtor's ability to produce revenue, and thereby have the resources necessary to retire the debt. For instance, if a farmer borrowed money from his bank and used those funds to purchase farming equipment, he would naturally need to use that equipment in the course and scope of his agricultural activities. But if the bank required the farmer to grant a security interest in the equipment under pledge, then the farmer would be forced to hand over the property. Without the equipment, he obviously would lack a significant tool necessary for his economic productivity (and thus his ability to repay the debt).

Over time courts and the legislature began to modify the law in order to address some of these difficulties. For instance, in the 1910s the so-called chattel mortgage was enacted, which quickly became a popular way to grant a security interest in movable property. The chattel mortgage was actually imported from the common law, but it dispensed with some of the less desirable rules governing pledge. Specifically, it allowed the creditor to maintain his security right without necessarily needing to maintain possession of the collateral. The legislature also enacted the Assignment of Accounts Receivable Act, which created a mechanism for creditors to take a security interest in the right to collect payment from an account debtor—a type of incorporeal movable right.

2. Post-1990 Law—Article 9 of the Uniform Commercial Code

While Louisiana was still using pledge and variously adopting a patchwork of other devices to deal with changing commercial demands for security, the law in this area, from a national perspective, was undergoing a sea change. First in 1962, and then again in 1999, scholars and practitioners under the aegis of the Uniform Law Commission and the American Law Institute came together to produce a new, unified statutory framework to simplify and replace the patchwork of security devices then existing across the United States so as to produce one clear, flexible, and modernized system for collateralizing personal property of any type. The result of this effort was Article 9 of the Uniform Commercial Code—often called the crown jewel of commercial law and one of the most successful and influential attempts at legal unification in modern history.

Louisiana, however, was the final state to enact Article 9 of the Uniform Commercial Code. With an effective date of January 1, 1990, the Louisiana Legislature adopted the uniform act in large part, although with a number of significant modifications and deviations, as Chapter 9 of Title 10 (the Commercial Laws). The enactment was driven by a public policy desire of the state to better compete regionally and nationally for investments and other commercial opportunities, as well as to better harmonize Louisiana's law governing secured transactions in movable property with the law of other states.

* * * * * *

Louisiana Chapter 9 (Part One): Creating and Perfecting the Security Interest

Henry Deeb Gabriel

35 Loyola Law Review 311, 312–16 (1989)

In April of 1988, Governor Roemer, on the advice of a strong contingency of Louisiana's financial community, proposed the adoption of Article Nine of the U.C.C. for Louisiana. Governor Roemer appointed Chancellor William Hawkland to chair a committee to study the feasibility of adoption and to prepare appropriate legislation. This was the first serious effort to make the Louisiana law of security rights conform with the law of the other forty-nine states, although the Louisiana Law Institute had commissioned and published a report on the feasibility of adoption twenty years ago.

Chancellor Hawkland, in a memorandum on behalf of the committee, set out four important reasons for the adoption of Article Nine in Louisiana. First, a lack of uniformity in the law of security rights created barriers to Louisiana's participation in markets that are basically national in character. Second, the adoption of Article Nine would reduce transaction costs related to obtaining security. Third, a wider variety of assets would be allowable as security under Article Nine than under previous law, thus expanding the potential base for credit. Finally, Article Nine would provide greater certainty between federal regulations and security rights law because the federal laws are written with the assumption that Article Nine is the state law governing security rights.

The scope of Article Nine and its effect on existing Louisiana law is quite limited. It essentially does not repeal any major sections of the Louisiana Civil Code, although it does supersede the Chattel Mortgage Act and the Accounts Receivable Act. Comparable acts existed in other states when they adopted Article Nine, and the transition was insubstantial in those jurisdictions.

Article Nine neither governs nor changes the law of secured financing of immovables except as it applies to fixtures. Furthermore, as adopted in Louisiana, Article Nine does not govern the financing of crops or timber; the present law of "crop pledge" and mortgage remains intact. The Louisiana version of Article Nine also explicitly excludes the secured financing of motor vehicles as to both dealer inventory and consumer purchases. In addition, under the new legislation, secured lenders are not required to adopt new methods of secured financing unless they wish to do so. Collateral mortgages and accounts receivable financing remain viable financing tools.

Notably, the validity of security devices created and recorded prior to the effective date of the new legislation is preserved. The new filing provisions, however, must be met for the re-inscription of a security device when that event occurs after its effective date. But even in that case, the security device will continue to be governed by the former law under which it was created.

Perhaps the most important legislative decision was to decline from adopting the self-help provision of section 9-503, which is the law in the other states. The self-help provisions of section 9-503 allow a secured party "the right to take possession of the collateral . . . without judicial process if this can be done without breach of the peace." Under the Louisiana version of Article Nine, the secured party must resort to the existing executory process to gain possession of the collateral unless the debtor voluntarily relinquishes possession.

* * * * * *

B. Brief Overview of UCC Article 9

Before diving in to the various non-uniformities, it is important to know some basics about how the Article 9 system works. This discussion is by no means exhaustive. The Article 9 system is extensive and merits a lengthier description, which we do not undertake in this casebook.

As a general matter, the actual process of confecting a security interest under this system is done in two-steps. First is "attachment." This is the way in which the security interest becomes effective between the parties to the contract of security itself (usually the debtor and the creditor, although it is possible for a non-debtor third party to serve as the person providing the collateral). There are a number of requirements governing this step, including typically the execution of a contract called the "security agreement" that sets forth some basic information about the transaction.

The next step is "perfection." This is the process whereby the security interest that was created by "attachment" becomes effective against third persons. This often involves, as one might surmise, a filing into a particular registry (although not the traditional conveyance or mortgage registry). However, sometimes it is possible to "perfect" the security interest without filing—but rather by giving the creditor possession or control of the collateral. Sound familiar? This is the same concept at play from the original law of pledge. And lastly, in rare cases perfection happens automatically upon attachment.

The precise rules for attachment and perfection are affected by what type of category the collateral falls into. UCC Article 9 divides up movable property by a limited number of broad categories (i.e., inventory, equipment, accounts, general intangibles, investment property, etc.). Generally speaking, all types of movable property fall into one of these neatly defined silos. So it is important to know what category the property falls into because that will often dictate which attachment and perfection rules govern.

Last but not least, the way in which a creditor can enforce his security interest changes depending on which category the property falls into. Sometimes it is necessary to obtain a judgment from a court or otherwise seek the assistance of a government official like a sheriff or marshal. However, at other times the collateral can be easily accessed by the creditor without involving legal officers. Again, knowing the correct category is key.

C. Louisiana's UCC Article 9 Non-Uniform Provisions

Unlike many other states that adopted Article 9 of the UCC, Louisiana did a certain level of picking and choosing from the model act. Some of this was done in an effort to ensure that the new system fit (both theoretically and from a linguistic perspective) with the state's unique civilian tradition. But Louisiana also made changes based on the experience of other states. Louisiana was the last of the 50 states to enact UCC Article 9. Although this may suggest a certain level of intransigence, it actually had its benefits. The legislature had the advantage of ascertaining what worked and what did not in the other states where Article 9 had already been enacted. Thus, Louisiana could pick the best parts, and reject or modify others that had proved problematic.

Because of this approach, a number of provisions in Louisiana's account of Article 9 (what we call "Chapter 9") diverges from the uniform version of the statute. In some ways these variances have aided the legislature in maintaining the state's civil law tradition and in in others it has helped, through the wisdom of time, to strike the correct balance between creditors and debtors.

To that end, the following are excerpts from a law review article by James Stuckey, the reporter of the Uniform Commercial Code Committee of the Louisiana State Law Institute, who oversaw a major revision of Chapter 9 in 2001. An overview of the major differences between Louisiana Chapter 9 and the uniform version of Article 9 is what follows.

* * * * * *

Louisiana's Non-Uniform Variations in U.C.C. Chapter 9
James A. Stuckey
62 Louisiana Law Review 793 (2002) (citations omitted)

I. Introduction

Louisiana was the last of the fifty states to adopt Article 9 of the Uniform Commercial Code, which took effect in Louisiana on January 1, 1990, long after the other states and the District of Columbia. Ironically, in that same year, a comprehensive revision and restatement of Uniform Commercial Code Article 9 commenced. After a decade long process, Revised Article 9 was promulgated by the National Conference of Commissioners on Uniform State Laws and The American Law Institute in 1999.

Louisiana's former Chapter 9 was adopted with multiple changes from the uniform model version of former U.C.C. Article 9. Recognizing that non-uniformity, and due to the complexity and length of the proposed legislation, when revised U.C.C. Article 9 was first introduced in the Louisiana Legislature it was referred to the Louisiana State Law Institute for study, redrafting and the addition of comments. After a two-year process of committee meetings and Institute Council sessions, a modified version of U.C.C. Article 9 containing

Louisiana non-uniform variations was recommended by the Louisiana State Law Institute to the Legislature for the 2001 regular session. With one substantive amendment made in the Senate Committee on Judiciary A, this legislation was enacted, effective July 1, 2001. This legislation is known officially as the Uniform Commercial Code-Secured Transactions, and is referred to in this article as "Chapter 9." . . .

II. Definitions

A. Louisiana Definitions

. . . Section 9-102 in Chapter 9 is by necessity non-uniform for several reasons. First, Louisiana has not enacted Articles 2 and 2A of the U.C.C. [dealing with sales of movables and the lease of movables], nor is their adoption likely in the foreseeable future. As a result, Chapter 9 excludes eleven definitions relating to U.C.C. Articles 2 and 2A, and instead includes Louisiana definitions for most of those terms in a new non-uniform Subsection 9-102(d).

. . . [D]efinitions are added to translate the common law terminology used in U.C.C. Article 9 to fit within the language of Louisiana's civil law property concepts and principles. Thus, "intangible" is defined to mean "incorporeal," "personal property" to mean "movable property," "real property" to mean "immovable property and real rights therein," and "tangible" to mean "corporeal." . . .

. . . A definition of "collateral mortgage note" is used to permit the inclusion of special non-uniform provisions pertaining only to collateral mortgage notes in Chapter 9, and to restrict their application to collateral mortgages encumbering Louisiana immovable property. At the request of the Law Institute Council a non-uniform definition of "local law" was added. "Local law" is a term used in U.C.C. Article 9 without definition to mean the substantive law of a particular jurisdiction and not its choice-of-law rules. Definitions of "mineral rights," "recorded timber conveyance," and "titled motor vehicle" are included in Chapter 9 for convenience in drafting.

B. Agricultural Matters

. . . [S]tanding timber owned separately from the land is in many instances within the scope of revised Chapter 9, even though not a farm product under

Chapter 9. This result arises from multiple provisions in Chapter 9. The definition of "goods," in combination with the new definition of "recorded timber conveyance," reproduces the substance of former Chapter 9 pertaining to timber. Standing timber is immovable, but trees cut down, whether carried off or not, are movables. Nonetheless, the precise intersection between immovable and movable property can be difficult to elucidate, and timber is no exception. Under Chapter 9, the interest of a debtor other than a landowner in standing timber that is to be cut and removed under a recorded timber conveyance is classified as goods, and may be encumbered under Chapter 9. The definition of "recorded timber conveyance" is new in Chapter 9, although it reproduces the substance of former Chapter 9. This term is used in revised Chapter 9 in the definition of "goods," pertaining to the circumstances in which standing timber is made movable by anticipation. This aspect of the treatment of timber in Chapter 9 did not change Louisiana law. Additional non-uniform language in former Chapter 9 was omitted as unnecessary and implicit, but with no intent to change Louisiana law.

If standing timber is not cut and removed within the time period provided for in the recorded timber conveyance, the standing timber ceases to be "goods" and any security interest granted in the standing timber will automatically terminate. Chapter 9 is more explicit than former Chapter 9 in providing that standing timber which is made movable by anticipation is within the scope of Chapter 9. Section 9-109(a)(1) provides that standing timber that constitutes goods (that is, the interest of a non-landowner in standing timber that is subject to a recorded timber conveyance) is subject to Chapter 9. A similar non-uniform clarification is added to Section 9-109(d)(11)(F).

The fourth definition pertinent to agricultural matters is "agricultural lien." As discussed below, Chapter 9 includes agricultural liens within its scope. This definition varies from U.C.C. Article 9 by substituting the term "lien," which is a non-uniform defined term in Chapter 9. This definition also changes U.C.C. Article 9 with respect to the lessor's privilege, in order to bring all Louisiana lessor's privileges on farm products within the scope of the definition. Louisiana does not restrict the lessor's privilege only to the movable effects of the tenant. The Louisiana lessor's privilege also includes the movables of a subtenant or third party on the leased premises. Thus the definition in Chapter 9 is modified so as to not require that the debtor be the direct tenant. In addition, the definition does not restrict the lien in favor of the furnisher of goods or services only to furnishers in the ordinary course of business. That requirement in U.C.C. Article 9 is not contained in all of Louisiana's statutes creating such privileges.

C. Other Modifications to U.C.C. Article 9 Definitions

1. Debtor

The definition of "debtor" in Chapter 9 is substantively uniform. However, the result from this uniform definition may be different in Louisiana from many other states. Louisiana is a community property state. The term "debtor" is defined in relation to property, rather than the secured obligation. The definition specifies that the debtor is a person having an interest in the collateral. Thus, as under former Chapter 9, each spouse is a debtor as to community property collateral, even if only one spouse acts alone to encumber the collateral with the security interest. Each debtor is entitled to the protections afforded under Chapter 9. . . .

III. Scope

In the first of several significant variations, Chapter 9 brings into its scope several kinds of property that reside outside of U.C.C. Article 9. . . . The additional types of collateral included within the scope of Chapter 9 are consumer deposit accounts, consumer tort claims, judgments, and life insurance policies. Additionally, Chapter 9 contains special provisions pertaining to collateral mortgage notes and to public finance transactions. . . .

A. Deposit Accounts

. . . U.C.C. Section 9-109(d)(13) excludes deposit accounts in a consumer transaction from the scope of U.C.C. Article 9. . . . Chapter 9 is uniform with U.C.C. Article 9 in most respects regarding deposit accounts, including the choice of law governing perfection and priority of security interests in deposit accounts under Section 9-304. However, because Chapter 9 includes consumer deposit accounts within its scope, Section 9-304 has a broader application than U.C.C. Section 9-304. Thus, the choice of law rule of Louisiana governing perfection and priority of a security interest in a consumer deposit account makes it clear that this inclusion of consumer deposit accounts within the ambit of Chapter 9 applies only when Louisiana is the depositary bank's jurisdiction. . . .

Chapter 9 does change the definition of "deposit account" from former Chapter 9 to correspond to the interplay of deposit accounts and instruments in U.C.C. Article 9. Former Chapter 9 excluded "an account evidenced by a certificate of deposit" from the definition of deposit account. The revised definition of "deposit account" in Chapter 9 goes further and specifically excludes all accounts evidenced by an instrument.

The definition of the term "instrument" in Chapter 980 and in U.C.C. Article 9 is broader than the definition of that term in U.C.C. Article 3, which includes only negotiable instruments. Under U.C.C. Article 9 and Chapter 9, an "instrument" is defined as "a negotiable instrument or any other writing that evidences a right to the payment of a monetary obligation . . . and is of a type that in the ordinary course of business is transferred by delivery with any necessary endorsement or assignment." Thus, under the new definition an uncertificated certificate of deposit is a deposit account if, and because, there is no writing evidencing the bank's obligation to pay. On the other hand, a non-negotiable certificate of deposit is a deposit account only if it is not an "instrument," i.e., a question that turns on whether the non-negotiable certificate of deposit is "of a type that in ordinary course of business is transferred by delivery with any necessary indorsement or assignment." . . .

B. Tort Claims

. . . [A]ll tort claims [are] eligible [as] original collateral. Once again, this addition in scope is accomplished in Chapter 9 by deletion from U.C.C. Article 9, which limits its scope to commercial tort claims. Indeed, Chapter 9 omits and reserves the definition "commercial tort claim" because Chapter 9 applies to all tort claims and there is no need to refer in the Louisiana statute to commercial tort claims specifically. Chapter 9 goes beyond former Chapter 9 in including specific provisions pertaining to security interests in tort claims, both by following U.C.C. Article 9 and by adding non-uniform provisions. . . .

D. Life Insurance Policies

Chapter 9 [includes] within its scope a transfer of an interest in or an assignment of a claim under a policy of life insurance. This inclusion is created by removing life insurance policies from U.C.C. Article 9's general exclusion of all insurance policies. The treatment of life insurance policies in former Chapter 9 was derived from Louisiana Civil Code Article 3158, which had formerly governed pledges of life insurance policies. In contrast, most, if not all, other states deal with the pledge of life insurance policies outside of U.C.C. Article 9.

. . . Chapter 9 provides that the only method of perfecting a security interest in a life insurance policy is to obtain control under Section 9-107.1. Filing is neither necessary nor effective. . . .

Chapter 9 continues the requirement in former Chapter 9 of written consent of the beneficiary of the insurance policy in certain cases if the beneficiary is not the insured or his estate.

The concept of possession of the life insurance policy as a method of perfection has been suppressed. Modern commercial practice is that life insurance companies do not attribute legal consequences to possession of a sole "original" life insurance policy. Moreover, the requirement of possession is not practical as applied to an interest in a group life insurance policy.

The definition of "general intangible" in Chapter 9 explicitly excludes life insurance policies. This exclusion prevents the general rules of creation, perfection, and priority applicable to general intangibles from applying to life insurance policies. Instead, specific rules under Chapter 9 apply to the creation, perfection, and priority of a security interest in a life insurance policy. . . .

Chapter 9 adds a non-uniform Section 9-329.1 governing priority of security interests in a life insurance policy, modeled upon the priority rules for deposit accounts in Section 9-327. Chapter 9 also adds a non-uniform provision in Section 9-208(b)(6) imposing a duty upon a secured party who has control of a life insurance policy to terminate under appropriate circumstances.

E. Collateral Mortgage Notes

For purposes of Chapter 9, a collateral mortgage note is an instrument. However, the definition of investment property excludes collateral mortgage notes in order to prevent the rules applicable to the creation, perfection, and priority of security interests in investment property from applying to collateral mortgage notes. Similarly, in multiple places in Chapter 9, collateral mortgage notes are expressly excluded from many rules pertaining to creation, perfection, and priority which are otherwise applicable to instruments generally.

Most importantly, Chapter 9 reproduces longstanding Louisiana law requiring possession of a collateral mortgage note for perfection. While Chapter 9 follows U.C.C. Article 9 in changing the law to permit perfection by filing with respect to instruments generally, Chapter 9 varies to exclude collateral mortgage notes in that respect. Without this variation, a financing statement covering instruments might have the unintended effect of giving the secured party a mortgage upon the debtor's immovable property.

. . . Because a collateral mortgage note is by definition secured by a mortgage on Louisiana immovable property and because filing is not an appropriate method of perfection as to collateral mortgage notes, Chapter 9 includes this special choice of law provision to prevent another state's laws from governing perfection and priority of a security interest in a collateral mortgage note. Chapter 9 is the sole source of law governing perfection, the effect of perfection or non-perfection, and the priority of a security interest in a collateral mortgage note.

A security interest in a collateral mortgage note requires a specific description of the collateral mortgage note for attachment. Chapter 9 does not change traditional Louisiana law with respect to the priority of collateral mortgages derived from the pledge and possession of a collateral mortgage note. Under Section 9-322(f)(6), the general priority rules under Section 9-322 are subject to Louisiana Revised Statutes 9:5551 with respect to collateral mortgages. This statute preserves the longstanding Louisiana rule governing the ranking of a collateral mortgage in instances in which the debt owed to a pledgee of a collateral mortgage note is reduced to zero, but debt secured by the pledge is incurred later, with no interruption in the possession of the collateral mortgage note. . . .

G. As-Extracted Collateral

The term "as-extracted collateral" is a definition new to U.C.C. Article 9, but does not reflect a change in the law. The term refers to minerals and related accounts resulting from the sale of minerals at the wellhead or minehead to which special rules for perfecting security interests apply. Chapter 9 carries forward Louisiana's non-uniform variations, made to mesh Chapter 9 with Louisiana's mineral law.

The definition of "as-extracted collateral" is modified in Chapter 9 to substitute Louisiana terminology from Louisiana's mineral law for common law language, and reproduces the language used in former Chapter 9. The definition uses the term "mineral rights," which is a non-uniform definition added in Chapter 9. . . . Mineral rights are defined under Chapter 9 to be immovable property, but also specifically include net profit interests, which in fact may or may not be immovable property interests under the Louisiana Mineral Code.

The definition of "accounts" in Chapter 9 contains a non-uniform addition, including within "accounts" rights to payment arising under mineral rights, even if such rights to payment are characterized as rentals under Louisiana law. The exception to this inclusion is rentals payable to a landowner or mineral servitude owner. A corresponding change is made in the scope provision in Section 9-109, to include these rights to payment under mineral rights within the scope of Chapter 9 and the definition of accounts.

Louisiana's non-uniform filing rules apply to as-extracted collateral. Under Chapter 9, filings pertaining to as-extracted collateral are made in the regular Uniform Commercial Code records, not the mortgage records for immovable property, even though immovable property descriptions are attached. Also, Chapter 9 continues the Louisiana system in permitting financing statements covering as-extracted collateral to be filed in any parish selected by the filer, rather than only in the parish where the pertinent immovable property is located.

Pertaining to minerals upon severance, Chapter 9 omits and reserves Subsection 9-320(d). Subsection 9-320(d) is included in U.C.C. Article 9 to provide a rule in those states in which a mortgage encumbers minerals both before extraction and after extraction. Neither part of that rule is law in Louisiana.

IV. Creation

A. Description

U.C.C. Section 9-108(e) lists several types of collateral which require greater specificity when described in a security agreement. For these types of collateral, description only by type of collateral using the statutory U.C.C. definitions is an insufficient description in a security agreement for purposes of creating a security interest. The purpose of requiring greater specificity of description is to prevent debtors from inadvertently encumbering certain property. . . .

Chapter 9 adds more collateral types to its Subsection (e). Because Chapter 9 includes all tort claims and not just commercial tort claims, this requirement necessarily applies to all tort claims. In addition, this section's requirement of more specific description is applied in Chapter 9 to life insurance policies, judgments, beneficial interests in a trust, interests in an estate, and collateral mortgage notes. It was considered appropriate policy to require such collateral to be described with greater specificity than, for instance, picking up a judgment or an interest in a trust or estate merely by reference to "all general intangibles." . . .

B. After-Acquired Collateral

. . . U.C.C. Article 9 makes after-acquired property clauses in a security agreement ineffective as to two types of collateral: certain consumer goods and commercial tort claims. Chapter 9 is uniform with respect to the after-acquired consumer goods provision. However, Chapter 9 applies the after-acquired property clause restriction to all tort claims, and also to security interests in a judgment, a life insurance policy, a beneficial interest in a trust, an interest in an estate, or a collateral mortgage note. The consequence is that under Chapter 9, in order for a security interest to attach to a tort claim, a judgment, a life insurance policy, a beneficial interest in a trust, an interest in an estate, or a collateral mortgage note, such collateral must be in existence when the security agreement is authenticated. . . .

The combined effect of Sections 9-108 and 9-204 is that an after-acquired collateral clause in a security agreement will not reach future tort claims, judgments, life insurance policies, beneficial interests in a trust, interests in an estate or collateral mortgage notes. . . .

D. Repledge by Secured Party

U.C.C. Section 9-207 deals with the rights and duties of a secured party having possession or control of collateral. . . . Under U.C.C. Article 9, if the secured party repledges collateral, the debtor's right to redeem is unimpaired as against the debtor's original secured party, but nevertheless may not be enforceable as against the new secured party. Indeed, in the vast majority of cases where repledge rights are significant, the security interest of the second secured party will be senior to the debtor's interest under U.C.C. Article 9. . . . U.C.C. Article 9 leaves the burden on the debtor to restrict this right in its agreement with the secured party. These rules follow common law precedents which apply unless the parties otherwise agree. The merits of the expanded right of repledge afforded by U.C.C. Article 9 are debatable.

Chapter 9 rejects this approach. Non-uniform Subsection 9-207(c) in Chapter 9 provides that a secured party's repledge is subject to and on terms that do not impair the debtor's right to redeem the collateral, unless otherwise agreed by the parties. Thus, under Chapter 9 the burden is on the secured party, rather than the debtor, to provide different treatment in the security agreement. This change is consistent with Louisiana civil law principles. . . .

V. Perfection by Filing

A perfected security interest is an attached security interest that will prevail over a competing creditor, including a trustee in bankruptcy having the status of a lien creditor on the commencement of the debtor's bankruptcy. There are three primary ways in which an attached security interest may be perfected. A security interest may be perfected by filing, the secured party's taking possession of the collateral or, in certain cases, control. In a few instances, U.C.C. Article 9 provides that a security interest may be perfected automatically upon attachment.

The primary method of perfection is for the secured party to file a proper financing statement in the appropriate Uniform Commercial Code filing office. For most security interests, perfection either is permitted or is mandatory by filing. Chapter 9 has multiple non-uniform changes regarding perfection by filing, resulting in a significant variation from U.C.C. Article 9.

A. Filing System

Section 9-501 of Chapter 9, governing filing of financing statements in Louisiana, is entirely non-uniform. Chapter 9 continues the unique filing system adopted by former Chapter 9. In Louisiana, a financing statement may be filed in the Uniform Commercial Code records of the Clerk of Court in any parish, or if in Orleans Parish with the Recorder of Mortgages, without regard to the location of the debtor or the collateral within the state. Each parish is linked by computer to the office of the Louisiana Secretary of State, which maintains a master, state-wide computer index of all Uniform Commercial Code filings. This system is not an alternative suggested in U.C.C. Article 9, but is fully consistent with the policy of central filing strongly promoted by U.C.C. Article 9. This Louisiana system combines the principal advantage of state-wide filing, which is ease of searches and access to information, with the convenience of local filing offices.

The Louisiana Secretary of State is not a "filing office." It accepts no filings of Uniform Commercial Code records, nor does that office perform searches. Instead, search requests are processed by the Clerks of Court and in Orleans Parish by the Recorder of Mortgages. This system has worked exceedingly well in Louisiana since its adoption in 1990. Louisiana has avoided the serious time delays encountered by states which have adopted pure central filing, with a solitary office handling all Uniform Commercial Code filings and searches in a state.

Chapter 9 also carries over other derogations of Louisiana's filing system from former Chapter 9. One such difference from U.C.C. Article 9 pertains to real property related filings covering fixtures, as-extracted collateral (minerals), or timber to be cut. Chapter 9's filing system follows former Chapter 9 in placing fixture filings and filings of financing statements covering as-extracted collateral or timber to be cut in the regular Uniform Commercial Code records. Unlike U.C.C. Article 9, such filings are not made in the mortgage records for immovable property, even though immovable property descriptions are attached. Also, unlike U.C.C. Article 9, Chapter 9 follows former Chapter 9 in permitting these initial filings to be made in any parish selected by the filer, regardless of the location of the pertinent immovable property within the state. Accordingly, in Louisiana a "fixture filing" does not require the filing of a separate financing statement. One financing statement may be effective to perfect a security interest in both ordinary collateral and fixtures. The same is true with respect to as-extracted collateral or timber to be cut.

. . . Chapter 9 also carries forward the rule from former Chapter 9 requiring all subsequent filings to be filed in the same parish in which the pertinent original financing statement was filed.

B. Rejection

Chapter 9 varies significantly from U.C.C. Article 9 on the authority of the filing officer to reject a tendered filing. U.C.C. Subsection 9-520(a) makes it mandatory for the filing officer to reject the filing for the reasons set forth in U.C.C. Section 9-516(b). However, under Chapter 9 the authority of the filing officer to reject a Uniform Commercial Code filing is discretionary, rather than mandatory. Nonetheless, like U.C.C. Article 9, Chapter 9 provides an exclusive list of grounds upon which the filing office, in its discretion, may reject a filing. The Louisiana approach of discretionary authority is consistent with former Chapter 9. The critical point of emphasis is that Chapter 9 limits this discretionary authority to the exclusive list of reasons set forth in Subsection 9-516(b).

Chapter 9 varies from other filing provisions of U.C.C. Article 9. U.C.C. Subsection 9-516 (d) deals with a filing office's unjustified refusal to accept a record. Under U.C.C. Article 9, an improperly rejected filing is considered filed. However, a financing statement that is communicated to the filing office but which the filing office refuses to accept provides no public notice. Louisiana's public records doctrine necessitates that Chapter 9 reject this approach. Therefore, Subsection 9-516(d) is omitted and reserved in Chapter 9. Such an approach will not prejudice creditors because under Louisiana's filing system a filer has a choice of sixty-four filing offices for Uniform Commercial Code filings, one in each parish. In the rare event that a filing officer in Louisiana improperly rejects a filing, the Louisiana filer has the easy option of filing in another parish. . . .

2. Property Description

Subsection 9-516(b)(3)(D) is omitted and reserved in Chapter 9, because the determination of the sufficiency of property descriptions in Louisiana is not the task of filing officers. The responsibility for the sufficiency of information contained in Louisiana filings is with the filer, not the filing officer.

C. Fixtures

Chapter 9 is significantly non-uniform in the provisions pertaining to fixtures. . . .

Under U.C.C. Article 9, fixtures are goods that have become so related to real estate that an interest in the goods arises under applicable real estate law. But fixtures are still goods. The uniform definition of "goods" includes "fixtures," even though goods are defined as things that are movable when a security interest attaches. A security interest under U.C.C. Article 9 (i) may be created in goods that are fixtures already or (ii) may continue in goods that become fixtures. There is an exception for goods that are ordinary building materials incorporated into an improvement on land. No security interest in them exists under Chapter 9 or U.C.C. Article 9. . . .

In stark contrast, Chapter 9 carries forward from former Chapter 9 a fundamentally different approach to security interests in fixtures, consistent with long established Louisiana legal principles relating to property and chattel mortgages. In Louisiana, a security interest cannot be created in goods that already have become fixtures. The definitions of "fixtures" and "fixture filing" in Chapter 9 are significantly non-uniform, as is the pertinent portion of the definition of "goods." Even the scope provision in Chapter 9 is non-uniform, with Subsection 9-109(a)(1) providing that Chapter 9 applies "as to fixtures only if the security interest has been perfected by a fixture filing when the goods become fixtures." These definitions, in combination with the non-uniform language in the scope provision in Subsection 9-109(a)(1), the fixtures provisions in Subsection 9-334(a), and the non-uniform filing provisions in Chapter 9 Part 5, establish the four major variations of Chapter 9 as it applies to fixtures.

First, in order for a security interest in fixtures to exist and continue, a fixture filing must be made before the goods become fixtures, i.e., component parts. Second, a security interest may not be retained under Chapter 9 in consumer goods that become component parts of immovable property. This is because by definition a consumer good cannot become a "fixture." Third, fixture filings under Chapter 9 are not filed in the immovable property records, but instead are filed in the regular Louisiana Uniform Commercial Code records. Fourth, the remedies applicable to fixtures are narrower under Chapter 9.

1. Component Parts

Chapter 9's definition of fixtures utilizes the terminology and principles pertaining to "component parts" in the Louisiana Civil Code. In Chapter 9, goods "includes fixtures but only if they were movable when a fixture filing covering them was made." Thus, unlike U.C.C. Article 9, under Chapter 9 the secured party's fixture filing must be made prior to the goods becoming component parts in order for the security interest to be preserved. This requirement reproduces the substance of former Chapter 9.

This timing requirement continues the substance of former Chapter 9 as well as Louisiana's former chattel mortgage statutes. Language from the former chattel mortgage statutes and former Chapter 9212 that, "[a]s to a secured party with a security interest in fixtures perfected by a fixture filing, the fixtures shall remain movables, and no sale or mortgage of the immovable property shall affect or impair the priority of the security interest," has been omitted as conceptually incorrect on the first point and unnecessary and implicit on the second. The omission does not change Louisiana law.

2. Consumer Goods

Chapter 9 reproduces former Chapter 9's exclusion of consumer goods from classification as fixtures. Except for manufactured homes, a Chapter 9 security interest may not be retained in consumer goods that become component parts of immovable property. A consumer good cannot become a "fixture" under Chapter 9 even though it has become a component part under Louisiana property law.

Manufactured homes are not dealt with as fixtures, but instead are encumbered either as titled motor vehicles under Chapter 9 as supplemented by the Louisiana Manufactured Home Property Act or as component parts of immovable property following a declaration of immobilization made under that statute.

3. Filing

Chapter 9 continues the special Louisiana filing rule under former Chapter 9 with respect to fixture filings. Unlike U.C.C. Article 9, fixture filings in Louisiana are not filed in the immovable property mortgage records, but instead are filed in the regular Uniform Commercial Code records. Accordingly, in Louisiana a "fixture filing" does not require the filing of a separate financing statement. One financing statement may be effective both to cover ordinary collateral and also to be a "fixture filing."

Consistent with the principles described above, Chapter 9 contains a non-uniform variation regarding purchase-money security interest fixture filings. U.C.C. Article 9 permits a purchase-money security interest fixture filing to be effective for priority purposes if the fixture filing is made within twenty days after the goods become fixtures. In Chapter 9, a fixture filing by definition is "made before the goods become fixtures." Accordingly, Subsection 9-334(d)(3) omits the twenty day rule entirely.

4. Remedies

The remedies available to a secured party having a security interest in fixtures is also significantly non-uniform. U.C.C. Section 9-604 significantly changes the former law in other states as to the remedies available to a secured party. U.C.C. Article 9 overrules cases in other states holding that a secured party's only remedy after default is the removal of the fixtures from the real property. U.C.C. Article 9 permits the secured party to sell the fixtures in place or use self-help to render the fixtures inoperative but left in place.

In contrast, Chapter 9 omits and reserves these provisions. The only remedy applicable to fixtures under Chapter 9 is judicial sale by the secured party. Section 9-604 is modified to eliminate any right, or implication thereof, of the secured party to self-help action with respect to fixtures, except in the very narrow circumstances set forth in Section 9-609. Section 9-604 also carries forward a non-uniform provision from former Chapter 9 authorizing a secured party to demand separate appraisal of the fixtures where the immovable property is sold in foreclosure proceedings by a mortgagee or other encumbrancer. . . .

There is another non-uniform provision in Chapter 9 pertaining to the relative priority of a secured party's fixture security interest and a mortgagee's mortgage of the pertinent immovable. Section 9-334(h) reproduces the variation in former Chapter 9 that omits the requirement that a mortgage indicate that it is a "construction mortgage" in order to have priority afforded thereto.

D. Manufactured Homes

Chapter 9 varies from U.C.C. Article 9 with respect to manufactured homes in order to preserve existing Louisiana law. Under Louisiana law, manufactured homes are encumbered either as titled motor vehicles under Chapter 9 as supplemented by the Louisiana Manufactured Home Property Act or as component parts of immovable property following a declaration of immobilization. Although Chapter 9 contains the defined term "manufactured home," both the definition and its use are non-uniform.

. . . In U.C.C. Article 9, the term "manufactured home" is used only in the definition of "goods," in the fixtures provision in Section 9-344, and in U.C.C. Section 9-515. Under U.C.C. Subsection 9-334(e)(4), a security interest noted on the manufactured home's certificate of title will have priority over the interests of competing real estate claimants, even if the manufactured home has already become a fixture and no fixture filing is filed in the real property records. In addition, the other fixture priority rules also apply to manufactured homes. If the state statute does not require notation on the certificate of title for perfection, then U.C.C. Section 9-515 permits an ordinary financing statement in a "manufactured-home transaction" to be effective for thirty years.

In contrast, under Chapter 9, security interests in manufactured homes are not perfected by the filing of ordinary financing statements. Instead, the security interest is noted on the certificate of title. Accordingly, the thirty-year rule in U.C.C. Article 9 is omitted in Louisiana as unnecessary. A security interest noted on a certificate of title remains effective until terminated.

More importantly, in Chapter 9 the term "manufactured homes" is instead used in the non-uniform provisions pertaining to fixtures. These non-uniform provisions in Chapter 9 exclude manufactured homes from being fixtures, pursuant to exclusionary language in the definition and other operative provisions. Thus the priority rules of the Louisiana Manufactured Home Property Act are left in effect, and U.C.C. Subsection 9-334(e)(4) is omitted and reserved in Chapter 9.

E. Titled Motor Vehicles

. . . U.C.C. Section 9-311 exempts from its filing requirements transactions governed by state certificate-of-title statutes covering motor vehicles and the like. Chapter 9 continues former Chapter 9 in omitting this exclusion. In Louisiana, the method of perfecting a security interest in automobiles and other titled motor vehicles is provided in Chapter 9 itself. These filings are made with the Department of Public Safety and Corrections of the Office of Motor Vehicles, unless the collateral is held as inventory for sale or lease as discussed below. It should be noted that in Louisiana financing statements covering titled motor vehicles are required to contain additional descriptive information, and filing is effective only if later validated by the secretary.

F. Interest in an Estate

Chapter 9 contains a clarifying exclusion in its scope provision pertaining to security interests in an interest in an estate. Subsection 9-109(c)(5) provides that Chapter 9 does not apply to the extent that the rights of a successor in an estate are interests in real property. This exclusion simply makes more express the general applicability of the exclusion in Subsection 9-109(d)(11), stating that Chapter 9 does not apply to the creation or transfer of an interest in real property. Civil Code Article 872 provides that the estate of a deceased means the property, rights, and obligations that a person leaves after his death.

VI. Perfection by Control

. . . Chapter 9 does contain two non-uniform provisions pertaining to collateral in which a security interest may be perfected by control. First, Section 9-107.2 governs situations where control of the collateral is subject to some condition. Under this statutory provision, an agreement by the depository bank, securities intermediary, letter of credit bank or similar pertinent party to comply with the secured party's instructions suffices for "control" of the pertinent collateral even if such party's agreement is subject to specified conditions, e.g., that the secured party's instructions be accompanied by a certification that the debtor is in default. This provision makes express a concept that is implicit in U.C.C. Article 9 and in U.C.C. Article 8. It should be noted that if the condition is the debtor's further consent, the statute explicitly provides that such agreement would not confer control.

. . . Second, as discussed above, Chapter 9 allows for perfection of a security interest in a life insurance policy by "control." In reality, this control is somewhat more implicit than the control achieved with respect to a deposit account or investment property, where control means that the parties have agreed expressly that the secured party can direct disposition of the collateral. Under Section 9-107.1, control of an insurance policy is achieved simply by the life insurance company's bare acknowledgment of the security interest, without the further requirement of an express agreement to follow the secured party's directions pertaining to the life insurance policy.

VII. Priority

Chapter 9 contains several important non-uniform provisions pertaining to priority in the areas of security interests in crops, the priority of security interests versus privileges, and purchase-money security interests. . . .

B. Priority Versus Privileges

One of the most significant variations in Chapter 9 is its non-uniform provision expressly dealing with the relative priority among conflicting security interests and liens in the same collateral. . . .

Chapter 9 adds a non-uniform provision of major importance in Subsection 9-322(h). Under Subsection 9-322(h), a security interest has priority over a conflicting lien, other than an agricultural lien, in the same collateral except as otherwise provided in Chapter 9 or except to the extent the lien is created by a statute that provides otherwise. This provision continues prior Louisiana law, although it states the result in strikingly clear fashion. Thus, as a general rule a security interest has priority over a conflicting lien in the same collateral, regardless of perfection.

There are, however, three exceptions to this rule. The first is when the conflicting lien is an agricultural lien, as discussed above. The second exception is found in Chapter 9 itself, in Section 9-333. Section 9-333 deals with possessory liens and, although reworded in Chapter 9, is substantively uniform. The third exception is where the statute creating the lien expressly provides that the lien has priority over the security interests. There are multiple examples of statutes which provide that certain privileges have priority over certain security interests. In addition, other statutes provide that the statutory privilege has priority over all security interests.

C. Consumer Purchase-Money Security Interests

Section 9-103 reproduces a change made in former Chapter 9 from former U.C.C. Article 9. Chapter 9 applies its rules in Section 9-103 to consumer goods transactions in the same manner as all other purchase-money security interest transactions. Former Chapter 9 contained a non-uniform addition which preserved purchase-money security interest status notwithstanding cross-collateralization. U.C.C. Article 9 has adopted this Louisiana rule for non-consumer good transactions, rejecting the "transformation" rule in some states' jurisprudence under which any cross-collateralization destroys the purchase-money status entirely. Chapter 9 goes further and continues the rule under former Chapter 9 that the principles in this section apply to all purchase-money security interest transactions, consumer and commercial. Chapter 9 rejects the approach of U.C.C. Article 9, which expressly leaves it to the courts to fashion a rule applicable to consumer-goods transactions. Under Louisiana civil law, such decisions are appropriately made by legislation, not by judge-made common law.

VIII. Third Parties

A. Purchasers

. . . Chapter 9 contains several non-uniform provisions pertaining to the rights of purchasers. First, Chapter 9 varies from U.C.C. Article 9 with respect to the requirements that a buyer, lessee or licensee of collateral must meet in order to take free of a security interest or agricultural lien. Section 9-317 deals with the rights of such parties versus unperfected security interests. Subsections 9-317(b), (c) and (d) omit the requirement contained in U.C.C. Article 9 that such buyer, lessee, or licensee act without knowledge of the security interest or agricultural lien in order to take free of the unperfected security interest. This omission is consistent with the Louisiana public records doctrine, which is predicated on filings and not knowledge. The Louisiana rule is that actual knowledge by third parties of an unrecorded interest is immaterial. Proper filing is alone dispositive. This policy promotes judicial efficiency by facilitating proof in contested cases.

Second, Section 9-320 of Chapter 9 also omits the requirement contained in U.C.C. Article 9 that a buyer of consumer goods buy without knowledge of the security interest in order to take free of a perfected security interest. Subsection 9-320(b) applies to buyers of goods that the debtor-seller holds as "consumer goods." The omission of this requirement that the buyer act without knowledge of the security interest is a change in Louisiana law. The reason for this deletion is both to give greater protection to the consumer buyer and to align this provision with the public records doctrine. In reality, this provision deals with purchase-money security interests in non-titled consumer goods, which are perfected automatically without filing. If the secured party does file, all buyers take subject to the security interest. . . .

C. Anti-Assignment Provisions

. . . U.C.C. Article 9 continues former law by rendering ineffective a clause restricting the creation or enforcement of a security interest in an account or a general intangible. U.C.C. Article 9 also renders ineffective an anti-assignment clause affecting payments under other chattel paper or promissory notes. In addition, and more importantly, U.C.C. Article 9 renders ineffective a provision of law that would prevent the attachment, perfection, or enforcement of a security interest in accounts or chattel paper. Finally, and of critical importance, U.C.C. Article 9 renders ineffective a clause in any general intangible or any provision of law relating to any general intangible, even if not for money due or to become due, that prevents a security interest from attaching and becoming perfected, so long as the rights of the account debtor or other party imposing the anti-assignment clause or provision of law are not disturbed. . . .

. . . Chapter 9 makes two substantive additions. First, Chapter 9 adds in each section a provision preventing that section from overriding anti-assignment provisions in statutes pertaining to government benefits, such as pensions, worker's compensation, unemployment compensation and public assistance, as well as statutes providing for crime victim reparation payments or lottery payments. Second, each section adds a provision preventing that section from overriding anti-assignment provisions in, among other things, structured settlements. These provisions were not part of the bill recommended by the Louisiana State Law Institute, but instead are the result of an amendment drafted and proposed by the American Insurance Association in Senate Committee on Judiciary A.

D. Banks

U.C.C. Article 9 provides that unless a secured party has control over a deposit account, which requires the depositary bank's agreement, the depositary bank has no obligation to deal with the secured party with respect to the deposit account. Furthermore, a depositary bank has no obligation to enter into a control agreement with a secured party relating to the deposit account, even if the debtor customer requests. Chapter 9 adds an additional new non-uniform Section 9-343, to clarify that the joinder by a depositary bank in a control agreement does not in and of itself constitute a waiver or subordination of the bank's security interest in the deposit account, unless that control agreement specifically so provides.

E. Life Insurance Companies

As discussed above, Chapter 9 contains a significant variation from U.C.C. Article 9 by including life insurance policies as eligible collateral. Although that inclusion carries forward prior Louisiana law, Chapter 9 contains a new Section 9-344 pertaining to the rights of life insurance companies. Section 9-344 is modeled on similar provisions pertaining to the rights and duties of persons in possession of collateral, including the duties of a person who voluntarily acknowledges that it holds possession for a secured party's benefit and the rights and duties of a depositary bank and securities intermediary. A life insurance company is not obligated by Chapter 9 to enter into a control agreement with a secured party even if the debtor-insured so requests. An insurer who does agree to allow "control" does not thereby assume any duty to such secured party. . . .

G. Tortfeasors

Chapter 9 contains several non-uniform provisions pertaining to security interests in tort claims. First, as discussed above, Chapter 9 includes all tort claims, even consumer tort claims, within its scope.

Second, Subsection 9-411(c) removes the creation and enforcement of security interests in litigious rights, including tort claims, from the application of Civil Code Article 2652. The policy underlying Civil Code Article 2652 is to prevent parties from trading in and attempting to profit from lawsuits. The rights of a secured party under Chapter 9 in a tort claim or other litigious right is limited to the secured debt otherwise incurred, and does not involve the negative consequences of independently trafficking in tort claims or other lawsuits.

IX. Remedies

The fourth major variation in Chapter 9 from U.C.C. Article 9 is in the area of remedies and damages. There are several important non-uniform remedies provisions in Chapter 9.324 Some are carried forward from former Chapter 9, while others were added in response to new provisions in U.C.C. Article 9. Although not the most significant, the variation which receives the most attention is the absence in Chapter 9 of a general authorization of self-help repossession of collateral by secured parties.

A. Self-Help

Louisiana has long had an established public policy against self-help action by creditors with respect to corporeal property. That public policy remains firmly in place in major portions of Louisiana law. The prohibition on self-help action by landlords except in instances of abandonment is unquestionably established in Louisiana lease law. Unlike most other states, Louisiana mortgage law does not provide for any non-judicial foreclosure remedies by a mortgagee of immovable property. There has been no significant movement to alter the prohibitions on creditor self-help in these areas of Louisiana law.

There has been, however, a continuing push by the finance industry to obtain a broader self-help right of repossession of collateral as part of Louisiana's former Chapter 9. This concerted effort is driven by concerns linked to the quintessential American consumer collateral—the automobile. It is the significant cost, in delay and expenses, inherent in Louisiana's procedures for judicial seizure and sale of automobiles in defaulted automobile finance loans that fuels the continued push for self-help repossession.

Bills have been introduced to grant an authorization of self-help repossession in every Louisiana non-fiscal legislative session for over a decade. None of these legislative efforts have been successful, however, largely due to the vehement opposition by Louisiana sheriffs. A major reason for their opposition, admitted or not, is the significant loss of revenue sheriffs would suffer due to a loss of or decrease in the foreclosure business. The political tension between the finance industry lobby and the Louisiana sheriffs has led to several attempts at legislative compromise, with enactments of an expedited judicial seizure and sale process short of self-help repossession. But those legislative attempts at compromise solutions have not had real practical success to date.

In recognition of this political context, there was an express policy decision by the U.C.C. Committee of the Louisiana State Law Institute and by the Institute Council not to change significantly the provisions of former Chapter 9 as they pertain to self-help repossession. Former Chapter 9 was the source of the language used in Chapter 9 authorizing a very limited right of self-help action by secured parties. The intent of the revised language in Chapter 9 is to provide for this narrow authorization of self-help repossession in more precise language.

Section 9-609 of Chapter 9 contains fundamentally different language from U.C.C. Article 9. There was no intent by use of this non-uniform language to introduce broad or prevalent self-help repossession by subterfuge or indirection. After default, a secured party in Louisiana may take possession of the collateral only (1) after the debtor's abandonment, or the debtor's surrender to the secured party of the collateral, or (2) with the debtor's consent given after or in contemplation of default.

The concepts in the first exception of abandonment and surrender are well understood. Both terms come directly from former Chapter 9. Surrender involves the voluntary yielding of the collateral by the debtor, and is not easily misconstrued. Surrender is a bilateral contractual act and occurs only through consent and mutual agreement of both parties.

Abandonment, on the other hand, is a unilateral act whereby the debtor voluntarily relinquishes all right and possession of the collateral, with the intention of not reclaiming it. Abandonment includes both the intention to abandon and an external act by which the intention is carried into effect. Thus, in determining whether a debtor has abandoned the collateral, the debtor's intention is the critical inquiry. Abandonment differs from surrender in that the debtor gives up the collateral with the intention terminating his ownership, but without vesting it in any other person.

The second exception, contained in Subsection 9-609(a)(2), provides for self-help repossession with the "debtor's consent given after or in contemplation of default." The language of this exception was carried over from former Chapter 9, and there was no intent to significantly broaden the availability of self-help repossession in Chapter 9. The purpose behind Subsection 9-609(a)(2) is to permit a debtor to consent to a secured party's self-help repossession only in two narrow circumstances, each of which is tantamount to a debtor's decision actively to surrender collateral to the secured party due to such circumstances. The purpose of allowing the debtor's consent, in addition to the debtor's surrender, is solely to permit the creditor to act where the debtor has the full intent to surrender the collateral, but is not willing to take the active step of delivery himself.

The phrase "after default" should be understood to require the debtor's consent while an uncured default exists. For example, in the case of a debtor who has missed a payment on his automobile loan, and in responding to a call from the automobile finance company says, "I have lost my job, and I can't make any more payments. You can come get the car, it's in my driveway." Such self-help authorization by the debtor is limited to the time for which the debtor remains in default, and is not a blanket general authorization of self-help repossession for any future circumstance. Upon cure of the default, the debtor's authorization is automatically revoked and must be granted again by the debtor in connection with a subsequent, unrelated default.

In addition to consenting to self-help "after default," Subsection 9-609(a)(2) permits the debtor to consent to self-help repossession "in contemplation of default." This provision should not be read more broadly than in that context. The debtor's consent is to be in specific expectation of a probable and proximate default, and to reasonably prompt self-help action by the secured party in response thereto. For example, the situation may arise where a debtor who has not yet missed a payment tells the secured party in the middle of the week, "I am broke and now unemployed, and there is no way I will make my loan payment on Friday. You can come get the car, it's in front of my apartment." The debtor's "contemplation of default" is of an anticipated likelihood of an imminent and identifiable default. The debtor's specific consent, and the secured party's self-help action based thereon, are authorized only in connection with that default, and are simply in substitution for the debtor's acting to surrender the collateral at that time.

Indefinite consent to a secured party's repossession is not authorized by Chapter 9. The debtor's consent can be neither indefinite in duration, nor indefinite as to its justifying cause. The debtor may not grant consent to self-help in general anticipation of the possibility that a default will occur. Consent to self-help also may not be given for a prolonged period. Thus, consent may not be given at the time the secured interest is created, except in extremely rare circumstances. Also, consent under Section 9-609 is not authorized to be given after a default occurs but with respect to another eventual default which is not then identifiable and probable.

Consent to self-help may be verbal. If necessary, of course, the existence of such consent must be proved in the normal manner. Whether or not secured parties are willing to rely on verbal consent alone is a business decision. Also such consent inherently includes a duty on the secured party to proceed without breach of the peace as a part of the obligation of good faith.

In keeping with the narrow and restricted treatment of self-help repossession in Section 9-609, other provisions of Chapter 9 have been similarly modified. U.C.C. Subsection 9-609(b) is omitted and reserved in Chapter 9. U.C.C. Subsection 9-609(c) provides that a secured party may require the debtor to assemble the collateral and make it available at a place designated by the secured party. Although this provision was contained in former Chapter 9, it was not enforced or utilized to the author's knowledge in Louisiana and is omitted and reserved in Chapter 9. U.C.C. Subsection 9-603(b), which establishes the standard of "breach of peace" for permitted self-help repossession, is omitted in Chapter 9 because U.C.C. Subsection 9-609(b) is omitted.

Subsection 9-602(6) is non-uniform in Chapter 9, providing that the restrictions on self-help repossession may not be varied, waived or avoided by contractual choice of law provisions or other agreement of the parties.

As discussed previously, Section 9-604 dealing with remedies applicable to fixtures is non-uniform in Chapter 9. In other states, U.C.C. Article 9 expands prior law to permit the secured party to sell the fixtures in place, or to use self-help to render the fixtures inoperative but left in place. The intent is to legislatively overrule cases in other states holding that a secured party's only remedy after default is the removal of the fixtures from the immovable property. Chapter 9 omits and reserves Subsection 9-604(b). The only remedy in Louisiana under Chapter 9 applicable to fixtures is judicial sale by the secured party. . . .

* * * * * *

NOTES AND QUESTIONS

Although outside the scope of Article 9, it is worth mentioning that Louisiana does allow a limited form of true "self-help" in the context of vehicle financing. This comes in the form of the Additional Default Remedies Act (Louisiana Revised Statutes §§ 6:965-969), which permits certain types of creditors to repossess motor vehicles through a licensed repossession agent, provided that the debtor has defaulted on at least two consecutive payments. However, not just any creditor can take advantage of this process. Rather, only those financial institutions licensed and regulated by the commissioner of financial institutions or licensed and regulated under the laws of the United States can take advantage of its provisions. If the creditor qualifies, then it has the authority under the statute to take possession of the collateral without any judicial process, provided repossession can be accomplished without a breach of the peace. A breach of the peace is defined as unauthorized entry into a closed dwelling or an oral protest by the debtor. Moreover, the creditor can undertake this action without losing his rights to a deficiency judgment.

From the description above it should be evident that the self-help remedy provided by the Additional Default Remedies Act is indeed quite narrow. It is available only with certain types of collateral and is available only to certain types of licensed creditors holding a security interest in that collateral. Repossession can occur only if it can be achieved without a breach of the peace, which is broadly defined.[1] Further, the repossession must be made only by a licensed repossession agent. In other words, the ability of creditors to take matter into their own hands is still very much prohibited.

D. The Law of Pledge

With that overview and understanding, it is easy to see how the popularity and user-friendly nature of the Article 9 system has rendered the law of pledge a bit of an antique. While it remains in the Civil Code, it has largely been supplanted by the express provisions of Chapter 9 of the Louisiana Commercial Laws. Indeed, there are very few types of movable property that are actually still susceptible to pledge.

1. The 2015 Reform of the Law of Pledge

Nevertheless, the few types of property that remain susceptible to pledge are fairly important to everyday commercial transactions. Because of this—and because there may be new types of property that arise in the future for which Article 9 does not provide a path for collateralization—the Louisiana legislature, under the guidance of the Louisiana State Law Institute, undertook a wholesale update to the law of pledge—effective January 1, 2015. This effort was headed by one of the co-authors of this casebook, David Cromwell—the reporter of the Security Devices Committee of the Law Institute.

2. Overview of Pledge

The following is an excerpt from a law review article written by Professor Michael Rubin. It provides a summary of the most important aspects of the 2015 reform, including a helpful discussion of the rules governing the pledging of rights to leases and rents of an immovable.

---

[1] *See* La. Rev. Stat. § 6:965 (1992) ("(1) "Breach of peace" shall include but not be limited to the following: (a) Unauthorized entry by a repossessor into a closed dwelling, whether locked or unlocked; (b) Oral protest by a debtor to the repossessor against repossession prior to the repossessor seizing control of the collateral shall constitute a breach of the peace by the repossessor.").

* * * * * *

Ruminations on the Louisiana Law of Pledge

Michael H. Rubin

75 LOUISIANA LAW REVIEW 697, 698 (2015)

On January 1, 2015, Act 281 of the 2014 Louisiana legislative session took effect. Drafted by the Louisiana State Law Institute, the Act amends, revises, and reworks not only the Civil Code articles concerning the rules on pledge as a form of real security, but also the articles setting forth the basic principles of personal liability and security for loans. It also deals, in part, with judicial mortgages.

Practitioners will find that, although many basic pledge concepts remain the same, there are a number of new rules, new procedures, and, in some cases, new prohibitions.

The Background of the Louisiana Law of Pledge

There are numerous historical antecedents for the Louisiana law of pledge, including an Egyptian tradition of pledging a mummy to secure a loan, Greek and Roman law, and the Bible.

Although there is an ongoing scholarly debate about whether Louisiana owes more of its civilian tradition to France or Spain, there is no dispute that, at the time the entire Civil Code was revised in 1870 following the Civil War, only 19 of its more than 40 articles on pledge were either direct translations of provisions of the Code Napoleon or dealt with the same subject matter. Nonetheless, because the previous Louisiana Civil Code of 1825 was written in both French and English (with French being the original language and English being the translation), and because French law at the time influenced the redactors of the 1825 Civil Code, many Louisiana courts have looked to the works of French commentators to aid in understanding the pledge provisions. Once the 1870 Civil Code articles on pledge were enacted, they remained almost completely unchanged until the 2014 legislative session.

When Louisiana adopted its version of UCC 9 in 1990, many of the security interests that previously had been controlled by the Civil Code pledge articles were superseded by the UCC provisions. The 1870 Civil Code pledge articles remained in effect, however, because there were some real security assets not covered by Louisiana's version of UCC 9.

In the quarter of a century since Louisiana adopted UCC 9, there has evolved a need to revisit the Civil Code pledge articles. The Legislature enacted the Louisiana State Law Institute's draft proposal in its entirety, and the current revision to the pledge articles completely rewrites this section of the Civil Code.

Some of the changes made by the 2014 legislation alter prior law and introduce new concepts. For example, Act 281 of 2014 allows non-recourse loans secured by a pledge. It abolishes antichresis, which is the pledge of immovable property. It alters the rules on how a creditor can obtain a secured position in a landlord's lease or rents as well as the rules regulating the rights of landlord, creditor, and tenant, and it moves these rules from the Revised Statutes to the Civil Code. It affirms the enforceability of a "negative pledge" but prohibits a payment obligor from restricting the right of the payment obligee to encumber the payment stream. . . .

III. The Limited Scope of Assets that Can Be Pledged

Prior to 1990, the Civil Code pledge provisions were extremely broad and applied to "every corporeal thing, which is susceptible of alienation," items classified as "incorporeal movables," and "a claim on another person." With the advent of Louisiana's adoption of UCC 9 in 1990, however, creditors who wanted to secure loans with the vast majority of items that formerly could be pledged had to employ the UCC's rules and procedures.

The changes made by Act 281 of 2014 include an exclusive listing of assets subject to pledge. Under New C.C. art. 3142, the "only things" that can be pledged are movables "not susceptible of encumbrance by security interest," a "lessor's rights in the lease of an immovable and its rents," and "things made susceptible of pledge by law."

Among the things "made susceptible of pledge by law" are property insurance on immovables and certain mineral payments.

A. A Pledge of Property Insurance on Immovables

The 2014 amendments changed portions of the Civil Code Ancillaries to make it clear that a pledge is the proper mechanism to grant a mortgage creditor a real security right in insurance on immovable property. Thus, property insurance is one of the assets New C.C. art. 3142 makes "susceptible of pledge by law."

B. A Pledge of Mineral Payments by an Owner of Land or a Holder of a Mineral Servitude

New C.C. art. 3172 clarifies the law on how to encumber mineral lease bonus payments payable to a landowner or holder of a mineral servitude. This article specifies the only kind of mineral payments susceptible of pledge. These are pledges by "the owner of land or holder of a mineral servitude" on "bonuses, delay rentals, royalties, and shut-in payments arising from mineral leases, as well as other payments that are classified as rent under the Mineral Code."

The contract of pledge must specifically describe the mineral interests being pledged. As the Comments to this article note, a "mere statement that all leases and rents of the immovable are pledged will not suffice for the pledge to encumber mineral payments."

Note that New C.C. art. 3172 does not apply to mineral payments owing to those who are neither a landowner nor a holder of a mineral servitude. . . .

VII. The Permissible "Negative Pledge" and a New Prohibition

New C.C. art. 3163 changes Louisiana law. It invalidates clauses that restrict the rights of a payment recipient to encumber the payment obligation. Yet, it permits the continued enforcement of the traditional "negative pledge."

A "negative pledge" is a contractual provision that does not grant a creditor any security in an asset but which allows the creditor to demand immediate repayment of a loan if one or more described assets are encumbered by the debtor. "Negative pledges" are routinely used in loan documentation, not only in Louisiana but also throughout the country. It is one of the many non-payment default clauses lenders use to assure that borrowers maintain sufficient assets to repay the loan.

Two examples based on the Comments to New C.C. art. 3163 may be helpful in explaining the distinction that the article draws between permissible "negative pledges" and impermissible restrictions.

Example #1. Landlord owns immovable property leased to Tenant. Landlord enters into a contract with Creditor that does not grant Creditor any pledge of the rental income arising from the property; however, Landlord agrees in the loan documents that it will not pledge rights to the rental income to any person or entity and, if it does so, such an action will violate the loan agreement allowing Creditor to declare a default and immediately demand the full amount of the loan.

This type of clause is a "negative pledge" permitted by New C.C. art. 3163. The reason that this provision is permitted and not prohibited by New C.C. art. 3163 is that the provision is extraneous to the lease, which is the contract under which payments "are or will become due"; further, Creditor is not a party to the lease.

Example #2. The facts are the same as in Example #1, but Tenant has insisted on inserting into the lease a provision prohibiting Landlord from pledging the Tenant's rents.

New C.C. art. 3163 prohibits the enforcement of this provision because it is contained in the lease, which is the contract under which the payments "are or will become due"; moreover, Tenant is "a party" to the lease.

Another distinction between this type of prohibited clause and a permitted "negative pledge" is that the latter does not encumber any property and does not invalidate the pledge; it merely operates to define a non-monetary default allowing a loan to be accelerated.

The public policy distinctions between a permitted "negative pledge" and a clause prohibited by New C.C. art. 3163 are understandable. Allowing enforcement of a contract by which Tenant has sought to prohibit Landlord from pledging rent would relieve Tenant of any rent obligation to anyone other than Landlord and would lessen the value of the rental income stream, which is a primary source of collateral that lenders use to secure loans on commercial properties.

The prohibition in New C.C. art. 3163 applies to more than just agreements between a landlord and tenant. It applies to all payment obligations outside the scope of UCC 9 where an obligee is ostensibly prevented by contract from pledging the obligor's contractual payments to the obligee.

VIII. Modifications, Terminations, and Substitutions of Pledged Obligations

New C.C. arts. 3164 through 3167 create a series of related principles governing the effect of an amendment, modification, or substitution of pledged obligations. The source of these rules is found not in prior Civil Code articles but rather in UCC 9 and in the superseded statute governing the assignment of rents.

Under the amended Civil Code articles, if a pledged obligation is modified or terminated, or if a new obligation is substituted, then the "agreement is effective against the pledgee without his consent" if this is done prior to the obligor having been given notice of the pledge. On the other hand, if the obligor of the pledged obligation has been given written notice of the pledge, a subsequent "agreement modifying or extinguishing the pledged obligation is without effect against the pledgee unless made with his consent." The 2014 amendments also permit the pledgor and pledgee to agree that an event of default occurs if there is a modification, termination, or substitution of the pledged obligation.

Although Part IX of this Rumination covers leases in more detail, a series of examples involving modification, termination, and substitution of a lease illustrates the rules these amended articles articulate. Each of these examples assumes (unless otherwise stated) that the rights of Landlord (the pledgor) in the lease had been "fully earned."

Example #3: Landlord and Tenant entered into a written lease dated February 1, 2015; the lease was properly recorded in the parish public records. The lease is for five years and requires monthly rental payments of $5,000.

Landlord owed Creditor $1 million on a line-of-credit loan. To secure the loan, Landlord pledged to Creditor the Landlord's rights to collect rent under the lease. The pledge was made March 1, 2015, and recorded in the appropriate public records, but Tenant was not notified of the pledge. It turns out that Tenant had not made any rental payments to Landlord in February or March. On April 1, 2015, Landlord and Tenant modified the lease. In exchange for Landlord forgiving the two missed rental payments, the Lease was shorted by two months.

Under C.C. art. 3164, because Tenant had not been notified of the pledge by either Creditor or Landlord, the modification was effective against Creditor. On the other hand, if Creditor had an agreement with Landlord that any modification of the lease would be an event of default, then under New C.C. art. 3166, Creditor may declare a default in the $1 million loan the pledge secures.

Example #4. The facts are the same as in Example #3, above, except that rather than modifying the lease on April 1, 2015, Landlord and Tenant agreed in good faith to terminate it because Tenant was suffering cash-flow issues.

In this instance, the result is the same as in Example #3. Because Tenant had not received notice of the pledge prior to the termination, the termination was effective against Creditor. Nonetheless, if Creditor had an agreement with Landlord that termination of the lease would be an event of default, Creditor may declare a default in the $1 million loan the pledge secures.

Example #5. The facts are the same as in Example #4, above, except that rather than just terminating the lease on April 1, 2015, Landlord and Tenant agreed in good faith to cancel the five-year $5,000/month lease because not only did Tenant have cash flow difficulties but also because Tenant had found Retailer who agreed to sign a new lease with Landlord on the same space, with the new lease extending for five years for a rent of $4,800/month ($200 less per month than Tenant had agreed to pay under its lease). On April 1, 2015, Landlord and Tenant canceled Tenant's lease, and Landlord and Retailer entered into the new lease.

Under New C.C. art. 3164, the substitution of a "new contract" is effective against Creditor because Tenant had not been notified in writing of the Landlord's pledge. The pledge continues on the rent under the lease between Landlord and Retailer. As in the prior examples, Creditor may declare a default in the $1 million loan if the loan documents prevented substitution of a new lease.

Note, however, that this example may not occur in the real world, because typically a pledge of rents would encompass all the rents arising from the building. In such instances, Retailer's lease would be subject to the pledge by contract regardless of whether the termination of Tenant's lease was effective against Creditor.

Example #6. The facts are the same as in Examples #3 and #4, involving a modification or termination on April 1, 2015, of the February 1, 2015 lease between Landlord and Tenant. In this Example #6, however, Creditor notified Tenant in writing on March 25, 2015, of the pledge to Creditor. Thus, Tenant had notice of the pledge prior to the April 1, 2015 modification or termination dealt with in the prior examples.

Under New C.C. art. 3169, the "pledge of the lessor's rights in the lease of an immovable and its rents" is "effective as to the lessee from the time that he is given written notice of the pledge." Because the Landlord's rights had been "fully earned" and because Tenant had received written notice, New C.C. art. 3164 requires that unless Creditor consents, the modification or termination "is without effect" against Creditor. Because Creditor had not been asked about the modification or termination and had not consented, Creditor may seek to require Tenant to pay Creditor $5,000/month for the full five years under the original lease provisions.

The rule of New C.C. art. 3164 applies only if both written notice to Tenant had occurred and the lease obligations had "been fully earned by the pledgor's performance." It is anticipated that there may be litigation requiring interpretation of the phrase "fully earned." The Comments to New C.C. art. 3164 appear to invite courts to consider by analogy the jurisprudence dealing with similar provisions of UCC 9.

To illustrate the issues that may arise, assume in this Example #6 that Creditor claims that the modification or termination had no effect because Landlord was not in default in his obligations under the lease with Tenant. On the other hand, assume Tenant asserts as a defense that Landlord's rights were not "fully earned" because the heating and cooling equipment had failed on March 23, 2015 (two days before the notice from Creditor to Tenant was given), because the equipment had not worked properly since then, and because Landlord had failed to remedy the situation despite repeated requests from Tenant. Tenant's assertion is that, because Landlord's performance under its lease obligations was in default and Landlord's rights were "not fully earned," the written notice Creditor had given came too late under New C.C. art. 3164.

Tenant may not seek to have Creditor correct the heating and cooling deficiencies because, under New C.C. art. 3167, in the absence of Creditor's "assumption" of these obligations in a contract with Landlord, "the existence of a pledge does not impose upon the pledgee [here, Creditor] liability for the pledgor's acts or omissions, nor does it bind the pledgee to perform the pledgor's obligations."

Assume further that Creditor seeks to counter Tenant's assertion concerning Landlord's failure to fully perform by pointing to a provision in the lease purporting to obligate Tenant to pay rent every month, regardless of Landlord's failure to maintain the systems that provide electricity, heating, and cooling to the premises.

As can be seen, this may become an area where Louisiana courts will have to adjudicate what the phrase "fully earned" means.

Example #7. The facts are the same as in Example #6 with one alteration. Creditor gave written notice of the pledge to Tenant on March 25, 2015, but the failure of the heating and cooling equipment occurred one day later, on March 26, 2015.

Now, Creditor may claim that because, at the time of the notice, the heating and cooling equipment was working properly, Landlord's rights had been "fully earned" for past-due rent at the time notice to Tenant was given. Thus, Creditor may argue that the modification or termination was not enforceable against Creditor. . . .

IX. The Pledge of a Lessor's Rights in a Lease of an Immovable and Its Rents

In connection with leases, the 2014 pledge amendments apply only to the lease of immovables. The Louisiana Lease of Movables Act deals with movables. Movables that are leased can be encumbered by a security interest under UCC 9, and the rents from such movables can be subjected to a UCC 9 security interest.

Prior to the 2014 amendments, a creditor who wished to obtain security on a lease of an immovable or its rents had to use the provisions of former Louisiana Revised Statutes section 9:4401, a complex and much-amended provision entitled "conditional or collateral assignment of leases and rents." These statutory rules have been moved to the Civil Code and are now dealt with by New C.C. arts. 3168-3175 as well as by amendments to the registry articles of the Civil Code.

The 2014 amendments apply not only to the pledge of rents by a lessor, but also to the pledge of rents by a sublessor. Although the 2014 amendments track the former provisions of section 9:4401 in a number of respects, they change the prior law by requiring all pledges of leases of immovables and of the rentals of such leases to be recorded in the mortgage records. The amendments change the law to permit an inferior pledgee to collect rent without accounting to a superior pledgee. The amendments prohibit a judicial sale of a pledged lease or of pledged rents. The amendments also clarify the law concerning a pledge of items classified as "rent" under the Louisiana Mineral Code.

A. What Can Be Pledged in a Lease of Immovables

The landlord of immovables may mortgage the immovable. The landlord may grant a lease of an immovable and obtain by operation of law a lessor's privilege on the property of tenants and subtenants on the leased premises, as well as a limited right to pursue these items when they have been removed from the premises. The tenant may mortgage the lease.

If a creditor, however, wants to obtain a security interest in the landlord's lease or in the rental stream, the only way to do so is through a pledge.

New C.C. art. 3168 permits a landlord to pledge the entirety of a single lease, all the leases on a specified immovable, all the rents under one or more leases, or just some of the rents under one or more leases. As the Comments to this article note, the "scope of what is pledged is a matter of contract between the parties."

B. How the Pledge Is Made Effective Between the Parties, to the Tenant, and to Third Parties

A pledge of a lease of an immovable or its rents is made effective only by execution of a written contract between the pledgor and pledgee. An act of pledge may be a separate document or it may be contained in a mortgage. An act of pledge does not need to be witnessed or notarized, and the pledgee does not have to sign it. It should be noted, however, that if an act of pledge is not in authentic form, it is not "self-proving." Many attorneys prefer to use authentic acts for documents that are to be recorded in the public records.

The written contract "must state precisely the nature and situation of the immovable and must state the amount of the secured obligation or the maximum amount of secured obligations that may be outstanding from time to time." The Comments to New C.C. art. 3168 note that description requirements are "identical" to those required for describing immovables subject to a mortgage.

A pledge of a lease or its rents is effective against third parties only if it is recorded in the mortgage records of the parish where the immovable is located. This rule applies regardless of whether the pledge is contained in a mortgage or a separate act of pledge. This is a change from the pre-2014-amendment law, where acts of "assignment" of leases were recorded only in the conveyance records, but acts of assignment of leases contained in a mortgage were recorded only in the mortgage records. The 2014 amendments continue to recognize that a pledge of leases may be contained in a mortgage.

Regardless of whether or when the pledge is made effective against third parties, however, a lessee is affected only from the point of time it receives a written notice of the pledge.

C. The Length of the Effect on Third Parties of a Pledge of Leases or Rents

The 2014 amendments incorporated the rules of a pledge of leases or rents into the rules concerning how long mortgages affect third parties. This is appropriate, considering the fact that such pledges are often contained in mortgages and because all such pledges are now recorded in the mortgage records.

If the act of pledge reflects that the obligation it secures is due in less than nine years, or if it cannot be ascertained from the act of pledge when the obligation it secures is due, the effect of recordation continues for ten years from the date of the document. If the act of pledge reflects that the obligation it secures is due nine years or more from the date of the document, the effect of recordation is six years from the maturity date of the obligation. Acts of timely reinscription preserve the original effective date for an additional ten years from the date of reinscription.

Example #8. Landlord and Tenant entered into a lease of an immovable on June 1, 2015. On June 15, 2015, Landlord and Creditor entered into a loan agreement; Landlord signed a negotiable note payable in three annual installments, the first installment due July 15, 2016, and the last installment due July 15, 2018. On June 15, 2015, Landlord and Creditor also entered into a written act of pledge of the lease and all rents under the lease. The act of pledge contained all the necessary terms and conditions and described the note it secured as well as the payment provisions of the note. Creditor, however, did not record the act of pledge in the appropriate parish mortgage records until August 1, 2015.

The result is that the pledge did not begin to affect third parties until it was recorded on August 1, 2015. It will cease affecting third parties on June 15, 2025. The reason is because the note is due in less than nine years from its date, and third parties are affected for ten years "from the date" of the contract of pledge, not ten years from the date of the lease, and not ten years from the date of recordation of the act of pledge.

Even though the effect of recordation of the pledge continues until June 15, 2025, the note itself may prescribe in 2023 (five years from its due date)

unless acknowledged or unless prescription has been interrupted. A pledge may interrupt prescription under the "constant acknowledgment rule."

What third parties can and cannot ascertain from the public records is essentially the same as the rule applicable to mortgages. Third parties cannot ascertain from the public records how much, if anything, has been paid on the note the pledge secures and cannot ascertain whether prescription has been interrupted or whether the note has prescribed because of non-payment. Thus, third parties examining the public records must assume the worst-case scenario, which is that the note has not prescribed. Under the Louisiana public records doctrine, third parties are entitled to rely upon the absence of a timely reinscription of the pledge.

Example #9. The facts are the same as in Example #8, except that the June 15, 2015, note is due in eleven years, not three years, with the last installment due July 15, 2026, and the act of pledge recites these provisions of the note.

As in Example #8, the act of pledge will affect third parties from the date it was recorded in the parish mortgage records (August 1, 2015) but now, under New C.C. art. 3358, the pledge will continue to affect third parties until July 15, 2032, "six years after the latest maturity date described in the instrument."

Example #10. The facts are the same as in Example #9, except that on December 1, 2031, Creditor reinscribes the act of pledge in the parish mortgage records.

Assuming that the act of reinscription contains the information required by New C.C. art. 3362, the reinscription is timely because it is made prior to July 15, 2032, and the effects of recordation will continue until December 1, 2041, ten years from the date of the timely reinscription.

D. What Happens When a Landlord Pledges the Same Lease or Rents to Multiple Creditors

The 2014 amendments recognize that a landlord of immovables may pledge the same lease or rents to multiple creditors. New C.C. art. 3173 deals with the rights of superior and inferior pledgees.

New C.C. art. 3173 "changes the law by generally permitting an inferior pledgee to collect rent from the lessee without a duty to account to a superior pledgee for the rent collected." Analogous rules are found in UCC 9.

Two examples may help explain some of these new pledge rules.

Example #11. The facts are similar to those in Example #8, above: June 1, 2015, lease of immovable between Landlord and Tenant, and June 15, 2015, loan agreement between Landlord and Creditor and act of pledge.

Unlike Example #8, however, the act of pledge between Landlord and Creditor was recorded in the appropriate parish mortgage records on June 15, 2015. A few weeks later, on July 1, 2015, Landlord and Bank, a new lender, entered into another act of pledge of the same lease, and Bank recorded the act of pledge on that same date in the parish mortgage records. Bank is an inferior pledgee because the pledge to it was recorded after the recordation of the pledge to Creditor.

In this Example #11, Creditor, the superior pledgee, did not notify Tenant of its June 15, 2015, act of pledge. On July 2, 2015, however, the inferior pledgee, Bank, notified Tenant of its act of pledge. Pursuant to the notification Tenant received, Tenant sent the monthly payments for August, September, and October 2015 to Bank as each payment became due.

It is not until October 2015 that Creditor became aware of Bank's act of pledge and of Tenant's payments to Bank.

Under New C.C. art. 3173, Bank "is not bound to account" to Creditor for the rent collected because Creditor had not notified Tenant of Creditor's pledge and directed Tenant to make payment to Creditor. Thus, Bank is not liable to Creditor to repay any of the amounts Bank collected from Tenant. This is a change in the prior law.

Moreover, if Bank had taken the rental payments and put them in a deposit account, Creditor's claims to such amounts would be trumped by Bank's rights, because in this example Bank had no duty to account to Creditor for the monthly rent collected as it accrued.

Example #12. The facts are the same as in Example #11, above, except that, on July 2, 2015, when inferior pledgee Bank notified Tenant of its act of pledge, Bank convinced Tenant to pre-pay the rent for August, September, and October 2015.

Pursuant to New C.C. art. 3173, while Bank may keep the August 2015 rent, Bank must account to Creditor (the superior pledgee) for rent Bank "collects more than one month before it is due." Thus, Bank would be liable to Creditor for the pre-paid rent for September and October.

E. What a Pledgee of Rents or Leases May Do

A pledgee of leases or rents may give written notice to the tenant to pay directly to the pledgee. There is no statutory prohibition preventing the pledgee doing this even before the pledgor is in default on the obligation the pledge secures, and New C.C. art. 3160 expressly authorizes such actions. Often, creditors like to receive and control the rent stream in what is sometimes referred to as a "lock-box" arrangement, although if the "lock-box" consists of a deposit account with a financial institution, there may be others with claims on the account.

Merely recording an act of pledge of leases or rents in the mortgage records, however, does not obligate the tenant to do anything unless and until the tenant receives a written notice from the pledgee directing the tenant to render performance to the pledgee.

New C.C. art. 3174 prevents a pledgee from filing suit to sell the pledged lease or rents. It prevents a judicial sale of the pledged lease or rents. It prohibits a pledgor and pledgee from agreeing to a judicial sale.

The only things the pledgee can do under the 2014 amendments are to (a) give notice to the tenant to make the rental payments to the pledgee and, if tenant fails to do so, seize the rents in the hands of the lessee; (b) pursue identifiable cash proceeds of rent; and (c) demand an accounting from an inferior pledgee who either has collected pre-paid rent or who has collected rents with the knowledge that this payment "violated written directions given to the lessee to pay rent to the holder of the superior pledge."

F. Right of Pursuit of Identifiable Cash Proceeds of Rent

The 2014 amendments continue the prior rule permitting a pledgee of rent of an immovable to pursue the identifiable cash proceeds of the rental payments in the absence of an agreement to the contrary between pledgor and pledgee. The term "identifiable cash proceeds of rent" is more limited than the prior provisions of old Louisiana Revised Statutes section 9:4401(F); however, the phrase does encompass "money, checks, deposit accounts, or the like."

If there are multiple pledges of rent, a superior pledgee may pursue the identifiable cash proceeds that the inferior pledgee has placed into its deposit account if the inferior pledgee has "an obligation to account for the collections" under New C.C. art. 3173.

New Louisiana Revised Statutes section 9:4402(b) also clarifies the respective rights of the pledgee and the depositary institution into which the identifiable proceeds are placed.

* * * * * *

NOTES AND QUESTIONS

1. In the context of granting a security interest in the right to collect payments related to minerals, Chapter 9 and the law of pledge interact. As noted in Civil Code article 3172, a landowner or the holder of a mineral servitude has the ability under the law of pledge to grant a security interest in his right to collect mineral payments. However, you'll recall that Chapter 9 also defines when an "account" can constitute payments related to mineral rights. There is no overlap, however—Chapter 9 carves out a type of mineral right payment for itself and pledge does the same.

If the right at issue relates to mineral lease bonus payments (or delay rentals, royalties, and shut-in payments) due to a landowner or a holder of a mineral servitude, then the law of pledge governs the collateralization process. However, if the right at issue relates to mineral payments due to a person *other than* a landowner or holder of a mineral servitude, then Chapter 9 governs the collateralization process—under the theory that these payments constitute an "account." There is no cross-over or opportunity to double up on security.

2. Not discussed above is the ability to grant a security interest in crops—known as the agricultural lien in UCC terms. Louisiana has a number of non-uniform provisions, particularly in light of the 2010 revision to the law governing agricultural privileges, when it comes to such encumbrances. More information about how agricultural privileges fit into the Chapter 9 system—as well as how Louisiana law varies from the uniform approach—will be provided in Chapter 5.

Chapter 4
The Law of Mortgages

A. In General

See La. Civ. Code arts. 3278–3286

Few great commentators have summed up the importance of the mortgage better than Marcel Planiol, the famed civil law scholar, when he declared: "The mortgage is the most important of the real securities, from the enormous amount of capital which it guarantees, and by the value of the landed property which it burdens. It can therefore be said that the establishment of a good system of mortgages is an economic and a social question of the first magnitude."[1] Indeed, the mortgage is perhaps the best known of all the security devices, both in Louisiana and beyond.

Broadly speaking, a mortgage is "a nonpossessory right created over property to secure the performance of an obligation." La. Civ. Code art. 3278. The concept is entirely similar at common law. The basic right that a mortgage grants is the ability of the mortgagee to have the mortgaged property seized and sold under the law and thereby use the proceeds from the sale in satisfaction of the debt that the mortgage secures. Importantly, mortgages, like all security devices, are accessory rights. They cannot endure without the existence of the underlying obligation they secure. When the principal obligation no longer exists—because it was extinguished, for instance, due to confusion, performance, or compensation, or when its enforcement is barred by prescription—then the mortgage right also ceases to exist.

The following excerpt gives an idea of the device's history and how it is distinguished from similar security devices over property. Interestingly, while

[1] Marcel Planiol, *Treatise on the Civil Law* 472 (1939) (1959? trans. by the La. St. L. Inst.).

many of the concepts and terminology that govern and pervade the law of mortgages in Louisiana are thought to be imported from the common law, the earliest origins of the institution find their place at Roman law.

* * * * * *

A TREATISE ON THE LAW OF MORTGAGES 1–4 (Boston ed. 1828)
JOHN JOSEPH POWELL

[The mortgage], as practiced with us, seems to owe its introduction more immediately to the Roman law, which distinguished between things pledged or hypothecated and things mortgaged.

. . . The striking distinction . . . between a mortgage of lands or goods, and a pawn of goods, is, that in the former case, the mortgagee has, after the condition forfeited, an absolute interest in the thing mortgaged, where the pawnee has but a special property in the goods, to detain them for his security. A mortgage is a pledge, and more; for it is an absolute pledge, to became an absolute interest, if not redeemed at a certain time: a pledge is a deposit of personal effects, not to be taken back but on payment of a certain sum, by express stipulation, or the course of trade to be a lien upon them. . . .

* * * * * *

As the passage above explains, the law of mortgage, despite its significant development under the English common law, originated in the Roman law. Thus, a great deal of the policies and origins of the law of mortgage can be found in the writings of French and civilian commentators. Although Powell speaks of the mortgage as a form of absolute pledge, the concept of mortgage is distinct from that of pledge proper, as you learned in the preceding chapter. As you will read below, a mortgagee need not have possession of the property in order for the mortgage to be effective.

The excerpts below are taken from a treatise on the civil law by Planiol. Like any endeavor, an appreciation of the mortgage of the present requires an understanding of the mortgage of the past. The history of the mortgage tells the story of its development and how it has evolved over time to accommodate not only changing economic winds, but also shifting social forces regarding the balance between the rights of creditors and debtors.

* * * * * *

2 Traite Élementaire de Droit Civil, pt. 2
(La. State Law Inst. trans., 1959) (12th ed. 1939) (Fr.)
Marcel Planiol & Georges Ripert

The mortgage is a real security which without presently dispossessing the owner of the property hypothecated, permits the creditor at the due date to take it over and have it sold, in whatever hands it is found, and to get paid from the proceeds by preference to the other creditors. . . .

HISTORY OF THE FRENCH MORTGAGE REGIME

The characteristic features of the Roman system were the following:

(1) The mortgage was established by simple consent. This was remarkable derogation of the principle according to which real rights were specially constituted and could not be established "by consent alone."

(2) The mortgage would be established on movables as well as on immovables and the mortgage on movables gave the right of pursuit to the creditor.

(3) Mortgages were concealed. No publicity warned third parties of their existence.

(4) General mortgages were allowed.

PERIOD OF THE VERY ANCIENT FRENCH LAW

The mortgage regime such as the compilations of Justinian show us, was not practiced in Gaul during the Roman domination. The opinion of Paul, which had a great vogue in our regions, did not speak of the *hypotheca* [mortgage], but only of the *pignus* [pledge]. . . . A multitude of ancient acts indicate the form in which immovables were, for a long time, used by us as a means of credit: it was by the constitution of pledges. . . . A remarkable transformation happened later. The several authors of the 13th and of the 14th centuries did not know the pledge in full ownership, giving the creditor the right to sell. For them the pledge of an immovable was what we today call antichresis; it is a simple pledge of the revenues or fruits; the debtor remains owner of his property and the pledgee does not have the right to dispose of it.

REAPPEARANCE OF THE MORTGAGE

The introduction of the mortgage into our law was not the effect of a direct borrowing, made at one time from the Roman law. It first appeared in the 13th century under the name of obligation *bonorum*. At this time the only means a creditor had to execute on the property of the debtor were long and difficult procedures; in certain regions, in Picardy, for example, he was only permitted to seize the movables and the fruits of immovables. Afterwards, by a special agreement the debtor declared that he obligated all his property as security of the debt and permitted the creditor to sell to pay himself.

It was this "obligation of property" which in the 16th century took the Roman name "*hypotheca*" and it was really the equivalent of [the mortgage].

THE MORTGAGE SYSTEM DURING THE 17th AND 18th CENTURIES

The French hypoethcary regime had abandoned the Roman principles on two important points:

(1) The mortgage of movables had disappeared. . . .

(2) The mortgage could not longer result from a simple private contract. A public notarial or judicial act was necessary.

On two other points, on the contrary, the Roman principles were preserved:

(1) The mortgage could be general and burden all of the property of the debtor.

(2) The mortgage was secret: means of publication had not yet been devised.

MORTGAGES UNDER THE CIVIL CODE

When the project of the [Code Napoleon] was submitted to the courts, the magistrates of the ancient regime, who were still in the majority, pronounced themselves against the new system of the law of Brumaire; only nine courts of appeal asked to have it retained. . . . At the Council of State also the majority appeared favorable to the traditional regime. The section on legislation was divided; there were two reports to the contrary to each other, the one of Bigot du Preameneu in favor of the secret mortgage, the other of Real in favor of publication. . . . The partisans of the secret mortgage urged the extreme simplicity of the ancient law; the law of Brumaire appeared to them contrary to the ancient law and the liberty of contract; the custom of pledging and the royal edicts were attached by them as feudalism. However, the principle of publicity won out. Its success seemed to be due principally to the efforts which the Court of Cassation made to defend it. . . .

* * * * * *

Another important aspect of the mortgage is that it, like with the rest of property law, is subject to the general rule of *numerus clausus*. This means broadly that property rights are of a limited class and that parties are not free to create by contract new rights that the law does not otherwise provide. In Louisiana, the best approximation to this is the notion that parties are not free to create new real rights through contract. Rather, only those real rights established by law are permitted. A mortgage is one of those few rights, and the Civil Code sets forth an exclusive list of those things that are subject to being mortgaged.

See **La. Civ. Code art. 3286**

Of those items listed in Civil Code article 3286, it is worth taking note of the ability of a lessee of an immovable to mortgage his rights in the lease. Such real security is often called a leasehold mortgage (a name derived from the common law), or the mortgage of a predial lease. Under these types of transactions the only thing the borrower has to offer as collateral is his interest in the lease of the immovable property, since it is the lessor who owns the actual immovable property and therefore is the only person with the power to encumber it (thus the legal maxim: *Nemo dat quod non habet*—"no one gives what he doesn't have"). In a leasehold mortgage transaction in which the lessee does not own the building or other constructions located on the leased property, it is only the contract rights provided under the lease that are mortgaged, and thus this is the only right that can be foreclosed upon in the event of a default. Therefore, a party who acquires the right at the foreclosure sale acquires only the rights of a lessee in the property. The lessor's rights are generally unaffected. Consider the following case dealing with leasehold mortgages.

* * * * * *

CARRIERE v. BANK OF LOUISIANA
702 So. 2d 648 (La. 1996) (ON REHEARING)

KIMBALL, Justice.

ISSUE

We granted the writ in this case to determine the respective rights and obligations of a lessor and the purchaser at a Sheriff's sale of the lessee's mortgaged "leasehold estate" and the improvements located thereon. Because we find the original lessee in mortgaging his "leasehold estate" mortgaged only his right of occupancy, use and enjoyment under the lease, as opposed to his entire interest in the lease, we hold that the purchaser owes no rent to the lessors under the lease. Furthermore, we find the lessors' claim for unjust enrichment is without merit (1) because there was justification under the law and under contract for the enrichment which inured to the benefit of the purchaser of the "leasehold estate" at the Sheriff's sale, and (2) because the lessors had available to them another remedy at law. Finally, because the "step in the shoes" provision in favor of the mortgagee in the lease is a separate, optional remedy for the mortgagee in the event of the lessee's default on the lease and the mortgagee herein elected to foreclose on the mortgaged collateral instead of availing itself of the "step in the shoes" provision, we hold the bank's use of the premises as a restaurant after acquiring the premises at the Sheriff's sale did not constitute a "step[ing] in [to] the shoes" of the lessee by the mortgagee under the lease. Instead, the bank's actions in operating the premises as a restaurant after acquiring the premises at the Sheriff's sale is a proper exercise of its right of occupancy, use and enjoyment under the lease. We therefore reverse the judgment of the court of appeal and dismiss plaintiffs'/lessors' case.

FACTS AND PROCEDURAL HISTORY

On April 23, 1982, plaintiffs/lessors, Richard P. Carriere and his wife, Shirley Hartmann, (hereinafter "Carrieres") owners of a commercially zoned tract of land located at 2712 N. Arnoult Road in Metairie, Louisiana, entered into a five-year ground lease with Frank Occhipinti, Inc. (hereinafter "Occhipinti"). The lease between the Carrieres and Occhipinti specifically contemplated the development of a restaurant by Occhipinti on the Carriere's land. To this end, in addition to provisions concerning lease payments, liability for taxes, and insurance requirements, provisions concerning the construction of improvements on the land by the lessee and the lessee's ownership thereof, the lease contained an option in favor of the lessee to renew the lease for two consecutive five-year terms, the reversion of any improvements constructed by the lessee on the leased premises to the lessor upon termination of the lease, the right of the lessee to mortgage the leasehold estate, an option in favor of the lessor to sell the land to the lessee, an option in favor of the lessee to purchase the land from the lessor, and liability of assignees and/or successors of the lease.

[The following are the relevant clauses contained in the lease:

[2. *CONSTRUCTION OF IMPROVEMENTS:* LESSEE anticipates constructing at its sole cost and expense, improvements to include a building, driveways and parking area (herein referred to as "Improvements") in accordance with the Plans and Specifications annexed hereto. . . .

[5. *LESSEE'S COVENANTS:* The LESSEE covenants and agrees that during the term of this Lease and for such further time as the LESSEE, or any person claiming under it, shall hold the demised premises or any part thereof;

[(G) Upon termination of this Lease, either by lapse of time or otherwise, to surrender, yield and deliver up the demised premises in such condition as it shall then be, subject to the provisions of paragraph 8 hereof. . . .

[8. *RIGHT TO MAKE ALTERATIONS, TITLE TO AND REMOVAL OF IMPROVEMENTS:* LESSEE may make or permit any Subleasee (sic) to make alterations, additions and improvements to the demised premises from time to time and all of such alterations, additions and improvements, including those which may be constructed by LESSEE in accordance with Paragraph 2 hereof, shall be and remain the property of the LESSEE or Sublessee, as the case may be, at all times during the term of this Lease and any extensions or renewals thereof. . . .

Upon termination of the Lease, for any reasons whatsoever, LESSEE shall return to LESSOR, without cost to LESSOR, the leased ground with such improvements or structures that may have been erected thereon during the term of this Lease, by LESSEE and to convey and vest in LESSOR, title to such buildings, improvements or structures, free and clear of any liens, rights, title, interest, claim or demand whatsoever and to deliver to LESSOR such instrument of title or Deed which LESSOR may reasonably require conveying to LESSOR and vesting in LESSOR, title to such improvements, buildings or structures.

[5. *LESSEE'S COVENANTS:* The LESSEE covenants and agrees that during the term of this Lease and for such further time as the LESSEE, or any person claiming under it, shall hold the demised premises or any part thereof; . . .

[(G) Upon termination of this Lease, either by lapse of time or otherwise, to surrender, yield and deliver up the demised premises in such condition as it shall then be, subject to the provisions of paragraph 8 hereof. . . .

[10. *MORTGAGING OF LEASEHOLD ESTATE:* In the event that LESSEE shall mortgage its leasehold estate and the mortgagee or holders of the indebtedness secured by the leasehold mortgage shall notify the LESSOR in the manner hereinafter provided for the giving of notice of the execution of such mortgage and name and place for service of notice upon such mortgagee or holder of indebtedness, or holders of indebtedness from time to time. . . .

[(B) Such mortgagee or holder of indebtedness shall have the privilege of performing any of LESSEE's covenants hereunder or of curing any default by LESSEE hereunder or of exercising any election, option or privilege conferred upon LESSEE by the terms of this Lease. . . .

[(E) No liability for the payment of the rental or the performance of any of LESSEE's covenants and agreements hereunder shall attach to or be imposed upon any mortgagee or holder of any indebtedness secured by any mortgagee upon the leasehold estate, all such liability being hereby expressly waived by LESSOR.]

After entering into the lease, Occhipinti obtained financing for the construction of his restaurant from Gulf Federal Savings and Loan Association (hereinafter "Gulf Federal") by pledging[2] both his "leasehold estate" and the improvements which would be built with the loan proceeds on the leased land. However, before Gulf Federal would actually commit to such financing, it demanded amendments to the lease to insure its position as mortgagee would be protected. The lease was therefore amended on January 10, 1983 to add Gulf Federal in its capacity as "LENDER" as an intervenor in the lease, stating "[t]he parties are desirous of amending said GROUND LEASE in order to induce LENDER to finance the project and its improvements by making a loan to the LESSEE." The amendment to the lease also added the lender as an additional insured for purposes of both liability and destruction of the premises and improvements, and also added, *inter alia,* provisions concerning the lender's ability to exercise the lessee's rights under the lease and limitations upon the lender's obligations under the lease, the lender's ability to exercise the lessee's option to purchase the land, subordination of any mortgage by the lessor of the land to the mortgage of the leasehold estate, and the continued existence of the lender's mortgage until satisfied regardless of termination of the lease or a change in ownership of any improvements constructed by the lessee.

[The relevant amendments to the lease are as follows:

> [5. LESSOR and LESSEE agree that the LENDER shall be permitted, at its option, to "stand in the shoes" of the LESSEE and to exercise, on behalf of the LESSEE or itself, all options and rights, and to fulfill all duties and requirements, and to pay any obligations, charges or expense encumbered upon LESSEE to pay. However, the exercising of these rights and meeting these obligations shall not be mandatory on the part of LENDER but shall be optional.
>
> [8. Article 8 is hereby amended to include the following sentence: "Except that the said improvements shall remain subject to the LENDER's mortgage until said mortgage is fully paid."

---

[2] You will notice that courts, including the one here, use the term "pledge" loosely. It is often casually utilized to refer to the granting of any kind of secured interest in property (i.e., "he pledged the real estate to the bank to secure the loan"—meaning he granted a mortgage to the bank over the property). This should not be confused with the technical meaning of the term "pledge," which is a distinct type of security device, as discussed in Chapter 3.

> [15. The parties agree, however, that any leasehold mortgage to LENDER shall require the LESSEE pledge and mortgage all rights and title it may have to the premises and to its leasehold interest and allow said LENDER to exercise all of LESSEE's rights, to stand in LESSEE's place, and to take over from LESSEE in the event of either a default on said indebtedness or if in the opinion of LESSEE it must act to protect its interests in the leasehold. Nothing contained in this article or in any other part of the lease shall operate to prevent the LENDER from so exercising its right to protect its security interests in the premises.
>
> [19. The parties hereby agree to all of the above as witnesses (sic) by their signatures below and acknowledge that Gulf Federal Savings and Loan Association of Jefferson Parish, the LENDER herein appears only to enforce its rights and said LENDER shall have no obligation under this lease except as set out and limited above.]

After the above amendments to the lease were instituted, Gulf Federal issued the proceeds of the loan to Occhipinti and he thereafter constructed a building and parking lot on the leased premises and began operating the facility as a restaurant. In 1987 Occhipinti refinanced the loan from Gulf Federal with Bank of the South ("BOS"). As part of this refinancing, an additional amendment to the lease was made on June 26, 1987, to substitute BOS as the lender and to provide the lessee with an additional option to extend the lease for another five-year term beyond the two five-year options to extend which had been granted in the original lease. This "buyout" of Gulf Federal as the lender by BOS also explicitly incorporated all of the terms and conditions of the original lease and the prior amendments thereto. Therefore, while Occhipinti was, at the time of the refinancing, still in the last year of the original five-year term of the lease, he now had three successive options to extend the lease through October of 2002. By virtue of a subsequent merger between BOS and the Bank of Louisiana in New Orleans ("BOL"), BOL became the holder of the collateral mortgage[3] and note given by Occhipinti and the successor in interest to BOS' position as lender under the lease. [In refinancing the loan with the Bank of the South, Occhipinti had borrowed $1,200,000.00. The loan was secured by a collateral mortgage on

[3] The collateral mortgage is a type of mortgage that, in effect, allows for an indeterminate future advance obligation to be secured by immovable property. It will be discussed in more detail later in this chapter.

Occhipinti's leasehold estate on the Carriere's land, and included all of the buildings and improvements located thereon.]

In 1988, Occhipinti filed for Chapter 11 bankruptcy, which was thereafter converted to a Chapter 7 bankruptcy proceeding on March 28, 1989. In January, 1989, Occhipinti ceased making rental payments due under the ground lease and also failed to pay the 1988 property taxes on either the land or the improvements, as required by the lease. Occhipinti also ceased making mortgage payments to BOL. In May, 1989, the trustee administering the Occhipinti bankruptcy estate rejected the ground lease and dismissed from the bankruptcy proceedings the leasehold improvements as assets of value to the bankruptcy estate. As a result of Occhipinti's failure to make the lease payments or pay the property taxes, the Carrieres issued a notice of default to Occhipinti on June 12, 1989, and, when the default was not timely cured under the terms of the lease, a notice to vacate the premises on July 7, 1989. Copies of both of these notices were sent to BOL in accordance with the terms of the lease. Thereafter, on July 19, 1989, the Carrieres filed suit to terminate the lease and evict Occhipinti from the premises. Less than a week later, on July 25, 1989, BOL filed suit for executory process, foreclosing on the Occhipinti note and collateral mortgage. At a Sheriff's sale on September 20, 1989, BOL purchased the mortgaged property, i.e., the "leasehold estate" and the improvements. The Carrieres then amended their suit for eviction to add BOL as a defendant, demanding the lease be declared terminated and the premises vacated.

On January 8, 1990, the district court rendered judgment in favor of the Carrieres, declaring the lease terminated and ordering BOL to vacate the premises. BOL appealed the judgment, claiming that as it was now the owner of the improvements constructed on the Carriere's land by Occhipinti by virtue of its purchase of the improvements at the Sheriff's sale, it could not be evicted from its own property. The court of appeal agreed and, finding the lease to still be in effect, reversed the judgment of the trial court:

> We hold that, as to the Bank of Louisiana, the Carrieres were not entitled to terminate the lease and evict it. . . . We expressly do not rule on the ownership of the property. Disputes as to ownership of property must be adjudicated in an ordinary proceeding and not in a summary eviction proceeding. [Citation omitted]. Nor do we rule on Bank of Louisiana's mortgage rights, as evidence pertaining to that

> issue is not in the record. In addition, neither the right of the Carrieres to rental payments, if any, nor the right of Bank of Louisiana, if any, to exercise the option to extend the lease is before us. These are issues which must be resolved in other proceedings. . . .

The Carrieres filed the instant suit on March 7, 1991, seeking rental payments and the payment of property taxes by BOL from the date of the foreclosure sale at which BOL had purchased Occhipinti's "leasehold estate" and the improvements. However, on BOL's motion, the trial court granted BOL summary judgment and dismissed the Carrieres' suit. On appeal by the Carrieres, the court of appeal vacated the judgment of the trial court and remanded for trial on the merits. . . .

After a trial on the merits, the trial court entered judgment in favor of the Carrieres in the amount of $398,032.05, representing rents and property taxes from the date of BOL's purchase of the "leasehold estate" and improvements at the Sheriff's sale, and attorney fees in the amount of $55,000.00. BOL appealed the judgment of the trial court and, on appeal, the court of appeal concluded "that the bank, by purchasing the lease and the building, and by operating the property as a restaurant, exercised its option to 'step into the shoes' of the lessee" and therefore became bound as the lessee and could "no longer take advantage of those articles in the lease governing the rights of the lender." . . . The court of appeal therefore affirmed the trial court award of damages for rents and property taxes. However, because BOL had not had an opportunity to contest the reasonableness of the attorney fees evidence, the court of appeal vacated that portion of the trial court award and remanded the matter to the trial court for consideration of the reasonableness of the attorney fees award. Id. at p. 13, 662 So. 2d at 497–98. On application by BOL, we granted the writ to consider the correctness of the court of appeal's decision. . . .

Thereafter, this court rendered an opinion affirming the judgment of the court of appeal. . . . Upon application by BOL, we granted the instant rehearing to reexamine our initial resolution of this matter. . . .

LAW

In Louisiana, a lease is a synallagmatic contract by which one party ("lessor") binds himself to grant to the other party ("lessee") the enjoyment of a thing during a certain time, for a certain stipulated price which the other party binds himself to pay. La. C.C. arts. 2669, 2674; *Potter v. First Federal Savings & Loan,* 615 So. 2d 318, 323 (La. 1993). The lessor's and lessee's duties *ex contractu* are set forth in the parties' contract of lease; in Title IX of the Civil Code, *Of Lease,* art. 2669 *et seq.*; and in Title III of the Civil Code, *Obligations in General,* art. 1756 *et seq. Potter,* supra at 323. The Civil Code, however, while defining and governing the relationship of the parties to a lease, still leaves the parties free to contractually agree to alter or deviate from all but the most fundamental provisions of the Code which govern their lease relationship. . . .

Along these lines, it has also been long established in Louisiana that the right of occupancy, use and enjoyment possessed by a lessee by virtue of a lease may be severed from the lessee's obligation to pay rents under the lease. . . .

Finally, where the parties to a lease intend to agree that one of the parties shall subordinate one or more of his codal rights to the rights or interests of the other party, such subordination must be specific and unambiguous. *T.D. Bickham,* 432 So. 2d at 230.

Though the right to possess, occupy or use the land of another may exist by virtue of agreement or by operation of law, it is axiomatic that one possessing, occupying or using the land of another must have a *legal right* of one type or the other to such possession, occupation or use. *See* Title II of the Civil Code, *Ownership,* art. 477 *et seq.* In this regard, though the Civil Code explicitly provides that buildings and other constructions permanently attached to the ground may belong to a person other than the owner of the ground, *see* La. C.C. arts. 491 and 493, the Code further provides that when such an owner no longer has the *right* to keep them on the land of another he must, upon written demand of the owner of the ground, remove them within 90 days after such written demand. La. C.C. art. 493. If the owner of such buildings or other constructions fails to timely remove them, the owner of the ground acquires ownership of such buildings or other constructions with no obligation to compensate the former owner. Id.

Applying the above precepts, a lessee who has availed himself of his statutory right to mortgage his interests in his lease may mortgage either: (1) his entire lease, which includes all of the lessee's rights, duties and obligations under the lease, including the obligation to pay rents; or (2) only his right of occupancy, use and enjoyment under the lease. If the lessee mortgages his entire lease, defaults on the mortgage, and the mortgagee forecloses, the purchaser at the Sheriff's sale becomes the owner of the lease, i.e., the lessee, and acquires all of the lessee's rights, duties and obligations under the lease, including the obligation to pay rent. As such, absent a specific and unambiguous subordination by the lessor, he acquires the original lessee's obligation to pay rents and he also acquires, in addition to the original lessee's right of occupancy, use and enjoyment, any and all other rights which the original lessee held, such as options to extend the lease and options to purchase the land from the lessor. If, on the other hand, the lessee mortgages only his right of occupancy, use and enjoyment, defaults on the mortgage, and the mortgagee forecloses, the purchaser at the Sheriff's sale becomes the owner of only the original lessee's right of occupancy, use and enjoyment under the lease, while the original lessee/mortgagor retains the obligation to pay rents. If, in this situation, the original lessee/mortgagor also defaults on his obligation to pay rents, the owner of the right of occupancy, use and enjoyment, absent a specific and unambiguous subordination in favor of such an acquirer by the lessor, may, should the lessor thereafter cause the lease to be terminated for the original lessee's non-payment of rents, lose his right to remain on the leased premises. In this situation, if there are also improvements on the land which were owned by the original lessee/mortgagor that are now, by virtue of the original lessee/mortgagor's default and the subsequent foreclosure and sale, owned by the purchaser at the Sheriff's sale, the lessor will be free, in accordance with La. C.C. art. 493, to demand, in addition to the purchaser's vacation of the land, removal of such improvements within ninety days.

DISCUSSION

In the instant suit, the Carrieres, as landowners and lessors, maintain the prior suit between themselves and BOL resulted in a final judgment that the lease is still in effect. As such, the Carrieres argue BOL, by virtue of its actions in occupying the leased premises after acquiring the collateral mortgaged by Occhipinti at the Sheriff's sale, has exercised its right under the lease to "step in the shoes" of Occhipinti, has thereby become the lessee, and is now responsible for rents and taxes under the lease. Alternatively, the Carrieres maintain they are, in any event, entitled to an award in unjust enrichment for BOL's rent-free occupation of their land.

In contrast, BOL first asserts that the court of appeal's statements in the prior suit between the Carrieres and BOL that the lease is still in effect are mere *dicta,* such that this court must now pass on BOL's contentions that the lease was either terminated prior to foreclosure by virtue of the Carrieres' letters to Occhipinti regarding default and termination or by the trustee's rejection of the lease in Occhipinti's bankruptcy, or was terminated by virtue of the foreclosure itself. Alternatively, BOL maintains that as only a right of occupancy, use or enjoyment was mortgaged by Occhipinti and therefore acquired by BOL at the Sheriff's sale, it has no obligation under the lease to pay rents to the Carrieres. BOL also asserts that the "step in the shoes" provision in the lease is optional, not mandatory, and that as it never exercised its option under the lease to "step in the shoes" of Occhipinti, it does not owe rents to the Carrieres pursuant to that provision of the lease. Finally, BOL maintains that as the Carrieres cannot meet the requirements for an award in unjust enrichment and, further, that as BOL has not been unjustly enriched in any event, no such award is warranted.

The Prior Suit

In the instant case, the court of appeal found its prior decision in the previous suit between these parties to be "law of the case" as to the issue of the existence of the lease after BOL's foreclosure and subsequent purchase at the Sheriff's sale. . . .

In the previous suit, the Carrieres filed a "Petition To Terminate Lease and for Possession of Premises" against Occhipinti, seeking termination of the lease and eviction of Occhipinti from the premises. After BOL filed suit for executory process against Occhipinti, foreclosed on the mortgage, and purchased the collateral at the Sheriff's sale, the Carrieres amended their petition to name BOL as an additional defendant as BOL was now the owner of Occhipinti's interest and the occupier of the premises. After trial on the merits the trial court rendered judgment in favor of the Carrieres, declaring the lease terminated and ordering BOL to vacate the premises. BOL appealed the judgment. . . .

After reviewing the lease, its amendments, and the record below, the court of appeal stated: "We hold that, as to the Bank of Louisiana, the Carrieres were not entitled to terminate the lease and evict it. However, with regard to Bank of Louisiana's argument that rejection of the lease by the trustee in bankruptcy had the effect of terminating the lease and, with it, the Carrieres' rights, we hold that the lease agreement continues in effect until it is terminated or expires. . . ."

After considering the pleadings filed in the previous suit and the court of appeal's decision, we find the court of appeal properly considered the existence of the lease to be at issue in BOL's appeal of the trial court's judgment terminating the lease and ordering BOL to vacate the premises. We also find the court of appeal considered and thereafter rejected BOL's contentions that the lease had been terminated by virtue of either the Carrieres' letters of default and termination to Occhipinti, the bankruptcy trustee's rejection of the lease and improvements as assets of the bankruptcy estate, or BOL's foreclosure. As such, the judgment of the court of appeal holding "the lease agreement continues in effect until it terminates or expires," *Carriere,* 570 So. 2d at 46, constitutes a final judgment as to these matters, and they cannot now be re-litigated in the instant case.

The Mortgage: Right of Occupancy or Entire Interest in Lease

Though the court of appeal decided in the previous suit that the lease agreement continued in effect, and we have decided herein the court of appeal's decision constitutes a final judgment as to that issue, that decision does not resolve the primary issue raised in this case, i.e., does BOL owe the Carrieres rents for its occupation of the Carrieres' land. Occhipinti ceased making rental payments in January of 1989. BOL purchased the collateral which Occhipinti had mortgaged on September 20, 1989, at the Sheriff's sale. Regarding any liability for rental payments which BOL may have had as mortgagee during that time period for rental payments, the lease specifically addresses this issue and states:

> (E) No liability for the payment of the rental or the performance of any of LESSEE's covenants and agreements hereunder shall attach to or be imposed upon any mortgagee or holder of any indebtedness secured by any mortgage upon the leasehold estate, all such liability being hereby expressly waived by LESSOR.

Thus, BOL is clearly not liable as mortgagee for rental payments which Occhipinti failed to make from January of 1989 until September 20, 1989.

We turn now to the issue of whether or not BOL, as the third party purchaser at a Sheriff's sale of the mortgaged "leasehold estate" and improvements located thereon, is liable to the Carrieres for rental payments which Occhipinti failed to pay subsequent to September 20, 1989. Resolution of this issue requires a determination not made in the previous suit or in the instant suit in the courts below as to what, exactly, was mortgaged by Occhipinti. BOL could not acquire anything more at the Sheriff's sale than that which was mortgaged by Occhipinti. As a result, depending on the nature of the collateral mortgaged and thereafter acquired by BOL, the lease continued in effect after the judgment in the previous suit with either Occhipinti retaining the obligation to pay the Carrieres rents under the lease, or BOL, by virtue of its acquisition of the collateral at the Sheriff's sale, also acquiring the obligation to pay the Carrieres rents under the lease.

In the June 26, 1987, mortgage to BOS, Occhipinti mortgaged "THAT LEASEHOLD ESTATE created and existing by virtue of a Ground Lease by and between . . . [the Carrieres and Occhipinti]." Beyond this initial description of that which is mortgaged, the mortgage goes on to declare:

> All rights, duties and obligations of the *mortgagor* and *mortgagee* as provided for in the Ground Lease dated Aril 23, 1982, between Shirley Hartman, wife of/and Richard P. Carriere, lessors and Frank A. Occhipinti, Inc., Lessee registered at COB 1029, Folio 580 in the Parish of Jefferson, State of Louisiana and the amendments to Ground Lease are incorporated into and made part of this act of Mortgage as if copied herein in extenso for all purposes. (Emphasis added).

Although the parties failed to describe that which was mortgaged as "THAT RIGHT OF OCCUPANCY, USE AND ENJOYMENT created and existing by virtue of a Ground Lease by and between" the Carrieres and Occhipinti, they nevertheless explicitly chose to describe that which was mortgaged as something other than Occhipinti's entire lease, instead describing it as "THAT LEASEHOLD ESTATE created and existing by virtue of a Ground Lease." Notably, Occhipinti did *not* mortgage "THAT GROUND LEASE by and between [the Carrieres and Occhipinti]."

First, we are unwilling to impose a requirement that, as a matter of law, only by the use of the phrase "THAT RIGHT OF OCCUPANCY, USE AND ENJOYMENT" may the parties to a mortgage create a mortgage of less than the entire interest of the lessee. Second, in our view, the mortgage at issue herein, in using the phrase "THAT LEASEHOLD ESTATE created and existing by virtue of a Ground Lease," neither explicitly states nor reasonably implies that a mortgage of Occhipinti's entire lease is intended or even contemplated by the parties. Instead, we conclude the use of the phrase "leasehold estate" as opposed to "THAT GROUND LEASE" or "THE LEASE" or "THE ENTIRE LEASE" connotes a mortgage of something less than Occhipinti's entire interest in the lease is being mortgaged.

Further, the additional mortgage paragraph quoted, supra, does nothing more than incorporate into the mortgage the rights, duties and obligations of the mortgagee and mortgagor, *vis-à-vis each other,* contained in the lease and its amendments. In addition, this conclusion is supported by Paragraph 15 of the first amendment to the lease, which amended Paragraph 19 of the original lease. The amendment, in pertinent part, states:

> The parties agree, however, that any leasehold mortgage to LENDER shall require the LESSEE pledge and mortgage all rights and title it may have to the premises and to its leasehold interest and allow said LENDER to exercise all of LESSEE's rights, to stand in LESSEE's place, and to take over from LESSEE in the event of either a default on said indebtedness or if in the opinion of LESSEE it must act to protect its interests in the leasehold. Nothing contained in this article or in any other part of the lease shall operate to prevent the LENDER from so exercising its right to protect its security interests in the premises.

This carefully drafted amendment requires the lessee to mortgage all of his *rights* to the lender under any leasehold mortgage, but omits reference to lessee's *obligations* under the lease. As the lender consistently required throughout the lease, however, the lease also explicitly states that "[n]othing contained in this article or in any other part of the lease" would operate to prevent the lender from electing to foreclose on the collateral.

We therefore hold the use of the phrase "THAT LEASEHOLD ESTATE created and existing by virtue of a Ground Lease" in the description of that which was mortgaged creates a mortgage by Occhipinti of only his right of occupancy, use and enjoyment. As such, BOL, when it purchased Occhipinti's mortgaged collateral at the Sheriff's sale following foreclosure, acquired ownership only of the building and other constructions on the leased premises and Occhipinti's right of occupancy, use and enjoyment under the lease with the Carrieres. The obligation to pay the Carrieres rents under the lease therefore remained with Occhipinti, and the Carrieres cannot now recover rents under the lease from BOL, the third party purchaser at a Sheriff's sale of the mortgaged collateral.

Unjust Enrichment

The Carrieres argue they are entitled to an award in unjust enrichment for BOL's rent-free occupation of their land. . . .

In the instant case, the Carrieres are not entitled to recover rental payments and property taxes from BOL under the theory of unjust enrichment because BOL's "enrichment" and the Carrieres' "impoverishment" were not "without cause" under Article 2298 and our case law. By its very terms, Article 2298 excludes from recovery those cases wherein the "enrichment results from a valid juridical act or the law." Likewise, prior to the adoption of this Article, this court stated repeatedly that one of the prerequisites for recovery under the theory of unjust enrichment was an absence of justification or cause for the enrichment or impoverishment. "[O]nly the unjust enrichment for which there is no justification in law or contract allows equity a role in the adjudication." . . .

Although there was arguably an enrichment on the part of BOL and an impoverishment on the part of the Carrieres, it was one justified under the law. As previously explained, when BOL purchased Occhipinti's mortgaged collateral at the Sheriff's sale following foreclosure, it acquired ownership only of the building and other constructions on the leased premises and Occhipinti's right of occupancy, use and enjoyment under the lease with the Carrieres. The obligation to pay the Carrieres rents under the lease therefore remained with Occhipinti. By operation of law, BOL has never been legally obligated to pay the Carrieres rental payments and property taxes and was legally entitled and, indeed, intended, as purchaser of the mortgaged collateral, to receive the "enrichment" resulting from its purchase of Occhipinti's "leasehold estate" without the attendant obligation to pay rents.

Not only was there justification in the law that BOL be enriched by not having the obligation to make rental payments, but there is also justification for such result in "a valid juridical act" as referred to by Article 2298 and signed by the Carrieres. The Carrieres agreed to, and the lease itself authorized, the mortgage of the "leasehold estate," which we have explained constitutes a mortgage of only the right of occupancy, use and enjoyment possessed by the lessee by virtue of the lease and does not include the lessee's obligation to pay rents under the lease. There can be no dispute that the very essence of a mortgage is that upon the failure of the obligor [Occhipinti] to perform the obligation that the mortgage secures [making loan payments to the mortgagee], the mortgagee has the right to "cause the property to be seized and sold in the manner provided by law and to have the proceeds applied toward the satisfaction of the obligation in preference to claims of others". La. C.C. art. 3279. The Carrieres should have contemplated that their agreement in the lease to allow Occhipinti to mortgage the "leasehold estate" included the possibility that Occhipinti would fail to make the loan payments, the mortgagee would foreclose on the mortgaged property securing the loan, and a third party would purchase the "leasehold estate" or right of occupancy, use and enjoyment at a Sheriff's sale without having the obligation to pay rents. Indeed, it was intended that such a result occur should there be a foreclosure. The Carrieres' impoverishment in this case resulted from Occhipinti's failure to pay them rental payments and the taxes on the property, not from any action by BOL as third party purchaser of the mortgaged collateral.

It is well-settled that the subsidiary remedy of unjust enrichment requires fulfillment of all five of the recognized conditions in order to succeed. *Edwards,* 636 So. 2d at 903. However, in addition to there being "justification" or "cause" for the enrichment and the impoverishment which precludes the application of unjust enrichment in this case, we note there was another remedy at law available to plaintiff which was to proceed against Occhipinti for his failure to pay rent. Irrespective of whether or not there is a judgment terminating the lease, a lessor can still file a suit against a lessee on the lease contract seeking past rental payments due. This action prescribes in three years under La. C.C. art. 3494. The Carrieres had a remedy under the law for their impoverishment and that remedy was pursuing an action against the person liable to them under the law for the rental payments—Occhipinti. Whether or not they could have been successful in that action because of Occhipinti's bankruptcy is not a factor which should considered with respect to the third party purchaser of the "leasehold estate" who acquired that "leasehold estate" at a Sheriff's sale without the attendant obligation to pay rent. The existence of a "remedy" which precludes application of unjust enrichment does not connote the ability to recoup your impoverishment by bringing an action against a solvent person. It merely connotes the ability to bring the action or seek the remedy. That the party whom the Carrieres authorized in the lease to mortgage only the right of occupancy, use and enjoyment while retaining the obligation to pay rent might file for bankruptcy and be unable to make rental payments is a risk attendant to every business transaction, and the impoverishment to the Carrieres which resulted therefrom does not justify a finding that BOL was unjustly enriched.

The record reflects that no option to extend the lease for the 1992–1997 term had been exercised, and that the lease did not otherwise remain viable after its expiration in October 1992. The Carrieres are not entitled to rental payments from BOL for the period of time prior to October 1992 for the aforementioned reasons. After the lease terminated, the bank's status was that of owner of an immovable separate from the land's ownership. It no longer enjoyed the right of occupancy, use and enjoyment under the lease because the lease no longer existed. The Carrieres are not entitled to unjust enrichment resulting from BOL's rent-free occupation of the buildings on their property after October 1992 because there existed another remedy at law available to plaintiff which would have terminated BOL's enrichment and the Carrieres' impoverishment. The Carrieres had the right to issue a written demand under La. C.C. art. 493, requiring the bank to remove its building and other improvements permanently attached to the ground at the instant they believed the owner of the building no longer had the right to be on their separately owned land. If within ninety days that removal had not been achieved, the lessor would have acquired ownership of the bank's separately owned building and other permanently attached improvements. This remedy at law was not seized upon by the lessor. Thus, the Carrieres, not having availed themselves of a remedy at law are precluded from recovery on an unjust enrichment theory for the bank's occupancy of their property for the period subsequent to the lease's expiration.

The "Step In The Shoes" Provision of the Lease

Finally, though the court of appeal in the instant case failed to specifically address the nature of the collateral mortgaged by Occhipinti and, hence, the nature of BOL's occupancy of the Carrieres' land, the court nevertheless held that BOL, after acquiring the leasehold estate and improvements at the Sheriff's sale, had tacitly availed itself of the "step in the shoes" provision of the lease and had therefore become the lessee, such that it was now obligated as the lessee under the lease to pay the Carrieres rents. *Carriere,* 95–212 at 13, 662 So. 2d at 497. More specifically, the court of appeal found BOL's actions in operating the premises as a restaurant after acquiring the leasehold estate and improvements constituted an exercise by BOL of the "step in the shoes" option contained in the lease. Id. We disagree.

The "step in the shoes" provision contained in the lease is optional on the part of the lender, not mandatory, and under the explicit terms of the lease exists as an entirely separate remedy from foreclosure as an available alternative for the lender in the event of a default under the lease by the lessee. As such, in the event of a default on the part of the lessee such as, in the instant case, a failure to pay rents, the lender had the option under the lease to either "step in the shoes" of the lessee or to foreclose on its collateral. In the instant case, BOL, as lender, elected to foreclose on its collateral and later acquired that collateral at the Sheriff's sale. As previously determined herein, the collateral acquired by BOL at the Sheriff's sale was Occhipinti's right of occupancy, use and enjoyment under the lease, along with the improvements constructed on the leased premises by Occhipinti. Therefore, BOL, in operating the building it now owned as a restaurant on premises on which it had a legal right to occupy, did not thereby "step in the shoes" of the lessee. Instead, BOL was appropriately exercising its right to occupy the leased premises, with Occhipinti retaining the obligation to pay rents.

CONCLUSION

Under the specific mortgage at issue in this case, we find the original lessee, Occhipinti, mortgaged to BOS only his right of occupancy, use and enjoyment under his lease with the Carrieres. As such, when BOL, as successor to BOS's interest, foreclosed upon the mortgage and subsequently acquired the collateral at the Sheriff's sale, it acquired only Occhipinti's right to occupy, use and enjoy the leased premises, along with the improvements constructed by Occhipinti on the leased premises, with Occhipinti retaining the obligation under the lease to pay rents to the Carrieres. As such, BOL does not owe the Carrieres rents while it possessed the premises.

Further, because there was justification under the law and under contract for the enrichment which inured to the benefit of the purchaser of the "leasehold estate" at the Sheriff's sale, and because the lessors had available to them another remedy at law, the Carrieres' claim for unjust enrichment is without merit. Finally, BOL's operation of the premises as a restaurant after acquiring the leasehold estate and improvements at the Sheriff's sale did not constitute a "step[ping] in[to] the shoes" of the lessee by BOL under the lease. Instead, BOL, as the owner of the improvements and Occhipinti's right of occupancy, use and enjoyment under the lease, was free to use the premises as a restaurant so long as the lease remained in effect. REVERSED.

CALOGERO, Chief Justice, concurring.

When this case was before us on original hearing, the majority held that the Carrieres were entitled to recover under the terms of the lease agreement because BOL had "stepped into the shoes" of the lessee, thereby obviating the issue of whether the Carrieres could have recovered under a theory of unjust enrichment. I concurred in the original opinion because I agreed that the plaintiffs were entitled to recovery, but I concluded that the basis of that recovery was unjust enrichment, not the terms of the lease agreement as the majority held.

On rehearing, however, the opinion presents an in depth analysis of the unjust enrichment issue, and this analysis has prompted me to side with this majority. Unjust enrichment is an available recourse provided that all five of the following requirements are met: (1) an enrichment; (2) an impoverishment; (3) a connection between the enrichment and the impoverishment; (4) absence of justification of cause for the enrichment and the impoverishment; and (5) no other remedy at law available to the plaintiff. Failure to satisfy any one of these criteria will preclude recovery. I now believe that there was justification both under the law and the contract of lease for the enrichment which enured to the benefit of the purchaser of the leasehold estate at the sheriff's sale. The plaintiffs therefore have not satisfied the fourth criterion. I am not sure that I agree with the majority's assertion that the fifth criterion was also not satisfied. However, this concern of mine is irrelevant as there existed a justification or cause for the enrichment and corresponding impoverishment, and that in itself is enough to bar their recovery under unjust enrichment.

Therefore, upon further consideration, while unjust enrichment initially seemed a viable remedy for the plaintiffs, I must now concede that the majority is correct that it is not, and for this reason I concur.

LEMMON, Justice, concurring.

The critical issue in this case is whether amended Paragraph 8 of the lease, which as originally written merely overrode statutory provisions regarding ownership of improvements, constituted a subordination agreement by which the lessors agreed to subordinate their rights under the lease (including the right to collect rent) to the Bank's right to full payment of the mortgage indebtedness.

Generally, priorities between leases and mortgages depend upon the order of recordation, but priorities can be changed by a subordination agreement. 2 Grant S. Nelson & Dale A. Whitman, *Real Estate Finance Law* § 12.9 (3d ed. 1994). When it is advantageous to do so (as, for example, to induce a lender to provide construction financing to a desirable lessee), the lessor in a recorded lease may agree to subordinate the lease to a future mortgage that is necessary for the lessee to construct improvements on the leased property. However, the lessor who thus alters his or her priority position must do so with the realization that it may become necessary to pay off the mortgage in order to regain the rights to the land if the lessee defaults on the mortgage.

In the present case, when Occhipinti defaulted on the mortgage payments and the Bank acquired by foreclosure Occhipinti's building and Occhipinti's leasehold interest in the land, the Bank had the right to occupy the property, and Occhipinti had the separate obligation under the lease to pay rent. However, in the absence of a subordination agreement, the Bank could occupy the property only as long as someone paid the rent, and the Bank would have had to pay the rent in order to preserve its right of occupancy; otherwise, the lessors could terminate the lease and exercise their ninety-day notice rights under La. Civ. Code art. 493 to require removal of the improvements or to acquire ownership thereof.

The amended Paragraph 8 was a subordination agreement. If the lessors, when neither Occhipinti nor the Bank made payments due under the lease after September 1989, had issued a ninety-day letter under Article 493, the Bank still had its rights under the Paragraph 8 subordination provision to full payment of the indebtedness secured by the mortgage, minus the amount credited in the foreclosure sale. The Bank's foreclosure extinguished its rights under the mortgage against Occhipinti, the owner of the building and the leasehold interest, but did not extinguish the right to full payment of the indebtedness that the Bank contractually extracted from the lessors in consideration for extending credit to the lessee to improve the lessors' property.

While the lessors suggest that Bank's foreclosure somehow relieved them of their obligation under the lease to which the Bank was a party, the Bank's exercising its rights to foreclose and acquire ownership at the sheriff's sale of Occhipinti's leasehold interest and Occhipinti's building did not cancel or impair the Bank's real rights under the subordination agreement. The foreclosure did not extinguish the underlying indebtedness to which the lessors subordinated their reversionary rights under the lease. The result of the Bank's becoming an owner of the building situated on the lessor's land, however, was significant in that it re-triggered the applicability of La. Civ. Code art. 493. However, the lessors and Occhipinti had expressly altered Article 493's usual result by providing in the original Paragraph 8 that full ownership of the building Occhipinti constructed with the lessors' consent would revert to the lessors on termination of the lease. Moreover, the crucial amendment to Paragraph 8 of the lease had added the subordination provision by which the lessors agreed that their contractual reversion rights would be primed by the Bank's rights to full payment of the indebtedness. By contracting to amend Paragraph 8, the lessors altered their rights that would have flowed from Article 493. As a result of this amendment, the lessors could not exercise any rights otherwise available under Article 493, inasmuch as they had agreed that the improvements would remain subject to the contractual provision requiring full payment of the indebtedness to the Bank.

I therefore concur in the dismissal.

KNOLL, Justice, dissenting.

The majority holds that the use of "That Leasehold Estate," when construed with other provisions in the mortgage, unambiguously created only a mortgage of the right of "Occupancy, Use and Enjoyment" under the lease, with none of the attendant obligations. The majority then concludes BOL purchased only the right of "Occupancy, Use and Enjoyment" at the sheriff's sale, while the obligation to pay rent remained with the bankrupt Occhipinti.

While I agree in theory, that the right to occupy property under a lease is severable from the obligation to pay rent, I respectfully disagree with the majority's conclusion that the parties to this mortgage in fact separated these elements of lease, and included only the rights of "Occupancy, Use and Enjoyment" in the mortgage. I find that the separation of the rights and obligations under a lease is a rare and archaic situation which should arise only when explicitly provided by the parties.

I find no support in the record for the proposition the proposition that the term "That Leasehold Estate" included only the benefits flowing from the lease without any of the attendant obligations. In the case *sub judice,* the parties to the mortgage made absolutely no mention that less than the full lease was subject to the mortgage. In fact, and as noted in the majority opinion, the parties to the mortgage expressly incorporated "[a]ll rights, duties and obligations of the mortgagor [Occhipinti] and mortgagee [BOL] as provided for in the Ground Lease . . . and the amendments to the ground lease . . . as if copied herein in extenso for all purposes." Since *all duties and obligations* of Occhipinti under the ground lease were *expressly* incorporated into the mortgage for *all purposes,* it is unreasonable to imply that the obligation to pay rent was *impliedly* excluded because of the description of the mortgaged right as "That Leasehold Estate" rather than "That Ground Lease."

In Blacks Law Dictionary, a "Leasehold" is defined as an "estate in real property held by lessee/tenant under a lease. . . . The asset representing the right of the lessee to use the leased property." In the case *sub judice,* the "asset representing the right of the lessee to use the leased property" is the *lease itself.* The "estate in real property" held by the lessee "under the lease" is his right to use the property *conditioned on the payment of rent.* The "Leasehold Estate" exists only by virtue of the ground lease, which necessarily includes the performance of the lessee's obligations. *See* La. Civ. Code art. 2710.

The simple realities of the creditor /debtor relationship also demand that the entire lease be mortgaged. It is only reasonable to assume that a debtor who cannot make the payments of interest and principal to his creditor will likewise be unable to make his rent payment to the lessee. In such a situation, if the only collateral securing the indebtedness is a mortgage on the right of "Occupancy, Use and Enjoyment," then these rights would be void for nonpayment of rent contemporaneous to the lender's foreclosure on the mortgage. These rights would be worthless as collateral.

In the instant case, BOL was financing a construction loan on property that was not owned by the debtor. Therefore, BOL took a mortgage on the separately owned building, and a mortgage on the only thing that allowed the building to be separately owned from the land, namely the lease. The mortgage on the lease was the only way BOL could protect its investment in the building, since without the lease, BOL would have to removed its building, presumably with a significant loss in its value as collateral.

When Occhipinti did in fact default, BOL successfully argued that it could not be evicted since the lease was still in effect. Now, in this subsequent suit for rent under the terms of the *existing* lease, BOL conveniently asserts that it only foreclosed on a right of occupancy, and that it has been justifiably occupying the property rent free, since the lessors have not yet sued the bankrupt Occhipinti for termination of the lease. BOL is playing a game of "hide the ball" in the courts, and has only asserted this arcane division of rights and obligations under the lease in order to recoup some of the losses from an ill-advised loan by avoiding rent rightfully owed to lessors.

I find that BOL purchased the entire lase at the sheriff's sale, along with all rights and obligations. When it foreclosed on the mortgage and purchased the collateral at the sheriff's sale, it no longer held the position of "lender" under the lease, but by purchasing all rights and obligations formerly held by Occhipinti, it succeeded Occhipinti as "lessee." Although BOL did not "step into the shoes" under the terms of the lease itself, by purchasing all the lessee's interest and by occupying the leased premises, it effectively became the lessee. Therefore I find that BOL should be held liable for the rent provided in the lease.

NOTES AND QUESTIONS

1. What do you think of the law stated in this case? In other words, what do you make of the idea that one may not only mortgage his entire interest as lessee under the lease of an immovable, but may also mortgage only some parts or aspects of said interest (i.e., only the right to use, enjoyment, and occupancy). Should a creditor be able to take a security interest in only the benefits derived

from a right and none of the duties or obligations of it? Is this fair to the lessor who is only able to collect rent from, as in the *Carriere* case, a bankrupt lessee? Along those lines, would it be possible for a creditor to take a mortgage over immovable property but limit its interest to only the rights related to the property but none of the duties of ownership? What policy implications exist here?

2. To what extent can the holding of the case be explained by the lessor's agreements made to accommodate the mortgage transaction, such as the subordination agreement to which Justice Lemmon refers in his concurrence? In other words, if the lessor had made no agreements in favor of the mortgagee concerning the mortgage of the lessee's rights under the lease, would the outcome of the case have been the same?

There are three types of mortgages in Louisiana. The first is the conventional mortgage, which is a mortgage established by contract between the mortgagor and the mortgagee. The second type is the legal mortgage that arises by operation of law, and the third is the judicial mortgage, which comes about through the rendering and recording of a judgment against a particular debtor. The first type—the conventional mortgage—is a special mortgage in that it can only encumber specific property of a mortgagee. According to Roman law and in France up until the Revolution, it was possible to grant a mortgage over all of one's property. The law of 11 Brumaire Year VII during the French Revolutionary period, however, changed this rule. From that point onward, as is the case in Louisiana today, a person may grant a mortgage only over specific property susceptible to mortgage. Conversely, legal and judicial mortgages are general in nature, in that they encumber all of the property of the debtor susceptible of mortgage.

B. Conventional Mortgages

See La. Civ. Code arts. 3287–3298

Although not impossible, it is unusual for an individual to be able to acquire immovable property without obtaining a loan—particularly for residential property. This is because very few individuals have cash on hand in a sufficient amount. Similarly, even those with sufficient cash may nonetheless desire to finance the transaction due to low interest rates or other economic incentives. Conventional mortgages help facilitate these transactions. They can be used in connection with obtaining a loan from a third party, such as a bank or other financial institution, or in facilitating a credit sale where the seller finances the transaction by allowing the buyer to make installment payments toward the purchase price over a period of time.

A conventional mortgage is simply a mortgage that is created by agreement of the parties. In other words, it is a form of consensual security due to the fact that the mortgagor agrees to grant the mortgage over his property and the mortgagee agrees to accept said encumbrance as security for the performance that he is due.

1. Effectiveness Between the Parties

As with many other types of juridical acts, the effectiveness of the contract of mortgage between the parties is separate and apart from the effectiveness of the contract of mortgage against third persons. This distinction is of the utmost importance, since the ranking and priority of a mortgage vis-à-vis competing mortgages usually depends on the timing of its effectiveness against third persons. Nevertheless, prior to the mortgage becoming binding on third parties it must be effective as between the mortgagor and mortgagee themselves.

i. Requirements

Civil Code art. 3288 sets forth the rules for making a mortgage effective between the parties. First, the contract of mortgage must be in writing because it purports to convey an interest in immovable property. Second, the document must be signed by the mortgagor (the person who is granting the mortgage). Note that the mortgagee (the secured creditor) need not sign the mortgage contract. Rather, the law provides that the mortgagee's consent to the mortgage is presumed, due to the fact that the existence of the mortgage in his favor naturally inures to his benefit because it provides security for the performance that he is owed.

Third, the mortgage must "state precisely the nature and situation of each of the immovables or other property over which it is granted." Civ. Code art. 3288. Bound up in this language, which originated in the French Revolutionary reform referred to above, is a rich body of jurisprudence where courts have variously upheld and rejected descriptions of property as being sufficient for purposes of granting a mortgage. A sufficient property description, based on jurisprudence and custom, is a specific type of description of property and, when used, certainly meets the requirements of Civil Code art. 3288. Recognized types of legal property descriptions in Louisiana include descriptions that make reference to the U.S. Public Lands Survey, metes and bounds descriptions, descriptions by reference to adjoining estates, and descriptions that make reference to recorded subdivision plats.

* * * * * *

LOUISIANA REAL ESTATE TRANSACTIONS (West 2000)
PETER S. TITLE

§ 2.1 Legal Descriptions

The description of real estate is very important, because in order for real estate to be conveyed or mortgaged, it must be sufficiently described. A description of real estate that is adequate for the purposes of sales or mortgages is often called its "legal" description. A legal description of property definitely locates the property and is sufficient to locate the property without oral testimony.

§ 2:4. Overview

Descriptions of property in Louisiana may be by reference to official governmental surveys, metes and bounds or plats of subdivision. Legal descriptions often combine the three forms of descriptions.

§ 2.5 Governmental Surveys

Rural property is generally described by the rectangular United States Public Land System (USPLS) adopted by the federal surveyors in subdividing the Louisiana public lands in the early 1800's. By Act of Congress on March 2, 1805, two years following the Louisiana Purchase, the Surveyor General of the United States was directed to send surveyors of the United States to survey and subdivide the vacant public lands. The official government surveys resulting from those surveys create, and do not merely identify, the boundaries. Where public lands were disposed of by the government to the State of Louisiana or to private persons according to lines appearing on the official plat of government surveys approved by the Surveyor General, the location of the lines as shown on the official plat is controlling. *State v. Aucoin*, 206 La. 787, 20 So. 2d 136 (1944); *State v. Ward*, 314 So. 2d 383 (La. Ct. App. 3d Cir. 1975) (surveys of public lands).

§ 2:11. Metes and bounds

Metes are lengths such as feet, yards and rods. Bounds are boundaries, either natural or artificial. A typical metes and bounds description draws a "picture" of the property beginning with reference to a public and recognizable point, known as the "commencing point." The description then expresses the distance from the commencing point to a point, the "point of beginning" of the parcel itself that is being described. The boundaries of the parcel are then outlined from the point of beginning by distances and often also by courses, or by reference to natural or artificial monuments. A "monument" is a physical structure which marks the location of a corner or other survey point. A "natural monument" is a natural object such as a lake, stream or stone. An "artificial monument" is a man-made object such as a street or surveyor's marker. Courses, also known as bearings or azimuths, are compass directions with reference to a meridian. Thus, a "metes and bounds" description describes a parcel of land by reference to courses and distances and/or by reference to natural or artificial monuments. Metes and bounds descriptions are often combined with descriptions referring to government surveys or to plats of subdivisions.

§ 2:13. Plats of subdivision

Common in urban areas is the description by reference to the plat of subdivision, by square (or block) and lot. Plats or maps of subdivisions are most commonly found in residential areas which have been subdivided by commercial developers, although platted subdivisions can be used in rural areas as well. *Banta v. Federal Land Bank of New Orleans*, 200 So. 2d 107 (La. Ct. App. 1st Cir. 1967).

* * * * * *

In drafting a mortgage it is optimal to use one of the legal description of the property described above. Indeed, when a lender or title insurance company is involved, a legal description will almost always be required. Louisiana jurisprudence is flush with cases where courts have had to determine whether a particular description of property met the requirements of Civil Code art. 3288.

The following seminal case from the Louisiana Supreme Court illustrates nicely the variety of property descriptions that courts have upheld and rejected in the context of the mortgage.

* * * * * *

METCALFE v. GREEN
74 So. 261 (La. 1916)

MONROE, Chief Justice.

The jurisprudence of this court is well settled, and well founded, to the effect that article 3306 of the Civil Code, which declares that it is necessary to the validity of a conventional mortgage that it should "state precisely the nature and situation" of the mortgaged property, is sufficiently complied with if the description identifies the property with reasonable certainty and is of such a character as not to mislead, or keep in the dark, creditors of the mortgagor or other persons having an interest.

In *City Bank v. Denham*, 7 Rob. 40, 41, it was said:

> The defendant cannot complain that he has been misled by the erroneous description of the lot. . . .The lot was described with sufficient certainty, and in a manner not calculated to mislead or deceive any one.

In *Ells v. Sims*, 2 La. Ann. 254, it was said:

> The land is described as situate on the Mississippi river, in the parish of Concordia; boundaries are stated, and the expression "my land," especially in the absence of any evidence showing the ownership of other land by Sims, is fairly comprehensive of the entire tract. . . . The question is whether, under the circumstances any one contracting with Sims, or in anywise trusting him, . . . would have been misled or kept in the dark by the omission to state the township, range and section, and the quantity of acres in Sims' tract. We think not; and are of opinion that in this case there has been a fair compliance with the requisition of law, that the mortgage and its registry shall "state precisely the nature and situation' of the property."

In *Baker v. Bank of Louisiana*, 2 La. Ann. 371, the act of mortgage which was the subject of litigation described the mortgaged property as:

> A certain tract of land, or parcel of ground, with the improvements thereon, situate, lying and being in said parish, on the bayou Tunica, being the land and plantation purchased by the said Samuel Wimbish, at the probate sale of Samuel Davis, deceased, containing five hundred acres.

The court said:

> We consider the description sufficient. It states the parish, a stream on which the property lies, the number of acres, and the use made of the property, and recites the origin of Wimbish's title.

In *City National Bank v. Barrow*, 21 La. Ann. 396, it appeared that the mortgaged property was described as:

> Her entire landed interest in the aforesaid parish of West Feliciana, situated on and adjacent to the Mississippi river, and composed of 3,800 acres of land more or less, as per acts of sale to be found at my [the parish recorder's] office in the town of St. Francisville, parish aforesaid.

It was said by the court:

> The description is inartificial, but it can hardly be said to be insufficient. In the first place it declares the object mortgaged to be "her entire landed interest in the parish of West Feliciana"; in the second place it is stated to comprise 3,800 acres, more or less; in the third place it is stated to be on and adjacent to the Mississippi river; and finally it refers to certain titles of the mortgagor to be found in the office of the recorder, and to which we will again allude. . . .

Thereafter, alluding to the titles, in answer to the contention that, at the date of the mortgage, there were four patents calling for 1,269.66 acres which were not in the recorder's office, the court said:

> We think this position untenable. The mortgagor hypothecated her entire landed interest in the parish, and at the time she owned the

> lands embraced in the four patents. She described it as embracing about 3,800 acres, and the amount of the eight tracts corresponds with that portion of the description. We regard the reference, "as per acts of sale," etc., not as limiting the previous portion of the description, but as merely explaining it, pro tanto.

In *Consolidated Association v. Mason*, 24 La. Ann. 518, the description in dispute was:

> *Une terre de cinque arpents de face, limitrophe à la ville de Monroe, sur quarante arpents de profondeur, dont cinquante arpents sont cultiver en coton et mais, le surplus étant en trois actions.*

And the court said of the property so described:

> The situation of the property was adjoining or bounding the town of Monroe, and of such a shape, quantity and position as to inform any reasonable man of ordinary experience examining the public records for incumbrances on Mr. and Mrs. Mason's property, where the land was which they mortgaged, etc.

In *Roberts v. Bauer*, 35 La. Ann. 454, it appeared that the mortgaged property was described as "un vaste terrain a l'encoignure des rues Orléans et Bourbon." The court quoted from *Troplong* (Hyp. et Priv. No. 536):

> *Il ne faut pas apporter esprit trop minutieux dans l'exigence de ces conditions. Il suffit que les parties aient employé telle ou telle désignation qui ne laisse pas de doute sur l'identité do l'immeuble*

and held that the description was a fair compliance with the law.

In *Dickson v. Dickson*, 36 La. Ann. 870, it was held (quoting the syllabus):

> Where in an act of mortgage the property mortgaged is first described by legal subdivisions and these subdivisions are then declared to compose a certain plantation, giving the name thereof and otherwise sufficiently describing it apart from the subdivisions mentioned, *held* that the mortgage rested on the plantation and that parol evidence was admissible to show that the description by the legal subdivisions

was erroneous and that said numbers did not, in whole or in part, compose the plantation.

In *Bryan v. Wisner*, 44 La. Ann. 832, 11 South. 290, it was held (quoting from the syllabus):

> If a portion of the description would mislead, it must be read with, and controlled by other parts which explain it; and an error in a description by legal subdivisions may be cured by other descriptive designations of the property in the conveyance, which leave no doubt of the particular tract that was intended to be sold.

* * * * * *

NOTES AND QUESTIONS

After reading *Metcalfe v. Green*, can you come up with a precise formulation of a rule for describing property such that the description is sufficient for purposes of granting a mortgage? Would a municipal address suffice? What if it was a municipal address, plus other identifying markers or indicators as to the location of the property? Does it matter whether the property is located in a rural, suburban, or urban area? Could you use a Google Maps printout to describe the property?

A point worthy of note deals with the interaction of so-called omnibus descriptions and descriptions that are sufficient to support the creation of a mortgage. Omnibus descriptions are those that purport to convey all of the property that the grantor owns within a certain broad area (i.e., within the state, parish, or municipality). Without a doubt, an "omnibus description does not provide adequate notice to third parties." *See Williams v. Bowie Lumber Co.*, 38 So. 2d 729, 731 (La. 1948). In the context of a contract of sale, however, courts have routinely held that omnibus descriptions are sufficient to make the sale effective as between the buyer and the seller. *See Dickerson v. Scott*, 476 So. 2d 524 (La. App. 1st Cir. 1985); *Snow v. MacDonnell*, 378 So. 2d 611 (La. App. 3d Cir. 1979); *Daigle v. Calcasieu Nat. Bank in Lake Charles*, 9 So. 2d 394 (La. 1942). But that rule does not seem to apply in the context of the granting of a mortgage. As the court in *Noel v. Noel* noted:

> All of those cases involved the rights of third persons and they are authority only for the proposition that a sale with an omnibus description does not supply notice to third persons who acquire an adverse interest in the lands. This was clearly pointed out in *Daigle v. Calcasieu Nat. Bank*, supra, where we remarked that, whereas Articles 3306 [current article 3288] and 3307 [current article 3288] of the Civil Code require precise description as one of the essentials for the validity of a conventional mortgage, there is no specific article of the Code with such a prerequisite as to sales.

Based upon the language of the court above, would one be able to make an argument that an omnibus description should be valid to support a mortgage as between the parties? How are property descriptions in the context of sales different from those in the context of mortgages? Does the Civil Code suggest different results? Since a mortgage is inherently a right of preference against third persons, would a mortgage that is effective only between the parties be of much utility? In any event, would it even matter if the mortgagee foreclosed on the property and there were no competing security rights in that property with which to deal?

The fourth and final requirement of the contract of mortgage is that it must state the amount of the obligation it secures, or, alternatively, it must state the maximum amount of the obligations that may be outstanding at any time. The phrasing of this final requirement accomplishes a number of ends, which are discussed at length below. Suffice it to say for now that this requirement provides that the mortgage must state a precise numerical amount that represents the maximum amount that the mortgage will secure.

ii. Type and Scope of Secured Obligations

Importantly, a mortgage need not (although it almost always does) secure an obligation to repay money. While a mortgage securing the obligation to repay a loan is the most pervasive type of secured obligation, it is not the only one that a mortgage may secure. Rather, a mortgage can secure any obligation (to do, to give, or not to do). As such, Civil Code article 3293 states, that "[a] conventional mortgage may be established to secure performance of any lawful obligation, even one for the performance of an act. The obligation may have a term and be subject to a condition."

If the obligation so secured is one that is not for the payment of money, the law requires that the mortgage stipulate a sum that would be commensurate with the damages that would be expected for a failure to perform. Civil Code article 3294 provides that "[a] mortgage that secures an obligation other than one for the payment of money secures the claim of the mortgagee for the damages he may suffer from a breach of the obligation, up to the amount stated in the mortgage." Thus, if a mortgage is given to secure an obligation to build, the mortgage must state an amount that is equal to the damages that the secured creditor would suffer if the debtor breached. No matter what, a numerical amount must be stated.

Lastly, while a conventional mortgage is typically granted to secure an obligation of the mortgagee, it is also sometimes used to secure the obligation of a third party. In other words, although the mortgagor provides the security, the principal obligor is actually a different person. For instance, Borrower desires to obtain a loan from Lender, but has no property to provide as collateral. However, Borrower's friend, Owner, has a tract of immovable property that Lender is willing to accept as collateral for the loan. Lender advances the funds to Borrower, and in connection with the loan Owner grants a mortgage over his immovable property to secure Borrower's obligation to repay the loan to Lender. Importantly, the only recourse that Lender has against Owner is to foreclose on the property. Lender does not have any personal rights against Owner—indeed, Owner is not the obligor and owes no performance to Lender in connection with the loan at all. Therefore, in the event of a default, Lender can sue Borrower personally and can foreclose on the property, but cannot obtain a personal judgment against Owner. In such a case, the liability of Owner is said to be *in rem* rather than *in personum*.

The *in rem* mortgage is important in a number of respects. Consider a variation on the hypothetical above: Lender desires to loan funds to Borrower. Borrower owns a tract of immovable property that he will provide as security for the loan, and Lender agrees that in the event Borrower defaults Lender's only recourse will be to foreclose on its mortgage over the property. Lender stipulates that Borrower will not have any personal liability on the loan. This, too, is called an *in rem* mortgage, and it is specifically sanctioned under Civil Code article 3297: "The mortgagee's recourse for the satisfaction of an obligation secured by a mortgage may be limited in whole or in part to the property over which the mortgage is established." Admittedly it is not often that a bank advances funds to a residential borrower and allows the borrower to escape any personal liability—even with real security provided. However, one instance where such a transaction often arises is when the loan proceeds will be used to construct a real estate development and the repayment of the loan is guaranteed by a government program. The Department of Housing and Urban Development and its subagency, the Federal Housing Administration, offer a number of programs whereby the government will insure a loan made by a HUD-approved lender in furtherance of a real estate development that aligns with certain federal housing goals. Also, permanent financing for large-scale, multi-million dollar commercial developments are often "collateral only" loans with no requirement that the developer incur personal liability. In both cases, the lender's focus is rather on the collateral and ensuring that it is of adequate value, rather than the solvency of the borrower himself.

iii. Pignorative Contracts/Disguised Mortgages

Lenders have at various points throughout history attempted to use contract law to obtain something similar to, but better than, a mortgage. Parties have from time to time confected agreements that simulate a mortgage but, by being denominated and constructed differently than one, attempt to escape the requirements and limitations of mortgage law. Contracts that in substance are mortgages, but are named and structured as something else, are called pignorative contracts. They are similarly known in Louisiana as simulations and are sometimes sham transactions.

Consider the following case that illustrates perhaps the most well-known of the pignorative contracts: the mortgage disguised as a sale with a right of redemption.

* * * * * *

LATIOLAIS V. BREAUX
98 So. 620 (La. 1923[4])

ST. PAUL, Justice.

This is an action to have an alleged sale of land with right of redemption (*vente à réméré*) declared a mere pignorative contract (common-law mortgage);

[4] The opinion was written in 1923; rehearing was denied in 1924.

the difference being this, that in sales with right of redemption the purchaser becomes the owner of the property sold, subject only to the right of the vendor to reacquire the property (C. C. 2567, 2575 to 2578), whilst in pignorative contracts the nominal vendor continues to be owner and the nominal purchaser has only a pledge or mortgage for his debt, which he must enforce in the usual way. *Collins v. Pellerin*, 5 La. Ann. 99.

Redemption sales have therefore been a fruitful source of litigation in this state. As to which the following cases may be listed, without exhausting the catalogue, to wit; (citations to 22 cases omitted).

I.

The leading case on the subject is *Marbury v. Colbert*, 105 La. 467, 29 South. 871. That case lays down the rule that—

> Redeemable sales of immovable property, unaccompanied by delivery of the thing sold, will be considered, as between the parties, in the absence of evidence to the contrary, as mere contracts of security, and the vendee out of possession may take this position equally with the vendor.

It was further laid down that in order to constitute a real sale the vendee must not only take actual possession, but must also have given 'reasonably adequate consideration.'

In his dissenting opinion, Mr. Justice Provosty (29 South. 872) reviews all the authorities up to that time, and points out that until then parol evidence had never been admitted (over objection urged) to vary, as between the parties, the express terms of the written agreement, or to affect the title to the real estate. But the rule was none the less laid down as above, and has been adhered to ever since.

In *Butler v. Marston*, 145 La. 41, 81 South. 749, it was pointed out that—

> Except as throwing light on what was probably the intention of the contracting parties, inadequacy of price is no more injurious to a redemption sale than to an out and out sale.

In *Bonnette v. Wise*, 111 La. 855, 35 South. 953, it was held that where the purchaser went into actual possession, mere inadequacy of price would not alone suffice to convert a redeemable sale into a simple contract of security, and that—

> The remedy, where the price paid is less than one-half of the value of the immovable estate sold, is by action of lesion.

In *Bagley v. Bourque*, 107 La. 395, 31 South. 860, it was held essential in order to state a cause of action (to have a redemption sale declared a mere contract of security) that plaintiff should allege that the purchaser never took actual possession.

Hence the one test by which to determine whether a contract evidences a real sale with right of redemption, or a mere contract of security, has ever since been whether the purchaser has gone into actual possession. (Citations to six cases omitted.)

II.

We think the rule, as thus stated, and as adhered to by this court, is sound in law, simple of comprehension, and easy of application. It avoids the necessity of attempting to reconcile the always conflicting testimony of the parties, where perchance each may be telling the truth as to his own intentions; and thus leaves the contract to be interpreted by facts readily proved and in accordance with the well-settled rule of law that a contract is to be interpreted according to the manner in which the parties themselves have executed it. C. C. art. 1956 (no current article).

III.

From the foregoing it results that the title of the purchaser is perfected by the delivery of actual possession. If that delivery takes place before the delay for redemption has expired, the vendor, of course, preserves his right of redemption. But if the vendor delivers the property after the delay for redemption has expired, obviously the sale then becomes absolute. By such delivery the vendor acknowledges that the thing belongs to the purchaser, and he cannot thereafter be heard to deny the latter's title thereto.

And this court has already so decided twice. In *Levy v. Ward*, 32 La. Ann. 784, 789, it was held that when a vendor, allowed to remain in possession under a sale with right of redemption, leased the property from the purchaser after the expiration of the delay for redemption, this established and acknowledged the purchaser's ownership and right of possession of the property; so that neither the vendor nor his heirs could ever afterwards question it. In *Jackson v. Lemle*, 35 La. Ann. 855, 857, 858, the vendor, left in possession under a sale with right of redemption, leased the property from the purchaser after the delay for redemption had expired; and the court held that such leasing of the property from the purchaser by the vendor was conclusive of his forfeiture of the right to redeem and an irrevocable admission of the purchaser's title to, and ownership of the land.

IV.

We now need only apply the foregoing principles of law to the case at bar; the facts of which, as we find them, being as follows:

> Plaintiff, being indebted to defendant for some $1,900 on various accounts, and being unable to pay, sold his land to defendant for $2,000; defendant paying the difference in cash. A counter letter was executed by which defendant was to have the right to redeem within two years for $2,360; being admittedly the purchase price with two years' interest added at 8 per cent. Plaintiff was to receive, and did receive, the revenues of the property during said two years. At the expiration of the two years plaintiff leased the property from defendant, the consideration for the lease being a share in the crops raised. Plaintiff swears he did not lease the land from defendant; but defendant swears that plaintiff did lease it, and the latter is corroborated by two witnesses, apparently disinterested. The trial judge found for defendant; and we see no reason to disturb his finding. The case comes squarely within the doctrine laid down in *Levy v. Ward* and *Jackson v. Lemle*, supra; and this makes it unnecessary to consider other points raised by counsel. . . .
>
> The judgment appealed from is therefore affirmed.

* * * * * *

NOTES AND QUESTIONS

For what reasons might a lender try to create a transaction like that described in *Latiolais v. Breaux*? What benefits might the creditor, the debtor, or both receive in such a transaction? Moreover, what types of borrowers are most likely to enter into these credit arrangements? Are all sales with rights of redemption attached to them absolutely prohibited?

Interestingly the problem of pignorative contracts is not unique to Louisiana. Rather, the common law has also had to deal with these types of transactions.

* * * * * *

Disguised Real Estate Security Transactions as Mortgages in Substance
Roger A. Cunningham & Saul Tischler
26 RUTGERS L. REV. 1 (1972)

Ever since the English Chancellors regularly began to allow redemption of mortgages after default, creditors have sought ways to have real property serve as security free from any right in the debtor to redeem. As one writer put it, "[T]he big idea is to find a form of a transaction that will have the practical effect of security, yet will be held not to be a security but to belong to a wholly different jural species and so be held immune from security law."

Creditors may use two devices to create real property security without appearing to enter into a security transaction. A creditor may require his debtor to grant him land by absolute deed, under oral agreement or tacit understanding that he will reconvey only if the debtor pays the debt when due. Alternatively, a creditor may obtain from his debtor an absolute deed to real property and execute to his debtor some sort of written agreement (almost invariably withheld from public record) to reconvey the property to the debtor upon receiving payment of the debt. The written agreement to reconvey may take the form of an option to repurchase, an unconditional contract obligating the grantee to reconvey and the grantor to repurchase, or a lease back to the grantor with an option to repurchase at or before the end of the lease term. Some such options or contracts provide for the deposit in escrow of a deed of reconveyance.

The use of an absolute deed to secure a debt, with or without a written collateral agreement for reconveyance upon satisfaction, is designed to eliminate the "grantor's" equity of redemption and the necessity of foreclosure if the debtor defaults. The written instrument, whether option to repurchase, contract to reconvey, or other arrangement, usually contains provisions making time "of the essence" and merely had an "option" to repurchase or was unconditionally obligated to do so forfeiting the grantor's right in case he fails to exercise the option or tender payment under the contract within the time limited.

Besides avoiding the expense and delay involved in foreclosure, the creditor often expects to gain other advantages by securing his interest with an absolute deed rather than a regular mortgage. These other advantages include the right to possession of the land prior to default, the right to possession of chattels severed from the land by the debtor or third parties, preventing the debtor from encumbering the land with further mortgages or judgment liens, and the possibility of enlarging the creditor's security interest to cover future advances to the debtor without the execution of a new security instrument.

Under the old system of separate law and equity courts, law courts would not entertain an action to establish that an absolute deed had been given as security for a debt though equity courts had long done so. It is now well settled, however, that any deed which is absolute on its face but intended at the time of its execution to be mere security for a debt will be regarded as a mortgage in substance. Since in the past only equity courts would entertain suits to establish that an absolute deed had been given as security for a debt, the term "equitable mortgage" is frequently used to describe disguised real property security transactions. The term "equitable mortgage" has not been confined, however, to "cases in which the interest in the property in the hands of the creditor is the full legal ownership and the aid of equity is necessary to cut it down to a security interest and to establish the rights of the debtor as a mortgagor." The term has also been used toe describe a creditor's interest where his "only interest . . . in the property for security purposes is an equitable one." . . .

It is important to keep in mind that the crucial question is not whether the parties to a deed absolute on its face intended to create the relation of mortgagor and mortgagee, but whether they intend the deed to stand as security for a debt. Where parties cast their deed in the form of an absolute conveyance instead of a mortgage, they do not intend to create the relation of mortgagor and mortgagee. Thus, the real issue is whether the circumstances are such as to justify treating the transaction as a mortgage in substance though the parties did not so intend. If the purpose of a conveyance was security, it will be treated as a mortgage even though the parties may have agreed or understood that the debtor should have no right to redeem. The right to redeem after default is an inseparable incident of the mortgage relationship and, as with ordinary mortgages, the parties cannot contract against its exercise where their relationship is in substance that of mortgagor and mortgagee.

* * * * * *

Another concept that can resemble a mortgage—at least at first glance—is the resolutory condition,[5] which is codified at La. Civ. Code art. 2561. This concept is not, however, one that creditors confect in an attempt to circumvent the laws of mortgage. Indeed, resolutory conditions are not security devices at all. Rather, it is a concept that arises from obligations principles whenever there is a sale of property—be it movable or immovable—and the price has not yet been paid, although ownership has been transferred. Since we are discussing the law of mortgage, we will confine our discussion of the resolutory condition only to sales involving immovables.

Consider the following two cases and observe how the law of mortgages and the law of resolutory conditions work together, although being separate and distinct from one another.

* * * * * *

[5] Although the pre-1985 law called the right of the obligee to dissolve the contract for non-performance a "resolutory condition" and, indeed, many practitioners still call it by this name, it is not really a condition. The 1985 revision to the law of obligations attempted to correct this misnomer, but the term still persists. In our context, it is really the seller's right to dissolve for non-performance, rather than the happening of a future uncertain event.

LOUIS WERNER SAW MILL CO. v. WHITE
17 So. 2d 264 (La. 1944)

ODOM, Justice.

This is a suit to enforce the resolutory condition. Revised Civil Code, Articles 2045 (current article 1767), 2046 (current article 2013), 2047 (current article 2013). The facts are not disputed. Only a question of law is involved.

According to the agreed statement of facts, the Louis Werner Saw Mill Company, on June 23, 1930, sold 80 acres of land in Ouachita Parish to E. J. White for $800, of which amount $400 was paid in cash. It was agreed that the balance of the purchase price, $400, would be paid one year from the date of the sale, or on June 23, 1931.

To represent the balance of the purchase price, the vendee gave his note, due in one year, secured by mortgage and vendor's lien on the land sold. The act of sale containing the mortgage and privilege was duly recorded in both the conveyance and the mortgage records of the Parish of Ouachita on June 25, 1930. In the act of sale and mortgage, the vendee agreed that he would not alienate, deteriorate, or encumber the property to the prejudice of the rights of the vendor. The balance of the purchase price, $400, was never paid by White, the purchaser, or by anyone else.

On November 12, 1940, which was more than 10 years after the sale of the land and the recordation of the mortgage but less than 10 years from the maturity of the note representing the credit portion of the price, E. J. White sold the property to his daughter for the purported consideration of $100.

This suit was instituted by the original vendor, Louis Werner Saw Mill Company, against the original vendee, E. J. White, on June 10, 1941, which was more than 10 years after the recordation of the mortgage and vendor's lien but less than 10 years after the maturity of the note representing the credit portion of the purchase price.

The purpose of the suit was to dissolve the sale, or set it aside, for the non-payment of the deferred portion of the purchase price. The suit was instituted against E. J. White, the original purchaser of the property, and his defense was that he had sold the land on November 12, 1940, and that "this sale was made more than five years after the due date of the mortgage note and more than ten years after the granting of the mortgage by your respondent to the plaintiff and, therefore, your respondent specially pleads the prescription of five and ten years."

There was judgment in the district court in favor of the Louis Werner Saw Mill Company and against the defendant E. J. White, "rescinding and dissolving that certain sale from Louis Werner Saw Mill Company to E. J. White, dated June 23, 1930," and decreeing that "Louis Werner Saw Mill Company have and recover said land, free from any mortgages, claims, liens, encumbrances or sales of said land or a portion thereof by the defendant, E. J. White; and more particularly that sale by E. J. White to Miss Willie Evelyn White, dated the 12 day of November, 1941 [1940]."

The plaintiff appealed to the Court of Appeal, Second Circuit. The Court of Appeal reversed the judgment of the district court, its decree reading as follows:

> For the reasons herein assigned, the judgment appealed from is annulled, avoided and reversed; plaintiff's demand is hereby rejected and its suit is dismissed at its cost.

Thereupon the plaintiff applied to this court for writs, which were granted.

Counsel for plaintiff and counsel for defendant filed in the record an agreed stipulation of facts, and in Paragraph VII of that stipulation it is agreed that:

> . . . based on the aforesaid statement of facts, the sole point of law involved in this case is whether or not the resolutory condition in an act of sale can be enforced ten years after the date of the recordation of the mortgage but within ten years of the maturity date of the mortgage note, where the property has been sold to a third party more than ten years after the recordation of the mortgage but within ten years of the maturity of the note.

The plaintiff's purpose in bringing this suit was not to enforce the contract of sale but to dissolve it, to set it aside. As the Court of Appeal said, "The note is not sued upon. There is no demand nor prayer for the enforcement of the mortgage and privilege." The suit is one to enforce the resolutory condition.

This court has repeatedly and consistently held that the right to dissolve or set aside a sale for the non-payment of the purchase price is an independent, substantive remedy which is in no wise dependent upon the existence of a mortgage or a privilege. As Judge Spencer said in the case of *Stevenson v. Brown*, 32 La. Ann. 461:

> A demand in resolution is a demand for the property itself, and embraces in it the abrogation of any and all alienations and encumbrances placed upon it by the vendee.
>
> In that case, the court said further:
>
> The fact that the vendor has lost, or not preserved, his vendor's lien, or mortgage, presents no sort of obstacle to the exercise of this right of resolution.
>
> . . .

In the case of *Heirs of Castle v. Floyd*, 38 La. Ann. 583, this court, speaking through Judge Watkins, said:

> In our opinion the two remedies of the vendor--one for the enforcement of the contract and the other for the resolution of it--are diametrically opposed, in the very nature of things.
>
> A suit to enforce the vendor's lien is an affirmance of the contract; while a suit for the resolution of it must be preceded by the restitution of the purchase notes and such part of the price as shall have been paid to the vendee, and same is a condition precedent to institution of the suit. . . .

There are other cases in which this court held emphatically, as was held in the above cited cases, that the right of a vendor to "resolve", or "dissolve", a sale for the nonpayment of the purchase price is an independent, substantive remedy which is in no wise dependent upon the existence of a mortgage or privilege. The rule announced in these cases has never been questioned, so far as we know. Nor can it be, we think, because it is rooted in, and grows out of, articles 2045 (current article 1767), 2046 (current article 2013), and 2047 of the Revised Civil Code (current article 2013), which articles are found under the heading "Of the Resolutory Condition." The remedy prescribed by these articles is to have the contract "dissolved" in case either party to it defaults or fails to comply with his engagements. The remedy afforded by these articles to a vendor who has not received the purchase price of the thing sold, in whole or in part, has no connection whatever with, but is diametrically opposed to, the remedy which he has under other articles of the Code for the enforcement of the contract. . . .

The failure of the vendee to pay the price is a "dissolving condition," or a "resolutory condition"; it is an event which gives to the creditor an absolute right to sue for the dissolution of the sale. This right is inherent in all credit sales. It is grounded upon the just and equitable principle that the vendee should not be permitted to withhold the price and keep the things. The contract of sale "is an agreement by which one gives a thing for a price in current money, and the other gives the price in order to have the thing itself." Revised Civil Code, Article 2439. The principal obligation of the buyer is "To pay the price of sale." Revised Civil Code, Article 2549. When the vendee fails to pay the price, he defaults on his obligation, the contract is breached, and the vendor may, under the articles of the Code, sue for its dissolution. The effect of the dissolution is to place "matters in the same state as though the obligation had not existed." The vendor gets the property back, and the vendee is discharged from his obligation to pay the price. If he has paid part of the price, that which he has paid is restored to him. . . .

In the case of *School Directors v. Anderson*, 28 La. Ann. 739, this court, following the ruling in *Templeman v. Pegues*, 24 La. Ann. 537, held that the resolutory action is prescribed only by 10 years, and that "the prescription of the notes given as evidence of the price does not affect that right of action, the right to dissolve not being an accessory to but different from the right to enforce the payment of the price, having its origin in the failure to pay the price, and resting on the principle of justice that the vendee should not retain both the thing and the price."[6]

In the case of *Latour v. Latour*, 134 La. 342, 64 So. 133, it was held that "An action to annul a sale for nonpayment of the price is barred by the prescription of ten years, which, in cases of credit sales, begins to run from the maturity of

[6] One should take note of the fact that the law has changed in this regard. Since the 1995 revision to the law of sales, the right to dissolve for the buyer's nonperformance now prescribes when the note prescribes. *See* Civil Code art. 2561.

the first installment" (citing *Gonsoulin v. John I. Adams & Co.*, 28 La. Ann. 598, and *George v. Knox*, 23 La. Ann. 354, 355).

This court has repeatedly and consistently held that the action to dissolve a sale for the non-payment of the purchase price accrues at the moment the buyer defaults on the payment of the credit portion of the price. In the recent case of *Louisiana Truck & Orange Land Co. v. Page*, 199 La. 1, 5 So. 2d 365, it was held that a suit to set aside a sale of real estate for non-payment of the purchase price is a personal action and is prescribed by 10 years. . . .

In the case at bar, the vendee's note representing the credit portion of the price was dated June 23, 1930, and was payable in one year, or on June 23, 1931. The note was never paid. Therefore the default occurred on June 23, 1931. The suit to dissolve the sale was filed on June 10, 1941, or within the prescriptive period of 10 years. Therefore, under the jurisprudence of this state, the judgment of the district court which dissolved the sale was correct.

But the Court of Appeal, Judge Hamiter dissenting, reversed the judgment. . . .

The Court of Appeal has, we think, erred in its interpretation of the article of the Code as amended.

. . . Article 2561 of the Code relates exclusively to the right to dissolve or set sales aside. The right to dissolve or set sales is in no sense related or akin to the accessory right of mortgage, which, according to the plain terms of the Code, aids in the enforcement of contracts. See Articles 3279 (no current article), 3282 (current article 3280), and 3284 of the Revised Civil Code (current articles 3278 and 3282). The action to enforce the resolutory condition, or to dissolve the contract, not only is different from, but is diametrically opposed to, the action to enforce the contract.

Under the amendment, the right to dissolve is available to the holder of the credit, or any part of it, without the necessity of a formal subrogation of that right to such holder or holders by the original vendor of the property and holder of the credit. The amendment makes the "right of dissolution," or right to dissolve, "an accessory of the credit representing the price." This means that the right is attached to, and accompanies, the credit into whatever hands it may pass. One of the definitions of the word "accessory" given by Webster's New

International Dictionary is "an adjunct or accompaniment," and it is in that sense in which the word is used in the amendment. That is the sense in which it was used in *Swan v. Gayle*, supra. The right to dissolve is now an appendage of the credit, in the sense that it is attached to, and follows, the credit. . . .

For the reasons assigned, the judgment of the Court of Appeal is reversed and set aside, and the judgment of the district court is affirmed; all costs to be paid by defendant E. J. White.

* * * * * *

ROBERTSON v. BUONI
504 So. 2d 860 (La. 1987)

DIXON, Chief Justice.

This is a suit to dissolve a sale of immovable property. By act of sale and assumption dated April 7, 1982, Elouise N. Robertson sold Mr. and Mrs. Joseph Buoni a piece of real property identified as Lot 20, Section D, Elmwood Subdivision, now known as Northbrook Subdivision, in Jefferson Parish, Louisiana. At trial, Ms. Robertson testified that the Buonis agreed to assume the balance of the existing mortgage held by Jefferson Savings & Loan, pay an $8,000 deposit and execute a promissory note in Ms. Robertson's favor for $40,000 representing the balance of the purchase price. The note provided for the payment of $7,000 on or before July 7, 1982, and $6,000 each year thereafter payable on April 7th. Ms. Robertson did not receive any payment after the initial $8,000, and when she attempted to collect, she learned the Buonis had left the area. The property at issue was no longer in her name on the public records, and the Buonis appeared as the record owners with only plaintiff's mortgage to Jefferson Savings & Loan Association encumbering the property. In an effort to avoid foreclosure because she had no funds with which to bid on the property, Ms. Robertson continued to make the mortgage payments. At the time judgment was rendered in the trial court, Ms. Robertson had paid taxes and mortgage installments for approximately three and one-half years after the sale.

Ms. Robertson sued, and an attorney was appointed as curator ad hoc for the absentee defendants. Attempts to locate the defendants were unsuccessful, and the matter proceeded to trial with Ms. Robertson as the lone witness. The promissory note, but not the act of sale, was introduced and admitted into evidence. The trial court declined to dissolve the sale, quoting at length from *Waseco Chemical & Supply Co. v. Bayou State Oil Corp.,* 371 So. 2d 305 (La. App. 2d Cir. 1979), cert. denied 374 So. 2d 656 (La. 1979), a case concerning dissolution of a mineral lease, and concluding that Ms. Robertson failed to meet her burden of proof in not providing the court with sufficient information to determine whether dissolution was warranted under Waseco. The court of appeal affirmed with one dissent, 494 So. 2d 563 (La. App. 5th Cir.1986), citing the devastating financial effect such a dissolution could have on an innocent third party purchaser. The dissenter objected to the court's speculation about the existence of a third party purchaser. . . .

The Louisiana Civil Code provides several remedies for a vendor who has not received payment of the purchase price. Under C.C. 3249 and C.C. 3271, the vendor has a privilege on things sold for payment:

> Creditors who have a privilege on immovables, are:
>
> 1. The vendor on the estate by him sold, for the payment of the price or so much of it as is unpaid, whether it was sold on or without a credit.

. . . Additionally, under C.C. 2561 and 2562, the unpaid vendor has the right to demand dissolution of sales by judicial process. This vendor's privilege and the right of dissolution are clearly distinguishable from and independent of each other. *Sliman v. McBee,* 311 So. 2d 248 (La. 1975); *Stevenson v. Brown,* 32 La. Ann. 461 (1880); *United States v. Maniscalco,* 523 F. Supp. 1338 (E.D. La. 1981); *Toler v. Toler,* 337 So. 2d 666 (La. App. 3d Cir. 1976). Enforcement of the vendor's privilege is "an affirmation of the contract" whereas the exercise of the right of dissolution places "matters in the same state as though the obligation had not existed." Yiannopoulos, *Real Rights in Louisiana and Comparative Law: Part I,"* 23 La. L. Rev. 161, 230, quoting *Heirs of Castle v. Floyd,* 38 La. Ann. 583, 587 (1886) and *Louis Werner Saw Mill Co. v. White,* 205 La. 242, 252, 17 So. 2d 264, 268 (1944). In the sale of immovables, the resolutory action of dissolution exists against the original purchaser and also third persons acquiring real rights or title to the property. 23 La. L. Rev. 161 at 232, fn. 334. *See also United States v. Maniscalco,* supra.

In Litvinoff, *7 Louisiana Civil Law Treatise, Book 2* at 508 (1975), the author cautions against casual dissolution of contracts, and states that the remedy of contract dissolution is not to be regarded as a convenient way for a party to unburden himself of the contract. The dissolution of the contract must be pronounced by the court, which must determine whether the rendering of only partial performance by the obligor, plus the delay attending a possible completion, or the failure to perform an accessory obligation, warrants dissolution. Litvinoff suggests several factors to be considered that were adopted by the Waseco court. These include the extent and gravity of the failure to perform alleged by the complaining party, the nature of the obligor's fault, the good or bad faith of the parties involved, and also the surrounding economic circumstances that may make the dissolution opportune or not. Litvinoff, supra at 509.

In *Sliman v. McBee,* supra, we addressed the issue of judicial dissolution of a contract of sale of an immovable. Among other pertinent facts and issues, in that case the agreed purchase price was $78,000, in part payment of which the purchaser paid $5,000, and executed four promissory notes for the remainder. There was no mortgage accompanying the sale. We applied C.C. 2045 which at that time read:

> The dissolving condition is that which, when accomplished, operates the revocation of the obligation, placing matters in the same state as though the obligation had not existed.
>
> It does not suspend the execution of the obligation; it only obliges the creditor to restore what he has received, in case the event provided for in the condition takes place.

(In the 1984 revisions of the articles on obligations, C.C. 2045 was incorporated into C.C. 1767.) We also applied C.C. 2561 and held that the vendor was entitled to dissolution of the sale on account of the purchaser's default in full payment of the purchase price, and held the vendee to be entitled to restoration of any partial payment. . . .

Ms. Robertson had an action under C.C. 2561, C.C. 2562 and Louisiana jurisprudence to seek dissolution of the sale when full payment of the price was not made, in spite of the fact that she failed to obtain a mortgage. The remedy afforded by C.C. 2561 is in no way dependent upon the existence of a security device such as a mortgage or a privilege. *Sliman v. McBee,* supra; *Hollanger v. Hollanger Rice Farms,* supra; *Stevenson v. Brown,* supra and *Toler v. Toler,* supra. Applying the Litvinoff suggested factors to the present case, it can be determined from Ms. Robertson's unrebutted testimony that the extent and gravity of the failure to perform is quite extreme. Failure to perform has caused Ms. Robertson to lose her property and her equity in such property, and to suffer substantial financial losses as she pays off the mortgage and taxes and legal fees for this action. Second, the nature of the obligor's fault—failure to pay—goes to the very heart of the purpose of the contract. Third, the good or bad faith of the parties must be considered, and it is unrebutted that Ms. Robertson is in good faith. On the other hand, the Buonis have defaulted on their obligation and have left the area without notifying Ms. Robertson. Litvinoff states that a fraudulent intent on the part of the obligor is not necessary to produce dissolution. "Any failure to perform involving some fault on his part suffices for this purpose, . . ." supra at 509-510. Leaving the area without notice or payment to Ms. Robertson constitutes more than "some fault." No economic circumstances have been shown in this case that would make dissolution inopportune. Conversely, the facts that the Buonis have not made any mortgage payments or paid any taxes on the house for the last three and one-half years when the house is in their name, and that Ms. Robertson has assumed these responsibilities, show economic circumstances that would make dissolution quite opportune. From the evidence presented, judicial dissolution of the sale is a warranted and just remedy.

The court of appeal's speculation of the presence of a third party purchaser of the property is reasonable, but is not a valid cause for denial of the remedy of dissolution of a sale of immovables. The right to dissolution of a sale of an immovable for nonpayment is not contingent on the absence of a third party purchaser. A vendor seeking dissolution of the sale may do so even after the property has left the hands of the original purchaser. *Stevenson v. Brown,* supra; 23 La. L. Rev., supra at 232 and cases cited therein. . . .

For these reasons the judgments of the courts below are reversed, and there is now judgment in favor of Elouise Neilson Robertson and against Joseph and Geraldine Buoni decreeing the sale of April 7, 1982, from Ms. Robertson to Mr. and Mrs. Buoni dissolved and of no effect, at the cost of defendants.

DENNIS and COLE, JJ., concur.

LEMMON, J., concurs and assigns reasons.

I do not necessarily agree with the broad proposition that a seller's right to dissolve the sale for non-payment of the purchase price under La. C. Cr. P. art. 2561 always exists against a third person who has subsequently acquired ownership. When a sale of immovable property has been recorded, the seller's right to dissolution, as against a subsequent purchaser, may depend on whether the recorded original sale indicates that the price has or has not been paid.1 A. Yiannopoulos, 2 Louisiana Civil Law Treatise-Property § 165 (2d ed. 1980).

Since the record in the present case does not contain the original sale, plaintiff arguably has not proved her right of dissolution as against a subsequent purchaser. However, the present litigation is solely between the original seller and the original purchasers, and plaintiff-seller is entitled to a judgment of dissolution as against these defendants.

* * * * * *

NOTES AND QUESTIONS

The resolutory condition and the vendor's privilege are found in all credit sales. Moreover, typically the sale transaction will include a conventional mortgage as well. In all cases it is important to understand the differences among the three. The mortgage is a type of consensual security in which both the debtor and the creditor agree to its granting. In the case of a vendor's privilege, this security right arises by operation of law without the consent of the buyer of the property. Lastly, the resolutory condition is not a security device at all, rather it is a concept found in the obligations principles of the Civil Code. Nevertheless, the resolutory condition can mimic many of the features of a security device in that it gives the seller/creditor recourse against the debtor with regard to the property—with a mortgage it is through foreclosure and with a resolutory condition it is through dissolution of the sale.

With a resolutory condition, the effectiveness as to third parties when the thing being transferred is immovable depends upon recordation and the information contained in the act of transfer. For instance, a credit sale whereby the recorded instrument of conveyance fails to indicate that the full purchase price was not paid at the closing will cause the resolutory condition to have effects only between the buyer and the seller, but not as to third persons. If the seller wants to ensure that the resolutory condition will bind third persons (such as a person to whom the original buyer might subsequently convey the property) then she must be sure that the act of sale includes a statement to the effect that the purchase price has not been paid, or that this is a credit sale. Mere recordation is not enough. Recordation plus the proper disclosure in the document itself is necessary to make the seller's right to dissolve for nonperformance binding on third persons.

2. Effectiveness as to Third Persons

Even more important than making the mortgage effective between the parties is making it effective as to third persons. At the heart of this concept is the public records doctrine and the laws of registry. Consider the following core code articles:

***See* La. Civ. Code arts. 3355, 3338.**

i. Recordation

While not overly complex, the rules governing recordation do require careful study. For the law governing the effects of recordation, timing of filing and how it is determined, as well as related matters, *see* **La. Civ. Code art. 3346-56.**

Another important concept that plagues lawyers and law students alike is the duration of the effects of recordation. As with most all recorded instruments, the effects granted by the laws of registry do not, on their own, last forever. The law of mortgages is no different and conventional mortgages in particular are subject to a somewhat complex set of rules that can serve as a trap for the unwary lawyer. The rules are found in C.C. arts. 3357 and 3358:

***See* La. Civ. Code arts. 3357-3358. *See also* La. Civ. Code art. 3361 regarding amendments to a mortgage.**

ii. Reinscription

***See* La. Civ. Code arts. 3362-3365**

iii. Cancellation

***See* La. Civ. Code arts. 3366-3368**

3. Types of Obligations Secured by Mortgages

The types of obligations that can be secured by a conventional mortgage have a storied history in Louisiana. As commercial transactions became more complex, and credit relationships became more sophisticated in terms of the legal tools that underpinned them, Louisiana's law of mortgages was forced (sometimes uncomfortably) to evolve to meet changing market needs. As discussed below, one can divide mortgages into three categories based upon the type of obligations that they secure.

The easiest mortgage to understand is the *single-advance mortgage loan* whereby a single, finite, and one-time amount of money is advanced to the debtor and is secured by a mortgage. This is the type of mortgage arrangement that is the hallmark of residential loans in the United States. The second type is the *determinate future advance mortgage loan*. In this case the creditor agrees to advance a certain finite amount of money to the borrower, but agrees to make the advance over time as the borrower requires. These are sometimes called non-revolving or non-fluctuating lines of credit, and construction loans are the most common examples of these. Once the bank advances the total amount of the loan (even though it is given over to the borrower in installments or "tranches"), no additional monies are handed over.

The final type—and the most complex—is the *indeterminate future advance mortgage loan*, or as it is more commonly called: the revolving line of credit or the fluctuating line of credit. These loans operate much like typical credit cards whereby the borrower has a set amount he is able to spend at any give time. When the borrower repays a certain amount, he is able to "free up" that amount to borrow again. Consider the following case that illustrates the importance of knowing which type of obligation the mortgage secures.

* * * * * *

THRIFT FUNDS CANAL, INC. v. FOY
260 So. 2d 628 (La. 1972).

SANDERS, Justice.

We granted certiorari in this mortgage foreclosure to review the judgment of the Court of Appeal, holding that the 1968 note and mortgage of Thrift Funds

Canal, Inc., the foreclosing creditor, primed a 1966 note and mortgage of First National Life Insurance Company. We affirm the judgment.

On February 14, 1963, First National Life Insurance Company loaned Leroy M. Foy $10,000.00. Foy executed a mortgage note payable to First National in the amount of the loan, bearing 6% Per annum interest from date and payable in monthly installments of $84.39. The note was paraphed for identification with a real estate mortgage describing the note and securing it. The mortgage was duly recorded on February 18, 1963. Foy made payments on the mortgage note and, by December 20, 1966, had reduced the principal to $8,227.83.

On that date, Foy obtained a second loan from First National. He gave a promissory note for $3,000.00, payable in 120 monthly amortized installments of $33.31 each. On its face, the note appears to be unsecured, but on the back is the following inscription signed by Foy and his wife:

> This note is secured by a mortgage executed under date of 2-14-63 together with the said mortgage note. It being understood that the mortgage and note shall remain in full force and effect as collateral security to this note.

On December 19, 1968, Foy gave a second mortgage on the same property to Thrift Funds Canal, Inc., securing a note in excess of $16,000.00. This mortgage was recorded on December 27, 1968.

Thrift Funds brought foreclosure proceedings against Foy on its 1968 mortgage note. Thus, at the time of foreclosure, the court was required to evaluate three alleged incumbrances:

> (1) The 1963 $10,000.00 note in favor of First National secured by a recorded mortgage, on which there was a balance due of $6,736.92;
>
> (2) The 1966 $3,000.00 note in favor of First National allegedly secured by the 1963 mortgage, on which there was a balance due of $2,368.83; and
>
> (3) The 1968 $16,000.00 note in favor of Thrift Funds secured by a recorded mortgage, on which there was a balance due of $13,000.00

The question presented is whether Thrift Funds' second mortgage primes First National's 1966 note as secured by the earlier mortgage. The resolution of this question has important implications for the law of security devices.

In Louisiana, a conventional mortgage is an accessory security device. LSA-C.C. Art. 3284; *Louis Werner Saw Mill Co. v. White*, 205 La. 242, 17 So. 2d 264 (1944); *Blappert v. Succession of Welsch*, 192 La. 173, 187 So. 281 (1939). It is founded upon a principal debt, which it secures, and when the principal debt is extinguished, the mortgage disappears. LSA-C.C. Arts. 3285, 3411(4); *Lacoste v. Hickey*, 203 La. 794, 14 So. 2d 639 (1943); *Rhys v. Moody*, 163 La. 1039, 113 So. 367 (1927).

Despite the accessory principle, however, Article 3292 of the Louisiana Civil Code authorizes a mortgage to secure a future debt. This provision enhances the commercial utility of the mortgage as a security device.

For analysis, conventional mortgages may be divided into three classes: (1) a mortgage for a specific debt, (2) a mortgage for future advances, and (3) a collateral mortgage. A mortgage for a specific debt is a mortgage given to secure a particular, existing debt. *See Lacoste v. Hickey*, supra. A mortgage for future advances is a mortgage given to secure a debt not yet in existence. *See* LSA-C.C. Arts. 3292, 3293.

A collateral mortgage is a mortgage designed, not to directly secure an existing debt, but to secure a mortgage note pledged as collateral security for a debt or a succession of debts. The mortgage is usually drawn in favor of future holders, represented by a nominal mortgagee. For convenience in pledging, the companion promissory note is usually payable to bearer on demand. The maker may reissue the note from time to time. . . .

First National relies upon its 1963 first mortgage to secure the later note executed by LeRoy Michael Foy. The mortgage recites that Foy is indebted to First National in the sum of $10,000.00, which First National has "this day loaned" to mortgagor; that mortgagor has given a specially described $10,000.00 note to First National; and that to secure the payment of the "above described note," Foy mortgages certain property "in favor of First National Life Insurance Company, and to enure to the use and benefit of any and all future holders of said note." The mortgage is accepted by First National Life Insurance.

The record reflects that First National advanced to the debtor the full amount stipulated contemporaneously with the execution of the mortgage.

Clearly, the mortgage cannot be classified as a collateral mortgage. It evidences and directly secures an existing debt, a money loan, and possesses none of the formal characteristics of a collateral mortgage.

First National contends, however, that specific language in the mortgage broadens it into a mortgage for future advances, relying especially upon the following default clause:

> (I)n any of said events, The said mortgage note, or notes, in principal and interest, And all other indebtedness secured hereby shall, at the option of the holder of said mortgage notes, immediately become due and payable, anything to the contrary notwithstanding, and it shall be lawful for, and the mortgagor herein does hereby authorize the mortgagee Or any future holder of the mortgage note, or notes, to cause all and singular the property hereinabove described, to be seized and sold under executory process issued by any competent court with or without appraisement, at the option of the mortgagee Or any future holder or holders of the within described mortgage note, to the highest bidder for cash, the said mortgagor hereby confessing judgment in favor of said mortgagee or any future holder of the mortgage note or notes, for the full amount thereof, together with all interest, attorney fees, insurance premiums, costs and expenses.

Specifically, First National argues that the clause provides for plural notes, indebtedness other than the $10,000.00 loan, and recognizes the rights of future holders.

Although the argument seems plausible upon first impression, it lacks real substance. The language relied upon appears in that portion of the mortgage describing the rights of the mortgagee when default occurs. The alternative language, Mortgage note, or notes, was designed to adapt this portion of the mortgage to plural notes executed with and described in the mortgage. . . . It must be noted that all portions of the mortgage form have not been adapted to plural notes, but this circumstance does not bar the above construction.

The phrase *any future holder* does no more than recognize that the mortgage note may be negotiated and held by someone other than the mortgagee at the time of default.

The phrase *other indebtedness secured hereby* refers, not to future notes, but to the allowable expense items that may be incurred by the mortgagee in protecting its security: taxes, insurance premiums, and attorney fees. An earlier paragraph in the mortgage makes this construction quite clear. It provides that the mortgage secures "said Note and Attorney fees, taxes and premiums of insurance."

It is true that, in order to secure a future debt, a mortgage need not express on its face that it is given for future advances. It may be phrased as security for an existing debt, when no debt in fact exists, and yet secure a later debt in accordance with the intention of the parties. *Hortman-Salmen Co. v. White*, 168 La. 1057, 123 So. 711 (1929); *Collins v. His Creditors*, 18 La. Ann. 235 (1866); *Pickersgill & Co. v. Brown*, 7 La. Ann. 297 (1852); 25 La. L. Rev. 789, 791 (1965).

In *Hortman-Salem Co. v. White*, supra, this Court held:

> It is true that the full amount of the loans was not advanced in money to White by plaintiff in either case at the date of the recordation of the mortgage, although the recorded acts of mortgage state that such advances had been made in fact.
>
> This is unimportant, however, in our opinion, as it is well settled, as stated in the syllabus of *Pickersgill & Co. v. Brown*, 7 La. Ann. 297, that: "Mortgages, under the hypothecary system of Louisiana, may be given to secure debts having no legal existence at the date of the mortgage. It is not essential, in such a mortgage, even with respect to third persons, that is should express on its face, that it was executed to secure future debts. It may be described as a security for existing debts, and yet used to protect those which, in contemplation of the parties, were to be created at a future time."

We find nothing in the present record, however, to show that, when the first mortgage was executed, the parties intended that it secure future advances. Quite to the contrary, the record reflects that it was designed only to secure an existing debt, a loan made contemporaneously with the execution of the mortgage.

First National strongly relies upon *Pickersgill & Co. v. Brown*, supra. That case, however, is inapposite. There, though phrased altogether in terms of an existing debt, the mortgage was actually given partly for an existing debt and partly for later advances. The later advances were in fact made. Since the excess mortgage security had been reserved for future advances and those advances made, the court properly recognized the mortgage as one for future advances.

We conclude that the present mortgage is one for a specific debt.

When the present mortgage is thus construed, the case is reduced to a narrow question of law: After an installment note secured by a mortgage for a specific debt has been partially paid, can the mortgagor by inscription on a later note secure that note by the earlier mortgage to the prejudice of other mortgagees? We think not.

After a mortgage note for a specific debt has been paid, the mortgage is extinguished. No later advance on the note can revive the mortgage. LSA-C.C. Arts. 3285 (current articles 3278 and 3279), 3411(4); *Baton Rouge Wood Products, Inc. v. Ezell*, 251 La. 369, 204 So.2d 395 (1967); *Lacoste v. Hickey*, supra; *Mente & Co. v. Levy*, 160 La. 496, 107 So. 318 (1926); *Hibernia Nat. Bank v. Succession of Gragard*, 109 La. 677, 33 So. 728 (1903).

Article 3285 of the Louisiana Civil Code declares: "(I)n all cases where the principal debt is extinguished, the mortgage disappears with it."

When partial payment is made of a mortgage installment note for a specific debt, the payment of the installments extinguishes the note Pro tanto. At the same time, the payment reduces the debt burden upon the mortgage. Thereafter, the debt burden cannot be increased to the prejudice of junior mortgages. . . .

In the present case, First National received the 1966 note after the balance on the original mortgage note had been reduced to about $8,000.00. The debtor continued his payments thereafter. Under the law, the debtor's inscription on the new note could effectuate no increase of the debt burden bearing upon the mortgage to the prejudice of other mortgagees. We hold, therefore, as did the

Court of Appeal, that the mortgage of Thrift Funds, the foreclosing creditor, primes the 1966 note of First National Life Insurance Company.

For the reasons assigned, the judgment of the Court of Appeal is affirmed; all costs in this Court are taxed against First National Life Insurance Company.

* * * * * *

The need for mortgages that secure indeterminate future advances has led to the creation of one of the most interesting and creative legal institutions in Louisiana law—specifically, the collateral mortgage package. For much of the state's history the typical mortgage contract could only secure a single advance or a determinate future advance, but the mortgage could not secure indeterminate future advances limited only by a maximum outstanding amount at any give time. The theory was that once the entire loan amount had been advanced and repaid, the mortgage was automatically extinguished due to there no longer being a principal obligation (i.e., an obligation to repay a debt). Any new amounts that were loaned would need a new mortgage that would, in turn, receive a new priority ranking.

However, commercial interests demanded this type of device, and so Louisiana lawyers devised a way to use the mortgage, in combination with a pledge, to accomplish the feat: the collateral mortgage. The following case illustrates this ingenious and distinctively Louisiana security device.

* * * * * *

DIAMOND SERVICES CORP. v. BENOIT
780 So. 2d 367 (La. 2001)

CALOGERO, Chief Justice.

We granted this writ primarily to resolve a conflict among the courts of appeal over whether the maker of a collateral mortgage note is personally liable beyond the value of the mortgaged property when the collateral mortgage note is pledged to secure the debt of a third party. After reviewing the applicable law, we conclude that, within the context of the collateral mortgage package, the maker of a collateral mortgage note is not personally liable beyond the value of the mortgaged property when the collateral mortgage note is pledged to secure the debt of a third party. Accordingly, we reverse the court of appeal's holding to the contrary.

FACTS AND PROCEDURAL HISTORY

On May 7, 1993, William Davenport signed two hand notes to obtain lines of credit for his corporation, International Diving and Consulting, Inc. The first hand note was in favor of Morgan City Bank and Trust Company (MC Bank) for $350,000.00. The second hand note was in favor of the plaintiff, Diamond Services Corporation, in the amount of $300,000.00. Davenport signed as guarantor on both hand notes.

On the same date, the defendant, Delores N. Benoit, a friend solicited by Davenport, executed documents comprising two collateral mortgage packages. The first collateral mortgage package was in favor of MC Bank, and consisted of a mortgage on Benoit's 410.92-acre tract of land in Acadia Parish, a collateral mortgage note or *ne varietur* note for $350,000.00, and a pledge of that collateral mortgage note to secure the $350,000.00 MC Bank hand note signed by Davenport. The second collateral mortgage package was in favor of Diamond Services. It consisted of a mortgage on the same 410.92-acre tract, a collateral mortgage note for $300,000.00, and a pledging document, entitled "Security Agreement (Possessory Collateral)," pledging the $300,000.00 collateral mortgage note to secure the $300,000.00 Diamond Services hand note signed by Davenport. Benoit did not sign either of the hand notes executed by International Diving and guaranteed by Davenport.

Eventually, International Diving and Davenport defaulted on both hand notes. . . . In December 1996, MC Bank filed for executory process in Acadia Parish on its $350,000.00 collateral mortgage note, attempting to seize and sell Benoit's 410.92-acre tract. However, in May 1997, MC Bank assigned to Diamond Services all of its rights in the MC Bank hand note, the MC Bank collateral mortgage note, and its petition for executory process against Benoit filed in Acadia Parish. Substituted as party plaintiff, Diamond Services caused Benoit's tract to be sold, netting $116,157.28, which was applied to the outstanding balance on the MC Bank collateral mortgage note. Thereafter, Diamond Services filed a supplemental petition against Benoit for a deficiency judgment on the MC Bank collateral mortgage note.

Regarding the Diamond Services hand note, because neither International Diving nor Davenport had made any payments on that note, Diamond Services filed a separate petition against Benoit in Lafayette Parish on its own $300,000.00 collateral mortgage note. Both suits were consolidated in Acadia Parish. In her answer to the lawsuits, Benoit denied personal liability. . . .

Diamond Services and Benoit both filed motions for summary judgment, with Diamond Services alleging that it was entitled to a deficiency judgment as a matter of law against Benoit as the maker of both collateral mortgage notes, and with Benoit alleging, among other things, that the maker of a collateral mortgage note is not personally liable, and that there was mutual error on the part of the parties as to the extent of her liability. The trial court in July 1999 denied Diamond Services' motion and granted Benoit's, finding that Benoit was not personally liable on either the MC Bank collateral mortgage note or the Diamond Services collateral mortgage note. . . .

The court of appeal affirmed in part, reversed in part, and remanded. . . . [W]ith regard to the Diamond Services collateral mortgage note, the court of appeal reversed the trial court's finding of mutual error, finding that Diamond Services' intentions and the terms of that note were indistinguishable, and thus any error as to Benoit's understanding of her personal liability exposure regarding that note was unilateral, not mutual. Id. Further, the court of appeal held that Benoit, as the maker of the collateral mortgage note pledged to secure the indebtedness of another, was personally liable for the debt, and that such personal liability was limited to the lesser of the face amount of the collateral mortgage note and the amount owed in connection with the hand note. Id. at 28. . . .

DISCUSSION

We granted Benoit's writ application to resolve a conflict among the circuits regarding whether the maker of a collateral mortgage note pledged to secure the indebtedness of a third party is personally liable on the collateral mortgage note beyond the value of the mortgaged property. *Diamond Services Corp. v. Benoit,* 00-0469 (La.4/20/00), 759 So. 2d 768. As Amicus Curiae acknowledges, the issue of the personal liability of the maker of a collateral mortgage note pledged to secure a third party's hand note is an "unclear and confusing area of the law." Amicus Br., p. 7. Although there have been several conflicting court of appeal opinions, the precise legal question has not been addressed, or resolved, by this court.

I.

The collateral mortgage, though now recognized by statute, is a form of conventional mortgage that was developed by Louisiana's practicing lawyers and has long been recognized by Louisiana courts. *Levy v. Ford,* 41 La. Ann. 873, 6 So. 671 (La.1889); *Merchants' Mut. Ins. Co. v. Jamison,* 25 La. Ann. 363 (La. 1873); *Succession of Dolhonde,* 21 La. Ann. 3, 1869 WL 4559 (La. 1869). The collateral mortgage arose out of the need for a special form of mortgage to secure revolving lines of credit and multiple present and future cross-collateralized debts for which there was no provision in the Civil Code. David S. Willenzik, *Future Advance Priority Rights of Louisiana Collateral Mortgages: Legislative Revisions, New Rules, and a Modern Alternative,* 55 La. L. Rev. 1, 7 (1999). The collateral mortgage was designed "to create a mortgage note that can be pledged as collateral security for either a pre-existing debt, or for a debt created contemporaneously with the mortgage, or for a future debt or debts, or even for a series of debts." Max Nathan, Jr. & H. Gayle Marshall, *The Collateral Mortgage,* 33 La. L. Rev. 497 (1973). One advantage it holds for creditors is that liabilities are ranked from the date of the original pledge of the collateral mortgage note (assuming the mortgage has been recorded), rather than from the date of the individual, subsequent advances. Further, the creditor is able to secure multiple present and future loans and obligations on a cross-collateralized basis.

This Court discussed the fundamentals of a collateral mortgage in *First Guaranty Bank v. Alford,* 366 So. 2d 1299, 1302 (La.1978), as follows:

> A mortgage is an accessory right which is granted to the creditor over the property of another as security for the debt. La. Civ. Code arts. 3278, 3284. Mortgages are of three types: conventional, legal and judicial. La. Civ. Code art. 3286. Within the area of conventional mortgages, three different forms of mortgages are recognized by the Louisiana statutes and jurisprudence: an "ordinary mortgage" (La. Civ. Code arts. 3278, 3290); a mortgage to secure future advances (La. Civ. Code arts. 3292, 3293); and a collateral mortgage. *See Thrift Funds Canal, Inc. v. Foy,* 261 La. 573, 260 So. 2d 628 (1972). Unlike the other

> two forms of conventional mortgages, a collateral mortgage is not a "pure" mortgage; rather, it is the result of judicial recognition that one can pledge a note secured by a mortgage and use this pledge to secure yet another debt.
>
> A collateral mortgage indirectly secures a debt via a pledge. A collateral mortgage consists of at least three documents, and takes several steps to complete. First, there is a promissory note, usually called a collateral mortgage note or a "*ne varietur*" note. The collateral mortgage note is secured by a mortgage, the so-called collateral mortgage. The mortgage provides the creditor with security in the enforcement of the collateral mortgage note.
>
> Up to this point, a collateral mortgage appears to be identical to both a mortgage to secure future advances and an ordinary mortgage. But a distinction arises in the collateral mortgage situation because money is not directly advanced on the note that is paraphed for identification with the act of mortgage. Rather, the collateral mortgage note and the mortgage which secures it are *pledged* to secure a debt.

366 So. 2d at 1302 (emphasis in original).

Pledge is an accessory contract by which one debtor gives something to a creditor as security for the debt. . . . Invariably, the thing given as security for the debt is a movable, in which case the contract is more accurately called pawn. . . . A person may give a pledge not only for his own debt, but also for that of another. . . .The pledge secures only that debt or debts contemplated in the contract between the pledgor and pledgee. . . .

A collateral mortgage is not a "pure" mortgage; instead, it combines the security devices of mortgage and pledge into one. . . . It is important to remember that the collateral mortgage does not directly secure a debt; instead, the collateral mortgage device "is designed to create a mortgage note for a fictitious debt that can be pledged as collateral security for a real debt." . . . *see also* David S. Willenzik, *Louisiana Secured Transactions,* § 2:13 (2000) ("The borrower's mortgage secures a fictitious collateral mortgage note, which is payable to bearer on demand. The collateral mortgage note is then pledged under a collateral pledge agreement to secure the borrower's true indebtedness under one or more hand notes."). Because the mortgagor, after executing the collateral mortgage and the collateral mortgage note, then pledges the collateral mortgage note as security for a debt, usually represented by a separate hand note, the collateral mortgage package combines the security devices of pledge and mortgage. . . .

II.

The dispute in this case centers around the obligation that arises from the making of the collateral mortgage note when that note is pledged to secure the debt of a third party represented by a hand note executed by that third party. Our courts of appeal have differed in resolving disputes in this area, yet this court has not spoken on the issue. The lack of resolution at this level prompted our writ grant.

The Third Circuit in *Bank of Lafayette v. Bailey,* 531 So. 2d 294 (La. App. 3 Cir.), *granted in part,* 533 So. 2d 5 (La.1988), was the first Louisiana court to suggest that the collateral mortgage note, when pledged to secure the debt of a third party, might create a personal obligation that exposes the maker to liability above and beyond the value of the mortgaged property. In *Bailey,* a husband and wife executed a collateral mortgage of immovable community property and a collateral mortgage note in the amount of $250,000, which they later pledged to secure any indebtedness of the husband up to $250,000. The husband defaulted on a subsequently executed hand note, resulting in a seizure and sale of the mortgaged property and a deficiency judgment against the wife for the unsatisfied portion of the hand note. Finding the wife personally liable for the deficiency, the *Bailey* court held that "the collateral mortgage note being pledged for an obligation evidenced by the hand note executed by the [husband] bound both in solido, for the payment of that obligation up to the full amount of the collateral mortgage note." 531 So. 2d at 298 (citing *Zibilich v. Rouseo,* 157 La. 936, 103 So. 269 (1925); *Chaffe v. Whitfield,* 40 La. Ann. 631, 4 So. 563 (1888)). . . .

In *Concordia Bank & Trust Co. v. Lowry,* 533 So. 2d 170 (La. App. 3 Cir. 1988), *rev'd in part on other grounds,* 539 So. 2d 46 (La.1989), the Third Circuit again addressed the issue of the personal liability of the maker of a collateral mortgage note and seemingly made explicit the rationale underlying its holding in *Bailey:* the maker of the collateral mortgage note is personally liable thereon and her liability is not limited to the value of the mortgaged property. In *Lowry,* six family members executed a collateral mortgage and a $100,000 collateral mortgage note, which was pledged to secure the future indebtedness of any of the mortgagors. One member executed a hand note in the amount of $61,859.67, but later defaulted on that note, thereby resulting in a judgment of $74,453.14 against the six makers of the collateral mortgage note. The judgment as to the appellants, three of the six family members, was taken by default upon their failure to answer the lender's suit. . . .

Notwithstanding our writ grant and partial reversal in *Bailey,* and Judge Foret's concurring reasons in *Lowry,* the Third Circuit in *Merchants & Farmers Bank & Trust v. Smith,* 559 So. 2d 845, 847 (La. App. 3 Cir.), *writ denied,* 563 So. 2d 865 (La.1990), reiterated its position that the maker of the collateral mortgage note is personally liable for the indebtedness sued upon, up to the full amount of the collateral mortgage note. . . .

Contrary to the Third Circuit's stance on the issue, the Second Circuit takes the view that the maker of the collateral mortgage note is liable only up to the value of the mortgaged property. *Commercial Nat'l Bank v. Succession of Rogers,* 628 So. 2d 33 (La. App. 2 Cir.1993). In *Succession of Rogers,* three men executed a hand note in the amount of $350,000. Two days later, the three men and their wives executed a collateral mortgage and note in the amount of $500,000, which was pledged to secure the hand note. The lender foreclosed on the mortgage. The sheriff's sale of the property netted $148,529.27. The lender then unsuccessfully petitioned for a deficiency judgment.

In affirming that ruling, the Second Circuit rejected the Third Circuit's position and held that the maker of a collateral mortgage note who does not execute the hand note has no liability beyond the value of the mortgaged property. *Succession of Rogers,* 628 So. 2d at 36-37. To reach a contrary result, the court noted, it would have to find that the wives had executed both a pledge of the mortgaged property and a personal guaranty of payment of the underlying indebtedness and any future advances made. The court reasoned that the bank could have personally obligated the wives by requiring that they sign the hand note as co-makers or that they execute some other document guaranteeing payment of the underlying debt and expressing an intent to be personally bound. Id. at 37.14

The Fifth Circuit also takes the view that the maker of a collateral mortgage note is not personally liable on such note when it is used to secure the debt of a third party. In *Bank of New Orleans & Trust Co. v. H.P.B., Jr. Development Co.,* 427 So. 2d 486 (La. App. 5 Cir.1983), the maker of a collateral mortgage note also signed the back of the hand note. However, the court noted that the collateral mortgagor "executed the back of the hand note only to effectuate the pledge of the collateral mortgage note secured by the collateral mortgage, as recited, and [the collateral mortgagor] did not execute or endorse as a co-maker or solidary surety." Id. at 490. "In other words, [the collateral mortgage] was *in rem* and [the collateral mortgagor] had no *in personam* liability." Id.

Furthermore, at least one federal court, after an in depth assessment of all Louisiana cases and law review articles on point, has held that the maker of a collateral mortgage and collateral mortgage note is not personally liable beyond the value of the mortgaged property when the collateral mortgage note is pledged as security on behalf of a third party. *Pontchartrain State Bank v. Lybrand,* 799 F. Supp. 633 (E.D. La.1992). . . .

Granted, the Louisiana Third Circuit in a trilogy of cases has expounded on the issue of the extent of the maker's liability on a collateral mortgage note pledged to secure the debt of a third party. However, the Louisiana Second Circuit, the Louisiana Fifth Circuit, and the United States District Court for the Eastern District of Louisiana—one might say a majority of the courts that have addressed the issue—have concluded that such a note generally does not create personal liability beyond the value of the mortgaged property, absent some additional document or agreement that provides for such liability.

III.

Early commentators discussing the collateral mortgage package understood that the collateral mortgage note itself did not represent the indebtedness; instead, the collateral mortgage note was merely pledged to secure the actual indebtedness. In 1973, Max Nathan and Gayle Marshall explained:

> the *"ne varietur"* note is not the indebtedness at all: the *"ne varietur"* note, rather, is only to be used as collateral, the security that is pledged to the creditor to secure another note. The true indebtedness is the debt that the collateral mortgage *"ne varietur"* note is pledged

> to secure. Thus, while the *"ne varietur"* note is generally a note payable on demand, it does not represent a specific debt . . . the terms and conditions of the hand note represent the indebtedness and govern the payment schedule for the borrower.

Nathan and Marshal, *The Collateral Mortgage,* 33 La. L. Rev. at 505.

Professor Crawford was even more explicit, stating that "[t]he collateral mortgage note itself represents no obligation or indebtedness at all." William E. Crawford, *Forum Juridicum, Executory Process and Collateral Mortgages, Authentic Evidence of the Hand Note?,* 33 La. L. Rev. 535, 536 (1973).

It was only after some courts of appeal began to ascribe qualities of a negotiable instrument to the collateral mortgage note that the opinions of certain commentators evolved to suggest that the collateral mortgage note is a separate debt instrument that creates a personal obligation beyond the value of the mortgaged property. For example, Max Nathan and Anthony Dunbar in 1988, relying on *Central Bank v. Bishop,* supra, and *Central Progressive Bank v. Doerner,* supra, posited:

> It is now quite clear that the *ne varietur* note is not a meaningless piece of paper. The note is indeed an enforceable obligation even though it does not represent the indebtedness of the borrower. No primary obligation is brought into existence by the mere execution of a collateral mortgage and a *ne varietur* note. The enforceability as well as the ranking of the mortgage depends upon "issuance" (the pledge of the ne varietur note). Nonetheless, the ne varietur note is a separate, viable negotiable instrument that may give rise to personal liability on the part of the maker.

Max Nathan, Jr., and Anthony P. Dunbar, *The Collateral Mortgage: Logic and Experience,* 49 La. L. Rev. 39, 41-42 (1988); . . .

While we agree that the enforceability of the collateral mortgage note depends upon the pledge of that note, we do not agree that the *Bishop* and *Doerner* cases jurisprudentially changed, or even more fully explained, the original nature and purposes of the collateral mortgage package in regard to the issue presented to us today. That issue, as previously set forth, is whether the maker of the collateral mortgage note is personally liable beyond the value of the mortgaged property when the note is pledged to secure the obligation of a third party. The fundamental error in the reasoning of the Third Circuit and the arguments of respondent in this case is the misunderstanding that the collateral mortgage note is "just like any other promissory note." The collateral mortgage note itself is not a separate debt instrument; nor is it just like any other promissory note. As we stated in *Alford:*

> That the collateral [mortgage] note was in effect a negotiable bearer instrument, a matter which we initially found troubling, is of no moment. It was not a debt instrument, but a security device, a pledge instrument.
>
> *Alford,* 366 So. 2d at 1303. . . .

A collateral mortgage note standing alone is virtually meaningless, as it has no intrinsic value and evidences no debt or obligation actually owed by or to anyone. Only when viewed in the context of the entire collateral mortgage package, with all of the component parts present, does the collateral mortgage note take on meaning. . . . As we explained in *Bozorg,* the collateral mortgage note is a "fictitious debt that can be pledged as collateral security for a real debt." 457 So. 2d at 671. Therefore, the collateral mortgage note differs from a typical promissory note in that, on its own, it does not represent any indebtedness by the maker.

The origins and purposes behind the evolution of the collateral mortgage support our view that the collateral mortgage note was not conceived as being a separate enforceable instrument like other promissory notes. The collateral mortgage device evolved in the nineteenth century to provide a flexible mechanism by which revolving lines of credit and other future obligations could be secured. . . . This security device was developed by practitioners in order to overcome limitations that then existed in the codified mortgage to secure future advances. . . . The collateral mortgage package was designed "to create a mortgage note that can be pledged as collateral security for either a pre-existing debt, or for a debt created contemporaneously with the mortgage, or for a future debt or debts, or even for a series of debts." Id. Hence, the collateral mortgage note was not envisioned as a separate, enforceable promissory note, but was created as a component part of the entire collateral mortgage mechanism, providing flexibility in securing future advances while allowing creditors to make those advances safely and without fear of being primed by intervening creditors because of the retroactive ranking to the date of issuance or pledge of the collateral mortgage note. Id. . . .

IV.

Nor do we find any support for the proposition that the collateral mortgage note creates a personal obligation beyond the value of the mortgaged property in the recent adoption of the Uniform Commercial Code, Article 9, and the corresponding changes to Louisiana securities law. By Act 135 of 1989, the legislature enacted into law a modified version of Article 9 of the Uniform Commercial Code (U.C.C.) as Chapter 9 of the Louisiana Commercial Laws. La. Rev. Stat. 10:9-101 *et seq.* As a general rule, Article 9 applies to contractual security interests affecting personal or movable property, including the pledge of a real estate mortgage note, that are entered into or granted on or after January 1, 1990. La. Rev. Stat. 10:9-102; Acts 1989, No. 135, § 12. However, security interests affecting real estate or immovable property, including collateral real estate mortgages, are excluded from coverage under Article 9, and are subject to other statutory authority. La. Rev. Stat. 10:9-104(j). Since Article 9 applies only to the pledge of the collateral mortgage note, and not to the mortgage of real property, commentators have noted that it has limited application to the post 1989 collateral mortgage security device. . . . We can find nothing in Article 9 of the Louisiana U.C.C. that addresses the extent of the liability of the maker of a collateral mortgage note pledged to secure the debt of a third party.

Act 137 of 1989, known as the U.C.C. Implementation Bill, was designed to facilitate implementation of Article 9 of the U.C.C. by amending various existing Louisiana security device laws to clarify that these laws would continue to apply to then outstanding transactions and security interests. . . . Yet, the legislature clearly recognized the special creature of the collateral mortgage, and therefore continued the juridical invention of the collateral mortgage by providing for it by statute. *See* La. R.S. 9:5550 *et seq.* This legislative definition, however, does not implicate the extent of the liability of the maker of the collateral mortgage note pledged to secure the debt of another.

In La. Rev. Stat. 9:5550(1), a "collateral mortgage" is described as "a mortgage that is given to secure a written obligation, such as a collateral mortgage note, negotiable or nonnegotiable instrument, or other written evidence of a debt, that is issued, pledged, or otherwise used as security for another obligation." La. Rev. Stat. 9:5550(1). This definition of a collateral mortgage certainly recognizes that the paraphed collateral mortgage note is a "written obligation"; however, it does not necessarily follow that the collateral mortgage note must be a negotiable promissory note. A collateral mortgage may secure a "negotiable or nonnegotiable instrument or other written evidence of a debt, that is issued, pledged, or otherwise used as security for another obligation." La. Rev. Stat. 9:5550(1). Although the legislature codified many of the rules applicable to collateral mortgages that were previously found only in case law, Willenzik, *Louisiana Secured Transactions,* § 2.14, we do not find any indication in either Act 137 of 1989 or its legislative history that the legislature intended to rewrite collateral mortgage law or to provide that a collateral mortgage note is to be treated the same as any other negotiable instrument, when there are inherent differences between a collateral mortgage note and other notes.

V.

. . . With these principles in mind, we decide today that personal liability beyond the value of the mortgaged property does not generally arise on the collateral mortgage note when the note is pledged to secure the obligation of a third party.

. . . The strength of the authority on this issue leads us to conclude that, for well over a hundred years, this practitioner-created and judicially recognized "hybrid" security device, the collateral mortgage and the subsequent pledge of the collateral mortgage note, has customarily not, absent some additional agreement, brought into play the personal liability of the maker of the collateral mortgage note, beyond the value of the property mortgaged, when the note is pledged to secure the debt of another.

Furthermore, the facts of the instant case, we believe, are typical of collateral mortgage packages used by Louisiana's practicing attorneys. Here, as in the ordinary collateral mortgage situation, the parties understood that the liability of the maker of the collateral mortgage note, paraphed *ne varietur* to identify it with the act of collateral mortgage, does not extend beyond the value of the mortgaged property when the note is pledged to secure an obligation of a third party. Attorney Andrew Reed, who prepared the collateral mortgage packages for both MC Bank and Diamond Services, testified that the documents he drafted were not documents he would use to bind the maker of the collateral mortgage note personally beyond the value of the mortgaged property. Reed, with twenty-three years of legal practice in banking and real estate law in Louisiana, confected each collateral mortgage package at the direction of his clients, in this case MC Bank and Diamond Services, respectively. Reed explained that, had his clients and he desired to make Benoit personally liable, beyond the value of the mortgaged property, for the obligations of International Diving and Davenport, he would have had Benoit execute an additional document, such as a continuing guaranty, or have her endorse the hand note or sign the hand note as a co-maker. Reed was not directed by either MC Bank or Diamond Services to obtain liability on the collateral mortgage notes beyond the value of the mortgaged property. Consequently, he did not prepare documents to achieve that objective. Instead, Reed used standard forms for the collateral mortgage package, believing that additional documents would be necessary to impose personal liability upon Benoit.

The actions of both MC Bank and Diamond Services further establish that the collateral mortgage documents before us were not confected to impose liability upon Benoit beyond the value of the property. The bank did obtain an appraisal of the 410.92-acre tract of land in Acadia Parish, and the property was valued at $119,000.00 at the time the mortgages and notes were executed. However, neither the bank nor Diamond Services (which knowingly took a secondary position on the mortgage) required Benoit to provide a financial statement or otherwise determined whether she had sufficient resources to satisfy the full amounts of the two collateral mortgage notes, totaling $650,000.00, executed by her that day. This inaction suggests that neither lender expected that the collateral mortgage packages as confected by Attorney Reed would impose liability upon Benoit beyond the value of the property mortgaged. . . .

CONCLUSION

We conclude that, within the context of the collateral mortgage package, the maker of a collateral mortgage note, paraphed *ne varietur* for identification with the act of collateral mortgage, is not personally liable beyond the value of the mortgaged property when the collateral mortgage note is pledged to secure the debt of a third party, absent some additional agreement so binding the maker of the collateral mortgage note.

* * * * * *

Louisiana Future Advance Mortgages—A 20-Year Retrospective
David S. Willensek
75 Louisiana Law Review 613 (2015)

A. History and Purpose

Louisiana collateral mortgages originated in the mid-19th century out of the commercial necessity for an enforceable security device that could encumber both immovable and movable property and that could secure multiple loans, revolving lines of credit, and performance obligations with retroactive ranking priority vis-a-vis potential competing third persons back to the time the mortgage instrument was originally recorded in the parish mortgage records. At that time (again the mid-19th century), and continuing until January 1, 1992, when the 1991 comprehensive revisions to the mortgage articles of the Louisiana Civil Code first took effect, Louisiana ordinary conventional mortgages were able to secure only one-time extensions of credit evidenced by a promissory note paraphed *ne varietur* for identification with the mortgage. Ordinary conventional mortgages were not able to secure multiple loans, revolving lines of credit, and other present and future cross-collateralized indebtedness because of the then-Civil Code rule that the lien of a conventional mortgage is automatically reduced on a pro tanto, dollar-for-dollar basis as principal payments were made under the secured mortgage note.

Recognizing that the lack of an enforceable open-end Civil Code mortgage instrument had the effect of inhibiting economic growth, certain innovative commercial lawyers of the mid-19th century reasoned that, although the Civil Code did not permit mortgages to directly secure multiple loans, revolving lines of credit, and other present and future cross-collateralized debt, the pledge articles of the Civil Code, namely articles 3103 and 3125 of the 1825 Code, contained no such limitation. These two 1825 articles, when read together, provided that a Civil Code pledge could secure any lawful obligation up to the maximum amount stipulated in the pledge agreement. The innovative commercial lawyers who first came up with the concept of a collateral mortgage further reasoned that, by having a mortgage secure a promissory note payable to bearer on demand, and then pledging that note to secure the real intended indebtedness, a mortgage could indirectly secure multiple loans, revolving lines of credit, and other present and future cross-collateralized indebtedness up to the maximum amount agreed to by the parties.

Thus, the future advance Louisiana collateral mortgage was created as a creature of commercial necessity and of the ingenuity of lawyers of the mid-19th century. As discussed in Part V of this Article, collateral mortgages are still being used today notwithstanding that Louisiana law now offers a more modern and less-risky alternative open-end mortgage instrument in the form of a multiple indebtedness mortgage.

B. How Future Advance Louisiana Collateral Mortgages Work

. . . Typically, there are four documents in a collateral mortgage package: (1) a collateral mortgage under which the mortgagor grants a mortgage on the mortgagor's immovable property; (2) a collateral mortgage note payable to bearer on demand; (3) a collateral pledge/UCC security agreement; and (4) one or more hand notes or other writings evidencing the debtor's true indebtedness. The primary security interest in a collateral mortgage arrangement is the UCC pledge of the collateral mortgage note, which secures the mortgagor's (or third-party obligor's) true indebtedness. The collateral mortgage is an accessory, secondary security interest that directly secures the pledged collateral mortgage note and that indirectly secures the true indebtedness represented by one or more hand notes or other evidence of indebtedness. The way a collateral mortgage works is that the mortgagor grants the collateral mortgage in favor of the mortgagee to secure payment of the collateral mortgage note. The mortgagor then simultaneously pledges or grants a UCC possessory security interest in the collateral mortgage note and delivers the pledged note into the secured party's possession to secure the debtor's (or third-party obligor's) true indebtedness. Assuming that (a) all of the requirements for perfection of a UCC possessory security interest in the pledged note are fully satisfied and remain satisfied at all pertinent times, (b) the collateral mortgage note is not allowed to prescribe, and (c) the ten-year inscriptive period of the mortgage is not allowed to lapse, then the lien of the accessory collateral mortgage will be entitled to retroactive ranking priority vis-a-vis potential intervening creditors back to the time that (i) the mortgage was originally recorded, (ii) the collateral mortgage note was delivered in pledge to the secured party, or (iii) the secured party initially funded the loan or issued a binding loan commitment to advance funds to the borrower at a later date, whichever is the last to occur.

C. 1990 Changes in Governing Law

Prior to January 1, 1990, pledges of Louisiana collateral mortgage notes were subject to the pledge articles of the 1870 Louisiana Civil Code, most notably including former Civil Code article 3158, which permitted a pledged collateral mortgage note to secure multiple loans, lines of credit, and other present and future obligations of the mortgagor (or third-party obligor) on an open-end, cross-collateralized basis. This assumed that the debtor's collateral pledge agreement contained a broad, expansive definition of the secured indebtedness to encompass not only the loan and note for which the collateral mortgage was being initially granted, but also any and all other related and unrelated loans, extensions of credit, and obligations that the debtor (or third-party obligor) may then and thereafter owe to or incur in favor of the secured party and its successors and assigns, of every nature and kind whatsoever, all up to a maximum stipulated dollar amount. This expansive definition of the secured indebtedness is sometimes referred to as a "cross- collateralization," "dragnet," or "gorilla" clause and was the key contractual provision that allowed pre-1990 pledges of collateral mortgage notes and accessory collateral mortgages to secure multiple present and future debts and other obligations.

1. Louisiana UCC Article 9 Applicable to Post-1989 Louisiana Collateral Mortgages

Louisiana collateral mortgage law significantly changed on January 1, 1990, when the Louisiana version of UCC Article 9 first took effect. As of that date, pledges of Louisiana collateral mortgage notes were no longer subject to the pledge articles of the Louisiana Civil Code and instead became exclusively subject to Louisiana UCC Article 9. Additionally, the various collateral mortgage cases that previously applied to pre-1990 collateral mortgages. . . .

Now to be sure, some practitioners and legal scholars may argue that, as a result of the 2001 enactment of Revised Louisiana UCC Article 9, all then-outstanding pledges of collateral mortgage notes, including pre-1990 pledges of collateral mortgage notes granted before January 1, 1990, became subject to Revised Louisiana UCC Article 9. This contrary position is based on the fact that the 2001 comprehensive revisions to UCC Article 9 were made retroactively applicable to all then-outstanding secured transactions falling within the scope of Revised UCC Article 9, including secured transactions which (prior to July 1, 2001) were excluded from coverage under the UCC.

The question raised is what difference does it make whether the Civil Code articles on pledge or Revised Louisiana UCC Article 9 apply to pre-1990 pledges of Louisiana collateral mortgage notes? In truth, it makes very little difference because only a relatively small number of pre-1990 Louisiana collateral mortgages remain outstanding as of this date, some 25 years after Louisiana UCC Article 9 first took effect. The vast majority of pre-1990 collateral mortgages have been either fully paid and satisfied or refinanced and replaced with substitute mortgages.

2. The Louisiana Collateral Mortgage Statute

Another significant 1990 change in the law applicable to Louisiana collateral mortgages was the enactment of the Louisiana collateral mortgage statute. Prior to the collateral mortgage statute taking effect on January 1, 1990, Louisiana collateral mortgages were jurisprudential in nature and subject to unpredictable and sometimes inconsistent interpretation and application by practitioners and the courts. The drafters of the 1989 UCC Implementation Bill sought to codify the law of collateral mortgages and thus make the law more certain and predictable. . . .

* * * * * *

Over time the collateral mortgage became more and more cumbersome, particularly when compared to the mortgage contracts that could be confected in other states. In order to maintain competitiveness, the legislature, with the guiding hand of the Louisiana State Law Institute, passed Civil Code article 3298 in 1991 to help alleviate the need to draft so many different documents in order to create a mortgage that could secure indeterminate future loan advances.

***See* La. Civ. Code art. 3298.**

However, despite legislative approval of a simpler way to confect a mortgage securing an indeterminate future advance loan, many Louisiana banks and lawyers were hesitant to leave behind the tried-and-true collateral mortgage device in favor of the new *future advance mortgage* (also called the *multiple indebtedness mortgage*). Many believed that despite the legislature sanctioning such a concept, Louisiana courts would deem it ineffective for the same reasons that courts prior to the collateral mortgage rejected using an ordinary mortgage to secure revolving lines of credit. Over time, the practice of using the article 3298 mortgage became more accepted, but a number of lending institutions and lawyers insisted on the continued use of the collateral mortgage due to the fact that there had been no definitive ruling on the validity of the multiple indebtedness mortgage. That is, until 2011. Read carefully the two cases that follow, particularly the *KeyBank v. Perkins Rowe Associates* case.

* * * * * *

IN RE HARI AUM, LLC

2011 WL 2746149 (E.D. Bankruptcy Ct. 2011)

JERRY A. BROWN, Bankruptcy Judge.

This matter was commenced by the complaint of First Guaranty Bank ("FGB") against the debtor, Hari Aum, LLC, doing business as Deluxe Motel (the "debtor" or "Hari Aum") to determine the validity, amount and extent of FGB's lien against the Deluxe Motel located in Slidell, Louisiana. A counterclaim was filed by the debtor, and the adversary was set for trial on May 9, 2011. The parties filed cross motions for summary judgment. At the hearing on the cross motions on April 4, 2011 the court determined that there were no issues of fact requiring a trial and instead required the parties to submit additional briefs on the legal issues involved in the case. Having read the briefs and considered the arguments of counsel, and for the reasons set forth below in this memorandum opinion, the court finds that the Multiple Indebtedness Mortgage recorded by FGB is valid, and that the Deluxe Motel property secures both the loan FGB made to the debtor and the loan FGB made to Mississippi Hospitality Services, LLC. . . .

II. Background Facts

The relationship between the Suresh "Sam" A. Bhula ("Bhula") and FGB appears to have begun in 2005, when the debtor, a limited liability company, which was wholly owned by Bhula, borrowed $1.8 million to finance the purchase of the Deluxe Motel in Slidell, Louisiana. To evidence and secure this loan, the debtor, through its 100% shareholder, sole officer and managing member, Bhula, signed both a promissory note and a Multiple Indebtedness Mortgage ("MIM") dated January 27, 2005. On that same date, the debtor also signed a commercial security agreement giving FGB a security interest in all equipment, furniture, fixtures, and an assignment of rents and leases in the Deluxe Motel property. The MIM was properly recorded in St. Tammany Parish, Louisiana on February 1, 2005.

The relationship between Bhula and FGB expanded in 2006, when Bhula obtained a commitment letter from FGB, dated May 31, 2006, by which FGB agreed to finance the purchase of a hotel in Hattiesburg, Mississippi through a new entity to be formed. Thereafter, Bhula formed a second limited liability company, Mississippi Hospitality Services, LLC ("MHS") in which Bhula was the 100% shareholder, sole officer and managing member. The loan which FGB agreed to make to MHS was for $4.9 million and was secured by a deed of trust that was properly recorded in Forrest County, Mississippi, on June 19, 2006. MHS also entered into a commercial security agreement with FGB dated June 16, 2006, giving FGB a security interest in all inventory, equipment, general intangibles, consumer goods and fixtures, and an assignment of rents and leases for the Hattiesburg property. The commitment letter specifically states that the Deluxe Motel in Slidell, Louisiana, and the 160 unit motel in Hattiesburg were to serve as collateral for the loan to the new limited liability company. Nothing in the other documents executed by Bhula in 2006 in connection with the MHS loan that were entered into evidence shows that any specific steps were taken to encumber the Deluxe Motel property as security for the MHS loan at that time. The MIM, however, does clearly state that it was a mortgage securing future indebtedness.

On April 21, 2009, FGB refinanced both the debtor's $1.8 million loan and MHS's $4.9 million loan. New promissory notes were signed by Bhula on behalf of each of the limited liability companies as well as a commercial guaranty personally obligating Bhula on the Hari Aum loan. On that same date, Bhula also executed two other documents: A Limited Liability Company Resolution to Grant Collateral ("Resolution"), and an Acknowledgment of Existing Multiple Indebtedness Mortgage ("Acknowledgment").

Thereafter, both MHS and Hari Aum defaulted on making their respective loan payments, and on August 12, 2010, Hari Aum filed a Chapter 11 petition for reorganization. Through this adversary proceeding, the parties seek the court's determination of whether the debtor's property, i.e., the Deluxe Motel, serves as security for only the loan between Hari Aum and FGB, or whether it also serves as collateral for the loan between MHS and FGB.

III. *Legal Analysis*

The parties ask the court to consider three separate but related issues in this matter: 1) Does the MIM allow FGB to secure future loans without further recording any additional paperwork associated with those loans; 2) Was Bhula authorized to pledge Hari Aum's property to secure the debt of MHS; and 3) If the first two questions are answered in the affirmative, do the documents here effectively accomplish the granting of a security right against Hari Aum's property to secure the MHS loan? The court answers all three of these questions affirmatively for the following reasons.

A. The Multiple Indebtedness Mortgage

The Louisiana Civil Code was amended in 1991 to update Article 3298, which took effect on January 1, 1992, and now provides that a mortgage may secure future obligations. In Louisiana a conventional mortgage may be established only by written contract. No special words are necessary to establish a conventional mortgage.

A contract of mortgage must state precisely the nature and situation of each of the immovables or other property over which it is granted; state the amount of the obligation, or the maximum amount of the obligations that may be outstanding at any time and from time to time that the mortgage secures; and be signed by the mortgagor.

Although Article 3298 took effect in 1992, no Louisiana court has yet issued a published opinion interpreting its provisions. Thus, guidance for this court is furnished by the language of the Article itself and its comments and legislative history. Additionally, the court consulted the excellent law review article, David S. Willenzik, *Future Advance Priority Rights of Louisiana Collateral Mortgages: Legislative Revisions, New Rules and a Modern Alternative,* 55 La. L. Rev. 1 (1994), which provided the following guidance:

> If a multiple indebtedness mortgage is properly executed and filed, and if the mortgage contains broadly drafted future advance/cross-

> collateralization language, then any and all present and future extensions of credit and other obligations the borrower may obtain from or incur in favor of the mortgagee, or its successors and assigns, while the mortgage remains effective, will be secured by the mortgage up to the maximum dollar limitation stipulated in the mortgage agreement, with retroactive priority rights over intervening creditors dating back to the time the mortgage originally was filed in the public records.
>
> The requirements for a multiple indebtedness mortgage are as follows: 1) It must be granted in favor of a specifically named and designated mortgagee; 2) It should contain no reference to the pledge of a collateral mortgage note; 3) It should define the secured indebtedness to include present and future indebtedness; 4) It should contain a maximum amount of secured indebtedness; 5) It should reference Louisiana Civil Code Article 3298; 6) It should contain language spelling out the procedures under which it may be cancelled; and 7) It should not have a note paraphed for identification with the mortgage.21

The court finds that the MIM recorded in St. Tammany Parish meets all of the requirements for a valid multiple indebtedness mortgage set forth by the Louisiana Civil Code. Insofar as it relates to any transactions between Hari Aum and FGB, the MIM secures any loans between FGB and Hari Aum from the date of its recordation, February 1, 2005, up to $50 million. Under the Louisiana Civil Code, it is not necessary for a party who has a properly recorded multiple indebtedness mortgage, such as the bank has here, to record promissory notes evidencing additional loans made under the multiple indebtedness mortgage in order to have those subsequent loans take priority over intervening creditors so long as the total amount of the loans does not exceed the maximum amount stated in the multiple indebtedness mortgage.

Under the practice that existed prior to the change to Article 3298 it was not necessary to record or file the note or other evidence of loans made after the recordation of the collateral mortgage. Nor was it necessary to supplement or amend the collateral mortgage if the subsequent advances did not make the loan exceed the total amount of the collateral mortgage. As noted in the Revision Comments–1991:

(a) As the Expose des Motifs more fully explains, this Article and certain supplemental legislation adopted with it (R.S. 9:5555–5557), is intended to provide a direct and convenient substitute for the so-called collateral mortgage, which in recent years has become widely used, and to permit a person to mortgage his property to secure a line of credit, or even to secure obligations that may not then be contemplated by him except in the broadest sense of an expectation that he may some day incur an obligation to the mortgagee. The supplemental legislation also facilitates the granting of mortgages to secure obligations that are not evidenced by a note paraphed for identification with it. See R.S. 9:5555–5557 (1991).

(b) The expression in Paragraph A that "a mortgage may secure" is intended to emphasize that a mortgage securing future obligations is not a distinct or different form of mortgage. A mortgage may secure existing obligations; obligations contemporaneously incurred with the execution of the mortgage or specific identifiable or particular and limited future obligations; or general and indefinite future obligations; or any combination of them. The matter is one of contract, not law, and the provisions of this Title regulating mortgages are equally applicable in each case.

If the prior practice did not require an additional recordation when a future advance was made and if the amendment to Article 3298 and the statutory provisions for a MIM were to make the securitization of future loans easier and more adaptable to modern day financing, it is difficult to understand Hari Aum's arguments that another note or an amendment to the MIM was necessary for the Deluxe Motel in Slidell to serve as security for the FGB loan to MHS. As Willenzik has noted, "the major advantage of the multiple indebtedness mortgage . . . is that [it] is much easier and simpler to use. To create a multiple indebtedness mortgage, the borrower must execute only one document, the multiple indebtedness mortgage agreement itself." . . .

IV. *Conclusion*

For the reasons set forth above, the court grants FGB's motion for summary judgment and denies the debtor's motion for summary judgment. The court finds that the Deluxe Motel property secures both FGB's loan to the debtor and FGB's loan to MHS. The court further finds that the SBA's loan is junior in priority to the FGB loans.

* * * * * *

KEYBANK NAT'L ASSOC. v. PERKINS ROWE ASSOCIATES, LLC
823 F. Supp. 2d 399 (M.D. La. 2011).

JAMES J. BRADY, District Judge.

. . .

I. FACTUAL BACKGROUND

The owners of the development—Perkins Rowe Associates, LLC, Perkins Rowe Associates II, LLC, and related entities (collectively, "Perkins Rowe owners")—contracted with several general contractors to build different portions of the development at different times.

The first general contractor, Lemoine Company ("Lemoine"), was tasked with building a medical office building ("MOB") and also providing site work on Tract A–5, a separate portion of the Perkins Rowe property. (Lemoine Contracts, Doc. 402–1, pp. 2–3, 58–61). The relevant contracts were recorded in the East Baton Rouge Parish property records on August 25, 2003 (medical office building) and April 1, 2004 (site work). (Id., pp. 3, 69). Lemoine recorded a bond for the MOB contract but not for the site work contract. (Id., p. 69). Lemoine recorded notices of substantial completion of these projects on October 15, 2004, and January 26, 2005, respectively. (Id., pp. 75, 77).

On September 14, 2005, a mortgage on certain parts of the Perkins Rowe property was recorded in favor of Wachovia Bank, N.A. (Wachovia Mortgage, Doc. 394–3, p. 5). The maximum principal amount of the mortgage was $200 million. (Id., p. 6). The following day, an engineer filed a "no work" affidavit in the property records, stating that "no work regarding the improvement of the property had begun at the site and no materials had been furnished to said site within the past six (6) month period." (Id., p. 40). However, the engineer noted that existing improvements "consisting of roadway paving, sanitary sewer and storm drainage collection system and associated utilities exist." (Id.).

On April 25, 2006, another mortgage on Perkins Rowe was recorded in favor of JTS Realty Services, L.L.C. (JTS Realty Mortgage, Doc. 394–3, p. 45). The parties agree this mortgage covered Block M of the development. (ThornCo Memo. in Supp., Doc. 392–2, p. 30; ThornCo Reply, Doc. 408, p. 21; KeyBank Memo. in Opp., Doc. 402, p. 17, n. 48). The maximum principal amount of the mortgage was $20 million. (JTS Realty Mortgage, Doc. 394–3, p. 45). A similar "no work" affidavit was filed by an engineer the next day. (Id., p. 70).

On June 9, 2006, Perkins Rowe executed promissory notes payable to Wachovia and JTS Realty—the Wachovia note for $1,000 and the JTS Realty note for $10,000—both of which became due on June 1, 2007. (Promissory Notes, Doc. 394–3, pp. 2, 42).

On July 17, 2006, Echelon Construction Services, LLC ("Echelon") recorded several contracts and bonds for construction in Blocks A, D, E and F of Perkins Rowe. (Block A contract, Doc. 402–3; Block D contract, Doc. 402–3; Block E contract, Doc. 402–4; Block F contract, Doc. 402–4).

On July 21, 2006, both Wachovia and JTS Realty assigned their notes and mortgages to KeyBank, and KeyBank recorded the assignments the same day. (Doc. 394–3, pp. 72, 78). KeyBank then consolidated the notes (Consolidated Note, Doc. 394–3, p. 84) and the mortgages (Consolidated Mortgage, Doc. 394–4, p. 2) into new documents, each consolidation claiming it "amended, restated and consolidated" the previous documents.

Specifically, the KeyBank note states that it combined the Wachovia and JTS Realty notes "so that together they evidence a single indebtedness in the aggregate principal amount of this Note . . . but this Note does not extinguish or constitute a novation with respect to the indebtedness evidenced thereby. . . ." (Doc. 394–3, p. 87, ¶ 5). The KeyBank note cites the construction loan agreement between Perkins Rowe and KeyBank and shows a principal indebtedness of $170 million. (Id., p. 84).

The KeyBank mortgage states in part that the prior Wachovia and JTS Realty mortgages "are hereby amended, restated and consolidated by this Mortgage and the provisions of the Original Mortgages, as amended, restated and consolidated by this Mortgage constitute the full, true, complete and correct Mortgage between the parties with respect to" the Perkins Rowe property. (Doc. 394–4, pp. 26–27, ¶ 8.10). The consolidated mortgage shows a maximum principal amount of $500 million. (Id., p. 6, ¶ 1.2).

On November 15, 2006, Echelon recorded contracts without bonds for construction of Blocks B and C of Perkins Rowe. (Block B contract, Doc. 402–5; Block C contract, Doc. 402–6). On February 23, 2007, it also recorded a contract without bond for construction of Block H. (Block H contract, Doc. 402–7).

In February 2007, ThornCo was hired as a subcontractor by general contractor Echelon on Blocks A–H of the Perkins Rowe development. (*See* Statement of Undisputed Facts, Doc. 392–1, ¶ 17–19; Thornton Deposition, Doc. 392–12).

On October 18, 2007, the Perkins Rower owners terminated a different general contract, EMJ Corporation, for its work on Block G, and Echelon proceeded to work on Block G without a contract, recording a certificate of substantial completion on November 29, 2007. (*See* Doc. 402–7 (notice of termination and certificate of substantial completion)).

In December 2007 and February 2008, ThornCo recorded construction liens totaling over $2 million for unpaid work on Blocks A–H. (Statement of Undisputed Facts, Doc. 392–1, ¶ 20; *see also* ThornCo Liens, Doc. 392–7). ThornCo eventually filed suit in state court, wherein a consent decree recognized the validity of the liens. (Statement of Undisputed Facts, Doc. 392–1; *see* Consent Judgment, Doc. 392–7, pp. 27–31). ThornCo received payment for its work on Blocks A, D, E and F, but the liens on Blocks B, C, G and H remain unsatisfied. (ThornCo Reply Brief, Doc. 408, pp. 16–17, 23, n. 24). It is undisputed that ThornCo's outstanding liens are all located on property originally secured by the Wachovia mortgage.

II. DISCUSSION

. . .

1. Governing Law on Louisiana Mortgages

A mortgage is a nonpossessory right created over property to secure the performance of an obligation. La. C.C. art. 3278. A mortgage is accessory to the obligation it secures. La. C.C. art. 3282. Historically, to secure an obligation that had not yet arisen, parties in Louisiana were forced to resort to a collateral mortgage, but the legislature in 1991 altered the code to reflect a new iteration of a conventional mortgage—the mortgage to secure future obligations. "A mortgage may secure obligations that may arise in the future." La. C.C. art. 3298(A). This authorization did away with the collateral mortgage requirement that the adjoining obligation supporting the mortgage be paraphed for identification to the mortgage. La. C.C. art. 3298(C).

This new version of mortgage has remarkable vitality, as the code envisions this mortgage exists from its creation "until it is terminated by the mortgagor or his successor" or "extinguished in some other lawful manner." La. C.C. art. 3298(E). The mortgagor may terminate the mortgage by giving "reasonable notice to the mortgagee when an obligation does not exist" or has not been incurred. La. C.C. art. 3298(D). In other words, absent affirmative termination of the mortgage by the parties or by operation of law under Article 3319, the mortgage may continue indefinitely. *See* La. C.C. art. 3298, comments (e)-(f) (explaining duration of mortgage absent termination or legal extinguishment). Thus, "the mortgage is fully in existence, though its enforcement may be conditional." Id., comment (f). Moreover, "[a]s to all obligations, present and future, secured by a mortgage, *notwithstanding the nature of such obligations or the date they arise,* the mortgage has effect . . . as to third persons from the time the contract of mortgage is filed for registry." La. C.C. art. 3298(B) (emphasis added).

This provision "declares that a mortgage securing future obligations has the same effect and priority it would have if the obligations were in existence when the contract of mortgage was entered into." Id., comment (c). It is the burden of the mortgage holder to prove the effective date of the mortgage as to third parties. *Tex. Bank of Beaumont v. Bozorg,* 457 So. 2d 667 (La. 1984).

KeyBank maintains the assignment of the Wachovia and JTS Realty mortgages to it were valid, the obligations which those mortgages secured were existent, and the subsequent consolidation of them into the KeyBank mortgage nonetheless allows it to relate back the effective dates of the consolidated mortgage to the recordation dates of the original mortgages. Because the mortgage holder bears the burden of proving the effective date of the mortgage, the Court must evaluate whether the assignment and consolidation caused KeyBank to lose any rights Wachovia held in its mortgage.

La. C.C. art. 2642 expresses a general policy which broadly supports assignment rights. La. C.C. art. 2645 makes clear that assigning a promissory note also transfers the mortgage securing the note. *See* id., comment (b). Louisiana law supports the proposition that an assignee stands in the shoes of the assignor. *N.S.Q. Associates v. Beychok,* 659 So. 2d 729, 734 (La. 1995). If the assignment is valid, then, KeyBank stands in the shoes of Wachovia and JTS Realty, respectively, for purposes of enforcing the mortgages. ThornCo contests both the validity of the assignments and also disputes the existence of any underlying obligation which would have supported the Wachovia mortgage. The Court treats each argument in turn.

2. Did Wachovia Assent to the Mortgage?

ThornCo argues that Wachovia never signed the mortgage and thus never gave assent to be bound. Louisiana law, however, does not require the mortgagee to sign the mortgage because consent is presumed and acceptance may be tacit. La. C.C. art. 3289. ThornCo also argues that it can overcome this evidentiary presumption of consent because there exists no affirmative act indicating consent by Wachovia, citing *Southern Enterprises, Inc. v. Foster,* 203 La. 133, 13 So. 2d 491, 494 (1943). It is difficult to find support for the proposition that Wachovia did not assent to the mortgage. This is borne out by the *Expose de Motifs,* a publication that accompanied passage of Act No. 652 of the 1991 regular session of the Louisiana Legislature, which included among its provisions La. C.C. arts. 3289 and 3298. The *Expose* explains that Article 3289 did not require a mortgage to be signed by the mortgagee because it was simply codifying a "widely accepted commercial practice." *Expose de Motifs* III.A, *available at* LA LEGIS 652 (1991) (Westlaw citation).

Even assuming *Foster's* requirement of an affirmative act to manifest consent to a mortgage remains good law, the Court finds the requirement met. The mortgage was recorded in the property records. (Doc. 402–1, p. 38). Wachovia received a promissory note which its mortgage secured, which was signed by a Wachovia representative. (Doc. 394–3, pp. 2–3).3 ThornCo cannot overcome the strong presumption in favor of consent provided for in Article 3289, and thus no genuine dispute of material fact exists.

3. Is Wachovia's Alleged Failure to Lend Money a Failure of Cause?

ThornCo argues the Wachovia mortgage could not be legally established because no obligation ever existed for which the mortgage could serve as security. Comment (a) to La. C.C. art. 3298 clarifies that a mortgage to secure future obligations remains valid "even to secure obligations that may not then be contemplated by [the mortgagor] except in the broadest sense of an expectation that he may some day incur an obligation to the mortgagee." This mortgage thus survives attack for failure of cause unless it can be shown that no expectation of an eventual obligation existed at the time the mortgage was signed, or perhaps arguably ceased to exist at some time after the mortgage was entered. ThornCo asserts this failure occurred because Wachovia never intended to loan any money to Perkins Rowe following Hurricane Katrina. (ThornCo's Reply Brief, Doc. 408, p. 15 (citing Spinosa's deposition testimony)).

While Wachovia does not appear to have loaned money, negotiations were ongoing. KeyBank was also negotiating with Perkins Rowe at the time, and eventually they were assigned Wachovia's mortgage and thereafter loaned money. Undoubtedly the hurricane altered the landscape for construction loans in post-storm Baton Rouge, but the mere failure to lend prior to the assignment to KeyBank does not mean the possibility of lending had been wholly eradicated.

ThornCo simply cannot point to any evidence during this interval which shows Wachovia and Perkins Rowe ceased having a broad expectation that they might someday reach agreement on the terms of a loan. Both parties cite the sealed deposition testimony of Joseph T. Spinosa, who served as a representative for both JTS Realty and the Perkins Rowe defendants during the course of the project. (KeyBank Memo. in Opp., Doc. 402, p. 14 (quoting Spinosa testimony)). The context of his statements, as KeyBank points out, makes clear that Wachovia and Perkins Rowe were engaged in substantial, ongoing negotiations about loan terms.

While ThornCo argues KeyBank had already essentially reached terms on a loan with Perkins Rowe, making the Wachovia loan unnecessary, that contention is simply irrelevant. The inquiry here relates to the intentions of the Perkins Rowe owners and Wachovia. Securing additional funding from KeyBank would not have precluded Wachovia from eventually lending. Until Wachovia assigned its interests to KeyBank, no evidence indicates it had forsaken the possibility of lending. ThornCo has not shown Wachovia and the Perkins Rowe owners ever wholly ceased to expect to incur a future obligation, and thus its failure of cause argument has no merit.

4. Were Wachovia's Mortgage and Note Mere Simulations?

ThornCo next argues that the note and mortgage were simply simulations devoid of legal effect. La. C.C. art. 2026 defines absolute simulations as contracts wherein "the parties intend that their contract shall produce no effects between them." However, even absolute simulations may be given effect if a third person has relied on a public record. La. C.C. art. 2028, comment (b). In this case, ThornCo attacks as a simulation the note and mortgage Perkins Rowe entered into with Wachovia. Yet it is readily apparent that KeyBank relied on the recorded documents when it received the assignments from Wachovia. Simulations cannot defeat good faith creditors and bona fide purchasers. *See* La. C.C. art. 2026, comment (c); La. C.C. art. 2028, comment (b).

More importantly, though, as the Court discussed previously, the parties did intend their contract to produce effects when it was entered. The intended effect of the mortgage was to secure the future obligations the parties expected to be created, namely, the construction loan for the Perkins Rowe development. While Wachovia's loan never came to fruition, no evidence exists which tends to show the parties never intended the note and mortgage to have legal effect.

5. Was Wachovia's Note a Sham Obligation?

ThornCo focuses most of its argument on this contention, and it is one that deserves attention. ThornCo asserts the Wachovia note did not create real obligations such that the later assignment of the note was merely a sham transaction. ThornCo thus asserts that, without a valid note underlying the mortgage, the mortgage assignment from Wachovia to KeyBank cannot stand, and KeyBank must thus rely on the date of the issuance of the consolidated note and mortgage. In this scenario, ThornCo's liens would prime the KeyBank mortgage.

ThornCo is certainly correct that Louisiana jurisprudence has long held a mortgage only provides security to the extent there is an underlying obligation to secure. It points to a line of cases which all, in one way or another, support that point of law. Article 3298 declares a policy demanding recognition of a mortgage at its date of recordation, regardless of when the obligation is actually incurred. Of course, the obligation must eventually arise for the mortgage to be enforceable. The Wachovia promissory note satisfies that requirement. While ThornCo argues no evidence exists that funds were ever lent, it cites no authority which establishes the handing-over of money as a prerequisite to incurring an obligation. Once the note was entered, Wachovia was obligated to advance the funds. The Wachovia mortgage was thus retroactively triggered and became effective for all purposes. Once Wachovia effectuated the assignment of the note and the mortgage, KeyBank stood in its shoes. KeyBank consolidated the Wachovia mortgage into a single writing, combining that mortgage with the JTS Realty mortgage. KeyBank executed a construction loan and advanced additional funds under the consolidated mortgage, which increased the amount of security the mortgage provided as the indebtedness of the Perkins Rowe defendants grew. These actions did not change the nature of the mortgage, either in its original or consolidated form, and they simply reinforce the underlying obligation incurred from the start via Wachovia's promissory note.

6. Was KeyBank's Consolidation of the Assigned Interests a Novation?

ThornCo also argues that the assignment and consolidation of the notes and mortgages by KeyBank really constituted a novation. "A novation is the extinguishment of an existing obligation by the substitution of a new one." La. C.C. art. 1879. Novations cannot be presumed and must be shown by clear and unequivocal evidence. La. C.C. art. 1880. Thus, the burden of establishing a novation rests with the party asserting novation. *Scott v. Bank of Coushatta,* 512 So. 2d 356, 360 (La. 1987). A change in the parties to an obligation is provided for in La. C.C. art. 1882, which covers subjective novations. It states that novation takes place only where "a new obligor is substituted for a prior obligor who is discharged by the obligee." La. C.C. art. 1882. Comment (d) to that article mentions a consideration worth repeating.

> *[N]ovation by substitution of a new obligee is not provided for because the effects of such a novation are readily achieved through an assignment of credit.* In modern law, the general acceptance of the notion of transmissibility of obligations has made novation by substitution of an obligee obsolete. (emphasis added).

This precept is confirmed by La. C.C. art. 2645, which allows for an assignment of a note with a concomitant assignment of a mortgage. As comment (b) to La. C.C. art. 2642 states, "an assignment is valid even without the debtor's consent, since, as a general rule, the identity of the creditor should be immaterial to the debtor who owes the performance involved."

ThornCo, however, points to *White Co. v. Hammond Stage Lines,* 180 La. 962, 158 So. 353 (1934) as authority for its position that the assignment and consolidation created a novation. In that case, White Co. sold two busses and a Cadillac sedan to Hammond Stage Lines, receiving a vendor's lien and a chattel mortgage on each, represented by a promissory note on each as well. 158 So. at 353–54. After Hammond Stage Lines became in arrears on its payments, White Co. consolidated the debts on the three vehicles into one note. Id. at 354. White Co. then asserted vendor's liens and chattel mortgages on five vehicles—the three it had sold to Hammond Stage Lines plus two more busses which appeared to have already been owned by Hammond Stage Lines. Id. at 353–54. The consolidation also included a new notarial act of sale of the five vehicles. Id. at 354.

The Louisiana Supreme Court held that a novation had occurred because it inferred the parties' objective intent was to extinguish the former indebtedness from the three vehicles White Co. originally sold to Hammond Stage Lines and replace it with a consolidated note which evidenced a new indebtedness. Id. at 356. The most convincing aspect, the Court found, was the sale of the five vehicles as evidenced by the notarial act of sale adjoining the new, consolidated note. Id. This could only be done by having the debtor, Hammond Stage Lines, convey the vehicles on which it owed money back to the creditor, White Co., who then reconveyed the vehicles back to Hammond Stage Lines. Id. In that way, White Co. gained additional collateral in the form of two new vehicles over which it could assert a security interest which it could not have on the old notes. Id. The combination of these actions amounted to convincing evidence that led the court to hold a landlord's lien, acquired after the original, separate notes (and attendant security interests) but before the consolidated note (with the expanded collateral), outranked White Co. Id.

Slightly different circumstances compelled the same court to hold the opposite only three years later. In *Union Bldg. Corp. v. Burmeister,* 186 La. 1027, 173 So. 752 (1937), the Louisiana Supreme Court distinguished *White Co.,* holding that no novation occurred. *Burmeister* concerned the sale of beauty parlor equipment to the defendant, who executed two notes and two chattel mortgages on the equipment to secure her payment. 173 So. at 753. After about three months passed, in order to satisfy a subsequent holder of her notes, the defendant executed a new note and chattel mortgage which added her debt from the prior two notes together and combined the equipment subject to the previous chattel mortgages into a single chattel mortgage. Id. at 753–54.

The *Burmeister* court found no intention to novate, either in the written agreements or through a promise by the creditor to return the original notes. Id. at 755. The court implied that the subsequent consolidation in *Burmeister* did not add to the security already held by the chattel mortgage holder, unlike the transaction in *White Co.* Id. Most importantly, the court credited the representation by the note holder that it never intended a novation when it obtained the combined note and chattel mortgage. Id. The court also found significant the fact that the original notes, in addition to the combined note, were produced by the company seeking payment under them. Id.

This case appears to follow the facts of *Burmeister* much more closely than the facts of *White Co.* Here, KeyBank already held by assignment the rights to the collateral described in the Wachovia and JTS Realty mortgages. When it consolidated the assigned notes, KeyBank and Perkins Rowe agreed that the consolidated note did "not extinguish or constitute a novation with respect to the indebtedness evidenced thereby. . . ." (Doc. 394–3, Ex. 9, ¶ 5). Thus, the most important consideration—the intent of the parties—clearly weighs against finding a novation. Moreover, unlike *White Co.,* no evidence exists here showing an additional round of conveyances between the creditor and debtor. As comment (g) to Art. 1881 notes, *White Co.* was correctly decided because the "opposite conclusion would have allowed the mortgagee to increase his security at the expense of another secured obligee." KeyBank here is not increasing its security interest in Perkins Rowe solely through the consolidation, as was attempted in *White Co.* Rather, KeyBank obtained the mortgages and notes from Wachovia and JTS Realty by valid assignment, then simply consolidated them into a single note and single mortgage. Each consolidation by KeyBank was merely an "execution of a new writing," which is exactly the type of "[m]ere modification of an obligation, made without intention to extinguish it, [that] does not effect a novation." La. C.C. art. 1881.

7. Does Amending the Assigned Interests Create a New Obligation?

ThornCo argues that the amendments to the consolidated note create new obligations such that the consolidated note (and thus the consolidated mortgage) cannot relate back to the original Wachovia note and mortgage. The original Wachovia mortgage secured a maximum aggregate principal amount of $200 million. The consolidated KeyBank mortgage secured a maximum aggregate principal amount of $500 million. However, the KeyBank consolidated note contained a maximum amount of only $170 million, which is less than the amount secured by the original Wachovia mortgage.

La. R.S. 9:5390(B) provides that amendments and modifications to security agreements are valid, but may rank from the date of the amendment's recording *if the amount of indebtedness increases.* The Wachovia mortgage allowed it to secure future obligations of up to $200 million. The Wachovia note and KeyBank's consolidated note in the amount of $170 million, added to the JTS Realty note in the amount of $10,000, did not increase the amount of secured principal indebtedness of the Perkins Rowe defendants beyond the $200 million maximum aggregate principal stated in the original Wachovia mortgage. This Court has already found that the amounts advanced under the KeyBank note amounted to $161,432,275.40 in principal. (Ruling on Right to Foreclose and Enforce Payment Guaranty, Doc. 397).

La. R.S. 9:5390 does not stand as an impediment to the validity of KeyBank's consolidated note and mortgage, especially when viewed in light of Article 3298. The Court finds the amendments and modifications to the previous notes and mortgages were not invalid and did not defeat KeyBank's right to use the date of the original Wachovia mortgage to determine its priority position. The Wachovia mortgage stated the maximum principal amount of the secured debt as $200 million, and KeyBank's obligations never surpassed that amount. Therefore, La. R.S. 9:5390 is not implicated here.

The Court therefore finds KeyBank received a valid assignment of interests from Wachovia and properly consolidated the Wachovia note and mortgage with the interests KeyBank received from JTS Realty. KeyBank's mortgage, as it pertains to ThornCo's liens.

* * * * * *

NOTES AND QUESTIONS

1. Do these two cases resolve any lingering apprehensions about using the multiple indebtedness mortgage under Civil Code article 3298? Did the court leave open any possible questions or raise any new issues that might be problematic in real estate transactions in the future?

2. You will recall from the introductory discussion in Chapter 1, as well as from numerous cases in this chapter, that a mortgage is an accessory security right. *See* La. Civ. Code art. 3282; *Thrift Funds Canal, Inc. v. Foy*, supra. Accordingly, a mortgage automatically follows an assignment of the obligation that it secures. *See* La. Civ. Code arts. 2645 and 3136. A corollary to this principle is that a mortgage, like other accessory rights, is insusceptible of assignment *separately* from the obligation that it secures. Under the facts of *Keybank*, the original mortgagee had never lent any money to the mortgagor, or even bound itself to do so, nor was any underlying obligation outstanding at the time the mortgage was assigned or at any previous time. What, then, was the underlying obligation that was assigned? Was it necessary that an underlying obligation exist at the time of the assignment in order for the assignment to have effect or for the assignee to enjoy the same retroactive ranking to which the original mortgagee would have been entitled? Or does *Keybank* stand for the proposition that the assignee of a multiple indebtedness mortgage is entitled to retroactive ranking to the date the mortgage was recorded, even in the absence of an underlying obligation at the time of the assignment, so long as the original mortgagee and the mortgagor had never abandoned the "broad expectation that they might someday reach agreement on the terms of a loan"?

3. On the basis of two alternative theories, the court in *In re Hari Aum* found that the multiple indebtedness mortgage involved in that case secured not only a loan made to the mortgagor but also a loan that the mortgagee made to an affiliate of the mortgagor. First, under the terms of the Acknowledgment of Existing Multiple Indebtedness Mortgage that the mortgagor signed, the mortgagor agreed to be personally liable for the loan made to the affiliate. Accordingly, this liability was simply one of the many types of obligations of the mortgagor included among the expansive description of secured obligations in the mortgage. The second theory was that, by virtue of the Acknowledgment of Existing Multiple Indebtedness Mortgage, the mortgagor "pledged" the mortgage as security for the loan made to the affiliate. The court drew an

analogy between the "pledge" of a multiple indebtedness mortgage and the pledge that is involved with a collateral mortgage. Does this analogy hold? Is a mortgage itself (as opposed to the obligation secured by a mortgage) ever susceptible of being given in pledge? Even if it were, how could a mortgagor, who is after all the obligor rather than the obligee under a mortgage, successfully give it in pledge?

When a collateral mortgage is used as security, the collateral mortgage is not itself "pledged"; rather, what is "pledged" is the collateral mortgage note, which is in turn secured by the collateral mortgage. The collateral mortgage, being an accessory to the collateral mortgage note, then follows the pledge of the collateral mortgage note and becomes enforceable by the pledgee to the extent of the underlying indebtedness secured by the pledge. *See* La. C.C.P. art. 696. As discussed in Chapter 3, since the enactment of Chapter 9, a collateral mortgage note is technically no longer pledged but instead is made the subject of a security interest under the Uniform Commercial Code. However, the same result still obtains, because the Uniform Commercial Code provides that the attachment of a security interest in an obligation secured by a mortgage or other lien on personal or real property also includes the rights to the mortgage or other lien. *See* La. R.S. 10:9-203(g).

4. Transfer of Mortgages

In today's commercial world it is quite common for secured creditors to sell their rights in a mortgage loan to a third party. Indeed, the entire secondary mortgage market is based on these transactions. As Civil Code article 3312 states, "A transfer of an obligation secured by a mortgage includes the transfer of the mortgage." It is often said in property law that "the mortgage follows the note" and that the two are, in essence, inseparable from one another. This concept makes sense when one considers the accessory nature of the mortgage itself. If the mortgage is ever severed from the obligation that it secures, the mortgage cannot continue to exist. A great deal of litigation occurred in the wake of the 2007–2008 financial crisis whereby one party acting in concert with the mortgagee—usually the Mortgage Electronic Registration Systems (MERS)—claimed the right to foreclose on the mortgage, even though it could not show that it had rights to the underlying debt. But while this concept of the mortgage following the note was reinvigorated through foreclosure litigation since 2008, the civil law has always made clear that the mortgage and the principal obligation go together. Civil Code article 3282 makes clear that the "[m]ortgage is accessory to the obligation that it secures." Thus, unless a specific law provides otherwise, "the mortgagee may enforce the mortgage only to the extent that he may enforce any obligation it secures." Id.

***See also* La. Civ. Code art. 3313**

Be mindful that although parties often refer to the transfer described above as a "sale of the mortgage," in fact the thing that is really being transferred is the secured obligation. Indeed, no third party would be interested in purchasing a mortgage without also purchasing the debt itself (i.e., the right to collect on the debt in the event of non-payment). Since most mortgage loans are evidenced by a promissory note, it is the transfer of the note that is essential to the transfer of a conventional mortgage. This should bring to mind the laws of negotiability (including bearer paper and order paper) as well as the requirements and significance of being a holder in due course. Of fundamental importance when dealing with a negotiable instrument is to remember the distinction between being the owner of the note and being the holder of the note. Only the holder of the note has the right to enforce it (and thereby the ability to foreclose on the mortgage that secures it). Owning a negotiable instrument secured by a mortgage, but not being the holder of the instrument, renders the mortgage useless.

Consider the following code articles that build upon the concept of transfers of the mortgage loan and accompanying security.

***See* La. Civ. Code arts. 3356; 1826(B).**

5. Transfer of Mortgaged Property

Although it occurs with less frequency than in cases where the secured obligation is transferred, parties will occasionally transfer the property that is subject to the mortgage. This would be a case whereby the transferor would not be the creditor (as in the case discussed above), but rather would be the owner of the mortgaged property (usually the mortgagor).

i. In General

The most important concept to understand here is that the transfer of the property from one party to another does not in any way terminate or diminish the effects of the mortgage on that property. Rather, the mortgage—like all other real rights—follows the property into the hands of the new owner (provided it was recorded). Thus, the transferee, although not the debtor himself, becomes the owner of the property that is encumbered by the mortgage to secure the debt of another (usually his transferor). Here, the original debtor remains obligated on the secured obligation. The new owner of the property is not and does not become (absent some agreement to the contrary) an obligor under the debt. Nevertheless, he will naturally have an interest in assuring that the secured obligation is performed, lest he lose his property in a foreclosure of the mortgage. Today, most mortgage contracts provide that the mortgagor's transfer of the mortgaged property without the mortgagee's consent is a default, giving the mortgagee the right to foreclose.

ii. Third Possessors

The new owner (the transferee of the mortgaged property), however, is not without rights. The Civil Code defines him as a "third possessor" and provides a number of rules relative to his position vis-à-vis the property, the mortgagee, and the mortgagor. Such a person is analogous to a purchaser of immovable property encumbered by a recorded lease who takes the property "subject to" the lease, rather than one who takes it and "assumes" the lease. If the transferee assumes the mortgage indebtedness, he is not a third possessor.

***See* La. Civ. Code art. 3315-3318.**

6. Termination of Conventional Mortgages

***See* La. Civ. Code art. 3319.**

For the relevant prescriptive periods applicable to the obligations secured by mortgages, *see* La. Civ. Code art. 3494(3) (for loans not evidenced by a promissory note); La. Civ. Code art. 3498 (for promissory notes).

* * * * * *

SCOTT v. CORKERN
91 So. 2d 569 (La. 1956)

McCALEB, Justice.

Plaintiffs, heirs of Mrs. Viola M. Scott, instituted this suit against Mrs. Ruby Jones Corkern, widow of Dr. Ronald E. Corkern, individually and as natural tutrix of her two minor children, on five promissory notes executed by the late Dr. Corkern in favor of the late Mrs. Viola M. Scott totalling $2,300, each note bearing 4% Interest from its date. Plaintiffs are claiming the sum of $5,029.20, this being the alleged amount of the principal and interest due on the notes, plus attorney's fees.

Plaintiffs' petition, as amended, alleges that on August 27, 1929, Mrs. Viola M. Scott entered into a contract with R. G. Corkern and his son, Ronald E. Corkern, whereby Mrs. Scott agreed to loan funds for the purpose of financing the medical education of Ronald E. Corkern up to the amount of $2,500 during the four years following the date of said agreement and that, to secure the payments of said loans, Ronald E. Corkern pledged and/or assigned unto Mrs. Viola M. Scott a certain life insurance policy in the amount of $2,000, issued by the Pan-American Life Insurance Company on the life of Ronald E. Corkern, with the designation of Mrs. Scott as beneficiary. Pursuant to the terms of the agreement, loans were made from 1929 through 1934 in the total amount of $2,300.

To this petition defendant, appearing individually and as tutrix of her two minor children, interposed a plea of prescription of five and ten years in which she denied that the aforesaid insurance policy had ever been pledged to Mrs. Scott to secure the payment of the notes and averred that it remained at all times in the physical possession of her late husband. After a trial on this plea, the judge, being of the opinion that the action was barred by the prescription of five years, dismissed the suit. Plaintiffs have appealed.

In this Court, plaintiffs are asserting that the insurance policy of Dr. Corkern was pledged to Mrs. Scott as security for the payment of all amounts for which he would become indebted to Mrs. Scott under the agreement of August 27, 1929, and that, this being so, prescription has never accrued on the obligations sued on as the existence of the pledge operated to suspend or interrupt the running of prescription. In this connection, we take notice at the outset of plaintiffs' indefinite allegation in their amended petition that the insurance policy was "pledged and/or assigned to the said Mrs. Viola M. Scott. . . ." In view of their contention here, we take it that plaintiffs have either abandoned or at least are not pressing the claim that the policy was assigned to Mrs. Scott for it is obvious that, if it was assigned, the policy became her property and could not be regarded as a pledge effecting an interruption of prescription.

The contracts of pledge and assignment are entirely different and produce varied legal results. Assignment or transfer of credits and other incorporeal rights is a species of sale and is treated as such in our Civil Code, being found in Chapter 12 of Title VII ("Of Sale"). Article 2642 of the Civil Code provides that delivery of an assignment takes place as between transferrer and transferee by the giving of title. Accordingly, a vesting of title in the transferee is essential to an assignment. *See Strudwick Funeral Home v. Liberty Ind. Life Ins. Co.*, La. App., 176 So. 679 and authorities there cited.

On the other hand, a pledge is another sort of contract, having characteristics completely diverse to those of an assignment. It is dealt with under a separate title (Title XX) of our Code and is essentially a contract of security, being defined in Article 3133 (current article 3141) as "a contract by which one debtor gives something to his creditor as a security for his debt." This is the antithesis of an assignment (in which title passes) for, in the contract of pledge, the debtor retains the title of the thing which he places, either actually or constructively, in the hands of his creditor as security for the payment of the debt. *See* Article 3166 of the Civil Code. Hence, it is impossible to have an assignment and a pledge of the same thing at the same time. And this, notwithstanding the recent decision to the contrary of the Court of Appeal, Second Circuit, *In re Pan American Life Insurance Company*, 88 So. 2d 410, a concursus proceeding for the determination of the ownership of the proceeds of the same insurance policy involved herein, where it was held that the agreement between Dr. Corkern and Mrs. Scott was a contract of assignment as well as a pledge of the policy.

An examination of the contract between Mrs. Scott and Dr. Corkern leaves no doubt whatever that it is a contract of pledge. It provides, in substance, that Mrs. Scott, Dr. Corkern and his father have entered into an agreement whereby Mrs. Scott is to lend the younger Corkern up to $2,500 to enable him to obtain a medical education and that he is to give his promissory notes for the particular amounts that are advanced and that, "in order to secure the payment of the sums advanced to him. . .", he will make Mrs. Scott beneficiary in a policy of life insurance carried by him in the Pan American Life Insurance Company in the sum of $2,000; that he would continue to pay the premiums thereon and not do any act that would decrease the cash or loan value of the insurance without the consent of Mrs. Scott, who agreed to reimburse his parents or his closest heirs any amount she would receive in the event of his death in excess of the amount loaned him. In conformity with his promise, Dr. Corkern wrote the insurance company enclosing the policy and effected a change of beneficiary from his mother to Mrs. Scott, directing that the policy be returned to the First National Bank of Oberlin, Louisiana, "with instructions to just hold in escrow as they have already been advised concerning this transaction." The policy was delivered to the bank by the insurer in accordance with these instructions.

In this Court, defendant does not contest that the agreement effected a pledge of the insurance policy. However, her counsel maintains that the pledge was extinguished by the occurrence of certain events by which Dr. Corkern obtained possession of the pledged policy, which was found in his safe deposit box after his death. It appears that the holder of the policy, First National Bank of Oberlin, became insolvent during the years of depression and was closed and placed in receivership. No information is available as to the whereabouts of the pledged insurance policy during the time the bank was being liquidated. Upon inquiry after the liquidation was completed, the office of the Comptroller of the Currency, which had supervised the affairs of the bank during its receivership, advised that all books, records and papers had been destroyed under proper authority on January 30, 1940, and that it had been unable to find any reference to the policy.

Mrs. Scott died on March 1, 1948, and Dr. Corkern died on February 20, 1953. When the bank box of the latter was opened in his succession proceedings, the policy of insurance was found therein but no one knows how or when he obtained possession of it. Mrs. Scott's name still appeared thereon as beneficiary.

It is the position of defendant's counsel, as we understand it, that the pledge was extinguished when Dr. Corkern came into possession of the policy. Contra, plaintiffs contend that Dr. Corkern's possession was a precarious one in which he was acting as a trustee for the pledgee, Mrs. Scott.

We find plaintiffs' position is sustained by applicable authorities. *See Jacquet v. His Creditors*, 38 La. Ann. 863; *Foote v. Sun Life Assur. Co. of Canada*, La. App., 173 So. 477 and cases there cited, particularly *Conger v. City of New Orleans*, 32 La. Ann. 1250, where this Court, in determining the validity of a pledge of stock owned by the City in a railroad company, which had never been delivered by the City to the plaintiff but which was perpetually pledged in favor of the bondholders by Act 109 of 1854, said:

> Possession, though essential to the validity of the pledge, need not be always in the creditor. It is sufficient that the thing pledged be in the possession of one occupying ad hoc, the position of a trustee. The debtor himself may, in some cases, be considered as such trustee and be given possession of the thing by him pledged, provided his tenure be precarious and clearly for account of the creditor. The Louisiana doctrine is in perfect accord with both the common, the Roman and French laws. (Citing a long list of authorities and commentaries from various jurisdictions in support of the statement).

Thus, it is manifest that the mere circumstance that the pledged insurance policy was found in the possession of the pledgor does not justify the conclusion that the pledge was extinguished and, in the absence of any evidence showing that the parties intended that the pledge be terminated or even that the pledgor considered it terminated, it will be presumed that the possession of the pledgor was precarious or as an agent pro hac vice.

Since we find the pledge to have been presumptively extant between the parties, we next inquire as to the effect of the pledge on the running of liberative prescription on the debt evidenced by the notes. It is the well-settled jurisprudence of this state that prescription does not run in favor of the debtor whose debt is secured by a pledge, and that it remains interrupted, as long as the thing pledged is in the possession of the pledgee. . . . While several cases state that prescription does not run during the existence of the pledge since the pledge itself is a standing acknowledgment of the indebtedness, . . . the proper view is that it is not the contract or act of pledge that interrupts prescription but rather the detention by the pledgee of the thing pledged, such possession serving as a constant acknowledgment of the debt and hence a constant renunciation of prescription. *See Police Jury v. Duralde*, supra; *Conger v. City of New Orleans*, supra; *Citizens' Bank v. Hyams*, supra; *Liberty Homestead v.*

Pasqua, supra; *Pelican State Bank v. Bogle*, supra and Article 3520 (current article 3464) of the Civil Code.

And it is plain, for reasons given earlier in this opinion, that physical possession of the pledge need not be in the creditor himself, it being sufficient that it be in someone who holds for the account of the creditor, even the debtor himself, provided his tenure be precarious and clearly for the account of the creditor.

Since we find in the case at bar that Dr. Corkern held the pledged policy as trustee pro hac vice for Mrs. Scott, as evidenced by the fact that during his unexplainable possession of it he did no act with respect thereto which could be considered inconsistent with the pledge agreement, the running of prescription on the promissory notes was continuously interrupted at least until his death in 1953 and, therefore, the suit is not barred by prescription.

Accordingly, the judgment appealed from is reversed; the exception of prescription is overruled and the case is remanded for further proceedings in accordance with law and consistent with the views herein expressed. The costs of this appeal are to be borne by defendant.

* * * * * *

NOTES AND QUESTIONS

What is the policy that underlies the rule in *Scott*? The rule played a significant role in the days of the collateral mortgage package. Would the same rule still apply when the creditor takes a possessory security interest under UCC Article 9 in the collateral mortgage note? What if the creditor's way of taking possession of movable collateral was by taking control, as would be the case for deposit accounts?

7. Defenses to Enforcement

There are a number of defenses that the mortgagor and other parties may raise against a party seeking to enforce a mortgage (i.e., foreclose). *See* **La. Civ. Code arts. 3282; 3295.**

However, take note of the language in Civil Code article 3296. When the holder of an obligation secured by a mortgage is immune to the assertion of defenses to the enforcement of the obligation, the article provides the holder with the same immunity to the assertion of those defenses against the enforcement of the mortgage itself. The comments to the article specifically reference the ability of a holder in due course to ignore personal defenses raised by the debtor.

***See* La. Civ. Code article 3296.**

8. Comparison to Non-Louisiana Mortgages

Louisiana has always taken a very conservative approach when it comes to mortgage law, requiring that a mortgagee proceed through a judicially controlled process when seeking to foreclose. However, other states have taken a different approach. A number of other jurisdictions have security contracts that produce the general effects of a mortgage, but are structured differently and provide a wider array of rights and benefits to mortgagees.

The deed of trust (sometimes called the deed of trust mortgage or the mortgage with a power of sale) is one of the most common and popular types of mortgage-like security devices. Although initially rejected by most English courts, they grew in popularity and general acceptance in the United States as early as the late 1700s. In such transactions the lender makes a loan to the borrower and, in return, the borrower executes a deed (act of sale) conveying specific immovable property to a person designated as the trustee. The deed itself is then held by the trustee for the duration of the loan.

There are a number of significant features of the deed of trust that differ from the mortgage. First, there are three parties involved in the transaction (the mortgagor, the mortgagee, and the trustee) rather than the typical two (mortgagor and mortgagee). Second, the transaction looks like a conveyance, but is really just a security device. At common law it is said that equitable title stays with the borrower even though he has executed a deed conveying the property to the trustee. This is mostly done for historical reasons that are particular to the English common law's feudal system of land. Third, although the deed of trust is initially filed into the public records, at the end of the term of the loan, assuming there has not been a default, the trustee cancels the deed of trust by transferring legal title to the property back to the borrower. However, in the event the borrower defaults, the true benefits of using the deed of trust (rather than a mortgage) arise. The trustee is allowed to foreclose on the property and thereby himself sell it on behalf of the lender to the highest bidder—with no court proceeding required.

A few things are worthy of note here: The foreclosure sale is conducted by the trustee (not an officer of the court or other public official). Also, there is no need for the lender to get a judgment against the borrower prior to having the trustee commence these proceedings. The law does provide a few protections to the borrower, in that he is typically entitled to notice, publication of the trustee's sale, and a period of delay between default and the trustee's sale. Otherwise his interest in the property (in the form of equitable title) is foreclosed (i.e., terminated) at the time the auction takes place. Parties come to the trustee's sale and bid on the property, with the highest bidder being entitled to a deed conveying the property to him. When available, lenders prefer to use the deed of trust to secure their loans because of the diminished time and expense involved in foreclosing on the property and reaping the value of the collateral. About twenty-two out of the 50 states allow for deeds of trust, including Louisiana's neighbors—Texas and Mississippi.[7]

So why doesn't Louisiana allow for the deed of trust? Louisiana has always had a historical aversion to the ability of a lender to foreclose on the property of the borrower without going through some sort of judicial process. The ability to foreclose non-judicially is often called "self-help," and the civil law has traditionally abhorred self-help remedies due to the abuses that they invite and the possibilities of unfairness to the borrower. To this day Louisiana still does not allow self-help in the contract of mortgage (and hardly anywhere else in the law for that matter). Although dealing with movables, the following case gives you a sense of the attitude of Louisiana courts when it comes to self-help.

* * * * * *

[7] Deed of trust jurisdictions include Alabama, Alaska, Arizona, California, Colorado, Connecticut, the District of Columbia, Idaho, Maryland, Mississippi, Missouri, Montana, Nebraska, Nevada, North Carolina, Oregon, Tennessee, Texas, Utah, Virginia, Washington, and West Virginia.

ALCOLEA v. SMITH
90 So. 769 (1922)

MONROE, Chief Justice.

This is an appeal from a judgment rejecting plaintiff's demand for certain jewelry on his paying $1,200, for which amount it was pledged to defendant, or, in default of its surrender, for $3,500, shown to be considerably less than its value; the circumstances out of which the suit has arisen being as follows:

On September 25, 1915, by authentic act executed in New Orleans, plaintiff acknowledged that defendant had loaned him $1,200, and defendant acknowledged that he "had in his possession three diamond rings; one diamond stick pin; three sets of diamond earrings; one diamond valliere;" and it was agreed that those articles were to be returned to plaintiff, upon the payment within 360 days of the amount loaned, free of further interest or other charges (a discount of $200 having been deducted from the $1,200 in the making of the loan). It was further agreed that, if plaintiff should fail to redeem the property so pledged, within the delay specified, defendant should become the owner of it, and that in the meanwhile defendant should not be responsible for its loss by fire. It appears from the evidence that when, in September, 1916, the loan was approaching maturity, plaintiff called at defendant's office in New Orleans with a view of making a settlement, and, finding that defendant was absent, caused a telegram to be sent him by some one in the office, and on September 16, plaintiff himself wired defendant as follows:

> The contract regarding the diamonds that I have with you expires on September 19. Have called at your office several times this week to settle this matter with you, as per agreement of September 25, 1915. Your office advised me that you are in Colorado and, at my request, telegraphed you, on Thursday and Friday of this week, regarding the matter. Other friends of mine are ready to pay you the $1,200.00 and take over the diamonds on the 19th, therefore, inasmuch as you are not here to close the transaction, this is to notify you that, in no way, are the diamonds to revert to you, as per the contract mentioned, due to the fact that I am now ready and willing to pay over the money coming to you. Please advise me, by wire, as to when you will return, and it will also be necessary for you to write me, guaranteeing that

> the contract will be extended until the date of your return to this city. Return address 738 Audubon Building-Rafael Alcolea Grunewald Hotel Sept. 17, 1916, W. U. Tel. Co.

On September 18, 1916, defendant wired some one in his office as follows:

> Telegram just received to-day. Am not stopping Albany. Advise Alcolea will either extend or give to him upon my arrival, whichever suits him best. Stop. Diamonds Whitney vaults, and I have key, so cannot do anything until my return.

Defendant returned to New Orleans about noon on October 3, and telephoned to an office which plaintiff frequented, requesting that plaintiff call on him on that afternoon or the next morning; and plaintiff called the next morning (which was Wednesday, October 4, 1916) at 9 o'clock, when, according to his understanding of the conversation, defendant gave him four days in which to pay the $1,200 and redeem the diamonds; and plaintiff admits that he did so. . . .

Since the edict of Constantine annulling and prohibiting what was known as the lex commissoria and the stipulation in the contract of pledge which it authorized, whereby, in default of payment by the pledgor, the thing pledged became the property of the pledgee without further action on his part, such stipulations have been prohibited in all countries where the civil law prevails, and the prohibition has long since become part of the common law, the commentators on both systems agreeing that they are contra bonos mores and oppressive; that they involve the abuse of the power of the strong over the weak, represent odious speculations by those who have money, at the expense of those who need it, and are unconscionable. *Denis on Contracts of Pledge*, c. XXIV, p. 253 *et seq.*, citing Troplong, *Nantissement*, § 379 *et seq.*; Pothier, *Nantissement*, § 18; De St. Joseph, *Concordance des Codes Civiles*, p. 109; Merlin, *Rept. verbo 'Gage'*; C. N. 2578; *Story on Bailments*, § 345; *Kent's Com.* vol. 2, § 583; *Jones on Pledges*, § 553; Rev. Civ. Code La. art. 3132; *Russell v. Southard*, 12 How. 139, 13 L. Ed. 927; *Peugh v. Davis*, 96 U. S. 337, 24 L. Ed. 775; *Pritchard v. Elton*, 38 Conn. 434.

Article 3132 (current article 3140?) of the Civil Code of 1825 was an adoption in *totidem verbis* of article 2578 of the Code Napoléon, and reads as follows:

> Art. 3132. The creditor cannot, in case of failure of payment, dispose of the pledge, but may apply to the judge to order that the thing shall remain to him in payment for as much as it shall be estimated by two appraisers, or shall be sold at public auction, at the choice of the debtor.
>
> Any clause which should authorize the creditor to appropriate the pledge to himself, or dispose thereof without the aforesaid formalities, shall be null.

In the revision and re-enactment of our Code in 1870 the article quoted was given the number 3165 and reads:

> Art. 3165 (3132). The creditor cannot, in case of failure of payment, dispose of the pledge, but when there have been pledges of stocks, bonds or other property, for the payment of any debt or obligation, it shall be necessary before such stocks, bonds, or other property so pledged shall be sold for the payment of the debt for which such pledge was made, that the holder of such pledge be compelled to obtain a judgment in the ordinary course of the law, and the same formalities in all respects shall be observed in the sale of property so pledged as in ordinary cases; but in all pledges of movable property, . . . it shall be lawful for the pledgor to authorize the sale or other disposition of the property pledged, in such manner as may be agreed upon by the parties, without the intervention of Courts of Justice; provided, that all existing pledges shall remain in force and be subject to the provisions of this act.
>
> Any clause which should authorize the creditor to appropriate the pledge to himself, or dispose thereof without the aforesaid formalities, shall be null.

The article thus quoted was amended and re-enacted by Act 9 of 1872, and the last paragraph (beginning, 'Any clause which should authorize, etc.) was omitted, but the act contains no repealing clause.

Commenting upon that statute, Prof. Denis (*Denis on Contracts of Pledge*, pp. 255, 256) has this to say:

301. Under the provisions of this law, it is the common practice now in Louisiana to stipulate in all acts of pledge that the pledgee shall have the right, in case of nonpayment, to sell the pledge at public or private sale, with or without notice, to buy it in, and so forth. But could the pledgee by virtue of the law which makes it lawful for the pledgor to authorize the sale or other disposition of the thing pledged, stipulate that it shall become his property without sale and without appraisement, though its value may be greater than the amount of the debt, as is ordinarily the case? This question has yet to be answered. It is likely that it will be answered in the negative. The prohibition contained in the article of the Civil Code of Louisiana is one of public order, as we have seen. The act of 1872 cannot be presumed to have been leveled at it, in providing that it shall be lawful for the pledgor to authorize the sale or other disposition of the property pledged in such manner as may be agreed on by the parties, without the intervention of courts of justice. Such an indirect and implied re-establishment of the *lex commissoria* would be against all the rules of legislation.

302. The common law has adopted from the civil law the wise and humane principles of the edict of Constantine. . . . In this respect the two systems seem to be on a par. Judge Story says: "If a clause is inserted in the original contract providing that, if the terms of the contract are not strictly fulfilled at the time and in the mode prescribed, the pledge shall be irredeemable, it will be of no avail. For the common law deems such a stipulation unconscionable and void, upon the ground of public policy, as tending to the oppression of debtors."

During the (almost) 50 years which have elapsed since the passage of the act of 1872, and the (almost) 25 years since the publication of Prof. Denis' work, the precise question here at issue has been neither presented to, nor decided by, this court. Cases have been argued, submitted, and decided in which, the litigants having so agreed, the rights of pledgees to sell pledged property otherwise than under judgments obtained against the pledgors have been recognized, and the provisions of the act of 1872 upon that subject and to that extent have more than once, been applied. Louisiana, etc., *Co. v. Bussey*, 27 La. Ann. 472; *Carr v. La. Nat. Bank*, 29 La. Ann. 259; *Lafitte, Dufilho & Co. v.*

Godchaux, 35 La. Ann. 1161; *Smith v. Shippers' Oil Co.*, 120 La. 640, 45 South. 533. But until now it seems never to have occurred to any one engaged in the business of lending money on pledges or to their legal advisers that the lawmakers of this state intended by the adoption of the statute in question to revive a law and practice which by imperial authority were abrogated some 1,400 years ago, and of which nothing better has since been said than that they were obnoxious to good morals, odious, oppressive, and unconscionable. . . .

[T]he courts will read into every contract of pledge, whether it be there expressed or not, the stipulation that the pledgor shall have the right to redeem the pledged property, and that the pledgee shall not appropriate it to himself. *See Jones on Pledges*, § 553, and authorities heretofore cited.

It is no doubt true that, after the debt for which the pledge is given has fallen due, the parties may lawfully agree that the pledgee may keep the pledge in satisfaction of the debt, but there was no such agreement in this case.

The plaintiff (pledgor) herein was ready to pay the debt at maturity, but the defendant (pledgee) had left the state and was not ready to deliver the pledged property and receive the payment. He returned to New Orleans when it suited his convenience, and, having notified defendant to call on him, informed him, when he called, that he would give him four days within which to make the payment, following that information a day or two later with a written notice sent to plaintiff on a half holiday that the delay so accorded would expire at 6 o'clock that day (Saturday). Plaintiff appeared on the following Monday and tendered payment, which defendant refused. Having failed to provide for the surrender of the pledged property and the receipt of the payment upon the day fixed by the contract, we are at a loss to understand where he obtained the authority so peremptorily to fix the exact day and hour outside of the contract when plaintiff should settle with him and he with plaintiff. It occurs to us that, as the matter then stood, plaintiff was entitled to a hearing on that subject. It is quite certain, in any event, that plaintiff never did agree, after the maturity of debt, that defendant should appropriate the pledged property to its payment. Whether the last tender made by him was within the four days allowed by defendant is, therefore, immaterial.

For the reasons thus assigned:

It is ordered that the judgment appealed from be annulled, and that there now be judgment in favor of the plaintiff, Rafael Alcolea, and against the defendant, Hugh F. Smith, condemning said defendant to surrender and deliver to plaintiff the jewelry described in the petition, within three days after this judgment shall have become final upon plaintiff's tendering and paying to him the sum of $1,200. It is further ordered that, in default of his delivering said jewelry as thus ordered, defendant be condemned to pay plaintiff the sum of $3,500. It is further ordered that defendant pay all costs.

* * * * * *

NOTES AND QUESTIONS

1. Although Louisiana has remained hostile toward self-help generally, the law does now allow for it in certain situations. As discussed in a prior chapter, Louisiana allows limited self-help in the case of automobiles using a licensed repossession agent. *See* La. Rev. Stat. §§ 6:965-967. The law of pledge also allows a form of self-help in instances where the collateral takes the form of the rights to leases and rents of an immovable. *See* La. Civ. Code arts. 3159, 3174. There are yet still other limited examples. In light of these, might there be a compelling reason to support Louisiana adopting a deed of trust or similar type of security instrument for immovable property? Are there any safeguards that the legislature could put in place to mitigate against lender abuse and to protect borrowers? Have safeguards in other states been effective? *See* UCC § 9-609; *see also Salisbury Livestock v. Colorado Central Credit Union*, 793 P. 2d 470 (Wyo. 1990); *Marine National Bank v. Airco*, 389 F. Supp. 231 (W.D. Pa. 1975).

2. Constantine's edict of January 31, 326, voided agreements whereby ownership of property would transfer automatically upon default to the creditor, the edict ironically expressing the hope that the future would hold no memory of clauses of that nature. *See De Commissoria Rescindenda*, Constantine Augustus Jan. 31, 326, cited and translated by Pharr, *The Theodosian Code* 65 (1952). As the court in *Alcolea* discusses, the Louisiana Civil Codes of 1825 and 1870 both contained an express prohibition on the creditor's appropriation of a thing given in pledge, but the express prohibition was deleted in an amendment made in 1872 to authorize extrajudicial sales to enforce pledges. The recent enactment of the title on security in the Civil Code codified, in new Article 3140, Louisiana's longstanding prohibition of agreements of forfeiture. The article

applies the prohibition not just to pledges but to all forms of real security. Thus, a mortgage may not provide that ownership of the mortgaged property transfers to the mortgagee upon default.

3. In French law, the prohibited forfeiture, known as the *pacte commissoire*, was until recently prohibited in the contract of pledge by former article 2078 of the Code Civil: *Toute clause qui authoriserait le créancier à s'approprier le gage ou à en disposer sans les formalités ci-dessus est nulle.* [Any clause which would authorize the creditor to appropriate to himself the pledge or to dispose of it without the formalities provided above is null]. The jurisprudence permitted the *pacte commissoire* in a subsequent agreement. However, art. 2348 of the Code Civil of France (2006) now specifically allows the parties to provide in a contract of pledge for forfeiture upon default: *Il peut être convenu, lors de la constitution du gage ou postérieurement, qu'à défaut d'éxecution de l'obligation garantie le créancier deviendra propriétaire du bien gagé.* [It can be agreed, in the formation of the pledge or subsequently, that upon default in performance of the secured obligation the creditor will become owner of the thing pledged.] The same article further provides that the amount by which the value of the thing pledged exceeds the debt must be paid to the debtor or inferior pledged creditors. Articles 2459 and 2460 contain similar provisions applicable to mortgages, but the former article nullifies any such stipulation in a mortgage burdening the debtor's principal residence.

4. The second paragraph of Civil Code Article 3140 invalidates an agreement by a debtor, in advance of default, to make a *dation en paiement*. This paragraph expands the holding of *Guste v. Hibernia National Bank in New Orleans*, 655 So. 2d 724 (La. App. 4th Cir. 1995), *writ denied* 660 So. 2d 852 (La. 1995), which found to be absolutely null a debtor's *dation en paiement* that was held in escrow under an agreement providing for its release from escrow if the debtor defaulted in the future under the act of credit sale whereby he had purchased the property.

C. Legal Mortgages

A legal mortgage is a security device that "secures an obligation specified by law that provides for the mortgage." *See* La. Civ. Code art. 3299. In other words, these are mortgages that are established by operation of law, rather than by consent of the mortgagor and mortgagee. One creates a legal mortgage simply by "complying with the law providing for it." Civ. Code art. 3301. Some of the most common examples of the legal mortgage are those that secure the obligations that a curator or tutor owes to his interdict or minor.

Unlike the conventional mortgage (which can only be a special mortgage), legal mortgages are general mortgages such that they encumber all of the immovable property of the obligor. *See* La. Civ. Code art. 3285, cmt. b.

***See* La. Civ. Code art. 3360.**

D. Judicial Mortgages

Judicial mortgages share a significant feature with legal mortgages in that they encumber all of the present and future immovable property that the judgment debtor owns in the parish in which the judicial mortgage is recorded. The judicial mortgage is a significant debt collection tool for unsecured creditors who obtain a judgment against their debtors.

1. Requirements for Creation/Recordation

A judicial mortgage is created "by filing a judgment with the recorder of mortgages" in any parish in which the judgment debtor owns immovable property. All of the debtor's immovable property within that parish will then be encumbered by a judicial mortgage. Thus, a prudent judgment creditor will discover in which parishes the judgment debtor owns or is likely to subsequently purchase immovable property and file the judgment in all of those parishes. Notably, recordation not only makes a judicial mortgage effective against third persons, it is the very mechanism by which the judicial mortgage is created.

2. Reinscription and Prescription

Once again, it is necessary for even a creditor with a judicial mortgage to be mindful of the obligation to reinscribe. However, unlike with a conventional mortgage, different durational periods apply and, importantly, there is a two-step process involved in maintaining the effects of registry when it comes to the judicial mortgage.

***See* La. Civ. Code art. 3359. *See also* La. Code of Civ. Pro. art. 2031 (for how to revive a judgment).**

E. Ranking of Mortgages

One of the most important aspects of being a mortgagee is knowing where you rank vis-à-vis other holders of security. A mortgagee, however secured he may be and however diligent he has been about reinscribing, will have little recourse or hope of loss recovery if he occupies an inferior position to other creditors and when the collateral is of insufficient value to satisfy the debts owed to all upon a sale.

1. Contests Between Mortgagees

Louisiana Civil Code article 3307(3) states that "[t]he mortgagee is preferred to the unsecured creditors of the mortgagor and to others whose rights become effective after the mortgage becomes effective as to them." Thus, the general rule is that mortgages rank chronologically based on the time of filing. In order words, mortgages generally follow the legal maxim: first in time, first in right.

There is one exception to this however, when dealing with collateral mortgages. *See* Louisiana Revised Statute § 9:5551. A collateral mortgage ranks from the later of perfection of a security interest in the collateral mortgage note or the date of recordation of the collateral mortgage. Because Article 9 provides that perfection cannot occur until a security interest has attached, and because attachment requires the giving of value, a collateral mortgage, unlike a future advance mortgage under Civil Code article 3298, cannot attain ranking until value has been given. This rule is, for all practical purposes, the same as the rule prior to 1990, which required the "issuance" of the collateral mortgage note (which meant that it had to be validly pledged).

Civil Code article 3307(3) is not absolute and must be read *in pari materia* with other articles of the Civil Code, including articles 3186 and 3274. As we shall see in a later chapter, the general rule, subject to many exceptions, is that privileges are preferred to mortgages, irrespective of the order of effectiveness against third persons.

2. Contests Between Mortgagees and Article 9 Creditors

Since Article 9 deals with the granting of security interests in movable property, it might strike one as strange to discuss a contest between an Article 9 secured party and a mortgagee. However, because an Article 9 interest can be granted in a fixture, which is attached to immovable property, this dispute can come up quite often. In Article 9 parlance, fixtures are those things that are originally movable, but become immovable under La. Civ. Code arts. 463, 465, 466, and 467.

In such a contest between a fixture-secured party and a mortgagee, Louisiana Revised Statute § 10:9-334(c) states that the general rule is that "a security interest in fixtures is subordinate to a conflicting interest of an encumbrancer or owner of the related real property other than the debtor." Thus, the general rule is that the mortgagee's interest primes that of the creditor with the security interest in the fixture. However, this is just the general rule and it admits a number of exceptions. Importantly, if the Article 9 secured party perfects his interest by making a fixture filing (which includes doing so prior to the time the movable becomes a fixture) before the mortgage is recorded, then the Article 9 secured party will prime the mortgagee. *See* Louisiana Revised Statute § 9-334(e). Other exceptions apply for PMSIs and for instances where the mortgagee gives his consent. *See* Louisiana Revised Statute § 9-334(d) & (f).

F. Overview of Mortgage Finance

Mortgage finance is of great importance in the United States because homeownership has played such a huge role in the country's public policy discourse over the past century. As such, the government is extremely active in mortgage markets and in the real estate finance system. As a general matter, there are two important concepts that should be mastered when talking about mortgage finance: mortgage originations and the secondary mortgage market. A mortgage is originated when a bank or other financial institution makes a loan to a borrower in exchange for the execution of, among other things, a note and a mortgage on immovable property to secure repayment. In days of old lenders would keep their loans "on the books" and thereby accept payments from the borrower until the debt was retired (i.e., the obligation was extinguished through performance). This period, mostly during the early 1900s and prior to then, was a time when personal and professional relationships between individuals in the community and the local bank often played a significant role in the credit relationship.

However, shortly after the Great Depression there was a national push to increase homeownership. To make that happen the government undertook a muscular federal initiative geared toward opening mortgage credit markets to more would-be homeowners. This resulted in the creation of the Federal Housing Administration (FHA) and its mortgage loan insurance program (essentially, a guarantee to banks that if they made loans to borrowers who met certain qualifications then the federal government would bear the brunt of any default that resulted thereafter). The FHA program was very popular and remains so today.

The other big concept is the secondary mortgage market. Many banks and financial institutions that originate mortgage loans have no intention of keeping these assets on their books. Rather, they intend to sell the loans to investors and other third parties at a discount. This is called the secondary mortgage market. By selling the loans and obtaining capital in the immediacy (rather than collecting payments over the term of the loan), the bank can turn around and make more loans to borrowers and therefore widen the scope of available credit in the marketplace. There are a number of parties who purchase mortgage loans—including pension funds, depository institutions, and insurance companies—from the banks who make them, but the most important of these purchasers are the so-called government sponsored entities (GSEs). These are Fannie Mae and Freddie Mac. The basic goal of these entities, which were originally created by Congress but have variously over time become more or less private entities, was originally to address the perceived lack of credit opportunities across the country's socio-economic spectrum. In other words, at one point most Americans could not get a home loan. Fannie Mae and Freddie Mac were created to help change that.

Although initially created with a more limited scope, today Fannie Mae and Freddie Mac mostly purchase conventional mortgages on the secondary market that are considered "conforming" (meaning that they meet certain underwriting criteria). Their importance can hardly be understated. By all accounts the GSEs have been integral in oiling the wheels of the housing market. Through their own loan originations and through the purchasing of mortgages on the secondary market, Fannie and Freddie's total assets increased from $78 billion in 1980 to $3.6 trillion in 2003. In fact, by 2010, these two entities owned or guaranteed about half of all outstanding residential mortgages in the United States.

Related to the secondary market is the sale of mortgage-backed securities. Some financial institutions (including Fannie Mae and Freddie Mac) purchase large numbers of mortgage loans from various originators and pool them together in a single entity or trust. The trust then issues certificates or securities (like stock or bonds) that investors can purchase. The investors then derive income from their purchase of interests in the pool of mortgage loans. As borrowers make payments on their loans, those amounts are passed on to the investors, much in the way a company makes dividend payments to their shareholders. These investments are called mortgage-backed securities (MBS), and they can vary depending upon whether the mortgage loans are for commercial (commercial mortgage-backed securities—CMBS) or residential (residential mortgage-backed securities—RMBS) purposes.

There is much more to learn and understand about mortgage finance, particularly since the advent of the Dodd-Frank Wall Street Reform and Consumer Protection Act of 2010 and the accompanying creation of the federal agency known as the Consumer Financial Protection Bureau. However, for purposes of this course, it is enough to know that although the mechanics of confecting a loan secured by an interest in immovable property may be simple enough, there is a much more complex and very important financial structure that these basic rules support.

Chapter 5
The Law of Privileges

A. In General

***See* La. Civ. Code arts. 3133-34; 3185–89**

Louisiana's use of the term *privilege* to denote a form of security is unique in American law. The term, taken from the French word *privilège* found in the Code Napoléon without any attempt at translation, descends from the Latin word *privilegium*, a combination of *privus + legis,* signifying law made for private or particular interests.

A privilege in Louisiana is similar in many respects to the form of security known in other states as a *lien*, which itself is a word of French origin conveying the sense of a relationship or connection. Indeed, there are innumerable instances in Louisiana statutes and jurisprudence in which the word *lien* is used when a privilege is technically intended. Louisiana practitioners probably use the term *vendor's lien* as frequently, if not more so, than the correct term *vendor's privilege*. For the sake of uniformity, Chapter 9 of the Louisiana Uniform Commercial Code consistently employs the model term *lien* but contains a non-uniform definition in La. R.S. 10:9-102(d)(9) making that term, when it appears in Chapter 9, synonymous with a privilege upon movable property.

Article 3186 of the Louisiana Civil Code, which was borrowed *verbatim* from the Code Napoléon, provides that "*[p]rivilege* is a right, which the nature of a debt gives to a creditor, and which entitles him to be preferred before other creditors, even those who have mortgages." A privilege is thus a preference established by legislation and is an exception to the general rule of Article 3134 that the proceeds of the sale of an obligor's property are distributed ratably among his creditors. Privileges cannot be granted contractually; they can arise only by operation of law based upon the nature of the debt.

The Civil Code classifies privileges as either general or special. The general privileges operate on all property of the debtor, or, in some cases, on all of the debtor's movables or all of his immovables. Other privileges are special; that is, they operate only on specific property.

* * * * * *

2 TRAITE ÉLEMENTAIRE DE DROIT CIVIL, PT. 2
(La. State Law Inst. trans., 1959) (12th ed. 1939) (Fr.)
MARCEL PLANIOL & GEORGES RIPERT

2545. Confused State of Existing Privileges

Although the notion of privilege was simple in Roman law, it has become uncertain and confused in modern law; they have brought together under this single name things quite different, to such an extent that it is today impossible to give to privilege a self-contained and unified theory; it is necessary to proceed by the way of analysis, and to choose from the confused mass.

In reality only the general privileges have preserved the nature of the ancient privilege; the special privileges on immovables are veritable mortgages which are privileged in the sense that they benefit out of turn. As to special privileges on movables, they are rights, varied in their origin, which have come to be confounded under the name of privileges, because they all give to a creditor a right of preference.

2546. Current Definition

The law defines the privilege as "a right that the nature of the claim gives to a creditor to be preferred to other creditors, even to those who have mortgages" (Art. 2095). The articles following say how the privileged creditors exercise their right of preference:

(1) What if there is a conflict between several different privileges? "The preference is governed by the different nature of their privileges" (Art. 2096)

that is to say according to the degree of favoritism which the law accords to each of them.

(2) Suppose there is a conflict between several creditors having the same privilege? These creditors are "in the same rank," as says Art. 2097, are "paid concurrently" (same). Each one of them receives only a proportional share of his credit, if there is not enough to pay all.

* * * * * *

Real Rights in Louisiana and Comparative Law: Part 1

A. N. Yiannopoulos

23 LOUISIANA LAW REVIEW 161, 222 (1963)

The question of the juridical nature of privileges and their classification as personal or real rights has prompted exhaustive discussion and controversies in the literature of civil law. In the French Civil Code, privileges are dealt with in a subdivision of Title XVIII, Book III, devoted to "Privileges and Mortgages." The Louisiana Civil Code, Book III, Title XXI, deals with privileges and the following Title XXII in the same book is devoted to mortgages. Apart from this systematic arrangement, which tends to distinguish between privileges and mortgages, the relevant articles in the Louisiana Civil Code follow in the main the arrangement and substantive content of the corresponding articles in the French Civil Code.

The Louisiana Civil Code establishes the general rule that "the property of the debtor is the common pledge of his creditors, and the proceeds of its sale must be distributed among them ratably, unless there exist among the creditors some lawful causes of preference" (Article 3183). Such "lawful causes of preference" are privileges and mortgages (Article 3183). Privilege is defined as "a right, which the nature of a debt gives to a creditor, and which entitles him to be preferred before other creditors, even those who have mortgages" (Article 3186). Privileges may exist on movables, immovables, or both (Article 3189). Privileges on movables may be "either general, or special on certain movables" (Article 3190). General privileges on movables are enumerated in Article 3191 and special privileges in Article 3217. Privileges on immovables may also be general or special; the Code does not say so expressly but this is apparent in the light of detailed provisions. Thus, Article 3249 enumerates as special privileges on immovables the vendor's privilege, the privilege of those furnishing labor and supplies, and the privilege of those "making or repairing levees, bridges, ditches, and roads on the land." Article 3252 enumerates general privileges which attach both to movables and immovables.

* * * * * *

Ranking Problems of Chattel Mortgages and Civil Code Privileges in Louisiana Law
Joseph Dainow
13 Louisiana Law Review 537 (1953)

In the civil law, the transactions which are intended to provide security for the fulfillment of a principal obligation are usually classified as being in the nature of either personal security (suretyship) or real security (pledge, mortgage). A privilege, which is one of the Louisiana security devices, gives a particular creditor precedence before other creditors; however, it does not fit into either of these two categories, although it comes closer to the latter than the former.

Generally speaking, all a person's property assets can be sought out by his creditors for the payment of his debts, and the general rule is that the creditors share ratably if the proceeds are insufficient to pay them all. The whole subject of privileges in the Civil Code is introduced, as an area of exception to the general rule of proration, by the concluding phrase of Article 3183, ". . . unless there exist among the creditors some lawful causes of preference."

The effect of this exemption from proration gives the privileged creditor an assurance of payment in full even if the ordinary creditors get nothing. In this respect, the Civil Code privilege constitutes a security device.

The subject matter of privileges is *stricti juris,* and no privilege can be claimed without an express text of law either in the Civil Code or in a statute. That is, privileges arise exclusively by the operation of law, and by reason of the nature of a debt. The determination of which debts shall carry a privilege is purely and simply a matter of legislative policy decision and the purpose is to make this automatic security device accompany the transaction so favored.

Reasons for Privileges

In the case of every single privilege, there is necessarily a policy objective which warrants an exception to the general rule of proration among creditors. The reasons are seldom stated, but it is apparent that in many instances the privilege is created in order to help a prospective debtor get credit which is not otherwise likely to be extended to him.

In some instances, the interest which needs the special automatic protection of the privilege is that of the creditor, such as the servant, the clerk, and the artisan. These persons are presumably dependent upon their personal earnings for their daily living.

A number of the Civil Code privileges must be considered as having been established in the ultimate general interest, despite the fact that a certain creditor gets the immediate advantage. In this category are the funeral charges, the expenses of the last illness, and to some extent the law costs for the administration of justice.

The privilege of the lessor does not have to be considered as established exclusively in favor of the lessor, because this security device may well be the supporting reason for a lease which might not otherwise be granted. Likewise, the privilege of the vendor may give as much help to the purchaser who needs credit as it is an encouragement to business. And so on.

* * * * * *

IN RE GREEN
516 B.R. 347 (E.D. La. 2014)
***aff'd.* 793 F. 3d 463 (5th Cir. 2015)**

JANE TRICHE MILAZZO, District Judge.

Before the Court is an appeal by Riverbend Condominium Association, Inc., from a decision of the United States Bankruptcy Court for the Eastern District of Louisiana. The decision of the bankruptcy court is AFFIRMED for the following reasons.

BACKGROUND

The facts in this case are undisputed. Torrance Tremayne Green ("Debtor"), the debtor in bankruptcy, is the owner of a condominium in Riverbend Condominiums in New Orleans, Louisiana (the "Condominium"). The Condominium is subject to the Louisiana Condominium Act (the "Act") and the Condominium Declaration of Riverbend Condominiums (the "Declaration"), which is recorded in the public records of Orleans Parish. The Declaration grants the Riverbend Condominium Association ("Riverbend" or "Creditor") the right to assess dues for the general maintenance of the complex and file a lien against condominium owners who become delinquent on those dues. The Act includes a similar provision granting a condominium association a privilege for unpaid sums assessed by the association.

Debtor fell behind on assessments owed to Riverbend. Subsequently, Riverbend filed a lien affidavit in the mortgage records of Orleans Parish and then obtained a default judgment against Debtor for $23,303.72.

After the judgment was obtained, Debtor filed Chapter 13 Bankruptcy. Riverbend filed a Proof of Claim in the bankruptcy proceeding and was recognized as a secured creditor by the Chapter 13 Trustee. Debtor filed a Motion to Avoid Riverbend's Lien on the grounds that after deducting the balance of the first mortgage and the Louisiana homestead exemption, there was only $8,000 left to which Riverbend's lien could attach.

The bankruptcy court bifurcated Riverbend's claim, finding that the $8,000 residual value in the Condominium constituted a secured claim, while the remainder was unsecured. Riverbend filed a Motion for New Trial and, pursuant to 11 U.S.C. § 1322(b)(2), alleged that its claims could not be bifurcated because its lien is a security interest. 11 U.S.C. § 1322(b)(2) states that a bankruptcy plan may "modify the rights of holders of secured claims, other than a claim secured only by a security interest in real property that is the debtor's principal residence." It is undisputed that the Condominium is Debtor's principal residence and thus, if Riverbend's lien is a security interest, it cannot be bifurcated pursuant to the anti-modification provision of 11 U.S.C. § 1322. On this matter of first impression in Louisiana law, the bankruptcy court held that Riverbend's lien is a statutory lien, not a consensual security interest, and thus the prohibition in 11 U.S.C. § 1322 does not apply. Riverbend appeals this holding and alleges that the bankruptcy court erred in finding that its lien is statutory. . . .

LAW AND ANALYSIS

The classification of a condominium lien is an issue of first impression under Louisiana law. Pursuant to the Bankruptcy Code, there are three types of liens: (1) statutory liens, (2) judicial liens, and (3) security interests. A statutory lien is a lien that arises "solely by force of a statute on specified circumstances or conditions." A "judicial lien" is a lien "obtained by judgment, levy, sequestration, or other legal or equitable process or proceeding." The term "security interest" means a lien that is "created by an agreement." Riverbend alleges that the condominium lien in question is a security interest and thus cannot be bifurcated pursuant to the anti-modification provision; Debtor contends that the bankruptcy court was correct in finding that the condominium lien is a statutory lien, to which the anti-modification provision does not apply. This Court agrees with the bankruptcy court and holds that a condominium lien is a statutory lien.

The root of the parties' disagreement stems from the fact that the authority by which Riverbend acquired a security interest in Debtor's condominium was present in both the law and the condominium declaration. Specifically, the Louisiana Condominium Act states that a condominium association "*shall* have a privilege on a condominium parcel for all unpaid or accelerated sums assessed by the association." It further requires that in order to preserve the privilege, the association must file a claim of privilege in the mortgage records of the parish in which the condominium is located and must notify the delinquent owner by sworn detailed statement of its claim at least seven days prior to the filing. This filing preserves the privilege for one year from the date of the filing, and the creditor must record a notice of filing of suit within that year to maintain the privilege.

The Declaration essentially repeats the law set forth in the Act. Creditor argues that by filing the Declaration into the mortgage records it has somehow transformed its statutory privilege into a consensual security interest. This Court disagrees for the following reasons.

Under Louisiana law, there are two types of security devices that pertain to immovable property: privileges and mortgages. The Declaration does not satisfy the creation requirements of either. The first, a "privilege," is a nonconsensual device that arises as a matter of law. The Louisiana Condominium Act grants a condominium association a special privilege in a debtor's condominium for amounts owed to the association. A "privilege is a right, which the nature of a debt gives to a creditor, and which entitles him to be preferred before other creditors, even those who have mortgages." While the term "privilege" is unique to Louisiana law, it is synonymous with the term "statutory lien," which is used outside of Louisiana. "[A] privilege arises only if and to the extent the law says it does; the law must be express, and privileges are interpreted strictly against the claimant."

In light of the legal nature of privileges, Creditor's attempt in the Declaration to give itself a privilege is ineffective. A privilege arises only by law and thus can never be created by the consent of the parties. The inclusion of the above quoted language in the Declaration could *not* have given Creditor a privilege. If the Louisiana Condominium Act did not expressly provide Creditor with a privilege in Debtor's Condominium for unpaid association fees, Creditor's attempt to take a secured interest in the Condominium based on privilege would have been ineffective.

Because the Declaration could not have given Creditor a privilege in the Condominium, the only other possibility is that it gave Creditor a mortgage, which is a consensual security interest in immovable property. In order to create a conventional mortgage, the parties must execute a written contract, which must be signed by the mortgagor, state the amount secured, and describe the immovable property. Creditor has provided no evidence that any of the above occurred. Indeed, Creditor argues only that the Declaration became binding upon third parties when it was filed in the mortgage records and thus became binding upon Debtor when he purchased the Condominium. This is insufficient to create a consensual security interest. "Because of their very nature and function, security devices should be strictly construed." An attempt to create a consensual security interest without any of the requisite requirements, especially the signature (and thus express consent) of the mortgagor, cannot be valid.

In short, the parallel inclusion of a reproduction of the Louisiana Condominium Act into the Declaration had no effect. In acquiring a secured interest in Debtor's property, Creditor was relying solely on the privilege granted to it by the Act. Indeed, it took all steps required by the Act to preserve that privilege, including filing a verified claim of privilege into the mortgage records in the parish where the Condominium is located and bringing suit within one year of filing. The fact that a creditor must take certain subsequent steps to preserve a privilege does not affect the fact that the privilege *arises* "solely by force of a statute." Because a privilege arises as a matter of law, it is, by definition, a statutory lien. Thus, because Creditor's lien on Debtor's Condominium is based on the privilege granted to it by the Louisiana Condominium Act, it is a statutory lien. "[A] Louisiana privilege is *not* a 'security interest.' " Accordingly, the anti-modification provision of 11 U.S.C. § 1322 does not apply. The bankruptcy court did not err in bifurcating Creditor's claim into secured and unsecured portions, and its decision is affirmed.

* * * * * *

NOTES AND QUESTIONS

1. The privilege arising under the Louisiana Condominium Act, found at La. R.S. 9:1123.115, is an example of a special privilege created by statute. Similar privileges arise under the Louisiana Time Sharing Act and the Louisiana Homeowners Association Act. *See* La. R.S. 9:1131.22 and La. R.S. 9:1145 *et seq*.

2. An important concept central to the notion of privileges is that they arise only by operation of an express provision of law and cannot be granted contractually. *See, e.g., Southport Petroleum Co. of Del. v. Fithian*, 13 So. 2d 382 (La. 1943); *In re Liquidation of Hibernia Bank & Trust Co.*, 162 So. 644 (La. 1935); *State v. Miller*, 126 So. 422, 428 (La. 1930); and *Succession of Rousseau*, 23 La. Ann. 1 (1871). For a case involving an extreme, and perhaps misguided, allegiance to this rule, *see Lewis v. Kubena*, 800 So. 2d 68 (La. App. 4th Cir. 2001), in which the court found that the words "I hereby grant a lien against the proceeds of this case" were ineffective to grant the creditor any rights in the proceeds in question because a lien or privilege cannot be created by contract. Should the quoted language have been considered sufficient to create a Chapter 9 security interest?

3. Might the result of *In re Green* have been different if the condominium unit owner had actually signed the condominium declaration?

* * * * * *

SOUTHERN SAVINGS ASSOCIATION

v.

LANGFORD LAND CO.

372 So. 2d 713 (La. App. 4th Cir. 1979)

BOUTALL, Judge.

This case involves a dispute as to the rights of a lessee and an option holder to the proceeds of a judicial sale after a superior creditor has foreclosed upon the property.

On May 1, 1974, Langford Land Company leased property located at 611 Bourbon Street in New Orleans to Oscar Stafford and included within the lease an option to purchase. Stafford assigned this lease to Crater Corporation, which then assigned it to Southern Marigold, Inc., one appellant in this action. Feelgood's Fotos, the other appellant, occupied a portion of the premises under a sub-lease specifically excepted in the assignment to Southern Marigold. Prior to this lease, a first mortgage had been placed on the property in favor of Southern Savings Association. Subsequent to the assignment, Langford executed a collateral mortgage in favor of Continental Bank, appellee herein.

On January 5, 1978, the property was seized and sold at public auction pursuant to a petition for executory process, filed by the first mortgagee, Southern Savings Association, for an amount exceeding the debt owed on the first mortgage. Continental Bank, the second mortgage holder, requested that the excess be paid to them. Southern Marigold then intervened asserting that the recorded option in the assigned lease afforded it rights superior to that of the holder of the subsequently recorded mortgage to the proceeds. Feelgood Fotos also intervened asserting that its claim as sub-lessee to the surplus proceeds primed the claim of the second mortgagee. Continental Bank responded by filing exceptions of no cause of action against the intervenors. The trial judge maintained the exceptions dismissing both interventions. From this judgment, both intervenors appealed.

Appellant Southern Marigold contends that the recorded lease and option to purchase which it held on the property constitutes a privilege on the proceeds which affords appellant greater rights than the holder of a subsequently recorded collateral mortgage. Appellant argues that the obligation arising from the option confers a real right on the optionee and that, therefore, its relative ranking as to other real rights, namely the two mortgages, is determined by time of recordation.

Appellant accurately points out that a validly exercised option results in a binding contract to sell giving either party the right to specific performance or an action for damages for breach. See Civil Code Article 2462. Since the first mortgagee has exercised his rights of seizure and sale, however, before an actual exercise of the option by the intervenors, the remedy of specific performance is no longer available to appellant. Where rights of others have intervened and full compliance with a contract for delivery of an immovable is impossible, courts will deny relief of specific performance and relegate the party to an action for damages. *See Thompson v. Thompson*, 211 La. 468, 30 So. 2d 321 (1947). What is at issue here is the distribution of the proceeds of a judicial sale. Regardless of any rights on the property held under its lease, appellant now merely occupies the position of an unsecured creditor as to the proceeds and is primed by secured creditors unless it can establish some basis for preference. It has an unliquidated claim for damages for breach of contract.

Civil Code Article 3184 states that:
"Lawful causes of preference are privilege and mortgages."

Civil Code Article 3185 states that:
"Privilege can be claimed only for those debts to which it is expressly granted in this Code."

A reading of the listed privileges reveals that the Code contains no privilege for the breach of an option contract or an agreement of sale. See Article 3249. Appellant, therefore, has no claim to the proceeds of this sale which is superior to that of the holder of a valid mortgage. Privileges are *stricti juris* and must be strictly construed. *See* Article 3185, supra and *Econo-Car International, Inc. v. Zimmerman*, 201 So. 2d 188 (La. App. 4th Cir. 1967). The operative effect of a privilege may never be extended by implication or analogy to any situation not explicitly contemplated by the statute creating it. *Martinez v. Therma-King Sales & Service*, 346 So. 2d 798 (La. App. 1st Cir. 1977).

We reject appellant's contention that it is a holder of a real right entitled to equal ranking with the mortgage holders to claim the proceeds of the judicial sale. Real rights are distinguished as either principal or accessory. Principal real rights pertain to the substance of a thing which is placed to the service of the holder of the right, while accessory real rights pertain to the pecuniary value of the thing. Rights of preference may be attached by law to any right, whether personal or real. See Yiannopolos, *Real Rights in Louisiana and Comparative Law: Part 1,* 23 Louisiana Law review 161 (1963). Examples of accessory real rights are mortgage, pledge and privileges on immovables.

The Louisiana Civil Code affords a preference to the accessory real right of mortgage and affords certain other rights a privilege attached to the real right, such as the special privileges on immovables created by Article 3249. Since the Legislature has granted no preference to one in appellant's position, appellant has no right to claim the proceeds of a judicial sale ahead of a statutorily preferred creditor, even if appellant's right to purchase could originally have been considered a principal real right.

The only other issue before us is whether the leases held by both intervenors create a preference to the proceeds of the sale. There is jurisprudence in Louisiana holding that a judicial sale in satisfaction of a mortgage dissolves any lease entered into subsequent to the mortgage. *See Board of Commissioners v. Hibernia Bank in New Orleans*, 52 So. 2d 771 (Orl. App. 1951); *Thompson v. Flathers*, 45 La. Ann. 120, 12 So. 245 (1893). Further we cannot see that a lessee has any more of a privilege to the proceeds than does an option holder. Any recourse which the lessees have is against the lessor. There is no support for the contention that the lessees are entitled to the proceeds of the judicial sale in preference to a mortgage holder.

The allegations of the petitions of both intervenors fail to state a cause of action upon which relief may be granted.

For the above reasons, the decision below is affirmed at intervenors' cost.

AFFIRMED.

* * * * * *

NOTES AND QUESTIONS

1. What is meant by the court's observation that privileges are *stricti juris*?

2. The court cited jurisprudence to the effect that a foreclosure upon a mortgage dissolves any lease entered into subsequent to the mortgage. Is it technically correct that a foreclosure dissolves a subsequently recorded lease? *See* La. Civ. Code art. 2711 (2004).

3. Could the lessee have protected itself against the claims of the second mortgagee by itself obtaining a mortgage upon the property subject to its lease? If so, was a separate act of mortgage necessary, or could a mortgage have been stipulated in the lease? *See* La. Civ. Code arts. 3293-94. *But see Mott v. EZ Money, Inc.*, 131 So. 3d 117 (La. App. 4th Cir. 2013), holding that a "special mortgage" clause contained in a bond for deed contract to ensure the seller's performance of the contract was a "conditional mortgage" and was therefore not entitled to constitutional protection under *Mennonite Board of Missions v. Adams*, 462 U.S. 791 (1983).

4. In practice, a lessee protects himself against the risk of a foreclosure upon a priming mortgage by obtaining from the mortgagee a non-disturbance agreement under which the mortgagee agrees that any purchaser at the foreclosure sale will be obligated to honor the lessee's right to possess the leased premises so long as the lessee does not default under the lease.

B. General Privileges

See La. Civ. Code arts. 3190-3214; 3252

The Civil Code creates general privileges securing funeral charges, law charges, expenses of the last illness, and the wages due to household servants and tutors, embracing both movables and immovables alike. In addition, those who have supplied household provisions to the debtor and his family during the last six months are granted a general privilege upon only the debtor's movables.

All but the first three of these privileges are archaic and rarely, if ever, asserted today.

The privilege of the needy surviving spouse, which is a general privilege on both movables and immovables, was first established by Act 255 of 1852 and later incorporated into the Civil Code of 1870 in Article 3252.

Statutory law has established other general privileges, such as "tax liens" on all of a tax debtor's property securing delinquent tax obligations. *See* La. R.S. 47:1577.

1. For Funeral Charges

* * * * * *

2 TRAITE ÉLEMENTAIRE DE DROIT CIVIL, PT. 2
(La. State Law Inst. trans., 1959) (12th ed. 1939) (Fr.)
MARCEL PLANIOL & GEORGES RIPERT

2556. Privileged Credits

The law having made nothing precise, everything has been disputed. Two principal questions are:

What should be admitted as funeral expenses? Formerly the jurisprudence was very magnanimous; it even allowed the benefit of the privilege, to the expenses of mourning of the widow and of the domestics (Caen, 15 July 1836, S.37.2.229); this rule is generally condemned by the modern authors (Aubry et Rau, 5th Ed., t. III, § 260, note 11).

There is also a tendency not to admit as privileged anything but the expenses strictly necessary for the burial (transportation of the body and burial) to the exclusion of the expenses of the religious ceremony (Laurent, t. XXIX, Nos. 357 *et seq.* Trib. Seine, 16 Jan. 1885, D.87.2.119; 15 Nov. 1889, S.90.2.47). But in general the expenses of the religious ceremony are considered as included in the funeral expenses, provided, however, that they are in relation with the social condition and the apparent fortune of the deceased (Paris, 9 Feb. 1887, D.87.2.119, S.87.2.40).

According to the jurisprudence the privilege of funeral expenses does not extend to the construction of a monument, however modest it may be (Trib. Seine, 6 May 1873, D.75.3.8), nor to the purchase of a cemetery plot.

Whose death does the law have in mind? It is generally admitted that the privilege of funeral expenses takes place, not only when it is the debtor himself who died, but even during his life, when the person buried was of a person living at his expense and without personal fortune, such as his children. The motive for this is that these expenses should be paid by the debtor.

It is in error that Laurent (t. XXIX, No. 329) restricts the privilege to the person of the debtor; it is equally erroneous for other authors to extend it to persons who do not live at the expense of the debtor.

* * * * * *

ALTER

v.

O'BRIEN

31 La. Ann. 452 (1879)

The opinion of the court was delivered by DEBLANC, J.

From the 7th of September to the 10th of October, 1877, Mrs. O'Brien and two of her children died, and—after their death—Charles E. Alter caused to be seized and sold, and—at the sale—purchased, for less than the claim which he had against defendant, the real estate mortgaged by the latter to secure said claim.

Mrs. O'Brien left nothing, and the property thus mortgaged and sold belonged to the community which existed between her and her surviving husband. He and that community are insolvent, and Francis Johnson—an undertaker—claims to be paid by preference, and out of the proceeds of the sale to Alter, the expenses incurred for the burial of Mrs. O'Brien and her children.

The district court maintained Johnson's opposition, but for exclusively the amount which he claims for the burial of the deceased wife. From that decree

Alter appealed, and—in answer to his appeal—Johnson prays that the decree be amended, by allowing the whole of the account on which he based his third opposition.

Does Johnson's claim for funeral expenses rank that of Alter, the mortgagee?

The Code expressly provides that *privilege* is a right, which the nature of a debt gives to a creditor, and which entitles him to be preferred before other creditors, *even those who have mortgages*—C. C. 3186 (3153). Funeral charges are secured by a privilege which extends alike to movables and immovables. C. C. 3252 (3219.) Though the lessor's right on the movables found on the place leased, is of a higher nature than a mere privilege—C. C. 3218-(3185)—that extraordinary right yields to the privilege for the funeral expenses *of the debtor and of his family*, when there is no other source from which they can be paid. C. C. 3257 (3224).

This is just: were it not for the privilege which the law allows to those who dig the grave, furnish the coffin and drive the hearse, many a lifeless frame, deprived of sepulture, would rot in unnoted or forsaken homes. Were it not for that privilege, when Death enters a city and knocks at every door—watchful and indefatigable as it is, Charity would inevitably be unequal to the increased task which—otherwise—would be imposed upon it.

In whomsoever may be the title to the property, whether in the husband or the community, howsoever encumbered it may be, the proceeds of the sale of the property can—under no circumstances—be applied to the satisfaction of a conventional mortgage, to the exclusion of the funeral expenses incurred, not only for the debtor, but for his family, when—in the language of the Code—there is no other source from which they can be paid.

> "Ce privilege"—according to the most eminent of the French commentators—"a été introduit: 1. dans l'interêt des mœurs publiques, qui auraient été blessés si le corps d'un homme insolvable fut resté sans sépulture; 2. dans l'interêt de la salubrité publique, qui eut été compromise si le corps n'eut pas été enseveli. . . . Les motifs qui ont fait admettre ce privilège, l'interêt de la décence et de la

salubrité publiques, existent, soit qu'il s'agisse de l'ensevelissement de débiteur, de ses enfants et proches parents."

Troplong, *Privilèges et Hypothèques*, vol. 1, No. 132.

Paul Pont, *Privilèges et Hypothèques*, vol. 1, p. 47.

Mourlon, *Examen du C. N.* vol. 3, p. 502.

Gilbert, *Codes Annotés*, p. 912.

The objection that the funds retained by the sheriff under the order granted on the third opposition, can be paid but to the representative of Mrs. O'Brien's succession, which is not represented in this suit, is not tenable. As between Johnson and Alter—two of the creditors of an insolvent community—the right of preference claimed by the former was properly passed upon and determined in the jurisdiction wherein the latter proceeded to enforce his mortgage.

At the death of Mrs. O'Brien, she and her husband owned no separate estate, and the whole of the property belonging to the community which heretofore existed between them, was insufficient to satisfy its liabilities. The common property was sold, purchased by Alter, and—less a fraction—he kept, as a creditor, the proceeds of that sale. There never was in the succession of Mrs. O'Brien, there no longer is in or of the community a single right or effect upon which to administer. Johnson alone is entitled to a sum which was claimed by him, which was due and allowed to him—to which no succession is entitled, which was not allowed to, and is neither claimed by or for any succession, and that sum retained to satisfy his demand, can be paid but to him.

It is—therefore—ordered, adjudged and decreed that the judgment appealed from is amended, and that Francis Johnson recover—out of the proceeds of the sale from the sheriff to Charles E. Alter, and in preference to the latter, the sum of three hundred twelve dollars and fifty cents: the costs of the appeal to be paid by Alter—and, as thus amended, the judgment of the lower court is affirmed.

Dissenting Opinion.

MANNING, C. J.

The interest of a wife in the community property, as owner, begins only after all the debts of the community are paid. If the community is insolvent, the wife has no succession *quoad* the community property. Neither the wife nor her heirs, she being dead, have any but a contingent and eventual interest in the community, and until the final discharge of the debts for which the community is liable, it cannot be known whether this contingent interest will ever become an absolute right. *Hawley v. Crescent City Bank*, 26 Annual, 230, and authorities there reviewed. *Gally v. Dowling*, 30 Annual, 323.

The husband, O'Brien, had mortgaged this property during the existence of the community. The mortgage debt was not wholly satisfied by its sale. There was therefore no residuum, and the wife, having no separate property, had no succession to be affected by privileges of any kind.

The undertaker's claim for the funeral expenses of herself, and her children, is a sacred debt, enforceable against the surviving husband and father, but there is no succession property upon which it can operate. The relation of the husband to the community property differs in many respects from that of the wife. He is its head and master. He can mortgage and alienate it. Upon his death, the community being insolvent, it is treated as his succession, and the privileges established by law rest upon it, and will be recognized.

But were it otherwise, how can a privileged creditor of the wife's succession proceed in his own name against a fund that was never brought into her succession, and subject it to the payment of his claim? According to the Opponent's theory, his claim is against her succession, and therefore he must prefer it against the representative of that succession. The mortgage creditor of the husband is certainly not that representative.

The only foundation, upon which the claim can rest as a privilege, is the fact that the property sold was in whole or in part succession property of the wife. It is only as a privilege that it can rank a mortgage. When the Code assigns priority of rank to funeral expenses upon succession property over certain other claims, it necessarily means the funeral expenses of the owner of the property.

If this property belongs to the succession of the wife, Alter is not administering it, and the only person who could claim of him that part of the fund which belongs to her succession, would be its representative, who would have to distribute it under the orders of the probate court.

I think the Opposition should be dismissed.

* * * * * *

NOTES AND QUESTIONS

1. It is a common misconception that privileges exist for the primary purpose of benefitting those creditors whose claims are privileged. As this case and others below illustrate, the benefit to the creditor, though real, is incidental to the underlying policy justification for the existence of most privileges: providing the debtor with credit that would otherwise not be readily available to him.

2. Is the holding of the case that the privilege for funeral expenses extends not just to the funeral of the debtor himself but also to funeral expenses of members of his family defensible? The articles of the Civil Code establishing the privilege are not clear on this point, in contrast to Article 3204, which expressly provides that the privilege for the expenses of the last illness extends to the last sickness of the debtor's children. Based on this difference, as well as the rule that privileges are *stricti juris*, Professor Daggett argues that there is no basis for extending the privilege for funeral charges to funerals of the debtor's children. Daggett, *Louisiana Privileges and Chattel Mortgage* § 146 (1942). She also makes an interesting counterpoint to the court's policy justification for the privilege for funeral charges: "On the other hand, unsavory whispers are heard from time to time that there are those who under the guise of rendering assistance at a time of sorrow and disorganization use this privilege as an entering wedge for gaining possession of the small holdings of the ignorant and helpless." Id. at § 141.

3. The case demonstrates the application of the general rule of Article 3186 of the Civil Code; a privilege allows its holder to be preferred even over a creditor holding a pre-existing mortgage.

* * * * * *

SUCCESSION OF HOLSTUN
141 So. 793 (La. App. 2d Cir. 1932)

McGREGOR, J.

This is a contest among the creditors of an insolvent succession over the proceeds of the sale of succession property, raised by oppositions to the account of the dative testamentary executor.

Miss Fay Holstun, a resident of Bienville parish, whose succession is involved herein, died testate in the city of Shreveport on June 25, 1930, and her will was probated by the judge of the Second district court two days thereafter. The heirs of the deceased were her mother, brothers and sisters, and nephews and nieces. In her will she bequeathed all of her property, both real and personal, to four of her nephews and nieces, and no objection was raised by any of the other heirs to this disposition of her property.

Soon after his appointment, the executor discovered that the succession was insolvent and that the property would be insufficient to pay the debts of the deceased. In due course of administration the property was all sold under orders of the court as the law directs, and the executor prepared and filed an account which included a tableau of the debts of the succession and asked for authority to pay them according to the rank he had assigned to each.

The oppositions of the two appellants are identical and present serious questions for determination. The items opposed are as follows:

> "a. Claim of Harry Holstun for expenses paid on account of last illness, with legal interest from demand, $406.30.
>
> b. Claim of Harry Holstun for expenses of tombstone for Fay Holstun, with interest, $103.53.
>
> c. Claim of Mrs. Ada H. Peyton, for expenses paid, with legal interest from demand, $164.85.

d. Claim of Frank C. Holstun, for expenses paid, with legal interest from demand, $32.55.

e. Claim of Mrs. Annie Lou Jones for expenses paid, with legal interest from demand, $69.30.

f. Claim of Telephone Company for bill made during last illness and death of Miss Fay Holstun, $18.00."

The last of the above items was very properly disapproved by the lower court as a privileged claim and was transferred to the list of ordinary claims. All the other items were approved by the court and recognized and ranked as privileged claims. It is from this decision that the two opponents have appealed.

The opponents object to the allowance of any of the above as privileged claims on the alleged ground that Harry Holstun, who paid them, was not formally subrogated to the rights of those to whom he paid the several amounts. It is true that subrogation is necessary in some instances where heirs, relatives, or strangers pay certain claims against the succession. For instance, the law provides that wages of servants and the salaries of secretaries, clerks, and other agents shall enjoy privileges. These naturally arise and accrue during the lifetime of those who owe them. It is clear that no one except those enumerated in article 2161 of the Civil Code would be subrogated to these privileges upon payment without a conventional subrogation. Counsel are laboring under a misapprehension of the real status of the various items. They represent expenses incurred by claimant, Harry Holstun, a brother of the deceased, on account of the last illness of his sister. It would be a narrow construction of the law, indeed, to hold that the sanitarium bill must be held in abeyance until the settlement of the estate of the deceased, on account of whom the bill was incurred, and that a brother or other close relative could not bear or incur that expense with assurance that he would have a privilege for the sum so expended, in case of death, unless he was formally subrogated to the rights of the sanitarium at the moment of payment. When Harry Holstun paid the first sanitarium bill of $33 for his sister, she was still alive and there may have been no thought or expectation of her ultimate death; but since he did pay the bill as and when he did, he is entitled to be reimbursed, as the sum so paid was a part of the expenses of her last illness. As a matter of fact, he, himself, incurred the expenses and furnished the services of the sanitarium to her. The same line of reasoning applies also to expenses incurred by Harry Holstun for the purchase of a shroud from Hearne Dry Goods Company, as well as to the expense of digging the grave and furnishing the casket. Therefore, the contention of the opponents that Harry Holstun is not entitled to have these various claims paid as privileged claims, on the ground that he has not been subrogated to the rights of those who received the money from him, is unsound.

Another objection urged against the items representing the sanitarium bills is that they were not recorded. In support of this contention, counsel cite Civil Code, art. 3274; *Succession of Elliott v. Elliott*, 31 La. Ann. 31; and *Succession of Rhoton*, 34 La. Ann. 893. Article 3274 of the Civil Code provides that:

> "No privilege shall have effect against third persons, unless recorded in the manner required by law in the parish where the property to be affected is situated."

Article 3276 of the Civil Code provides that:

> "The charges against a succession, such as funeral charges, law charges, lawyers' fees for settling the succession, the thousand dollars secured in certain cases to the widow or minor heirs of the deceased, and all claims against the succession originating after the death of the person whose succession is under administration, are to be paid before the debts contracted by the deceased person, except as otherwise provided for herein, and they are not required to be recorded."

These two articles, 3274 and 3276 of the Civil Code, are discussed in the case of the *Succession of Elliott v. Elliott*, 31 La. Ann. 31, and in ruling that physician's bills for service rendered during the last illness are not privileged unless recorded, the court said:

> "The accounts though large, are fully proven to be at customary rates. The Civil Code declares that no privilege shall have effect as against third persons unless duly recorded. Art. 3274, C. C.
>
> "However unreasonable this provision is when applied to cases like this, still it is the law, and is binding on this court. We know no law

> excepting or exempting such claims from the necessity of this registry. These claims can not be ranked therefore as privileged. We apprehend that claims which arise after the death of a party, and in the administration of his estate, and which the law classes as privileged, need not be recorded, since registry is without effect, after decease; and by giving the privilege under these circumstances the law manifestly intends to exempt them from registry. *See, also*, R. C. C., Art. 3276, so providing."

The case of *Succession of Elliott v. Elliott*, is cited with approval in *Succession of Rhoton*, 34 La. Ann. 893. So that, if articles 3274 and 3276 of the Civil Code, as interpreted in these two cases, were the latest expressions of the law on the subject, it would seem that counsel are right in contending that expenses of last illness are not privileged claims unless recorded. In spite of the interpretation of these two articles so as to require the recordation of claims for expenses of last illness to entitle them to the privilege accorded by law, there was a strong view to the contrary, that article 3276, under the proper interpretation, exempts these claims from recordation in that they are included in the term "charges against a succession," and that the reference to funeral charges, law charges, etc., is illustrative and not definitive. But be that as it may, in the Constitution of 1898 the matter was settled by the enactment of article 186, which reads as follows:

> "No mortgage or privilege on immovable property shall affect third persons, unless recorded or registered in the parish where the property is situated, in the manner and within the time as is now or may be prescribed by law, *except privileges for expenses of last illness* and privileges for taxes, State, parish, or municipal; provided, such tax liens, mortgages, and privileges, shall lapse in three years from the 31st day of December, in the year in which the taxes are levied, and whether now or hereafter recorded." (Italics ours.)

In interpreting this clause of the Constitution, this court, in the case of *Dinnat v. Succession of B. T. Lewis*, 8 La. App. 820, has held specially that sanitarium and hospital bills are properly classified as expenses of last illness. This same article is cited in the case of *Bauman v. Armbruster*, 129 La. 191, 55 So. 760, 761, to the effect that expenses of last illness are not now required to be recorded in order to be ranked as privileged claims.

> "Funeral charges rank *first* among the general privileges on movables. Civ. Code, art. 3252. If the movables are insufficient, such charges ought to be paid out of the product of the immovables belonging to the debtor in preference to all other privileged and mortgage creditors. Civ. Code, art. 3289. Funeral charges and other claims originating after the death of the *de cujus* are not required to be recorded. Civ. Code, art. 3276. Article 186 of the Constitution of 1898, in declaring that no mortgage or privilege on immovable property shall affect third persons unless duly recorded, simply repeats the provisions of the Civil Code, and adds to the list of exceptions contained in article 3276 privileges for 'expenses of last illness' and privileges 'for taxes.' In other words, article 186 of the Constitution places such privileges on the same plane as claims originating *after the death* of the *de cujus*, which the Civil Code has never required to be recorded, "since registry is without effect, after decease." *Succession of Elliott v. Elliott*, 31 La. Ann. 37."

This same provision is found in the Constitution of 1921, in article 19, § 19, which reads as follows:

> "No mortgage or privilege on immovable property, or debt for which preference may be granted by law, shall affect third persons unless recorded or registered in the parish where the property is situated, in the manner and within the time prescribed by law, *except privileges for expenses of last illness, privileges arising upon the death of the owner of the property affected,* and privileges for taxes, State, parish and municipal; provided such tax liens, mortgages and privileges shall lapse in three years from the 31st day of December, in the year in which the taxes are levied, and whether now or hereafter recorded.
>
> "Privileges on movable property shall exist without registration of same except in such cases as may be prescribed by law." (Italics ours.)

So that, under the law as it now stands, bills incurred for expenses of last illness, such as hospital and sanitarium bills, are not required to be recorded in order to be ranked as privileged claims. Therefore the opposition to those items on the account which represent expenses incurred for sanitarium bills are without merit.

Another objection raised to the claim of Harry Holstun for the burial expenses is that, since the succession is insolvent, $200 is the maximum amount allowable on account of funeral charges. This is a valid and legal objection, and the opposition must be sustained to that extent. Civ. Code, arts. 3193, 3194.

The last item on the account that is opposed is the claim of Harry Holstun for $102.75, the price of a monument erected over the grave of deceased. There is no law or jurisprudence allowing a claim of this nature against an insolvent estate, either as a privileged or an ordinary claim, so this opposition to the allowance thereof is valid and must be sustained.

* * * * * *

NOTES AND QUESTIONS

1. Those providing funeral or mortuary services rarely rely today on the general privilege for funeral charges. What do you feel is the reason for this? Does the privilege nonetheless still have utility as protection for heirs or others who pay the decedent's funeral expenses?

2. The case observes that both the Civil Code and Article XIX, Section 19 of the 1921 Constitution excuse the privilege for funeral charges from recordation requirements, even insofar as it affects immovables. The latter provision continues in force today in the Constitution Ancillaries. What if the funeral charges were incurred not for the owner himself but instead for a family member, as in *Alter v. O'Brien*? If the owner is still living at the time funeral charges for a family member are incurred, would these provisions nonetheless excuse recordation?

3. In *Succession of Foulkes*, 12 La. Ann. 537 (1857), the court implicitly held that the reduction of the privilege for funeral charges to the maximum amount permitted by the Civil Code must be affirmatively requested, and the court cannot make the reduction in the absence of a request.

2. For Law Charges

* * * * * *

2 TRAITE ÉLEMENTAIRE DE DROIT CIVIL, PT. 2
(La. State Law Inst. trans., 1959) (12th ed. 1939) (Fr.)
MARCEL PLANIOL & GEORGES RIPERT

2552. Principle

When the expenses were made to liquidate (transform into money) the property of the debtor, these expenses should be levied on the sums thus obtained; the law declares them privileged (Art. 2101 par. 1).

These expenses are not always judicially incurred; they include also a certain number of extrajudicial expenses, such as expenses of seals and inventory.

On the other hand, there are privileged in this title not only the expenses incurred for liquidating the property of the debtor and for distributing the price to his creditors, but also those made to preserve or to recover certain property in the interest of creditors: such are the expenses of a revocatory action (Art. 1167), those of a revendication exercised against a third person on behalf of the debtor (Art. 1166), or expenses or a sequestration. (Cass. Civ., 27 Nov. 1912, D.1913.1.96, P. and S. 1913.1.89).

2553. Restriction

If the law charges are privileged, it is because they are useful to the creditors. This reason has brought about a restriction of the privilege in certain cases: if there is a creditor for whom the expenses claimed were not useful, they are not privileged against him. That happens in the case of the lessor with regard to the procedure for ratable distribution; the lessor has the right to have his privilege determined by a referee without waiting for the accomplishment of this procedure (Art. 661 C. Proc. Civ.); the expenses of the distribution are therefore not made in his interest, and his credit is not primed by them; these expenses are paid, says the law, before any credit "other than those for rent due to the lessor" (Art. 662 C. Proc. Civ.).

This rule should apply not only to the expenses of distribution (of which the law speaks), but for an even stronger reason, to the expenses of bankruptcy or of judiciary liquidation made in the interest of the mass of the creditors (Alger, 23 Feb. 1893, D.94.2.542, S.93.2.175). The lessor suffers only the taking of those expenses which were useful to him, such as those of seals and of inventory (Paris, 27 March 1824, Dalloz, Répert., Vo. *Privilèges* and *hypothèques*, No. 169, S.25.2.193. Comp. Riom, 24 Aug. 1863, D.63.2.161.

2623. Generality of the Rule

In every case where expenses are necessary to transform into money the assets of the debtor, their amount should first be subtracted from the price obtained, before any creditor is paid, whether he be a privileged or a mortgage creditor.

2624. Character of this Priority

Everyone recognizes this priority of law charges; but what they ordinarily do not see is that it is not the effect of a privilege. When one speaks of privilege, one necessarily speaks of a conflict between the creditors of the same debtor; law charges are not a debt of the person whose property has been sold. They are due by the pursuing creditors. It is the creditors who have caused these expenses and who are debtors for them; the deduction to which they agree is only a convenient way to pay for them; but if the expenses exceed the amount obtained by the pursuits, they are personally responsible for them.

The Roman jurisconsults were not deceived about this, and they never classed judicial expenses among the privileged credits, even though these expenses were certainly paid first. There had to be weakening of the juridical mind in the Middle Ages in order to classify this deduction as a right of the same nature as the privileges.

* * * * * *

ROUSSEAU

v.

CREDITORS

17 La. 206 (1841)

Appeal from the court of the first judicial district.

This case arises on an opposition made by Guiseppe Giordano, to the homologation of the tableau of distribution filed by the syndic of the creditors in this case.

The opponent alleges that besides his mortgage claim, he is a privileged creditor of the insolvent's estate in the sum of $55.62, for clerk's and sheriff's fees, by him advanced in a certain suit in which he had judgment for costs against said insolvent. He prays that the tableau be so amended as to allow this sum as a privilege debt, and also for some other claims.

The district judge in rendering judgment stated the case thus: "The question presented for consideration in this case is, whether the privilege granted to law charges by the Code extends to all cases, which the insolvent may have been condemned to pay in the various suits against him previous to his failure; or whether such privilege be confined to the costs incurred in the *concurso.*" There was judgment denying this as a privilege claim, and overruling the opposition. The opposing creditor appealed.

Simon, J. delivered the opinion of the court.

The only question submitted to our consideration in this case, is whether under the Louisiana Code, the privilege granted to law charges ought to be extended to such costs as may have been occasioned by the prosecution of suits against an insolvent debtor previous to his failure? or whether such privilege ought to be limited to the costs incurred in the *concurso*, and for the benefit of the mass of creditors?

Under the Old Civil Code, as early as 1812, the jurisprudence of this court had repeatedly recognized that the *law charges* contemplated by the art. 73, page 468, were *taxed costs*. 2 Martin, 264; 5 Id. 468; that general professional services rendered by an attorney were no part of the privileged *law charges* or *taxed costs*. 2 Id. 242; 3 Id. 282. And in the case of *Turpin v. His Creditors*, 7 Id. 54, it was held again that the costs of suits against an insolvent, previous to his failure, were privileged on his estate. The point was thus so well settled that it had become a well known rule, under the old Code, that taxed costs of every kind were entitled to the privilege allowed under the denomination of *law charges*.

The Louisiana Code has re-enacted the same provisions with regard to *law charges*, arts. 3158 and 3219; and were these articles to be made exclusively the subject of this investigation, there would be no difficulty in maintaining our former jurisprudence. But it is contended by the counsel for the appellee that our law on this subject has undergone very material changes and modifications by the enactment of the articles 3162, 3163, 3164, and 3165, contained in the section 2, under the head of law charges; and that the general interpretation heretofore given by this court to the art. 73, p. 468, of the Old Code, and the construction of the arts. 3162 and 3163, are now restrained by the art. 3164, from which it is evident that the privilege in cases of insolvency ought to be allowed to those costs only which are incurred for the general benefit of the creditors. The art. 3162 is in these words: "Law charges are such as are occasioned by the prosecution of a suit before the court. But this name applies more particularly to the costs, which the party cast has to pay to the party gaining the cause. It is in favor of these only that the law grants the privilege." This, in our opinion, gives a clear definition of what the law means by "*law charges,*" and indicates the extent of the privilege by which their recovery is secured. The art. 3163 explains how and to what extent the privilege is to be enjoyed, and limits it to such costs as are taxed according to law, and such as arise from the execution of the judgment. So far, these new laws agree with our former jurisprudence, and would be rather considered as confirmatory of the repeated decisions of this court, unless modified or further restrained by the subsequent articles. The art. 3164, relied on by the appellee, is as follows: "The costs for affixing seals and making inventories for the better preservation of the debtor's property; those which occur in cases of failure or cession of property for the general benefit of creditors, such as fees to lawyers, appointed by the court to represent absent creditors, commissions to syndics; and finally, costs incurred for the administration of estates, which are either vacant or belonging to absent heirs, enjoy the privileges established in favor of law charges." And it is urged that this last article shows the restricted sense of the privilege granted by the preceding ones. We think differently; it seems to us that this art. 3164, far from restricting the privilege, has been passed for the purpose of extending it to such claims as would not be comprised in the general definition of law charges given by the art. 3162, as most of those claims have nothing to do with the prosecution of suits before the courts, and relate more particularly to the costs incurred in such estates as are administered for the benefit of a *concurso* of creditors. This art. does not say that the costs therein mentioned shall be *the only costs* entitled to enjoy the right of privilege established in favor of *law charges* or *judicial expenses*, and in our opinion it would be absurd to give it such construction as to defeat the right recognized by the provisions contained in the two previous articles. Besides, this is also sufficiently explained by the art. 3165, from which it is clear, under the well known rule *"exclusio unius est inclusio alterius,"* that the creditor is entitled to enjoy the privilege, when the costs which he claims are *taxed costs*, or *are included* among those mentioned in the preceding articles.

It is therefore ordered, adjudged and decreed, that the judgment of the district court be annulled, avoided and reversed, that the opposition filed by G. Giordano to the tableau of distribution filed by the syndic be maintained, so far as he claims to be placed on the said tableau as a privileged creditor for the *taxed costs* therein mentioned, and that the said tableau be amended accordingly, the costs in both courts to be borne by the insolvent estate.

* * * * * *

NOTES AND QUESTIONS

1. *Friend v. Graham's Administrator*, 10 La. 438 (1836) held that debts of a succession are of a higher dignity than, and are to be paid before, those of the decedent. Thus, the fees of an attorney employed by the heirs to remove a purported curator of the estate inured to the benefit of the entire succession, including both the creditors and the heirs, and it was proper to charge the fees of the attorney against the succession, although the services were rendered at the request of some of the heirs.

2. In *Succession of Lauve*, 18 La. Ann. 721 (1866), the administrator of a succession proposed to deduct succession charges from funds realized from the sale of certain immovable property subject to a vendor's privilege and certain

other immovable property subject to a special mortgage. Citing *Friend v. Graham's Administrator*, the court observed that succession charges inuring to the benefit of all parties concerned are of higher dignity than, and except in exceptional cases are to be paid before, those of the deceased. The court apparently held, however, that Art. 3234 of the 1825 Civil Code (Art. 3267 of the 1870 Civil Code) is an exception to this rule, and the holder of the vendor's privilege could therefore not be charged with general privileges or succession charges. The mortgage creditor, on the other hand, was required to bear the general privileges and succession charges from the proceeds of the sale of his mortgaged property.

3. *Succession of Wells*, 24 La. Ann. 162 (La. 1872) involved the issue of whether an executor's commission and attorney's fees paid to an attorney to protect the rights of the succession in various suits were privileged claims. One of the creditors opposed the claim of privilege, contending that the attorney's fees did not inure to the benefit of all parties in interest and that the attorney's services certainly did not inure to the benefit of the objecting creditor, since most of the litigation had been carried on against him. Nonetheless, the court held that all persons interested in a succession are benefitted by legal services in defending the rights of successions, inasmuch as there can be no settlement of the succession until all contests relative to debts claimed against the successions or to the rights of the succession to property have been determined. The fees of attorneys for services of this nature and the commissions of the executor are debts of the succession and, being of a higher dignity than the debts of the deceased, must be paid by preference.

4. As security for their professional fees, the law now provides a special privilege in favor of attorneys on "all judgments obtained by them, and on the property recovered thereby." La. R.S. 9:5001. The statute affords this special privilege priority over all other privileges and over all Chapter 9 security interests.

3. For Expenses of the Last Illness

* * * * * *

2 Traite Élementaire de Droit Civil, pt. 2
(La. State Law Inst. trans., 1959) (12th ed. 1939) (Fr.)
Marcel Planiol & Georges Ripert

2557. Origin of the Privilege

This privilege did not exist in Roman law. It arose from a false interpretation given by the commentators to two Roman laws (Code, Bk. III, tit. 31, law 4; tit. 44, law 3), which do not accord a privilege, but simply an action in repetition to the heir when it is he who has paid from his own pocket the expenses of the sickness of the decedent. Domat does not speak of this privilege; Pothier considers it as a simple application of the privilege of funeral expenses (*Procédure civile,* No. 481). The origin of this privilege tells us the value to be accorded to the affirmations of modern authors who declare that this privilege was instituted by an idea of humanity.

2558. Definition of the Last Malady

Under the Code, what should be understood by "last sickness"? Is it the last in date, the most recent, that which preceded the bankruptcy or the insolvency of the debtor or the last in his life, that which preceded the death? According to tradition and the whole of the texts, there is no doubt about this last conclusion: the last sickness for which the privilege is accorded is the one from which the debtor died (Cass., 21 Nov. 1864, D.64.1.457, S.65.1.25; Cass., 27 June 1892, D.92.1.376, S.92.1.360). But that did not suit the doctors who wished to enjoy the same privilege when the debtor, still living, became insolvent, and they attacked the law by raillery: "Isn't it ridiculous, they said, when the maladroit doctor, who loses his patient is privileged while the good doctor, who saves his life, is recompensed by the suppression of the privilege?" The doctors succeeded in obtaining from the Chambers a law which conceded them a whole series of favors. This law (30 November 1892) by its Art. 12 modified Art. 2101(3), by adding to the words "expenses of the last sickness" the words: "whatever may have been its termination" which decided the question in a sense contrary to the former jurisprudence.

* * * * * *

SUCCESSION OF WHITAKER
7 Rob. 91 (La. 1844)

MARTIN, J.

The appellant complains of a judgment which allows his claim for medical services to the testator, but denies any privilege therefor, the court being of opinion, that the testator died in consequence of having been shot; while the appellant contends, that he died of the sickness during which he was attended by him; and this is the only question which the case presents for our solution. The testimony shows, that the testator's disease was such, that the appellant's services could only tend to the mitigation of his sufferings, but could not have prevented a fatal termination. It appears, that the wound which he received from a pistol shot was the immediate cause of his death.

The Civil Code, art. 3158, gives a privilege for all charges of whatever nature, occasioned by the last sickness. If the Code contained no explanation of this article, there is no doubt the appellant would be entitled to the privilege; but art. 3166, informs us, that "the last sickness is considered to be that of which the debtor died." It is, therefore, clear, that the physician has no privilege on the estate of a testator who did not die from sickness; and the appellant's counsel, in his brief, tells us, that *"he was shot dead by some unseen and unknown hand."*

The Judge of Probates did not err.
Judgment affirmed.

* * * * * *

NOTES AND QUESTIONS

1. Considering the text of Civil Code Articles 3190-3201, is there room to argue that "the last sickness" means the debtor's most recent sickness, even if it does not result in his death?

2. Suppose that the pistol shot, rather than being delivered by "some unseen and unknown hand," was instead fired by the patient who, out of

despondency over a terminal illness, took his own life. Could it then be said the terminal illness was the patient's "last sickness"?

3. Considering that the purpose of the privilege is to allow the debtor to obtain medical treatment that might not otherwise be available to him, does it make good policy sense for the privilege to be lost by the fortuity of death from an unforeseen intervening cause?

4. By an express provision in Civil Code Article 3204, the privilege also exists for the expenses of the last sickness of the debtor's children.

5. *Succession of Elliott v. Elliott*, 31 La. Ann. 31 (La. 1879) held that the privilege for the expenses of the last illness was subject to the requirement of recordation despite the fact that, in cases where it was the debtor himself who died, the expenses of the last illness constitute "claims against the succession originating after the death of the person whose succession is under administration" exempted from recordation by Civil Code Article 3276. Albeit in dicta, *Succession of Holstun,* supra, found that Article XIX, Section 19 of the Constitution of 1921 (now the Constitution Ancillaries) specifically exempts privileges for expenses of the last illness from the requirement of recordation.

* * * * * *

PELICAN STATE ASSOCIATES, INC.

v.

WINDER

219 So. 2d 500 (La. 1969)

FOURNET, Chief Justice.

This case is now before us on a writ of certiorari granted in accordance with Article 7, Section 11 of the Louisiana Constitution of 1921, 252 La. 178, 210 So. 2d 56, on the application of Pelican State Associates, Inc., pointing out that the judgment of the Court of Appeal for the First Circuit, in direct conflict with the decision of the Second Circuit in the case of *Dinnat v. Succession of Lewis*, 8 La. App. 820, reversed the judgment of the lower court that recognized the expenses incurred by the decedent in the month preceding his death while in Our Lady of the Lake Hospital to be expenses of last illness and as such, a privileged debt against the property of the estate removed from the category of ordinary debts subject to the prescription of LSA-Civil Code Article 3538. La. App., 208 So. 2d 355.

The facts of this case are not in dispute and are as stated by the Court of Appeal, to-wit: "Decedent, John Robinson, died in Our Lady of the Lake Hospital on June 11, 1952, having been admitted to the hospital about one month prior to that date. At the time of his demise, decedent's account with the hospital amounted to $1,034.26, and consisted of charges for room and board, x-ray and laboratory services, drugs, dressings, oxygen, blood typing and transfusion charges. His succession was opened on June 23, 1952, and the executor qualified in April, 1958. On January 11, 1961, decedent's account was assigned to plaintiff and this action was instituted against the succession the next day, or about eight and one-half years after Robinson's demise. The executor filed a general denial to the plaintiff's petition." The sole heir and legatee, Joyce Fay Robinson Brewer, intervened pleading the prescription of three years under Civil Code Article 3538, which was overruled by the trial judge; and, after trial on the merits judgment was rendered in favor of plaintiff as prayed for.

It is apt to observe that the privilege accorded for expenses incurred during the last sickness of the deceased is especially recognized and granted on movables of the estate (LSA-Civil Code 3191), as well as on both movable and immovables. (LSA-Civil Code 3252), "The last sickness is considered to be that of which the debtor died; . . ." LSA-Civil Code 3199; and "The expenses of the last sickness comprehend the fees of physicians and surgeons, the wages of nurses, and the price due the apothecary for medicines supplied by him to the deceased for his personal use during his last illness." LSA-Civil Code 3202.

In resolving the identical issue presented for our consideration, i.e., that expenses incurred in a hospital for the last illness of the deceased not being specifically enumerated in article 3202 as an expense of last illness, is not within the scope of the definition and is, therefore, not a privileged claim under articles 3191 and 3252, the Court of Appeal for the Second Circuit in *Dinnat v. Succession of Lewis*, supra, held, "In our opinion Article 3202 is not definitive but illustrative. This is shown, we think, in the use of the word 'comprehend,' which is used as the equivalent of 'such as,' and these latter words, when used to give some example of a rule, are never exclusive of other cases which that rule is made to embrace,' pointing out, 'The Standard Dictionary gives as a definition of 'comprehend,' 'to include; comprise; enclose; encompass.' Webster defines it as 'to contain; to embrace; to include.' 'To take in or include; to take in by construction or implication; to comprise; to imply'."

The Court of Appeal in reversing the judgment of the district court refused to follow the decision of the Second Circuit in the case of *Dinnat v. Succession of Lewis*, supra, holding, "The debt sought to be recognized herein as a privileged expense of the last illness cannot be so recognized because it is not included by positive and unequivocal statement in the definition of these expenses as expounded by Article 3202, . . . " and, therefore, found it was not necessary to decide whether such bills are exempt from liberative force of Article 3538 as held by the lower court, but concluded the debt was prescribed as "on all other accounts" under article 3538 inasmuch as more than three years had elapsed from the death of John Robinson and the filing of this suit.

While we agree with the conclusion of the court of appeal that plaintiff's claim is prescribed, for reasons hereinafter stated, we cannot agree with its conclusion that the claim under consideration here is not an expense of last illness.

We are in full accord with the view expressed in the opinion of the Court of Appeal that a privilege, being an extraordinary preference granted in derogation of rights common to all, is subject to the rule of *stricti juris* and that articles 3191, 3252 and all other related articles must be considered *in pari materia* in determining the scope of the privilege.

We think when reading all the pertinent articles above referred to it is clear that the redactors of our code intended to encompass and to include any necessary expense incurred during the last illness of decedent to be privileged debts subject only to specific limitations therein. See LSA-Civil Code Articles 3200, 3201. We, therefore, agree with the conclusion of the Second Circuit Court of Appeal in the Dinnat case that "article 3202 is not definitive but illustrative." We are supported in this conclusion by the unequivocal language in article 3191 which provides as one of the privileged debts on movables, "charges, *of whatever nature*, occasioned by the last sickness." (Emphasis added.)

The foregoing is not only consonant with the very words of article 3202 as demonstrated in the *Dinnat* case but is also in keeping with conditions of he times. The existence of hospitals as we know them today were few, if any, at the time of the adoption of our code. It is not strange therefore that it was omitted in the illustrative list comprehended as those of last illness. In other words, it is clear the redactors of our code did not intend to so limit the scope of the term "expenses of last illness" as to include only those listed in article 3202, but rather as pointed out hereinabove when considered in the light of the several pertinent articles it was intended to encompass and include any expense incurred during the last illness of the decedent except where specifically limited. It, therefore, follows that whatever charges may come about in this vast and complex cycle of our modern civilization and all its progressive ramparts in treating of the sick, it will be included within the privilege provided for as expenses of last illness. In fact, in this day and modern time we can think of no more logical service to be utilized for treating of the last illness than the hospitals with the most modern and scientific equipment and where treatment that is needed is furnished by our leading technicians, surgeons and nurses as well as other services as x-rays, laboratory tests, oxygen, blood typing which are performed by either the physicians, nurses or their staff. Our redactors would have been short sighted indeed if they had failed to envision this progress for the future.

This brings up for consideration whether this claim is prescribed under LSA-Civil Code Article 3538 as urged in intervenor's plea of prescription.

Counsel for plaintiff contends that the redactors of our Civil Code, while creating the privilege on the estate of the deceased for expenses of last illness, created in the same article other privileges to be paid in the order specified therein, but in establishing a prescriptive period for certain expenses and charges that are encompassed in the last illness they did not specifically prescribe a period for the expenses of last illness as a whole. However, counsel claims the courts have supplied the jurisprudence which governs the subject, i.e., holding that such expenses are a privileged charge against the estate and so long as the estate is not settled, the heirs hold the property subject to such charge.

While it is true that expenses of last illness are not listed as one of those actions that are barred by the prescription of three years under article 3538, a mere reading of the article will readily disclose that the redactors of our code in preparing a draft thereof and our law makers in adopting the same, while specifically listing certain actions, in their wisdom provided for a general cause to cover all such actions "on all other accounts" which encompasses the claim under consideration here. Consequently, by the extinction of the debt by prescription, the privilege, as an accessory thereto, becomes extinct also. LSA-Civil Code Article 3277.

* * * * * *

NOTES AND QUESTIONS

1. The listing of privileged expenses in Civil Code Article 3202 appears narrow indeed, particularly when viewed in light of the varied charges that can arise from modern medical treatment. On the issue of the scope of expenses of the last illness that are secured by the privilege, Professor Daggett was of the view that "one would hardly think that the framers of the Code intended to cramp the future resources of medical science by the enumeration of items in Art. 3202." Daggett, *Louisiana Privileges and Chattel Mortgage* § 140, at pp. 547-48 (1942). As the case demonstrates, she was ultimately proved to be correct.

2. Louisiana law now provides a health care provider, hospital, or ambulance service a special privilege upon the net amount payable to an injured person, whether by judgment or settlement, from another person on account of his injuries. This privilege, which is subordinate to that of the attorney under La. R.S. 9:5001, secures the reasonable charges of the privilege holder and, unlike the general privilege provided by the Civil Code, is not limited to expenses of the last illness. *See* La. R.S. 9:4751 *et seq.*

* * * * * *

SUCCESSION OF BARRY
236 So. 2d 660 (La. App. 4th Cir. 1970)

BARNETTE, Judge.

Dr. Robert A. Robinson, a physician, has appealed the second time from a judgment dismissing his opposition to the account and tableau of distribution filed by the testamentary executrix of the Succession of Denis A. Barry. The opponent, appellant, is seeking recovery of the sum of $4,640 alleged due him for professional services rendered the deceased from May 18, 1960, to date of his death, December 8, 1963. The executrix's tableau of distribution filed April 2, 1965, did not include Dr. Robinson's claim. He filed an opposition on April 13, seeking to have his claim included for payment. The first dismissal of his opposition was appealed, and we reversed and remanded. *See Succession of Barry*, 185 So. 2d 53 (La. App. 1966). Pursuant to our order of remand the opposition was again heard by the trial court and was again dismissed. The present appeal is from that second judgment of dismissal.

We have examined the memoranda proffered in evidence and find that none of the charges for services allegedly rendered the decedent meet the requirements of LSA-C.C. arts. 3199 and 3200 to come within the privilege of expenses of last illness. Those articles are as follows:

Art. 3199.

> "The last sickness is considered to be that of which the debtor died; the expenses of this sickness enjoy the privilege."

Art. 3200.

> "'But if the sickness with which the deceased was attacked and of which he died, was a chronic disease, the progress of which was slow and which only occasioned death after a long while, then the privilege shall only commence from the time when the malady became so serious as to prevent the deceased from attending to his business and confined him to his bed or chamber."

It is apparent that the decedent had a heart condition of long standing and also complications involving the liver and spleen. There is also a notation in the proffered memoranda of rectal hemorrhage and one of oral surgery. Treatments for these alleged conditions run from May 16, 1960, to December 4, 1963, and cover hospital and office visits, house calls and treatments away from home while on trips. The final entry is: "Dec. 8, 1963 Passed suddenly while sitting in back seat of car in yard." From this review we must conclude that the decedent's death followed at least three years of chronic illness and there is no proof that "the malady became so serious as to prevent the deceased from attending to his business and confined him to his bed or chamber." LSA-C.C. art. 3200. The proffered evidence is to the contrary. Even assuming arguendo that the parol evidence proffered should have been admitted, it would fall short of proof (1) that the illness for which Dr. Robinson treated the decedent was the illness of which he died, LSA-C.C. art. 3199; and (2) it fails to meet the test of LSA-C .C. art. 3200.

In *Pelican State Associates, Inc. v. Winder*, [219 So. 2d 500 (1969)] the Supreme Court held that LSA-C.C. arts. 3200 and 3201 and related articles must not be given such a narrow and strict interpretation as to exclude any necessary expense incurred during the last illness. It recognized the vast changes which have taken place in modern times in the treatment of the sick and held that hospital expenses in connection with the last illness are embraced within the privilege. There is no conflict in our conclusion with this rationale.

The foregoing provisions of the Civil Code contemplate that a person who is not prevented because of the seriousness and confining nature of his illness from attending to his own business may be held personally accountable. This intention is reflected again in the next article which refers to sickness which "prevented him from attending to his affairs," and in any event the privilege can extend no more than one year before the decedent's death. LSA-C.C. art. 3201. It is only after he has reached the point of inability to attend to his business that the physician and others rendering service in his last illness are given the special privilege against his estate. Humanitarian considerations underlie the granting of this privilege of high rank in favor of those to whom claims are due for services rendered in time of need. In the event of death the physician and others rendering those services are assured that their charges will not be treated as ordinary debts with less favorable chance of payment. This obvious intent is to make it less likely that one will be deprived of much needed service because of doubtful means of payment.

Plaintiff's claim is for services extending back more than three years during all of which time the decedent was capable of attending to his business. The expense incurred for medical treatment was a personal debt as distinguished from a charge against decedent's estate.

The judgment appealed is affirmed at appellant's cost.

Affirmed.

* * * * * *

NOTES AND QUESTIONS

1. The preceding two cases demonstrate the very limited reach of the privilege for expenses of the last illness. As the excerpt from the writings of Planiol above recites, Article 2101 of the Code Napoléon, from which Article 3191 of the Louisiana Civil Code of 1870 was borrowed, was amended in 1892 to allow a privilege for expenses of the last illness, whatever its outcome (See now Article 2331 of the French Civil Code).

4. For the Surviving Spouse and Minor Children

The privilege of the needy surviving spouse is sometimes known as the "widow's homestead" because the original purpose of the privilege, as stated in the title of the 1852 legislation creating it, was to provide a homestead for the widow and children of deceased persons. However, the text of the statute did not tie the privilege in any manner to a homestead, thus leading to an unsuccessful constitutional challenge that the statute differed from its title. *See Succession of Lanzetti*, 9 La. Ann. 329 (1854). The privilege still exists today in Article 3252 of the Civil Code but is of little utility, in view of its limitation to only one thousand dollars. It remains of continued interest chiefly because the provisions of that article and of Article 3254 subordinating it to vendor's privileges while making it superior to all other debts has created numerous vicious circles of priority, which are discussed in the next chapter.

One of the most significant cases to discuss the privilege of the surviving spouse in modern times is *Washington v. Washington*, 127 So. 2d 491 (1960), which rejected a claim that the privilege was lost after the widow failed to file a timely suit for separation of patrimonies. That decision, which also touched upon important issues involving the nature of privileges as real rights and the exceptions to the recordation requirement that generally applies to privileges on immovables, will be considered in the section of this chapter on privileges to effect separation of patrimonies.

* * * * * *

SUCCESSION OF WHITE
29 La. Ann. 702 (1877)

J. G. White died in Bossier parish in July 1876. His widow was appointed administratrix of his succession, and the property was sold by her under an order of the parish court for the payment of debts. The sales were made in December of same year, and about the time of the last sale, the widow removed to Texas, and has not returned.

On March 2d 1877, a tableau was filed for her, ranking the debts of the deceased, and of the succession, upon which her widow's claim of one thousand dollars is placed. Lane, an acknowledged creditor, opposes it. The succession is confessedly insolvent.

There is no doubt that the widow was in necessitous circumstances at, and after her husband's death, and at the time of filing the tableau. The opponent insists upon the authority of *McCoy's* case, (26 Annual 686.) that the condition of the widow at the time the claim is made must determine her right. This is in direct conflict with the dictum of *Gimble v. Goode*, (13 Annual 352); also *Suc. Marx*, (27 Annual 99.) that the right of the widow and of the minor children of a decedent to the portion secured to them under the act of 1852, vests in them at the moment of the death of the deceased, and their condition then, and not at any subsequent time, is the test of the rightfulness of their claim. We think this is the sounder doctrine, and is more in harmony with the manifest intent of the act, which was to ward off from the widow and young children of one recently dead, the misery of unmitigated destitution, and to cover, as with a shield, these helpless mourners from the pitiless shafts of poverty, at the moment when the protecting arm of the husband and father was made powerless by death.

It is also contended by opponent that whatever may be the time that controls the right of the necessitous widow, if she does not reside in this State at the time her portion is formally demanded, she will not be entitled to receive it. On the other hand we are referred to a reported case, *Suc. of Christe*, (20 Annual 383.) wherein it was ruled that a surviving necessitous widow, who had never been in the State, was entitled to the benefit of the act of 1852, a dictum we do not approve.

As the right of Mrs. White accrued at the moment of her husband's death, her subsequent removal from the State did not annihilate it. She was a resident of Louisiana during the coverture, and at its termination, and may well be considered as falling within the designation of "its own widows," used in *Stewart's* case (12 Annual 89.) when applying a different principle.

The opponent argues that as the widow in this case has only the usufruct, if she is permitted to take the money out of the State, the minor children may be deprived of the benefit which the act secures to them. To this suggestion it may be answered, 1. that it does not concern the creditor what becomes of the money if it be once ascertained and determined that it does not belong to the fund which he can make available to the payment of his debt. And 2. we have no power to compel the widow to give security for the production of the money at her death. She is the mother of the minors and hence their natural tutrix.

The legislature has not thought proper to protect the interests of the minor further than they are in the Act which created this special provision for them, although twenty-five years of experience under it must have presented cases not unlike the present, and it is not for us to supply any omission which may be discovered in practically applying it.

Judgment affirmed.

* * * * * *

NOTES AND QUESTIONS

1. *Succession of Marc*, 29 La. Ann. 412 (1877), which is reproduced in the following chapter, held that the privilege of the surviving spouse exists in favor of a former concubine who married the decedent only twelve days before his death. *Veillon v. LaFleur's Estate*, 110 So. 326 (La. 1926), and *Gee v. Thompson*, 11 La. Ann. 657 (1856), held that a widow is entitled to claim the privilege even

after a legal separation, and regardless of her faithfulness to her husband. The privilege is not lost even on account of her living with another man at the time of her husband's death. *Danna v. Danna*, 161 So. 348 (La. App. 1st Cir. 1935).

2. The fact that the widow is able to work, and actually resumes work shortly after the death of her husband, does not rob the widow of her privilege, for to hold otherwise "would place a premium upon shiftlessness." *Succession of Kuntz*, 179 So. 623 (La. App. Orl. Cir. 1938).

3. *In the matter of Succession of Geisler*, 32 La. Ann. 1289 (1880), held that the privilege may be claimed only against the succession of the deceased father, not the succession of the deceased mother. A century later, this holding was legislatively overruled by Act 711 of 1979, which changed the word "widow" in Civil Code articles 3252 and 3254 to "surviving spouse" and the words "the deceased husband or father" to "the deceased spouse or parent."

4. *Stewart v. Stewart*, 13 La. Ann. 398 (1858), held that, in cases where the surviving spouse or minor children, individually or collectively, own more than $1,000 in assets, the privilege is unavailable. Moreover, the privilege is not necessarily a full $1,000 but only the difference between $1,000 and the amount of the assets held by the surviving spouse and minor children. When this limitation is viewed in the context of present day reality, the privilege seems both anachronistic and in consequential.

5. Civil Code Art. 3276 expressly exempts the privilege of the surviving spouse from recordation requirements. Article XIX, Section 19 of the Constitution Ancillaries does as well, since the privilege is one that arises "upon the death of the owner of the property affected."

* * * * * *

SUCCESSION OF VIVES
35 La. Ann. 371 (1883)

The facts are these:

Adolph Vives died in 1870 and his wife, Eleanor Hébert, in 1871. Emile Poché, administrator of their successions, filed his final account of his administration. In this account, after paying certain privilege debts, he proposed to turn over the balance to the heirs of the deceased.

These heirs were all majors, except the three children of Cecelia Vives, who died before her parents.

In the proposed distribution, the minors were to receive one-fourth of the estate, the share of their deceased mother, and the three major heirs each a like portion.

The administrator, in proposing this distribution, proceeded on the hypothesis that the widow of Adolphe Vives, Eleanor Hébert, being in necessitous circumstances at the death of her husband, became entitled to one thousand dollars from his estate, and which sum became hers absolutely, and on her death was transmitted by inheritance to her heirs, majors and minors alike.

The account was opposed by the creditors, on the ground that the heirs of Eleanor Hébert—neither the major nor minor heirs—were entitled to any part of said sum. That the same had never come into the possession of the necessitous widow, and if it had, that she would have possessed only as usufructuary, and at her death it would not descend to her children who survived her, because they were all of age, and her grandchildren, though minors, were not entitled under the law to receive the same.

The Act of 1852, after providing that the widow or minor children of a deceased person left in necessitous circumstances may claim from his estate $1,000, further declares in these words:

> "The surviving widow shall have and enjoy the usufruct of the money so received from her husband's succession during her widowhood, afterwards to vest in and belong to the children or *other descendants* of said deceased."

The case of the succession of John Durkin, reported in 30 An. 669, was quite similar to the instant one. There the father and husband died. The widow survived him but a short time, without receiving or claiming the portion of the estate reserved to her as widow in necessitous circumstances. Upon her death it was claimed by her children of age. Their claim thereto was rejected. In the opinion therein delivered, Chief Justice Manning being the organ of the Court, referring to this Act of 1852, uses the following language:

> "The 'children,' meant throughout the Act, are those descriptively mentioned in the first clause as 'minor children' of a deceased person, for whose benefit alone the bounty provided by the Act was intended. Of course, we understand the word 'children' here as having the largest import, and as including grandchildren and other descendants."

Considering that the statute provides, in so many words, that upon the death of the widow and usufructuary the money "shall vest in and belong to the children or *other descendants* who are minors," we conclude that the above construction of the law was the proper one. And so concluding, we are of opinion that upon the death of a widow in necessitous circumstances, her own children being all of age, her grandchildren, then minors and also in necessitous circumstances, are entitled to receive what she, their grandmother, could legally claim from the succession.

This was the opinion also of the Judge of the lower court; and finding no error in his judgment, it is affirmed with costs.

* * * * * *

NOTES AND QUESTIONS

1. Civil Code article 3506(8) defines "children" to include not only a person's immediate offspring but also "descendants of them in the direct line." If the words "minor children" at the beginning of the last paragraph of Civil Code article 3252 were intended to include minor grandchildren, why does the last sentence of the paragraph refer to "children and other descendants"? Is this simply the product of inartful drafting, or does it provide a basis for interpretation of the meaning of "minor children" at the beginning of the paragraph?

2. The courts have had substantial difficulty in formulating a rule governing the issue of whether and under what circumstances grandchildren have the

right to assert the privilege of the needy surviving spouse. Citing dicta in *Succession of Durkin*, 30 La. Ann. 669 (1878), *Succession of Vives* held that minor grandchildren of a deceased widow could assert the privilege against major heirs of the husband's succession. In *Succession of Watzke*, 72 So. 423 (La. 1916), the wife had predeceased the husband, and the court held that minor grandchildren were not permitted to claim the privilege, because the word "children" does not include grandchildren.

* * * * * *

SUCCESSION OF TACON
177 So. 590 (La. 1937)

ROGERS, Justice.

This is an intestate succession, in which the widow of the deceased opposed the administrator's final account. This account shows assets amounting to $4,312.52 and privileged and ordinary debts amounting to $768.77. Opponent claimed the marital fourth, and, in the alternative, her rights and titles to her lawful portion of the estate. The administrator moved to dismiss the opposition, on the ground that opponent's claim to the marital fourth could not prevent the payment of the debts of the succession. The motion prevailed in the district court, the trial judge holding that in order to properly claim her marital fourth the widow must proceed by separate action against the heirs after settlement and liquidation of the succession. On appeal the judgment was annulled, this court holding that the widow was not required to proceed in the manner pointed out by the trial judge and that her pleadings were sufficient to entitle her to claim not only the marital fourth, but also, in the alternative, to claim $1,000, or her widow's homestead, as a widow in necessitous circumstances. Accordingly, the case was remanded for the purpose of having the widow's opposition tried and determined on all the claims therein set up. *Succession of Tacon*, 186 La. 418, 172 So. 513.

After the case was remanded to the district court, the widow filed a supplemental and amended opposition to the administrator's account, in which she specifically asserted her right to $1,000, or widow's homestead, as a widow in necessitous circumstances, claiming a lien and privilege on the assets of the succession for the payment of that amount. The opposition as amended was heard in the district court, and again was dismissed by the trial judge. From that judgment, opponent is prosecuting this appeal.

On the retrial of her opposition, the widow, considering it would be to her advantage to do so, abandoned all her claims, except the one for the $1,000 homestead as widow in necessitous circumstances. The administrator insists that she could not do this, and that her opposition must be restricted to the claim for the marital fourth.

We find no merit in the contention of the administrator. The law gives the opponent, as widow in necessitous circumstances, the right to claim the marital fourth, Civ. Code, art. 2382, or the right to claim the $1,000 widow's homestead, Civ. Code, art. 3252. She may assert either, but not both, of those rights. We see no reason why she may not assert that one of the rights which will be more advantageous to her and afford her more protection. In our opinion, the assertion of either right is not dependent upon the solvency or the insolvency of the succession.

The statement is correct that the marital fourth is taken from a solvent succession or the heirs. Obviously, if the succession is insolvent, there is nothing for the claimant to take. The statement is also correct that the widow in necessitous circumstances enjoys a preferential claim for $1,000 in an insolvent succession. The statement literally taken does not say that the widow's claim for $1,000 cannot be set up in a solvent succession. If such be its implication, then we think that the statement is erroneous.

A privilege is a right which the nature of the debt gives the creditor, and which entitles him to be preferred before other creditors, even those who have mortgages. Civ. Code, art. 3186.

There must be a debt or obligation where a privilege exists. The privilege arises from the nature of the debt or obligation, from which, however, it is entirely distinct. A privilege is an incident to the debt or obligation which it secures, and it is also a remedy therefor. But, while the debt or obligation may be enforced with the aid of the privilege, it may also be enforced if circumstances warrant without such aid. In a solvent succession there is no necessity for asserting the privilege protecting the widow's homestead of

$1,000. It is only where a succession is insolvent that the necessity arises for asserting such privilege. But, whether the succession be solvent or insolvent, the widow in necessitous circumstances is entitled to the preferential claim for $1,000 to be paid out of the assets of the succession.

It is not so important that article 3252 of the Civil Code is to be found under the title treating of "Privileges" and not in that portion of the Code covering "Successions" or "Marriage Contracts," as it is that the codal article itself creates the debt or obligation in favor of the widow in necessitous circumstances as well as the privilege by which that debt or obligation is secured.

The preferential right granted the widow in necessitous circumstances to claim a homestead of $1,000 out of the succession of her deceased husband is not derived from the Spanish or French laws. Neither does it appear in the Digest of Civil Laws of the Territory of Orleans adopted in 1808, nor is it embodied in the articles of the Civil Code of 1825.

The right was originally created by Act. No. 255 of 1852. The statute was enacted, as shown by its title, "To provide a homestead for the widow and children of deceased persons." The first section of the act provides: "That whenever the widow or minor children of a deceased person shall be left in necessitous circumstances and not possess in their own right property to the amount of one thousand dollars, the widow or legal representatives of the children, shall be entitled to demand and receive from the succession of their deceased father of husband, a sum which added to the amount of property owned by them or either of them, in their own right, will make up the sum of one thousand dollars, and which said amount shall be paid in preference to all other debts, except those for the vendor's privilege, and expenses incurred in selling the property." The second section of the act provides: "That the surviving widow shall have and enjoy the usufruct of the money so received from her deceased husband's succession, during her widowhood, afterwards to vest in, and belong to the children or other descendants of said deceased."

Act No. 255 of 1852 was reproduced in article 3252 of the Civil Code of 1870. It was also reproduced in the Revised Statutes of 1870 in section 2885 under the head of "Privilege," and in sections 1693 and 1694 under the head of "Homestead and Exempted Property."

Article 3252 of the Civil Code was amended by Act No. 17 of 1917, Ex. Sess., and by Act No. 242 of 1918. These amendments merely provide that debts ranking the widow's homestead claim shall be the vendor's privilege on both movables and immovables and debts secured by conventional mortgages, as well as the expenses incurred in selling the property.

Act No. 255 of 1852 provides that: "The widow (in necessitous circumstances) or the legal representatives of the (minor) children shall be entitled to demand and receive from the succession of the deceased husband or father, a sum which added to the amount of property owned by them or either of them, in their own right, will make up the sum of one thousand dollars." Following this provision is another provision declaring: "Which amount (an amount up to $1000.) shall be paid in preference to all other debts, except those for the vendors privilege, and expenses incurred in selling the property." These statutory provisions were embodied *ipsissimus verbis* in article 3252 of the Civil Code and also in sections 1693 and 2885 of the Revised Statutes. And they are not changed in the codal article by the amendments thereof, except that the ranking vendor's privilege is declared to embrace both movables and immovables, and conventional mortgages are made to prime the widow's homestead.

Thus, it will be seen that the original statute, the article of the Code and the sections of the Revised Statutes in which it is reproduced, first create the debt or obligation of the succession (solvent or insolvent) of a deceased husband to his necessitous widow up to the sum of $1,000; and then, secondly, secure the payment of the debt or obligation by according it a privilege over "all other debts" of the succession, except those secured by the vendor's privilege and expenses of selling the property. The privilege established by law for the security of the debt or obligation created by law is of particular value to the necessitous widow when used as a remedy for enforcing the debt or obligation due her by an insolvent succession. But this does not preclude her from asserting her preferential right when the debt or obligation is due her by a solvent succession.

There are no children of opponent's marriage, and it is not disputed that she is in necessitous circumstances and is not possessed of any property in her own right. In these circumstances, she is entitled to recover from the succession of her deceased husband the full amount of $1,000 allowed by law as her widow's homestead.

For the reasons assigned, the judgment herein appealed from is annulled, and it is now ordered that the opposition of Mrs. Leonora Dupuy Tacon to the final account of Marcel L. Tacon, administrator of the succession of Edward L. Tacon, be maintained to the extent of her claim for the widow's homestead. It is further ordered that opponent as widow in necessitous circumstances be recognized as a privileged creditor of the succession of Edward L. Tacon for the sum of $1,000, and, accordingly, that she be placed on the administrator's account as a creditor of the succession for $1,000, which amount is to be paid opponent out of the assets of the succession of Edward L. Tacon, in preference to all other debts, except those for the vendor's privilege on movables or immovables, debts secured by conventional mortgages, and the expenses of selling the property, if there be any. All the costs of this proceeding to be borne by the succession.

* * * * * *

NOTES AND QUESTIONS

1. The "marital fourth" mentioned in the case is the marital portion, which is now provided for in Civil Code Articles 2432 through 2437.

2. The case holds that a surviving spouse in necessitous circumstances is entitled to claim either the marital portion or the privilege of the surviving spouse, and that the availability of the latter is not dependent on the solvency or insolvency of the succession. *See* Note, 12 Tulane L. Rev. 639 (1938).

3. How does the privilege of the surviving spouse differ from the marital portion? Is the marital portion a preference that can be asserted against creditors of the decedent's estate?

C. Special Privileges

***See* La. Civ. Code arts. 3216-17; 3249**

1. In General

In contrast to general privileges, special privileges operate only on specific property. The Civil Code establishes only two special privileges upon immovables: the privilege of the vendor and the privileges of architects, contractors, and others involved in the construction and repair of houses, buildings, and other works. The latter category of special privileges has been wholly supplanted by those established under special legislation known as the Private Works Act, which is discussed in a later chapter. With respect to movables, the Civil Code establishes quite a number of special privileges, among them the privilege of a lessor upon movables of the lessee located on the leased premises; the privilege of a vendor upon the thing sold; and the privileges of the artisan, depositor, innkeeper, carrier, and farm laborer. Statutes have added innumerable other special privileges.

Article 2292 and 3511 of the Code of Civil Procedure establish a special privilege in favor of a seizing creditor upon the property seized, whether movable or immovable. This privilege supplements whatever other security the seizing creditor may hold, such as another privilege or a mortgage or security interest.

Any attempt to list, much less treat, all of the special privileges would be a massive endeavor. An incomplete listing of the special privileges created by statute on movables appears in Chapter 1 of Code Title XXI of Title 9 of the Louisiana Revised Statutes of 1950, among them the moss gatherer's privilege that has been a perpetual source of both amusement and bewilderment for generations of Louisiana law students. The cases below illustrate the scope and operation of special privileges that are more commonly encountered in practice.

* * * * * *

2 Traite Élementaire de Droit Civil, pt. 2 (La. State Law Inst. trans., 1959) (12th ed. 1939) (Fr.) Marcel Planiol & Georges Ripert

2583. Definition

A privilege is special when it gives the right of preference on one or several determined things; if such things are movables, the privilege is movable.

2584. Origin

The special privileges on movables were unknown in Roman law, it was the French law that invented them little by little: they were formed slowly under the influence of changes made in other institutions. The first of these changes was the separation of executory proceedings which became radically distinct depending upon whether if they bore on movables or on immovables; the movables were seized separately and discussed before the immovables, which was never the case in Roman law. Their fate being from then on independent, one can understand the formation of new customs and new conceptions regarding them, and how the notion of a special privilege on movables could have come into being. It found the ground quite prepared for its birth. Its cause was the suppression of the right of pursuit resulting from the mortgage of movables, a suppression which was the consequence of Germanic ideas on devolution and the revendication of movables. When this double change was accomplished, it was found that, in the execution on movables, there were only simple rights of preference: real securities themselves no longer gave the right of pursuit. Since then, by an abuse of language easily understood among the practitioners, the indifferent appellation of "privileges" was given to all the causes of preference on movables, whatever was their true nature. This confusion is complete in Pothier, but it is considerably older.

Our ancient authors employed the word "privilege" with the broad sense we give to the expression "right of preference." Their synonymous use is very noticeable in Domat, in the passages where he speaks of the pledge, the mortgage, and the privileges.

2585. Later Development

Once the notion of a specialized privilege was created, that is to say, a simple right of preference limited to certain things, and as this new concept was in itself comprehensible and useful, they set about creating new cases. After having lived for a long time under the ancient traditions with which the law seemed satisfied simply by altering and transforming them, it entered into a productive phase: a certain number of privileges of recent institution were created under the form of special movable privileges, and have never been anything else. The oldest example of the creation of this kind is the privilege which was introduced in 1580 in the Coutume de Paris for the benefit of the seller on time (infra, No. 2606).

In addition, an old general privilege of Roman law has been retained in modern law, but only as a special privilege: it is the privilege given for the expenses of preserving the thing.

* * * * * *

2. The Lessor's Privilege

***See* La. Civ. Code arts. 2707-10; 3217(3); 3219**

i. In General

Under the regime of the Civil Code of 1870, the right accorded to the lessor was "of a higher nature than mere privilege." La. Civ. Code art. 3218 (1870). The lessor was given not only a privilege but also an implied pledge and right of retention under Article 2706. Moreover, the lessor's rights extended not just to the property of the principal lessee, but also to property of a sublessee to the extent that the sublessee was indebted to the principal lessee at the time the lessor exercised his rights. La. Civ. Code art. 2706 (1870). In addition, under Article 2707, the lessor's right of pledge extended to property owned by other third persons "contained in the house or store by their own consent, express or implied," provided that such property was not "transiently or accidentally" on the premises.

* * * * * *

CASE
v.
KLOPPENBURG
27 La. Ann. 482 (1875)

TALIAFERRO, J.

The plaintiff having a judgment against Kloppenburg and Schneider *in solido* and another against Schneider alone, caused executions to issue, and proceeded to seize the entire contents of a barroom or drinking saloon kept by Schneider at the corner of Gravier and Baronne streets. Mrs. Lenes, claiming to be the owner of the building in which this saloon is kept, and alleging that she leased the ground floor of the same to Schneider for the purpose of keeping a coffeehouse, filed a petition of opposition to the plaintiff's seizure, on the ground that she has by law the lessor's privilege upon all the effects of her lessee thus seized, and that she has also by law the right of pledge on the same; that the seizures made by the plaintiff are violative of her said rights, and are wrongful and injurious, and will inflict upon her irreparable loss and injury. She prayed that the plaintiff be restrained by injunction from proceeding with the said seizure, and that she recover from the plaintiff two hundred and fifty dollars as special damages for attorney's fees, reserving her right of action against the said parties for the recovery of all damages, loss or injury she may hereafter sustain from the illegal acts and proceedings of the plaintiff in the premises. The plaintiff filed an exception to the opponent's right to an injunction, and took a rule upon her to have it dissolved. Judgment was rendered in favor of the opponent perpetuating the injunction, releasing the seizure, and awarding the opponent one hundred dollars special damages as attorney's fees. From this judgment the plaintiff has appealed. . . . We understand the position of the opponent to be, that she maintains the right to keep in her possession the effects in controversy, without molestation as a subsisting pledge for the payment of her rent, and that the property so subject to her privilege can not be legally removed from the premises, or in any manner disposed of before her demand for rent is paid. This right is claimed under several articles of the Civil Code, and especially under articles 2705 and 3218. Article 2705 declares that the lessor has for the payment of his rent, and other obligations of the lease, a right of pledge on the movable effects of the lessee, which are found on the property leased. Article 3218 provides that "the right which the lessor has over the products of the estate, and on the movables which are found on the place leased for his rent, is of a higher nature than mere privilege. The latter is only enforced on the price arising from the sale of movables to which it applies. It does not enable the creditor to take or keep the effects themselves specially. The lessor on the contrary may take the effects themselves and retain them until he is paid." The opponent's right, it is held, is sustained by the jurisprudence of the State, and we are referred to the case of *James Robb v. William F. Wagner*, 5 An. 111, and to *Arick v. Walsh & Boisseau et al.*, 23 An. 605. The expressions used in the two articles of the Code make it that the lessor's rights are secured by more than a privilege, and we must interpret these articles so as to protect the lessor's right fully over the movable effects subject to his privilege in order that such effects may be wholly and entirely subjected to the payment of the lessor's rent to the exclusion of every inferior privilege. But there are higher privileges than those of the lessor. Take for example the privilege of the laborer on the crop grown on the plantation of the lessor cultivated by a lessee who owes his landlord rent for it. To the laborer who produces the crop the law accords the first privilege on the crop. Shall we say that the lessor may detain the products of the plantation until the laborer pays him the sum his lessee owes him for rent before he can enforce his first privilege upon those products? In such a case we apprehend the proceeds of those products would have to be distributed according to law if they were insufficient to pay both privileges. If they sufficed to pay only the laborer's privilege the lessor would receive nothing.

It is a trite maxim that the property of a debtor is the common pledge of his creditors; by which we understand that every creditor has the right to look to the property of his debtor for the payment of his debt. Where the law creates privileges in favor of certain creditors on the property of the common debtor, it leaves to the creditors not preferred their residuary rights whatever they may be against the property of the debtor, notwithstanding the privileges imposed upon it, and they may exercise those rights subsidiarily to those enjoyed by the preferred creditors; and the reason of this right is obvious, for the value of the property may exceed in amount the debt of the privileged creditor and leave something for the ordinary creditor. It seems to us that the interpretation of the articles of the Code referred to, contended for in behalf of the opponent tends to ignore this well settled principle which accords to all creditors the equal right to pursue the property of the common debtor. The terms used in article 3218 of the Civil Code require a more liberal construction than the one offered in defense of the opponent's claim. The right of the lessor to detain the movables subject to his privilege until his rent is paid is not incompatible with the right of an ordinary creditor to enforce his rights against the same property without depriving the lessor of any portion of his debt for rent. The payment spoken of in that article does not necessarily mean payment of the lessor's debt by the adverse creditor before the latter is permitted to proceed against the property. There are weighty objections to such an interpretation. The value of the property could not well be ascertained except by a sale of it. It might pay only a part of the lessor's debt, it might pay all of it, or it might pay more than all of it. Again, the creditor seeking to enforce his claim (in this case the plaintiff is a judgment creditor) might be unable to advance the amount of the lessor's debt for rent, and thus by his poverty be debarred from pursuing a legal right which if enforced would realize money sufficient to pay the lessor in full and leave a surplus for himself. But it is argued on the side of the opponent that a seizure of the effects of the lessee subject to the lessor's privilege is an interference with his rights of detention of the property, and if permitted would greatly deteriorate the value of the effects subject to his pledge, because by the use of them in the establishment of the lessee, they would yield a greater revenue and be a subsisting security to the lessor for his rent; whereas, by a sale of them a far less value would be realized. These are considerations that can not be taken into view in determining the legal rights of the parties. The elements for such an estimate are few and simple. The lessee owes the lessor a certain sum of money for rent of a coffeehouse, for which he is entitled to a privilege on all the movable property of the lessee in that establishment, consisting of his outfit, stock in trade, and paraphernalia of every kind used in carrying on the business he is engaged in. The lessor is entitled to the proceeds of that property if sold, to the extent of his debt for rent, if so much is realized by the sale. If a less sum is made he takes it all. He can not prevent a sale of the property on the pretense that it would not bring the amount of his debt. No right of his is violated by a sale made in the exercise of a legal right of another against the property. If the lessor's right is preserved, if his debt is paid in whole or in part only, if the entire proceeds of the property subject to his privilege are insufficient to pay it all, he has no just ground to complain. His rights can only be exercised concurrently with the rights of others on the same property. His assumption of the right of detention of the property continuously unless his entire privileged debt is paid, would put the rights of others in abeyance and destroy that condition of equality before the law that all are entitled to occupy in asserting their rights in the courts of the country.

Our conclusion is that the injunction was illegally issued, and that the plaintiff's remedy was by third opposition, claiming her priority of privilege on the proceeds of the property seized and subject to the lessor's privilege.

Mr. Justice Morgan concurs in this opinion.

LUDELING, C. J., dissenting.

It is contended that notwithstanding the lessor's rights, the plaintiff may seize and sell the property, and that the lessor must assert his right against the proceeds.

If the lessor had only a privilege to secure his rents, the position would be correct. But the Code says: "The right which the lessor has over the product of the estate, and on the movables which are found on the place leased, is of a higher nature than a mere privilege. The latter is only enforced on the price arising from the sale of movables to which it applies. It does not enable the creditor to take or keep the effects themselves. The lessor, on the contrary, may take the effects themselves, and detain them until he is paid." 3218.

In *Robb v. Wagner*, 5 An. 111, it was decided that a lessor had "a lien and right of detention upon the property on the premises for the security of his rent. The lien was his property, and as valuable to him as if he were the owner of the property itself; and no sheriff or marshal, under execution against a third person, had any right to take away the property before paying the landlord." The same principle was recognized in *Arick & Walsh v. Boisseau*, 23 An. 605.

The case of *Tanner v. Succession of Pearce* is not in point. The organ of the court in that case said: "The only question which this case presents for our solution is, whether the lessor or the overseer has the superior privilege on the crop of a plantation leased to the defendant." And the court decided that the overseer's privilege was superior. The court, it is true, said afterwards: "The right of detention, which is part of the lessor's remedy, affords him, to be sure, much greater security; but, like the pledgee, and the creditor having only a privilege, he must have the thing subject to the lien sold in the manner provided by law. When this takes place, if a conflict should arise in consequence of adverse claims on the same fund, a distribution must be made pursuant to that chapter of the Code which treats of the order in which privileged creditors are to be paid." This is true as to the privilege of the lessor, but what becomes of the greater right given him by the article, the right "to take the effects themselves and detain them until he is paid"; which the court says, in the case of *Tanner v. Succession of Pearce*, "affords him, to be sure, much greater security?" How does it afford him additional security if, to enforce payment of his debt, he must give up this right of detention, which is higher than a privilege, and only assert his privilege on the proceeds of the sale? The language of the Code is plain, and I think the legislators meant what it declares. "The lessor, on the contrary, may take the effects themselves and detain them until he is paid." *Sic scripta est lex*. I therefore dissent in this case.

* * * * * *

NOTES AND QUESTIONS

1. The 2004 revision of the law of lease suppressed the lessor's implied pledge and right of retention and relegated the lessor to a mere privilege. *See* La. Civ. Code art. 2707 (2004).

2. The court held that the lessor was not entitled to an injunction against the seizure by the seizing creditor but instead had the remedy of asserting the superiority of her privilege through a procedural device then known as a third opposition (*See now* La. C.C.P. art. 1092, allowing a third person claiming a mortgage or privilege on property seized by another to assert his claim by intervention). Ordinarily, a sheriff's foreclosure sale does not extinguish any real charge that is superior to the right of the seizing creditor. *See* La. C.C.P. 2372. Suppose that the lessor failed to assert her claim by intervention but instead allowed the property subject to her privilege to be sold in execution of the writ obtained by the seizing creditor. Would her lessor's privilege survive the sheriff's sale? *See Liquid Carbonic Corp. v. Leger*, 169 So. 170 (La. App. 1st Cir. 1936), infra.

ii. Rights Against Sublessees and Other Third Persons

In the 2004 revision of the law of lease, the rules governing the lessor's privilege over property of a sublessee were essentially preserved, except that the prior rule to the effect that the sublessee could not make payment in anticipation of his rent was discarded. *See* La. Civ. Code art. 2708. As a significant departure from the 1870 Code, Article 2709 of the revision completely removed the lessor's privilege over goods of a third person other than the sublessee. Under that article, the lessor may nonetheless seize a third person's movable found on the premises unless the lessor knows that the movable is not the property of the lessee. The third person is permitted to recover the movable by establishing his ownership prior to the judicial sale and, if he fails to do so, the movable may be sold as though it belonged to the lessee.

* * * * * *

HENRY ROSE MERCANTILE & MFG. CO.

v.

STEARNS

159 La. 957 (1925)

OVERTON, J.

Plaintiff leased to defendant, who was doing business under the tradename of the Stearns Wagon Company, certain premises in the city of Shreveport. Montgomery Ward & Company, the intervener herein, under the name of the Hummer Plow Works, entered into a contract with Stearns, in which it was agreed that the former would ship to the latter carload lots of implements, wagons, and other equipment handled by it; that Stearns would store the goods to be shipped in his place of business, in the city of Shreveport, and would display samples of them there to prospective purchasers and the public; that Stearns should have the right to sell any of the goods to be shipped at prices not less than those to be quoted by intervener from time to time; that he should settle, in cash, for the goods sold by him on the first of each month at the prices fixed by intervener, that, in addition, he should furnish intervener monthly with a list of all of its goods on hand at the time of making the statement; and that intervener, as well as Stearns, should have the right to sell any part of the goods so shipped. The contract did not contemplate that intervener should pay storage on the goods. It did contemplate, however, that Stearns, for his expense and trouble in handling the goods, should receive the difference between the prices fixed by intervener and those to be obtained by him for such of the goods as he might sell.

Intervener made shipments under the contract entered into by it. Stearns received the goods, paid the freight on them, and stored and displayed them in his place of business, which he had rented from plaintiff.

After the shipments were made, Stearns fell considerably in arrears with his rent, and in February, 1921, about 7 months after his contract with intervener had been entered into, owed his landlord, the plaintiff herein, something over $1,100. As a result of his failure to pay his rent, plaintiff brought suit against him for the rent then due and for that to mature, and caused to be provisionally seized all of the property found on the leased premises, including such of the goods as remained on hand that intervener had shipped.

Intervener then filed this intervention. In that pleading it claims ownership of the goods shipped by it, and seized under the writ of provisional seizure, and claims that these goods were only transiently on the leased premises, and for that reason were not subject to the lessor's privilege. . . . The intervention was tried, and judgment was rendered, recognizing, in effect, intervener to be the owner of the property claimed by it and provisionally seized, but decreeing the property to be subject to the lessor's privilege asserted by plaintiff, and ordering the property sold, to satisfy the claim of that company, for rent. The appeal on the intervention is now before us.

There is no serious dispute as to the ownership of the goods, claimed by intervener and seized in this case. They belong to intervener. The real question is whether the goods are subject to the lessor's privilege asserted against them, and if so, to what extent.

Article 2705 of the Civil Code provides, in part, that:

> "The lessor has, for the payment of his rent, and other obligations of the lease, a right of pledge on the movable effects of the lessee, which are found on the property leased."

Article 2706 of the Code provides, in part, that:

> "This right of pledge includes, not only the effects of the principal lessee or tenant, but those of the undertenant, so far as the latter is indebted to the principal lessee, at the time when the proprietor chooses to exercise his right."

Article 2707 provides that:

> "This right of pledge affects, not only the movables of the lessee and underlessee, but also those belonging to third persons, when their goods are contained in the house or store, by their own consent, express or implied."

And article 2708 provides that:

> "Movables are not subject to this right, when they are only transiently or accidentally in the house, store, or shop, such as the baggage of a traveler in an inn, merchandise sent to a workman to be made up or repaired, and effects lodged in the store of an auctioneer to be sold."

In our opinion this case is governed by the case of *Goodrich v. Bodley*, 35 La. Ann. 525. The facts in that case are very similar to those in the present one. It was held, to quote the syllabus, which correctly states the ruling of the court, that:

> "The goods of a third person found in a leased store, where they had been consigned by their owner to the lessee, to be sold by the latter at a price fixed by the owner, with the understanding and agreement that the lessee or consignee could keep, as his compensation, all that he could obtain above the inventoried prices, and that no rent or storage was due by the owner, will be affected by the lessor's privilege, and are liable to the latter's seizure for unpaid rent due by the lessor."

And in the body of the opinion, the court, after deciding that, under the facts of the case stated, it was clear that the intervener could not be considered an undertenant, within the meaning of article 2706 of the Civil Code, quoted above, said:

> "It is equally clear that the goods were not transiently or accidentally in the store, as the evidence shows that they were to remain there until sold at the invoice prices, and hence the provisions of article 2708 of our Civil Code cannot be successfully invoked by intervener."

The only difference between the facts in the foregoing case and those in the case at bar, in so far as we are able to perceive, is that the intervener in the case cited apparently did not reserve the right to sell at will from the goods placed by him in the hands of the defendant, and kept in the leased premises, whereas, in the case at bar, the intervener expressly reserved that right. However, the reservation of that right has no important bearing on the case; the question being whether the goods were transiently in the leased premises, and, in determining that question, it is a matter of no importance whether intervener or defendant, or both, had the right to sell the goods.

In the case at bar the evidence shows that the goods were placed in defendant's place of business with the consent of intervener, to be there sold and to remain there until sold, and hence, as said in the *Goodrich Case*, from which we have quoted, the provisions of article 2708 of the Civil Code cannot be invoked by intervener, for the goods were not transiently in the premises within the intendment of that article.

Intervener also urges that, in the event we hold that the goods were not on the leased premises transiently, then we should hold that the case is governed by article 2706 of the Civil Code, quoted above, which limits the lessor's right of pledge to the amount that the undertenant is indebted to the lessee at the time the lessor exercises his right against the lessee. In this connection it may be said that the word "undertenant," as used in article 2706 of the Civil Code, is not used in its broad sense, but is synonymous with the word "underlessee." *University Publishing Co. v. Piffet*, 34 La. Ann. 602. It may be also observed, in the same connection, that one who pays storage for the safe-keeping of his goods in a warehouse, or other place, is regarded as a sublessee within the meaning of the same article of the Code. *Vairin & Co. v. Hunt*, 18 La. 498. In the *University Publishing Co. Case*, supra, quoting the syllabus, which correctly states the finding and decision of the court, it was held that:

> "The goods of a third person contained in the leased house by his consent, under an agreement with the lessee that no rent or other consideration was to be paid for the occupancy, are not the goods of an 'undertenant,' and are affected by the landlord's pledge."

In the case at bar there was no agreement by intervener to pay defendant anything for the occupancy of the premises and no agreement to pay storage. To the contrary, the contract clearly contemplated that no rent or storage should be paid by intervener. Intervener, however, takes the position that the profits, which defendant was supposed to make from the sale of the goods, stand in lieu of a storage charge, and have the effect of making the contract one of storage or sublease. It may be said, however, that this position is untenable. The hope of making these profits cannot be said to constitute, or be the equivalent of, a price or consideration for storage, or for a sublease, nor was it intended that the hope, or even the profits, should be. The real object of the contract was not to provide for storage, but for the sale of the goods. *See University Publishing Co. v. Piffet*, supra, and *Goodrich v. Bodley*, supra.

Intervener also relies on article 3260 of the Civil Code. That article of the Code gives, by necessary implication, to one who deposits movables in the hands of a lessee, a preference on the things deposited and found in the leased premises, superior to that of the lessor, provided it be proved that the lessor knew that the things deposited did not belong to his tenant. Intervener contends that it deposited the goods in the hands of defendant, within the meaning of that article, and that plaintiff knew that the goods did not belong to his tenant. While intervener alleged no such claim in its intervention, yet we may say that, in our view, the article cannot be successfully invoked by intervener. This is so, because there was no deposit made within the meaning of the article. The deposit, referred to by the article, is that defined by law as being an act by which a person receives the property of another, binding himself to preserve it and return it in kind. Civil Code, art. 2926. In this instance, it was not the intention that the property, placed in defendant's hands, should be preserved by defendant and returned to intervener. The intention was that it should be sold, and it was placed in defendant's hands for that purpose.

For the foregoing reasons our conclusion is that the property in question is subject to the lessor's privilege, under article 2707 of the Civil Code, quoted above; it being the property of a third person, placed in the leased premises with the consent of such person, and coming within none of the exceptions provided by law.

* * * * * *

NOTES AND QUESTIONS

1. Would the case be decided differently after the 2004 revision of the law of lease?

2. Interestingly, the 2004 revision of the law of lease, when coupled with the 2003 revision of the law of deposit, may have an unexpected effect on the rights of a lessor against the property of persons who, for compensation, store their goods with a warehouse or other storage facility. Under the 1870 Code, a contract of deposit was always gratuitous. A number of cases thus held that one who pays storage for the safekeeping of his goods in a warehouse or other place is regarded as a sublessee insofar as the lessor's privilege is concerned and thus has only limited exposure to the seizure of his property. *See University Publishing Co. v. Piffet*, 34 La. Ann. 602; *Vairin v. Hunt*, 18 La. 498. *See also Burn Planting Co. v. Goldman Landing Co.*, 112 So. 662 (La. 1927). However, with the 2004 revision of the lease articles, the movables of a third person who is not a sublessee are not subject to the lessor's privilege, and the third person is thus now treated more favorably than a sublessee. Moreover, under the 2003 revision of the law of deposit, a deposit can now be onerous as well as gratuitous. *See* La. Civ. Code art. 2928 (2003). Thus, those who store their goods with a warehouse or similar storage facility might now contend that they are not sublessees (whose goods are to a limited extent exposed to the lessor's privilege) but rather depositors, and that their goods are now wholly free of any privilege in favor of the lessor of a leased storage facility.

iii. Right of Pursuit

Article 2710 provides that the lessor may exercise his privilege for 15 days after the movables subject to the privilege have been removed from the leased property, but only if they remain the property of the lessee and can be identified. Thus, either alienation of the movables by the lessee, or their removal from the leased property for more than 15 days, will cause a loss of the privilege.

* * * * * *

DESBAN

v.

PICKETT

16 La. Ann. 350 (1861)

LAND, J.

The plaintiff, the lessor of the defendant, provisionally seized certain household furniture, after its removal from the leased premises, and after its sale to the intervenor, for the payment of rent due him.

Judgment was rendered in favor of the intervenor, and the plaintiff has appealed.

The evidence shows that the plaintiff was aware, that the furniture was being removed and delivered to the intervenor, and although present, neither asserted any privilege on the furniture, nor made any objection to its removal and delivery.

The lessor has a right of pledge on the movable effects of the lessee, which are found upon the property leased, and may even seize them within fifteen days after they are taken away, if they continue to be the property of the lessee, and can be identified, for the payment of his rent. C. C. 2675, 2679. But in this case, the furniture had ceased to be the property of the defendant before the seizure was made; and the sale and delivery of it to the intervenor extinguished the lessor's right of privilege. The right of seizure, after the removal, is made to depend on the continued ownership of the lessee.

The evidence is insufficient to establish any fraud on the part of the intervenor, in the purchase of the furniture. The plaintiff had an opportunity of preserving his rights, but by his silence and non-action lost them.

There is no error in the judgment of the lower court; the plaintiff was not entitled to a personal judgment against the defendant, because there was neither a personal citation served on her, nor answer filed by her.

It is, therefore, ordered, adjudged and decreed, that the judgment be affirmed, with costs.

* * * * * *

NOTES AND QUESTIONS

1. Civil Code Article 2710, as revised in the 2004 revision of the law of lease, preserves the rule that there is no right of pursuit once the property has been transferred to a third person, even though 15 days have not yet elapsed since removal. The text of the article provides that the 15-day right of pursuit exists only if the goods "remain the property of the lessee and can be identified."

3. The Artisan/Repairman's Privilege

The artisan's privilege, which is presently provided for in the second numbered paragraph of Civil Code Article 3217, first appeared in the Civil Code of 1825. It has been supplemented by the statutory privileges that are now found in La. R.S. 9:4501 and La. R.S. 9:4502. As the cases below reflect, the Civil Code privilege and the statutory privileges are independent, and neither limits the other.

i. Civil Code Privilege

See **La. Civ. Code arts. 3217(2)**

* * * * * *

GAYARRE
v.
TUNNARD
9 La. Ann. 254 (1854)

CAMPBELL, J.

The petitioner alleges that on the 9th of September, 1852, the defendant, *W. F. Tunnard*, though thereto demanded, refused to deliver the possession of a four wheeled carriage belonging to him; and that he detains the same illegally and maliciously. He prays for the restitution of the carriage, and for $1,000 damages for its detention. The defence is a general denial, and a special denial that his conduct towards petitioner has been malicious or illegal; alleging that the suit of plaintiff is malicious and ungrounded in law, and brought with the intent of annoying and harassing him; he claims damages in reconvention. The case was tried by a jury, and in conformity with their verdict, a judgment was rendered in plaintiff's favor, decreeing the return of the carriage and sentencing defendant to pay twenty-five dollars as damages, and the costs of suit.

From the judgment and fine rendered, this appeal has been prosecuted.

The facts of the case as disclosed by the record, are substantially as follows: Plaintiff, on the morning of the 9th of September, sent his carriage to the shop of defendant, who is an artisan, to be repaired. The repairs were made, and are proved to be worth two dollars, the sum charged. Defendant refused to deliver to plaintiff the carriage, until he should be paid this sum. This plaintiff refused to do, but proffered to and actually did deposit with *Dufroc*, Mayor and Justice of the Peace of Baton Rouge, the sum demanded, subject to the claim of defendant upon his establishing his right to it. The money thus deposited was never demanded by defendant, and was withdrawn on the 14th of the same month by plaintiff.

The defendant maintaining, that under the Article 3184 of the Civil Code, he had the right to keep possession of the carriage until payment of the price of repairs, has excepted to the charge of the Judge, who instructed the jury that defendant had no such right, but that it should have been delivered up immediately on demand, and that the jury consequently were bound to render a verdict in favor of plaintiff for the carriage, and for such damages as they might consider he had suffered by its detention.

We think the court erred in charging the jury, that defendant had no right to detain the carriage until payment for the repairs was made. The right necessarily results from the second paragraph of Article 3184 of the Civil Code, which expressly accords this privilege to "the debts of a workman or artisan, for the price of his labor, on the movable which he has repaired or made, if the thing continues still in his possession."

This rule—the artisan's *droit de retention*—is derived from the Roman Law, (*See* Voet cited *Trop. Priv. et Hyp*. vol. 1, No. 264,) and is analogous to the particular lien given in like cases by the common law, which their writers define to be "the right to retain the property of another for a charge on account of labor bestowed upon it," (2 Kent Com. 634,) which right, as has been held by their courts, continues while the possession is retained, but is lost by a voluntary surrender. *Holly* v. *Hungerford*, 8 Pick. 73. *Moore* v. *Hitchcock*, 4 Wend. 292.

In *Jordan* v. *James*, 5 New Ham. 88, it was held that the possession of the object on which the lien is claimed to operate, is the very essence of the lien. It was necessary for the plaintiff before demanding the possession of his carriage judicially, either to have paid the charge for repairs, or, in case he deemed it excessive, to have made to the defendant a tender of such sum as the repairs were reasonably worth, and the Judge should so have instructed the jury.

We must not be understood as intimating that the law accords no other remedy to the artisan, than that which results from the right of retention, or that the exercise of this right precludes the artisan from enforcing his privilege by a sale of the thing, as in other cases of privilege. The two remedies may exist together, and are not inconsistent with each other, and a decision of that question is not necessary in the present case.

It is therefore ordered, adjudged and decreed, that the judgment of the District Court be avoided and reversed; and that there be judgment in favor of the defendant as in case of nonsuit; that the costs of both courts be paid by the plaintiff and appellee.

C. Gayarre, for re-hearing:

It is true that Art. 3184 says, that a workman has, for repairs done, a privileged claim on the object so repaired, when in his possession.

But, in the very next Article, 3185, the Legislator has declared in the clearest terms, that privilege gives no right of detention; that this right must originate from something more than a privilege, and that it is actually more than a privilege.

What was granted in Art. 3184?—a mere privilege founded on a mere contingency—not the right of detention, which is more than a privilege; and not the right to compel payment extra-judicially, which is infinitely more than the right of detention as guaranty or security, until payment can be enforced judicially.

This appellee begs leave respectfully to refer the court to said Article 3185 of the Civil Code, but to which the attention of the court was not invited with sufficient clearness—no doubt through the appellee's fault—and on which the verdict and judgment in the court below rested altogether.

Art. 3185 says: "The right which the lessor has over the products of the estate, and on movables which are found on the place leased for the rent, is of a higher nature than mere privilege. The latter is only enforced on the price arising from the sale of movables to which it applies. It does not enable the creditor to take or keep the effects themselves specially. The lessor, on the contrary, may take the effects themselves and retain them until he is paid."

Appellee further invites the court to the examination of the following considerations:

> Art. 3152, Civil Code, says: "privilege can be claimed only for those debts to which it is expressly granted in the Code."

Therefore, if privilege cannot be presumed, it follows that the right of detention, (which, according to Art. 3185, is more than a privilege,) can much less be presumed, and must be specially given.

Art. 3184, relied on by defendant, gives, it is true, and in specific terms, a privilege to the workman, but no right of detention—which is not the consequence of privilege, but more than a privilege, according to the express declaration contained in Art. 3185. What is more than a privilege cannot be a consequence of it. If it is more than a privilege, it cannot be implied as proceeding from it, for the obvious reason that, when two things are of different dimensions, the one which is larger cannot be supposed to have been contained in the smaller.

But if our Civil Code says, that no privilege can be presumed, and that it must be specially given, the next question is, what is a privilege?—not according to the Roman law, or to the common law, but according to our Code, which permits none to be presumed, and which recognizes the existence only of such as it grants and defines. It is therefore of no consequence to ascertain what privileges or liens were granted by the Roman law, or the common law, when our Code has spoken on the subject. Our Code refers to its own definitions for what it grants, and not to other systems of jurisprudence.

But what is a privilege according to the Code of Louisiana? Is it anything like what is understood as such by those who have studied the Roman law? Or is it what is called a lien at common law? Is it the right of detention as guaranty? Is it more than that? Is it the right of detention to compel payment? No, for Art. 3153 of the Civil Code, defines what a privilege is, and says: "Privilege is a right which the nature of a debt gives to a creditor, and which entitles him to be preferred before other creditors, even those who have mortgages."

This is all that a privilege is in Louisiana, whatever it may be in those countries where the Roman law and the common law prevail, unless something be added to it by some other provisions of law, as in a few cases in which that addition is made, in special and guarded terms.

If Art. 3184, when granting privileges to the above mentioned creditors, had conceded, as a necessary corollary, the right of detention, where was the necessity of granting such a right, in a special form, in the subsequent articles I have quoted? The inevitable inference seems to be, that the framers of the Civil Code meant that Art. 3184 should give no right of detention, but a mere privilege, such as is defined in Art. 3153, and conferring no more rights than those therein mentioned. It seems also, that the omission of granting to the workman or artisan the right of detention, when the like was subsequently superadded to privilege by the legislator, in favor of certain creditors to whom privilege had also been granted in said Art. 3184, shows that the legislator intended to confer no such right on the workman or artisan. But, not satisfied with having carefully abstained from using any words of doubtful import, and, as if he anticipated, however, a possible misconstruction of Art. 3184, the legislator said, in the very next Article, 3185, that privilege gives no right of detention-and that the right of detention is more than a privilege.

I respectfully suggest that the above article means only this: That certain creditors therein mentioned have, in virtue of the privilege granted to them and defined in Art. 3153, the right to be paid in preference to other creditors, whether or not the articles on which they have a privilege are in their hands: but that an exception is made, in relation to the artisan, who has a right to be paid in preference to other creditors only as long as the article on which the privilege exists continues in his hands. It is a diminution—a curtailment of the privilege granted to the other creditors—and not an enlargement of it—not something more than a privilege—not the right of detention as security—and much less is it the right of detention to compel payment extra-judicially, as the court supposes; and if it be an extension of privilege, it is only an extension of what was granted. And what was granted in said Article 3184? Why—no more than the right of being paid in preference to other creditors—and not the right of detention—not the right of enforcing payment for an unliquidated claim against the owner of the object detained—which is a right of a different nature—nay—which far from being a right, would be a monstrosity. Such a thing is nowhere granted to a workman either by our Code or by any of our statutes.

In conclusion, I humbly beg leave to call the attention of the court to the following considerations:

That the right of detention forcibly and inevitably confers a privilege; but that privilege does not confer the right of detention;

That the right of detention, which is granted in certain cases merely as a security for debt, does not give impliedly the right to compel payment extrajudicially;

That according to the express will of the legislator, privilege is never to be inferred; and that, consequently, much less is the right of detention to be presumed. What shall I say of the right assumed by a creditor to compel payment without resorting to a court of justice!

Re-hearing refused.

* * * * * *

NOTES AND QUESTIONS

1. From the fact that the Civil Code limits the enforcement of the artisan's privilege to movables remaining in the artisan's possession, the court infers that there is a right of retention in his favor. To reach this result, the court primarily cites common law authorities.

2. Do you find persuasive the argument, urged on rehearing, that the Civil Code expressly affords the lessor a right of retention but makes no mention of a right of retention in favor of the artisan?

3. The Civil Code expressly provides a pledgee with a right of retention. La. Civ. Code Art. 3220 (1870); La. Civ. Code Art. 3156 (2014). A right of retention is also expressly granted to the holder of a privilege for preservation expenses as well as an innkeeper, in both instances premising the right of retention upon an implied pledge. *See* La. Civ. Code Art. 3225 and 3233 (1870).

4. Unlike codes found in some other civilian jurisdictions, the Louisiana Civil Code contains no set of articles expressly treating the subject matter of the right of retention, which is viewed by some authorities as a distinct form of security. There are, however, numerous instances in which the text of the Louisiana Civil Code either grants or implies a right of retention. *See, e.g.,* La. Civ. Code Art. 529 (expressly granting a right of retention to a possessor in good or bad faith before revendication of a thing); Art. 580 (expressly granting the naked owner a right of retention until the usufructuary makes reimbursement of expenses), Art. 627 (expressly granting a usufructuary a right of retention pending reimbursement of expenses); Art. 1268 (expressly granting a right of retention in cases of collation of an immovable): Art. 2022 (implying a right of retention by justifying a party to a contract in refusing to perform if the other party has failed to perform); Arts. 2293 and 2297 (in the case of *negotiorum gestio*, perhaps implying a right of retention through the incorporation of the mandate articles); Art. 2487 (granting a seller for cash the ability to refuse delivery until the price is paid); Art. 2613 (granting a seller of movables represented by a bill of lading an express right of retention); Art. 2614 (allowing a seller of movables the right to stop them in transit): Art. 2532 (expressly granting the buyer in a redhibition case a right of retention); Art. 2599 (expressly granting a right of retention in the case of lesion); Art. 2939 (expressly granting a right of retention to a depositary);

and Art. 3004 (granting a limited right of retention to a mandatary). For a discussion of the history, nature, and operation of the right of retention under French law, *see* 2 Marcel Planiol & Georges Ripert, *Traité Élémentaire de Droit Civil*, pt. 2, Nos. 2514-36 (La. State Law Inst. trans., 1959) (12th ed. 1939)(Fr.).

* * * * * *

COZZO

v.

ULRICH

14 Orl. App. 137 (La. App. Orl. 1916)

His Honor, JOHN ST. PAUL, rendered the opinion and decree of the Court, as follows:

This controversy involves the question whether or not plaintiff has an artisan's lien upon a certain automobile, and if so, whether or not same is superior to the vendor's lien claimed by the third opponent, Peter Kaul, Jr.

The automobile was sold and delivered by Kaul to Ulrich, and part of the price is still due and unpaid.

The machine being out of order Ulrich sent Cozzo to repair it, and Cozzo, with the help of a workman made the repairs at a cost of $125, ten dollars of which represents materials furnished and the rest labor done.

The repairs were made upon the machine, whilst the same lay in the premises of Ulrich, and when Cozzo took the machine upon the street to try it, it was forcibly (though not violently) taken from his possession.

We are of opinion that as long as an artisan or workman is actually at work making or repairing a movable object, the same continues in his possession within the meaning of Art. 3217 C. C. granting such artisan or laborer a lien for his compensation, even though the object be allowed to remain on the premises of the owner who has employed him.

For all laws must be interpreted according to the rules of common sense, and so as to carry out the manifest legislative intent. And it is quite clear that the purpose of the Code was to secure the artisan's compensation by a lien upon the object until by delivering same to the owner, he manifests an intent to relinquish his lien and trust entirely to the credit of the owner. Nothing in the law requires that the laborer should remove the object from the premises, and in cases where the object is bulky it would seem unreasonable to do so.

Indeed the somewhat analogous articles of the Code on the lease of labor, (C. C. 2758, 2759, 2760, 2761) show us that when the work is by the job, delivery to the owner cannot be made before the work is finished, until which time the object remains at the risk of the workman.

For the same reasons, and by the same analogies, we think the artisan's lien covers not only his labor, but also the material by him furnished, for it is clear that the law, by putting the thing at the risk of the artisan until its delivery, treats him more as the owner of the object than as having a mere claim thereon.

Likewise we think for the same reasons, that the lien exists not only in favor of an artisan who does the work with his own hand, but in favor of one who has contracted for the work, though he may have had it done by another; for the fact is that to the extent of the labor done and materials furnished he is to be considered as owner of the object.

We do not think the case of *Guion v. Brown*, 6 An., 112, at all applicable here.

That concerned a matter of general privilege and not a special privilege giving a right of detention or pledge as in this case.

For an artisan has a right of pledge (*Gayarre v. Tunnard*, 9 An., 254), and the presumption is that there has been added to the value of the object, the full value of the materials furnished and labor done thereon.

We likewise think that the artisan's lien is superior to the vendor's privilege, for the reason that the vendor's right is a mere privilege, or right of preference, whilst the artisan's lien is a right of pledge, which includes the right to retain the object until payment (9 An., 254).

The judgment appealed from seems to us correct and should be affirmed.

Judgment affirmed.

* * * * * *

NOTES AND QUESTIONS

1. This case is a sequel to *Cazzo v. Ulrich*, 13 Teiss. 257 (Orl. App. 1916), which, despite the variances in the spelling of the plaintiff's name, involved the same parties and arose out of the same set of facts. In the earlier case, the court held that the fact that the repairman was forcibly dispossessed of the automobile he was repairing did not deprive him of his privilege. Though the opinions do not state who took possession of the automobile from the repairman, an inference might be made that it was a vendor or his agent who did so.

2. Civil Code Article 3217(2) grants the privilege to an artisan "for the price of his labor." Do you find persuasive the court's holding that the privilege also extends to amounts due to the artisan for materials he furnishes? Does this holding comport with the rule that privileges are *stricti juris*?

ii. The Statutory Privileges

See **La. Rev. Stat. 9:4501-02**

* * * * * *

HART ENTERPRISE ELECTRICAL CO.
v.
STEWART
168 So. 791 (La. App. Orl. 1936)

JANVIER, Judge.

Hart Enterprise Electrical Co., Inc., claiming to be the owner of two electric motors which, at the time of the filing of the suit, were in the possession of defendant, S.J. Stewart, prayed for judgment decreeing it to be the owner of the said motors, and, at the same time, prayed for and obtained a writ of sequestration under which the civil sheriff for the parish of Orleans seized the said motors and took them into his possession.

Stewart denied plaintiff's ownership of the motors and averred that the true owner thereof, to wit, Consolidated Mills, Inc., had, some two years previously, contracted with him for the sale of the said motors and had authorized him to take them into his possession and clean and repair them so that they might be sold by him, and had stipulated that out of the proceeds of the sale, it, the said owner, should receive $125, the balance to be retained by Stewart.

In a reconventional demand the said defendant alleged that he had repaired the motors at a cost of $150, and he prayed that they be returned to him and that "there be judgment in his favor on the amount demanded." In the alternative, he prayed for judgment condemning plaintiff, the Hart Enterprise Electrical Co., Inc., to pay him $150, the amount of his bill, and that his lien and privilege on the motors be recognized.

In the court, a qua, there was judgment in favor of plaintiff recognizing it as the owner of the motors and dismissing the reconventional demand of Stewart. The latter has appealed.

The record shows the following facts:

On July 13, 1933, Consolidated Mills, Inc., authorized Stewart to take possession of the two motors and to clean and "put them in saleable condition" and to then sell them and remit to it $125.

On August 23, 1935, Stewart had not sold the motors, and, on that day, Consolidated Mills, Inc., contracted to sell them to the present plaintiff corporation and gave to it a letter directed to Stewart and authorizing him to deliver the said motors to the plaintiff corporation. The motors had been cleaned and made salable by Stewart, who, in removing them to his shop and doing the work on them, had expended for labor $93.65 and for material $6, making a total for labor and material of $99.65. The record further shows to our satisfaction that a proper charge for profit and supervision and overhead on such a job would be $49.82, which is the amount which Stewart added to his bill and which amount made a total of $149.47 instead of $150 as originally claimed.

The present status of the controversy is that Stewart maintains that he should be paid the amount of his bill, and that his lien and privilege should be recognized and that he should be permitted to retain possession of the motors under his privilege which exists, under article 3217, C.C., as we shall hereafter show, only so long as he has possession.

He has no interest in questioning the validity of the sale by the original owner, Consolidated Mills, Inc., to Hart Enterprise Electrical Co., Inc. The sale, so far as he is concerned, was a valid and complete one, and the letter of the former directing him to deliver the motors to the latter is sufficient evidence of ownership so far as he is concerned. If he is entitled to a lien and privilege, and if that lien and privilege still existed at the time of the sequestration, then it is of no concern to him that the original owner has sold the motors, because no sale could divest his lien. The sale of an article which is encumbered with a lien or privilege necessarily is made subject to the lien or privilege. It would be a worthless lien which could be removed by sale.

The real question is whether or not there is a lien, and if so what is the amount of it.

Stewart contends that it results from article 3217 of the Civil Code and that according to that article it exists so long as "the thing continues still in his possession."

Plaintiff, on the other hand, asserts that if Stewart, at any time, was entitled to a lien and privilege it came into existence solely as a result of Act No. 209 of 1926, and that by the very terms of that act it expired "ninety (90) days from the date of making of such repairs. . . ."

It is the contention of plaintiff, the Hart Enterprise Electrical Co., Inc., that the act of 1926, to which we have referred, has application to all cases where repairs to machinery are made by one who operates a garage or place where automobile trucks or other machinery are repaired, and that such shop or garage operator is entitled only to the lien created by the act of 1926, which lien expires 90 days from the date of the making of the repairs.

Stewart contends, however, that the lien granted by the act of 1926 is in addition to that which is granted by article 3217 of the Code, and that the two liens are not in any way in conflict. He maintains that it was the purpose of the framers of the act of 1926 to permit one who makes such repairs to deliver the article repaired to the owner without immediately losing his lien thereon.

It is evident that under article 3217 of the Code the moment the repairman delivers the repaired article to the owner the lien no longer attaches to it, and we believe that it was a realization of this fact which prompted the framers of the act of 1926 to create in favor of the repairman a lien for a limited period even after the delivery of the repaired article.

In the instant case the motors remained in the possession of Stewart. Therefore, under the view which we take, his lien subsisted until the seizure by the sheriff, and, in fact, subsisted during the period of the seizure and still subsists because a lienholder is not deprived of his lien when the article on which the lien bears is judicially sequestered. It is argued that in any event Stewart is not entitled to a lien for the entire amount of his claim because article 3217 of the Code, which recognizes the lien, limits it to "the price of his labor, on the movable which he has repaired or made." But it has been held by this court in *Cozzo v. Ulrich*, 14 Orleans App. 137, that "the artisan's lien covers not only his labor, but also the material by him furnished."

It has been decided that in such case, as this, although there may be no question concerning the ownership of the article on which the artisan is entitled to a privilege, he may, nevertheless, retain possession of the article and force the sale thereof in order that he may be paid out of the proceeds. *See Gayarre v. Tunnard*, 9 La. Ann. 254. There the Supreme Court expressly and squarely held that to the artisan there are afforded, by article 3184 of the Civil Code (now article 3217), two methods of procedure which are not conflicting. In the first place, he may retain the article until his bill is paid and in the second place, if it is not paid, he may proceed to have the article sold under his privilege.

In another branch of the case of *Cazzo v. Ulrich*, reported in 13 Orleans App. 257, we said:

"It will thus be seen that possession is of the essence of the privilege, and that the privilege is lost at the same time as the possession. This was the basis of the opinion in *Gayarre v. Tunnard*, 9 La. Ann. 254.

Therefore, defendant is entitled to retain possession of the motors under his privilege.

It is therefore ordered, adjudged, and decreed that the judgment appealed from be, and it is, amended, and that the lien and privilege and right of retention of S.J. Stewart, defendant, plaintiff in reconvention, on the two motors sequestered, be, and it is, recognized up to the sum of $149.47, with legal interest from judicial demand, and it is further ordered, adjudged, and decreed that the writ of sequestration be, and it is, dissolved at the cost of plaintiff-appellee.

* * * * * *

NOTES AND QUESTIONS

1. This case demonstrates the independence of the two alternative privileges granted under the Civil Code and the Revised Statutes. The expiration of the period provided by the statute for the enforcement of the statutory repairman's privilege does not deprive the artisan of his Civil Code privilege upon things that remain in his possession.

2. An interesting aspect of this court's opinion is the cavalier manner in which it dealt with the effect of the sale to the plaintiff of the repaired articles while they remained in the repairman's possession. Without any apparent recognition of the rule that a privilege normally terminates upon the debtor's alienation of the thing subject to the privilege, the court held that the "lien" survived the sale, for "[i]t would be a worthless lien which could be removed by sale." The court's expansive language, which was not even limited to the particular privilege involved in the case, would, if taken literally, transform every privilege into a real right following the property into the hands of third persons. Could the court's holding nonetheless be justified by an argument

that the statement of Civil Code Art. 3217(2) that the artisan's privilege continues for so long as "the thing continues still in his possession" creates an exception to the general rule that a privilege is lost upon the debtor's alienation of the thing subject to the privilege? Alternatively, could an argument be made that the transfer of the thing while in the artisan's possession was ineffective against him under Civil Code Article 518, which provides that transfer of ownership of a movable is effective against third persons when possession is delivered to the transferee and, until that occurs, creditors of the transferor can seize it?

3. The extent to which privileges constitute real rights that survive the debtor's alienation of the thing subject to the privilege is discussed at length in a later section of this chapter.

* * * * * *

THOMPSON CHEVROLET CO.

v.

BLANCHARD

131 So. 630 (La. App. 2d Cir. 1930)

ODOM, J.

On or about April 3, 1930, an automobile belonging to the defendant, Blanchard, was seized and ordered sold under a writ of seizure and sale in the case styled *C. J. Goodwin v. W. C. Blanchard*, No. 7845, on the docket of the Fifth district court for the parish of Richland. On or prior to the date of sale this plaintiff intervened in the suit by way of third opposition, claiming the proceeds of the sale by virtue of an alleged superior lien and privilege on the automobile for labor and parts furnished in the repair of the car.

Plaintiff attached to and made a part of its petition an itemized account showing that the labor account for making the repairs amounted to $34.35 and that the value of the material and parts used in connection therewith was $78.81.

The lien and privilege the plaintiff asserts is claimed under a special statute, Act No. 209 of 1926, p. 337, which provides that those making repairs upon automobiles, trucks, etc., "shall have a lien and privilege upon the automobile, truck, or machine so repaired or for which such repairs were made or parts furnished or made and for the labor performed upon same, for a period of ninety (90) days from the date of making of such repairs or parts or performing such labor, said period to run from the last day such repairs or parts are made or labor performed when the repairs done, parts made or labor performed require more than one day to complete." Section 1.

Plaintiff's itemized account, attached to and made part of its petition, shows that the first item charged thereon is dated November 16 and the last December 22. Its first step to enforce its lien and privilege was on April 25 of the following year, more than ninety days after the last item was charged.

C. J. Goodwin, plaintiff in the original suit, filed *in limine* an exception of no cause of action, and, from the judgment sustaining the exception, intervener has appealed.

The act above cited under which intervener claims to have a lien and privilege on the automobile repaired provides in specific terms that those making such repairs "shall have a lien and privilege upon the automobile . . . for a period of ninety (90) days . . . said period to run from the last day such repairs or parts are made or labor performed when the repairs done, parts made or labor performed require more than one day to complete."

Intervener's petition affirmatively shows that the last day on which labor was performed or parts furnished was more than ninety days prior to the date of its filing. It therefore follows necessarily that intervener had no privilege on the car or its proceeds when the intervention was filed and its alleged privilege asserted, and, further, that, as intervener did not pray for judgment against defendant, Blanchard, and as the only purpose of the intervention was to have the privilege recognized, the petition of intervention sets out no cause of action, and the judgment sustaining the exception was proper. As an alternative demand, intervener asks, in case the court should hold that it has no lien and privilege on the automobile repaired under the special statute above cited, that it be accorded the privilege allowed by law to vendors upon the parts and material furnished by it and used on the car. Under intervener's allegations it cannot be held that it has a privilege as vendor upon the materials and parts furnished for defendant's car. While it is true that in paragraph 2 of the petition it is alleged that a portion of the total amount charged is for "parts and accessories fully itemized and described on the annexed sworn account, sold and delivered to defendant by petitioner," yet the petition when considered as a whole and in connection with the account which is made part of it shows that the parts and material were not in fact sold to defendant, but were used in repairing the automobile. The pleading shows that the contract entered into by plaintiff and the defendant, Blanchard, was for the repair of the automobile.

The word "repair," when used as a verb, as defined by Webster, means to restore to a solid or good state after decay, injury, dilapidation, or partial destruction. Intervener was employed by defendant to repair this car after it had been wrecked and practically destroyed. To restore the car to solid good order, plaintiff necessarily had to use material and parts. The car could not have been repaired or restored to good order without them, and therefore the furnishing of the material and parts was an incident to and a part of the repair contract. The furnishing of parts and material used in connection with the repair of an automobile does not convert a repairman into a vendor. The relationship of vendor and purchaser does not arise under such circumstances.

The purpose of the above-cited statute is to protect mechanics who furnish labor and materials for the repair of automobiles, trucks, etc., and has reference to repair contracts only. The act contemplates that material and parts may have to be used as an incident to such contracts, and creates a lien on the car repaired not only for the work done, but for the value of the parts and materials as well. But that lien exists for a period of ninety days only. As that period had lapsed when this intervention was filed, the plaintiff or intervener has no privilege under the act.

For the reasons assigned, the judgment appealed from is affirmed, with all costs.

* * * * * *

NOTES AND QUESTIONS

1. Why did the repairman not assert the artisan's privilege under Civil Code art. 3217(2)?

2. Given that the courts have held that the statutory repairman's privilege is independent of and supplements the artisan's privilege granted by the Civil Code, why did the statutory repairman's privilege not also supplement the Civil Code vendor's privilege?

3. Suppose that the automobile owner had bought the needed materials and parts on credit from the repairman with the intention of installing them himself, but then returned a day later asking the repairman to install them for an additional charge. Might a vendor's privilege have arisen under those circumstances, and, if so, what amounts would it secure?

* * * * * *

WOOLDRIDGE PRODUCTION COMPANY, LTD.

v.

GOLDSTREAM CORPORATION

827 So. 2d 1211 (La. App. 2d Cir. 2002)

GASKINS, J.

The defendants, Goldstream Corporation, Jerry L. Whitton, Gerald D. Whitton, and Bobby G. Whitton, appeal a trial court judgment ordering them to pay $43,548.30 to the plaintiff, Wooldridge Production Company, Ltd., and rejecting the defendants' claims against the plaintiff. For the following reasons, we amend, and as amended, affirm the trial court judgment.

FACTS

Goldstream Corporation (Goldstream) is operated by Jerry L. Whitton, Gerald D. "Doug" Whitton, and Bobby G. Whitton. Wooldridge Production Company, Ltd. (Wooldridge) is operated almost exclusively by Mark Wooldridge, although his brother, Maury Wooldridge, previously worked in the business. This case is a suit on open account by Wooldridge and involves a dispute over the terms of an agreement between the parties.

In 1996, Goldstream had oilfield equipment that was not being used in south Louisiana, including a Bowen power swivel, triplex pump, Cameron QRC blow-out preventer, Wheatley plunger pump, two small tanks, two pipe threaders, two pumping units, a power tong, air slips, Martin Decker weights, a

Ford engine, and a big rig tank. Also, at some point, Goldstream owned a 1977 Wilson 42 B rig. Goldstream enlisted the aid of Wooldridge in going to south Louisiana, bringing the equipment back to Wooldridge's facility in Caddo Parish, and refurbishing it.

The parties agreed that the plaintiff would refurbish the equipment, would use or rent it, and would retain the revenue until the cost of repairs was recovered. Then Wooldridge would receive half the income from the equipment and Goldstream would be entitled to the remainder. At this point, the agreement was not reduced to writing. Wooldridge claimed that invoices for the repair work were periodically furnished to Goldstream. The defendants asserted that they did not receive invoices regarding the cost of repairs.

The power swivel and triplex pump were refurbished and were used to some extent by Wooldridge. Other items were not repaired. Two small tanks were not salvageable and were cut up for scrap. As the work progressed, the dispute over the terms of the agreement surfaced. At one point, Goldstream submitted a letter to Wooldridge, purporting to set forth the terms of the agreement. This letter was not signed by the plaintiff.

In January 1997, Goldstream presented Wooldridge with another letter, providing for Wooldridge's recovery of out-of-pocket costs for the repair of the equipment by the use of it in the plaintiff's well servicing business. According to the letter, any repairs of the equipment after reconditioning would be the responsibility of Wooldridge. Wooldridge was given the right of first refusal on purchasing the equipment. Wooldridge would be required to provide Goldstream with a total cost for the initial repair and reconditioning and to provide payout status on a monthly basis. Wooldridge would be obligated to carry insurance on the rig and related equipment. According to Goldstream, after making some modifications, Mark Wooldridge signed the agreement, but failed to furnish a signed copy to Goldstream. Mr. Wooldridge claimed that he did not agree to pay for repairs to the equipment after the initial refurbishing and did not agree to maintain insurance on it. Mr. Wooldridge denied signing the letter and stated that he could not find a copy of it in his files.

In October 1997, Goldstream wrote Wooldridge that it did not have a signed agreement or payout status and informed Wooldridge that it had five days from the date of the letter to exercise the right of first refusal to purchase the equipment. The parties were able to come to an agreement whereby Wooldridge purchased the 1977 Wilson 42-B rig for "$45,000, less liens of $13,042.13."

On January 22, 1998, a demand letter was sent by Wooldridge to the defendants requesting payment for the expenses of retrieving and refurbishing the equipment. The defendants responded, denying the amount owed and claiming entitlement to additional credits. The defendants also offered to sell the equipment to Wooldridge, but the plaintiff declined.

On February 6, 1998, Jerry Whitton and Gerald Whitton sent demand letters to the plaintiff for payment of compressor and pump rentals and for engineering and supervision services. The invoices supporting these charges were later shown to have been fabricated by the defendants.

The present lawsuit was filed by Wooldridge on February 12, 1998 for a money judgment, to recognize a privilege and for a writ of sequestration. Wooldridge alleged that beginning in November 1996, it provided goods and services to the defendants to repair equipment. Wooldridge claimed that Goldstream owed $83,000.46 on open account and sought to have its repairman's lien recognized under La. R.S. 9:4502. It asked for a writ of sequestration on the equipment without the necessity of furnishing security. The writ of sequestration was granted on February 17, 1998.

Goldstream answered, denying that it owed anything to Wooldridge, and claiming that the charges were wrongfully incurred. In its reconventional demand, Goldstream sought credit for use of the equipment by the plaintiff. . . . Goldstream further claimed that Wooldridge's writ of sequestration was wrongfully granted.

On October 25, 2001, the trial court issued a written ruling. The court found that there was an enforceable agreement between the parties for Wooldridge to retrieve and refurbish the defendants' equipment from south Louisiana. The court concluded that the defendants owed Wooldridge $43,548.30. . . . The court recognized that Wooldridge had a privilege on the property under La. R.S. 9:4502 and La. C.C. art. 3217. It also held that the defendants did not have a valid claim for loss of use of the equipment. Wooldridge was given the right to retain possession of the equipment until the judgment is paid by the defendants.

The defendants appealed the trial court judgment. They claim that the trial court erred in finding that they are indebted to Wooldridge for $43,548.30, in failing to allow them appropriate credit as deductions from any sums owed to Wooldridge, and in enforcing Wooldridge's lien against the equipment.

WRIT OF SEQUESTRATION

The defendants assert that the trial court erred in denying its request to dissolve the writ of sequestration, thereby enforcing what the defendants term an "invalid and unenforceable lien." The defendants contend that Wooldridge's writ of sequestration should have been dissolved for failure to post a bond or security as required by the court. The defendants also argue that Wooldridge has not had the uninterrupted possession of the equipment as required by La. R.S. 9:4502. The defendants note that Wooldridge destroyed or disabled some of the equipment without permission. According to the defendants, under La. C.C.P. art. 3506, they are entitled to damages and attorney fees for dissolution of the writ of sequestration. They seek to have this matter remanded to the trial court for a determination of appropriate damages and attorney fees. These arguments are without merit.

Failure to Furnish Security

As found by the trial court, Wooldridge exercised its right to a repairman's privilege regarding the equipment under La. R.S. 9:4502 and La. C.C. art. 3217. La. R.S. 9:4502 provides in pertinent part:

> A. (1) Any person engaged in the making or repairing of movable goods, . . . equipment, . . . machinery, or movable objects or movable property of any type or description, has a privilege on the thing for the debt due him for materials furnished or labor performed. This privilege is effective for a period of one hundred twenty days from the last day on which materials were furnished or labor was performed, if the thing affected by such privilege is removed from the place of business where such labor was performed or materials furnished;

> provided that if the thing affected by such privilege remains in the place of business of the person who furnished such materials or performed such labor, such privilege continues as long as such thing remains in such place of business.
>
> B. This privilege may be enforced by the writ of sequestration, without the necessity of the creditor furnishing security therefor, if the debtor is first given ten days' written notice by registered mail, and the exemptions from seizure granted by R.S. 13:3881 shall not be applicable to objects or property subject to this privilege for purposes of enforcing this privilege.
>
> C. In addition to the remedy above granted, when the thing affected by the privilege remains in the place of business of the person having such privilege and the debt due thereon remains unpaid for more than ninety days from the date on which the last labor was performed or last material was furnished, the holder of such privilege may sell such property at private sale and without appraisement, after advertising such property for ten days as provided by law in case of judicial sales of movables. . . .

La. C.C. art. 3217 provides in pertinent part:

> The debts which are privileged on certain movables, are the following:
>
> 2. The debt of a workman or artisan for the price of his labor, on the movable which he has repaired or made, if the thing continues still in his possession.

Pursuant to these articles, Wooldridge obtained a writ of sequestration. The first writ was granted in February 1998 and did not require security. The second writ was issued in April 1998 and required the posting of security. The defendants contend that, because the record does not show that the security was furnished, the writ should be dissolved. They contend that under La. C.C.P. art. 3501, the plaintiff was required to furnish security for the payment of damages the defendants may sustain if the writ is wrongfully obtained.

We note that the defendants failed to raise in the trial court the issue of failure to post security. In their post-trial brief, the defendants argued that the writ of sequestration should be dissolved because Wooldridge wrongfully possessed the property, failed to prove its claim against the defendants, and destroyed or damaged some of the equipment. At no point did the defendants raise the issue of failure to furnish security. As a general rule, appellate courts will not consider issues raised for the first time on appeal. *Geiger v. State Department of Health and Hospital,* 2001-2206 La. 4/12/02), 815 So. 2d 80, and cases cited therein. Accordingly, because the defendants have not previously raised this argument, it is not now properly before this court.

We further note that, under La. R.S. 9:4502, the repairman's privilege may be enforced by a writ of sequestration without the necessity of furnishing security. Arguably, pursuant to this statute, the posting of security was not necessary in this case. However, because this issue is not properly before the court for review, we do not reach consideration of this issue.

Uninterrupted Possession

The defendants further argue that the writ of sequestration should be dissolved because the plaintiff was not in uninterrupted possession of the equipment as required by La. C.C. art. 3217. They argue that the use of the equipment on other parties' wells interrupted the possession by the plaintiff.

The statutory privilege in La. R.S. 9:4502 is supplemental to the codal privilege granted artisans and repairman by La. C.C. art. 3217(2). *Thompson v. Warmack,* 231 So. 2d 636 (La. App. 3d Cir. 1970). To enforce the codal privilege, the repairman has the right to retain possession until paid. Unlike the statutory privilege, the code privilege requires uninterrupted possession to be enforceable. *Thompson v. Warmack,* supra.

In this case, the trial court found that Wooldridge was seeking to enforce both the statutory and codal privileges. As stated above, uninterrupted possession is not necessary to enforce the statutory privilege. However, under the facts of this case, even under the codal privilege, the plaintiff had uninterrupted possession. The equipment, on a few limited occasions, was used on customers' wells and they were charged for its use. In all instances, Wooldridge was in control of the equipment. We do not see that using the equipment in the manner intended by the agreement between the parties constitutes an interruption of possession.

* * * * * *

NOTES AND QUESTIONS

1. The plaintiff in the case asserted both the Civil Code privilege and the statutory privilege under La. R.S. 9:4502, and the court apparently recognized both. Was the claim asserting the statutory privilege timely? If so, why did the court feel it necessary to address the issue of whether the plaintiff continued to have possession for purposes of maintaining the Civil Code privilege?

2. Both the Civil Code privilege and the statutory privilege can be enforced by a pre-judgment seizure pursuant to a writ of sequestration, but in the case of the statutory privilege the requirement of furnishing a bond in order to obtain the writ is excused.

4. Privileges for Expenses of Preservation and Carrier's Charges

***See* La. Civ. Code arts. 3217(6) and (9); 3224-26; La. Rev. Stat. 9:4601; La. Rev. Stat. 10:7-207 and 7-209**

* * * * * *

2 Traite Élementaire de Droit Civil, pt. 2
(La. State Law Inst. trans., 1959) (12th ed. 1939) (Fr.)
Marcel Planiol & Georges Ripert

2590. Origin

The Roman law gave a privilege to those who made advances for the purpose to repairing, to preserving or to reconstructing, either a house or a ship (Dig. Bk. XLII, tit. 5 fr. 24, § 1, fr. 26).

2591. Transformation

Since Roman times this privilege has undergone two changes: (1) instead of being a general privilege on all the property, as the ancient *"privilegia exigendi,"* it became specialized, bearing exclusively on the thing ameliorated or preserved; (2) instead of applying only to houses and ships, it is accorded for the expenses of preserving anything whatsoever; Art. 2102(3) speaks in terms as general as possible of the "preservation of the thing" (Cass. Civ., 14 Feb. 1900, D.1900.1.175, S.1900.1.176; 3 Nov. 1925, D.1926.1.49, S.1925.1.353). Curtailed on one side; it is extended on another.

* * * * * *

POWERS & CO.

v.

SIXTY TONS OF MARBLE

21 La. Ann. 402 (1869)

WYLY, J.

This is a proceeding *in rem* to recover the amount of storage due the plaintiffs, keepers of a warehouse, on sixty tons of marble, and to enforce their privilege thereon.

The marble was shipped from Boston in December, 1860, by unknown parties, and consigned to Cavanaugh and Cully, at this place, who refused to pay the freight and accept the consignment. Thereupon the same was hauled by the plaintiffs to their warehouse and stored at the request of the captains or consignees of the vessels which transported it.

The owners appear to have abandoned the property, never having offered to pay the freight and storage and to take possession of the same.

On ninth February, 1867, plaintiffs sued to recover the amount due them and to enforce their privilege and pledge on the marble which still remained stored in their warehouse, the court appointing a curator *ad hoc* to represent the absent owners.

George W. Hynson & Co. as ship agents and consignees intervened and claimed the amount due for freight, primage and average on said marble, with a privilege, as they allege, superior to that of plaintiffs.

On the trial the court rendered judgment in favor of plaintiffs for the amount claimed by them, to be paid by privilege and preference out of the proceeds of the sale of the marble, and in favor of the intervenors for the amount claimed by them without privilege.

The intervenors have appealed.

The claims of these creditors are fully established. The owners of the marble owe the full amount of freight due the intervenors, and they also owe the full amount claimed by plaintiffs for storage.

The only question to determine is, which one of these creditors has the superior privilege on the marble or its proceeds?

The intervenors contend that under article 3213 Civil Code they have a privilege on the goods for the freight, the same not having been delivered to the consignees, nor passed into third hands. That having stored it, the marble, in effect, remained in their hands.

They contend the court erred in allowing the plaintiffs a privilege; that a privilege for storage is no where allowed by our laws.

Plaintiffs' claim is for the preservation of the thing. Under articles 3191, 3192 and 3193 of the Civil Code a party is entitled to recover the expenses incurred for the preservation of the property which he has in his possession, "whether in deposit, loan or otherwise;" and he has a right of pledge by which he may, until reimbursed, retain the property.

The evidence in this case establishes that the charges of plaintiffs are reasonable for taking care of and preserving the property which had been placed in their hands for storage.

In our opinion the court did not err in giving plaintiffs preference to be paid out of the proceeds of the thing preserved by them. The intervenors had the first privilege on the marble for the freight had they seen fit to keep it in their own custody till they were paid. But after permitting it to remain in storage with the plaintiffs for so many years where they placed it, they cannot complain if their privilege must yield to the superior rights of those who have preserved the thing for so long a period.

We think the court erred in not recognizing the privilege of the intervenors on the property in contest, but that their privilege is inferior to that of plaintiffs. C. C. 3229.

It is therefore ordered that the judgment appealed from be amended by allowing the intervenors a privilege next in rank to the plaintiffs to be paid out of the proceeds of the sale of the marble, and as thus amended that the judgment be affirmed.

It is ordered that plaintiffs pay costs of this appeal.

* * * * * *

NOTES AND QUESTIONS

1. Civil Code Article 3225 grants a creditor who incurred expenses for the preservation of a thing both a privilege in the nature of an implied pledge and a right of retention.

2. Civil Code Article 3224 conditions the existence of the privilege upon the creditor's possession of the thing preserved. Where a creditor claiming a privilege for preservation expenses never had possession of the property in question, he is entitled to no privilege. *Boylan's Detective Agency & Protection Police v. Brown & Company*, 102 So. 417 (La. 1924).

3. Does this case stand for the broad proposition that the privilege for preservation expenses always outranks the privilege for carrier's charges?

4. By what rationale did the court rank the warehouse's privilege for storage charges above that for carrier's charges? Was it on account of the implied pledge and right of retention that the Civil Code gave to the warehouse for preservation expenses? Was it the fact that the warehouse had possession of the goods? Was it because the warehouse's preservation efforts came after the carrier's privilege had already risen and therefore inured to the benefit of the carrier? Was it because the carrier appears to have contracted for the

storage by delivering the goods to the warehouse? Or did the court simply apply the ranking rule of Article 3229 of the Civil Code of 1825 in preference to that contained in Article 3232 (*see now* La. Civ. Code Arts. 3262 and 3265 (1870))? The extent to which the factors just enumerated are applied in ranking privileges on movables is explored in detail in the next chapter.

5. A statutory privilege for carrier's charges now exists under La. R.S. 9:4601 in favor of a person in the business of hauling. By the text of that statute, the privilege is subordinate to vendor's privileges, previously perfected security interests, and the rights of a bona fide purchaser to whom possession was delivered and who paid the price without previous notice of the existence of the privilege for carrier's charges. The statute does not purport to rank the privilege against other privileges, but an argument can be made that they are made inferior by omission from the list of priming encumbrances in the statute.

6. La. R.S. 10:7-207 provides that "[a] carrier has a lien on the goods covered by a bill of lading or on the proceeds thereof in its possession for charges after the date of the carrier's receipt of the goods for storage or transportation, including demurrage and terminal charges, and for expenses necessary for preservation of the goods incident to their transportation or reasonably incurred in their sale pursuant to law." Under Section 7-207(b), the lien is effective against any person who permitted the bailor to have control or possession of the goods unless the carrier had notice that the bailor lacked authority. The carrier loses the lien on goods that it delivers or unjustifiably refuses to deliver. As will be discussed in the following chapter, La. R.S. 10:9-333 grants priority over Chapter 9 security interests to possessory liens securing payment or performance of an obligation for services or materials furnished with respect to goods when effectiveness of the privilege depends upon the person's possession of the goods. Because the existence of the carrier's lien under Section 7-202 is dependent on the carrier's continued possession of the goods, the lien has priority over Chapter 9 security interests, so long as the requirements of Section 7-207(b) are satisfied.

7. La. R.S. 10:7-209 supplements the preservation privilege available to a warehouse under Civil Code Article 3224. The warehouse loses its Chapter 7 privilege on goods that it delivers or unjustifiably refuses to deliver. The warehouse's Chapter 7 lien is not effective against a person who, before

issuance of a document of title covering the goods, had a perfected security interest in the goods, unless the secured party delivered or entrusted the goods or any document of title covering the goods to the bailor or the bailor's nominee with certain enumerated powers over the goods. Thus, even though the warehouse's Chapter 7 lien is a possessory lien, it does not benefit from the priority ordinarily granted to possessory liens under Section 9-333, because Section 7-209 "expressly provides otherwise" within the meaning of Section 9-333. Would the privilege under Civil Code Article 3224 nonetheless have priority?

5. The Depositor's Privilege

***See* La. Civ. Code arts. 3217(5); 3222-23**

* * * * * *

LONGBOTTOM'S EXECUTORS

v.

BABCOCK

9 La. 44 (1836)

BULLARD, J., delivered the opinion of the court.

The testamentary executors of Joseph Longbottom, deceased, being ordered by the Court of Probates to file an account of their administration, an account and tableau were after some delay filed, to which numerous oppositions were made on various grounds, by creditors of the estate. The court, after hearing evidence and argument, gave judgment sustaining some of the oppositions and overruling others. The executors appealed.

One of the opposing creditors and appellees, Cotton Henry, prays that the judgment below may be so amended as to allow his claim for one thousand one hundred dollars to be paid by privilege, as for a special deposite, that sum being found in the store of the deceased.

The evidence in the record shows that the deceased was the attorney in fact of Cotton Henry, during his absence from the State, and that before his departure he had given his agent a check on one of the banks for one thousand three hundred dollars, to be disbursed on his account, and that the sum of one thousand one hundred dollars was found in the store of the deceased at the time of his death. But there is no evidence to show that this sum is the same money received by the testator. Article 3189, relied on by the opponent, requires, in order that the depositor may exercise his right of privilege, proof of the identity of the thing deposited. It is of the essence of deposite that the depository should be bound to keep the thing deposited and restore it in kind to the depositor. In this case the money appears to have gone into the hands of Longbottom as the agent of Cotton Henry. He was bound to account for it, but not to restore it in kind. He did disburse a part of it for the use of his principal. We therefore think the court acted correctly in rejecting the opponent's claim as a privileged one.

* * * * * *

NOTES AND QUESTIONS

1. The first paragraph of Civil Code art. 3222 states categorically that he who deposits a thing in the hands of another still remains the owner of it. To that extent, the depositor's privilege does not seem to partake of the nature of a true privilege, which an owner ordinarily cannot hold over his own property. The idea of a preference appears in the second paragraph of the article, which provides that the depositor's claim to the thing deposited is preferred to the claims of the other creditors of the depositary.

2. The depositor does hold a true privilege if the depositary has disposed of the thing and is owed money from the disposition. In that event, Civil Code article 3217(5) grants the depositor a privilege on the price due on the sale of the thing deposited.

* * * * * *

IN RE LOUISIANA SAVINGS BANK & SAFE DEPOSIT CO.
40 La. Ann. 514 (1888)

TODD, J.

The Louisiana Savings Bank & Safe Deposit Company was placed in liquidation in June, 1879. On the 16th of June, 1887, the liquidators or commissioners filed their second provisional account. . . . Oppositions were filed to the account by the heirs of Royal A. Porter, deceased. . . . From an adverse judgment these opponents have appealed.

Opposition of the Porter heirs. Upon the settlement of the succession of Royal A. Porter, the father of these opponents, their distributive shares were found to be in the aggregate $9,866.15, which sum was deposited in the Louisiana National Bank to the credit of the succession of the deceased. On the 12th of June, 1878, under an order of the Second district court of New Orleans, this fund was withdrawn from the bank mentioned, and deposited in the Louisiana Savings Bank, where it drew interest, which was paid to the executrix. On the 31st of May, 1879, an order of the same court was rendered, directing the withdrawal of said funds from the savings bank, and the investment thereof by the tutrix in United States bonds. On the 4th of June thereafter, this order was presented to the president of the bank, who, after a short delay to ascertain the correctness of the order, informed the tutrix that no United States bonds could then be purchased in New Orleans, but that he would take the money, and send it to Washington city, and there purchase the bonds for the heirs. To this the tutrix agreed, and surrendered her bankbook, and received two certificates of deposit, one for the shares of the two younger heirs, and the other for the oldest, who had then been emancipated, accompanied by the assurance of the president of the bank that these certificates would be exchanged for the bonds as soon as they arrived, which it was stated would be about the 7th of July. The bonds never came, the investment was never made in fact, and the bank failed; closing its doors on the 30th of June. It possessed, at the time, in cash, $32,639.42, which went into the hands of the commissioners. On the account of the commissioners these heirs are placed thereon as ordinary creditors. They claim, however, by reason of the facts recited above, that their deposit was a special deposit, entitling them to be paid by preference over all creditors; and this is the sole question relating to this opposition to be determined. The contention of the opponents rests entirely on the hypothesis that there was an actual deposit made on the 4th of June, 1879. The actual deposit was really made in June, 1878, and in point of fact from that time continuously the fund was in the possession of the bank, after the proposed investment of the fund of the bonds as before. From the time of the actual deposit of the money in June 1878, the heirs or their tutrix were never in possession of their money. There was an order of court, it is true, requiring the fund to be invested in United States bonds, but the fund was not withdrawn for the purpose of this investment; and, although there was a promise on the part of the president of the bank to make this investment or purchase the bonds for the parties, it was never done by him, and the money remained in the bank as before. The issuing of the certificates, even coupled with the promise of the president to invest in the bonds, and the purpose of the depositors to effect the investment, did not change the *status* or condition of the fund, and convert the original irregular deposit of 1878 into a real or special deposit. We cannot, under any reasonable view of the circumstances, construe this deposit as the real or special deposit, as contended for by the opponents. A deposit, as defined by the Code, "is an act by which a person receives the property of another binding himself to preserve it, and return it in kind." Civil Code, art. 2926. "The depositary cannot make use of the thing without the express or implied consent of the depositor." Id. art. 2940. "The depositary ought to restore the precise object which he has received." Id. art. 2944. "The only real deposit is that where the depositary receives a thing to be preserved in kind, without the power of using it, and on the condition that he is to restore the identical object." Id. art. 2963. "He who deposits a thing in the hands of another still remains the owner of it"; "consequently his claim to it is preferred to that of the other creditors of the depositary, and he can demand the restitution of it, . . . if the thing reclaimed be identically the same which he deposited." Id. art. 3222. The deposit thus specifically described in the foregoing article is claimed by opponents to be the kind of deposit that was made by them in the savings bank; and upon this claim exclusively their case rests. It will be seen that the essential conditions of the deposit, a real or special deposit, is that the thing deposited can be identified. In this case, $9,866, in no particular or designated kind of money, was placed in the bank in June, 1878. In June, 1879, the bank failed, having in its vault, in money, $32,639. That the fund deposited more than a year before could be identified and taken from these moneys found in the bank would certainly seem impossible; and even that any of this original fund remained, and made part of this balance found, was highly improbable. Yet this identification is essential. In the case of *Longbottom's Ex'rs. v. Babcock*, 9 La. 50, opposing creditors to the executor's account claimed the privilege on account of the special deposit, as follows; "The evidence in the record shows that the deceased was the attorney in fact of Cotton Henry during his (Henry's) absence from the state, and that before his departure he had given his agent (the deceased) a check on one of the banks for $1,300, to be disbursed in his account, and that $1,100 was found in the store of the deceased at the time of his death.

But there is no evidence to show that this sum is the same money received by the testator. Article 3189 [now 3222] requires, in order that the depositor may exercise his right of privilege, proof of the identity of the thing deposited must be made. It is of the essence of the deposit that the depositary should be bound to keep the thing deposited, and restore it in kind to the depositors. In this case the money appears to have gone into the hands of Longbottom as agent of Henry. He was bound to account for it, and not to restore it in kind. He did disburse a part of it for the use of his principals. The court properly rejected the claim as a privilege." The case The case of *Matthews v. McKenzie*, 10 La. Ann. 342, is confirmatory, and even more strongly illustrative of the same principle. We quote from their decision: "The money was counted and debited to the depositary simply as so much cash. Special or real deposits are usually sealed up, and not counted by the banker, and are to be returned in kind. The box or package containing the real deposit is indorsed with the depositor's name, and is put away by itself in the vault, there to remain till demand by the owners, and checks cannot be drawn against it." In view of the above, it is plain that the issuing of the certificates of deposit in this case cannot be regarded as changing in anywise the character of the deposit, as contended for by opponent's counsel. A certificate is given as evidence of the amount standing to the credit of the depositor. The main object of such certificate is to afford satisfactory evidence of such credit, and to enable the depositor to utilize the credit by drawing checks against or upon the amount so deposited; whereas, it is seen from the authority last cited that, if it be a special or real deposit, checks cannot be drawn upon it. The counsel for opponents claim that the identification of the fund was sufficient, because the bank, when it failed, had in its possession cash exceeding in amount the deposit. We have before adverted to the extreme improbability that any part of this money was part or parcel of the funds originally deposited; but the authority of the case in 9 La., above cited, is, as we have seen, directly opposed to such contention. It is true that authorities from other states were cited by the counsel of the opponents that undoubtedly supported their argument, and especially on this particular point, but they belong to a different system, and were the enunciations of equity courts, relating to trusts, express or implied, and to trust funds. While they are authority entitled to respect, we cannot yield to them in the face of the positive declarations of our written law, and the settled jurisprudence under it. The claim was properly construed to be an ordinary debt of the bank, and the privilege rejected.

* * * * * *

NOTES AND QUESTIONS

1. Civil Code Articles 3260 and 3261 give the depositor's privilege preference over all other privileged debt, except for the privilege in favor of a lessor who is unaware that the thing deposited does not belong to the lessee. Though these articles might appear to provide considerable protection to a depositor, they are of limited benefit where the thing deposited is fungible, since Article 3222 requires that the "thing reclaimed be identically the same which he deposited." The jurisprudence has held that this means that the privilege is extinguished if the thing deposited is commingled with others of like kind such that the identity of the thing deposited is destroyed. As the case above reflects, in that event the depositor is treated as a general creditor who shares pro-rata with the other creditors of the depositary. *See also Daugherty v. Canal Bank & Trust Co.*, 158 So. 366 (La. 1935) and the cases cited therein.

2. Is the subordination of the depositor's claim to the privilege of a lessor who was unaware of the depositor's ownership still of any relevance? Recall that, following the 2004 revision of the law of lease, the lessor's privilege no longer attaches to things of a third person, other than a sublessee, found on the leased property.

3. When a warehouse or any other person fails to pay an agricultural producer for agricultural or dairy products, La. R.S. 9:5021, added by Act 461 of 1968, grants the producer a "special privilege" on all movable and immovable assets of any insolvent or bankrupt debtor "for the amount of payments for agricultural and dairy products due them, not exceeding six months payments for such products which shall have accrued prior to the adjudication of the insolvency or bankruptcy." Although the statute uses the term "special privilege," what it actually creates is a general privilege since it affects all movable and immovable property of the debtor. This privilege ranks ahead of all other privileges, debts, charges, or claims, except for taxes, bona fide vendor's privileges, laborer's privileges, lessor's privileges, and mortgages recorded before the purchase of the agricultural and dairy products. No reported case has ever applied the statute.

6. The Vendor's Privilege

i. In General

See **La. Civ. Code arts. 3217(7); 3249(1)**

The vendor's privilege has been a coveted and powerful form of security throughout Louisiana's history. It gives the seller the right to be satisfied from the proceeds of the thing sold with preference over other creditors of the buyer. It attaches automatically to anything that is sold—movable or immovable, corporeal or incorporeal. It is a matter of substantive right incident to a contract of sale and not a mere remedy for enforcing its execution. A vendor's privilege arises only from a sale, and not from other kinds of transactions, such as a building contract. Thus, there must be a transfer of ownership for a price. A vendor's privilege does not arise from a loan transaction by which the purchaser borrows the money to be used to purchase the property.

The vendor's privilege secures not only the price itself but also interest accruing on the price, attorney's fees stipulated in the obligation representing the purchase price, and any other monetary obligation of the purchaser undertaken in the sale transaction.

As the cases below reflect, the rules applicable to the vendor's privilege on movables differ markedly from those that apply to the vendor's privilege on an immovable.

* * * * * *

2 TRAITE ÉLEMENTAIRE DE DROIT CIVIL, PT. 2
(La. State Law Inst. trans., 1959) (12th ed. 1939) (Fr.)
MARCEL PLANIOL & GEORGES RIPERT

2604. Protection of Vendor and Roman Law

The privilege of the vendor has its first origin in the Roman law, although the ancient legislation never dreamed of attributing a privilege to a vendor. To tell the truth it had no need for it: he was still better protected though in another fashion. Generally, as long as the price was not paid, the vendor remained proprietor of the thing sold: *"Venditae vero res et traditae non alitea emptori acquiruntur quam si is pretium solverit*" (Institutes Bk. II, tit. I, No. 41); he could therefore revendicate it and take it back.

By exception, the ownership passed to the buyer even though the price was not yet paid: (1) when the vendor had received a guaranty such as a faithswearer; (2) when he trusted the faith of the buyer, by giving him credit and by giving him a term for payment. They said then "*res abirt in creditum,*" and the vendor despoiled of his property was nothing more than an ordinary creditor.

It is from the Roman action in revendication that the modern privilege of the vendor was derived.

2605. Original State of the French Law

For a long time France adhered to the ancient rules, reserving to the vendor the revendication of the sale without term, and relegating him to the personal action in the sale on term. Dumoulin and all the authors explain this right of the vendor by the application pure and simple of the Roman law; if he could revendicate, it was because he remained proprietor.

2606. Change in the XVI Century

If French law had done nothing more, the privilege of the vendor would not have existed, and we would still have the primitive rules. But in the XVI Century a new usage was introduced: the vendor on term, who was not protected by the common law, took his precautions; he delivered the thing under a precarious title or on a fictitious lease, so as to make a tradition which did not transfer the ownership. He thus placed himself in the same position as if he had not accorded a term to the buyer. Such usage was so general that the ancient Roman distinction, which made the protection of the vendor depend upon the absence of a term, was considered a "subtlety" (Lauriére, *Coutume de Paris*, t. II, p. 148) and to satisfy the practice a new article was added to the Coutume (Art. 177), at the time of the reformation of 1580. According to this article, "even when he [the vendor] gives a term, if the thing is seized with the debtor by another creditor, he can prevent the sale and is preferred on the thing to the other creditors. Observe the language of the new text: it gives to the seller on time a right of preference on the price coming from the execution on the movable. It is the first appearance of a veritable special privilege in our law.

This institution was then entirely new, contrary to all tradition. Also it is not astonishing that they hesitated for a long time as to the name to give to it. Pothier called it from time to time *hypothéque (Cout. d'Orleans*, on Art. 458, t. I, p. 687), and *privilége* (*Procéd. Civile*, No. 488, t. X, p. 140). Claude Ferriére speaks as Pothier, sometimes of privilege and sometimes of mortgage (*Coutume de Paris*, small edition, t. I, p. 386).

2608. Reasons

As long as the price is not paid the sale augments the patrimony of the buyer at the expense of the vendor: the latter has impoverished himself, he has alienated his property and has not yet received anything in exchange. The vendor has thus gratuitously augmented the common pledge of the creditors of the buyer; the latter can be paid with the property sold without the vendor being paid, they enrich themselves at his expense, which is unjust. The new property therefore can be veritably acquired by the buyer only by the payment of the price; in French legislation which admits the immediate transfer of the title, the privilege is necessary to prevent an inequity.

* * * * * *

DE L'ISLE

V.

SUCCESSION OF MOSS

34 La. Ann. 164 (1882)

The opinion of the Court was delivered by BERMUDEZ, C. J.

The only question presented on appeal in this case for determination, is simply:

Whether the payment of a mortgage debt, assumed by a vendee, as part of the price of sale, is or not secured by vendor's privilege on the property sold.

By Article 3126 of the Code of 1825, in force of the date of the sale and assumption, and which is Article 3249 of the R. C. C., it is clearly provided, that the payment of so much of the price of sale as remains unpaid, shall be secured by the vendor's privilege.

If the note now sued on were one subscribed by the purchaser, there would probably have arisen no difficulty, even as against the present plaintiff, who is not the vendor, but a mere holder and owner of a note of his, for having acquired the same through others, from the original mortgagee, by transfer and subrogation.

The objections made to the vendor's privilege claimed, are grounded upon the charge, that the amount claimed is not a *debt created* at the time of the sale, and due *to* the vendor, or to one of his authors; but that it is a debt which existed prior to the date of the purchase, in favor of one who was not a vendor and who was not a party to the act.

In demonstration of the soundness of this distinction, it is asserted, as a test, that if the creditor whose mortgage debt had been assumed as part of the purchase price, remained unpaid, he could not seek and obtain a resolution of the sale, in the exercise of the right vested in a vendor, by the reserve of the resolutory condition.

The privilege accorded for the payment of the unpaid price of sale, is one of great value, resting on considerations of the plainest equity. It would indeed be unjust to place an unpaid vendor on a footing of equality with the other creditors of the purchaser, and permit these to devour his substance; for it is only on the condition that the price of the thing sold has been paid, that the purchaser acquires an indefeasible title of ownership to the property, and that his creditors can be paid.

This privilege was unknown to the old Roman Law, as also was the resolutory condition. It is of Gallic creation. The modern civilians say that it adheres to the entrails of the thing. After delivery, the old Roman law abandoned the vendor selling on credit to the good faith or mercy of the purchaser, and declined a resolution of the sale in case of non-payment of the price, unless the *pactum commissarium* had been expressly stipulated.

It confers rights of a high character, superior to those which flow from a mortgage. It entitles the vendor, at his option, either to specific performance in exacting payment, or to a resolution of the sale and taking back the property, free from all encumbrance by the vendee. It protects him from contribution towards the expenses of the liquidation of the estate of the purchaser in case of his death, or insolvency. It shields him from the claim of a widow, of minor children, or of both for a homestead. It springs from the very nature of the contract of sale, of which it is a legal concomitant. It exists without stipulation, and adheres tenaciously to the thing sold. It is invariably considered as retained, unless renounced in language unmistakably clear, or by acts evidently designed to destroy effectually the presumption of its retention. It exists and continues until satisfaction, to secure the payment of the unpaid price, whether an entirety or a fraction. 3 A. 600; 4 A. 313; 32 A. 828.

It is the *price* which is protected by the privilege. By the sale the vendor increases the estate of the purchaser. It would be iniquitous to permit the property sold to become the prey of the creditors of the purchaser, without requiring, as a condition precedent, the payment of its costs. Laurent 30, p. 6, § 2; p. 18 § 16; Troplong, *Priv. and Hyp. on Art. 2096*, p. 25; on Art. 2103, p. 333.

The word *price* signifies the sum stipulated as the equivalent of the thing sold and also every incident taken into consideration for the fixing of the price, put to the debit of the vendee, and agreed to by him. Troplong, *Priv. and Hyp. on Art. 1552*, p. 65, No. 595; Laurent 30, p. 11, §§ 9, 10. Pont. *Priv. 1*, Tit. 28, §§ 190, 145, 187.

Both on principle and practically, it is a matter of indifference to the purchaser to whom the price be paid, whether to the vendor, or to his creditors, or to his beneficiaries. His obligation is to pay the price agreed upon, to whoever can, on payment, give him acquittance and discharge. His assumption to pay it to a third person, makes him personally liable to the creditor, on his acceptance of the assumption.

Where the purchaser assumes to pay a mortgage debt of the vendor, the creditor has the right of proceeding against him directly.

Where the mortgage debt has not been assumed it is so well secured that the suing creditor would rank the vendor of the previously mortgaged property. The creditor is under no obligation to accept the assumption, but he may do so until he has declined it. Duranton, vol. 10, Ed. Brux, 1134, p. 234, No. 26; Mourlon, vol. 3, p. 497, No. 1249; *Marcadé on Art. 2098*, p. 19, III No. 26; 2 N. S. 32; 12 L. 184; 8 A. 267, 758; 26 A. 618; H. D. 255; L. D. 442; 21 Wall. 123.

The debt due by the vendor in the present case and secured by preexisting mortgage on the property sold, became guaranteed by the vendor's privilege, the very moment that it was, by covenant, to form an integral part of the price of sale. The privilege was then created by law, not by the consent of parties, to secure the price thus made up and agreed upon; but it conditionally existed in favor of the mortgage creditor, who could either ignore or accept the assumption and stipulation. By the fact and at the instant of acceptance, that creditor acquired the right to ask payment of his debt with the vendor's privilege, as effectually as he could have done, had he been the holder of a note of the purchaser, furnished in settlement of the price of sale.

Whether by thus accepting the stipulation, he has lost a priority over the vendor, is a question not presented, and on which we express no opinion.

The doctrine presently announced may well hereafter be considered as a rule of property, which, in our mind, it has always been.

We do not think that it is material, for the determination of this case, to decide whether the plaintiff, instead of demanding specific performance, could have asserted the resolutory condition, and sought to enforce rights protected by it: whether he could or not, does not deprive him of the right of claiming the privilege of vendor, which was denied him by the court *a quo*. 12 A. 695; 24 A. 498.

We have given due attention and weight to the theory advanced and to the authorities invoked by the learned counsel for the defense, but, while we admit their respectability, we cannot recognize that they can receive any application or produce any effect in a case like the present one.

We think the District Judge erred in refusing to allow the privilege claimed.

It is therefore ordered and decreed, that the judgment appealed from be amended by inserting in the latter part thereof, a recognition of the vendor's privilege claimed in the petition, and that thus amended, said judgment be affirmed with costs.

Rehearing refused.

* * * * * *

NOTES AND QUESTIONS

1. In the excerpt quoted above, Planiol gives essentially the same justification for the vendor's privilege as the court in *De L'Isle*, but in language that evokes other concepts of the Civil Code: the unpaid vendor has gratuitously augmented the *common pledge* of the vendee's creditors, who are thus *unjustly enriched* at his expense. Because the sales articles of the French Civil Code—and of course the Louisiana code as well—force the immediate transfer of title to the vendee even though the price has not been not paid, the privilege is necessary to prevent an inequity. The vendor is privileged because he has augmented the patrimony of the vendee.

2. The case demonstrates that the vendor's privilege arises not just as security for the vendee's obligation to pay the balance of the price he owes to the vendor, but also from the vendee's assumption of an existing obligation of the vendor.

3. *Citizens Bank v. Succession of Cuny*, 38 La. Ann. 360 (1886), held that, where a vendee assumes a debt secured by an outstanding mortgage that burdens only a portion of the estate sold to him, the vendor's privilege thus created in favor of the mortgagee nonetheless burdens the entire estate. La. R.S. 9:5383 appears intended to alter this result, though the statute is awkwardly worded and written in a way that seems not to recognize that the assumption itself creates a new vendor's privilege.

* * * * * *

W. T. GRANT COMPANY

v.

MITCHELL

269 So. 2d 186 (La. 1972)

SUMMERS, Justice.

Lawrence Mitchell purchased a refrigerator, range, stereo and washer from W. T. Grant Company on an installment sales contract. When Mitchell defaulted in his payments, Grant instituted this suit in the First City Court of New Orleans for $574.19, the balance due on the contract.

Grant alleged its entitlement to "a vendor's lien and privilege" on the merchandise and that it "fears that said defendant will encumber or alienate same during the pendency of the proceeding. . . ." Accordingly, Grant alleged, the issuance of a writ of sequestration was necessary to protect its interest. La. Code Civ. P. arts. 3501, 3571.

In an attached affidavit Jerry Dunnegan, Grant's Credit Manager, verified the facts of the petition and affirmed that petitioner "has reason to fear and believe that the said defendant, Lawrence Mitchell, will encumber, alienate or otherwise dispose of the merchandise . . . during the pendency of these proceedings, and that a writ of sequestration is necessary. . . ." La. Code Civ. P. art. 3501.

The Judge of the City Court signed an order for the issuance of a writ of sequestration upon plaintiff furnishing bond in the amount of $1,125. La. Code Civ. P. art. 3574. On the same day bond was furnished, February 2, 1972, the writ of sequestration issued, and Mitchell was cited to answer within five days. On February 7, 1972, Mitchell's stove, refrigerator and electric wash tub were provisionally seized pursuant to the writ of sequestration.

Thereafter, on March 3, 1972, Mitchell's counsel filed a motion to dissolve the writ of sequestration, alleging that the refrigerator, stove and electric wash tub were exempt from seizure by any process whatsoever under Section 3881 of Title 13 of the Revised Statutes. The motion to dissolve was also based upon the assertion that Mitchell was denied due process of law in that he received no notice prior to the provisional seizure under the writ of sequestration nor was he afforded an opportunity to defend his rights to the personal property prior to the seizure. Mitchell also alleged his poverty and want of means and sought to proceed *in forma pauperis* as authorized by Article 5181 of the Code of Civil Procedure.

Mitchell's motion to dissolve and the application to proceed *in forma pauperis* were denied by the judge a quo, and a subsequent application for review to the Court of Appeal, Fourth Circuit was also denied. We granted review on Mitchell's application.

I.

Section 3881 of Title 13 of the Revised Statutes exempts from seizure the stove, wash tub and refrigerator "under any writ, mandate, or process whatsoever." This section was added to the Revised Statutes by Act 32 of 1960 to replace Article 644 of the Code of Practice when the latter was repealed, having been superseded by the Code of Civil Procedure. See Act 15 of 1960.

After its inclusion in the Revised Statutes, Section 3881 was amended in 1961 to remove all doubt that the wages, salaries, and other compensation of public employees and contractors were subject to garnishment. The second reason was to effectuate the recommendation of the Louisiana Sheriff's Association that the refrigerator used in a debtor's household be exempted from seizure. Act 25 of 1961; Comments by Henry G. McMahon to Section 3881. In all other respects the subject matter of Article 644 of the Code of Practice was unchanged by Section 3881.

This conclusion is further confirmed by the inclusion of Section 3881 in Chapter 18 of Title 13 of the Revised Statutes dealing with seizures in general. This chapter also contains enactments pertaining to execution of judgments under a writ of *fieri facias*; whereas a separate chapter (Chapter 20) in the same title collects the sections pertaining to provisional remedies (attachment, sequestration, etc.). If the compilers of the Revised Statutes, and the Legislature, intended that the exemptions of Section 3881 should apply to provisional remedies, it would have been more orderly and logical to include this section with the sections on that subject. Instead this exemption provision was included with those sections pertaining to seizures under *fieri facias*.

Article 644 of the Code of Practice was contained in Chapter 6, "Of The Proceedings in Execution of Judgments." Section 3 of that chapter dealt with "The Execution of Judgments Directing the Payment of a Sum of Money." Paragraph 1 of Section 3 pertained to the Writ of *Fieri Facias*. Article 644 falls under this heading. It is for this reason that the courts have held that Article 644 related to exemptions from seizure under the writ of *Fieri facias* only, refusing to allow the exemption against a provisional seizure to assert a lessor's privilege. *Ross v. Rosenthal*, 1 Orleans App. 203 (1904), *cert. denied* by Supreme Court June 30, 1904; *Benton v. Jarrett*, No. 2136 on the Docket of the Court of Appeal, Parish of Orleans, *cert. denied*. In *Stewart v. Lacoume*, 30 La. Ann. 157 (1878), commenting upon the effect of Article 644, this court said: "It is evident that the exemptions of property from seizure provided for by Art. 644 C.P. and by the Acts of 1872 and 1874, do not apply in favor of the lessees as against their lessors."

These results were based upon the proposition that the lessor's privilege established by Article 2705 of the Civil Code was not on the same subject matter as the exemptions of Article 644 "and the Code of Practice was framed exclusively with a view to judicial proceedings, and its provisions on the subject of general laws do not necessarily repeal those of the Civil Code that are contrary to, or inconsistent with them." *Ellis v. Prevost*, 13 La. 230 (1839). *See also Kay v. Furlow*, 178 La. 635, 152 So. 315 (1934); *Kyle v. Sigur*, 121 La. 888, 46 So. 910 (1908); *Ross v. Rosenthal*, 1 Orleans App. 203 (1904). In essence, the conclusion has been that exemptions from seizure under *fieri facias* were inapplicable to provisional remedies to assert privileges created by the Civil Code. On this basis we hold that the exemptions allowed by Section 3881 cannot be allowed against a provisional seizure by writ of sequestration to preserve a vendor's privilege.

II.

Article 3217 of the Civil Code announces that "The debts which are privileged on certain movables, are the following: . . . The price due on movable effects, if they are yet in the possession of the purchaser. . . ."

Article 3227 elaborates:

> He who has sold to another any movable property, which is not paid for, has a preference on the price of his property, over the other creditors of the purchaser, whether the sale is made on a credit or without, if the property still remains in the possession of the purchaser. . . .

The vendor's privilege on movables exist against the property sold as a substantive right incident to the contract of sale. *Johnson v. Bloodworth*, 12 La. Ann. 699 (1857); *State ex rel. Landry v. Broussard*, 177 So. 403 (La. App. 1937).

The privilege has been an integral part of the law of Louisiana since the adoption of the State's first code in 1808. Its practical importance has diminished somewhat since adoption of the Chattel Mortgage Act, the latter having been enacted principally to supply the commercial deficiency of the vendor's privilege, which in general does not follow the movable when it leaves the vendee's possession. Nevertheless, the vendor's privilege remains an important and valuable right in commerce. The formality, time and expense involved in executing and recording chattel mortgages often prevent their use, particularly on small, inexpensive chattels or where the vendor neglects or is prevented from using the chattel mortgage. Daggett, *Louisiana Privileges and Chattel Mortgages*, p. 91 (1942); Margolin, *Vendor's Privilege*, 4 Tul. L. Rev. 237 (1929).

As understood in our law, the vendor's privilege does not exist at common law. It is distinguished from the common law vendor's lien, which the vendor loses when he delivers possession of the article sold to the vendee. Daggett, Id.

The privilege exists upon the sound equitable principle that when the purchaser acquires the vendor's property, his estate is enriched. "It would indeed be unjust to place an unpaid vendor on a footing of equality with other creditors of the purchaser. . . . It would be iniquitous to permit the property sold to become the prey of the creditors of the purchaser without requiring, as a condition precedent, the payment of its cost. . . ." *De L'Isle v. Succ. of Moss*, 34 La. Ann. 164 (1882).

As defined by Laurent, Vol. XXX, p. 6, s 2; p. 18, s 16, the *raison d'etre* of the vendor's privilege is the enrichment of the purchaser's estate by the acquisition of the vendor's property. The right to the payment of the price has, therefore, always commended itself to the favorable consideration of courts.

Planiol gives this justification of the privilege:

> As long as the price is not paid the sale augments the patrimony of the buyer at the expense of the vendor; the latter has impoverished himself, he has alienated his property and has not received anything in exchange. The vendor has thus gratuitously augmented the common pledge of the creditors of the buyer; the latter can be paid with the property sold without the vendor being paid, they enrich themselves at his expense, which is unjust. . . . (Planiol, Vol. 2, No. 2608)

The privilege alone as defined by the Civil Code is of limited value. It is essentially a right without a remedy for its implementation. The machinery for its enforcement and protection is found in our procedural law. Louisiana has long recognized a need for several types of seizure before judgment. Today two are allowed: attachment and sequestration. Attachment is based upon some act, or anticipated act, of the debtor which would place the creditor at a disadvantage in the suit and which prompts the law to protect the creditor by permitting him to seize the debtor's property pending the suit, even though the creditor has no claim against the thing seized. Sequestration involves no intent on the part of the debtor to defraud, but it is founded upon a claim to the ownership or possession or a privilege on the property seized. La. Code Civ. P. Book VII, Special Proceedings, Title I, Provisional Remedies, Chapter 1, Attachment and Sequestration, Preliminary Statement.

Sequestration issues only when the grounds clearly appear by affidavit, and security is required for the payment of damages for wrongful issuance of the writ. La. Code Civ. P. 3501. It issues on the claim of ownership, right of possession or a mortgage, lien or privilege if it is within the power of the defendant to conceal, dispose of, or waste the property or the revenues therefrom, or remove the property from the parish during the pendency of the action. Id. art. 3571. In certain instances the court may on its own motion order the sequestration of property where the ownership is in dispute. Id. art. 3572. The seizure must not be excessive, id. art. 3505, and the defendant may by contradictory motion obtain its dissolution unless plaintiff proves the grounds. Or defendant may obtain the release of the property upon furnishing security. Id. art. 3507. Sequestration has only the effect of preserving the property pending judgment. Id. 3510. Plaintiff's security is not released until a final judgment is rendered in his favor. Id. art. 3512.

Against this background we consider Mitchell's due process contention. It is based upon the argument that to satisfy the requirements of due process defendant is entitled to prior notice and prior hearing before seizure. The contention is principally based upon the recent decision of the United States Supreme Court in *Fuentes v. Shevin*, 407 U.S. 67, 92 S. Ct. 1983, 32 L. Ed. 2d 556 (1972), and its companion case. There appellants were purchasers of household goods under conditional sales contracts. They challenged the prejudgment replevin provisions of the Florida and Pennsylvania law.

The Court declared these statutes worked a deprivation of property without due process of law insofar as they denied the right to a prior opportunity to be heard before chattels are taken from their possessor. However, in its reasons the Court said, "There may be cases in which a creditor could make a showing of immediate danger that a debtor will destroy or conceal disputed goods."

This clearly announced exception to the ruling, we feel, exists in the instant case. Aside from the quoted allegations of the petition and averments of attached affidavits, there is the irrefutable inference that the vendee has, by the act of buying itself, consented to the preservation of the vendor's privilege.

A purchaser can only be excused from the effects of the vendor's privilege by saying he was ignorant of its implications. To sanction such an excuse violates the most fundamental of all legal principles and negates law at its source. It is only one step from the conclusion that the purchaser is presumed to know the law to say that when the purchaser acquires property subject to the vendor's privilege, he is held to be cognizant of the remedies such a privilege affords to the vendor and the ancillary obligations of the purchaser. One of these remedies is the right to sequestration where the purchaser has defaulted in his payments.

Under Louisiana law, therefore, the purchaser's possession is precarious to this extent: He holds possession with the implied-in-law knowledge that he has acquired the right to possession, subject to the vendor's paramount right to seize the property without hearing should he default in his payments. This seizure, the law ordains, must be with security in favor of the debtor and can only continue until a final adjudication of the rights of the parties. In effect, when the purchaser acquires movables he consents to the privilege and its enforcement provisionally.

The vendor's privilege differs from the common law conditional sale in that, in the conditional sale, the vendor retains title, and he does not lose his right to recover the property after it leaves the possession of the vendee. It is different with the vendor's privilege. The vendor's privilege is lost when the vendee divests himself of possession. The prejudgment seizure is the only effective device which will preserve the vendor's rights against a reluctant debtor, pending the protracted delay incident to obtaining judgment. Sequestration is simply a device to which the parties to the sale have, in effect, agreed whereby the property may be preserved for the mutual benefit of the parties pending a determination of their rights.

The law of vendor's privilege in this state operates to favor the vendor and the vendee alike. The long history of vendor's privilege in Louisiana demonstrates that it enables the purchaser to acquire property he may otherwise be unable to buy as much as it induces the vendor to sell. Without the benefits accorded the vendor, it may well be concluded that in a substantial number of instances the possession and title to property would not be surrendered to prospective purchasers. Because of it, many impecunious citizens are enabled to acquire property to foster their livelihood and provide for their sustenance.

We can discern no violation of due process rights when the purchaser is fully informed by law of the remedies which may be invoked as an incident of the sale. . . .

For the reasons assigned, the ruling of the trial judge rejecting the motion to dissolve the writ of sequestration is affirmed, and the case is remanded to the trial court for further proceedings in accordance with law and the views herein expressed. The assessment of costs is to await the final outcome of the case.

DIXON, J., concurs in the result, but is of the opinion that *Young v. Geter*, 185 La. 709, 170 So. 240, is Contra and should be overruled. *Young v. Geter* gives too narrow a construction to Article 1, Section 11 of the Louisiana Constitution.

BARHAM, J., dissents for reasons assigned by TATE, J.

TATE, Justice (concurring in part and dissenting in part).

I fully concur in Parts II and III of the excellent majority opinion. However, on the basis of current legislative enactments and judicial interpretations, I cannot subscribe to the holding that a debtor's cooking stove and refrigerator are not expressly exempt from seizure under La. R.S. 13:3881.

This enactment is found within Title 13 ("Courts and Judicial Procedures") of the Louisiana Revised Statutes. It is found in Chapter 18 thereof, entitled "Seizures in General." La. R.S. 13:3881 exempts specified income or property "from seizure under any writ, mandate, or process whatsoever."

There is thus no statutory warrant for holding La. R.S. 13:3881, providing for exemptions from seizure under "any writ, mandate, or process whatsoever," applicable only to seizures under writs of *fi. fa*. Nor is there any practical reason for the distinction.

The exemption statute in question was enacted in 1960 in connection with the repeal of the old 1961 Code of Practice, especially Article 644 thereof. As did that former Article, the 1960 statutory provision exempts from seizure a major proportion of a debtor's wages, the tools and instruments by which he earns a living, and (pertinently) certain minimal household goods necessary to save a debtor from being without the means to eat or sleep. This statute unambiguously exempts from any seizure the present debtor's stove and refrigerator.

The writer initially believed that, despite this exemption from seizure, it did not apply to debts "for the purchase price of property or any part of such purchase price," by reason of Article 11, Section (4), La. Constitution of 1921. . . . However, this court expressly rejected a similar contention in *Young v. Geter*, 185 La. 709, 170 So. 240, 107 A.L.R. 608 (1936), a lead case. *See also Grayson v. Gray*, 207 So. 2d 916 (La. App. 2d Cir. 1968), to the same effect; *cf. also, Mounger v. Ferrell*, 11 So. 2d 56 (La. App. 2d Cir. 1942).

In *Young v. Geter* a landlord sought to enforce his lessor's privilege against certain property used by the tenant to earn his livelihood. Just as is the property presently seized, the tools there seized were exempt from seizure under the predecessor provision (Article 644, Louisiana Code of Practice of 1870) to La. R.S. 13:3881(2). This court expressly rejected the contention that provisions of Article XI, Section 2 applied so as to nullify the statutory exemption from seizure of property subject to the landlord's privilege. The court expressly held that the cited constitutional provision applied only to invalidate the claim of a right to the homestead exemption established by Article 11, Section 1, of the constitution—an exemption concededly not at issue here.

In refusing to hold the statutory exemption invalid against the claim of the lessor's privilege (a claim based like the vendor's privilege upon our Civil Code and the valid commercial and equitable purposes thereby embodied), this court expressly stated, 170 So. 242: "In order to advance the humane purpose of preserving to the unfortunate debtor and his family the means of obtaining a livelihood and thus prevent him from becoming a charge upon the public, it has become an almost universal rule that statutes creating an exemption should receive a liberal construction in favor of the debtor."

The ruling in *Young v. Geter* is controlling here. The broad statutory exemption to a debtor of minimal household furniture necessary for him to eat and sleep must be respected by the courts. As there stated, 170 So. 241, "the state has an interest . . . that families shall not be deprived by extravagance or misfortune of the shelter and comforts necessary to health and activity."

There is simply no legislative or constitutional exception from this exemption now in effect. However salutary the purposes of the legislatively created vendor's privilege, "it is hornbook law" that the legislatively created privilege may be legislatively made subject to 'such exemptions and limitations' as the legislature sees fit. *Young v. Geter* at 170 So. 242.

Arguably, perhaps, former Code of Practice Article 845 (1870; as amended in 1924) did provide a statutory basis for a claim that the statutory exemption from seizure did not apply to debts for the purchase price. *See Ferrell v. Jena Auto. Co.*, 16 So. 2d 548 (La. App. 2d Cir. 1943). However, Article 845 of the Code of Practice was repealed by the enactment of the 1960 Code of Civil Procedure. No subsequent enactment has afforded even the shadow of a basis for claiming that the statutory exemption from seizure of minimal household goods must not be respected by the courts.

The courts are not empowered to supply an exception to the broad exemption provided by the legislature in La. R.S. 13:3881, however equitable or wise we may deem such an exception. Perhaps the legislature in its discretion and wisdom may modify such exemption law, in the same manner as former La. Code of Practice Article 845 was modified (to except certain debts, such as the purchase price, from the exemption from any seizure); but it has not yet done so. Until then, the creditor's only remedy is to secure a contractual waiver of the exemption by chattel mortgage or otherwise.
For these reasons, I must respectfully dissent.

* * * * * *

NOTES AND QUESTIONS

1. The court invokes the policy justification that exists generally for most privileges: The existence of the privilege benefits the debtor by allowing him to obtain credit that would otherwise not be available to him. In the specific case of the vendor's privilege, its existence facilitates sales that otherwise would simply not occur, for without a privilege, the seller either would refuse to sell on credit or would insist upon other security.

2. The case illustrates the procedural advantage of a privilege: the right of the privileged creditor to have the property subject to the privilege seized, before judgment, under a writ of sequestration issued in accordance with La. C.C.P. art. 3501. Was it necessary for the vendor to allege that it had "reason to fear and believe" that the vendee would dispose of the goods during the pendency of the suit? *See* La. C.C.P. art. 3571.

3. Do you find persuasive the court's reasoning that the placement of the exemption statute in a chapter dealing with execution of judgments, rather than in a separate chapter pertaining to provisional seizures, means that the exemption statute does not prohibit a provisional seizure under a writ of sequestration?

4. A writ of sequestration allows a plaintiff to obtain a provisional seizure of property before judgment has been rendered in his favor. After obtaining a judgment that has become executory, the plaintiff must then obtain a writ of *fieri facias* to execute the judgment against the property that was seized. If the exemption statute cannot be used to oppose the provisional seizure of goods, but will later prevent its sale under a writ of *fieri facias*, is the provisional seizure of any utility?

5. The court's rejection of the vendee's constitutional due process arguments was affirmed by the United States Supreme Court in *Mitchell v. W. T. Grant Co.*, 416 U.S. 600 (1974), which held that the Louisiana statutory procedure of sequestration "effects a constitutional accommodation of the conflicting interest of the parties." 416 U.S. 607. In finding the Louisiana procedure constitutional, the Court cited the ability of the debtor to provoke an immediate hearing and dissolution of the writ unless the plaintiff proves the grounds upon which the writ was issued. *See* La. C.C.P. art. 3506. The Court also cited the substantive rule that a vendor's privilege will be lost if the buyer transfers possession, observing that it is "imperative when default occurs that the property be sequestered in order to foreclose the possibility that the buyer will sell or otherwise convey the property to third parties against whom the vendor's lien will not survive." 416 U.S. 609. In their dissent, Justices Stewart, Douglas, and Marshall argued that the Louisiana sequestration procedure is indistinguishable from the replevin procedure found unconstitutional in *Fuentes*

v. Shevin, 407 U.S. 67 (1972), and that "[t]he the only perceivable change that has occurred since *Fuentes* is the makeup of this Court." 416 U.S. at 635.

ii. Over Movables

***See* La. Civ. Code arts. 3217(7); 3227-31**

The vendor's privilege on movables, which is established by Article 3227 of the Civil Code, affords the seller automatic security in the form of a right to be preferred over other creditors of the buyer. Historically, the only other security device available to the seller of a movable was the pledge, but a pledge could be created only if the seller retained possession. In a day before recognition of chattel mortgages and certainly before security interests under the Uniform Commercial Code, the vendor's privilege allowed the seller to deliver possession and yet retain security. This same capability still exists today, regardless of whether the seller for some reason failed to arrange for the buyer on credit to grant him a consensual security interest under the Uniform Commercial Code. However, the sale must be a Louisiana sale; otherwise, no vendor's privilege arises under Louisiana law.

Article 3227(7) provides that the vendor's privilege subsists only so long as the movable remains in the possession of the immediate vendee. Thus, a vendor's privilege on a movable is lost when the vendee sells and delivers the thing to a second buyer. Because the vendor does not have a general privilege on the property of the vendee, he does not have a privilege on the cash price received by the vendee from the sale of the movable subject to his privilege, even though that sale causes the loss of his privilege. However, if the second sale is made on credit, the original vendor's privilege nonetheless continues to encumber the unpaid price owed by the second buyer. The vendor's privilege similarly continues to exist upon proceeds of the sale of the thing by a receiver and proceeds of the judicial sale of a thing while the proceeds are still in the hands of the court.

Immediately following Article 3227 are three obscure and somewhat enigmatic articles providing the seller with a right of restitution, a vestige of the Roman action in revendication to which Planiol referred in the excerpts above. At Roman law, no privilege existed in favor of the vendor; instead, the vendor remained the owner of the thing and, so long as he had not allowed the vendee a term for payment, could revendicate the thing sold if he was not paid. These three articles of the Civil Code permit the seller of a movable not sold on credit to reclaim the movable as long as it is still in possession of the purchaser, provided that the claim for restitution is made within eight days after the sale and the identity of the movable has not been lost. Nevertheless, this appears to be a seldom used remedy indeed, as these articles have not been applied or interpreted in any reported Louisiana case since 1881. The reason that the right of restitution is provided for immediately after the article that establishes the vendor's privilege on movables is that the right of restitution is designed to afford the unpaid seller a means of protecting his privilege against the risk of a second sale that would cause a loss of the privilege.

* * * * * *

2 TRAITE ÉLEMENTAIRE DE DROIT CIVIL, PT. 2
(La. State Law Inst. trans., 1959) (12th ed. 1939) (Fr.)
MARCEL PLANIOL & GEORGES RIPERT

2618. Rule of the Code

Modern law has reduced the privilege of the vendor to a simple right of preference, the right of pursuit being entirely eliminated. This is what Art. 2102(4) intended to express, in providing: "as long as they [the movable effects sold] are still in the possession of the debtor." What is the sense of this formula? It is borrowed from our ancient authors for whom "to be in the possession of the buyer" signified "not having been alienated by him." It is not therefore the fact of possession, but the fact of alienation which must be considered. This observation permits the resolution of some of the difficulties which arise.

2619. Difficulties

Two cases are to be distinguished:

(1) *The Buyer Is Still the Owner.* The thing can have passed materially into the hands of a third person, without the buyer having lost either the ownership or the possession; for example, it was loaned, deposited, given in pledge, etc. In such a case the privilege of

the vendor subsists, because the buyer is still possessor of the thing by the intermediation of another. However, according to the rules which will be given farther on, the vendor may be obliged to recognize the priority of the privilege of the pledgee.

(2) *The Buyer Is No Longer Owner of the Thing.* In this case if he has already delivered it after having resold it, everything is consummated; the privilege is extinct. But as long as the subsequent purchaser has not yet entered into possession, the question arises as to what becomes of the privilege of the original vendor. Most of the authors think that the privilege subsists intact, because the thing is still "in the possession of the buyer." I consider that opinion an error: the condition of the law is not fulfilled; the buyer, who has in turn become a vendor has lost the possession and is no longer a detainer for the account of another. It is said that the second buyer, not having been really put into possession, cannot protect himself by the maxim "In the matter of movables possession is equivalent to title." That is true, but this buyer has no need of it: he has something better than the material possession, he has the title by virtue of the purchase he has made, and he can revendicate the thing as his own, against the creditors of his vendor. As to the original vendor, he no longer has a right on the movable sold to a third person, because it has ceased to be a part of the patrimony of his debtor, and consequently of his common pledge; in order to seize it again in spite of the alienation thereof, he would have to have a right of pursuit which the law does not give him.

* * * * * *

DREYFOUS

v.

CADE

70 So. 231 (La. 1915)

MONROE, C. J.

The court of appeal, First circuit, has certified to this court, "for instructions," the question whether the petition in this case discloses a cause of action against the defendant Bellevue Planting Company.

"The substantial allegations of the petition," says the court, "in so far as they bear upon the issues presented in this appeal, are:

That petitioner, then engaged in retail business, sold and delivered to the said Overton Cade implements of husbandry and other articles and implements used in the cultivation of land, etc., as appear in the detailed exhibits annexed to the petition; that, in liquidation of said indebtedness, Overton Cade executed a promissory note to the order of petitioner for the sum of $601.38; that said note is still due and unpaid; that, before and during the period petitioner sold to said Overton Cade said implements of agriculture and articles of husbandry, the said Overton Cade was the owner of, and was cultivating, for his own benefit, a certain plantation, situated in the parish of Lafayette, known as Bellevue Plantation, and, in the cultivation thereof, used said implements of agriculture and articles of husbandry, up to the time of the sale of said plantation, hereinafter referred to; that on August 3, 1914, by act No. 46442, recorded in Book S-4, p. 107, of the recorder's office of the parish of Lafayette, said Overton Cade sold to the Bellevue Planting Company, a corporation organized under the laws of the state, domiciled and doing business in the parish of Lafayette, La., the said plantation, known as Bellevue Plantation, situated in said parish, together with the movables and immovables by destination thereon situated, and other things, all the agricultural implements, implements of husbandry (wagons, tools, etc.); that, at the time of the said sale of said plantation to the said Bellevue Planting Company, the implements and articles of husbandry, sold by petitioner as aforesaid, described in detail, and, on the dates and at the prices shown on Exhibit A, hereto annexed, and aggregating a total of $559.01, were on the said plantation and included in said sale and delivered therewith to the said Bellevue Planting Company. Petitioner has been informed, verily believes, and so alleges, that, at the time of said purchase of said plantation, the said Bellevue Planting Company, its officers and agents, well knew that the said agricultural implements and articles of husbandry, purchased by them as aforesaid, had been purchased by the said Overton Cade from petitioner, that the purchase price thereof had not been paid, and that your petitioner was then a creditor of the said Overton Cade for the purchase price thereof; that petitioner is entitled to a vendor's privilege on the said agricultural implements and articles of husbandry described in Exhibit marked 'A,' notwithstanding their use in the cultivation of the said plantation, the same having been purchased by the Bellevue Planting Company, well knowing that they had not been paid for, as aforesaid, and being still in the possession of the said Bellevue Planting Company. Wherefore, petitioner prays for judgment against Overton Cade (and the Bellevue Planting Company), etc., and that a vendor's privilege be recognized in his favor on those agricultural implements and articles of husbandry, described in Exhibit marked 'A,' and made part of the petition, to secure the payment of $559.01, the purchase price thereof, with interest at 8 per cent. from February 1, 1913, and 10 per cent. on the aggregate, as attorney's fees, notwithstanding the sale thereof to the Bellevue Planting Company, and that said implements and articles of husbandry be seized and sold by the sheriff of this parish at public auction, and according to law, in satisfaction of said sum of $559.01 with interest and attorney's fees, *pro tanto*, and petitioners paid out of the proceeds, by preference and right of priority over all the creditors of the said Overton Cade, and for general relief," etc.

To the foregoing application and statement of the case, "one of the members of the court" (of appeal), appends the following "suggestions, in favor of the correctness of the judgment appealed from," to wit:

"It must be observed that this is not a contest between two creditors of Cade against a third possessor. It is apparent that the present cannot be considered a revocatory action, for the reason that it is not alleged that Cade is insolvent nor that the Bellevue Planting Company bought, with knowledge, for the purpose of defeating the rights of plaintiff or to defraud him out of the alleged purchase price of the implements, both of which allegations are sacramental in the revocatory action. *Hicks v. Thomas*, 114 La. 223 [38 South. 148]; *Rownds v. Davidson*, 113 La. 1047 [37 South. 965]; C. C. art. 1971. If Overton Cade, the purchaser of the alleged implements, is solvent, and has sufficient property to satisfy an execution for the value of said implements, plaintiff has suffered no harm by the sale; hence, from this standpoint, plaintiff shows no cause of action. Nor can it be considered as the hypothecary action, proper, for the reason that plaintiff fails to allege that his privilege on the implements, which became immobilized by destination, when attached to the Bellevue Plantation for its service and improvement (C. C. art. 468), was recorded, and that said implements passed to the third possessor, the Bellevue Planting Company, subject to the said privilege. The alleged notice is not equivalent to registry (*McDuffie v. Walker*, 125 La. 152 [51 South. 100]; *Sorrell v. Hardy*, 127 La. 843 [54 South. 122]; *Washington v. Filer*, 127 La. 870 [54 South.

128]; *Haas v. Fontenot*, 132 La. 816 [61 South. 831]; *Parent v. First Nat. Bank*, 135 La. 254 [65 South. 233]. If, on the other hand, the implements continued to remain in the condition of movables, there was no necessity for registry (Const. art. 187); but the vendor's privilege lasted only so long as the property still remained in the hands of the purchaser, Cade (C. C. art. 3227). The vendor's privilege does not extend to personal property which has passed into the hands of a third purchaser, although such purchaser may have known of the embarrassed circumstances of his immediate vendor. *Hayes v. Crockett*, 7 La. Ann. 645. Vendor's privilege only remains so long as purchaser holds possession. *Willard v. Parker*, 7 Mart. (N. S.) 483; *Laughlin v. Ganahl*, 11 Rob. 143. *See, also, Payne & Joubert v. Buford*, 106 La. 87 [30 South. 263]. The vendor's privilege on sugar house machinery continues to exist as long as the machinery remains in possession of the purchaser. *Pratt v. Cecelia Sugar Company*, 135 La. 179 [65 South. 100]."

"To hold that a vendor's privilege on a movable follows it into the hands of a third person would seem to be judicial legislation, amending article 3227, C. C."

We have but little to add to the "suggestions" so offered. The Civil Code declares that:

> "The debts which are privileged on certain movables are the following: The price due on movable effects, if they are yet in the possession of the purchaser." Article 3217, No. 7.
>
> "He who has sold to another any movable property, which is not paid for, has a preference on the price of his property, over the other creditors of the purchaser, whether the sale was made on credit or without, if the property still remains in the possession of the purchaser," etc. Article 3227.
>
> "All sales, contracts and judgments, affecting immovable property, which shall not be so recorded" (i.e., recorded in the parish where the property is situated) "shall be utterly null and void except between the parties thereto," etc. Article 2266.

Act 63 of 1890 provides:

> "That any person who may sell the agricultural products of the United States in any chartered city or town of this state shall be entitled to a special lien and privilege thereon, to secure the payment of the purchase money for and during the space of five days only after the day of delivery; within which time the vendor shall be entitled to seize the same in whatsoever hands or place it may be found, and his claim for the purchase money shall have preference over all others. . . ."

Section 1804 of the Revised Statutes declares that:

> "If a debtor, who has voluntarily surrendered his property to his creditors, or has been proceeded against for a surrender, . . .shall purchase property for cash, the delivery whereof shall be made to him, and then shall dispose of the same without paying his vendor, . . . any such act shall be . . . presumptive evidence of fraud."

And section 825, R. S., and Acts 166 of 1894, 94 of 1896, and 114 of 1912, contain various provisions concerning the acquisition and disposition of property, with intent to cheat and defraud. In the instant case, there is no allegation of either insolvency or of intent to cheat or defraud, and the case is not within the exception (provided by Act 63 of 1890) to the rule enunciated in C. C. art. 3217, to the effect that the privilege of the vendor of movable property exists only so long as the property remains in the possession of the vendee. In *Burdeau v. Creditor*, 44 La. Ann. 20, 10 South. 399, this court, referring to the provisions in R. S. § 1804, concerning purchases, by an insolvent, for cash, and sales of the property without payment of the price, found occasion to say:

> "Certainly that provision of the law was not intended to apply to sales of property, or goods and effects, on terms of credit, . . . for it is a precept of our Civil Code that the vendor's lien on movable property is lost by a sale and delivery thereof to another."

And after quoting C. C. art. 3227, and citing certain adjudged cases, the opinion proceeds:

"Evidently, there is no prohibition against a sale being made by a vendee of goods which are purchased on credit; and no fraudulent intent can attach to the act, though his contract be thereby violated."

Our answer to the question here certified, then is: No.

* * * * * *

NOTES AND QUESTIONS

1. This case is an early example of the application of the rule that delivery of possession to a second buyer will cause a loss of the vendor's privilege on a movable. The court's holding that the vendor's privilege was lost even though the second buyer "may have known of the embarrassed circumstances of his immediate vendor" diverges from the views of most French writers, who maintain that the vendor's privilege is not lost when possession is delivered to a second buyer who knows of the existence of the privilege, because that second buyer is not in good faith and therefore is not protected by the doctrine under the French Civil Code of *la possession vaut titre*. This doctrine holds that, with respect to movables, possession is equivalent to title. The doctrine is of questionable effect in Louisiana and may not apply at all. *See* A. N. Yiannopoulos, 2 La. Civ. L. Treatise Series: Property § 232 (4th Ed. 2014); Tanya Ann Ibieta, Comment, *The Transfer of Ownership of Movables*, 47 La. L. Rev. 841 (1987).

2. Another factor behind the court's decision was that the equipment, with the plaintiff's knowledge, had become immovable by destination. Because the contract out of which the privilege arose was unrecorded, the court found that it became utterly null and void against the purchaser of the plantation under the rule of *McDuffie v. Walker*, 125 La. 152, 51 So. 100 (1909). The court's holding on this point was effectively overruled by subsequent jurisprudence to the effect that recordation of a vendor's privilege on a movable is not required for it to remain enforceable following its immobilization. *See Globe Automatic Sprinkler Co. v. Bell*, 165 So. 150 (1935). However, it is now questionable whether a vendor's privilege upon a movable, whether recorded or not, can ever survive immobilization in light of a still later holding of the Supreme Court in *American Creosote Company v. Springer*, 241 So. 2d 510 (1970). *See also Hyman v. Ross*, 643 So. 2d 256 (La. App. 2d Cir. 1994). *See* notes following

Cristina Inv. Corporation v. Gulf Ice Co., 55 So. 2d 685 (La. App. 1st Cir. 1951), infra.

* * * * * *

PIERSON
v.
CARMOUCHE
84 So. 59 (La. 1920)

PROVOSTY, J.

The Court of Appeal for the parish of Orleans has certified to this court for instructions the following question:

> "May a purchaser on credit of movable property validly give it in pledge to a third person, who knows that he has not paid the price (but is otherwise in good faith), so as to vest in the pledgee a right superior to that of the vendor, whose privilege thereupon ceases (?) by reason of the property having passed out of the possession of the vendee?"

We answer, Yes. In *Dreyfous v. Cade*, 138 La. 298, 70 South. 231, this question was very fully discussed, with full reference to authorities, and was decided in the affirmative.

The decisions which have appeared to our learned Brethren of the Court of Appeal to be opposed to this we have not found to be so in reality. They are *Compton v Dietlein & Jacobs*, 118 La. 360, 42 South. 964, 12 L. R. A. (N. S.) 174; *Fetter v. Field*, 1 La. Ann. 80; *Seelig v. Dumas*, 48 La. Ann. 1494, 21 South. 91; *Hewett v. Williams*, 48 La. Ann. 686, 19 South. 604; and *Bres & O'Brien v. Cowan*, 22 La. Ann. 438.

The first, *Compton v. Dietlein & Jacobs*, involved the "Misdemeanor in trade and commerce act," and the present case does not come under that act.

The next, *Fetter v. Field*, is not only not opposed but is strictly in line. The vendee shipped the goods and pledged the bill of lading, and the pledgee was preferred to the vendor, because the delivery of the bill of lading was a delivery of the goods, and by express provision of article 3227 of the Code the vendor's privilege continues to exist only so long as the property sold "still remains in the possession of the purchaser."

In *Seelig v. Dumas*, the suit was in damages, and was based on the fact that the property had not been sold to Theresa Hamilton but only leased, and that the purchaser from this lessee was aware of that fact. There was no attempt being made to enforce the privilege of the vendor. Very true, the court added that the suit in damages might have been maintained even though the property had been not leased but sold to Theresa Hamilton; but this was on the principle enforced in *Irish v. Wright*, 8 Rob. 428, that a person who fraudulently aids a debtor in placing his property beyond the reach of his creditors renders himself liable in damages to the creditors.

The other cases did not involve the privilege of the vendor but that of the furnisher of supplies on the crops of the year, as to which the Code, art. 3217, says that it rests not only on the crops but also on the proceeds thereof, and that it "shall not be divested . . . by any seizure and sale of the land while the crop is on it." It was under this provision of the Code that these decisions were rendered. See, also, *Weill v. Kent*, 52 La. Ann. 2139, 28 South. 295; *National Bank v. Sullivan*, 117 La. 163, 41 South. 480.

* * * * * *

NOTES AND QUESTIONS

1. When a thing burdened by a vendor's privilege is pledged and possession delivered to a pledgee, Planiol and most, if not all, other French writers maintain that the privilege persists, because the thing still belongs to the vendee and remains in his possession by virtue of the precarious possession exercised by his pledgee.

2. Was the court's holding that the vendor's privilege was wholly lost when possession was delivered to the pledgee, or that the vendor's privilege was simply outranked by the rights of the pledgee? The only support given by the court for its holding was its decision in *Dreyfous v. Cade*, supra, which involved a second sale (an alienation) and not a mere pledge by the purchaser.

3. Professor Yiannopoulos cites *Pierson v. Carmouche* for the proposition that "a pledge constituted on a thing subject to a vendor's privilege involves transfer of possession and terminates the privilege of the vendor." *See* Yiannopoulos, *Real Rights in Louisiana and Comparative Law*: Part 1, 23 La. L. Rev. 161, 226, n. 301 (1963). On the other hand, Professor Daggett appears to espouse the view that *Pierson v. Carmouche* should be interpreted as a ranking case rather than a case involving the outright loss of a vendor's privilege. *See* Daggett, *Louisiana Privileges and Chattel Mortgage* at § 51. *See also* Slovenko, *Of Pledge*, 32 Tul. L. Rev. 59, 69 (1958) (opining that the vendor's privilege is surely not lost when the vendee lends or bails the property).

* * * * * *

IN RE TRAHAN
283 F. Supp. 620 (W.D. La. 1968)
***aff'd* 402 F. 2d 796 (5th Cir. 1968)**

PUTNAM, District Judge.

This case presents for review the question of whether or not the vendor's privilege afforded to the seller of merchandise under the law of Louisiana (LSA-C.C. art. 3227) is a statutory lien valid against the trustee in bankruptcy under the Bankruptcy Act, Sections 1(29a), 67(b) and (c), and 70(c), as amended July 5, 1966, P.L. 89-495, 11 U.S.C.A. §§ 1(29a), 107(b) and (c), and 110(c). The Referee held that it was not and allowed the trustee's claim for costs to be satisfied in preference to that of the creditor, Beneficial Finance Company (hereinafter referred to as Beneficial).

Beneficial is the assignee of the note of a furniture store dealer who sold the bankrupt certain items of furniture on credit, with reservation of the vendor's privilege, on which there is a balance due of $299.10. The property was in the possession of the bankrupt at the time his petition was filed. *See*, Bankruptcy Act, Section 1(13); 11 U.S.C.A. § 1(13). Resolution of this case involves a consideration of the method of distribution of the assets of the bankrupt, provided for by the Bankruptcy Act, and of the nature of the Louisiana "vendor's privilege."

Decision of the case at bar depends in part upon federal law and in part on the law of Louisiana. It is the state law that determines the nature of the vendor's privilege; but it is the Bankruptcy Act which determines whether or not a right of that nature is a secured claim in bankruptcy.

This case hinges upon an interpretation and application of Sections 67(b) and (c)(1)(A) and (B), and 70(c) of the Bankruptcy Act. Section 67(b) of the Act provides that "statutory liens" will be recognized as secured claims in bankruptcy, so long as they are not excluded by the provisions of Section 67(c). Statutory liens are defined for the first time by Section 1 (29a), 11 U.S.C.A. § 1(29a), added by the 1966 amendment, as follows:

"'Statutory lien shall mean a lien arising solely by force of statute upon specified circumstances or conditions, but shall not include any lien provided by or dependent upon an agreement to give security, whether or not such lien is also provided by or is also dependent upon statute and whether or not the agreement or lien is made fully effective by statute." (As amended July 5, 1966.) . . .

Adhering to concepts of "mortgage" and "privilege." the Louisiana Civil Law system provides security devices to certain classes of persons which, in the common law, might be called liens. The vendor's privilege cannot be excluded from definitional coverage under Section 1(29a) merely because Article 3227 uses the word "privilege" instead of "lien"; the nature of privilege, though different from that of the common law lien, is close to that of a statutory lien; the concepts being similar, the words are often used interchangeably. Daggett, *Louisiana Privileges and Chattel Mortgages*, § 1 at p. 1, § 2 at pp. 4-5 (1942); Dainow, *Vicious Circles in the Louisiana Law of Privileges*, 25 La. Law Rev. 1, n. 1 (1964); Slovenko, *Of Pledge*, 33 Tul. Law Rev. 59, 60 (1958); 53 C.J.S. *Liens* § 1 d, p. 833; *Black's Law Dictionary*, "LIEN: Roman or Civil Law" (4 ed. 1951).

We conclude that a vendor's privilege meets the definitional requirements of Section 1(29a), because it is a "statutory lien" which arises by operation of law upon the happening of a specified circumstance. LSA-C.C. arts. 3186, 3227. It would not fall under the exclusionary provision of Section 1(29a), because it can not be created by agreement of the parties. It results from the nature of the debt and arises only by operation of law. LSA-C.C. art. 3185. Daggett, supra, § 37,

p. 96; Planiol, *Traite Elementaire De Droit Civil*, No. 2544, pp. 425-426 (11 ed. 1939, trans. Louisiana State Law Institute, 1959); Bonomo, *Saunder's Lectures on the Civil Code*, p. 503 (1925); Dainow, *Ranking Problems of Chattel Mortgages and Civil Code Privileges in Louisiana Law*, 13 La. Law Rev. 537, 545 (1953).

Having concluded that the vendor's privilege is a "statutory lien," as that term is defined by the Bankruptcy Act, we now turn to Sections 67 and 70(c) for resolution of the remaining issue before us. We have found no case law interpreting this recently amended section and applying it to the Louisiana vendor's privilege. The problem is res nova and requires our considered attention.

Because of circuity of liens resulting from the application of State law to determine the rank of statutory liens created by State legislatures in many fields, Congress felt a need to protect the order of distribution of proceeds of the bankrupt's estate as provided for in the Act; the 1966 amendments are the consequence. Statutory liens which do not meet the requirements of 67(c) are not given secured status; for the purposes of the Act, they are state-created priorities, not recognized in bankruptcy.

A statutory lien will be viewed as such a priority when (1) it does not become effective until the debtor is insolvent or his property is being distributed or liquidated, or (2) it does not become effective until another creditor seeks execution of a claim against the property (Section 67(c) (1)(A)), or (3) it would not be enforceable against a bona fide purchaser (Bankruptcy Act, Section 1 (5); 11 U.S.C.A. § 1(5)) on the date of bankruptcy, provided that if the lien is not invalid under Section 70(c), then the lienor may constructively seize the property (by filing notice with the court) or otherwise perfect the lien against the fictitious bona fide purchaser (Section 67(c)(1)(B)).

The Court must apply these tests to the vendor's privileges as that right is defined by the laws of Louisiana. And the hypothetical statuses given the trustee or "bona fide purchaser" are also governed by state law.

. . . .

> 1. Louisiana's Privilege and Sec. 67(c)(1)(A):
>
> Upon default in payment by the debtor, a vendor, in Louisiana, may sue for collection of the balance of the purchase price remaining unpaid; he may sequester the thing sold (LSA-C.C.P. art. 3571), and judgment will be with recognition of his vendor's privilege, to secure payment of the judgment. The privilege arises automatically upon the contract of sale, and it can be enforced by sequestration, judgment and sale at anytime following default. The privilege is enforceable regardless of whether the debtor is insolvent or his property is being distributed or liquidated, and whether or not the property has been seized by some other creditor seeking execution of a claim against it. Therefore, we conclude that the requirements of Section 67(c)(1)(A) are met by the vendor's privilege.
>
> 2. Louisiana's Privilege and Sec. 67(c)(1)(B):
>
> We now apply the "bona fide purchaser" test of Section 67(c)(1)(B). It is the settled law of Louisiana that a vendor may enforce his privilege only so long as the thing sold remains in the possession of the original vendee. LSA-C.C. arts. 3217(7) and 3227. If the original vendee resells the thing to a third party bona fide purchaser who takes possession, then the privilege of the vendor is lost. *Wilson v. Lowrie*, 156 La. 1062, 101 So. 549 (1924); *Burdeau v. His Creditors*, 44 La. Ann. 11, 10 So. 395 (1891); *United Furniture Stores, Inc. v. Rogers*, 14 La. App. 529, 129 So. 377 (1930); *Heard v. Noble*, 9 La. App. 153, 119 So. 479 (1928); *Robinson v. Tatum*, 7 La. App. 335 (1927).

Section 67(c)(1)(B) does not require the assumption that a "bona fide purchaser" be in possession of the thing sold which is subject to the vendor's privilege. Possession by the original vendee is a requisite for protection of the seller and the enforcement of his vendor's privilege under Louisiana law. And, at the time of filing the petition in bankruptcy by the bankrupt-vendee in this case, this was the reality of the situation between the parties. Under these circumstances the vendor (Beneficial) had the right under Louisiana law to seize or sequester the article sold to the bankrupt even if legal title had passed to a bona fide purchaser, provided there had been no actual delivery of the property to cause the loss of its security. *Continental Bank & Trust Co. v. Succession of*

McCann, 151 La. 555, 92 So. 55 (1922); *Flint & Jones v. Rawlings*, 20 La. Ann. 557 (1868). *See, Wilson v. Lowrie*, supra; *Alex Kuhn & Co. v. Embry & Pilcher*, supra. This result has been explained as follows:

> "The Louisiana courts follow the majority French view in consistently holding that a resale of the property by the vendee does not divest the original vendor of his privilege unless there has been actual physical delivery to the second vendee. (The author notes that a vocal minority (including Planiol) of the French commentators argue persuasively that the French Code would not support such a position.) However, the Louisiana Civil Code contains three pertinent articles which are not found in the French Code at all (La. Civ. Co. arts. 1922, 1923 and 2247 (see also, art. 2480)), and it may be that these articles give Louisiana more justification for this position than the French courts and commentators have. . . . Hence, it seems that if these three articles are read together with Article 3227 on the vendor's privilege, the phrase 'if the property still remains in the possession of the purchaser' might reasonably mean in the actual physical possession of the vendee, and the Louisiana courts are, therefore, logical and right in their interpretation of the article. This interpretation would be justified in Louisiana where the similar French interpretation (which is not supported by the above three additional articles) is not justified." Margolin, [*Civil Law: Vendor's Privilege*, 4 Tul. L. Rev. 239, at 249-251 (1929-30)]

Even assuming that the bona fide purchaser contemplated in Section 67(c)(1)(B) was in possession of the property, the first proviso of Section 67(c)(1)(B) would require a consideration of Section 70(c). And if the "statutory lien" is not invalid against the trustee "at the date of bankruptcy" under that section, and if it is required by applicable lien law to be perfected in order to be valid against a subsequent bona fide purchaser, it may nevertheless "be valid . . . if perfected within the time permitted by and in accordance with" such law. As is readily seen from the foregoing discussion, the time permitted Beneficial to perfect its lien was any time before the property left the bankrupt's actual possession. The second proviso of Section 67(c)(1)(B) makes filing of notice of its claim to the privilege by Beneficial, the equivalent of a seizure (under sequestration) of the thing subject to the privilege or "statutory lien."

The question then becomes whether or not the vendor's privilege is invalid against the trustee under Section 70(c). An examination of the "applicable lien law" (Louisiana law) requires the conclusion that the privilege is valid against the trustee.

In a distribution of the proceeds from the sale of the thing to which the privilege attaches, a creditor whose claim is secured by a vendor's privilege would come before a judgment creditor, or a creditor with a general lien on all of the bankrupt's property, or a creditor who had obtained an execution returned unsatisfied. *Converse, Kennett & Co. v. Hill & Co.— W. H. Letchford & Co.*, 14 La. Ann. 89 (1859); LSA-C.C. arts. 3183, 3267; LSA-C.C.P. arts. 1092, 2292, 2337, 2374, 2378, 3571; LSA-R.S. 9:2621.

The vendor's privilege, a special privilege on movables, is one of the most important and highest ranking security devices recognized in Louisiana. It has formed a cornerstone for credit in the economic structure of the mercantile trade in this State for centuries. It is not a spurious legal device to permit a debtor in failing circumstances to favor one creditor at the expense of another. Justice requires its recognition:

> "As long as the price is not paid the sale augments the patrimony of the buyer at the expense of the vendor; the latter has impoverished himself, he has alienated his property and has not yet received anything in exchange. The vendor has thus gratuitously augmented the common pledge of the creditors of the buyer; the latter can be paid with the property sold without the vendor being paid, they enrich themselves at his expense, which is unjust. The new property therefore can be veritably acquired by the buyer only by the payment of the price; in French legislation which admits the immediate transfer of the title, the privilege is necessary to prevent an inequity." Planiol, supra, No. 2608, p. 453. *See, Carlin v. Gordy*, 32 La. Ann. 1285 (1880).

Since the vendor's privilege meets the requirements of Section 70(c), and because Beneficial can enforce its privilege against a bona fide purchaser if the property is seized in the possession of the original vendee (by the filing of notice), it must be concluded that this privilege, a statutory lien, must be treated as a secured claim in bankruptcy. The case is remanded to the referee for treatment in accordance with this decision.

* * * * * *

NOTES AND QUESTIONS

1. In a per curiam opinion, the Fifth Circuit affirmed the district court's ruling. After the new Bankruptcy Code was adopted in 1978, the Fifth Circuit again ratified the *Trahan* holding in *Matter of Tape City USA*, 677 F. 2d 401 (5th Cir. 1982).

2. In reaching its holding, the district court in *Trahan* quoted extensively from a student comment, Margolin, *Civil Law: Vendor's Privilege*, 4 Tul. L. Rev. 239 (1929), in which the author, Bessie Margolin, outlined the majority view of the French commentators that a resale of the property by the vendee does not divest the original vendor of his privilege unless there is actual physical delivery to the second vendee, the views of Planiol and other members of the vocal minority notwithstanding. The court also cited her analysis that three additional articles found in the 1870 Louisiana Civil Code but not found in the French Civil Code (Articles 1922, 1923 and 2247) were even greater justification in Louisiana for the majority view of the French commentators that a vendor's privilege survives a subsequent sale by the vendee when unaccompanied by delivery. Those articles, the substance of which now appears in Civil Code art. 518, provided that the sale of a movable does not affect third parties until actual delivery of the object is made and that creditors of a seller may still seize a movable he has sold while it remains in his possession. In holding that the vendor's privilege survived the bankruptcy filing, the *Trahan* court placed great weight upon the argument that, because a sale unaccompanied by delivery is not effective against third persons, and because the seller's creditors, including presumably his own unpaid vendor, still have the right to seize his assets, the vendor's privilege should remain effective until delivery occurs.

3. Ironically, even though the *Trahan* court quoted her summation of the majority view of the French commentators in support of its holding, Margolin actually wrote that "the real right argument is weak and has been ably refuted by those commentators in the minority who say that a vendor's privilege is lost

by a resale even though there has been no delivery." She felt that a more convincing reason in support of the majority view was that the word "possession" in Article 2102 of the French Civil Code, which provides that the privilege exists only so long as the original buyer remains in possession, refers to *physical* possession. Those French commentators in the majority support this argument by citing the rule of *la possession vaut titre* under Article 2279 of the French Civil Code. As the argument goes, the unmodified use of the word "possession" in Article 2279 must plainly mean physical possession, and the article should be used to interpret what is meant by the same word in Article 2102. However, Margolin felt that the majority took an inconsistent view when confronted with the issue—faced by the Louisiana Supreme Court in *Pierson v. Carmouche,* supra—of whether a vendor's privilege is extinguished when the vendee enters into a pledge, loan or bailment of the thing sold. She points out that, in that case, the French commentators almost unanimously agree that the privilege is not lost, even though the vendee no longer has physical possession and exercises only civil possession.

4. Margolin favored a consistent "civil possession" theory of Article 3227 of the Louisiana Civil Code (as opposed to actual possession) because that theory would allow the object in question to be pledged, loaned, or bailed without destruction of the vendor's privilege. Consistently applied, this theory would, of course, mean that a privilege is lost if there is a sale to a purchaser who does not take immediate physical delivery. The second purchaser would have civil possession, and the original vendee's mere physical possession would be insufficient to maintain the vitality of the vendor's privilege. She asserted that this rule would make little practical difference, because the original vendor would still have the right to seize the property as a general creditor of his vendee under Article 1923 of the 1870 Code (*See now* La. Civ. Code art. 518). Do you agree that, if the vendor's privilege were extinguished by a second sale unaccompanied by delivery, there would be little practical difference because the original vendee's creditors could still have recourse against the thing sold? What if the original vendor found himself in competition with other creditors of the original vendee?

5. The issue of whether privileges on movables—the vendor's privilege included—can be viewed as real rights is discussed further in a later section of this chapter.

* * * * * *

SNELL

v.

HART JEWELRY CO.

14 Teiss. 94 (Orl. App. 1916)

His Honor, EMILE GODCHAUX, rendered the opinion and decree of the Court, as follows:

Plaintiff, a non-resident widow, sues to recover possession of certain jewels, her separate paraphernal property, which she left with defendant, a jeweler, to be reset, on or about January 1st, 1914.

Defendant does not seek to justify its retention of the jewels, admittedly still in its possession, because of any claim against same for work done or otherwise, but founds its refusal and failure to return the jewels on the following ground only, as its answer in substance states, to-wit:

That on October 10, 1914, that is, subsequent to the deposit of the jewels, plaintiff and her husband called at defendant's store, where plaintiff's husband purchased on credit one gold purse for $395.00, and then and there, in the presence of defendant's manager donated it by manual gift to plaintiff, his wife; that the husband has since died; that no part of the purchase price has been paid; that plaintiff took the purse subject to defendant's privilege for the purchase price under R. C. C. 1551, which provides that the donation passes to the donee subject to all charges, and that accordingly plaintiff is personally liable for the purchase price of the purse.

And the prayer of the answer is that plaintiff's demand be dismissed and that defendant have judgment in reconvention against her for $395.00, the price of the purse, with recognition of its vendor's privilege aforesaid.

Upon the trial the evidence established the facts alleged in the pleadings as above set out and there was judgment dismissing plaintiff's demand for the return of her jewels, and furthermore in favor of defendant decreeing it a personal judgment in reconvention against plaintiff for the price of the purse, with recognition [sic] of the vendor's privilege as prayed for.

The judgment is clearly erroneous and must be reversed in so far as it rejects plaintiff's demand for the recovery of her jewels. Defendant's retention of the jewels solely because of the existence of an alleged claim against her growing out of a concededly separate and distinct transaction, namely, the subsequent purchase of the purse, is wholly unjustifiable. The jewels were deposited with defendant for a particular purpose, its custody of them was of a fiduciary character, and it "cannot withhold the deposit on pretense of a debt due from the depositor on an account distinct from the deposit, or by way of offset." R. C. C. 2956, 2210.

Upon the reconventional demand, it was erroneous, as plaintiff correctly contends, to award a personal judgment against her for the price of the purse; for even should the contention be true that the purse passed to her subject to defendant's privilege as unpaid vendor, still there is no law which imposes upon her as donee a personal liability for the price. And this is particularly true in the case of the wife, whom the law jealously safeguards against the obligations of the husband.

Nor do we think that a vendor's privilege attached to the purse in the hands of plaintiff, notwithstanding the provisions of R. C. C. 1551 to the effect that a donation passes to the donee subject to all charges. That provision can have no application to a case such as this, where the vendor knows that the thing is purchased by the vendee avowedly as a gift to another, and where at the moment of purchase and in the presence of the vendor the contemplated donation is in fact made to the donee; for these circumstances give rise to an implied understanding between the parties that the vendor will not look to the thing for payment but will rely exclusively upon the personal responsibility of the purchaser. It is a tacit waiver of the privilege.

The judgment on the main demand is accordingly set aside and reversed, and it is now decreed that there be judgment in favor of plaintiff, Mrs. Agnes Pratt, widow of Harry C. Snell, and against the Hart Jewelry Company, defendant, ordering the latter to deliver to plaintiff within ten (10) days after this judgment becomes final and executory, the jewelry described in plaintiff's petition herein;

and in default of such delivery within the time prescribed, this decree shall stand and be final and executory as a money judgment in plaintiff's favor and against defendant in the sum of $250.00, with legal interest thereon from this date.

And upon the reconventional demand the judgment is set aside and reversed and it is now decreed that the reconventional demand be rejected.

It is further decreed that defendant pay all costs incurred in both Courts.

Reversed.

* * * * * *

NOTES AND QUESTIONS

1. Instead of finding that the seller had waived its right to a vendor's privilege, could the court have decided the case by the application of the rule that a vendor's privilege is lost when the immediate vendee no longer has possession of the thing sold?

2. In *Royal Oldsmobile Co., Inc. v. Yarbrough*, 425 So. 2d 823 (La. App. 5th Cir. 1983), an attorney's client, in the attorney's presence, purchased an automobile that the client immediately gave to him in payment of his fee. The client paid for the automobile with a check that was ultimately dishonored by the drawee bank. Holding that the dealership's vendor's privilege was lost when the vehicle left the hands of the immediate purchaser (the client), the court found that, even though the attorney was present at the dealership to help select the car and had the title placed directly in his name, he did not undertake to buy the automobile or to pay the purchase price; rather, he simply agreed to accept the car in payment of the debt due him by his client.

* * * * * *

ERMAN

v.

LEHMAN

47 La. Ann. 1651 (1895)

NICHOLLS, C. J.

In December, 1893, various attachments were taken against the defendant, Theodore Lehman, under which his stock of merchandise, liquor, etc., was seized by the civil sheriff. The attachments of Erman & Cahn and A. Erman were prosecuted to judgment, and the privilege resulting from their attachment was recognized. The stock was sold, and out of the proceeds the first attaching creditor was paid the amount of his judgment. The present contest is over the remainder of the proceeds; plaintiffs, as attaching creditors, claiming to be paid by reason of their privilege, while several other parties claim to be paid by preference over them on the proceeds of different articles which were sold, claiming the vendor's privilege thereon. Each of these last-named parties pointed out the property on which they claimed a privilege before the sale was made. Separate appraisements and sales were made, and the sheriff kept the proceeds of the different lots, thus pointed out, separate and distinct. After the sale, the sheriff filed in court an account, in which, after presenting the disbursements claimed to have been made, and the costs, and prorating them among the various parties, he prepared a proposed distribution of the funds according to the rights of parties as he understood them to be, and ruled all parties into court to show cause why the distribution should not be made in accordance therewith. . . .

By the sheriff's tableau he proposed to pay over to each of the parties claiming vendor's privilege the net proceeds arising from the sale of the articles on which the privilege was asserted. No objection was made in any quarter to the form of the proceeding. Erman & Cahn, plaintiffs in the original suit, opposed the sheriff's tableau of distribution, and the payment he proposed to make to the parties mentioned above, for the reasons: (1) That none of the said parties have any valid claim of indebtedness against the defendant; (2) that, if they have any valid claim, they have no lien, privilege, or rights whatever on the proceeds of the sales accounted for by the sheriff, the contracts for the sale of the merchandise sold by them to defendant not being Louisiana contracts, but having been made, entered into, and consummated out of the state of Louisiana, in states where the common law prevails; (3) that the goods sold, the proceeds of which were accounted for by the sheriff, have not been identified by the parties as being the goods alleged to have been sold by them to defendant, and are, in truth and in fact, not the goods so sold and unpaid for, as claimed; (4) that, in any and all events, opponents, being domestic and attaching creditors, with attachments priming all the sequestrations which the said parties obtained against the defendant, and by virtue also of their writ of *fi. fa.*, under which the proceeds were held by the sheriff, and of their lien and privilege resulting from the seizures under attachment and *fi. fa.*, are entitled to be paid by privilege, preference, and priority over and before any of the said parties, or any other creditors of the defendant, out of the proceeds. On the trial of the rule, the district court dismissed the opposition of Erman & Cahn, approved and homologated the sheriff's account and tableau, and ordered the funds to be distributed in conformity therewith. Erman & Cahn appealed. . . .

The first proposition which we will notice is that last advanced in plaintiff's brief, "that, in any and all events, they have a priority and preference of payment out of the proceeds of the property sold by the sheriff in this case, by reason of the privilege which they obtained under their attachment and their *fi. fa.*" The parties whose claims to privileges superior to that of the plaintiffs have been recognized by the district court, do not rest their right upon their sequestrations, but upon the fact that they are unpaid vendors of the various lots of articles which have been sold, and upon the proceeds of which they claim a privilege. It has been repeatedly decided that the privilege resulting from an attachment or a seizure is subordinated to privileges legally existing upon the property seized at the time of the attachment or seizure. The real contention of the appellants (one common to the case of all of the appellees) is that the court erred in applying the rule of law announced in *McLane v. His Creditors*, 47 La. Ann. 135, 16 South. 764, to the contracts which are involved in this litigation. They maintain that the facts bearing upon them bring them, relatively to the existence of a privilege, under the decision in *Claflin v. Mayer*, 41 La. Ann. 1048, 7 South. 139, "that the contracts were not Louisiana contracts, but were made, entered into, and consummated in states where the common law prevails." The syllabus in the *Claflin Case* reads as follows: "Where an agent in New Orleans, for nonresident dealers, has authority only to exhibit samples and receive orders, which he communicates to his principal for acceptance or rejection, held, that an order so transmitted was similar in every respect to an order to purchase, sent direct by the buyer to the seller, and, when accepted and filled and the goods delivered to the carrier and insured by the buyer, that it was a contract where said order was accepted and filled and the goods delivered." In the body of the opinion, the court, referring to the party who represented the vendors in Louisiana, said: "The agent's authority here was limited and restricted. He could not bind his principal, and his sole duty was to exhibit the samples, receive and forward orders for goods."

We find in the cases at bar an entirely different state of facts. The authority of the parties who represented the vendors here was not limited and restricted to exhibiting samples, and receiving and forwarding orders for goods for acceptance. On the contrary, when the interviews between Theo. Lehman and these various parties terminated, the situation was not that of parties waiting to see whether or not propositions for purchases, which were to be sent forward, would be accepted or not by principals residing in other states, and depending upon the action of those persons in order to determine whether contracts would be made or not, but of parties who had then and there made completed contracts of sale, the one as a purchaser, the others claiming to be authorized by their principals to make presently concluded sales, and so making them. There was no misunderstanding between the parties as to the attitude in which they respectively stood. Lehman did not deal with the representatives of the foreign houses as solicitors for those houses, forwarding orders for acceptance or rejection, but as agents of those houses, making present sales for them, and forwarding orders, not for acceptance or rejection, but in execution of concluded sales. The orders sent forward were sent forward solely because the articles which were the object of the sales were in other states, and required shipment. Had they been in New Orleans at the time of the interviews, delivery could have been called for there at once by Lehman. Under the evidence in the record there would have been no necessity for any communication between the different agents and their principals to justify the former in making a delivery. . . .

In the cases now before the court, the different agents did not assume the position of "drummers" or "solicitors." They took upon themselves the position of agents of the vendors, with full, present authority to sell absolutely and at once, and they were so dealt with by Lehman. We think they had ample authority to act as they did in making the sales; but were we to assume that they had transcended their authority, or disobeyed secret instructions in so doing, it would by no means follow, when their principals, called on to take action in respect to their New Orleans dealings, should affirm them, that the contracts are to be taken as contracts of the place of residence of the principals. On the contrary, the act of affirmance being of a sale made by the agent as one *in praesenti*, the act would stand affirmed as made, with its character as fixed by the parties to it when made. The ratification would give to the act all the force of an original authority in the agents to have sold at the time and in the manner and at the place they did. "*Omnis ratihabitio retrotrahitur et mandato priori aequiparatur.*" The contracts made by the Louisiana representatives of the houses were not submitted to their respective houses for "acceptance," but for "execution," as we have already stated, and the authority exercised by the agents in Louisiana to sell absolutely in that state was ratified (if ratification were needed), and acted upon before Erman & Cahn had acquired any rights in the premises. We think the contracts were Louisiana contracts, and the rights and obligations of parties controlled by the decision in *McLane v. His Creditors*, 47 La. Ann. 135, 16 South. 764. We are of the opinion that appellees have identified, with reasonable certainty, the property sold by them, and shown that it was struck by the privilege which they claimed thereon. We are of the opinion that the judgment appealed from is correct, and it is hereby affirmed.

* * * * * *

NOTES AND QUESTIONS

1. This case demonstrates the rule that only a Louisiana sale will give rise to a vendor's privilege. What factors did the court find relevant in determining that the sales contracts involved in the case were Louisiana contracts?

2. On this issue, *see also De La Vergne Refrigerating Mach. Co. v. New Orleans & W.R. Co.*, 26 So. 455 (La. 1899) (holding that, where a contract of sale made in New York contemplated delivery and testing of the movables in Louisiana, and the buyer's acceptance was dependent on the results of the test and the movables remained the property of the seller and at its risk until thus tested and accepted, the contract was a Louisiana sale creating a vendor's privilege). *Cf. Jones v. Bradford*, 353 So.2d 1348 (La. App. 3d Cir. 1977), which

appears to assume, without discussion, that a vendor's privilege arose from the sale of equipment in Mississippi and holds that the privilege continued to be effective after the equipment was subsequently removed to Louisiana without the seller's consent.

3. Under a modern conflicts of law analysis, the inquiry should focus upon whether Louisiana substantive law is applicable to the sale, rather than merely the situs of the thing sold or the parties. *See generally* Tooley-Knoblett and Gruning, 24 La. Civ. L. Treatise Series: Sales §§ 1:11-18 (2012).

4. In the case, the vendor's privilege came into conflict with a seizing creditor's privilege, which arose upon seizure of the goods by the sheriff. This privilege is now statutorily prescribed by Article 2292 of the Louisiana Code of Civil Procedure, which provides that a creditor, by the mere act of seizure under a writ of *fieri facias*, acquires a privilege that entitles him to preference over ordinary creditors. Under Article 3511, a creditor who seizes property under the provisional writs of attachment or sequestration also acquires a privilege from the time of seizure if judgment is ultimately rendered maintaining the attachment or sequestration. The case recognizes the longstanding rule that a seizing creditor's privilege is subordinate to privileges that existed upon the property seized at the time of seizure. Thus, the privilege of the seizing creditor ranked behind the previously existing vendor's privilege.

5. In *Board of Supervisors of Louisiana State University v. Hart*, 26 So. 2d 361 (La. 1946), the court held that a seizing creditor's privilege, when later recognized by judgment, relates back to the date of the seizure and is superior to any intervening encumbrances or purchases.

* * * * * *

CRISTINA INV. CORPORATION

v.

GULF ICE CO.

55 So. 2d 685 (La. App. 1st Cir. 1951)

ELLIS, Judge.

The Cristina Investment Corporation, plaintiff herein, brought foreclosure proceedings against the Gulf Ice Company, Inc., the defendant, under a mortgage it held against the real property of the defendant. The property securing the mortgage and vendor's lien notes was an ice manufacturing plant, which was seized and sold, but the amount of the sale was insufficient to satisfy the indebtedness sued upon.

Plaintiff's mortgage was dated April 28, 1949, and recorded May 28, 1949. On July 7, 1949, the Lilly Company sold to the Gulf Ice Co. a certain ice crusher, which was placed upon the premises upon which the plaintiff held the mortgage.

The Lilly Company, third opponent herein, prior to the date of the foreclosure sale, obtained an order directing the Sheriff to appraise and sell separately, and to hold the proceeds thereof, a certain ice crusherslinger which the Lilly Company had sold to the defendant and upon which it claimed a vendor's lien arising from a conditional sales contract executed and performed in this State.

The ice crusher was sold under the order obtained for $1,350.00 and the funds were held by the Sheriff subject to the disposition of the Court.

The District Court on the trial dismissed the rule and rendered judgment in favor of the plaintiff, Cristina Investment Corporation, and against the Lilly Co., third opponent, decreeing the proceeds from the sale of the ice crusher to be paid to the plaintiff.

From this judgment the Lilly Co., third opponent, has appealed.

There is a stipulation of facts in the record between the Cristina Investment Corporation and the Lilly Co., agreeing that: On July 7, 1949, the Lilly Company, a Tennessee corporation, sold to the Gulf Ice Company, one model 440, new ice crusherslinger complete with motor, hose and swivel nozzle. This machine was the same model and exactly similar to the model 440 machine illustrated on page 7 of the Link Belt Company's catalog, which catalog was introduced and filed as evidence. The sale was made under a conditional sales contract signed by both parties in the State of Louisiana and is filed in the record. The Gulf Ice Company did not make the payments as promised, and on March 22, 1951, was indebted to the Lilly Co. in the amount of $1,326.00 plus interest at 6% from March 22, 1951, until paid, and all costs and expenses incurred in the collection of said indebtedness. That the ice crusher was appraised separately from the other assets of the Gulf Ice Co. and was sold separately by the Sheriff at a valid judicial sale for the sum of $1,350.00, the proceeds of said sale to be held by the Sheriff subject to the disposition of the Court.

While we have not been favored with any written reasons for judgment, appellant's brief and appellee's supplemental brief state the trial Court was of the opinion the machine had become an immovable by destination and attached to the realty in such a manner it could not be removed without damaging the realty, and consequently, although sold subject to a vendor's lien, this privilege was out-ranked by the first mortgage and vendor's lien previously executed and recorded on the ice factory.

In Louisiana a vendor of movables is given the privilege for the unpaid price of the property sold as long as the property remains in the possession of the vendee and can be identified. Revised Civil Code, Articles 3227 and 3231.

The third opponent firstly urges the ice crusher did not become an immovable by destination but retained its character as a movable, and secondly, even though the movable property be incorporated into immovable property as the machine can be removed and reclaimed in substantially the same condition it was when sold, without serious or material injury to the immovable to which it is attached, that its vendor's lien primes the mortgage in question.

On the other hand, the appellee insists the crusher has become a permanent rigid installation, immovable by destination, and a component part of the ice manufacturing plant, continuously used in this business, and it cannot be detached without working material injury to the immovables covered by the mortgage which he claims and therefore out-ranks third opponent's vendor's lien and privilege.

First, we might mention that under the law of Louisiana, which does not recognize conditional sales, such contracts are considered outright sales vesting absolute title in the buyer, but a vendor's lien is thereby created when entered into and executed in Louisiana. *Graham Glass Co. v. Nu Grape Bottling Co.*, 164 La. 1103, 115 So. 285; *In re New Orleans Milling Co.*, D.C., 263 F. 254.

A leading case upon the questions involved in the case at bar is *Caldwell v. Laurel Grove Co., Inc.*, 1932, 175 La. 928, 144 So. 718, 721. There a Third party opponent vendor had sold to a plantation a lot of second hand rails, switches, and other related railroad supplies, and this material was all made into a railroad on the plantation's road-bed. A foreclosing mortgage creditor claimed the equipment, maintaining it had become immovable by destination and by nature, and that the vendor's privilege claimed by the opponent was extinguished. The District Court recognized the vendor's lien, the Court of Appeal reversed this holding, and the Supreme Court reinstated the judgment of the District Court upon application for writs, saying:

> "When the rails and other materials were sold to the owner of the plantation they were impressed with the vendor's privilege, and it is difficult for us to see how the privilege can be defeated by the use the vendee made of them, since they are not appreciably affected by such use. The rails and their accessories have not been converted into a new species of thing. They remain rails and railroad iron even though attached to the ties. They can be removed without affecting any independent rights of ownership in the soil or structure, for when they are removed the soil and the roadbed will remain in the same form and condition they were before the materials were attached thereto.
>
> We adhere to the jurisprudence established in the long line of cases . . . mentioned . . . to the effect that the unpaid vendor enjoys a real right in a thing sold to which the right of the purchaser is subordinated, so that, if the thing can be identified and reclaimed in substantially the same condition as when sold and without material

> injury to the structure to which it is attached, the vendor's lien is enforceable, even though the use of the structure may be temporarily impaired." . . .

Since the Caldwell case numerous decisions have followed the doctrine therein expressed. . . . All of these cases hold a mortgage on the real estate does not destroy the vendor's privilege on an immovable by destination placed on the property mortgaged as long as the object is complete in itself and can be removed without much damage. However, if the movable has become so incorporated thereto, or merged into the immovable property as to have become part and parcel of it, the vendor's privilege on the movable is lost. *Swoop v. St. Martin*, 110 La. 237, 34 So. 426; *Hibernia Bank & Trust Co. v. Knoll Planting & Mfg. Co.*, 133 La. 697, 63 So. 288; *Monroe Auto & Supply Co. v. Cole*, 6 La. App. 337; *St. Mary Iron Works v. Community Mfg. Enterprise*, 9 La. App. 743, 119 So. 564.

The problem to be solved here is, first, whether in fact the ice crusher became immovable by destination, and even if it did, was it still identifiable as such and could it be removed from the premises without "much damage." . . .

The record discloses the ice crusher, upon which relator claims his privilege, was used to crush ice after it was manufactured, and blew it into boats which moored at the plant's dock for this service. There does not appear to be the necessary attachment to the realty for us to consider the machine to have become an immovable by destination. The authorities upon this point are contrary to such a conclusion. However, a determination upon this point is not necessary even though the machine had become an immovable by destination, under the authority of *Caldwell v. Laurel Grove Co.*, supra, and other authorities cited as the vendor's lien and privilege was preserved against the mortgage creditor.

Here the machine was not in the building at all, and the only connection with the dock of the ice company were the blocks put in front of the wheels to keep the machine from rolling, and the angle irons pressed into the conveyor coming out of the ice plant, and electric wires running to the plant. It would seem the machine could be removed without any material injury to the real estate whatsoever.

Our Federal Courts have been presented with the same problem we find here on several occasions, where a vendor's lien has conflicted with the claim of a mortgage creditor on an object that has become immovable by destination. In *State Trust Co. v. De La Vergne Refrigerating Machine Co.*, 5 Cir., 105 F. 468, 476, a vendor asserted his privilege on cotton compresses against a real mortgage creditor. The Court quoted and discussed many Louisiana cases, especially *Lapene v. McCan & Son*, 28 La. Ann. 749, 751; *Carlin v. Gordy*, 32 La. Ann. 1285, and *Baldwin v. Young*, 47 La. Ann. 1466, 17 So. 8839 The Court, in deciding for the vendor against the mortgage creditor, said: "In *Walburn-Swenson Co. v. Darrell*, 49 La. Ann. 1044, 22 So. 310, *Hall v. Hawley*, 49 La. Ann. 1046, 22 So. 205, and [*Monroe Building and Loan*] *Association v. Johnston*, 51 La. Ann. 470, 25 So. 383, it is again held that the privilege of the unpaid vendor on the movable is not lost because it has been attached to the immovable. In each of these last three cited cases the contest was between the mortgage creditor and the vendor of the movable, but in neither is there any reference to any registry of the vendor's privilege as in any wise affecting the rights of the parties. The opinion of the court in *Baldwin v. Young*, supra, so far as it overrules and modifies *Gary v. Burguieres*, supra [12 La. Ann. 227], is vigorously attacked as obiter, because the case showed that the movables involved were sold under a contract that, until paid for, the vendor should be the owner of the thing sold, and registry *vel non* was not in question. So far as the necessity of registry was concerned, we think it depended on the determination of an issue as to whether quoad the vendor the movable sold has been so merged in the immovable that the vendor could no longer assert his privilege on the identical thing sold; and, to the extent that this question was involved, we cannot agree that the enlightened views so well expressed by Mr. Justice Miller, delivering the opinion of the court, were obiter; and, so far as anything favorable to appellant here can be claimed, because the sale in *Baldwin v. Young*, supra, was a conditional sale, we may inquire what substantial difference can be urged between a so-called conditional sale and an ordinary sale in which the vendor's privilege is preserved, so far as the right to recover the unpaid price is concerned? 'The privilege of the vendor is founded on the right of property. The payment of the price is essential to the vesting of an indefeasible title in the vendee.' *Carlin v. Gordy*, supra. Whether the sale be conditional or absolute, retaining the vendor's privilege, the vendor in each case may subject the thing sold to the payment of the unpaid purchase money; and in equity the results in each case are the same. In Louisiana it is well understood that, as against third persons, the vendor's privilege on an immovable must be recorded. Rev. Civ. Code, Art. 3274. *See* Act No. 45 of 1877. In substance, this has been the law since the Code of 1825. The variations have been with regard to the manner and time of registry. It is equally understood in Louisiana that the vendor's privilege on a movable is not lost by failure to record the same. This has been the law since the adoption of the constitution of 1879. The real question considered in the above-cited cases was, when, in favor of third persons and against the vendor, does a movable attached to land, tenement, or building become an immovable, or part thereof, by destination? And we understand the decisions of the supreme court of the state to be uniformly (except in *Gary v. Burguieres*, supra) to the effect that, so long as the price is unpaid, and the movable has not lost its identity, and can be separated from the land, tenement, or building to which it has been attached without injury to the immovable, as to the vendor it remains a movable, and he may subject the same to his vendor's privilege, the registry of the same being immaterial." *See Whitney-Central Trust & Savings Bank v. Luck*, 5 Cir., 231 F. 431; *Tangipahoa Bank & Trust Co. v. Kent*, 5 Cir., 70 F.2d 139.

Appellee also contends that the relator's privilege cannot prevail as it was not recorded.

In *Weiss v. Hudson Construction Co.*, 151 La. 1, 91 So. 525, 526, the vendor of a truck and automobile under an unrecorded bill of sale asserted his lien against the holder of a chattel mortgage on the vehicles which had been recorded after the sale. The Supreme Court decided the Chattel Mortgage Statute did not change the prior law derived from Articles 3186 and 3227 of the Civil Code, that a vendor's lien on a movable did not require recordation, and held that a subsequent recorded chattel mortgage was subservient to the lien. The language of the Court follows: "The General Assembly has never passed any general or special law by which a vendor's privilege on movable property is required to be recorded in order to have effect, either as between the parties or as to third persons. Until such a law is passed, a vendor's privilege once created will continue to exist without being recorded, until it is lost or superseded in some manner provided by law. The Civil Code declares the privilege to be a right, which the nature of a debt gives to a creditor, and which entitles him to be preferred before other creditors, even those who have mortgages. Article 3186. And he who has sold to another any movable property, which is not paid for, has a preference on the price of his property, over the other creditors of the purchaser, if the property still remains in the possession of the purchaser. C.C. art. 3227."

In *Baldwin v. Young*, 47 La. Ann. 1466, 17 So. 883, it was said: "The vendor of a movable is apprised by law that, without registry, he preserves a privilege on the thing sold. Civ. Code, art. 3227."

For the above reasons, the judgment of the lower court is hereby reversed and it is ordered, adjudged and decreed that there be judgment in favor of the third opponent as prayed for.

* * * * * *

NOTES AND QUESTIONS

1. Though the rule that a vendor's privilege on a movable will survive immobilization of the thing subject to the privilege might have appeared well-settled by the mid-twentieth century, the Louisiana Supreme Court appeared to chart an entirely new course in *American Creosote Company v. Springer,* 241 So. 2d 510 (1970), a case that did not even involve a claim of a vendor's privilege but instead presented a contest between a railroad company that had leased railroad track to the owner of an immovable under an unrecorded lease and a third party purchaser to whom this owner later sold the immovable. Deciding the contest in favor of the purchaser, the court held that the railroad track was an immovable by nature and passed with the sale. Even though *American Creosote Company* did not involve an unpaid vendor asserting a vendor's privilege, the court nonetheless expressly overruled *Caldwell v. Laurel Grove Co.*, 144 So. 718 (1932), which was cited extensively in *Cristina Inv. Corporation*. The court intentionally chose not to distinguish *Caldwell v. Laurel Grove Co.* on the basis of the status of the parties involved or other facts, because it felt that such a distinction would be invalid as to the "real" issue of whether the rails constructed into a railway became immovable by nature. As to that proposition, the court found that the two cases were irreconcilable, for "if a thing is immovable by nature, it is immovable as to everyone." What *American Creosote Company* implies with respect to the continued existence of a vendor's privilege on a movable following immobilization is not entirely clear. Given its

most expansive interpretation, the case supports the proposition, albeit in dicta, that the vendor's privilege is irretrievably lost upon immobilization, regardless of whether the movable subject to the privilege has retained its identity or can be removed without substantial injury to the immovable.

2. Is it true that "if a thing is immovable by nature, it is immovable as to everyone"? At the time *American Creosote Company* was decided, the Chattel Mortgage Law provided, in former La. R.S. 9:5357, that a thing subject to a chattel mortgage remained movable following attachment to an immovable insofar as the chattel mortgage was concerned. Another example of a thing being considered movable only as to designated persons is found in La Civ. Code art. 474, which provides that unharvested crops and ungathered fruits encumbered with security rights of third persons are movables by anticipation "insofar as the creditor is concerned."

3. Since *American Creosote Company*, the courts have only rarely had occasion to revisit the issue of loss of a vendor's privilege on a movable upon immobilization. In *Hyman v. Ross*, 643 So. 2d 256 (La. App. 2d Cir. 1994), perhaps the only case to consider the issue after the revision of Civil Code Article 466 in 1978, the court applied the "societal expectations test" under Article 466 to find that heating and air conditioning units sold to the owner of a hotel had become its component parts and were therefore encumbered under a mortgage previously granted upon the immovable. Although the seller of the heating and air conditioning units had moved for separate appraisal prior to the foreclosure sale of the immovable, the court found that the pre-existing mortgage attached to them and therefore outranked the vendor's privilege, with no citation to the previous jurisprudence involving vendor's privileges or any reasoning other than that the units had become component parts of an immovable that was subject to a previously recorded mortgage. Without specifically citing *American Creosote Company,* the court appears to have followed its implication that immobilization of a thing subject to a vendor's privilege necessarily implies a loss of the privilege.

iii. Over Immovables

See **La. Civ. Code arts. 3249(1); 3250-51**

The vendor's privilege on immovables affords greater rights and is much stronger than that on movables. When properly recorded, the vendor's privilege on immovables is unquestionably a real right, giving the vendor the right to assert his privilege even after the immovable has passed into the hands of a third person. As will be discussed in the following chapter, a vendor's privilege primes general privileges; thus, the unpaid seller is exempted from having to bear the general privileges, as mere mortgagees are forced to do. More importantly, timely recordation of the vendor's privilege causes it to outrank even previously existing mortgages against the vendee. This includes not only mortgages that may be recorded within the period of time prescribed for recordation of the privilege but also pre-existing mortgages, including previously recorded judicial mortgages bearing against the vendee's property. Cases involving these ranking issues are included in the following Chapter.

Because a vendor's privilege arises by operation of law, the concurrence of both spouses is not required to establish it, even if it encumbers community immovables.

A sale and resale of a thing made for the sole purpose of acquiring a vendor's privilege on the object is recognized under the law. For decades, building and loan associations used the sale-resale transaction for the express purpose of creating a vendor's privilege in the association's favor. Under this practice, the borrower, already the owner of the immovable, would sell it to the building and loan association, which then resold the property back to the borrower, reserving both the vendor's privilege provided by law and a conventional mortgage upon the immovable.

* * * * * *

PELICAN HOMESTEAD AND SAVINGS ASSOCIATION

v.

ROYAL SCOTT APARTMENTS PARTNERSHIP

541 So. 2d 943 (La. App. 5th Cir. 1989)

WICKER, Judge.

This is an appeal taken by the intervenors/appellants, Marguerite Lola Lopez, Joanne Lopez, and Steven A. Lopez, from an adverse judgment on a rule to show cause why their vendors' lien should not prime plaintiff/appellee's (Pelican Homestead and Savings Association) mortgage and why the proceeds from the sheriff's sale should not be required to satisfy their vendors' lien prior to satisfying Pelican's mortgage. We affirm.

Pelican initially filed suit against defendants, Royal Scott Apartments Partnership, William C. Boehmer, William T. Charbonnet and Nouvelle Vie Construction, Inc. seeking a recognition of its first mortgage on immovable property securing a defaulted promissory note as well as judgment in the amount of $397,737.96, plus interest, insurance and attorney's fees. The note was executed on January 23, 1985, in the amount of $400,000.00 before Malcolm A. Meyer, notary public.

A default judgment was rendered recognizing Pelican's first mortgage and awarding a money judgment as prayed. On May 23, 1988, Marguerite Lola Lopez, Joanne Lopez, and Steven A. Lopez filed an "intervention and rule to show cause." Made defendants in intervention were Pelican, Royal Scott Apartments Partnership and the sheriff of Jefferson Parish. Intervenors/appellants alleged they sold the property which is the subject matter of Pelican's original petition to Royal Scott Apartments Partnership on January 23, 1985, before notary, Malcolm A. Meyer. Pelican answered the petition for intervention, admitting this allegation.

Intervenors/appellants further alleged they have a vendors' lien which outranks Pelican's mortgage. Pelican denied there was a vendors' lien. Intervenors/appellants sought payment on a defaulted note executed by Royal Scott Apartments Partnership. Pelican answered admitting the existence of the note for $150,000.00 but denying information as to the default.

Intervenors prayed that a show cause order issue to the parties as to why intervenors should not be paid in preference to Pelican at the forthcoming sale resulting from seizure of the property. The show cause hearing was set on July 7, 1988. On July 1, 1988, Pelican filed a memorandum in opposition to intervenors' assertion that their vendors' lien was preserved following a recitation in the deed that the full purchase price had been paid in cash. Pelican further urged that if intervenors possessed such a privilege it was tacitly waived or renounced in their act of second mortgage. No reply memorandum was filed by movers-in-rule.

The rule to show cause was heard on July 7, 1988. The trial judge took the matter under advisement and rendered judgment on July 14, 1988. The only documents introduced into evidence were the following:

(1) The Act of Sale dated January 23, 1985, concerning the subject property indicating sale from intervenors/appellants to Royal Scott Apartments Partnership executed before notary, Malcolm A. Meyer. The act of sale contains the following provision:

> "*This sale is made and accepted for and in consideration of the price and* sum of FIVE HUNDRED THOUSAND AND NO/100 ($500,000.00) DOLLARS, Cash, which the said purchaser has well and truly paid, in ready and current money to the said vendors who hereby acknowledge the receipt thereof and grant full acquittance and discharge therefor."

(2) An act of mortgage executed on the same date by Royal Scott Apartments Partnership in favor of Pelican in the amount of $400,000.00. The act indicates the note is secured by the subject property and that the notary was Malcolm A. Meyer.

(3) A document styled "Second Mortgage by Royal Scott Apartments Partnership in favor of Bearer" executed on the same date before Malcolm A. Meyer, notary. The document contains the following provision:

> "Which said appearer declared and acknowledged that it is justly and truly indebted unto BEARER in the full and true sum of ONE

> HUNDRED FIFTY THOUSAND AND NO/100 ($150,000.00) DOLLARS, borrowed money, which the said BEARER has this day loaned and advanced to Royal Scott Apartments Partnership and for the reimbursement whereof Royal Scott Apartments Partnership has made and subscribed one certain Promissory Notes for the sum of ONE HUNDRED FIFTY THOUSAND AND NO/100 ($150,000.00) to the order of and endorsed by BEARER dated January 23, 1985."

The note is secured by the subject property. The act of mortgage additionally contains the following provision:

> *"Mortgagees hereby acknowledge that the mortgage granted herein is inferior and subordinate to that certain mortgage executed by Royal Scott Apartments Partnership (mortgagors) in favor of Pelican Homestead & Savings Association, in the amount of $400,000.00, as per act before the undersigned Notary Public, of even date herewith . . . and now to these presents personally came and intervened MARGUERITE LALA LOPEZ, JOANNE LOPEZ RICHARDSON, and STEVEN A. LOPEZ, who on behalf of any future holder or holders of said note hereby accept this act of mortgage."* [emphasis added]. . . .

The trial judge . . . rendered the following judgment based on the pleadings, memoranda and the evidence submitted:

IT IS HEREBY ORDERED, ADJUDGED AND DECREED that Pelican Homestead and Savings Association, as the first mortgage holder, is entitled to be paid at sheriff's sale with preference and priority over all creditors, including but not limited to intervenors' vendors' lien.

Intervenors have appealed that judgment and specify the following errors:

1. The trial court's judgment ordering that the proceeds of the judicial sale of the property be paid to the mortgage creditor in preference to Appellants' vendors' privilege for the balance of the purchase price was error. . . .

Pelican further urges that even assuming intervenors retained their vendors' privilege the privilege would still be primed by Pelican's first mortgage and its La. R.S. 6:830(H)(1) vendor's privilege.

La. R.S. 6:830(H)(1) provides in pertinent part:

> All mortgages executed upon immovable property in Louisiana in favor of associations organized and operating under the laws of the state shall have a rank equal to that of a vendor's privilege upon immovable property and shall have priority over all other liens, privileges, encumbrances, and mortgages upon the property, and the improvements and component parts thereon *which are recorded or arise in any manner subsequent to the date of recordation of the mortgage in favor of the association.* . . . [Emphasis added].

In *Home S. & L. Ass'n v. Tri-Parish Ventures,* 505 So. 2d 165, 167 (La. App. 4th Cir. 1987), our brothers in the fourth circuit explained:

> While LSA-R.S. 6:830 does create a vendor's privilege upon the mortgaged property, the privilege has priority only over those ". . . other liens, privileges, encumbrances, and mortgages upon the property . . . which are recorded or arise in any manner *subsequent* to the date of the recordation of the mortgage in favor of the association. . . ." LSA-R.S. 6:830(H)(1). [Emphasis added].

In the case at bar the intervenors' vendors' lien *arose* prior to the recordation of Pelican's first mortgage. Thus, La. R.S. 6:830(H)(1) does not apply. As explained in *De L'Isle v. Succession of Moss,* 34 La. Ann. 164, 166-67 (1881):

> It would indeed be unjust to place an unpaid vendor on a footing of equality with the other creditors of the purchaser, and permit these to devour his substance; for it is only on condition that the price of the thing sold has been paid, that the purchaser acquires an indefeasible title of ownership to the property, and that his creditors can be paid. . . . It springs from the very nature of the contract of sale, of which it is a legal concomitant. It exists without stipulation, and adheres tenaciously to the thing sold. It is invariably considered as retained, *unless renounced in language unmistakenly clear, or by acts evidently designed to destroy effectually the presumption of its retention.* . . . [Emphasis added]

It is the price that is protected by the privilege. By the sale the vendor increases the estate of the purchaser. It would be iniquitous to permit the property sold to become the prey of the creditors of the purchaser, without requiring as a condition precedent, the payment of its costs. [citations omitted].

The circumstances, however, support the trial court's conclusion that the vendors' privilege was waived.

Intervenors executed an authentic act in which they clearly stated they were executing "a mortgage [which was] inferior and subordinate" to Pelican's mortgage.

In addition, the act of sale recites that intervenors/vendors "hereby acknowledge the receipt thereof [of the cash] and grant full acquittance and discharge therefor." By its own terms, the above statement of "full acquittance and discharge" expresses that there is no privilege. Intervenors/vendors by these words discharged the purchasers from any debt owed to them. We conclude the language expresses a clear intent to waive the vendors' privilege. *De L'Isle,* supra.

The trial judge obviously found that the vendors' lien was waived in favor of Pelican's mortgage. The trial court's conclusion is further bolstered by the absence of any recordation of the vendors' lien so as to protect intervenors/vendors against third parties. La. R.S. 9:2721.

Accordingly, for the reasons stated the trial court's judgment in favor of Pelican decreeing that Pelican be paid at the Sheriff's sale with preference and priority over all creditors is affirmed at appellants' cost.

Affirmed.

* * * * * *

NOTES AND QUESTIONS

1. Did the recitation in the act of sale that the price had been paid constitute an outright waiver of the vendor's privilege, or did the recitation simply prevent the vendor from asserting his privilege against third persons?

2. Curiously, the court felt that its finding of waiver was bolstered by the absence of any recordation of the vendor's privilege. Should that fact alone, irrespective of the issue of waiver or subordination, have been sufficient to defeat the attempt of the vendors to assert their privilege to the prejudice of the building and loan association?

3. For a similar ruling concerning the effect of a statement in a recorded act of sale that the price has been paid, *see Alison Mtg. Inv. Trust v. BPB Contractors, Inc.*, 362 So. 2d 1203 (La. App. 4th Cir. 1978), holding that, where an act of sale recited that the vendor had been paid in full, even though the seller had in fact taken two promissory notes for a large portion of the purchase price, any vendor's privilege that the seller might have retained was subordinate to a mortgage executed in favor of a third-party lender, notwithstanding the fact that the lender's representative was present at the closing of the sale and knew that a portion of the purchase price had been paid in notes. The case cited *McDuffie v. Walker*, 51 So. 100 (1909), for the rule that even actual knowledge is not a substitute for the requirement to properly record privileges.

iv. As Compared to the Seller's Resolutory Condition

***See* La. Civ. Code arts. 2561-64**

In addition to the vendor's privilege, the unpaid vendor enjoys the right of dissolution of the sale in the event that the vendee fails to pay the price. The exercise of this right is, of course, antithetical to the vendor's privilege. With the exercise of the right of dissolution of the sale, the vendor undoes the sale and must return whatever portion of the price has been paid. Enforcement of the vendor's privilege, on the other hand, is an affirmation of the sale by which the vendor seeks to enforce the vendee's obligation to pay the price. The right of a vendor to seek dissolution of a sale upon non-payment of the price and the vendor's privilege are distinct remedies, neither of which is dependent on the existence of the other.

Another difference between the two alternative rights is recordation: where immovables are concerned, the vendor's privilege must be evidenced by a recordation in the mortgage records. On the other hand, the right of dissolution can be asserted against third persons without the necessity of recordation in the mortgage records, so long as the act conveying the immovable to the vendee does not reflect that the price was paid. The fact that the vendor has lost, or failed to preserve, his vendor's privilege presents no obstacle to the exercise of the separate right of dissolution.

Until the revision of the sales articles of the Civil Code in 1993, there was another interesting distinction between the vendor's privilege and the right of dissolution. Following prior jurisprudence, *Louis Werner Saw Mill Co. v. White,* 17 So. 2d 264 (La. 1944), held that the action to dissolve a sale for the non-payment of the purchase price is a personal action prescribed by ten years (*see now* Civil Code Article 3499), running from the moment the buyer defaults on the payment of the credit portion of the price. Applying the rule that the right of dissolution is independent of the vendor's privilege and is not dependent on the preservation of the privilege, the court reaffirmed earlier holdings to the effect that the right of dissolution may be exercised even if the notes given to evidence the price have prescribed. The rule established in *Louis Werner Saw Mill Co.* was ultimately altered in the 1993 revision of the law of sales: Under revised Article 2561, if an instrument is given to evidence the price, the right of dissolution now prescribes at the same time and in the same period as the instrument. The vendor's privilege, being an accessorial right, is also extinguished when the underlying obligation prescribes.

* * * * * *

SLIMAN

v.

MCBEE,

311 So. 2d 248 (La. 1975)

MARCUS, Justice.

By act of sale dated March 28, 1968, Florence Joseph Sliman sold to Hal D. McBee and Marilyn Sliman McBee (her son-in-law and daughter) certain described property located in the Indian Hills subdivision within the city of

Opelousas in St. Landry Parish. The agreed purchase price was $78,000.00, in part payment of which the McBees paid to the vendor $5,000.00 and for the balance thereof executed four promissory notes. The act of sale contained the following language:

> It is agreed between the parties that the notes . . . shall be and remain the personal obligation of the makers and their heirs, but no lien shall exist on the lots herein sold securing payment of said notes.

There was no mortgage accompanying the act of sale, which was recorded only in the conveyance records of the parish.

Exactly one year later, on March 28, 1969, Florence Sliman filed suit against the McBees, seeking recognition of her vendor's privilege on the property and its recordation in the mortgage records of the parish. By supplemental petition filed on June 3, 1969, Mrs. Sliman also sought cancellation of the sale for nonpayment of the purchase price on the ground that defendants were in default on payment of the first promissory note, which became due on May 1, 1969.

This lawsuit was settled by an act of compromise dated November 6, 1969, in which Florence Sliman agreed to a dismissal of her claims, including those set forth in the supplemental petition, with prejudice in exchange for payment of the first note by the McBees and their agreement to pay the balance due on the remaining notes according to a revised payment schedule. . . . Pursuant to this settlement, the parties moved for and obtained a judgment dismissing all claims with prejudice.

The McBees then executed three mortgages on the property to secure loans from the St. Landry Bank and Trust Company in the amount of $68,800.00. When they defaulted on their obligation to repay the loans, the bank instituted suit for collection of the amount due and recognition of its mortgages on the property. Florence Sliman intervened, seeking a money judgment on the remaining notes which were not paid when due, and recognition of her vendor's lien. The district court rendered judgment in favor of both the bank and Mrs. Sliman against the McBees in the full amounts claimed. However, finding that she had waived her right to a vendor's lien in the act of sale, the court refused to allow Mrs. Sliman a vendor's lien and ruled that her claim was secured only by the judicial mortgage that would result from her recordation of the judgment in the mortgage records. Mrs. Sliman appealed the ruling to the court of appeal, which affirmed the judgment of the district court. *St. Landry Bank & Trust Co. v. McBee*, 284 So. 2d 155 (La. App. 3d Cir. 1973). Her application to this court for a writ of certiorari to review the judgment of the court of appeal was denied. 287 So. 2d 188 (La. 1974).

The present suit against the McBees and the bank was filed during the course of the litigation instituted by the bank on the mortgage notes. In this suit, Mrs. Sliman seeks dissolution of the sale for nonpayment of the purchase price, alleging that she is entitled to a rescission of the sale and return of the property (with the exception of certain described lots that were sold with her written approval or ratification) free and clear of the mortgages held by the bank as a result of the McBees' default on the notes representing the purchase price. Additionally, plaintiff seeks a money judgment against the McBees in the amount of $15,662.53, which she alleges is the difference between the revenues they derived from the property and the amount they paid on the purchase price. After trial on the matter, judgment was rendered in favor of defendants, dismissing plaintiff's petition with prejudice.

Mrs. Sliman appealed the judgment to the court of appeal. In affirming the district court, the court of appeal found in the language of the act of sale not only a waiver by Mrs. Sliman of her right to a vendor's lien, but a waiver of her right to sue for dissolution of the sale for nonpayment of the purchase price as well. *Sliman v. McBee*, 300 So. 2d 585 (La. App. 3d Cir. 1974). We granted Mrs. Sliman's application to this court for a writ of certiorari to review the judgment of the court of appeal. 303 So. 2d 175 (La.1974).

The court of appeal determined that the language contained in the act of sale (quoted supra), in which Mrs. Sliman agreed that the notes given in payment of the purchase price were to remain a personal obligation and that no lien on the property would secure payment of the notes, constituted a waiver not only of her vendor's lien, but of her right to rescind the sale for nonpayment of the purchase price as well. Review of that ruling requires an understanding of the right of dissolution asserted by the plaintiff as well as application of the rules governing the interpretation of contracts.

The right of a vendor to rescind the sale on account of the vendee's default in payment of the purchase price rests in articles 2045-2047 and 2561-2564 of the Civil Code. Article 2045 provides:

> The dissolving condition is that which, when accomplished, operates the revocation of the obligation, placing matters in the same state as though the obligation had not existed.

It does not suspend the execution of the obligation; it only obliges the creditor to restore what he has received, in case the event provided for in the condition takes place.

This dissolving, or resolutory, condition is implied in all commutative contracts and takes effect upon the failure of either party to comply with his engagement and the demand for dissolution by the aggrieved party. La. Civil Code art. 2046 (1870).

Where the commutative contract is one of sale, the special rules governing the contract of sale must be consulted, in addition to the general principles announced above. Id. art. 2438. The principal obligation of the buyer is to pay the price of sale. Id. art. 2549(1). Upon his failure to do so, the vendor has two remedies available: one for the enforcement, or affirmance, of the contract and the other for its dissolution. The second right, asserted here by Mrs. Sliman, is an independent, substantive remedy available under article 2561 of the Civil Code that is in no way dependent upon the existence of a security device such as a mortgage or a privilege, which secures the first remedy of the seller, i.e., the enforcement of the buyer's obligation to pay the price agreed upon in the contract of sale.

Should the seller elect the second remedy and sue for rescission of the sale for nonpayment of the purchase price, the buyer's default ". . . operates the revocation of the (seller's) obligation . . . ," id. art. 2045, which, in a sale, initially consists of his delivery of the thing sold. Id. art. 2475. Accordingly, the seller may then sue for dissolution of the sale and return of the property. Id. art. 2561. The effect is to place all parties in the same position they occupied prior to the sale.

Clearly, then, in order for Mrs. Sliman to waive the separate and independent right to dissolve the sale upon the buyer's default in payment of the sale price, she must express her intent to relinquish that right in words that make specific reference to the action to dissolve as distinguished from the action to enforce the contract. In interpreting agreements, we are required to ascertain the true intent of the parties as evidenced by their choice of language. Id. art. 1945. Article 1947 directs that

> (t)erms of art or technical phrases are to be interpreted according to their received meaning with those who profess the art or profession to which they belong.

Accordingly, the terms used by the parties in the alleged waiver of legal rights must be construed in light of their legal significance.

In the act of sale, Mrs. Sliman agreed that the notes given by the McBees were to remain a "personal obligation" and that no "lien" would exist on the lots sold securing payment of the notes. Considered in view of their legal significance, the terms used in the act of sale cannot be said to evince an intent, express or implied, on the part of Mrs. Sliman to waive her right to dissolve the sale for nonpayment of the purchase price. As long as Mrs. Sliman held the credit representing the purchase price, two remedies, or courses of action, were available to her in the event the credit was not paid: she could either sue to enforce payment or sue to dissolve the sale. In agreeing that the notes would remain a personal obligation unsecured by a lien, Mrs. Sliman simply forfeited a device securing the buyer's obligation to pay, to which she would otherwise be entitled. She did not forfeit the right to enforce payment, much less the independent, alternative right of dissolution. Moreover, even if she had waived her right to enforce the obligation to pay the purchase price, waiver of one remedy in no way affects the other.

The only question that remains is whether the return of the property is to be free and clear of the mortgages given by the McBees to the bank to secure the loans made to them. The answer here is well settled. We stated in *Stevenson v. Brown*, 32 La. Ann. 461, 464 (1880) that "(a) demand in resolution is a demand for the property itself, and *embraces in it the abrogation of any and all alienations and encumbrances placed upon it by the vendee*." (Emphasis added.) The failure of the purchaser to pay the sale price causes the resolutory condition to take effect, which places matters in the same state as though the obligation had not existed. La. Civil Code arts. 2045-47, 2561 (1870). Thus, judicial dissolution of a sale for nonpayment of the price frees the property of all mortgages created by the purchaser. E.g., *Adler v. Adler*, 126 La. 472, 52 So. 668 (1910) and authorities cited therein.

CONCLUSION

Mrs. Sliman, the plaintiff herein, is entitled to a dissolution of the sale to the McBees, the defendants herein, on account of their default in full payment of the purchase price. As noted above, the effect of the dissolution is to place matters in the same state as though the obligation had not existed. The vendor gets the property back, and the vendee is discharged from his obligation to pay the price. If he has paid part of the price, that which he has paid is restored to him. . . .

Reversed and remanded.

DIXON, Justice (dissenting).

I respectfully dissent.

Although I concur with the majority's analysis of the law concerning resolutory conditions and vendor's liens, I note that the facts of this case require a different resolution of the case.

When a vendor waives his vendor's privilege in the act of sale and does not retain a mortgage on the property, there is no recordation of the retention of the right to resolution of the sale. This court has properly held that resolution of the sale does not depend on recordation. The French solved the problem created by the absence of recordation of the resolutory condition by enacting a provision in the law of recordation (Law of Recordation of 23 March 1885, Art. 7) which barred the exercise of the action of resolution after the extinction of the privilege. Louisiana does not have such a provision and, therefore, the conclusion that the action in resolution can be maintained even though no privilege exists in favor of the vendor plaintiff is correct.

The action to resolve the sale can be renounced by the vendor. Planiol states:

> "The action in resolution is extinguished by application of the general rules of law.
>
> "'. . . it may be extinguished either by the effect of a renunciation made by the vendor,
>
> "The renunciation which the vendor makes can be express or tacit. . . ."

Planiol, *Traite Elementaire De Droit Civil*, Vol. 2-Part 1, No. 1567, Louisiana State Law Institute Translation.

In this case the vendor expressly renounced the right to resolve the sale. As noted in the majority opinion the settlement agreement of the first suit stated:

> "All parties declare and acknowledge that with the exception of the hereinabove referred to notes, No. (sic) 2, 3, and 4, that any and all of the indebtedness which may exist be (sic) either party to the other *and any and all claims of every kind which either party may have against the other is hereby compromised and settled* and that neither party will make any claim against the other party for any matter or thing which may have arisen or happened prior to the execution of this agreement." (Emphasis added).

The resolutory condition is a right of the vendor. This vendor renounced all rights except the rights contained in the notes.

I would find that the resolutory condition was expressly renounced in the settlement agreement, and dismiss the suit.

* * * * * *

NOTES AND QUESTIONS

An acknowledgment in a recorded sale of payment of the price is sufficient to bar the seller from asserting either the vendor's privilege or right of dissolution to the prejudice of third persons. *See, e.g., City Bank & Trust*

Company v. Caneco Construction, Inc., 341 So. 2d 1331 (La. Ct. App. 3d Cir. 1977), holding that the seller was barred by both the parol evidence rule and the public records doctrine from seeking to enforce to the prejudice of a mortgagee either the seller's right to dissolve or its vendor's privilege, where the act of sale recited that the purchase price had been paid in full, rejecting arguments that the mortgagee, as the drawee bank, knew that a check given to the seller for the remaining balance of the purchase price had been returned for insufficient funds.

7. Agricultural Privileges

***See* La. Civ. Code arts. 3217(1) and (3); La. Rev. Stat. 9:4522–23; La. Rev. Stat. 10:9-109(a)(2).**

At the time Louisiana attained statehood in 1812, its law recognized only two privileges on crops: the privilege of the overseer on crops of the current year to secure payment of amounts due him for the current year and the immediately preceding year, and the privilege due for the rent of an immovable and the hire of slaves employed in working it. Act 70 of 1843 added a privilege for debts due for necessary supplies, making this privilege expressly subordinate to that of the overseer. Following the close of the Civil War, Act 195 of 1867 amended article 3184 of the Civil Code of 1825 by substituting a privilege for the wages of farm laborers in place of the previously existing privilege for the hire of slaves. The same act added a privilege for debts due for money advanced for the purpose of the purchase of necessary supplies and payment of necessary expenses. All agricultural privileges were ranked concurrently, except that the laborer's privilege was given first priority. The 1867 legislation was retained in the adoption of the Civil Code of 1870, and the privileges that it recognized are the same crop privileges that arise under the Louisiana Civil Code today. Special legislation has added additional privileges for debts for water furnished to grow crops and amounts due to threshermen, combinemen, and grain driers. *See* La. R.S. 9:4522–4523.

Privileges and other secured interests affecting crops are now ranked by a non-uniform provision of the Louisiana Uniform Commercial Code, La. R.S. 10:9-322(g), which is discussed in the following chapter.

* * * * * *

LOEB

v.

COLLIER

59 So. 816 (La. 1912)

SOMMERVILLE, J.

A. McCranie furnished the necessary supplies to enable Hezekiah Kendrick to grow his 1911 crop. Kendrick deposited with the Homer Compress Company a bale of cotton raised by him in 1911, and took a receipt for the same. J. R. Madden advanced Kendrick $17 on the warehouse receipt, and a week or 10 days thereafter bought the bale of cotton from Kendrick, paying the balance of the purchase price in money. On September 30, 1911, Madden sold this bale to Herman Loeb, a cotton buyer of Shreveport, through Loeb's agent, Palmer.

McCranie, setting up his privilege as a furnisher of supplies, sequestered the bale of cotton. Loeb claims ownership. The district court having rendered judgment sustaining McCranie's privilege, Loeb has invoked the supervisory jurisdiction of this court.

Privileges are in derogation of common right, and secret liens hamper commerce, hence privileges are strictly construed, and secret liens are not favored.

[2] C. C. art. 3217, provides:

> "That debts which are privileged on certain movables are the following:
>
> (1) . . . Debts due for necessary supplies furnished to any farm or plantation . . . on the crops of the year and the proceeds thereof."

It has been uniformly held that the purchaser of a growing crop is charged with presumptive knowledge of the privilege of the furnisher of supplies, and buys subject to such privilege (*Weill v. Kent*, 107 La. 322, 31 South. 761, and 52 La. Ann. 2139, 28 South. 295; *Garcia v. Garcia*, 7 La. Ann. 526; *Welsh v. Barrow*,

3 La. Ann. 133), and it was held in *National Bank of Commerce v. Sullivan (Oil Co., Intervener)*, 117 La. 163, 41 South. 480, that:

> "The privilege for advances conferred by Civil Code, art. 3217, is not confined to the growing crop, but bears upon the products after they are severed from the soil, and follows them into the hands of a purchaser, who, buying directly from the planter, is presumed to know that such privilege may or actually does exist."

In that case the intervener not only had bought directly from the planter, but had bought while the crop was in the ground, and for future delivery; besides, constructive knowledge of the existence of plaintiff's lien, the efforts of intervener, aided and abetted by the defendant, to 'run the crop off,' plainly disclose an actual knowledge of plaintiff's privilege.

The state of facts presented in the instant case is altogether different from that passed upon in the cases hereinabove quoted and relied upon by the respondent judge, and must lead to different conclusions. It may well be that when Madden bought from Kendrick he bought a portion of the crop and acquired the cotton *cum onere*, but surely in Madden's hands it was no longer a crop. It had become an article of commerce, had gone into the channels of trade, and was merchandise pure and simple.

Louisiana is an agricultural state, and its prosperity largely depends upon agriculture. To enable the farmer to make his crop, the privilege of the furnisher of supplies must be recognized, and must be adequately protected. This protection is assured by the enforcement of the privilege upon the crop, or, if sold, upon the proceeds thereof, and by charging the purchaser from the planter with knowledge that that crop is bought subject to any liens that may be upon it at the time of his purchase. As long as the agricultural product remains in the hands of the farmer or planter, it is a crop and nothing else; but, when his vendee parts with ownership the agricultural product can no longer be considered a crop, it has become merchandise; hence it necessarily follows that the lien is gone. If this were not true, it would be unsafe for any one at any time to buy from anybody a bale of cotton, a sack of rice, or a pound of sugar. If the lien rested on the thing until the furnisher of supplies has been paid, not only might cotton bought in open market from a merchant, and on shipboard, and for which a bill of lading had been issued and transmitted to the foreign buyer, be sequestered, but the rice in the family storeroom, the sugar or molasses on the breakfast table would be subject to sequestration by the unpaid furnisher of supplies. To entitle the lienholder to his writ, he would simply have to establish identity. Such an interpretation of the statute is not only not justified by the lawgiver's language, but would practically paralyze our entire commerce; that commerce being almost wholly of agricultural products.

It is therefore ordered, adjudged, and decreed that the judgment herein rendered by the district court on April 26, 1912, be annulled, avoided, and reversed, and that there now be judgment in favor of plaintiff, with costs of both courts, decreeing plaintiff to be owner of the bale of cotton described in his petition, free of any lien or privilege in favor of A. McCranie.

* * * * * *

NOTES AND QUESTIONS

1. As will be discussed in a later section of this chapter, as a general rule, privileges on movables are by their very nature simple preferences unaccompanied by a right of pursuit. Nonetheless, a number of early cases held that agricultural privileges follow crops into the hands of third persons, who were charged with presumptive knowledge of the existence of the privilege. *See, e.g., Nat'l Bank of Commerce v. Sullivan*, 41 So. 480 (1906); *Weill v. Kent*, 31 So. 761 (La. 1902); *Weill v. Kent*, 28 So. 295 (La. 1900). *Loeb v. Collier* limited the right of pursuit to only the first purchaser. Was this decision predicated primarily upon conceptual notions that a privilege is a mere right of preference, a belief that a crop is transformed into inventory when it leaves the hands of the farmer, or policy considerations of the disruptive effect that would flow from a right of pursuit against subsequent purchasers?

2. Louisiana's 2001 revision of Chapter 9 of the Uniform Commercial Code, in keeping with nationwide revisions of the model UCC, brought most aspects of agricultural privileges within the coverage of Chapter 9, except for the law governing creation of the agricultural privileges themselves. La. R.S. 10:9-109(a)(2). Thus, agricultural privileges, known in UCC parlance as agricultural liens, became subject to the filing and perfection rules of revised Chapter 9. Another interesting feature of the 2001 revision was its inclusion of agricultural liens within the scope of the general rule of the model UCC that a security

interest or *agricultural lien* continues in collateral notwithstanding the sale, lease, license, exchange, or other disposition of the collateral. *See* La. R.S. 10:9-315(a) (as enacted by Act No. 128 of 2001). With little fanfare, this revision appeared to abrogate the rule of *Loeb v. Collier*. Indeed, it effectively elevated agricultural privileges to the status of real rights. This change was reversed in 2010. As the 2010 comments to La. R.S. 10:9-315(a) indicate, the removal of references to agricultural liens in Section 9-315(a)(1) was intended to restore longstanding Louisiana law limiting the enforcement of agricultural privileges on crops after they have been sold.

3. Acting in response to the federal Food Security Act of 1985, which was designed to protect buyers of farm products, the Louisiana legislature in 1987 enacted La. R.S. 3:3651 *et seq.*, creating a central registry of all security devices establishing security interests in farm products. As revised in 2010, La. R.S. 3:3656(D) allows a buyer in the ordinary course of business to take free of unfiled agricultural privileges.

4. In 1987, when the Louisiana legislature created the central agricultural registry, the state had not yet adopted Article 9 of the Uniform Commercial Code, and there was no central filing office for security devices affecting any type of movable collateral. The 1987 Louisiana legislation specifically provided that a security device affecting farm products was ineffective against third persons unless the security device and an "effective financing statement" containing certain prescribed information were filed in the central agricultural registry. Act 123 of 1990, which was adopted after Chapter 9 of the Louisiana Uniform Commercial Code had become effective, provided for the transfer of the central agricultural registry to the secretary of state; however, the central agricultural registry was, and continues to be, separate from the master index maintained by the secretary of state of filings made under Chapter 9 of the Louisiana Uniform Commercial Code. *See generally* La. R.S. 10:9-519 to 9-526. An interesting feature of Louisiana's central agricultural registry is that, unlike the central agricultural filing systems created by a number of other states in response to the Food Security Act of 1985, Louisiana's registry serves the *dual* purpose of not only providing constructive notice to buyers in accordance with the federal act but also serving as the place where Uniform Commercial Code financing statements are filed in order to perfect security interests and agricultural liens in farm products against other secured parties, lien creditors,

and unsecured creditors of the debtor. The filing that is required, commonly known as a UCC-1F, is similar to an ordinary financing statement but includes additional information required by La. R.S. 3:3651 *et seq.*

5. For a comprehensive history of the evolution of secured interests in Louisiana crops, *see* L. David Cromwell, *Secured Interests in Louisiana Crops: The 2010 Legislative Revision*, 71 La. L. Rev. 1175 (2011).

* * * * * *

BAYOU PIERRE FARMS

v.

BAT FARMS PARTNERS, III

693 So. 2d 1158 (La. 1997)

KIMBALL, Justice.

We granted certiorari to determine whether Bayou Pierre Farms (Bayou Pierre), a Louisiana general partnership which contracted with Bat Farms Partners (Bat Farms), also a Louisiana general partnership, to pick all of the cotton grown by Bat Farms, qualifies as a laborer pursuant to La. R.S. 9:4521 and La. C.C. art. 3217 and would thus be ranked as the first privilege on the funds derived from the sale of that cotton now on deposit in the registry of the court. Though there were competing claimants for these funds, the district court, in accordance with La. R.S. 9:4521, ranked Bayou Pierre ahead of the other claimants. The court of appeal reversed, finding that Bayou Pierre was not a laborer and therefore was not entitled to a first ranking privilege on the funds on deposit in the registry of the court. For the reasons explained more fully below, we affirm the judgment of the court of appeal.

FACTS

On April 5, 1993, Bat Farms leased land in Natchitoches Parish from T.L. James Company, Inc. (T.L. James) at a rental of $55,000. Bat Farms leased this land to grow cotton and corn. The parties executed an agricultural security agreement on the crops. On April 13, 1993, to secure the land lease, the parties filed a UCC-1F form pursuant to La. R.S. 3:3651 *et seq.* and La. R.S. 10:9-101 *et seq.* . . .

After leasing the land from T.L. James, Bat Farms arranged a crop loan from Ag Services of America, Inc. (Ag Services) for $190,000. This loan was secured by an agricultural security agreement listing as collateral the crops on the land leased from T.L. James as well as crops on other leased lands. On May 3, 1993, to secure the loan, the parties filed a UCC-1F form pursuant to La. R.S. 3:3651 *et seq*. and La. R.S. 10:9-101 *et seq*.

T.L. James then sold the land subject to Bat Farms' land lease and equipment lease to Melrose Planting Company, Inc. (Melrose). T.L. James and Melrose agreed between themselves to a pro-rata distribution of the rents due under Bat Farms' lease. On July 12, 1993, to secure its interest, Melrose filed a UCC-1F form pursuant to La. R.S. 3:3651 *et seq*. and La. R.S. 10:9-101 *et seq*.

On July 28, 1993, by written contract, Bat Farms hired Bayou Pierre to pick the cotton grown by Bat Farms in Natchitoches Parish. Under the terms of the contract, Bayou Pierre, who is referred to as "Contractor" in the contract, was to receive ten cents per lint pound to pick the cotton the first time and if the cotton was required to be picked a second time, it was to receive twelve cents per lint pound. . . . By an act of crop pledge, Bat Farms granted Bayou Pierre a security interest in the cotton and its proceeds. On July 29, 1993, Bayou Pierre perfected its security interest by filing a UCC-1F form pursuant to La. R.S. 3:3651 *et seq*. and La. R.S. 10:9-101 *et seq*.

The cotton crop was raised, picked, moduled, ginned, baled, and sold. However, the proceeds were insufficient to satisfy all the claims of Bat Farms' creditors. Bayou Pierre, the first to file suit, petitioned for a writ of sequestration on the warehouse receipts or proceeds from the sale of the cotton and prayed that there be judgment recognizing its entitlement to $47,700 of the proceeds and attorney's fees. Melrose, T.L. James, and Ag Services each answered the suit and filed a reconventional demand against Bayou Pierre. A proliferation of cross-claims, third-party demands, and oblique actions followed. After the proceeds from the sale of the cotton, $124,412.05, were deposited into the registry of the court, T.L. James, Melrose, and Bayou Pierre filed motions for summary judgment and rules to rank the liens.

The district court granted T.L. James' and Melrose's motions for summary judgment and awarded them rent for the land in the amount of $55,000, plus interest and attorney's fees. . . . . The district court also granted Bayou Pierre's motion for summary judgment and awarded it $39,264.50 plus interest and attorney's fees. A final judgment was signed ranking the priorities of the liens in the following order in accordance with La. R.S. 9:4521:(1) Bayou Pierre; (2) T.L. James and Melrose; and (3) Ag Services.

T.L. James, Melrose, and Ag Services appealed the district court's judgment. The court of appeal affirmed the money judgments but modified the ranking order as follows: (1) T.L. James; (2) Ag Services; (3) Bayou Pierre; and (4) Melrose. According to the court of appeal, Bayou Pierre did not qualify as a laborer under La. R.S. 9:4521, thus it was not entitled to a first ranking privilege over the proceeds of the crop. The court of appeal determined that Bayou Pierre did not pick the cotton itself, rather, it only hired people who operated the mechanical cotton pickers that picked the cotton. By strictly construing La. C.C. art. 3217, the court of appeal concluded the laborer's privilege was intended to protect the workers who actually ran the machines that picked the cotton and not the contractor who hired the workers to pick the cotton. Thus, the court of appeal ruled that Bayou Pierre did not have a laborer's privilege and was not entitled to a first ranking privilege over the proceeds of the cotton crop.

We granted Bayou Pierre's application for certiorari, *Bayou Pierre Farms v. Bat Farms Partners, III, et al.,* 96-2826 (La. 1/24/97); 686 So. 2d 853, to determine whether Bayou Pierre qualified as a laborer entitled to a first ranking privilege under La. C.C. art. 3217 and La. R.S. 9:4521. La. Sup. Ct. R. X, § 1(a)(2).

LAW

All of the financing statements involved in this case were filed under both Louisiana's version of Article 9 of the UCC (La. R.S. 10:9-101 *et seq.*) and its laws regarding security devices affecting farm products (La. R.S. 3:3651 *et seq.*). La. R.S. 10:9-312(5) is the normal rule for ranking UCC interests and provides, in pertinent part:

> [p]riority between conflicting security interests in the same collateral shall be determined according to the following rules:

> (a) Conflicting security interests rank according to priority in time of filing or perfection. Priority dates from the time a filing is first made covering the collateral or the time the security interest is first perfected, whichever is earlier, provided that there is no period thereafter when there is neither filing nor perfection.

A parallel provision is found in Louisiana's farm products legislation, La. R.S. 3:3651 *et seq*. La. R.S. 3:3656(D) provides, in pertinent part:

> Except as otherwise provided in this Section, each effective financing statement and other statement shall become effective against third parties on the date and at the time it is filed with the filing officer.

Both La. R.S. 10:9-312(5) and La. R.S. 3:3656(D) provide that liens should rank in the order of their recordation. However, an exception to this normal ranking rule is found in La. R.S. 9:4521 and La. C.C. art. 3217. La. R.S. 9:4521 provides:

> As a specific exception to R.S. 9:4770 and R.S. 10:9-201, the following statutory privileges and perfected security interests as affecting unharvested crops shall be ranked in the following order of preference, provided that such privileges and security interests have been properly filed and maintained in accordance with the central registry provisions of R.S. 3:3651 *et seq*.:
>
> (1) Privilege of the laborer, the thresherman, combineman, grain driver, and the overseer.
>
> (2) Privilege of the lessor.
>
> (3) Perfected security interests under Chapter 9 of the Louisiana Commercial Laws in the order of filing, as provided by R.S. 3:3651 *et seq*.
>
> (4) Privilege of the furnisher of supplies and of money, of the furnisher of water, and of the physician.

La. C.C. art. 3217 provides, in pertinent part, that the following debts are privileged on certain movables:

> (3) The rents of immovables and the wages of laborers employed in working the same, on the crops of the year, and on the furniture, which is found in the house let, or on the farm, and on every thing which serves to the working of the farm.
>
> (9) The privileges granted by this article, on the growing crop, in favor of the classes of persons mentioned shall be concurrent, except the privilege in favor of the laborer, which shall be ranked as the first privilege on the crop.

Laws on the same subject matter must be interpreted in reference to each other. La. C.C. art. 13. When read *in pari materia,* La. R.S. 9:4521(1) and La. C.C. art. 3217(3) and (9) provide a first ranking privilege to a *laborer* for payment of *his wages.* The laborer's privilege for payment of his wages is subjected to a *stricti juris* interpretation. La. C.C. art. 3185; *Lumber Products, Inc. v. Crochet,* 244 La. 1060, 156 So. 2d 438 (La. 1963).

While this court has never directly addressed the issue of who qualifies as a laborer under La. R.S. 9:4521(1) and La. C.C. art. 3217(3) and (9), we have addressed the issue of who qualifies as a laborer entitled to the laborer's privilege under The Private Works Act, specifically, La. R.S. 9:4801(D) and La. R.S. 9:4812. *See Pringle-Associated Mortgage Corp. v. Eanes, et al.,* 254 La. 705, 226 So. 2d 502 (La.1969) (on rehearing). In *Pringle-Associated,* we held that a subcontractor who pays his own employees wages for labor performed on a building project does not become legally subrogated to his employees' superior laborer's privilege provided by La. R.S. 9:4801(D) and La. R.S. 9:4812. We reasoned in *Pringle-Associated* that "[t]o permit the subcontractors to invoke legal subrogation for the payment of their employees' wages would in effect award them a first ranking privilege for their own credit against the owner." Id. at 515.

DISCUSSION

Bayou Pierre complains the court of appeal erred in refusing to afford it the first ranking laborer's privilege on the crop proceeds deposited into the court registry. After a review of the entire record, the court of appeal rejected Bayou Pierre's argument, reasoning that it was not a laborer under a strict construction of La. C.C. art. 3217. Rather, the court of appeal determined that

Bayou Pierre was a contractor who was paid a contract price to pick the cotton and pay the wages of the workers who actually ran the machines that picked the cotton. We agree with the court of appeal's interpretation of La. R.S. 9:4521 and La. C.C. art. 3217.

Bayou Pierre is a partnership that entered into a contract with Bat Farms, whereby Bayou Pierre as the "Contractor" would receive compensation in return for supplying all the equipment and manpower necessary to pick the cotton grown by Bat Farms. This written contract also included a provision for payment of Bayou Pierre's attorney's fees if it was necessary for Bayou Pierre to retain an attorney to collect its fee due under the contract. The laborers hired by Bayou Pierre, the "Contractor," who actually operated the machines that picked Bat Farms' cotton, were paid their wages by Bayou Pierre. This contractual relationship is analogous to the subcontractor-laborer relationship analyzed by this court in *Pringle-Associated,* supra.

Applying a *stricti juris* interpretation to La. R.S. 9:4521 and La. C.C. art. 3217, we find the first ranking laborer's privilege applies only to a laborer for that laborer's unpaid wages. In this case, the laborers who actually picked the cotton were paid their wages. The plain wording of La. C.C. art. 3217 provides a first ranking privilege only to *laborers* for payment of their *wages.* Therefore, even if the laborers who actually picked the cotton had not been paid their wages, Bayou Pierre, as the employer of these laborers, is precluded by La. C.C. art. 3217 from claiming the laborer's privilege as that privilege belongs only to the laborers who actually picked the cotton and who were not paid their wages. Bayou Pierre contracted with Bat Farms to provide a service for Bat Farms in return for compensation; it is not a laborer who picked Bat Farms' cotton in return for wages. Thus, Bayou Pierre is not a laborer suing for payment of his unpaid wages; rather, it is a contractor suing for the amount due under a contract.

For the reasons expressed above, we find that Bayou Pierre is not entitled to a first ranking laborer's privilege under La. R.S. 9:4521 and La. C.C. art. 3217. Accordingly, we affirm the judgment of the court of appeal.

* * * * * *

NOTES AND QUESTIONS

1. The crop ranking statute applied by the court, La. R.S. 9:4521, was repealed in 2010 and replaced by a non-uniform provision of the Louisiana Uniform Commercial Code, La. R.S. 10:9-322(g). The basic ranking scheme was largely unchanged. Under La. R.S. 10:9-322(g), the agricultural laborer's privilege continues to have first-priority ranking ahead of all other agricultural liens and security interests, but the law now provides that it is automatically perfected. *See* La. R.S. 10:9-309(13).

2. Did the court's holding that the company that had contracted to pick the cotton, like the subcontractor in *Pringle-Associated Mortg. Corp. v. Eanes*, was not entitled to claim subrogation to the privileges of its laborers necessarily mean that the contractor was not itself entitled to a laborer's privilege under La. Civ. Code Art. 3217? In his dissent, Justice Traylor complained that the majority in effect re-wrote the ranking statute, by limiting those privileged creditors holding first-priority status (the laborer, the thresherman, combineman, grain drier, and the overseer) to individuals. As enacted in the 2010 revision, R.S. 10:9-322(g) made this limitation an express part of the statutory text. First-priority ranking under R.S. 10:9-322(g) is accorded to agricultural liens held by "agricultural laborers." That term is defined, by a non-uniform definition appearing in La. R.S. 10:9-102(d)(1), to include only "an individual holding agricultural liens securing payment of wages due him for labor he performed as a worker, thresherman, combineman, grain drier or overseer."

3. The court's opinion in *Pringle-Associated Mortg. Corp v. Eanes* is included in the chapter below on the Private Works Act.

D. Privileges to Effect Separation of Patrimonies

***See* La. Rev. Stat. 9:5011-16**

When an heir succeeds to the ownership of a decedent's property, the heir's patrimony, which has been thus augmented by that of the decedent, becomes subject to claims of two distinct masses of creditors—his own and the creditors of the decedent. La. R.S. 9:5011 *et seq.* allows each of these masses of creditors to assert, within a period of only three months after the decedent's death, a privilege upon a portion of the combined patrimony in preference to the other mass of creditors. The statute also provides a privilege for the decedent's particular legatees. As former Article 1445 of the 1870 Civil Code declared, the object of a separation of patrimony "is to prevent property, out of which a particular class of creditors have a right to be paid, from being confounded with other property, and by that means made liable to the debts of another class of creditors."

* * * * * *

2 TRAITE ÉLEMENTAIRE DE DROIT CIVIL, PT. 2
(La. State Law Inst. trans., 1959) (12th ed. 1939) (Fr.)
MARCEL PLANIOL & GEORGES RIPERT

2927. Summary Notion of the Benefit

When a person dies leaving an insolvent heir his creditors run the risk of not getting paid, for the property which their debtor possessed, is from then on confused with the property of the heir, and will be used to pay two masses of creditors, those of the deceased, and those of his heir. Then the creditors of the deceased who could perhaps have been paid integrally if their debtor had lived, are limited to a proportionate share by the competition of the creditors of the heir, who has, by hypothesis more debts than property. In order to protect them and to preserve the position they had during the lifetime of their debtor, the law permits them to demand the separation of the patrimonies, a particular benefit which prevents the creditors of the heir from competing with them on the property of the succession (Art. 878 and following).

2928. Question to Resolve

The benefit of the separation of patrimony resolves itself therefore into the right, for one of the two masses of creditors to be paid on the property of the succession by preference to the creditors of the other mass. It may be asked whether this right of preference constitutes a privilege.

Formerly this question could not arise: in the Roman theory, this result (preventing the competition of the two masses of creditors) was obtained by the aid of a fiction; it was assumed that the deceased was still living and that it was under his name that the property which he left was sold: *"Recesserunt a persona heredis . . . et quasi defuncti bona vendiderunt"* (Paul, *Dig. Bk.* XLII, tit. 6, fr. 5). The two masses of creditors were therefore considered as not having the same debtor; no relationship was possible between this benefit and the privilege, which assumes a conflict between the creditors of the same debtor.

With modern authors the memory of the Roman fiction was little by little effaced; by his acceptance, the heir has become the sole debtor of the two masses of creditors, and there is in reality a preference of one of two masses against the other. Under these conditions, the question arises as to whether this right of preference has not become a veritable privilege. It is well to limit the question to the immovables of the succession: if there is a privilege, it will be a privileged mortgage with all its consequences, so that the creditor exercising the action for the separation of patrimony will be able to seize the immovables coming from the succession, even after they have been alienated by the heir, that is to say, to exercise a right of pursuit, even though he was only a chirographic creditor during the life of the debtor.

* * * * * *

WASHINGTON

v.

WASHINGTON

127 So. 2d 491 (La. 1960)

On Rehearing

McCALEB, Justice.

The questions for decision herein arise out of the seizure of real property formerly belonging to a succession, under a writ of *fieri facias* in execution of a judgment obtained by plaintiff against the heirs of her former husband for the widow's homestead provided by Article 3252 of the Civil Code. The facts of the case are fully stated in our original opinion and will be repeated here only to the extent necessary to bring the legal problems into focus.

Isaac Washington, Sr., died in 1953. He had been married twice and was survived by plaintiff, his second wife, three children of his first marriage (one of whom died shortly thereafter leaving one child as her only heir) and two grandchildren. The main asset of his estate was his undivided one-half interest in a piece of improved real property which had been acquired during the existence of the first community. At the death of Washington's first wife, the children of that marriage inherited their mother's undivided one-half interest in the property subject to their father's usufruct. In 1954, these children and grandchildren opened the successions of Washington and his first wife, which they accepted unconditionally, and were put in possession of all the succession property by an ex parte judgment. Two days later one of the children, Isaac Washington, Jr., acquired from his co-heirs the piece of real estate above mentioned on which plaintiff had lived since her marriage.

Soon after his purchase, Washington, Jr., brought ejectment proceedings against plaintiff, who subsequently, filed the instant suit against the heirs of her deceased husband for recovery of the widow's homestead of $1,000, and other items of indebtedness, alleging that she was in necessitous circumstances at the date of her husband's death. Her claims were resisted by the heirs but, after a trial, judgment was granted in her favor for the widow's homestead less certain credits chargeable to her for rent of the premises involved after the death of her husband. The heirs did not appeal from this judgment and, when it became executory, plaintiff caused the real estate to be seized under a writ of *fieri facias*. Thereupon, Washington paid the amount of his virile share due under the judgment into the registry of the court and then proceeded by rule to have the seizure of his property set aside. At the hearing on this rule, plaintiff contended that she had a privilege on the real estate for the payment of the judgment recognizing her widow's homestead and that the seizure should not be released. The judge rejected this contention and released the seizure, stating that plaintiff must be held to have waived her privilege since she failed to claim it in her suit against the heirs and have it recognized in the judgment. Thereafter, plaintiff sought recognition of her privilege by supplemental petition filed in the original suit but this pleading was rejected by the judge. Then she appealed from the judgment rescinding the writ of *fieri facias* to the Court of Appeal, First Circuit, where the judgment was reversed, that court holding that plaintiff's failure to request recognition and enforcement of her privilege in the suit claiming the widow's homestead did not constitute a relinquishment and further that her legal privilege on the real estate of the succession was not affected by the prescription of 90 days pleaded by defendant, Washington, Jr. *See Washington v. Washington*, 116 So. 2d 125.

This writ of certiorari was granted to review the holding of the Court of Appeal. On first hearing, we concluded that plaintiff's privilege had become extinguished by her failure to institute a suit for a separation of patrimony within 3 months from the acceptance by the heirs of their father's succession.

During oral argument on rehearing counsel for Washington, Jr. reurged his contention, which was sustained by the district court, that plaintiff waived her privilege on the succession property by failing to have it recognized in her demand for recovery of the widow's homestead.

We find no merit in this point. The circumstance that plaintiff did not seek recognition of the privilege accorded her by Article 3252 of the Civil Code in her suit against the heirs cannot be viewed as a waiver of her right to claim this privilege at the time it became necessary and expedient to have it enforced. The property herein was lawfully seized under a writ of *fieri facias* and, while it is true that Washington, Jr. was personally liable for only his virile share of the judgment in plaintiff's favor, the property he acquired from the succession of his father by inheritance and purchase was burdened with plaintiff's legal privilege, which was not required to be recorded. We can think of no valid reason why plaintiff should be held to have lost her privilege because she did not seek judicial sanction of it when she sought recovery *in personam* from the heirs. There was no necessity for assertion of the privilege in that action; the law granted the privilege and failure to seek recognition cannot be rightly said to equate abandonment.

In *Perot's Estate v. Perot*, 177 La. 640, 148 So. 903, 904, the plaintiff sued for and obtained a personal judgment against the defendant for $96 for rent due on a store building. Plaintiff did not ask in those proceedings for recognition of the landlord's lien or obtain a writ of provisional seizure and no mention was made of the nature of the debt in the judgment rendered. Later a writ of *fieri facias* was issued under which the constable seized a lot of store fixtures in the leased building. Before sale was made, the party holding a chattel mortgage on the fixtures filed a third opposition and requested payment in preference to the seizing creditor out of the proceeds of the constable's sale. In answer to the third opposition, plaintiff averred that the judgment in favor of the estate was rendered on a claim for rent and asserted that the landlord's lien, although not claimed or recognized in the judgment, was superior to the chattel mortgage of the opponent. On the trial, these facts were proven and judgment was rendered rejecting the third opposition. Thereafter, the case reached this Court on writ of certiorari issued at the instance of the third opponent who complained mainly of the introduction of parol evidence to prove the landlord's lien at the trial of the third opposition. After review here the judgment was affirmed, it being observed that plaintiff's failure to ask for recognition of the landlord's lien in the suit in which the monied judgment for rent was obtained ". . . had no significance, one way or the other." The Court further said:

> "A plaintiff whose claim is secured by a lien does not waive his lien by failing to ask for recognition of it unless and until there is some necessity for having the lien recognized. If there is no demand for recognition of the lien, the judgment rendered for the debt, without mention of the lien, does not have the effect of a denial that the debt is secured by a lien. *Nalle v. Baird*, 30 La. Ann. (1148) 1150; *Battalion Washington Artillery v. St. Charles Skating Rink Co.*, 7 Orleans App. 431; *Cazzo v. Ulrich*, 13 Orleans App. 257; 34 C.J. 853, s 1265; 15 R.C.L. 977, s 452."

If, under the law, the debt creates a privilege or there is a conventional mortgage, such privilege or mortgage exists independently of the judgment rendered upon it. *See Parker v. Starkweather*, 7 Mart., N.S., 337; *Holmes v. Holmes*, 9 Rob. 117; *Gustine v. Union Bank of Louisiana*, 10 Rob. 412 and *J. Davidson Hill & Co. v. Bourcier*, 29 La. Ann. 841. Hence, in the instant case plaintiff was not obliged to pray for recognition of the privilege given her by law on all of the property of the succession until her right to sell the seized property securing the debt was questioned by Washington, Jr. at which time she properly asserted her preferential right and sought judicial recognition of it.

This brings us to a reconsideration of our decision on first hearing that plaintiff's privilege on the property of her deceased husband's succession was extinguished after expiration of three months from the acceptance of the succession by the heirs. In reaching this conclusion we relied on the 1935 decision of the Court of Appeal, First Circuit, in *Danna v. Danna*, 161 So. 348 and rejected the contrary ruling in 1938 of the Court of Appeal, Second Circuit, in *Beck v. Beck*, 181 So. 635, which the present members of the Court of Appeal, First Circuit, in ruling herein for plaintiff, believed to be a correct view of the law.

The *Danna* and *Beck* cases involved the same question presented here—i.e., whether the privilege granted to a widow in necessitous circumstances prescribes under Article 1456 of the Civil Code, if she fails to institute a suit for separation of patrimony within 90 days of the acceptance of the succession by the heirs. The affirmative conclusion reached in the *Danna* decision was predicated on the assumption that the codal provisions dealing with the separation of patrimony ". . . will not admit the existence of any preference after three months, ..."' (161 So. 351)

On the other hand, the opinion in the *Beck* case, after considering the stated purpose of a suit for separation of patrimony and the requirements essential for the maintenance of the action (Articles 1445 and 1457 of the Civil Code) concludes that the institution of such a suit is not essential in order to preserve a privileged debt.

Our further study of this case has convinced us of the soundness of the *Beck* decision and we are now of the opinion that the privilege accorded to the widow in necessitous circumstances does not prescribe by reason of her failure to sue for a separation of patrimony. The object of a separation of patrimony, as stated by Article 1445 of the Civil Code, "is to prevent property, out of which a particular class of creditors have a right to be paid, from being confounded with other property, and by that means made liable to the debts of another class of creditors." This being so, the period of three months allowed creditors for the institution of a suit for separation of patrimony is a prescription which affects only the right of succession creditors to institute such a suit. Indeed, that is all that Article 1456 prescribes for it states that "The suit . . . must be instituted within three months . . . ; after the expiration of this term, it (the suit) is not admitted." It cannot be justifiably construed as a prescription either of the debt or of the privilege created by law to secure the payment of the debt. An ordinary succession creditor who fails to institute an action for separation of patrimony within the time prescribed by Article 1456 incurs only the loss of his right to be paid out of the succession assets to the exclusion of the creditors of the heirs; he does not lose his right to recover from the heirs who accept the succession unless his claim is otherwise prescribed under positive provisions of law.

The holder of a privilege, defined by Article 3186 of the Civil Code to be a right which the nature of the debt gives the creditor entitling him to be preferred before other creditors, "even those who have mortgages," has no reason to seek a separation of patrimony. The law grants him preferential rights on the succession property, so there is no possibility of the creditors of the heirs priming his rights. If the debt itself has not prescribed, the privilege, which is an accessory right to secure payment, does not, in the absence of positive law on the subject, prescribe before the debt itself. Accordingly, since the widow's homestead claimed by plaintiff was recognized by final judgment in these proceedings, from which no appeal was taken, it necessarily follows that the privilege the law gave to secure preferential payment of that claim could not be avoided on the basis of prescription in the absence of a claimed statutory provision different from that applicable to the debt.

The codal article applicable to the case at hand is Article 3276, providing that succession charges, law charges, fees for settling the succession, the $1,000 secured in certain cases to the widow or minor heirs and all claims against the succession ". . . originating after the death of the person whose succession is under administration, are to be paid before the debts contracted by the deceased person, except as otherwise provided for herein, and they are not required to be recorded."

Plainly, since plaintiff's privilege on the property of the succession was not required to be recorded, it would be inappropriate to conclude that she lost the privilege because she did not file a suit for separation of patrimony and record her claim as a privilege against the real property seized under the writ of *fieri facias* within three months after the succession was opened.

SANDERS, J., concurs in the decree.

HAMITER, Justice (concurring in part and dissenting in part).

Assuming (but not conceding) that initially plaintiff was entitled to and enjoyed the widow's homestead privilege, I agree that it could affect no more than the undivided one-half interest in the seized real estate which Isaac Washington, Sr., owned when he died, the remainder having vested in the heirs of his first wife at the date of her death.

However, I do not agree that such privilege now affects the interest which Isaac Washington, Jr., purchased from his coheirs. As stated in the Louisiana Revised Civil Code ". . .all final judgments affecting immovable property shall be recorded in the parish where the immovable property is situated." Article 2265. "All . . . judgments affecting immovable property, which shall not be so recorded, shall be utterly null and void, except between the parties thereto. The recording may be made at any time, but shall only affect third persons from the time of the recording." Article 2266. "Privileges are valid against third persons, from the date of the recording of the act or evidence of indebtedness as provided by law." Article 3273. At the time of the mentioned purchase (it occurred more than ninety days after the death of Isaac Washington, Sr.) there was nothing of record evidencing plaintiff's claimed privilege or the indebtedness that it allegedly secured; and unquestionably Isaac Washington, Jr., who admittedly paid a good and sufficient consideration for his acquired interest, was a third person purchaser.

HAMLIN, Justice (dissenting).

I respectfully dissent from the majority opinion on rehearing in this matter for the reasons expressed in the original opinion of this Court, of which I was the author. October 5, 1960, and for the further reasons hereinafter set forth.

I have searched for and have been unable to find any provision of our law relating specifically to the prescription of the privilege granted a widow under Article 3252 of the LSA-Civil Code.

Article 21 of the LSA-Civil Code provides as follows:

> "In all civil matters, where there is no express law, the judge is bound to proceed and decide according to equity. To decide equitably, an appeal is to be made to natural law and *reason*, or received usages, where positive law is silent." (Emphasis mine.)

Reason dictates that a widow is able to decide immediately after the death of her husband whether she is in necessitous circumstances and will thereby feel the pinch of poverty; she should be able to decide within three months whether or not she will claim the privilege granted to her under Article 3252, supra. Justice demands that she should require recognition of her privilege within the same time as the Civil Code provides for the demand for separation of patrimony. She should not be permitted to hold a sword over the estate of her deceased husband for an unreasonable length of time and thereby subject many titles to real property to question.

Try as I will, I cannot perceive why title examiners should be compelled in many cases to require affidavits to the effect that the "widow's thousand" has been satisfied before finally passing upon the merchantability of a title. Property owners have enough burdens without adding this additional one to their travail.

* * * * * *

NOTES AND QUESTIONS

1. After the case was decided, the articles governing the privilege to effect separation of patrimonies were moved from the Civil Code to La. R.S. 9:5011-16.

2. This case illustrates the unique nature of the privilege to effect separation of patrimonies, which is designed to protect one class of otherwise unsecured creditors over another whose claims originally arose against a different obligor. To avail himself of this privilege, the creditor must assert it within three months after the decedent's death. On the other hand, where the creditor holds some other privilege, such as the privilege of the surviving spouse in the case, there is no need for that creditor to seek a separation of patrimonies, because the privilege he already holds continues to provide him with a preference. Thus, a creditor holding such a privilege need not assert it within three months.

3. Is the dissent's concern that title examiners will have to require affidavits of payment of the "widow's thousand" well founded? As the majority correctly observe, Civil Code Article 3276 excuses the privilege of the surviving spouse from the requirement of recordation, but both the majority opinion and the dissent appear to have lost sight of the fact that the privilege of the surviving spouse is a mere right of preference that does not survive the alienation of the immovable from the decedent's estate. On that point, the case has been severely criticized. *See* Vetter and Harrell, *Louisiana Creditors' Security Rights*, Vol. II (1988), p. 332. The extent to which privileges are real rights that survive

alienation from the debtor's patrimony is addressed in the following section of this chapter.

4. Commenting on the decision, Judge Alvin Rubin observed that "[t]he decision appears inescapably to imply that the unrecorded privileges for expenses of last illness and those arising on death of the owner of the property follow succession property into the hands of third persons, who purchase it in good faith from the heirs following a judgment sending the heirs into possession of the estate. It therefore is necessary for title examiners to satisfy themselves that these debts have in fact been paid if their clients are to be protected." Alvin B. Rubin, *Civil Code and Related Subjects: Successions*, 22 La. L. Rev. 317, 319 (1962).

E. Privileges as Real Rights

A privilege is a form of real security. This does not, however, mean that a privilege is necessarily a real right. In order to consider the interesting question of the status of privileges as real rights, it is necessary, of course, to know what is meant by the term, which is not defined in the Civil Code. In a comprehensive article on the subject written in 1963, excerpts from which appear below, Professor A. N. Yiannopoulos writes that the traditional definition of a real right in France is "said to involve subjection of a thing, in whole or in part, to the authority of a person by virtue of a direct relationship which can be asserted against the world." He concludes that real rights are ultimately distinguishable from personal rights in France by the presence of two essential attributes: *droit de suite* (the right of pursuit) and the *droit de préférence* (the right of preference). Privileges, of course, by their very nature always involve a right of preference. It follows then that a privilege can be classified as a real right only if it also entails a right of pursuit of the thing sold in the hands of third persons.

The definition of *privilege* contained in Article 3186 of the Civil Code has been criticized on the ground that it envisions merely rights of preference that exist upon property while in the debtor's patrimony and that the general privileges comprise the only category of privileges that truly fit within this definition. Nonetheless, the Civil Code establishes other privileges, such as the special privileges on immovables, which, when properly recorded, include a right of pursuit in addition to a mere right of preference and are therefore undoubtedly real rights.

* * * * * *

2 Traite Élementaire de Droit Civil, pt. 2
(La. State Law Inst. trans., 1959) (12th ed. 1939) (Fr.)
Marcel Planiol & Georges Ripert

2548. Veritable Privileges are Not Real Rights

The system of the law has another inconvenience: even though it does not say so expressly, the juxtaposition which it makes between the privileges and mortgages gives birth to the idea that privileges are real rights, as are mortgages. That is true for the special privileges on immovables, which are veritable mortgages (infra, Nos. 2886 and following); that is true also for the pledgee, who has the right of pledge and whose right of preference is not at all of the nature of privileges (supra, No. 2435). But for all the other privileged creditors, no real right exists. Only those are real rights which protect a person against all others in the total or partial possession of a thing. Such are ownership, usufruct, servitudes, emphyteusis, pledge; such is also the mortgage, because it tends to leave the thing to the creditor and authorizes the latter to transfer the ownership to another. In privileges there is nothing like that: it is a simple right of priority between creditors, a permit to come in out of turn in the division of the price, and it is thus that the law looks upon it in defining it "as a right which the creditor has to be preferred" (Art. 2095).

* * * * * *

Real Rights in Louisiana and Comparative Law: Part 1
A. N. Yiannopoulos
23 Louisiana Law Review 161, 222 (1963)

The question of the juridical nature of privileges and their classification as personal or real rights has prompted exhaustive discussion and controversies in the literature of civil law.

Mortgage is defined as "a right granted to the creditor over the property of the debtor for the security of his debt, and gives him the power of having the property seized and sold in default of payment" (Article 3278). The Code indicates that "mortgage is a species of pledge, the thing mortgaged being bound for the payment of the debt or fulfillment of the obligation" (Article 3279). Mortgages are distinguished as general or special (Article 3288) and as conventional, legal, or judicial (Article 3286). Conventional mortgages may be either general or special, depending on the agreement of the parties (Article 3290). Legal mortgages are general mortgages in the absence of legal provision to the contrary (Article 3328). According to Article 3329 "the creditors who have either a privilege or mortgage on immovables recorded according to law may pursue their claims thereon into whatever hands the immovables may pass, as provided in Article 2378, or in Articles 3721 through 3743, respectively, of the Code of Civil Procedure."

Commentators elaborating on corresponding provisions in the French Civil Code have reached at least three different conclusions concerning the juridical nature of privileges in general and the classification of each particular privilege as a personal or real right. According to one view *all* privileges are real rights. Under a second view privileges (other than the real rights of pledge and mortgage) are merely *causes of preference* attached to personal rights. Finally, according to a third view, privileges may be either personal or real rights depending on whether they bear on movables or immovables and on whether they are general or special privileges. Thus, it has been urged that special privileges on immovables are real rights (*hypotheques privilèges*) while special privileges on movables and general privileges on immovables are personal rights. It would seem that the controversy is without purpose. An analytically preferable approach is to regard privileges as accessorial rights of preference which may be attached by the law to any right, whether personal or real. This view is supported by Article 3186 of the Louisiana Civil Code, which declares that privilege is "a right which the nature of a debt gives to a creditor." Accordingly, a relevant question is which *privileged* rights are real and which personal.

In France, classification of privileged rights as personal or real is said to be determinative of the questions of divisibility of the privilege and of its enforcement in the hands of third parties. Courts in Louisiana, however, are seldom inclined to derive practical consequences from abstract classifications. The process is reversed and a privileged right can be classified as personal or real only in the light of its function. The special privileges on immovables created by Article 3249 of the Civil Code function as veritable mortgages and should be regarded as attached to real rights. All other privileges in the Civil Code whether bearing on movables or immovables are merely *causes of preference* incidental to personal rights. Similarly, some of the privileges created by special legislation are attached to real rights and others to personal rights.

* * * * * *

A. N. Yiannopoulos, 2 La. Civ. L. Treatise Series: Property § 237 (4th Ed. 2014)

The distinction between personal and real rights is a systematic generalization deeply embedded in the civilian tradition and known to all western systems of law. Yet, neither analytical jurisprudence nor civilian theory succeeded in furnishing generally acceptable criteria for this distinction and for the determination of the respective nature of personal and real rights. As a result, there is still much disagreement among jurists concerning the classification of certain rights as personal or real in contemporary legal systems. Classifications made by commentators, legislation, and jurisprudence are at times arbitrary and do not fit a consistent theory.

Real rights in Louisiana may be divided into those established by the Civil Code and those created by special legislation. Under the Civil Code real rights are ownership and the *jura in re aliena.* Ownership is a real right whether its object is a movable or an immovable. . . . Privileges under the Civil Code are causes of preference rather than real rights. However, the vendor's recorded privilege on the immovable sold is a veritable mortgage. The vendor's privilege on movables, and the lessor's privilege are merely causes of preference.

* * * * * *

SCARDINO

v.

WHITNEY MOSS TIE CO.

7 La. App. 427 (1st Cir. 1928)

LECHE, J.

Plaintiff seeks to have some 2,200 crossties, manufactured by defendant, recognized as affected with a lien and privilege to secure $536.63 advanced by him in money and supplies to enable defendant to manufacture the ties.

The T. J. Moss Tie Company intervened, claimed ownership of the ties, and contested the existence of plaintiff's alleged lien and privilege.

The trial court held that the evidence failed to show with clearness and certainty that the advances were used by defendant for the purpose of manufacturing the ties, refused plaintiff's demand, and adjudged intervenor to be the owner of the ties.

The evidence is clear to the effect that defendant was not an employee of intervenor, that the ties were manufactured by defendant for his own account, and that they were by him sold to intervenor; that delivery was made on the banks of Bayou Grosse Tete and that intervenor paid defendant the purchase price of the ties before they were seized by plaintiff. The evidence fails to show any privity between plaintiff and intervenor or any fraud or concealment on the part of intervenor towards plaintiff. According to the general tenor of the testimony, intervenor was an innocent third person and bought the ties in good faith. Under this state of facts, plaintiff's asserted privilege, if it did exist, could not follow the ties, a movable, into the hands of intervenor.

For this reason the judgment of the District Court should be affirmed.

ON APPLICATION FOR REHEARING

LECHE, J.

In the original opinion, the writer thereof said: "The evidence fails to show any privity between plaintiff and intervenor, or any fraud or concealment on the part of intervenor towards plaintiff."

This was mere surplusage and not necessary to a decision of the case, as plaintiff did not charge fraud or concealment in his answer to the petition of intervention of the T. J. Moss Tie Company, and therefore might have been omitted from the opinion without affecting the reasons upon which the opinion was based.

Plaintiff in his application for rehearing admits the correctness of all the facts stated in the opinion of this court, but contends that under Act 195, p. 382, of 1912, his alleged privilege followed the ties in the hands of intervenor after intervenor had purchased them from defendant. We see nothing in that act to justify that assumption. On the contrary, the last clause of the act, in Section 4, gives the privilege holder a right to seize the ties where they are about to be disposed of or removed from the parish. The obvious inference is that where the ties have been disposed of, as they were in this case, they may not be seized.

It must be kept in mind that this is not an action by a privileged creditor to avoid a sale as made in fraud of his rights. No fraud is alleged in plaintiff's answer to the intervention, and none was proved.

The only purpose subserved by a privilege on a movable is to give the privilege holder a preference over other creditors of the debtor. Movables are not affected by registry and the only instances in which privileges follow them, so far as we know, are in the case of the erection of buildings and in the granting of chattel mortgages. See the case of *Dreyfous vs. Cade et al.*, 138 La. 298, 70 So. 231, where the subject is thoroughly discussed.

Rehearing refused.

* * * * * *

NOTES AND QUESTIONS

1. The statutory privilege involved in the case, granted by Act 195 of 1912, secures amounts lent to enable a debtor to manufacture poles or cross-ties. *See now* La. R.S. 9:4621(2).

2. Did the court base its holding on the specific provisions of the statute establishing the privilege at issue, or rather upon notions generally applicable to privileges on movables?

3. In support of its rationale, the court cited *Dreyfous v. Cade*, which is reproduced in an earlier section of this chapter, a case involving the loss of a vendor's privilege upon a re-sale by the original vendee. Does the rationale of *Dreyfous v. Cade* apply generally to all privileges on movables, or rather to the unique characteristics of the vendor's privilege which, by the text of Civil Code Article 3227, continues for only so long as the movable remains in the immediate vendee's possession?

* * * * * *

LIQUID CARBONIC CORP.

v.

LEGER

169 So. 170 (La. App. 1st Cir. 1936)

DORE, Judge.

The plaintiff sold to Oscar Leger a certain soda fountain, together with all accessories, and, at the time of the sale, retained a vendor's lien, and the purchaser granted a chattel mortgage to secure the unpaid part of the purchase price. This sale and chattel mortgage act was promptly recorded prior to the installation of the soda fountain in the drug store operated by Leger. Thereafter the lessor of Leger brought suit against him for past-due rent, praying for a writ of provisional seizure. There was judgment against Leger as prayed for, with the recognition of the lessor's privilege. Thereafter a writ of *fieri facias* was issued, and all of the property as contained in the drug store was seized and advertised to be sold. All of the property seized was appraised by the intervener and third opponent and another druggist, and at the sale the sheriff sold the same in bulk or in globo. At the sale, in accordance with law, the sheriff read the certificate of mortgage, and upon which the chattel mortgage of the plaintiff was reported. The *procès verbal* clearly states that the sheriff made known to the prospective purchasers that the same was to be sold "subject to all mortgages and liens" in accordance with the certificate of mortgage. His deed of adjudication further sets forth that the property was sold subject to the mortgages with which the property was burdened and conditional that the purchaser or purchasers were to pay whatever portion of the price exceeded the amount of mortgages. In other words, that the purchaser or purchasers were buying the property *cum onere*. Some time after this sale, the present plaintiff instituted this suit by executory process to satisfy its claim, and Eloi Melancon, by intervention and third opposition, claimed the property free from all mortgages.

The third opponent bases his claim to the property by virtue of the said adjudication previously referred to, and further avers that he is the bona fide purchaser at the sheriff's sale; that, the property having been appraised in globo and having been sold en masse, even if the plaintiff herein had a vendor's lien and privilege or a chattel mortgage, the vendor's lien and all its mortgage rights were lost by the said sale in bulk. In answer to the demand of the third opponent, plaintiff sets up the defense that the third opponent was not a bona fide purchaser; that he had acted as appraiser of the said property; that the property was not definitely described so as to put plaintiff on guard that the property subject to its mortgage was to be sold; that it was contrary to the agreement had with the lessor, the seizing creditor, at which sale third opponent purchased said property; and that the third opponent purchased the property subject to the mortgage rights granted under the mortgage act.

There was judgment for the third opponent, and plaintiff has appealed.

The chattel mortgage on the soda fountain on which plaintiff seeks to foreclose was duly executed and recorded in the parish where the property is located. Under section 4 of Act No. 198 of 1918, the Chattel Mortgage Law, the recordation of this act of chattel mortgage on the property involved created a lien thereon in favor of the mortgagee from the time of filing the act for record, and this filing for record and its recordation served as notice to all persons of such mortgage, and created a lien on the property in favor of the mortgagee superior in rank to any privilege or lien arising subsequently thereto. The effect of the recordation of this chattel mortgage against this property had the same effect with regard to the debtor as the mortgage of any other property has under articles 3397 and 3399 of the Civil Code, viz., the debtor could not sell, engage, or mortgage the same property to the prejudice of the mortgage; if the mortgaged property goes out of the debtor's hands, the creditor can pursue it into whomsoever's hands he may find it, and the creditor has the right of being preferred in the payment of his claim out of the proceeds of the sale of the property in accordance with the rank of his mortgage.

The third opponent, Melancon, relies on a purchase by him at sheriff sale of the mortgaged property under a *fieri facias* issued against the mortgage debtor and under which the mortgaged property was seized and sold *in globo* with other movable property without any separate appraisement and sale of the mortgaged property. It is claimed by the third opponent that whatever lien and privilege the plaintiff had on the soda fountain by reason of its recorded chattel mortgage was lost by reason of this sale of the mortgaged property confusedly with other movable property under the *fieri facias* without a separate appraisement and sale.

A chattel mortgage, when recorded, is full and complete notice to the world of the existence of the lien against the property described in the mortgage. The debtor cannot sell or alienate the property to the prejudice of the chattel mortgage holder. The property passes to third persons *cum onere*. In the present case the record not only shows that third opponent had constructive notice of the existence of plaintiff's chattel mortgage on the soda fountain by reason of the public record thereof, but, in addition thereto, he had actual notice thereof from the fact that the sheriff read at the sale the certificate showing the mortgage, and announced that the purchaser bought the property subject to the mortgage. Under no theory can third opponent be classed as a purchaser in good faith and without notice. He took title to the property *cum onere*.

In making a sale of property under execution, the sheriff is required to procure and read at the sale a certificate showing the privileges and mortgages on the property offered for sale. Article 678 of the Code of Practice requires the sheriff to procure and read this certificate when he sells lands, "or other objects susceptible of being mortgaged." This means that he must procure and read this certificate on all property subject to a chattel mortgage. Under article 679 of the Code of Practice, if there exists any mortgage or privilege on the property put up for sale, it is made the duty of the sheriff to give notice that the property is sold subject to all privileges and mortgages thereon. This was done in the present case, and third opponent purchased the soda fountain subject to the lien and privilege thereon of plaintiff.

Furthermore, the courts of this state should note a difference between a privilege which confers a right of preference and one which also gives the additional right to follow the property on which it rests into the hands of a third person or persons. The articles of the Civil Code which give the right of preference are found in Book 3, title 21, beginning at article 3182 and ending with article 3277, and in which is to be found article 3228 relative to the sale en masse with other goods and the loss of privilege; while the right to follow the property on which the mortgage rests in the hands of a third person or persons is to be found in Book 3, title 22, beginning at article 3278 and ending with article 3411.

This distinction is marked by the French commentators in apt phrases. Under their nomenclature, privileges of the first class, which are by far the most numerous, confer a "*droit de preference*" only, while those of the second class confer in addition a "*droit de suite*." It is the holder of a privileged debt of the first class who is obliged to intervene by way of third opposition and to ask for a separate appraisement and sale of the property on which he has a privilege in order to preserve his rights when said property is seized *in globo* with other property of the debtor by a third person. The reason is obvious. In such case, the property passes to the purchaser free of encumbrances. The contest for preference is then fought out over the proceeds. But, if a creditor with a privilege on only a part of the property seized permits the sale of such property to be made *in globo* with other property of the debtor without having asked for the separate appraisement and sale of that part of the property on which his privilege bears, it becomes impossible to determine what proportion of the purchase price is to be allocated to the property on which he had a privilege with the consequence that his rights are lost. Mortgages, whether movables under the Chattel Mortgage Law, or immovables, under the Code, are a species of privilege and fall under the second classification. The mortgagee, under the Chattel Mortgage Law, or the holder of a special mortgage on immovables, is never required to intervene by way of third opposition in order to maintain his rights. That is so because his rights are not lost by the alienation, be it by public or private sale. The fact that his rights are not lost by private sale is so elementary that we need pay no further attention to the point. It is equally clear that his rights are not lost when the property on which his mortgage bears is sold under a *fieri facias*, for the reason that article 709 of the Code of Practice provides: "The hypothecary action lies against the purchaser of a property seized, which is subject to privileges or mortgages, in favor of such creditors as have said privileges and mortgages, in the same manner and under the same rules and restrictions as are applicable to a third possessor of a mortgaged property."

For the reasons herein set forth, it is ordered that the judgment of the court be annulled, reversed, and set aside; and that there be judgment herein in favor of plaintiff and against intervener and third opponent dismissing the intervention and third opposition, all at the costs of the said intervener and third opponent.

* * * * * *

NOTES AND QUESTIONS

1. As the case reflects, it is not only a private sale that will cause the holder of a privilege upon movables to lose his privilege; the same effect will result from a judicial sale, even if the sale is made at the instance of a creditor holding an inferior privilege or an unsecured creditor. In order to preserve his rights, the holder of the superior privilege must intervene to assert his rights to the proceeds from the sale. In any event, he has no right of pursuit against the property, even though his right is superior to that of the seizing creditor.

2. As discussed above in the section of this chapter on vendor's privileges, when a vendee retains physical possession of a movable after he has re-sold it, the privilege held by his vendor is preserved, even though the movable has been alienated from the original vendee's patrimony. It might be contended that this rule improperly transforms the vendor's privilege on a movable into a real right that survives a re-sale, so long as there is no delivery to the second buyer. Although there is certainly room for disagreement on that issue among French commentators, that objection would appear unfounded under the Louisiana Civil Code because of its rule, under Article 518, that transfer of ownership of a movable is effective against third persons when possession is delivered to the transferee and, until that occurs, creditors of the transferor can seize it. Thus, until possession is delivered to the transferee, the alienation that Planiol and others argue extinguishes the vendor's privilege is simply not effective as to third persons, including the transferor's unpaid vendor and other creditors, who may ignore the alienation altogether. Moreover, there is a justification for the survival of the privilege under these circumstances: Since all of the transferor's creditors continue to have recourse against the thing, a privilege is necessary so

that the unpaid vendor will still be preferred over the transferor's other creditors. It might be argued that, to the extent that this causes the vendor's privilege on a movable to function as a real right, it is a very limited and ephemeral one that owes its existence more to the rules on transfer of ownership of a movable than to the rules applicable to privileges. For a detailed discussion of this issue, see L. David Cromwell, *Vendor's Privilege: Adheret Vicerbus Rei*, 75 La. L. Rev. 1165 (2015).

F. Requirements of Recordation

***See* La. Civ. Code arts. 3271-76; 3338; 3354-67**

With limited exceptions, privileges on immovables must be recorded in the mortgage records to be effective against third persons. The exceptions include privileges for funeral charges and expenses of the last illness, as well as the privilege of the surviving spouse. In order for a privilege to enjoy a preference over previously recorded mortgages, it must be recorded within the period prescribed by Article 3274 of the Civil Code. If not recorded within that period, the privilege enjoys no preference over mortgages that were previously filed and has "effect against all parties from date of registry." Under the traditional French view, the untimely recordation of a privilege on an immovable causes it to "degenerate" into a mere mortgage and lose the effects of a privilege. As will be seen in the following chapter, Louisiana does not follow this rule: The late-filed privilege retains its effect as a privilege, except that it loses priority over previously recorded mortgages.

Privileges on immovables are subject to the same requirements of reinscription that apply to mortgages.

The law generally excuses the requirement of recordation of privileges on movable property, except where otherwise prescribed by law. An example of such an exception exists in the case of agricultural privileges, which, as we have seen, are subjected to the perfection rules of Chapter 9 of the Uniform Commercial Code. However, most special privileges on movables are mere rights of preference that are lost when the property subject to the privilege is alienated by the debtor. Recordation of a privilege on a movable generally does not cause it to follow the movable into the hands of a third person, nor does recordation of a privilege on a movable ordinarily give that privilege priority over an unrecorded privilege on the same movable. Again, an exception to this rule exists in the case of agricultural privileges subject to Chapter 9: Perfected agricultural privileges outrank those that are unperfected.

* * * * * *

La. Constitution Ancillaries, Article XIX, Section 19:

> No mortgage or privilege on immovable property, or debt for which preference may be granted by law, shall affect third persons unless recorded or registered in the parish where the property is situated, in the manner and within the time prescribed by law, except privileges for expenses of last illness, privileges arising upon the death of the owner of the property affected, and privileges for taxes, State, parish and municipal.. . .
>
> Privileges on movable property shall exist without registration of same, except in such cases as may be prescribed by law.

* * * * * *

Civil Code and Related Subjects: Security Devices
Joseph Dainow
22 LOUISIANA LAW REVIEW 322 (1962)

Privileges are a form of security device in Louisiana law and when they affect immovable property there is a close resemblance to mortgage. For mortgages, there is an inexorable rule that there must be proper recordation in order to affect third persons. For privileges which affect immovables, the same is generally true, but there are some exceptions. In the case of such an exception, the privilege attaches to the property just as if it had been recorded, and the lack of recordation does not abbreviate or limit the scope of the effectiveness of the privilege, even as against third persons. At this time, there is no question of sympathy for the property owners who have so many other burdens, or the title examiners who already have a fantastic job in comparison to the simple checking of titles under a Torrens system type of recordation. Neither is this the time for sympathy to the patient funeral director, the devoted doctor, or the necessitous widow. These policy considerations were all taken into account in the formulation of Article XIX, Section 19, of the

Constitution and Article 3276 of the Civil Code. Nevertheless, the so-called public records doctrine has taken such a strong hold on the minds of the legal profession that, with the aid of a little wishful thinking and a lot of legal pyrotechniques, there develops a blind spot which refuses to see the established exceptions.

The case of *Washington v. Washington,* with its several trials and a Supreme Court rehearing, reflects some of the foregoing difficulties and finally came out with what appears to be the correct conclusion, although there were many diverse contentions and opinions formulated in the total process.

The necessitous widow's claim and privilege for $1,000, together with the conditions governing its ranking, are set forth in Civil Code Article 3252; and it affects immovable as well as movable property. Article XIX, Section 19, of the Constitution and Article 3276 of the Civil Code specifically except this privilege from the recordation requirement. In the presence of the contemplated circumstances, the privilege comes into existence at the time of the husband's death.

If there were a recorded mortgage or vendor's privilege against this property at the time of the husband's death, there would be no question about such a mortgage or privilege being effective against the property even if it were conveyed in the succession settlement to a third person. Why then should there be so much resistance to the idea of the widow's homestead privilege being similarly effective? If this privilege had been recorded, there would of course be no objection; but since this privilege is excepted from the requirement of recordation it is just as effective as if it had the same benefits which recordation gives to those privileges and mortgages which do need it.

* * * * * *

NOTES AND QUESTIONS

1. The early case of *Morrison v. Trudeau,* 1 Mart. (n.s.) 384 (1823) interpreted an 1813 act of the legislature providing that "all liens, of any nature whatever, having the effect of a legal mortgage, which shall not be recorded agreeably to the provisions of this act, shall be null and void." Because conventional and judicial mortgages had already been provided for in the

statute, the court felt that the term "all liens" must have "meant something more than legal mortgages; there remained then no other liens to be acted on but privileges, and it was to embrace them these words were used; or else they were used to no purpose." Id. at 393. Thus, an unrecorded vendor's privilege was held ineffective against a creditor holding a mortgage granted by the vendee. Article 3241 of the Civil Code of 1825 explicitly required that privileges be recorded in order to affect third persons, and Article 3274 of the 1870 Civil Code, as well as Article XIX, Section 19 of the Constitution Ancillaries, also explicitly require recordation for privileges affecting immovables to have effect against third persons, though, as we have seen, there are exceptions in the case of privileges for funeral expenses and the expenses of the last illness, as well as the privilege of the surviving spouse.

2. *Washington v. Washington,* supra, should be re-read in the consideration of the exceptions to the requirement of recordation of privileges upon immovables.

3. As *Cristina Inv. Corporation v. Gulf Ice Co.,* supra, reflects, there is no requirement for recordation of privileges affecting movables, even when the movable becomes immobilized.

4. In *Reeves v. G. & G. Pumping Co.,* 151 So. 679 (La. App. 2d Cir. 1934), an unpaid seller of an air compressor, which held a properly recorded chattel mortgage, re-acquired ownership of the compressor by dation en paiement. Between the time of the original sale and the seller's reacquisition, the buyer had contracted with the plaintiff to transport the compressor to a location in an oilfield. The court held that the carrier's privilege was ineffective against third persons because it was unrecorded. The court cited no authority for the proposition that the privilege should have been recorded, nor does the opinion contain any indication of where the court felt recordation would have been appropriate. This rationale seems insupportable in view of the fact that there is no provision of law requiring recordation of the carrier's privilege, and Article XIX, Section XIX of the 1921 Constitution provides that privileges affecting movables are effective against third persons even without recordation. Are there nonetheless other grounds justifying the court's holding that the carrier's privilege could not be asserted against the buyer's transferee?

Chapter 6
The Rules of Ranking Privileges

A. In General

See La. Civ. Code arts. 3252-74

The ranking rules that apply to privileges are wholly different from those that govern mortgages. The ranking of one privilege against another is generally *not* governed by the order of recordation at all, but rather by the nature of the competing privileges involved. Privileges that are of the same rank are paid concurrently from the proceeds of the thing that they burden. The ranking of one privilege against another at times seems wholly arbitrary but is supposed to proceed from the legislator's decision that reasons of policy dictate that certain types of claims be paid in preference to others. Thus, the agricultural laborer's privilege on a crop is paid in preference to the privilege of the lessor. Similarly, the construction worker's privilege under the Private Works Act is preferred over that held by the supplier of building materials. However, the reasoning for the preference of one privilege over another is not always readily apparent, as when the privilege of a residential lessor upon movables of the lessee found at the residence is preferred to the privilege of the unpaid vendor who sold these same movables to the lessee.

It is well known that the ranking rules, particularly in the case of privileges on movables, are often inconsistent, thus resulting in myriad "vicious circles," in which one privilege outranks another, which it turn outranks a third privilege that is itself preferred to the first of these three privileges. Vicious circles can even involve four or more privileges given circular ranking by the statutes that create them.

Neither the Code Napoléon nor the Digest of 1808 contained extensive provisions ranking privileges. These rules were introduced in the Civil Code of 1825 and were retained, largely unchanged, in the Civil Code of 1870. Complex as they may at first blush appear, the ranking rules of the Civil Code can be reduced to a few guiding principles:

First, under Articles 3253 and 3266, where a general privilege affects both movables and immovables, it must be satisfied first from the movables of the debtor before resort is made to the immovables.

Second, general privileges on movables rank among themselves in the order prescribed by Article 3254. General privileges rank against special privileges on movables, and special privileges on movables rank among themselves, in accordance with the rules contained in Articles 3256 through 3265.

Third, if the debtor's movables are insufficient to satisfy the claims secured by general privileges, those remaining general privileges can be satisfied from the debtor's immovables. Under Article 3267, to the extent they operate upon immovables, the general privileges are outranked by special privileges.

Finally, provided that any applicable recordation requirements are satisfied within the time prescribed by Article 3274, Article 3186 effectively provides that both general and special privileges outrank mortgages on the debtor's immovables, even those recorded previously. A privilege that is not recorded within the time provided by Article 3274 will not enjoy this favored treatment: It will still be effective as a privilege, but it will be preferred only to those mortgages that become effective as to third persons after the privilege is recorded. Any loss that may arise from the payment of general privileges in preference to mortgages is borne by the mortgagee whose mortgage is "the least ancient," as provided by Article 3269.

A number of the ranking rules were illustrated by the cases contained in the preceding chapter, and those cases will not be included again in this chapter. *Alter v. O'Brien* was an application of the rule that general privileges arising under the Civil Code are preferred to mortgages. *Cozzo v. Ulrich* held that an artisan's privilege primes that of the vendor. *Powers & Co. v. Sixty Tons of*

Marble found that, at least under the facts of that case, the privilege for preservation expenses outranks that for carrier's charges, and the notes following the case discussed a number of ranking rules involving statutory privileges granted to carriers and warehouses. *Erman v. Lehman* mentioned the rule that a seizing creditor's privilege is subordinate to any other privilege that exists at the time of seizure. The ranking of Private Works Act privileges is treated in the following chapter.

* * * * * *

2 Traite Élementaire de Droit Civil, pt. 2
(La. State Law Inst. trans., 1959) (12th ed. 1939) (Fr.)
Marcel Planiol & Georges Ripert

2622. Silence of the Code

The ranking of privileges is considered one of the most difficult of the French law: but the analysis as to their origin which has been made above, to some extent indicates the nature of various privileges and greatly facilitates this task. The legislator is often criticized for not having ranked them himself, having given us only some indications of detail which are entirely insufficient. He seems to have passed over the difficulty without perceiving it; his silence, however, has had a favorable consequence; he has given time to the doctrinal writers to study this matter and to arrive at scientific solutions.

2637. Triple Principle of Special Privileges

All the special privileges can be put into three principal categories:

(1) *Pledge.* Certain creditors are privileged because they are provided with a thing which serves as security; this is what happens regarding the privileges derived from the pledge or the right of retention.

(2) *Putting of the Thing into the Patrimony of the Debtor.* Certain creditors are privileged because they have augmented at their expense the assets of the common debtor and have not received the equivalent which is due them. . . . The principal example of this category of privilege is that of the vendor, and which, to abbreviate, is often referred to as the "privilege of the vendor."

(3) *Preservation of the Thing.* Finally, the law declares privileged various creditors who have, at their expense, preserved the common pledge. We will call them "preservers of the thing."

2638. Conflict of a Secured Creditor and a Vendor

In principle, the preference should be given to the creditor having the thing. The possessor has the right to repel all the actions directed against him, when his possession is in good faith. As in the case of revendication, all the rights of preference are ineffective against him. The Code itself gives us an example in Art. 2102(4), par. 3: he who has sold objects to a lessee of a house or a farm does not exercise his privilege until after the lessor. Thus we have a secured creditor who is preferred to the creditor who has placed the thing into the patrimony of the debtor.

By exception the pledgee or the lessor will be primed by the vendor, if they were in bad faith in receiving the thing in pledge, that is to say, if they knew at the time that the price of it was still due. The rules on the possession of the pledge which are only an extension of Art. 2279, protect only the possessors in good faith (Vol. I, No. 2479). . . .

2639. Conflict Between Preserver of the Thing Pledgee or Vendor

The rank then becomes a question of date: if the expenditure for preservation was prior to the pledge or the sale, the creditor who incurred it will be primed by the pledgee or the vendor. If, on the contrary, the expenditure is subsequent to the sale or pledge, he will have priority because in making these expenditures he has preserved the pledge of the other creditors. It is therefore natural that the latter, who would have otherwise lost all his security, should suffer the deduction of the expenses which preserved it for him, while if the sale or the pledge is more recent, one cannot use the same reasoning: if the thing had not been preserved, the vendor would have sold nothing, and the pledgee would have gotten another pledge.

No. 2640. Conflict Between Privileges of the Same Title

Finally, if we suppose a conflict between two pledgees, between two vendors, or between two preservers of the thing, it is again between them a question of date as in the preceding case, but the priority is determined in a different manner according to the circumstances:

(1) *Between Successive Vendors.* It is the oldest who primes because he is himself creditor of the second for the price, and the latter for the third and so on.

(2) *Between Successive Pledgees.* It is still the first one who is preferred to the others because the pledge is a right of the same nature as the mortgage, and to him is applied the rule *"Prior tempore, potior jure."* Comp. supra, No. 2437.

(3) *Between Preservers of the Thing.* The most recent is preferred, for the same reason which gives him the priority against a pledgee or a prior vendor: he preserves the pledge of the others.

* * * * * *

Planiol's theories of the ranking of the privileges within each class and among classes have largely been accepted by modern French writers, whose views might be summarized as follows:

1. Preservation privileges rank in inverse chronological order, because the preservation performed by each of them inures to the benefit of all who have come before.

2. Among creditors holding an implied pledge, there is little opportunity for conflict unless a third party holds the thing for the benefit of more than one creditor. In that case, the rule of first in time, first in right applies.

3. Among two creditors whose privileges are based on augmentation of patrimony, such as two successive vendors, the first to arise primes, for the reason that the first seller is the creditor of the second seller for the unpaid price due to him. Also, this principle draws by analogy upon the rule ranking successive vendor's privileges upon immovables.

Between two privileges found within different classes, ranking is as follows:

a. *Preservation versus pledge*. Preservation privileges arising after the pledge prime, because they inured to the benefit of the pledgee. Preservation privileges arising before the pledge are inferior if the pledgee was unaware of them, because the pledgee is entitled to the benefit of the doctrine of *la possession vaut titre*.

b. *Preservation versus augmentation of patrimony.* The preservation privilege primes, regardless of when the preservation occurred. If it occurred after the vendor's privilege arose, it primes because the preservation inured to the benefit of the vendor as privilege holder. If it occurred beforehand, the preservation privilege still primes because it inured to the benefit of the vendor when he was owner.

c. *Pledge versus augmentation of patrimony.* The pledge primes by operation of the doctrine of *la possession vaut titre*, unless the pledgee was aware of the earlier privilege. In that event, the pledge is inferior.

In large measure, these principles find expression in Article 2332-3 of the French Civil Code, adopted in 2006. Under this article, the lessor's privilege, privilege for preservation expenses, and vendor's privilege are ranked as follows: first, the privilege for preservation expenses, when the expenses of preservation arose after the other privileges; second, the lessor's privilege, provided that the lessor did not know of the existence of the other privileges; third, the privilege for preservation expenses, when the expenses of preservation arose prior to the other privileges; fourth, the vendor's privilege; and last, the lessor's privilege, when the lessor was aware of the existence of other privileges. Among multiple privileges for expenses incurred for the preservation of the same movable, preference is accorded to the most recent. Among multiple vendors' privileges affecting the same movable, preference is given to the first vendor's privilege to arise. The article accords the innkeeper's privilege the priority of a lessor's privilege. Of course, these rules are not in effect in Louisiana, but they illustrate the application of doctrine to rank privileges in a modern Civil Code.

* * * * * *

Art. 3267 and the Ranking of Privileges,
Joseph Dainow
9 LOUISIANA LAW REVIEW 370 (1949)

The absence in the French Civil Code of such a chapter of rules and instructions for the ranking of privileges among themselves was a source of some consternation to the French commentators. Without going into extensive detail, it will suffice here merely to note the fact that one of the basic issues on which the early commentators reached opposing views was the question of ranking between the general privileges and special privileges. In addition to the two views which favored either one group of privileges or the other, there was the third view that neither one group nor the other group should have a fixed rule of priority for all situations, but that special solutions should be reached in each case of conflict.

The Louisiana codifiers faced this problem directly and worked out a solution of their own. They adopted as a fundamental principle that special privileges should have priority over general privileges bearing upon the same subject matter, and then in addition they proceeded to enunciate individual solutions for the possible conflicts between each of the special privileges and those general privileges with which it might compete. As a collateral proposition, they adopted the rule that where a privilege operated on both movable and immovable property, it should be exercised first against the movables before proceeding against the immovables.

An analysis of Articles 3254-3270 indicates the following division. Apart from the first and last articles—which open and close the chapter—the remainder break into two distinct groups: (1) Articles 3255-3265, which are focused on problems of conflict between privileges on movable property only, and (2) Articles 3266-3269, which are centered particularly upon the ranking of privileges affecting immovable property.

In Article 3254, the codifiers indicated their basic preference for special privileges on movables over the general privileges, but then they proceeded in Article 3255 to anticipate and provide solutions for the certain specific conflicts likely to occur between the special and general privileges, as well as conflicts among the special privileges themselves.

Thus, in Article 3256-3265 the codifiers carried out this purpose in relation to movables, and they followed closely the list of special privileges on movables which they set out in Article 3217. The first few articles deal with the privilege of the lessor and other privileges on crops and provide the solution for conflicts between these privileges and certain general privileges. Articles 3260 and 3261 deal with the conflict between the privilege of the depositor and other privileges. Article 3262 provides for the conflicts involving the privilege for the expenses of preservation. Article 3263 then deals with the vendor's lien; Article 3264 with the privilege of the innkeeper; Article 3265 with the privilege of carriers. This pattern follows very markedly the list of privileges which are enumerated in Article 3217. In each instance, the rule of the code is predicated on the general policy determination that special privileges prime all the general privileges *except* the ones expressly selected for priority in specific instances of conflict.

* * * * * *

B. Ranking Privileges Over Movables

1. Contests Between Privilege Holders

***See* La. Civ. Code arts. 3252-65.**

Like the Code Napoléon, the Digest of 1808 contained no rules ranking privileges; those rules were added in the Civil Code of 1825, which included an entire chapter dedicated to the topic. With little substantive change, those same rules were carried forward into the Civil Code of 1870. The doctrinal basis for many of the ranking rules can be found in the excerpts from Planiol quoted above or, as Professor Dainow asserts in the excerpts above, from the general proposition that special privileges should prime general privileges. Even a cursory reading of Articles 3254 through 3265 reveals that the hierarchy of ranking that they provide is often not linear and is riddled with exceptions and qualifications. The articles never attempt to rank all privileges at once, but instead rank two or three privileges against each other, with no obvious attempt at harmonization of all ranking rules. Of course, in many instances, it is not necessary to rank certain privileges against each other, for it might well be impossible for them to operate at once upon the same movable.

It is, perhaps, a fool's errand to attempt construction of a schematic diagram of the ranking rules that these articles provide, but the following discussion, which lists the various privileges in the order that they are effectively ranked by the Civil Code, might serve as a useful guide in understanding and applying the articles.

1. *Expenses of sale*, which are defined to be costs necessary or incidental to the sale of movables. *Moutolly v. His Creditors*, 2 Rob. 350 (1842). Articles 3256, 3262 and 3265 specifically provide that the lessor's privilege, the preservation privilege, and the carrier's privilege, respectively, are subordinate to the expenses of sale. Similarly, Articles 3254 and 3256 provide that the privilege of the surviving spouse is subordinate to the privilege for expenses incurred in selling property. Article 3264 makes the privilege of an innkeeper subordinate to law charges, which would include expenses of the sale.

The only privilege that has even an arguable basis for priority over the expenses of sale is the depositor's privilege, which, under Article 3261, "is not preceded by any other privileged debt, even funeral expenses," other than the cost of sealing and making inventories and the exception stated in Article 3260. That article provides that the depositor's privilege is subordinate to the lessor's privilege if the lessor did not know that the things deposited did not belong to his tenant. Since the lessor's privilege is always subordinate to the expenses of sale, as provided by Article 3256, one might infer that the depositor's privilege is thus also subordinate to expenses of sale. In any event, it would make little policy sense for that single privilege—in contrast to all others—to outrank the expenses of the sale. Nor would it make sense for the depositor's privilege to be inferior to the cost of seals and inventories (as Article 3261 expressly provides) but superior to the cost of the sale.

2. *Vendor's privileges, but only if the privilege of the surviving spouse is claimed*. Though the vendor's privilege usually has much lower priority, if the privilege of the surviving spouse is in play, then the vendor's privilege might have elevated priority under Articles 3252 and 3254, which give the vendor's privilege priority over the privilege of the surviving spouse. This is the solution Professor Dainow reaches to resolve what would otherwise be a vicious circle, discussed in a later section of this chapter. *See* Joseph Dainow, *Vicious Circles in the Louisiana Law of Privileges*, 25 La. L. Rev. 1 (1964). His reasoning is based upon the fact that Articles 3252 and 3254 were amended after the Civil Code was adopted. However, this elevated priority will apply only if the privilege of the surviving spouse is actually claimed. *See Succession of Hardy*, 122 So. 154 (La. App. 1st Cir. 1929).

3. ***Privilege of the surviving spouse.*** Articles 3252 and 3254 provide that the privilege of the surviving spouse has priority over all debts, except for vendor's privileges and the expenses of sale.

4. ***Privileges for preservation charges and carrier's charges***. Article 3262 provides that the privilege for preservation has priority over all other claims for expenses, with the sole exception of charges on the sale of the thing preserved. Similarly, Article 3265 provides that the privilege of carriers yields only to the charges that arise on the sale of the goods. However, this result is altered by the later amendments to Articles 3252 and 3254, which give priority to the privilege of the surviving spouse—and by extension to the vendor's privilege when the privilege of the surviving spouse is claimed.

There is no provision that ranks the preservation privilege and the carrier's privilege against each other. Apparently, therefore, they should rank concurrently under Article 3188. *See, however, Powers & Co. v. Sixty Tons of Marble*, reproduced in the preceding chapter.

5. ***The cost of affixing seals and inventory, but only to the extent of farming utensils.*** Under Article 3191, the cost of affixing seals and inventory are a type of law charge, which benefits from a general privilege under Articles 3191 and 3252 (referred to in the latter article as "judicial charges"). As a general rule, Articles 3257 and 3258 accord the lessor priority over all general privileges, except for funeral charges. However, Article 3259 provides that the lessor's privilege is subordinate to the vendor's privilege on farming utensils. Moreover, Article 3263 provides that the vendor's privilege in all instances yields to the charges for affixing seals and inventories. Thus, an inference can be drawn that, insofar as farming utensils are concerned, the cost of affixing seals and inventory has priority over the lessor's privilege and over other general privileges, including funeral charges that would normally have priority over law charges.

6. ***Vendor's privilege on farming utensils.*** As mentioned above, Article 3259 subordinates the lessor's privilege to the vendor's privilege on farming utensils. This is an exception to the general rule of Article 3263, which ordinarily ranks the vendor's privilege behind the lessor's privilege. The same article also provides that vendor's privileges rank above "the funeral and other expenses of the debtor."

7. ***Vendor's privilege on items other than farming utensils, but only if a privilege for funeral charges is involved.*** The ranking inference made here is the resolution of another vicious circle inherent in the Civil Code itself. As noted above, the vendor's privilege is ordinarily inferior to the lessor's privilege under Articles 3258 and 3263. However, the latter article gives the vendor priority over funeral charges, whereas Article 3257 provides that the lessor's privilege is primed by funeral charges. In his article on vicious circles from which excerpts are quoted below, Professor Dainow notes the existence of this vicious circle and concludes that the proper ranking is for the vendor to have priority, under this set of circumstances, over both the funeral charges and the lessor.

8. ***Privileges on current year's crops for seed, labor, and the wages of overseers and managers.*** Article 3259 ranks these privileges ahead of the lessor's privilege. However, to that extent, this article was superseded by Act 89 of 1886, which enacted a comprehensive scheme governing the ranking of agricultural privileges and crop pledges among themselves, displacing the ranking rules of the Civil Code. That act was a precursor of former La. R.S. 9:4521, which itself was repealed in 2010 and replaced by the crop ranking rules of La. R.S. 10:9-322(g), discussed below, affording priority to the lessor, provided that he has perfected his privilege by making a filing in the central agricultural registry.

9. ***Depositor's privilege, but only if the lessor has knowledge of the depositor's rights.*** Article 3261 provides that the depositor's privilege outranks funeral charges. If the lessor knows that goods belong to a depositor, then, under Article 3260, the depositor's privilege also outranks the lessor's privilege. If the lessor does not have such knowledge, inferior ranking is accorded to the depositor, as discussed below.

10. *Funeral charges*. Funeral charges are inferior to the depositor's privilege under Article 3260 (subject to the exception noted below). Although Article 3262 makes the vendor's privilege superior to funeral charges, Article 3257 provides that funeral charges prime the lessor's privilege. Moreover, under Article 3254, the privilege for funeral charges outranks all other general privileges.

11. *Lessor's privilege.* The rules cited above cover situations in which the lessor knows that goods are the property of a depositor. If the lessor is ignorant of that fact, then the lessor's privilege outranks the depositor's privilege under Article 3260. This rule may be of little continuing relevance, however, since the lessor's privilege no longer attaches to movables of a third person, other than a sublessee, found on the leased property.

As has already been observed, the vendor's privilege is ordinarily inferior to the lessor's privilege under Articles 3258 and 3263.

Article 3258, in tandem with Article 3257, gives the lessor priority over all general privileges with the exception of funeral charges.

12. *Depositor's privilege, if the lessor is ignorant of the depositor's rights.* As just stated, Article 3260 provides that, if the lessor is ignorant of the fact that the goods belong to a depositor, then the lessor's privilege outranks the depositor's privilege. (The reference to a "depositary" in the text of the article is a mistranslation of the French text and should be understood to mean the "depositor.") However, the lessor's privilege is always primed by funeral expenses under Article 3257. This creates the appearance of a vicious circle, because Article 3261 provides that the depositor's privilege outranks funeral expenses. However, upon closer analysis, there is in fact no vicious circle, because Article 3261 begins with the words "with the exception stated in the foregoing article." The "foregoing article" (Article 3260), which deals with the situation where the lessor is ignorant of the fact that things deposited did not belong to his tenant, gives the lessor priority over the depositor, and says nothing about the priority of the depositor over funeral charges. In other words, the priority given to the depositor over funeral charges in Article 3261 yields, by the express command of the article, to the priority that the lessor who is unaware of the depositor's rights enjoys under Article 3259.

Though Professor Dainow agrees, in the article cited in the section below on vicious circles, that Article 3260 must be given primacy, he does so for a different reason and also reaches the conclusion that funeral charges become subordinate to *both* the lessor's privilege and the depositor's privilege where Article 3260 applies. His belief that Article 3260 prevails is based upon the fact that it is later legislation (having been amended in 1871) rather than the fact that Article 3261 has textual reference to the exception stated in Article 3260. He concludes that, by operation of Article 3260, the result is to move the lessor ahead of the depositor, with the result that the lessor at the same time gains priority over the privilege for funeral charges, which would otherwise have precedence of the lessor.

13. *Vendor's privilege on items other than farming utensils, where no funeral charges are involved.* If no funeral charges are involved, then the vicious circle noted above is avoided, and the ordinary rule of Article 3263 ranking the vendor's privilege behind that of the lessor is operative.

The listing of the depositor's privilege above the vendor privilege in this discussion does not imply that the former outranks the latter. If the depositor himself owes money for the unpaid purchase price he deposits with another, he is the debtor with regard to that obligation and can certainly not prime the privilege of his own vendor by claiming a depositor's privilege on his own property.

14. *Other law charges.* Article 3254 ranks the general privileges. The highest ranking of these, that for funeral charges, has already been ranked above, as have law charges consisting of the expenses of sale and the cost of seals and inventories. This leaves the privilege for other law charges as the next ranking privilege.

15. *Remaining general privileges.* The remaining general privileges are ranked by Article 3254 in the following order: (i) expenses of the last illness, (ii) wages of servants, (iii) suppliers of provisions, and (iv) salaries of clerks and secretaries.

Curiously, that there is no provision of the Civil Code ranking the artisan's privilege arising under Article 3217(2). In *Cozzo v. Ulrich*, supra, the court held that the artisan's privilege has priority over the vendor's privilege, because the vendor has a mere privilege, while the artisan is entitled to a right of pledge that includes the right to retain the object until payment.

The preceding discussion addresses only the ranking rules contained within the Civil Code itself. The statutes creating the many special privileges upon movables often contain their own ranking rules, sometimes creating vicious circles, as discussed in a later section of this chapter.

* * * * * *

GARRETSON
v.
HIS CREDITORS
1 Rob. 445 (La. 1842)

MORPHY, J.

The syndic in this case, filed a tableau of distribution, showing the privileged claims and charges against the estate, and prayed to be authorized to pay the same in accordance therewith. The money to be distributed amounts to \$2,164.04, and is the proceeds of the sale of a stock of household furniture which the insolvent had in a house belonging to Nicholas Hoey, whose claim for rent is admitted to be fifteen hundred dollars. The law charges, including \$100 for wages due to a laborer, amount to no less than \$1,050.75, which sum is deducted on the tableau from the proceeds of the furniture, leaving, after reserving a sum of \$100 in the hands of the syndic, only \$1,013.29, to be applied to the payment of the house rent. A memorandum at the foot of the tableau, shows that the notes and accounts of the estate, were yet on hand to be collected. To this tableau, Hoey made opposition, claiming to be paid out of these proceeds, in preference to all the creditors therein set down. The judge below sustained his opposition, and ordered his claim to be paid in preference to all the creditors on the tableau, except the auctioneer for his commission and the incidental expenses of the sale of the movables, amounting to \$115.10. The balance in the hands of the syndic, he ordered to be distributed *pro rata*, among all the creditors for law charges. The syndic appealed.

The judge, in our opinion, decided correctly. The lessor is treated with peculiar favor by the Civil Code. In the language of article 3185, his right is of a higher nature than a mere privilege, the latter is enforced only on the price of the movables to which it applies; it does not enable the creditor to take or keep the effects themselves in kind; the lessor, on the contrary, may take the effects themselves, and retain them until he is paid; he has on them a right of pledge. Article 3223 provides, that the charges for selling the movables, subject to the lessor's privilege, are to be paid before the rent, because these charges procure the payment of the rent. The following article says, that when there is no other source, from which the funeral expenses of the debtor and his family can be paid, they have a preference over the debt for rent or hire, on the price of the movables contained in the house or on the farm; and article 3225 enacts, that the lessor has a preference on the price of these movables over all the other privileged debts of the deceased, such as expenses of the last illness, and *others which have a general privilege on the movables*. The debts having this general privilege on the movables, are enumerated in article 3158, and among them are the law charges. But if any doubt could remain, after the perusal of the above provisions of law, they must, we think, be removed by article 3237, which provides, that when the privileged debts on the movables and immovables cannot be paid entirely, either because the movable effects are of small value, or *subject to special privileges which claim a preference*, or because the movables and immovables together do not suffice, the deficiency must be borne proportionably among the creditors, but the debts must be paid according to the order above established, and the loss must fall on those which are of an inferior dignity.

By presenting his tableau before the collection of the notes and accounts due to the estate, the syndic has given rise to a conflict which perhaps should not exist, for *non constat* but that a sufficient sum may be collected to pay off the law charges, independent of the proceeds of the movables, subject to the appellee's privilege. Be this as it may, the judge has, in our opinion, taken a correct view of the lessor's right on the particular fund to be distributed by the tableau, as presented.

Judgment affirmed.

* * * * * *

NOTES AND QUESTIONS

1. The case holds that the lessor's privilege, being of a higher nature than a mere privilege and instead a right of pledge, yields only to those law charges necessary to obtain the sale of the property and to funeral charges, but has priority over other law charges and other general privileges. For other early cases to the same effect, *see Montilly v. His Creditors*, 2 Rob. 350 (1842), and *Succession of Devine*, 4 Rob. 366 (1843). *Accord, City Item Co-Op Printing Co. v. Phoenix Furniture Concern*, 32 So. 469 (La. 1902), holding that where a corporate receiver held at the same time goods that were subject to a lessor's privilege and goods that were not, the costs of provoking the sale should be taken first out of the funds derived from the sale of the goods that were not subject to the lessor's privilege.

2. As discussed in the preceding chapter, after the revision of the law of lease in 2004, the lessor's privilege no longer imports a right of pledge. Does it nonetheless still enjoy the favored ranking described in *Garrettson*?

* * * * * *

SUCCESSION OF CROTTY
116 So. 2d 74 (La. App. 1st Cir. 1959)

LOTTINGER, Judge.

The facts may be briefly re-stated as follows: Douglas L. Crotty, Sr. died intestate on February 14, 1954, leaving a surviving spouse and two minor children. The surviving spouse, Mrs. Gertrude Thelma Siers Crotty, qualified as tutrix of the minors and as administratrix of the succession. The inventory reflected only some items of household furniture, fixtures and appliances (which were stored with The Globe Storage Company, Inc.) the whole of which were appraised at the sum of $500. A petition was filed by the administratrix to sell the movables to pay debts of the succession, which were alleged to exceed the value of the assets. The Globe Storage Company, Inc. then filed a third opposition claiming preference of the proceeds of the sale over all other persons, including Court costs and attorney fees, up to $623.98. The trial judge sustained the opposition of The Globe Storage Company, Inc. hence the appeal.

It is admitted that the facts set forth in the third opposition are correct but it is contended that as the succession owes funeral charges, court costs and legal charges the matter is governed by LSA-C.C. Articles 3191 and 3276 and that, therefore, the claim of the warehouseman, The Globe Storage Company, Inc. is outranked by the privileges enumerated in the aforesaid articles.

The contention of the third opponent, on the other hand, is that it is accorded a privilege by virtue of the provisions of LSA-R.S. 54:27 and LSA-C.C. Articles 3224-3226 which privilege, under the authority of LSA-C.C. Article 3262, primes those set out in the Codal articles relied on by appellant.

LSA-C.C. art. 3191, which is found in Chapter 3, Section 1, entitled "Of General Privileges on Movables" of Title XXI of the Code, reads as follows:

> "The debts which are privileged on all the movables in general, are those hereafter enumerated, and are paid in the following order:
>
> 1. Funeral charges.
>
> 2. Law charges.
>
> 3. Charges, of whatever nature, occasioned by the last sickness, concurrently among those to whom they are due.
>
> 4. The wages of servants for the year past, and so much as is due for the current year.
>
> 5. Supplies of provisions made to the debtor or his family, during the last six months, by retail dealers, such as bakers, butchers, grocers; and, during the last year, by keepers of boarding houses and taverns.
>
> 6. The salaries of clerks, secretaries, and other persons of that kind.
>
> 7. Dotal rights due to wives by their husband (sic)"

The other code article relied on by appellant, LSA-C.C. Article 3276, which is found in Chapter 7, entitled "How Privileges Are Preserved and Recorded" of Title XXI, reads as follows:

> "The charges against a succession, such as funeral charges, law charges, lawyers' fees for settling the succession, the thousand dollars secured in certain cases to the widow or minor heirs of the deceased, and all claims against the succession originating after the death of the person whose succession is under administration, are to be paid before the debts contracted by the deceased person, *except as otherwise provided for herein*, and they are not required to be recorded." (Emphasis supplied.)

LSA-C.C. Articles 3224-3226, which grant to third opponent its privilege are found in section 2 entitled "Of the Privileges on Particular Movables" of Title XXI of the Code. LSA-C.C. art. 3262, which is found in the same Title under Chapter 6 thereof, entitled "Of the Order in Which Privileged Creditors are to be Paid," reads as follows:

> "The privilege of him who has taken care of the property of another, has a preference over that property, for the necessary expenses which he incurred, above all the other claims for expenses, *even funeral charges*; his privilege yields only to that for the charges on the sale of the thing preserved." (Emphasis supplied.)

We think it clear that the precise and specific provisions of the Codal articles relied on by the third opponent control over the general and overall provisions of those cited by appellant. The trial judge so held and, we think, correctly so. For the reasons assigned the judgment appealed from is affirmed.

Judgment affirmed.

* * * * * *

NOTES AND QUESTIONS

Does the case stand for the proposition that special privileges on movables always prime general privileges, or rather the proposition that the specific ranking rules found in the Civil Code Articles 3254-65 prime the more general rule of Civil Code Article 3191?

* * * * * *

INTERCITY EXPRESS LINES

v.

LITCHFIELD

174 So. 149 (La. App. 1st Cir. 1937)

DORE, Judge.

On December 7, 1934, plaintiff filed a suit against defendant Litchfield for damages to one of its trucks in the amount of $538.54, caused by a Ford car owned and driven by said defendant. As the defendant was a nonresident of the state, plaintiff secured an attachment under which the Ford car was seized.

On April 23, 1935, a judgment was rendered in favor of plaintiff for the amount claimed in rem against the attached automobile, and the attachment was sustained, recognizing the lien and privilege of plaintiff on the attached property resulting from the attachment, and ordering the property sold according to law.

On January 15, 1935, Leon Guarisco, the third opponent, filed a separate suit against Litchfield for $203.45, being the amount due third opponent for material and parts furnished and labor done in repairing said Ford automobile. A lien and privilege on the automobile repaired was claimed in the suit and a provisional seizure issued under which the car was again seized. On March 29, 1935, third opponent obtained a judgment in rem for the amount of his claim with recognition of his lien and privilege on the car for the repairs in accordance with Act No. 209 of 1926.

Third opponent had execution to issue on his judgment and the car was advertised for sale, whereupon plaintiff, which had in the meantime secured a judgment on its claim for damages as heretofore stated, instituted a separate suit against third opponent to have his judgment annulled on certain alleged grounds and also to enjoin the sale of the property under the alleged void judgment. From an adverse judgment, plaintiff took an appeal to this court where the judgment was affirmed in so far as it maintained the validity of third opponent's judgment against the car and recognized a lien and privilege thereon in his favor for the repairs made. *See Inter City Express Lines v. Guarisco*, 165 So. 727.

Plaintiff then caused a writ of *fi. fa.* to issue on its judgment and had the automobile seized and advertised for sale. Third opponent filed this intervention and third opposition in plaintiff's suit against Litchfield and claimed to be paid by preference and priority over plaintiff out of the proceeds of the sale of the car on the ground that his judgment and lien and privilege on the car for repairs recognized therein primed the lien and privilege in favor of plaintiff resulting from the attachment of the car on its claim for damages. The claim of third opponent was sustained and the sheriff was ordered to pay the amount of third opponent's judgment out of the proceeds of the sale of the car by preference and priority over the judgment of plaintiff. From this judgment, plaintiff has appealed.

Counsel for plaintiff relies for a reversal of the judgment appealed from entirely on his objection to the admissibility of the judgment and petition with annexed documents in the suit of third opponent against Litchfield, and the resulting lack of proof to support the preference and priority claimed by third opponent.

A judgment which decrees the existence of a debt and recognizes a lien and privilege on property of the debtor for the payment of the debt makes prima facie proof against a third party where the judgment is sought to be enforced on the property in which such third person has acquired an interest; but the third person is not precluded by such judgment from making an attack upon its legality or fraud in its procurement. *Lanata v. Planas et al.*, 2 La. Ann. 544; *Turner v. Luckett*, 2 La. Ann. 885. The plaintiff in its answer to the intervention and third opposition does not allege any fraud or collusion in the procurement of the judgment on which third opponent relies as a basis for his prior lien and privilege on the car, but, on the contrary, pleads an estoppel arising from an unsuccessful attack made by it on the legality of third opponent's judgment. It is true that plaintiff denies that third opponent has a valid judgment or that he has a valid lien and privilege on the car, but it failed to offer any proof to show that the lien and privilege of third opponent was invalid and not based on sufficient evidence.

The judgment offered by third opponent in his favor made out a prima facie case in support of his prior lien and privilege. It was not necessary for him to bring forward again all the evidence on which his judgment was based, otherwise it would be necessary for a person to produce over and over again all the testimony on which his judgment is based when enforcing that judgment and the rights created thereunder where a third person is affected. It is for that reason that the judgment makes a prima facie proof against a third person, and it is incumbent on such person to allege and prove that the debt and privilege recognized by the judgment were not due or legal. If the plaintiff had offered proof that third opponent did not have a just claim for repairs on the car by the same kind of evidence that the defendant Litchfield could have used in defense of the suit, it would then have been necessary for third opponent to produce evidence to support the judgment.

The lien and privilege recognized by the judgment in favor of third opponent for repairs on the automobile was created by the law, Act No. 209 of 1926, and rested on the property before it was attached in plaintiff's suit on an ordinary claim for damages. The privilege resulting from an attachment is subordinate to the privilege existing on the article and created thereon by law. Such a privilege is not affected by the attachment of the property. *See Erman & Cahn v. Lehman*, 47 La. Ann. 1651, 18 So. 650.

For these reasons, the judgment appealed from is correct and is hereby affirmed.

* * * * * *

NOTES AND QUESTIONS

1. Did the plaintiff's tort judgment itself create a judicial mortgage or a privilege upon the defendant's movable property?

2. This case is another illustration of the rule that a seizing creditor's privilege is subordinate to previously existing encumbrances. A judgment recognizing the pre-existing encumbrance is prima facie evidence of its validity but does not preclude the seizing creditor from proving otherwise.

3. Suppose two different repairmen have, successively, performed repairs on the same automobile. Neither has paid been, and both repairs were made within the last 120 days. How would the two repairmen's privileges under La. R.S. 9:4501 rank against each other? Would the result be changed if, after

the first repairs were made but before the second, a security interest in the automobile was perfected?

2. Contests Between Privileges and UCC Security Interests

***See* La Rev. Stat. 9:4770; La. Rev. Stat. 10:9-201; 9-322(h); 9-333.**

* * * * * *

FIRST NATIONAL BANK OF BOSTON
v.
BECKWITH MACHINERY CO.
650 So. 2d 1148 (La. 1995)

MARCUS, Justice.

Pursuant to La. R.S. 13:72.1 and Rule XII of the Supreme Court of Louisiana, the United States Court of Appeals for the Fifth Circuit has certified the following question of law to this court:

Which interest should have priority under Louisiana law: (1) a civil law "privilege" for suppliers of ship-building materials, thus giving Beckwith creditor priority rights, or (2) an earlier perfected UCC security interest, thus giving FNBB creditor priority rights.

As Rule XII, § 3 requires, the certificate includes a statement of facts showing the nature of the cause and the circumstances out of which the question of law arises:

This case revolves around the construction and financing of a towboat. In 1992, Viking Maritec, Inc. ("Viking") and Avondale Industries, Inc. ("Avondale") entered into a contract for Avondale to build a towboat for Viking in exchange for a purchase price of $2.8 million. Viking entered into a credit agreement with First National Bank of Boston ("FNBB") to finance the purchase price due Avondale and to pay for other equipment for the vessel. FNBB agreed to lend Viking up to $4.8 million, and Viking executed a construction note in favor of FNBB. Viking also executed a "Louisiana Ship Mortgage and Security Agreement," granting the bank under the provisions of La. Rev. Stat. Ann. 10:9–101—10:9–604 (West 1993) a security interest in the towboat and its materials and components. FNBB perfected the security interest by filing a UCC–1 financing statement in the proper office on August 6, 1992. The documents stated that the Ship Mortgage Law and the Louisiana UCC would govern the security agreement. In early 1993, Viking purchased from Beckwith Machinery Company ("Beckwith") engines and related machinery, which were incorporated into the tugboat.

Viking did not pay either Beckwith or FNBB. After its demand for payment was not answered, FNBB filed an action in federal district court to have the unfinished and undocumented towboat seized and sold. Beckwith intervened, seeking priority through the Louisiana Civil Code which gives privileges to certain classes of creditors, including suppliers of ship-building materials and equipment. La. Civ. Code Ann. art. 3237 (West 1952). FNBB filed a motion asking the court to give priority instead to its perfected UCC security interest.

On July 26, 1993, the district court rendered a decision formally ranking FNBB's security interest in the vessel ahead of Beckwith's materialman's privilege. Judgment was entered on September 3, 1993, giving priority to the bank's security interest. Beckwith appeals from that judgment. In its memorandum and order, the district court expressed considerable doubt as to whether the Louisiana legislature intended such a result.

The question certified to this court raises two issues: (1) whether the priority rules contained in Chapter 9 of the Louisiana Commercial Laws (Chapter 9) govern a ranking dispute between a materialman's privilege created pursuant to La. Civ. Code art. 3237(8) and a prior perfected security interest in the same goods created pursuant to Chapter 9; and (2) which of the foregoing interests has priority over the other.

Beckwith obtained a materialman's privilege on the engines and machinery sold to Viking and incorporated into the tugboat by operation of La. Civ. Code art. 3237, which provides in pertinent part:

The following debts are privileged on the price of ships and other vessels, in the order in which they are placed: . . .

8. Sums due to sellers, to those who have furnished materials and to workmen employed in the construction, if the vessel has never made a voyage; . . .

It is undisputed that this privilege is nonpossessory; that is, its existence does not depend on Beckwith's possession of the goods, nor does Beckwith have possession of the goods. Additionally, the facts as stated in the certificate indicate that FNBB perfected its security interest prior to the time Beckwith's privilege arose. The first issue we must decide is whether the ranking dispute between Beckwith's nonpossessory materialman's privilege and FNBB's prior perfected security interest is governed by the provisions of Chapter 9. This is a case of first impression in this state.

Louisiana enacted Article 9 of the Uniform Commercial Code (UCC) as Chapter 9 of the Louisiana Commercial Laws effective January 1, 1990, and was the last of all the states to do so. Section 10:9–102 indicates the subject matter of Chapter 9 and provides in pertinent part:

> (1) *Except as otherwise provided in R.S. 10:9–104 on excluded transactions*, this Chapter applies (a) *to any transaction (regardless of its form) which is intended to create a security interest in personal property or fixtures* including goods, documents, instruments, general intangibles, chattel paper or accounts;
>
> (2) This Chapter applies to *security interests* created by contract, including pledge, assignment, chattel mortgage, other lien or title retention contract, and lease or consignment intended as security. *This Chapter does not apply to statutory liens and privileges except as expressly provided herein. . . .*
>
> (4) As used in this Chapter the following terms have the following meanings when they refer to property that is located in this state and is subject to its law:
>
> (b) *"Lien" or "statutory lien" means a privilege created by the Louisiana Civil Code*, Louisiana Revised Statutes of 1950, or other statutory authority, other than a vendor's privilege on immovable property. (Emphasis added.)

The term "security interest" is defined in La. R.S. 10:1–201(37), which provides in pertinent part:

> "Security interest" means an interest in personal property or fixtures, created by contract, which secures payment or performance of an obligation. . . . *A lien or privilege created by the Louisiana Civil Code, the Louisiana Revised Statutes, or other statutory authority is not a security interest*. . . . (Emphasis added.)

Section 10:9–104(c) on excluded transactions states, in pertinent part: "The provisions of this Chapter do not apply . . . to a lien given by statute or other rule of law for services or materials *except as provided in R.S. 10:9–201 and 10:9–310 on priority of such liens. . . .*" (Emphasis added.) These provisions, when read together, mean that a Louisiana privilege is not a "security interest" for Chapter 9 purposes, and the provisions of Chapter 9 do not govern such privileges, *except* as provided in §§ 10:9–201 and 10:9–310 on priority. Therefore, while Chapter 9 does not govern the creation or existence of Louisiana privileges (because such privileges arise by operation of law without the necessity of complying with the provisions of Chapter 9), the *priority* of such privileges vis-a-vis security interests *is* governed by Chapter 9 to the extent provided in §§ 10:9–201 and 10:9–310.

Section 10:9–201 sets forth the basic priority rule of Chapter 9, and provides:

> § 9–201. General validity of security agreement
>
> Except as otherwise provided by this Title, a security agreement is effective according to its terms between the parties, against purchasers of the collateral and against creditors, *including those holding liens on property subject to this Chapter unless the statute creating the lien expressly provides to the contrary, and the lien depend on possession of the lien holder in which case the lien has preference to all security interests except those perfected before the lien arises.* Nothing in this Chapter validates any charge or practice illegal under any statute or regulation thereunder governing usury, small loans, retail installment sales, or the like, or extends the

> application of any such statute or regulation to any transaction not otherwise subject thereto. (Emphasis added.)

Section 10:9–310 provides:

> § 9–310. Priority of certain liens arising by operation of law
>
> When a person in the ordinary course of his business furnishes services or materials with respect to goods subject to a security interest, a lien upon goods in the possession of such person given by statute or rule of law for such materials or services, *or the holder of any other lien, the continued existence of which is dependent upon the possession of the goods by the lien holder,* takes priority over a perfected security interest unless the statute creating the lien expressly provides otherwise. (Emphasis added.)

Both of these provisions are nonuniform, in that they vary from the standard version of the UCC drafted by the American Law Institute and the National Conference of Commissioners on Uniform State Laws. Louisiana has added the language emphasized above to the standard versions. Louisiana is the *only state* which includes in its version of Article 9–201 language explicitly making the security interests effective against creditors holding *liens* on the same property. Louisiana is also the *only state* which specifically makes liens subject to the provisions of § 10:9–201 *in addition to* § 10:9–310. Louisiana does this by including a nonuniform reference to § 10:9–201 in § 10:9–104(c) (the section listing excluded transactions). No other state includes such a reference. To the contrary, the only UCC provision which other states specifically make liens subject to is Article 9–310. We believe the nonuniform language contained in § 10:9–104(c) combined with that in § 10:9–201, which states that a security agreement is "effective according to its terms . . . against creditors . . . holding liens on property subject to this Chapter. . . ." compels the conclusion that the Louisiana Legislature intended to bring *all priority disputes* between Chapter 9 security interests and Louisiana privileges within the scope of Chapter 9. Furthermore, we interpret the nonuniform language in these statutes to mean that all Louisiana privileges, both possessory and nonpossessory, are subordinate to perfected Chapter 9 security interests in the same property, *unless* those privileges fall within one of the limited exceptions giving them priority, which are contained later in § 10:9–201 and in § 10:9–310. Those exceptions will be examined next.

Section 10:9–201 provides, in pertinent part, that a security interest is effective against those holding liens on the property:

> *unless* the statute creating the lien expressly provides to the contrary, *and* the lien depends on possession of the lien holder in which case *the lien has preference* to all security interests except those perfected before the lien arises. (Emphasis added.)

Applying the language of this statute as written would lead to the following result: A lien is subordinate to a perfected Chapter 9 security interest, unless: (1) the statute creating the lien expressly provides to the contrary, *and* (2) the lien depends on possession of the lien holder. If these requirements are met, the lien has preference to all security interests except prior perfected security interests.

Section 10:9–310 is a very specific statute which only addresses the priority of a certain type of lien vis-a-vis a Chapter 9 security interest. That statute provides that a lien which meets one of the following criteria has priority over even a perfected security interest: (1) the lien is for services or materials furnished in the ordinary course of business with respect to goods which are in the possession of the lien holder; *or* (2) the existence of the lien is dependent upon the possession of the goods by the lien holder. A lien meeting either one of these criteria will have priority over a perfected security interest *unless* the statute creating the lien expressly subordinates it.

These two statutes give priority to certain types of possessory liens. However, when they are read together, two conflicts between them become apparent. First, § 10:9–201 states that a possessory lien has priority over a security interest, except a prior perfected security interest, *only if* the statute creating the lien gives it priority, but § 10:9–310 states that a possessory lien has priority over a perfected security interest *unless* the statute creating the lien subordinates it. Obviously, possessory liens not meeting the criteria of § 10:9–201 (because the statute creating them does not provide for their priority over security interests), will meet the criteria of § 10:9–310, because they are granted priority unless the statute creating them expressly takes it away. This conflict would render the exception granted in § 10:9–201 meaningless, because possessory lien holders would simply disregard § 10:9–201 and invoke the priority granted in § 10:9–310.

While courts must generally interpret statutes as written, statutes on the same subject should be construed in harmony and unnecessary conflict should be avoided. *State v. Piazza,* 596 So. 2d 817, 819 (La.1992). Courts should give effect to all parts of a statute, and not adopt a construction making any part superfluous or meaningless, if that result can be avoided. *Dore v. Tugwell,* 228 La. 807, 84 So. 2d 199, 204 (1955), *reh'g denied.* Additionally, "[t]he object of the court in construing a statute is to ascertain the legislative intent and, where a literal interpretation would produce absurd consequences, the letter must give way to the spirit of the law and the statute construed so as to produce a reasonable result." *Smith v. Flournoy,* 238 La. 432, 115 So. 2d 809, 814 (1959), *reh'g denied.*

Applying these principles of statutory interpretation, we hold that the provisions granting certain liens priority in § 10:9–201 must be construed to create two separate exceptions. First, a lien will be subordinate to a perfected Chapter 9 security interest unless the statute creating the lien expressly provides to the contrary. Second, a lien will be subordinate to a perfected Chapter 9 security interest unless the lien depends on possession of the lien holder, in which case the lien has preference to all security interests except those perfected before the lien arises. All other privileges are subordinate to perfected Chapter 9 security interests. This interpretation results from reading the exception clause in § 10:9–201 as follows: a security interest is effective against a lien on the same property "*unless* the statute creating the lien expressly provides to the contrary, *and [unless]* the lien depends on possession of the lien holder in which case the lien has preference to all security interests except those perfected before the lien arises." (Emphasis added.) We believe this interpretation is consistent with a reading of Chapter 9's priority rules as a whole, and with the intent of the legislature. While there is no legislative history commenting on these specific provisions, nor are there any Louisiana comments illuminating the reasons for the variations from the standard version of the UCC, we are convinced that the legislature intended to authorize the granting of express priority of *nonpossessory* liens over security interests in specific statutes.

The legislature's treatment of liens on unharvested crops in La. R.S. 9:4521 supports this proposition. That statute provides, as an express exception to the priority rule of § 10:9–201, that certain statutory privileges granted therein shall have priority over a perfected Chapter 9 security interest. These privileges are nonpossessory because the privilege holders do not have possession of the unharvested crops. Therefore, the legislature has created an express exception granting specific *nonpossessory* privileges priority over perfected Chapter 9 security interests. Reading the language of § 10:9–201 as a single exception with two conditions (instead of two separate exceptions) would not allow such a result, because it would only allow priority for possessory privileges. We reject that reading because we believe the legislature has the authority to enact exceptions to the priority rules of Chapter 9 for all types of privileges. We hold that § 10:9–201 contains two separate exceptions wherein a privilege may be granted priority over a perfected security interest, one of them being when the legislature expressly provides for such priority in the statute creating the privilege.

Having reconciled §§ 10:9–201 and 10:9–310 to the extent the facts of this case require, we must next decide if any of the exceptions granting Louisiana privileges priority over Chapter 9 security interests apply to the nonpossessory materialman's privilege held by Beckwith. The exceptions contained in § 10:9–310 only govern the priority of certain *possessory* privileges vis-a-vis perfected security interests. Since the privilege at issue in the present case is *nonpossessory,* § 10:9–310 does not apply. Additionally, the second exception contained in § 10:9–201 only governs possessory liens, so does not apply. That leaves the first exception in § 10:9–201, which subordinates a privilege to a perfected security interest unless the privilege is expressly granted priority in the statute which creates it. Therefore, we must determine if the statute creating Beckwith's privilege expressly grants it priority.

Civil Code article 3237(8) is the source of Beckwith's privilege. While that article does rank the various privileges created therein with respect to each other, it does not rank the materialman's privilege vis-a-vis a Chapter 9 security interest. However, Beckwith claims the legislature specifically acknowledged that this privilege had priority over all other claims in the Ship Mortgage Law (enacted in 1975); specifically in La. R.S. 9:5524(D). Beckwith further claims that, by the enactment of La. R.S. 9:5538 in conjunction with the enactment of

Louisiana's Chapter 9, the legislature explicitly provided for the priority of this privilege over a Chapter 9 security interest. Looking beyond the Civil Code article creating the privilege, without deciding if we may, we hold that the Ship Mortgage Law does not give an article 3237(8) materialman's privilege priority over a prior perfected Chapter 9 security interest. [The court's discussion of the provisions of the Ship Mortgage Law, which was effectively superseded by the adoption of Chapter 9 of the Louisiana Uniform Commercial Code effective January 1, 1990, is omitted].

Based on the foregoing, we conclude that neither the Civil Code article creating the privilege nor the Ship Mortgage Law expressly provides that the nonpossessory privilege at issue in the present case has priority over a prior perfected security interest. Therefore, since this privilege meets none of the exceptions contained in §§ 10:9–201 or 10:9–310 which would grant it priority, it is subject to the general rule of § 10:9–201, which subordinates a privilege to a perfected security interest. Therefore, FNBB's prior perfected Chapter 9 security interest has priority over Beckwith's nonpossessory materialman's privilege.

We recognize that the application of the provisions of Chapter 9 to resolve a priority dispute between a nonpossessory lien holder and a Chapter 9 security interest is a departure from the approach adopted by a majority of the states. However, this different treatment is due specifically and solely to the nonuniform language added by our legislature to §§ 10:9–104(c) and 10:9–201. While one of the general policies of the UCC is to "promote uniformity of the law among the various jurisdictions," this policy cannot govern when Louisiana's version of the UCC is nonuniform. Furthermore, Louisiana was the last of the 50 states to adopt Article 9 of the UCC. Therefore, our legislators had the advantage of studying the experience of the other states with their provisions before enacting them. "[L]aws are presumed to be passed with deliberation, and with full knowledge of all existing ones on the same subject. . . ." *City of New Orleans v. Board of Supervisors of Elections, Parish of Orleans,* 216 La. 116, 43 So. 2d 237, 247 (1949), *reh'g denied.*

Furthermore, we observe that the legislature's enactment of La. R.S. 9:4770 entitled "Conflicts in favor of Chapter 9 of the Louisiana Commercial Laws" as part of the UCC Implementation Bill provides additional support for our conclusion that priority disputes between Louisiana privileges and Chapter 9 security interests are governed by the provisions of Chapter 9. That statute provides:

> This Code Title (Code Title XXI of Code Book III, R.S. 9:4501 *et seq.*), Part 8 of Chapter 7 of the Louisiana Mineral Code (R.S. 31:146 through 148), and *Title XXI of Book III of the Louisiana Civil Code (Arts. 3182 through 3277)* shall be interpreted and applied consistent with Chapter 9 of the Louisiana Commercial Laws. *Other than as provided in R.S. 9:4521, any conflict between the priority ranking of privileges under this Title,* Part 8 of Chapter 7 of the Louisiana Mineral Code, and *under Title XXI of Book III of the Louisiana Civil Code with the priority ranking rules of Chapter 9 of the Louisiana Commercial Laws shall be resolved in favor of the priority ranking rules of Chapter 9 with regard to secured transactions subject thereto.* Whether a sale or lease was entered into before or after January 1, 1990, the rights of a vendor under Civil Code Articles 2561, 3217(7), and 3227 or of a lessor under Civil Code Articles 2705 and 3218 or Mineral Code Article 146 are subordinate to the rights of a secured party with a perfected security interest under Chapter 9 of the Louisiana Commercial Laws. (Emphasis added.)

While we find no conflict between article 3237 or the Ship Mortgage Law and Chapter 9 regarding the priority of the nonpossessory materialman's privilege at issue (because we find that the former two laws do not address such priority), the legislature's express resolution of any such conflicts in favor of Chapter 9 is a clear indication of the legislature's intent to favor perfected Chapter 9 security interests over nonpossessory Louisiana privileges.

As a final matter, we point out that our holding does not leave creditors like Beckwith without means to protect their interests. As a financing seller of engines used in the construction of the vessel, Beckwith could have obtained a "purchase money security interest" in these goods, La. R.S. 10:9–107(a), and could have achieved *superpriority* status. "A purchase money security interest in collateral other than inventory has priority over a conflicting security interest in the same collateral or its proceeds if the purchase money security interest is perfected at the time the debtor receives possession of the collateral or within thirty days thereafter." La. R.S. 10:9–312(4). Instead, Beckwith sold over $1.2 million in engines and equipment on an open-account basis.

JUDGMENT

For the foregoing reasons, we render the following judgment in response to the certified question:

A prior perfected Chapter 9 security interest created pursuant to La. R.S. 10:9–101 *et seq.* has priority over a nonpossessory materialman's privilege granted to a supplier of ship-building materials under La. Civ. Code art. 3237(8).

* * * * * *

NOTES AND QUESTIONS

1. As the case observes, the Louisiana Uniform Commercial Code contains non-uniform provisions ranking Chapter 9 security interests against privileges upon movable property. Among these was the originally enacted version of Section 9-201, quoted in the case. With skillful use of judicial legerdemain, the court effectively transformed the conjunction "and" into the disjunctive "or" in order to resolve the inconsistency that had existed within Chapter 9 as originally enacted.

2. Though Chapter 9 continues to have non-uniform provisions ranking security interests against privileges, the awkward internal consistencies were removed in its 2001 revision. Section 9-201 no longer makes specific references to creditors holding liens. Non-uniform Section 9-322(h) provides the general rule that a security interest has priority over a conflicting privilege except as otherwise provided in Chapter 9 or except when the statute creating the privilege expressly provides otherwise. Chapter 9 itself contains two provisions granting priority to privileges: Section 9-333, a substantively uniform provision giving priority to possessory liens securing payment or performance of an obligation for services or materials furnished with respect to goods when effectiveness of the privilege depends upon the person's possession of the goods, and Section 9-322(g), which is a non-uniform successor to former R.S. 9:4521, ranking security interests and privileges in crops.

3. Statutes giving complete or partial priority to privileges over security interests include R.S. 9:5001 (giving priority to an attorney's privilege over all security interests); and R.S. 9:4501 and 4502 (making repairmen's privileges subordinate to previously perfected security interests, thereby implying that they outrank later perfected security interests).

4. How does the artisan's privilege under La. Civ. Code Art. 3217(2) rank against Chapter 9 security interests?

5. As mentioned in the previous Chapter, a carrier's lien under La. R.S. 10:7-207 enjoys the priority accorded to possessory liens under Section 9-333, provided that the requirements of Section 7-207(b) are satisfied. The lien in favor of a warehouse under La. R.S. 10:7-209 is not entitled to the priority ordinarily granted to possessory liens under Section 9-333, because Section 7-209 "expressly provides otherwise" within the meaning of Section 9-333.

6. La. R.S. 9:4770 provides that vendor's privileges and lessor's privileges are subordinate to all Chapter 9 security interests, apparently even those that are unperfected. An important exception to this rule exists in the case of the lessor's privilege on crops, as discussed in the next section of this chapter.

3. Special Ranking Rules for Security Rights in Crops

***See* La. Rev. Stat. 10: 9-322(g)**

* * * * * *

DEPOSIT GUARANTY NATIONAL BANK
v.
CENTRAL LOUISIANA GRAIN CO-OP, INC.
737 So. 2d 167 (La. App. 3d Cir. 1999)

AMY, Judge.

The plaintiff bank filed a security agreement noticing third parties that it held a security interest in a corn crop. The defendant grain cooperative sold the crop to a third party and, from the proceeds, paid a harvester and hauler. The plaintiff filed suit asserting the defendant had converted these funds as the bank had filed a security agreement and the harvester and hauler had not filed notice of any privilege. The defendant maintained that there is no filing requirement for the privileges due to necessity and custom. The lower court found in favor of the defendant. The bank appeals. We reverse.

Factual and Procedural Background

The plaintiff, Deposit Guaranty National Bank (Bank), held a security interest, by way of a security agreement, in the 1996 corn crop of Laura Clement. This security interest included all products and proceeds of the crop. Furthermore, the bank recorded the requisite UCC-1F Effective Financing Statement with the West Carroll Parish Clerk of Court.

According to the stipulated facts submitted to the lower court in this matter, the defendant, Central Louisiana Grain Co-Op, Inc., stored and sold the secured corn crop. The instant matter arose when the defendant remitted the crop proceeds to the bank absent the harvest and hauling expenses paid to the individuals performing these functions. The parties' stipulated facts indicate that paying the expenses for harvesting, freight, or hauling from the proceeds of the crop was their customary practice in years past.

The plaintiff filed suit in September 1997, asserting that the defendant converted the harvesting/hauling funds as the bank's perfected security interest had been recorded, but any privileges of the harvester/hauler had not been filed. The matter was submitted to the lower court on stipulated facts in a jointly filed pre-trial statement. The statement was accompanied by memoranda from the parties. The lower court found in favor of the defendant concluding that any privilege of the hauler in this matter did not have to be filed in order to rank in priority above the perfected security interest of the bank.

The bank appeals assigning the following issues for review:

1. Is the appellant court bound by the findings of fact of the trial court?
2. Does Louisiana law require a thresherman/combineman to file an Effective Financing Statement as per La. R.S. 9:4521 and [La.] R.S. 3:3651 *et seq.* to perfect his lien in farm products to be given priority over a prior perfected security interest?

3. Does Louisiana law recognize a "hauler's privilege" for the payment of services of transporting the crop from the fields to the grain elevator and if so, is an Effective Financing Statement required to be filed as per La. R.S. 9:4521 and [La. R.S. 3:3651 *et seq.*, to perfect the same and to give said privilege a priority ranking over a prior perfected security interest in farm products?

Discussion

Findings of Fact

In its first assigned issue for review, the bank argues that the lower court's reasons demonstrate that the court found that the defendant, *itself,* harvested and transported the crop to its facilities thereby ranking the defendant as a privilege holder with priority. Contrary to this holding, the stipulated facts submitted to the lower court clearly indicate that the defendant stored and sold the crop and then paid the harvesting and hauling expenses to others.

Our review of the lower court's findings reveal no errors of fact requiring correction. As asserted by the bank, the stipulated facts, submitted by the parties jointly, clearly indicate that the defendant stored and sold the crop and then remitted harvest, hauling, and freight expenses to others. In the recitation of facts found in the lower court's reasons for judgment, the court states that the defendant "did disburse sums totaling $27,357.00 without consent or authorization of the plaintiff." Furthermore, the lower court found that "the funds were rightly disbursed as payment for services rendered which does not constitute conversion on the part of the defendant." In order to *disburse,* as found by the lower court, the defendant would obviously had to have had an outside party to whom the funds could be disbursed. Therefore, it is obvious the lower court recognized that the individual haulers and harvesters had been paid by the defendant. We find no meaningful error in the lower court's statement in summation wherein the court finds that "Defendant, Central La. Grain CO-OP falls within the ranks of those having first priority. Therefore, they are entitled to be paid first." Rather, it is obvious from a reading of the full text of the court's reasons that it is the privileges of the hauler and the harvester that are at issue.

We find this assignment to be without merit.

Filing of Financing Statement for Thresherman/Combineman

The bank argues that although Roger Clement, the harvester to whom funds were paid, did have a privilege in the corn crop proceeds, notice of the privilege was never filed with the Secretary of State through the local Clerk of Court. The bank contends La. R.S. 9:4521 clearly indicates that in order for a harvester's privilege to rank above the perfected security interest of the bank, notice of the privilege must have been properly filed. As no notice was filed in this matter, the bank argues that its own perfected security interest should have received priority over the harvester's privilege of Roger Clement.

The privilege of the harvester is created by virtue of La. R.S. 9:4523 which provides that "[t]hreshermen, combinemen and grain driers have a privilege for services rendered on the crop which they have threshed, combined or dried."

Essentially at issue in this assignment is the meaning of La. R.S. 9:4521 which ranks the priority of several specific privileges, including that of the harvester. La. R.S. 9:4521 provides as follows:

> As a specific exception to R.S. 9:4770 and R.S. 10:9-201, the following statutory privileges and perfected security interests as affecting unharvested crop shall be ranked in the following order of preference, provided that such privileges and security interests have been properly filed and maintained in accordance with the central registry provisions of R.S. 3:3651 *et seq.*:
>
> (1) Privilege of the laborer, the thresherman, combineman, grain drier, and the overseer.
>
> (2) Privilege of the lessor.
>
> (3) Perfected security interests under Chapter 9 of the Louisiana Commercial Laws in the order of filing, as provided by R.S. 3:3651 *et seq.*
>
> (4) Privilege of the furnisher of supplies and of money, of the furnisher of water, and of the physician.

Thus, the privilege of the harvester is given priority over a perfected security interest.

The bank asserts that the priority given to the harvester's privilege over the bank's perfected security interest is, according to the wording of the statute, effective *only* if the notice of the privilege "has been properly filed and maintained in accordance with the central registry provisions. . . ." The defendant contends that La. R.S. 9:4523, which creates the harvester's privilege, does not require that the privilege/lien be perfected. Rather, according to the defendant, such a reading of the statute is impractical and contrary to common practice.

In reasons for judgment, the lower court framed the issues before the court as follows:

> The issues before this court are: (1) whether or not it is required or even realistic to expect a hauler of crop and one involved in the harvesting of crop to file a perfected security interest on each agricultural product that they haul; (2) whether the funds in dispute were improperly disbursed by the defendant constituting a conversion on the part of the defendant.

In resolving these issues, the lower court first related the ranking of priorities found in La. R.S. 9:4521 and then found, in part:

> In the normal course of business a hauler is presumed to have a vested interest in the crop he hauls. Therefore, it does not appear practical nor is it customary for a hauler to place others on notice each and every time he transports a particular crop. It is the opinion of this court that the law does not intend to place such restraints upon regular commercial trading practices.

We agree with both the defendant and the lower court that requiring a harvester to file notice of the La. R.S. 9:4523 privilege appears contrary to both custom and conventional wisdom. Any perfected security interest in a crop, which is held by a bank, is worthless if the crop which it secures is not harvested. The crop, of course, will not be harvested if the harvester's payment is not assured. However, the law appears clear and such policy considerations are the province of the legislature. As urged by the defendant, La. R.S. 9:4523 does *not* indicate that notice of the harvester's privilege must be given. But, La. R.S. 9:4521 provides otherwise. The statute *clearly* states that the ranking of priorities, which places the "thresherman, combineman" above the holder of a perfected security interest, is applicable *"provided that such privileges and security interests have been properly filed and maintained. . . ."* (Emphasis added.) The privilege of Roger Clement, the harvester, was not filed.

Furthermore, in *Howard v. Stokes,* 607 So. 2d 868 (La. App. 2 Cir.1992), the second circuit reversed a judgment wherein a trial court ranked the privileges at issue as follows: 1) combineman's privilege, 2) lessor's privilege, 3) recorded crop pledge. The second circuit stated as follows with regard to the trial court's findings:

> In ranking the lessor's privilege and the combineman's privilege ahead of the recorded crop pledge, the trial court concluded that only a secured lender like Terrick, Inc., who had his security interest created in a written instrument, needed to file with the central registry in order to have his security interest ranked in the order of preference set forth in R.S. 9:4521. Because the law does not require the combineman's privilege or the lessor's privilege to be created in a written document, the trial court ranked these privileges ahead of the recorded crop pledge.

In so holding, the trial court overlooked pertinent provisions of Act 548 of 1989, effective August 22, 1989, prior to the 1990 crop year, which amended both the provisions of R.S. 3:3651, *et seq*. and R.S. 9:4521. Act 548 amended R.S. 3:3652(14) to define "security device" as a written instrument that established a creditor's security interest in farm products, or, *any pledge or privilege described in R.S. 9:4521, whether or not evidenced by a written instrument.* This change in the law made clear the legislature's intent for the term "security device" to include not only a written crop pledge established pursuant to the provisions of R.S. 9:4341, but also the privilege of the combineman and the privilege of the lessor, both of which are set forth in the provisions of R.S. 9:4521. Act 548 also added to R.S. 9:4521 the provisions concerning notice properly filed in accordance with R.S. 3:3651, *et seq*.

Further, Act 548 amended the provisions of R.S. 3:3656 to provide that the central registry would only accept and record written security devices accompanied by a related effective financing statement, *and effective financing statements alone for unwritten security devices described in R.S. 9:4521.* The changes to R.S. 3:3656 provided that only security interests as to which financing statements and written security devices were filed would be effective against third parties.

The definition of "security device" in effect at all pertinent times in this case included all three security interests at issue. Therefore, the trial court erred in reading the provisions of R.S. 9:4521 as applying only to the crop pledge. Because all three security interests were subject to the provisions of R.S. 9:4521 and R.S. 3:3651, *et seq.*, but only the crop pledge was recorded, only the pledge was effective against third parties and should be ranked first. Id. at 870.

We find the instant matter analogous. As only the bank's perfected security interest was recorded, it should have received priority in accordance with the rankings of La. R.S. 9:4521. We conclude that, under the facts presented here, the lower court erred in finding any privilege of the harvester ranked above the bank's security interest.

Hauler's Privilege

In this assignment of error, the bank argues that the lower court erred in finding the existence of a hauler's privilege. The bank maintains that no privilege is recognized in Louisiana law for the payment of services related to the transport of a crop from the field to the grain elevator. Furthermore, even if such a privilege exists argues the bank, the privilege must be recorded in order to receive priority over a perfected security interest according to La. R.S. 9:4521.

In the reasons for judgment, the lower court found as follows: "This court believes that the law did intend for a hauler to receive privileges in crop he hauls which would insure that he is paid with preference for his services." Although no statutory authority for such a privilege was provided by the lower court, the obvious wisdom of the lower court's finding is illustrated in the conclusion that crops which are not hauled from the field are worthless.

However, again, we are bound to apply the legislature's decision regarding the ranking of privileges.

Even if we were to find that a hauler's privilege has been specifically provided by statute, which we do not, this argument has been rendered moot by our above conclusion that any privilege enjoying priority over a perfected security interest must be filed per La. R.S. 9:4521. Therefore, we do not address this issue.

REVERSED AND RENDERED.

* * * * * *

NOTES AND QUESTIONS

1. If the harvester had filed an effective financing statement in the central agricultural registry, but only after the bank had already filed, which of them would have had priority under former La. R.S. 9:4521?

2. Would the case have been decided differently if the ranking rules of current R.S. 10:9-322(g) had been in effect at the time? Would it make a difference whether the harvester was an individual?

3. The court struggled to find the basis for a privilege in favor of the hauler, even though it agreed with "the obvious wisdom of the lower court's finding . . . that crops which are not hauled from the field are worthless." Can you cite a basis under the law for such a privilege?

* * * * * *

MEYHOEFFER

v.

WALLACE

792 So. 2d 851 (La. App. 2d Cir. 2001)

PEATROSS, J.

This appeal arises out of a dispute over the proceeds from the sale of crops grown in 1998 by farmer David Wallace on farm land located in Franklin Parish that Mr. Wallace leased from Dr. Klaus Meyhoeffer. Winnsboro State Bank & Trust Co., Inc. ("the Bank") had a security interest in the crops and crop proceeds granted to it by Mr. Wallace, under which it took possession of the entire 1998 crop proceeds. Dr. Meyhoeffer filed suit against Mr. Wallace and the Bank asserting his lessor's privilege and seeking the 1998 rental payment. The case was submitted on stipulated facts and the trial court held that the Bank's perfected security interest in the crop proceeds was superior to Mr. Meyhoeffer's lessor's privilege. Mr. Meyhoeffer's suit was, therefore, dismissed and he now appeals. For the reasons stated herein, we affirm.

FACTS

On January 27, 1993, David Wallace leased 530 acres of farm land in Franklin Parish from Dr. Klaus Meyhoeffer. The lease agreement stated the annual rental as "one-fifth (1/5th) of the [annual] crop or $32,000.00, whichever is greater." The lease was recorded in the conveyance records of Franklin Parish on January 31, 1995. In 1998, Mr. Wallace obtained a loan from the Bank, for which he granted a security interest in the crops and crop proceeds of the leased farm land. The Bank perfected its security interest by filing a financing statement (UCC 1F) in the Louisiana Agricultural Central Registry ("LACR"), as required by La. R.S. 3:3654. A UCC search revealed security interests in the crops (and proceeds therefrom), and various equipment belonging to Mr. Wallace, beginning with filings dated February 28, 1995, and continuing through February 17, 1998. The lease from Dr. Meyhoeffer was not filed in the LACR. When Mr. Wallace could not meet his obligation to the Bank and pay rent to Dr. Meyhoeffer in 1998, the Bank took possession of the proceeds from the 1998 crops and applied them to Mr. Wallace's debt.

ACTION OF THE TRIAL COURT

Dr. Meyhoeffer sued for 1998 rentals in the amount of $32,000, arguing that his lessor's privilege was superior to the Bank's security interest. The trial court disagreed and held that, since the Bank had taken the necessary steps to perfect its security interest in the crops and crop proceeds where Dr. Meyhoeffer had not (he did not file a financing statement or the lease in the LACR—only in the conveyance records of Franklin Parish), the Bank's interest in the property outranked Dr. Meyhoeffer's interest. Specifically, the trial court concluded that Dr. Meyhoeffer did not avail himself of the protection of La. R.S.

9:4521, which provides that the lessor's privilege outranks a perfected security interest only when the lessor's privilege is properly filed and maintained in accordance with the central registry provisions of La. R.S. 3:3651, *et seq*. As such, the trial court concluded that the Bank's perfected security interest outranked Dr. Meyhoeffer's lessor's privilege; and he was not, therefore, entitled to collect the rent for 1998 from the crop proceeds.

DISCUSSION

At the outset, we note that, in his petition, Dr. Meyhoeffer asserted a lessor's privilege on the "crops produced," and the proceeds therefrom, to secure payment of the rent. He further alleged that the Bank had constructive notice of the privilege and, therefore, should not have taken possession of the entire proceeds from the 1998 crops and should not have applied the entire crop proceeds to Mr. Wallace's loan. Nowhere in his petition did Dr. Meyhoeffer assert *ownership* of any portion or share of the crops or their proceeds.

After the trial court's ruling regarding the ranking of the interests, however, Dr. Meyhoeffer changed his argument for purposes of appeal, now asserting *ownership* of 1/5th of the crops under the lease. According to Dr. Meyhoeffer, since he retained ownership of 1/5th of the crops, Mr. Wallace did not have the authority to encumber this portion by granting a security interest in the same to the Bank and the Bank's retention of the proceeds from "his" 1/5th of the crops was improper. We acknowledge that this argument may have merit under certain circumstances; however, under the facts of this particular case and the terms of this particular lease agreement, as executed by the parties, we find Dr. Meyhoeffer's argument is without merit.

The lease

After careful examination of the lease, we conclude that Dr. Meyhoeffer did not retain ownership of 1/5th of the crops under the terms of the lease. First, the lease is the standard form Farmers Home Administration's ("FmHA") "Crop–Share Farm Lease." The standard provisions of the form lease seem to contemplate joint ownership of crops between lessor and lessee, as evidenced by sections B(7) and (8), which provide space for the parties to add agreements as to the buying and selling of "jointly owned property" and provide for the division of such jointly owned property on termination of the lease. The form lease also provides space for the parties to define the "place of sale or delivery" of a portion of the crops due lessor as rent under section D(1), regarding the sharing of costs and returns and, specifically, defining rental rates. It is not, however, the blank standard form lease we are called upon to examine.

In this case, we find that the parties intended for the rental on the farm land to be a cash sum rather than the physical "delivery" of 1/5th of the crops to Dr. Meyhoeffer as rent. We draw this conclusion from several provisions of the lease. First, in section B(7), which provides for the buying and selling of "jointly owned property," the parties have written in that "[t]enant sell at his choice." Second, in section B(8), regarding the division of jointly owned property on termination of the lease, the parties have written in "N/A," indicating that this section is not applicable to the parties' intentions or agreement. Third, in section D(1), where the rental rate is specified, the parties failed to provide a "place for sale or delivery" of any portion of the crops to the lessor, which indicates that the lessor did not intend to own or to ever take possession of any part of the crops. Finally, the rental rate itself states that the "[r]ent due after [h]arvest 1/5th (sic) or $32,000 whichever greatest." We believe that it was only "after harvest" that the lessee was obligated to pay rent and that, after the lessee exercised its right to harvest and after the crops were sold by lessee, the lessor was left with a claim for cash rent specified in the lease. Stated another way, we find that this agreement reveals that the parties intended that there be a cash payment to Dr. Meyhoeffer of at least $32,000 per year, to be made after the fall's harvest. In the event that 1/5th of the crop proceeds exceeded $32,000, Dr. Meyhoeffer was entitled to a cash payment of the value of 1/5th of the crop proceeds. If 1/5th of the crop proceeds was less than $32,000, Dr. Meyhoeffer was still entitled to $32,000 cash payment as rent. In this regard, we also find telling that, in his original petition, Dr. Meyhoeffer characterized the rental agreement between him and Mr. Wallace as follows:

> Under the terms of said lease, [Dr. Meyhoeffer] was entitled to rent in the amount of $32,000 at the very least, and in a greater amount if one-fifth ($^1/_5$) of the crops produced on the leased premises exceeded $32,000.

No provision of this lease contemplates physical possession or ownership of 1/5th of the crops by Dr. Meyhoeffer; and, according to the allegation in his petition, he intended to always receive a cash rent payment. Moreover, the practice of the parties supports this conclusion as well. Since the inception of this lease arrangement between Mr. Wallace and Dr. Meyhoeffer, the practice was that Mr. Wallace would sell the entirety of the crops (which the lease specifically authorizes him to do) and would then pay Dr. Meyhoeffer cash rent.

Dr. Meyhoeffer relies on three sources for support of his position that he retained ownership of 1/5th of the crops: section F(7)(b) of the lease; La. R.S. 9:3204; and *Guaranty Bank and Trust Company of Alexandria v. Daniels,* 399 So. 2d 790 (La. App. 3d Cir. 1981). First, section F(7)(b) of the lease provides as follows:

> Landlord subordination.—In consideration of loan(s) to be made by the Farmers Home Administration (FmHA) the landlord hereby subordinates in favor of the FmHA any lien the landlord now has or may acquire in or on: . . . (b) the crops, livestock increase and livestock products of the tenant (*except a lien on such property produced in any year for that year's rent*); . . . (Emphasis ours.)

Dr. Meyhoeffer argues that this provision, in which the lessor refuses to subordinate his lien on crop proceeds produced for rent, indicates that the lessee does not have the right to encumber that portion of the crops or proceeds. The fatal flaw in this logic, however, is that, if the lessor retains *ownership* of 1/5th of the crops, then the lessor would not have a lien on the crops to subordinate—he would own them. It is axiomatic that one does not have a lien on something one owns. To the contrary, we read this provision to apply to cases such as this, where the lessor does not retain ownership of the crops, but, rather, has a lien on the proceeds for the payment of rent. In this particular case, the lessor was not the only party with a security interest in the proceeds, hence, the ranking issue, which will be addressed later in this opinion. In summary, we find no support for Dr. Meyhoeffer's position in section F(7), or any other section, of this lease.

Second, in light of our conclusion regarding ownership of the crops, we find La. R.S. 9:3204 inapplicable to this case. That statute provides:

3204. Lessor's part of crop considered his property; disposition penalty.

In a lease of land for part of the crop, that part which the lessor is to receive is considered at all times the property of the lessor.

The lessee or any person acting with his consent who sells or disposes of the part of the crop belonging to the lessor shall be fined not more than one thousand dollars, or imprisoned for not more than one year, or both.

By its terms, 9:3204 applies to leases wherein a part of the crop is to be "received" by the lessor. As discussed above, the lease in the case *sub judice,* does not so provide, nor has such been the practice of the parties. We find, therefore, that the protection of 9:3204 is not available to Dr. Meyhoeffer.

We reach a similar conclusion regarding Dr. Meyhoeffer's reliance on *Guaranty Bank v. Daniels,* supra. In that case, the bank sued the tenant farmer under certain promissory notes secured by a pledge of crops. The landowners intervened and the court ultimately found that the tenant farmer did not have authority to pledge the crops because the lease made it clear that the landowners retained ownership of a portion of the crops. The rental rate under the lease read as follows: "LESSEE agrees to pay LESSOR a total rental of Twenty-five (25%) of all the crop or $150,000 whichever is more." Significantly, however, the lease in *Guaranty Bank v. Daniels* also had other provisions which indicated the landowners' retention of ownership, such as an agreement that the lessee could not in any way encumber or place a crop lien on the 25% of the "crop due LESSOR" and that lessor could sell his 25% at any time. As previously discussed, there are no similar provisions in the lease before us; and, therefore, we find *Guaranty Bank v. Daniels* to be clearly distinguishable from the present case.

As such, we find that Mr. Wallace owned all of 1998 crops and had the authority to sell and/or encumber all of the crops. We have already noted that the lease expressly gave Mr. Wallace the authority to sell the crops, as was his practice for all previous crop years. Further authority is found in the civil code in La. C.C. art. 474, Movables by anticipation, which provides as follows:

> Unharvested crops and ungathered fruit of trees are movables by anticipation when they belong to a person other than the landowner. When encumbered with security rights of third persons, they are movables by anticipation insofar as the creditor is concerned.

The landowner may, by act translative of ownership or by pledge, mobilize by anticipation unharvested crops and ungathered fruits of trees that belong to him.

Under this article, the 1998 crops were movables by anticipation which Mr. Wallace, as owner of the crops, was entitled to encumber. In addition, the crops were movables by anticipation insofar as the Bank was concerned once Mr. Wallace granted the Bank a security interest in the crops.

Notwithstanding our conclusion that Dr. Meyhoeffer did not retain ownership of 1/5th of the crops or the proceeds therefrom, we agree with him and the trial court that he did, however, enjoy a statutory lessor's privilege on the same. Our conclusions thus far, therefore, are (1) Dr. Meyhoeffer did not retain ownership of 1/5th of the crops or proceeds, but did enjoy a statutory privilege on the same and (2) Mr. Wallace had the authority to sell and encumber all of the 1998 crops. We will now address the trial court's conclusion regarding the ranking of Dr. Meyhoeffer's lessor's privilege and the Bank's perfected security interest in the crop proceeds.

Lessor's privilege and ranking of interests

The dispute in the case *sub judice* is over 1/5th of the cash proceeds from the sale of the 1998 crops and not the actual crops. In 1998, consistent with his usual practice, Mr. Wallace harvested and sold the crops. Thereafter, the Bank seized the proceeds of the crops and applied them to Mr. Wallace's indebtedness. La. C.C. art. 3217(3) establishes a lessor's privilege on "the crops of the year" for "[t]he rents of immovables," which clearly gave Dr. Meyhoeffer a lessor's privilege on the crops for payment of rent due. Further, La. C.C. art. 3218 elevates that privilege to a right, allowing the lessor to seize and detain the crops until the lessor is paid. Article 3218, Lessor's privilege, nature and extent, provides:

> The right which the lessor has over the products of the estate, and on the movables which are found on the place leased, for his rent, is of a higher nature than mere privilege. The latter is only enforced on the price arising from the sale of movables to which it applies. It does not enable the creditor to take or keep the effects themselves specially. The lessor, on the contrary may take the effects themselves and retain them until he is paid.

Louisiana law provides that the lessor must exercise his privilege while the crops are still on the lessee's premises or within 15 days after they have been removed from the premises, provided the crops still remain in the lessee's possession. La. C.C. art. 2709; *Carroll v. Bancker,* 43 La. Ann. 1078, 43 La. Ann. 1194, 10 So. 187 (La. 1891); *Bayou Pierre Farms v. Bat Farms Partners, III,* 95–1669 (La. App. 3d Cir. 5/29/96), 676 So. 2d 643, *aff'd,* 96–2826 (La. 5/20/97), 693 So. 2d 1158. We cannot discern from the record before us the exact dates of harvest and sale of the crops or the date on which Dr. Meyhoeffer made demand for the 1998 rent. In any event, we find that, since Dr. Meyhoeffer did not assert his privilege by seizing the unharvested or harvested crops within the required 15 days, his lessor's privilege over the *crops* was lost.

Assuming arguendo, without specifically deciding, that Dr. Meyhoeffer enjoyed a privilege on the *proceeds* of the sale of the 1998 crops which survived his failure to timely assert his right of pledge and detention over the *physical crops,* we agree with the trial court that the only means by which Dr. Meyhoeffer could have had a viable claim for the 1998 rent was if he had complied with the filing requirements of La. R.S. 9:4521. Filing would, in effect, have rendered him a secured party with a perfected security interest in the crop proceeds. *See Bayou Pierre Farms v. Bat Farms Partners, III,* supra. The issue presented in such situation would be whether Dr. Meyhoeffer's right in the proceeds of the crops outranked the Bank's security interest in the same.

Recall that the lease was recorded in the conveyance records of Franklin Parish, but was not filed in the LACR. The Bank argues that, since it is undisputed that Dr. Meyhoeffer did not take the necessary steps required for his lessor's privilege to outrank the Bank's security interest, the trial court was correct in ruling that the Bank's security interest was superior. We agree.

La. R.S. 9:4521, Rank of privileges and security interests in crops, provides as follows:

> As a specific exception to R.S. 9:4770 and R.S. 10:9–201, the following statutory privileges and perfected security interests as affecting unharvested crops shall be ranked in the following order of preference, provided that such privileges and security interests have been properly filed and maintained in accordance with the central registry provisions of R.S. 3:3651 *et seq.*:
>
> (1) Privilege of the laborer, the thresherman, combineman, grain drier, and the overseer.
>
> (2) Privilege of the lessor.
>
> (3) Perfected security interests under Chapter 9 of the Louisiana Commercial Laws in the order of filing, as provided by R.S. 3:3651 *et seq.*
>
> (4) Privilege of the furnisher of supplies and of money, of the furnisher of water, and of the physician.

The statute expressly provides that the lessor's privilege is superior to a Chapter 9 security interest, "provided that such privilege . . . ha[s] been properly filed and maintained in accordance with the central registry provisions of R.S. 3:3651 *et seq.*" In other words, to enjoy the superior ranking provided by 9:4521, Dr. Meyhoeffer had to have filed his lessor's privilege in the LACR; and it is undisputed that Dr. Meyhoeffer did not do so. Accord *Henry v. Pioneer Sweet Potato Co., Inc.,* 614 So. 2d 853 (La. App. 2d Cir. 1993); *Howard v. Stokes,* 607 So. 2d 868 (La. App. 2d Cir. 1992). It is also undisputed that the Bank properly perfected its security interest by so filing. Again, if Dr. Meyhoeffer retained a privilege over the proceeds in this case, we see no error in the trial court's conclusion that the Bank's perfected security interest would outrank that lessor's privilege.

* * * * * *

NOTES AND QUESTIONS

1. La. R.S. 9:3204, upon which the lessor attempted to rely in claiming ownership of a portion of the crop, is now supplemented by La. Civ. Code Art. 2677, which provides that, where the parties agree that the rent will consist of a

portion of the crops, that portion is considered at all times the property of the lessor.

2. Do you find the rationale by which the court distinguished *Guaranty Bank and Trust Company of Alexandria v. Daniels*, 399 So. 2d 790 (La. App. 3d Cir. 1981), to be persuasive?

3. Observing that the lessor's privilege is lost 15 days after the movable subject to the privilege is removed from the leased property, the court noted, but did not decide, the issue of whether the lessor's privilege extends to *proceeds* of the crops. Though Civil Code Article 3217(3) does not expressly mention proceeds, the courts have nonetheless given the lessor the right to pursue proceeds of crops, primarily on the basis of Article 2705 (1870) (*see now* Article 2707), granting the lessor a privilege on "the fruits produced during the lease of the land." *See Carroll v. Bancker*, 10 So. 187 (La. 1891); and *Vento v. Amici*, 159 So. 751 (La. App. 1st Cir. 1935).

4. As the case demonstrates, a lessor's privilege upon crops enjoys much more favorable treatment than a lessor's privilege upon other types of property, for the former outranks competing security interests provided that the lessor makes a filing in the central agricultural registry. *See now* R.S. 10:9-322(g); R.S. 9:4770. Would the result of the case have been altered if the lessor had filed a financing statement in the central agricultural registry after the filing of a financing statement in the bank's favor but before judgment was rendered against him?

5. The comprehensive revision in 2001 of Chapter 9 of the Louisiana Uniform Commercial Code occurred after the case was decided. Among other things, the revision brought agricultural liens, such as the lessor's privilege, within the ambit of Chapter 9. If a lessee who farms leased property in Louisiana is located in Mississippi, where must a financing statement be filed to perfect a security interest in the lessee's Louisiana crops? Where must a financing statement be filed to perfect a lessor's privilege upon the crops? *Cf.* La. R.S. 10:9-301(1) *with* La. R.S. 10:9-302.

6. In 2010, La. R.S. 9:4521 was repealed and replaced by a non-uniform provision of the Louisiana Uniform Commercial Code, La. R.S. 10:9-322(g). How does the new statute change the ranking of the lessor's privilege?

7. The court notes that the unharvested crops belonging to the lessee were movables by anticipation under La. Civ. Code Art. 474. Suppose that a mortgagee holding a mortgage upon the land had seized the land, including the crops, before they were harvested. Would the mortgage attach to the lessee's crops? Would it matter whether the lease was recorded? Would it matter whether the lease was recorded before or after the mortgage? *See Porche v. Bodin*, 28. La. Ann. 761 (1876), holding that a foreclosure upon a mortgage recorded before an agricultural lessee's lease did not divest the lessee of his crops, which "in no sense form[ed] part of the immovable." Id. at 763.

8. In a contest between a mortgagee and a lender holding a perfected security interest in growing crops, who would prevail? Would it matter whether the crops belonged to the mortgagor/landowner or to a lessee? *See* La. R.S. 10:9-334(i), providing that a perfected security interest in crops (but not an agricultural lien) ranks ahead of mortgages if the debtor has an interest of record in the real estate.

C. Ranking of Privileges Over Immovables

1. The Ranking of General Privileges Among Themselves

***See* La. Civ. Code arts. 3254**

* * * * * *

SUCCESSION OF CAMPBELL
40 So. 449 (La. 1906).

LAND, J.

It appears that Lewis Campbell died in the year 1904 in the parish of Vermillion, leaving a small estate and a widow and minor children in necessitous circumstances.

The succession was insolvent. The administrator filed a tableau of distribution, proposing to pay taxes, expenses of selling the property, and law charges, aggregating $267.23, and then to apply the remainder of the funds in his hands amounting to $771.02 to the payment of the homestead claim of the widow and minor heirs of the deceased. A claim of $193.50 for medical services during last illness was allowed and classed on the tableau as inferior in rank to the claim of the widow and minors. The physician filed an opposition to said tableau, alleging that his privilege was superior in rank to that of the widow and minors. There was judgment homologating the tableau as filed, and the opponent appealed to the Court of Appeal for the parish of Vermilion.

Upon the case as stated the judges of the Court of Appeal, finding a decided conflict in the jurisprudence of this state, have certified to us the following question, to wit:

> "Which should be paid by preference, the homestead claim of the widow and minors as carried on the tableau, or the claim of the physician for service rendered the deceased during his last illness?"

We are indebted to the district judge for his very thorough and able review of the legislation and jurisprudence on the subject-matter submitted to us for determination.

The act of March 17, 1852, provided that, whenever the widow and minor children of a deceased person should be left in necessitous circumstances, they should be entitled to demand and receive from the succession a sum which added to the amount of property owned by them or either of them in their own right would make up the sum of $1,000, said amount to be paid "in preference to all other debts, except those for the vendor's privilege and expenses incurred in selling the property." Laws 1852, p. 171, No. 255.

This act was embodied substantially in article 3252 of the Revised Civil Code of 1870, treating of privileges on movable and immovable; and article 3254, treating of the order in which general privileges are to be paid, was amended by adding the following paragraph, to wit:

> "The thousand dollars secured by law to the widow or minor children, as set forth in article 3252, shall be paid in preference to all other debts, except those for the vendor's privileges and expenses incurred in selling the property."

The words "all other debts" are in themselves broad enough to cover the "debts" which the article declares shall be paid in a certain order of preference, and their application to privilege debts is shown by the exception of vendor's privileges and expenses of sale. To hold that the words "all other debts" do not include the "debts" specified in article 3254 would be to subordinate the claim of the widow and minors, not only to funeral expenses, law charges, and expenses of last illness, but to "wages of servants," "supplies of provisions," and "salaries of clerks, secretaries, and others of that nature." And as special privileges as a general rule, prime general privileges, the claim of the widow and minors would be, under such a construction, reduced to a mere priority over ordinary creditors.

It seems evident that the words "all other debts" include all privileged debts or none at all. That all such debts were intended is shown by the special exception of two classes of privileged debts. The general rule must necessarily include things of the same class as those.

In no other cases has the precise issue now before the court been considered, but in a number of cases the court has announced the general doctrine that the widow's claim outranks all privileges, except that of the vendor and the expenses of selling the thing. *Quertier & Co. v. Hille*, 21 La. Ann. 429; *Succession of Heitzler*, 25 La. Ann. 116; *Durac v. Ferrari*, 26 La. Ann. 116; *Succession of Rawls*, 27 La. Ann. 560. In *Succession of Neguelona*, 52 La. Ann. 1500, 27 South. 964, the court, in discussing the rank of the vendor's privilege on immovables, said that the claim of the necessitous widow "is to be paid in preference to all other debts—those of the succession, as well as those of the deceased—except those for the vendor's privilege and expenses incurred in selling the property." In a recent case decided by this court the claim of the widow was ordered "to be paid out of the succession funds in preference to all other debts, except those for the vendor's privilege and the expenses of selling the property." *Succession of Duplain*, 113 La. 786, 37 South. 755. And in one more recent the distribution was made on the same basis of preference. *Succession of Peters*, 114 La. 952, 38 South. 690.

The confusion and conflict in our jurisprudence on this subject has arisen from the failure to recognize and enforce the plain meaning of the statute. To subordinate the claim of the necessitous widow, not only to funeral expenses, but to expenses of last illness and law charges, would in many cases throw her and her children penniless on the cold charity of the world, and thereby defeat the very object of the statute. Where the law makes no exception, courts should make none, and when the words of the law are clear and free from all ambiguity "the letter of it should not be disregarded under the pretext of pursuing its spirit." Civ. Code, art. 13.

We therefore hold that the claim of the necessitous widow is superior in rank to the claim of the physician for services rendered to the deceased during his last illness, and so instruct the judges of the Court of Appeal.

* * * * * *

NOTES AND QUESTIONS

1. The ranking of general privileges among themselves usually presents little difficulty, for they are expressly ranked by the text of Civil Code article 3254. However, the privilege of the surviving spouse, which as we have seen was not initially included among the general privileges of the Civil Code, has a special ranking rule in Civil Code articles 3252 and 3254.

2. *Succession of Campbell* holds that the words "all other debts" in Civil Code article 3254 includes both privileged and unprivileged debts. In 1918, several years after the case was decided, Article 3252 (but not Article 3254) was amended to make the privilege of the surviving spouse inferior to all conventional mortgages. As will be seen in a later section of this chapter, the general privileges of the Civil Code are ordinarily superior to all mortgages, conventional or otherwise. Does the 1918 amendment present any difficulty in ranking where a conventional mortgage, a privilege of the surviving spouse and some other general privilege are involved?

3. Civil Code Article 3254 ranks funeral expenses ahead of law charges, without differentiation between law charges incurred to sell the thing that generates the proceeds in question and other kinds of law charges. Should the privilege for funeral charges have priority over the law charges that are incurred in making the very sale that generates the proceeds that are available for disbursement to privileged creditors? On this point, *see* Joseph Dainow, *Ranking Problems of Chattel Mortgages and Civil Code Privileges in Louisiana Law*, 13 La. L. Rev. 537, 550 (1953): "It would thus appear that for ranking purposes the law charges consist of at least three groups, of which the costs indispensable to the liquidation of the assets are given the highest priority. No creditor at all can obtain his preferential payment until the debtor's property is transformed into money, so these costs are necessarily paid first of all, possibly even ahead of funeral expenses. The specific ranking provisions of the code expressly place funeral charges, ahead of law charges, but this may have to be taken to mean those law charges which were not incurred in the sale of the property. Otherwise, the officers of the court could refuse to incur the expense if it would be tantamount to their having to pay the funeral charges. On the other hand, the Louisiana codifiers, both in the 1808 and 1825 Civil Codes, reversed the order of the French Civil Code, which ranks all law charges ahead of funeral charges; and it may be that they really intended to rank funeral charges ahead of all law charges just as they stated in Articles 3191 and 3254."

2. The Ranking of General Privileges Against Special Privileges

***See* La. Civ. Code arts. 3267**

The ranking of general privileges against special privileges on an immovable is governed by Civil Code Article 3267, the meaning of which is obscured by two unfortunate drafting errors. The first few words contained in the article give the impression that the article is designed to rank the vendor's privilege on *movables* against other privileges; however, when the entire article is read, it is readily apparent that the word *movables* at the beginning of the article must have been used by mistake where *immovable* was actually intended. If the article were applied as written, then the vendor's privilege on movables would be ranked quite unnecessarily against general privileges on immovables. This article was not borrowed from the Code Napoléon, and for that reason, the error cannot be laid to a fault in translation. Both the French and English versions of the 1825 Code, which introduced the article, contained the same error. If this error is corrected in the interpretation of the article, its meaning is that special privileges on immovables, including the vendor's privilege, outrank general privileges other than those for fixing seals, making inventories, and law charges for things necessary to procure the sale of the thing subject to the specil privilege.

Professor Dainow wrote an entire article dedicated solely to the proof that the word *movables* in Article 3267 should be *immovables*. *See* Joseph Dainow, *Art. 3267 and the Ranking of Privileges*, 9 La. L. Rev. 370 (1949), excerpts from which appear above. He observes that, at the time of his writing, there was not a single decision predicated upon the application of the article to a vendor's privilege on movables. No such case appears to have arisen in the many decades since the time of his writing.

The English version of the article also contains an unrelated, though perhaps benign, error in translation from the French version of the 1825 Code: "privileged debts" should be "privileged creditors."

* * * * * *

MARSH

v.

HIS CREDITORS

11 La. Ann. 469 (1856)

LEA, J.

The question to be determined in this case is "What are the expenses which immovables subject to the vendor's privilege must contribute, under Article No. 3234 of the Civil Code where the remaining assets are insufficient to pay costs." The Article referred to provides that the vendor shall be paid from the price of the object affected in their favor in preference to other privileged debts of the debtor, even funeral charges, except the charges for affixing seals, making inventories, and others which may have been necessary to *procure the sale of the thing*. In this case the issue between the parties is what charges were necessary to "procure the sale of the thing." On the one hand it is contended that this claim embraces all the charges of the administration by the syndic, and on the other, that its application is to be restricted to those charges without which the sale could not have taken place. We think this latter construction most in accordance with the letter of the Article and the decisions interpreting it. We adopt, however, the ruling of our predecessors in the case of *Monrose* v. *His Creditors*, 2d Rob. 281, which includes the syndic's commissions upon the property sold as an expense of the administration resulting to the benefit of the vendor. It is conceded that the sheriff's, clerk's, notary's and appraisers' fees were necessary charges in procuring the sale, and as to these charges we consider the opposition withdrawn. It is, therefore, unnecessary for this court to pass upon their validity. To these we think the syndic's commission should be added, for the reasons before stated. Neither the fees of the counsel for the insolvent, nor of the syndic (far less that of the attorney of absent creditors) constitute a charge without which the sale could not have taken place. For a construction of an analogous Article of the Civil Code *see Garretson v. His Creditors*, 1st Robinson, 446, also Civil Code, 3223.

It is ordered that the judgment appealed from be reversed, that the opponent be placed on the tableau as a creditor in the sum of $3,335, with privilege upon the proceeds of the property referred to in his opposition above all others, except the fees of the sheriff, clerk, appraisers, notary, and the commissions of the syndic, and that in other respects the judgment be affirmed. It is further ordered that the costs of this appeal be paid by the appellee.

* * * * * *

NOTES AND QUESTIONS

1. The case construes Article 3234 of the 1825 Civil Code, the precursor of Article 3267 of the 1870 Civil Code.

2. Why does Civil Code article 3267 state expressly that the vendor's privilege outranks "even funeral charges"? Recall that, under Article 3254, the privilege for funeral charges primes that for law charges. Article 3267 makes the vendor's privilege superior to the former but inferior to at least some of the latter.

3. The Ranking of Special Privileges Among Themselves

The only two categories of special privileges upon immovables established under the Civil Code are vendor's privileges and the various construction privileges granted to architects, contractors, subcontractors, suppliers, laborers, and others under Civil Code Articles 2772 and 3249. As discussed in the following chapter, the construction privileges were ranked concurrently among themselves under Article 3272, but were not directly ranked against vendor's privileges. Instead, Article 3268 prescribed an appraisement procedure to divide the proceeds of the immovable between the vendor and those holding construction privileges. Those provisions, however, have now been superseded by the Private Works Act, which ranks privileges arising under its provisions against vendor's privileges, other privileges, and mortgages. Those ranking rules are considered in the following chapter.

The ranking of one vendor's privilege against another is governed by Civil Code Article 3251, which provides that they rank in the order in which the sales giving rise to them occurred. This is not at all surprising, given that, in the case of successive sales, the creditor with the later arising vendor's privilege is often the obligor who owes the unpaid price secured by the previous vendor's privilege, and he could certainly not be expected to outrank his own creditor.

Special privileges created by statute upon immovables are almost always subjected to their own ranking rules contained in the statute creating them. Usually, the special privilege is given the ranking of a mortgage: It outranks encumbrances that become effective against third persons after the special privilege is recorded but is subject to all encumbrances that were already effective against third persons at the time the privilege is recorded. *See, e.g.,* La. R.S. 9:1123.115(C), making a condominium association's privilege inferior to privileges and mortgages recorded against a condominium unit before recordation of the statement of its privilege. This is not, however, always the case. *See, e.g.,* La. R.S. 9:2781.1 and 2781.2, which create special privileges in favor of real estate brokers and appraisers but make these privileges inferior to all other validly recorded privileges and mortgage, whether recorded before or after notice of the broker's or appraiser's privilege.

4. The Ranking of Privileges Against Mortgages

i. In General

***See* La. Civ. Code arts. 3186; 3274**

As a general rule, the Civil Code provides that all privileges on immovables outrank all mortgages, irrespective of order of recordation. Article 3186 of the Louisiana Civil Code itself provides this rule of priority in the very definition of privilege. However, this general rule is subject to so many exceptions that it remains useful only as a point of departure in the analysis of a ranking problem. Even where the general rule applies to give a privilege priority over a mortgage, the privilege will enjoy this priority in most cases only if the act evidencing the privilege is filed for registry within a prescribed number of days, as required by Article 3274. If the act evidencing the privilege is not timely filed, the privileged creditor still holds a privilege, but that privilege takes its rank against mortgages from the date that the privilege is filed and loses its priority over previously recorded mortgages. As we have seen, however, some general privileges are excused from the requirement of recordation, and in those cases Article 3274 does not apply.

* * * * * *

BAUMAN
v.
ARMBRUSTER
55 So. 760 (La. 1911)

LAND, J.

J. G. Roche & Sons, undertakers, obtained judgment in solido against the succession of Grace Eggleston and F. W. Armbruster, her universal legatee, who had been sent into possession under an ex parte order of the court, for the sum of $326, with recognition of privilege for funeral expenses on all the property of the succession.

While said suit was pending, C. S. Bauman sued out executory process against all the real estate of the succession under a special mortgage executed by the decedent about a year prior to her death. The property was sold at sheriff's sale for $4,400, leaving a balance of some $1,100 due the mortgage creditor.

The sheriff, finding on the records the registry of several privileges against the property, among them the notice of suit and judgment of Roche & Sons, deposited the proceeds of the sale in the registry of the court, and cited the mortgage and privileged creditors to assert their respective claims against the fund. In the ensuing concursus, judgment was rendered in favor of Roche & Sons for $200. On appeal, the Court of Appeal increased said amount to $326, with legal interest thereon from judicial demand. The case is before us on a writ of review.

Mrs. Eggleston died February 9, 1909, and her will was probated one week later, and F. W. Armbruster was confirmed and qualified as executor. The inventory showed real estate appraised at $6,000 and movables at $2,499.60, including three rings, valued at $405, which were claimed by the universal legatee.

On February 26, 1909, the universal legatee, by a decree of the court, was sent into possession of all the property of the estate, after payment of the inheritance tax due thereon.

On March 9, 1909, Roche & Sons sued Armbruster and the succession to recover $640 for funeral expenses. This litigation continued until June, 1910, with the result above stated.

In May, 1910, Carl S. Bauman sued out executory process on the mortgage note held by him, and in due course the property was sold as above stated.

It appears that, on the day of the death of Mrs. Eggleston, the public administrator filed an application for the administration of her estate, and Roche & Sons took charge of the body of the deceased and rendered the usual funeral services. Roche & Sons took no steps to secure the payment of their claim until several weeks after Armbruster had been discharged as executor and sent into possession as universal legatee. Armbruster subsequently disposed of all the movables of the succession, on which Roche & Sons had a privilege for funeral expenses. Roche & Sons, now seek payment by preference out of the proceeds of the real estate specially mortgaged to Carl S. Bauman.

Funeral charges rank *first* among the general privileges on movables. Civ. Code, art. 3252. If the movables are insufficient, such charges ought to be paid out of the product of the immovables belonging to the debtor in preference to all other privileged and mortgage creditors. Civ. Code, art. 3289. Funeral charges and other claims originating after the death of the *de cujus* are not required to be recorded. Civ. Code, art. 3276. Article 186 of the Constitution of 1898, in declaring that no mortgage or privilege on immovable property shall affect third persons unless duly recorded, simply repeats the provisions of the Civil Code, and adds to the list of exceptions contained in article 3276 privileges for "expenses of last illness" and privileges "for taxes." In other words, article 186 of the Constitution places such privileges on the same plane as claims originating *after the death* of the *de cujus,* which the Civil Code has never required to be recorded, "since registry is without effect, after decease." *Succession of Elliot*, 31 La. Ann. 37.

The ex parte order sending the universal legatee into possession did not deprive Roche & Sons of their right as creditors to demand security or exact an administration of the succession, during three months from the date of such order. In other words, the succession was not closed by the ex parte order. *Succession of Hart*, 52 La. Ann. 364, 27 South. 69.

Roche & Sons, however, did not demand security of the executor or universal legatee, but limited their demands to a judgment against the succession and the universal legatee on his assumption of the debts thereof, with recognition of privilege on all the movables and immovables of the estate. Roche & Sons could have compelled the executor to give security. Civ. Code, art. 1677. They could also have required the universal legatee to give security. Civ. Code, art. 1012. They could also have sequestered the property, or enjoined the legatee from disposing of the same.

It is admitted that Roche & Sons were present in the parish of Orleans at the time of the sale of the movables belonging to the succession at public auction at the instance of the universal legatee, and made no objection thereto. thereto.

When the succession was opened, the movables were more than sufficient to pay Roche & Sons and all other creditors having a general privilege thereon. Under Civ. Code, art. 3269, Roche & Sons were bound to exhaust the movables before seeking payment out of the product of the immovables. The alleged insufficiency of the movables to pay the claim of Roche & Sons resulted from their failure to take the proper legal steps to enforce their privilege against the property. They had the legal right to demand an administration and security, or security of the universal legatee. They did neither, but sued the universal legatee on his assumpsit of the debts of the succession.

Roche & Sons, through their neglect having lost their recourse on a fund specially appropriated by law to the payment of their claim, and which was more than sufficient for such purpose, cannot be permitted to recoup their loss at the expense of the creditor holding a special mortgage on the immovables of the succession. Our learned Brothers of the Court of Appeal erred in holding that no duty rested on Roche & Sons to discuss and exhaust the movables of the succession. Their claim of privilege on the immovables is predicated on the *insufficiency* of the movables to satisfy their debt. Hence Roche & Sons bear the burden of showing that they could not have obtained payment out of the movables of the succession. This they have failed to do. . . .

In the case at bar the law pointed out the movables of the succession for discussion by Roche & Sons, before calling on the special mortgage creditor for contribution, and, if they have lost their recourse on said property by their remissness in commencing proceedings, they must bear the loss.

It is therefore ordered that the judgments of the Court of Appeal and of the district court be reversed, and it is now ordered that the fund in dispute be paid to Carl S. Bauman, and that Roche & Sons pay costs in all courts.

* * * * * *

NOTES AND QUESTIONS

1. The privilege for funeral charges embraces movables and immovables alike and is paid before the other general privileges. La. Civ. Code Art. 3191, 3252 and 3254. However, the law provides that those general privileges bearing upon both movables and immovables are to be satisfied first from the debtor's

movables. The case holds that an insufficiency of movables to discharge the undertaker's general privilege for funeral charges resulting from his own failure to take proper steps to enforce his privilege against the movables before they were alienated from the succession caused him to lose his right of privilege against the succession's immovables. For a more recent case to the same effect, *see Homeowner's Loan Corporation v. Succession of Brooks*, 180 So. 170 (La. App. 2d Cir. 1938).

2. Planiol is also of the view that a general privilege holder who is tardy in pressing his claim against the debtor's movables loses his right of preference over mortgages upon the immovables. *See* 2 Marcel Planiol & Georges Ripert, *Traité Élémentaire de Droit Civil*, pt. 2 (La. State Law Inst. trans., 1959) (12th ed. 1939)(Fr.), Nos. 2632-33.

3. At Roman law, mortgages were preferred to privileges; this was reversed with the adoption of the Code Napoléon. Can you articulate a policy reason for this reversal based upon the disparity in the relative amounts that each secures?

4. Funeral charges, like most general privileges, ordinarily have priority over previously recorded mortgages on immovable property. However, under the Uniform Commercial Code, a security interest primes most privileges, including the general privilege for funeral charges. Does this make good policy sense, particularly in view of the rule that general privileges are supposed to be satisfied first from the decedent's movables?

ii. The Rule of the Least Ancient Mortgage

* * * * * *

DEVRON

v.

HIS CREDITORS

11 La. Ann. 482 (1856)

MERRICK, C. J. (SPOFFORD, J., and LEA, J., dissenting.)

Eugene Rochereau & Co. appeal from a judgment homologating a tableau of distribution.

They are mortgaged creditors, and complain of the judgment on the following grounds, viz:

[Their] objection is, that the division of the privileges among the mortgage creditors, and charging them therewith *pro rata* is in direct opposition to the principles of the law of mortgages embodied in the Code. In support of this proposition the appellant cites Article 3236 of the Civil Code, and insists that the court ought to have charged the privileges against the proceeds of the property in the order in which it was mortgaged beginning with the *least* ancient and ascending in this order, so that the younger mortgages should be compelled to bear the loss, and not compel the older ones to bear any portion of the same.

To this it is replied, that the opponents are made to contribute to the privileged expenses by virtue of Art. 3236 C. C.; that the second paragraph of the Article speaks of the *creditor* who is to bear the loss, showing clearly its application or reference exclusively to different special mortgages on the same property; whereas, the first paragraph containing the rule of the law has invariably been construed to mean that it is not the *creditor* holding the mortgage, but the *property* on which the mortgage exists which is liable to the contribution. In support of this position counsel for appellees cite 5 M. 469, 6 M. 520; 10 L. R. 554, 18 L. R. 372; and 6 Rob. 268.

It may be remarked in regard to the first two of the authorities cited, that they were decided under the old Code, the provisions of which are not the same as the Code of 1825. In regard to the more recent cases the attention of the court does not appear to have been directed to Articles 3236 and 3237, which seem to us to be provisions directly in point. They read as follows:

"Art. 3236. With the exception of special privileges which exist on immovables in favor of the vendor, of workmen and the furnisher of materials, as declared above, the debts privileged on the movables and immovables generally, ought to be paid, if the movables are insufficient, out of the product of the immovables, and slaves belonging to the debtor, in preference to all other privileged and mortgaged creditors.

The loss which may result from their payment must be borne by the creditor whose mortgage is less ancient and so in succession, ascending according to the order of the mortgages or by *pro rata* contributions where two or more of the mortgages have the same date."

"Art. 3237. When the debts privileged on the movables and immovables cannot be paid entirely, either because the movables are of small value or subject to special privileges which claim a preference or because the movables and immovables together do not suffice, the deficiency must *not* be borne proportionally among the debtors (creditors), but the debts must be paid according to the order established above, and the loss must fall on those which are of inferior dignity." (*du rang inférieur.*) But it is contended that the foregoing Articles of the Civil Code apply to cases where the same property is affected by the all the mortgages, and that then only the loss must fall upon the junior mortgage and that where there are several pieces of property, the privilege attaches to them all and under the authorities cited they must bear the loss *pro rata*. The reason why there should be the distinction contended for between one or several immovables is by no means clear.

The first mortgage creditor having his mortgage upon a single immovable, would, in the event of insolvency, have the right to insist that the proceeds of the movables and unincumbered immovables should be exhausted before his fund should be required to contribute to the payment of the general privileged claims. Let us take another step; a second mortgage creditor acquires a right upon another immovable, and the debtor becomes insolvent. Here, this second mortgage creditor has the right in like manner to compel the application of the proceeds of the movables and unincumbered immovables to the payment of the general privileges before his fund shall be required to contribute. But suppose the movable and unincumbered immovables are insufficient to meet the privileged claims, and that the mortgaged property must contribute, and he were to call upon the senior mortgage creditor, to contribute to the payment of the privileges, would there be any want of equity in a reply to him, from the first mortgage creditor, to this effect: "Sir, when I took my mortgage, the very immovable, the proceeds of which you now claim, was liable, in the hands of my debtor, to be first exhausted for the payment of all general privileges before I could be called upon to contribute at all. You have acquired no greater right than the debtor had, who gave you the mortgage"?

The compilers of the Civil Code of 1825, having made no exception, appear to have adopted the view, that the proceeds of mortgaged property ought to be applied, whether there are one or several immovables, to the payment of the privileges in the order in which the property was mortgaged, commencing with the most recent, and thus ascending to the most ancient. This is also in harmony with Article 715 of the Code of Practice, which requires the holder of a legal or judicial mortgage, to discuss other property which the debtor has in his possession, and even that which he has alienated since the purchase, before requiring payment of a purchaser of property bought at Sheriff sale, which is subject to a legal or judicial mortgage. The reason announced by the lawgiver, in the same article, is: "Because the creditor who has a general mortgage, can only act against the property of which his debtor disposed, in the order in which the alienations have been made, beginning at the most recent and ascending to the most ancient."

Although the *property* contributes, and not the mortgage creditors, to the payment of the privileges, nothing prevents the appropriation of the proceeds of the mortgage property to the payment of the privileges in an inverted order from that in which the mortgages were created.

We consider the provisions of the Code clear and unambiguous, and that hitherto there has not been any interpretation placed upon the articles cited, which could weigh as an authority against what appears to us to be their obvious meaning.

The mortgages of *François Jartoux* and *Mrs. Devron*, being both junior to those of *Eugene Rochereau & Co.*, the property subject to the subsequent mortgages, must first contribute to the payment of the privileges, and the fund subject to the mortgage of *E. Rochereau & Co.*, can only be applied to the payment of the residue of the privileges, after the funds subject to the junior mortgages are exhausted.

SPOFFORD, J., (with whom concurred LEA, J.,) dissenting.

It appears to me, that the mode of contribution to debts, *privileged generally upon movables and immovables*, has been judicially determined in the cases of *Janin* v. *His Creditors*, 10 L. 554, and *Cazeau* v. *His Creditors*, 6 Rob. 268, in both of which cases the court must have had in view Articles 3236 and 3237 of our present Code.

The decision was, that the immovables, not the mortgage creditors, owed the contribution, and that the privileged debt aforesaid, must be borne by the immovables *pro rata*, according to the price which they produced respectively.

Nor does this interpretation seem to me to be opposed to the fair meaning of Articles 3236 and 3237.

The reference to different mortgages, according to their date, must be taken to refer to different mortgages upon the same thing.

Conventional mortgages, in due form, upon different things, are of equal dignity irrespective of their dates.

The argument, that the eldest mortgagee of a single immovable, looks to the fact, that the mortgagor has at the time other unincumbered immovables to respond first to the privileged claims in question in case of insolvency, would seem to imply that the mortgagor was bound not to alienate his other immovables, or, if alienated, that they would still be liable to contribute, when the opposite is the fact.

Until death or a declared insolvency, the privileged claims under consideration do not spring into existence. When they arise, I think they attach indifferently to all the immovables surrendered, and thus each must pay its quota. When there are two or more creditors, with mortgage upon the same thing, their rank is fixed by the Code.

On this point, I dissent from the opinion just pronounced.

* * * * * *

NOTES AND QUESTIONS

1. The case was among the first to apply the rule of Article 3236 of the 1825 Civil Code, the precursor of Article 3269 of the 1870 Civil Code. As the

court observes, even though the article speaks somewhat figuratively in terms of a contribution being made by the creditor, it is actually the property that contributes to payment of the general privileges, rather than the creditor himself.

2. The court's rationale was largely predicated upon the argument that the property encumbered under the "least ancient" mortgage would have been available for payment of general privileges at the time the earlier mortgage was granted. But is this argument convincing if the debtor did not then own that property but instead acquired it at some later time? *See Succession of Hautau*, 32 La. Ann. 54 (1880), in which the court rejected an argument that the rationale of *Devron* does not apply in cases where the property subject to the junior mortgage did not belong to the debtor at the time the earlier mortgage was granted.

3. Do you find persuasive the argument of the dissent that the reference in the article to different mortgages according to their dates must be taken to refer to different mortgages bearing upon the same thing, because conventional mortgages upon different things are of equal dignity irrespective of their dates?

iii. Ranking of the Vendor's Privilege

* * * * * *

PEDESCLAUX
v.
LEGARE
32 La. Ann. 380 (1880)

The opinion of the court was delivered by SPENCER, J.

On the 23d May, 1868, plaintiff obtained a judgment against her husband for $9,050, with legal mortgage, etc., also dissolving the community, and restoring to her the administration of her separate estate. This judgment was advertised, but no execution was ever issued thereon, or other steps taken to satisfy it.

On 3d April, 1869, her husband, Landry, bought from Mrs. Walker, by public act passed in New Orleans, a sugar plantation situated in Ascension parish, for $40,000, of which $10,248.36 was paid in cash, and for the balance the vendee assumed a pre-existing mortgage on the property, and gave notes at one and two years. The vendor reserved special mortgage and vendor's lien on the property to secure the credit part of the price. This act of sale and mortgage was recorded simultaneously in the conveyance and mortgage books of Ascension, on the 14th April, 1869.

Landry having failed to pay the price, the vendor's mortgage and privilege were foreclosed by Dr. J. C. Legaré, the holder of the notes, and the property was adjudicated to him in August, 1871, at less than the debt due. In August, 1876, Dr. Legaré sold the plantation to the defendant. About a year later (in 1877), the plaintiff commenced the present suit, which is an hypothecary action to subject said plantation to her legal mortgage.

The plaintiff's theory is, *that the law in force in April, 1869*, required, in order to preserve the vendor's lien, that the act of sale and mortgage should be recorded in the mortgage office "*on the day of the passage of the act*." And strangely enough, counsel for defendant has discussed this case at great length, upon that hypothesis.

When counsel agree as to what the facts of a case are, we feel obliged to accept their conclusions; but not so as to the law. We take the law from the Code, and not from the counsel. The Revised Civil Code of 1870 was adopted only on the 14th March of that year. The provisions of that Code, therefore, are inapplicable to this case, and we must look elsewhere for the law governing it.

Art. 3240 of the Code of 1825 provides that the vendor's privilege on immovables is "valid against third persons *from the date of the act*, if it has been duly recorded, that is to say, *within six days of the date, if the act has been passed in the place where the registry of mortgages is kept*, or adding *one day more for every two leagues* from the place where the act was passed to that where the register's office is kept."

This article was amended and re-enacted in 1868 (see Act No. 126, approved September 29th), so as to read as follows: "The privileges enumerated in the two preceding articles" (i.e., those of the vendor and of architects, etc.,) "are valid against third persons *from the date of the recording the act or evidence of indebtedness,* as provided in the foregoing articles." The "foregoing articles" referred to simply require these privileges to be recorded in the mortgage registry of the parish where the property is situated. They fix no time within which the recording is to be done, under pain of forfeiture of privilege, as did the original art. 3240, and as did art. 3274 of the Code of 1870, which has been amended by act of 1877.

There was not therefore in existence on the 3d April, 1869, any law fixing *a delay* within which registry must be made in order to preserve the existence of the vendor's lien. On the contrary, the act of 1868, above quoted, provided that that privilege *should be valid* against third persons *from the day it was recorded.* There was no law forfeiting the privilege. There was no law which authorized a court to say that where an act was passed on the third and recorded on the fourteenth, the privilege was not preserved. The plaintiff's claim is by no means an equitable one, in that it is an effort to appropriate to herself property which her husband bought and never paid for; and that to the prejudice of the vendor, who had not only a legal but moral right of revendication for this failure to pay. We are not disposed in the interest of such a demand to extend forfeitures of just rights by implication. Nothing short of a positive enactment would justify our holding plaintiff's claims to be superior to those of the vendor.

We have said that as between a mortgage and a privilege the question of priority of registry could not arise; that if the privilege existed at all it of necessity primes all mortgages as being higher in its nature. *Jacob v. Preston*, 31 An. 518.

The vendor's privilege in the case before us did exist and was preserved by the registry on the 14th April. No law declared its forfeiture for failure to register on the 3d April, 1869.

If we applied the rule of the original article 3240 of the Code of 1825, the registry on 14th April was seasonable, for it is more than ten leagues from New Orleans, where the act was passed, to the parish seat of Ascension, where the property was situated.

We hold, therefore, that the vendor's lien was in full force in 1871, and that the sale thereunder passed the property to the purchaser free of plaintiff's alleged mortgage.

This view dispenses us from considering the many intricate questions raised and discussed by counsel.

The judgment appealed from is affirmed with costs.

Rehearing refused.

* * * * * *

NOTES AND QUESTIONS

1. As mentioned earlier in this chapter, a privilege that is subject to the requirement of recordation is entitled to priority over previously recorded mortgages only if it is recorded within the delays provided by Article 3274.

2. Curiously, both counsel in *Pedesclaux v. Legaré* argued the case on the basis that the supposition that the law in force in April 1869, when the vendor's privilege arose, required the vendor's privilege to be recorded on the very day of the passage of the act in order to enjoy priority over a previously recorded mortgage. That law did not come in force until the adoption of the 1870 Code a year later. Article 3240 of the 1825 Code had imposed a delay for recordation of a vendor's privilege, but an 1868 statute removed the delay altogether. Thus, the court held that the vendor's privilege, by its very nature alone and irrespective of the time of its recordation, outranked the legal mortgage. The court observed, however, that even if it were to apply the original Art. 3240 of the 1825 Code, the same result would obtain, since the vendor's privilege was recorded in a seasonable manner based upon the time originally given under the 1825 Code for recordation.

3. By an amendment to Article 3274 of the 1870 Code made in 1877, the delays permitted for recording a privilege were lengthened: The period is presently 7 days if the property is located in the same parish where the act was passed; otherwise it is 15 days.

4. *Pedesclaux v. Legaré* involved a contest between a wife's legal mortgage upon her husband's property and a vendor's privilege arising out of his subsequent purchase of an immovable. The legal mortgage constituted a general mortgage upon all of the husband's property, including the property he acquired in the purchase. More often, the general mortgage in conflict with a later arising vendor's privilege is a judicial mortgage resulting from the recordation of a money judgment. The cases below involve contests between vendors' privileges and previously filed judicial mortgages.

5. It is not a common occurrence for a vendor's privilege to be in contest with a previously recorded conventional mortgage, but that is not an impossibility. Suppose that a conventional mortgage is granted and recorded after the execution of the act of sale but before the act of sale is recorded. In that circumstance, which would have priority? What if the conventional mortgage were granted and recorded before the act of sale by which the mortgagor acquired the property was even executed? Would the conventional mortgage be valid? If so, would it have priority over the vendor's privilege?

* * * * * *

GIVANOVITCH

v.

HEBREW CONGREGATION OF BATON ROUGE,

36 La. Ann. 272 (1884)

The opinion of the Court was delivered by BERMUDEZ, C. J.

This is a contest for priority of payment out of the proceeds of the property of defendant, which was simultaneously sold under writs respectively issued by the contending creditors.

Marco Givanovitch claims that he is entitled to the vendor's privilege, while the heirs of Gallaugher insist that their judicial mortgage ranks the privilege thus claimed.

From a judgment in favor of the judgment creditors, the present appeal is taken.

The following are the facts established by the record:

On the eighteenth of July, 1872, a judgment in favor of F. V. Gallaugher stood recorded in the proper book, in the parish of East Baton Rouge, for $1,330, against C. Delacroix.

On the first of October, 1875, more than *three* years later, Givanovitch sold to Delacroix a piece of real estate in the same parish, part cash, part on time.

On September 12, 1876, Delacroix sold the same property to the Hebrew Congregation, who, in part consideration of the price, assumed Delacroix' debt to his vendor.

The act of sale by Givanovitch to Delacroix was recorded in the mortgage and privilege book on the twenty-first of September, 1876.

The sale by Delacroix to the Congregation was recorded in the same book, on the sixteenth of the same month and year, (September, 1876) five days before the registry of that of Giranovitch to Delacroix.

The judgment of Gallaugher was duly revived and reinstated and had full force and vitality, when the property herein was sold.

The question presented is simply: Whether the judicial mortgage securing Gallaugher's judgment recorded on July 18, 1872, shall or not take precedence over the privilege claimed by Givanovitch, whose act was recorded on September 21, 1876.

An attentive and thorough examination of the matter leaves no doubt in our minds, that the proceeds of sale must be first applied to the satisfaction of the judicial mortgage debt, which is *first* in point of time of registry, and that, whatever amount may thereafter remain, will have to be applied to the next ranking mortgage claim.

We think it needless to review and reannounce explicitly the authorities, deeming a mere reference to them amply sufficient, as we have taken the pains to re-examine them separately and find them clearly decisive of the issue.

They all accord that, unless the contract from which the vendor's or other privilege is claimed to arise, was recorded seasonably in the proper book of the mortgage office of the parish in which the real estate is situated, general mortgages previously recorded, and even certain liens, will take precedence and be satisfied according to their respective rank. 6 A. 162; 7 A. 65; 12 A. 178; 18 A. 143; 20 A. 79; 23 A. 286; 24 A. 610; 26 A. 80; 27 A. 290, 243, 405, 461; 28 A. 305, 534; 29 A. 116, 412; 30 A. 727, 833, 1007; 31 A. 284; 34 A. 923, 1131; 35 A. 829. The authority invoked of *de l'Isle v. Moss*, 35 A. 165, is well entitled to the respect which is claimed for it, but it cannot avail Givanovitch, as it recognizes in a vendor the privilege which secures payment of the price, with priority over the purchaser's creditors, only where the act mentioning it has been seasonably and properly recorded.

We find no error in the judgment appealed from, which is affirmed, with costs.

* * * * * *

NOTES AND QUESTIONS

1. *Givanovitch v. Hebrew Congregation* is a sequel to *Gallaugher v. Hebrew Congregation,* 35 La. Ann. 829 (1883), which arose from the same set of facts and involved a contest between the holder of a judicial mortgage and a third person who had purchased the immovable from the judgment debtor. The judicial mortgage was recorded long before the judgment debtor acquired the immovable in question and even longer before he sold it to the third person. However, the act of credit sale by which the judgment debtor acquired the property was not recorded until three days *after* recordation of the judgment debtor's sale of the property to the third person. The third person cleverly contended that the judicial mortgage never attached to the immovable, on the theory that a judicial mortgage cannot attach until the judgment debtor's title has been recorded and in this case, by the time the judgment debtor's title was recorded, he had already alienated the property in favor of the third person. Rejecting this contention, the court held that the Civil Code provides that no act affecting immovable property shall have any effect *against* third parties until deposited for registry. The law requiring registry is intended to protect the vendor's creditors and other third persons who do not know of the existence of an unrecorded transfer; it was never designed to prevent property from passing

from vendor to purchaser or to prevent general mortgages from reaching and encumbering immovables acquired under an unrecorded title. Thus, judicial and legal mortgages recorded against the purchaser encumber immovables from the very instant of purchase whether the purchaser's act of acquisition is recorded or not, but are subordinate to encumbrances existing on the property *against the vendor* at the moment of transfer.

2. In holding the vendor's privilege to be inferior to the pre-existing judicial mortgage against the purchaser, the court in *Givanovitch v. Hebrew Congregation* followed previous authorities to the effect that previously recorded general mortgages will take precedence over a vendor's privilege unless the contract from which the vendor's privilege arises is seasonably recorded in the mortgage records.

3. In *Ridings v. Johnson*, 128 U.S. 212, 9 S. Ct. 72, 32 L. Ed. 401 (1888), the United States Supreme Court considered the issue of whether a vendor's privilege recorded several years after the date of the sale, but simultaneously with the recordation of the contract of sale, granted the vendor a privilege. Citing both *Gallaugher* and *Givanovitch*, the Court held that even though the unrecorded act of sale passed title to the vendee such that he had the power to grant mortgages upon it, the vendor's privilege had no priority over mortgages granted by the vendee in the interim where the vendor's privilege was not recorded within the period of time required by Article 3274.

4. For a recent case holding that a vendor's privilege that is not timely recorded in the mortgage records does not outrank a previously existing judicial mortgage, *see Commissioner of Insurance v. Terrell,* 647 So. 2d 445 (La. App. 2d Cir. 1994), holding that where an act of sale did not mention a promissory note that had been given to evidence the unpaid purchase price or otherwise indicate that the sale was made on credit, but at the same time a mortgage was executed to secure this note, any vendor's privilege the seller might have had was not properly preserved by the recordation of the act of sale only in the conveyance records, and the vendor's privilege was therefore subordinate to a previously recorded judicial mortgage against the purchaser. The court rejected arguments that anyone looking at the recorded act of sale and mortgage should have seen that the transaction was in the nature of a credit sale and would have been put on notice of the existence of the vendor's privilege.

* * * * * *

LAWYERS TITLE INS. CORP.

v.

VALTEAU

558 So. 2d 1319 (La. App. 4th Cir. 1990)

Writ denied 563 So. 2d 260 (La. 1990)

WARD, Judge.

The issue in this appeal is whether a vendor's privilege on immovable property has preferential ranking over a previously recorded judicial mortgage recorded against the vendee of the property.

By an act entitled "Vendor's Lien" dated April 30, 1985, Robert L. Lucien sold immovable property in New Orleans to Joy Price, wife of/and Paul V. Spooner. The purchase price was $60,000.00, and Mr. and Mrs. Spooner gave Lucien a promissory note for $59,685.00 for the unpaid portion. The act recites that Lucien reserved and assigned the vendor's privilege and note to Mellon Financial Services Corporation # 7. In the same act Joy Price Spooner and Paul V. Spooner executed a mortgage to Mellon # 7 to further secure payment of the note, which was paraphed for identification with the mortgage.

Three years later, the Spooners defaulted and Mellon foreclosed on its *mortgage,* purchasing the property at sheriff's sale. The Civil Sheriff for the Parish of Orleans prepared the Process Verbal Deed which recited that the judicial sale was subject to a prior recorded judgment against Joy Price in favor of the Leon Godchaux Clothing Co., Ltd. dated October 1, 1980.

Lawyers Title Insurance Corporation, which had issued a title policy for Mellon insuring it against prior encumbrances, filed a petition for writ of mandamus to direct the Civil Sheriff to execute an Act of Correction of the Process Verbal Deed, to show that Mellon's vendor's privilege and mortgage had priority in ranking over the judicial mortgage in favor of Godchaux's. The Civil Sheriff answered opposing the mandamus. After trial on the merits the District Court issued its judgment directing the Civil Sheriff to reform the deed and ordering the Recorder of Mortgages for the parish of Orleans to cancel the Godchaux lien insofar as it related to the property acquired by Mellon.

The Civil Sheriff has appealed the District Court judgment rendered in favor of Lawyer's Title. The Civil Sheriff contends the District Court decision is at odds with this Court's decision in *Home Savings and Loan Association v. Tri-Parish Ventures, Ltd. No. 1,* 505 So. 2d 165 (La. App. 4th Cir. 1987). The Civil Sheriff argues the *Home Savings* decision means that a prior recorded judicial mortgage against the vendee ranks before a subsequent and later recorded vendor's privilege on the property purchased.

We affirm. Although this Court's decision in *Home Savings* is correct, the District Court was also correct in distinguishing that case from this case.

The *Home Savings* case originated from two separate suits for executory process to enforce notes and mortgages granted by Tri-Parish Ventures, Ltd., No. 1, in favor of Home Savings and Loan association. Tri-Parish purchased two separate pieces of property from third parties, and then granted mortgages to Home Savings. At the time Tri-Parish purchased the properties and when Tri-Parish granted the mortgages on the properties purchased by Tri-Parish, there was a judicial mortgage recorded against Tri-Parish.

The Home Savings security devices were conventional mortgages. Home Savings did not utilize the often used procedure of acquiring the property from the sellers and immediately selling it to the true purchaser for the unpaid purchase price. Home Savings was never a vendor and did not acquire a vendor's privilege granted by La. C.C. Art. 3249(1). Home Savings simply held mortgages which purportedly acquired the rank of a vendor's privilege by virtue of La. R.S. 6:830 H set out below.

After Tri-Parish defaulted on both loans, and after foreclosure, holders of judicial mortgages against Tri-Parish intervened, claiming priority in the distribution of funds from the judicial sale. Homes Savings claimed priority by virtue of its conventional mortgages which Home Savings contends were given the same ranking priority as vendor's privilege by virtue of La. R.S. 6:830 H and preferred over all mortgages. La. C.C. Art. 3186. This Court held the prior recorded judicial mortgage emanating from the *mortgagor* had priority in ranking, and quoted that part of La. R.S. 6:830 H(1) which gives those conventional mortgages the same status as a vendor's privilege, but preference only as to mortgages that arise and are recorded subsequently to the conventional mortgage.

The prior recorded mortgage against Tri-Parish obviously has preference over the conventional mortgage Tri-Parish granted to Home Savings, La. C.C. art. 3329. Tri-Parish as a debtor could not sell the property to others to the prejudice of the prior recorded mortgage, and if Tri-Parish and Home Savings went through the sale and resale procedure, the prior recorded mortgage against Tri-Parish would still have preference. La. C.C. art. 3397. Consequently, even if Home Savings by virtue of La. R.S. 6:830 H acquired a vendor's privilege, the prior recorded mortgage had preference. Therefore, arguably, the Home Savings Court need not have relied on La. R.S. 6:830 H(1) as authority for ranking. Harrell, *Developments in the Law, 1986-87, Security Devices*, 48 La. L. Rev. 477 (1987). Nonetheless, reliance on La. R.S. 6:830 H(1) was not misplaced.

If the purpose of La. R.S. 6:830 H was to give a conventional mortgage in favor of a homestead *full* equality as a vendor's privilege created by La. C.C. art. 3249, it failed. When there is a credit sale, and a vendor's privilege arises by virtue of Art. 3249, the vendor's privilege on the immovable sold is preferred over all other creditors of the *vendee* for the unpaid purchase price, even over prior judicial mortgages recorded against the *vendee*. La. C.C. art. 3186. La. R.S. 6:830 H(1) says that this mortgage is given a status as a vendor's privilege but is preferred *only* as to those judicial mortgages which arise and are recorded subsequent to its recordation. It does not differentiate between prior mortgages against vendor or vendee, and unlike Art. 3186 privileges, it is not preferred over prior judicial mortgages against the vendee. La. R.S. 6:830 H(1). Admittedly, Section H(1) conflicts with H(3):

H. (1) All mortgages executed upon immovable property in Louisiana in favor of associations organized and operating under the laws of the state shall have a rank equal to that of a vendor's privilege upon immovable property and shall have priority over all other liens, privileges, encumbrances and mortgages upon the property, and the improvements and component parts thereon which are recorded or arise in any manner subsequent to the date of recordation of the mortgage in favor of the association, including tax privileges of any nature and character, except ad valorem taxes on immovable property and assessments for paving. . . .

(3) The associations adopting the procedure set forth in this Section shall have all of the rights and privileges of a vendor to the same extent and in the same manner as if a sale to the association, and a sale by the association to a borrower had in fact been consummated, the intent of this Section being merely to provide an optional procedure without altering in any manner any of the rights accorded to, and obligations incurred by associations prior to the passage of this Section.

We are satisfied the *Home Savings* interpretation, which preferred the specific language of paragraph 1 over the general language of paragraph 3, is correct.

Although the *Home Savings* interpretation and decision is correct, that decision should not be interpreted to mean that all prior recorded liens, privileges, encumbrances, or mortgages are preferred over vendor's privileges created by La. C.C. art. 3249. Notwithstanding anything in *Home Savings,* only prior recorded liens, privileges, encumbrances and mortgages emanating from the *vendor* are preferred to vendor's privileges that arise from La. C.C. art. 3249, and a vendor's privilege given by that article has preference for payment of the purchase price over all liens, privileges, encumbrances and mortgages (excluding some taxes and paving liens) emanating from the *vendee,* even when those encumbrances are recorded before a credit sale is consummated and the vendor's lien is created. La. C.C. art. 3186. The jurisprudence has always held and the newly amended La. C.C. art. 3251 confirms that a timely filed vendor's privilege is superior in rank. Harrell, *Developments in the Law, 1986-87, Security Devices,* 48 La. L. Rev. 477 (1987). As explained in *De L'Isle v. Succession of Moss,* 34 La. Ann. 164, 166-67 (1881):

> "It would indeed be unjust to place an unpaid vendor on a footing of equality with the other creditors of the purchaser, and permit these to devour his substance; for it is only on condition that the price of the thing sold has been paid, that the purchaser acquires an indefeasible title of ownership to the property, and that his creditors can be paid. . . . It springs from the very nature of the contract of sale, of which it is a legal concomitant. It exists without

stipulation, and adheres tenaciously to the thing sold. It is invariably considered as retained, unless renounced in language unmistakenly clear, or by acts evidently designed to destroy effectually the presumption of its retention. . . .

"It is the price that is protected by the privilege. By the sale the vendor increases the estate of the purchaser. It would be iniquitous to permit the property sold to become the prey of the creditors of the purchaser, without requiring as a condition precedent, the payment of its costs. [citations omitted]."

The purpose of the vendor's lien is to prevent creditors of the vendee from appropriating the value of an increase in the assets of the vendee when the purchase price has not been paid and the vendee's patrimony has not in fact increased. *Harrell,* supra.

In this case when Lucien sold to Joy and Robert Spooner by means of a credit sale, a vendor's privilege was created by La. C.C. art. 3249. Lucien assigned this vendor's privilege to Mellon # 7. Although Mellon # 7 foreclosed on a conventional mortgage which resulted in seizure and sale, Mellon # 7 may assert its claim to preference by virtue of that vendor's privilege acquired from Lucien. Mellon's vendor's lien, at least to the extent of the unpaid part of the purchase price owed to Lucien, has preference over the previously recorded Godchaux judgment against Joy Price.

AFFIRMED.

* * * * * *

NOTES AND QUESTIONS

1. In holding that a timely filed vendor's privilege outranks a previously recorded judicial mortgage, the Fourth Circuit in *Valteau* was put to the task of explaining its prior ruling in *Home Savings & Loan Association v. Tri-Parish Ventures,* 505 So. 2d 165 (La. App. 4th Cir. 1987), a case that did not involve a true vendor's privilege arising from a sale/resale to and from a building and loan association but instead a vendor's privilege claimed by a building and loan association on the basis of La. R.S. 6:830H. The association's mortgage was in competition with a judicial mortgage that had been filed against the

association's borrower *before* the borrower acquired the property and mortgaged it to the building and loan association. Citing Civil Code Article 3273 to the effect that privileges are effective against third persons from the date of recordation, the court in *Home Savings* held that Article 3274 is simply a limited exception to this rule, "in which a grace period is given to the privilege holder over *intervening* mortgages only, where the act importing privilege is recorded within a very limited period after the date of execution." The court in *Home Savings* observed that a similar grace period was created for mortgages in favor of building and loan associations pursuant to the savings and loan association law; "however, the special ranking date, as in Louisiana Civil Code article 3274, affects intervening mortgages only." Later the court remarked that "[a] vendor's privilege which is preserved and perfected against third parties through recordation primes subsequent mortgages affecting the property." The court thus found that the holder of the previously filed judicial mortgage had priority. What is surprising about the court's holding is that it did not seem to be based upon an interpretation of La. R.S. 6:830, but rather upon an interpretation of those articles of the Civil Code applicable to all vendor's privileges.

2. Do you find the court's efforts in *Valteau* to distinguish its prior holding in *Homes Savings* convincing, or do you feel that the court should have candidly admitted that its reasoning, if not its holding, in the earlier case was in error?

3. In its opinion denying a writ application in *Valteau*, the Supreme Court limited the holding of the case to a mere statement that a vendor's privilege arising from a sale to a vendee outranks a prior recorded judicial mortgage *against the vendee*. The Supreme Court explained that the decision in *Home Savings* involved a situation in which a judgment debtor already owned the property *before* mortgaging it to the building and loan association in a refinancing transaction. For that reason, the prior recorded judicial mortgage against that judgment debtor outranked any vendor's privilege arising from his mortgage of the property in favor of the building and loan association. Nonetheless, the Supreme Court found that the Fourth Circuit's observations concerning the nature and effect of the vendor's privilege granted to building and loan associations under La. R.S. 6:830H were "clearly dicta" since there was no building and loan association involved in *Valteau*.

4. In 1989, Civil Code Article 3251, which ranks successive vendor's privileges among themselves, was amended by the addition of a provision that "as provided by Article 3186, and assuming timely recordation as provided in Article 3274, each such vendor is preferred to the previously recorded mortgages of his vendees and their successors." Acts 1989, No. 538. Was this an attempt to clarify the law after *Home Savings*? This is the amendment to which the court in *Valteau* refers in its statement that "[t[he jurisprudence has always held and the newly amended La. C.C. art. 3251 confirms that a timely filed vendor's privilege is superior in rank."

iv. Untimely Recordation; the Degeneration Principle

* * * * * *

2 Traite Élementaire de Droit Civil, pt. 2
(La. State Law Inst. trans., 1959) (12th ed. 1939) (Fr.)
Marcel Planiol & Georges Ripert

3148. Necessity for Inscription

Differing from general privileges for which an inscription is not necessary, special privileges are subject to a system of publicity: they must be inscribed, and the law even provides that this be done rapidly; for almost all, with one exception, it has fixed a delay within which the inscription should be taken.

3149. Role of the Delay

It is important to understand at once the nature and the effect of this delay: its expiration does not at all prevent the creditor from inscribing. A privilege can still be inscribed after the delay has elapsed, but its rank is not as good: the rank which belongs to it, in the series of creditors having a right of preference, ceases to be regulated by the law; it depends on the date of its inscription. Thus, one of two things may happen:

(1) The inscription was made within the delay. Even if it was the last day, it is not the date of inscription on which the rank of the creditor depends, who is classed at the rank that the law assigns to him in its quality of privileged creditor. His privilege is preserved.

(2) The inscription was taken after the expiration of the delay. As it is tardy, the privileged rank which the law gave it is lost, and the creditor has only a variable rank which depends on the date of the day it was inscribed. Its privilege is lost as such and it is nothing more than an ordinary mortgage.

Thus the delay fixed by the law is given to the creditor, not to inscribe as a mortgage creditor, but to preserve his privileged rank.

3150. Formula of Art. 2113

This rule of law is very clearly expressed in Art. 2113, thus:

> "All privileges which are required to be inscribed and as to which the conditions above prescribed to preserve the privilege have not been fulfilled, do not cease, nevertheless, to operate as mortgages, but the mortgage dates, with regard to third persons, only from the time of the inscriptions."

Ordinarily this disposition is summarized by saying that the privileges degenerate into mortgages, if they have not been inscribed within the legal delays. The law in effect does not exact other "conditions" for the preservation of privileges than the inscription within a certain delay.

3151. Conflict Between Privileges Degenerated into Mortgages

When several creditors provided with the same privilege (for example, co-partitioners) allow their privileges to degenerate into mortgages, and then make one after the other, tardy inscriptions, they must be considered as simple mortgage creditors. Consequently, Art. 2097, according to which creditors who have the same privilege concur with each other, ceases to be applicable to them, and the one who is inscribed first primes the others (Rouen, 24 Dec. 1866, D.67.1.211, S.67.1.122).

3152. Explanation of Art. 2106

The system of the law on privileges and on their preservation is therefore very simple and very clearly enunciated in the texts. Thus, there is no difficulty at present in explaining Art. 2106 which was the despair of certain commentators. One reads in this article: "Privileges only produce effect . . . if they are made public and only from the date of the inscription, with the following exceptions only." They tortured themselves trying to understand how a privilege, which according to Articles 2095 and 2096, is classified according to the quality of the credit can only produce its effect from the date of the inscription. Is not that effacing all the difference which separates the privilege from the mortgage?

It is not important to know all that has been written on this article. Nothing is more simple than this disposition: Art. 2106 commences by reproducing Art. 2 of the law of 11 Brumaire, Year VII, which says simply: "The privileges on immovables only take effect by their inscription," which is very clear, for that signifies: if you have a privilege and if you wish to avail yourself of it, inscribe it. To that brief formula the drafters of the Code added the words: "and counting from the date of the inscription," in order to observe that the effect of the privilege cannot be invoked by a creditor not yet inscribed. But it is evident that the purpose of this text is to determine the conditions of efficacy of the privilege, and not to return to the question of rank which the authors of the law had sufficiently regulated by Arts. 2095 to 2097. The title of the section of which 2106 forms a part proves it: it deals only with "how privileges are preserved," and not with the rank they should be given.

* * * * * *

SUCCESSION OF MARC
29 La. Ann. 412 (1877)

The opinion of the court was delivered by MANNING, C. J.

The sole contest in this case is between the creditors of the deceased, each of whom has a mortgage.

Soye, the older creditor, obtained executory process, under which the property specially mortgaged to him was sold, and it did not realize sufficient to pay his claim, after the costs of his process and the taxes were satisfied.

Gayarré's mortgage was on another property, and was subsequent in date to Soye's, and he had also the vendor's privilege upon it, retained in the same act which recited the mortgage. The sale of that piece of property was likewise insufficient to pay the costs, taxes, and his debt. The executrix has charged the general and special privileges, viz.: the funeral charges, and those of the last illness, and of law, and the widow's portion of one thousand dollars, to the fund derived from the sale of the two mortgaged properties indifferently, and they consume the whole of both.

Opponents deny that the widow is entitled to the gratuity of one thousand dollars under the act of 1852, because she was the concubine of the decedent until within twelve days of his decease, when their marriage took place, while he was in the presence of death, and without issue born of their previous concubinage.

The act of 1852 gives to the widow who is in necessitous circumstances the sum already mentioned, without qualifying her right to receive it by the condition that her previous life should have been blameless, or by limiting its operation to those whose married life should have lasted a specified time. Revised Statutes of 1870, section 1693. It is argued by one of the opponents that an interpretation of the statute which permits the widow of Marc to partake the beneficence provided by it, would be offensive to our moral sense, and that it could not have been in the contemplation of the Legislature to place a woman, who has thus disregarded religious and social duty, upon the same plane with the respectable and bereaved widow, whose condition attracted the regard and provoked the compassion of the law-maker.

It is very certain, however, that the law has not attached qualifications, nor imposed conditions upon the recipients of this legislative bounty, such as we are asked to supply and enforce in the present proceeding. Should we attempt to do so, omitting any mention of our want of authority, we must arrange this description of persons into classes, separated from each other by the purity or impurity of their ante-nuptial lives, or by the longer or shorter duration of the marriage which preceded the widowhood.

There are conditions, however, imposed by the statute which the claimant of this bounty must fulfill. The widow must be in necessitous circumstances, and the present claimant is indisputably in that condition. The sum to be received from the succession of her deceased husband must be such, as added to the amount of property owned by her, will make one thousand dollars. She had no property, but the rents of the mortgaged property occupied by her since her husband's decease are $325, and are deductible from her portion under the act. *Succession of Drum*, 26 Annual, 539. The residue is to be paid in preference to all other debts, except those for the vendor's privilege, and expenses incurred in selling the property, but the widow is entitled to the usufruct only of the sum specified in the act if there be children.

The opponent, Gayarré, had a vendor's privilege on the property sold under his mortgage, and claims its exemption from the widow's allowance, which is opposed by Soye for an alleged want of seasonable registry of the privilege. The copy of the act of mortgage contains also the retention of the vendor's privilege, and it was recorded in the mortgage office on the fourth of April, 1874, a few days after its execution. It is not pretended that any other mortgage exists, or existed on that property, and the objection of want of registry is therefore untenable as between these creditors.

Two rules relating to the rank of privileges and to the fund out of which they are payable, are well established. One is, that when the movables and unmortgaged property are insufficient to pay the privileges, they must be paid out of the fund arising from the sale of the property covered by the youngest mortgage, and, that being insufficient, the residue must come out of that next in age. *Devron's case*, 11 Annual, 482; *Succession of Cerise*, 24 Annual, 96; *Succession of Rousseau*, 23 Annual, 1.

The other is, that the destitute widow's portion primes all privileges created previous to the death of the party, except that of the vendor, but that it yields to funeral expenses, expenses of last illness, and law charges growing out of the administration and settlement of the succession. *Foulkes's Succession*, 12 Annual, 537; *Quertier v. Hille*, 21 Annual, 429.

Applying these rules to the case at bar, the widow of Marc, whose portion is reduced to six hundred and seventy-five dollars by her previous receipts from the succession, must be paid that residue out of the Soye-mortgage fund, and the general privileges, which are not satisfied by the sale of the movables, must be paid by the Gayarré mortgage as the least ancient.

The taxes and costs of sale of the Soye-mortgaged property are nearly one half of the sum at which it was adjudicated, and the residue is insufficient to pay the widow's portion, but the unpaid part of that residue can not be charged against the property affected by the vendor's privilege.

The taxes and costs of sale of the Gayarré-mortgaged property are more than half of the sum realized by its sale, and that residue must bear the burthen of such part of the general privileges as are not satisfied by the sum derived from the sale of the movables.

Where the husband dies without descendants, as in this case, the necessitous widow is not required to give security. She does not take the usufruct only of the sum secured to her, but its full ownership. *Succession of Hunter*, 13 Annual, 257; *Yarborough's Succession*, idem 378.

The reductions and alterations made by the lower court in the tableau are approved, and the funds must be distributed as directed by that court, except where amended or reversed by this decree, and it is accordingly so ordered, the costs of appeal to be paid by the two opponents and appellants in equal parts.

On Rehearing.

The opinion of the court was delivered by MANNING, C. J.

A rehearing of this cause has been granted on the application of the opponent, Charles Gayarré. The grounds urged by him for error are, that we subjected the fund, derived from the sale of the property upon which his vendor's privilege rested, to the payment of the general privileges, when these latter should have been charged to the Soye fund.

Upon a review of our opinion and decree, we find there was error in holding that his privilege existed, or could be enforced. A material alteration has been effected in the law applicable to this question by a radical change of two articles of the Civil Code.

Article 3240 formerly read as follows: "The privileges enumerated in the two preceding articles are valid against third persons from the date of the act, if it has been duly recorded, that is to say, within six days of the date," etc. It is numbered 3273 in the revisal, and reads: "Privileges are valid against third persons from the date of the recording of the act or evidence of indebtedness as provided by law."

Article 3241 formerly read thus: "When the act on which the privilege is founded has not been recorded within the time required in the preceding article, it shall have no effect as a privilege, that is to say, it shall confer no preference on the creditor who holds it, over creditors who have acquired a mortgage in the mean time, which they have recorded before it; it shall, however, still avail as a mortgage, and be good against third persons from the time of its being recorded."

That article is numbered 3274 in the revisal, and reads: "No privilege shall have effect against third persons unless recorded in the manner required by law in the parish where the property to be affected is situated It shall confer no preference on the creditor who holds it over creditors who have acquired a mortgage, unless the act or other evidence of the debt is recorded on the day that the contract was made."

The privilege mentioned in article 3238 (new number 3271), is one of those referred to: "The vendor of an immovable only preserves his privilege on the object when he has caused to be duly recorded at the office for recording mortgages, his act of sale in the manner directed hereafter, whatever may be the amount due him on the sale."

Formerly, and under the Code of 1825, the vendor of an immovable preserved his privilege if he had the act evidencing it recorded within six days of its date. Now, by the alteration, or rather substitution of a new article, that privilege is preserved against third persons only from the date when the act is recorded. As against mortgages recorded anterior to the registry of the privilege, this latter has effect as such only when recorded on the day of the date of the contract creating it.

The application of these new articles of the Code to the present case sensibly affects the opponent, who claims exemption from contribution to the general succession privileges by reason of his holding a privilege superior to them. We are compelled to hold that he has no privilege whatever, as against third persons, since the act which conferred upon him, or preserved, the vendor's privilege, was not recorded upon the day the sale was made. And this is what was meant by the counsel of Soye when the loss of the privilege was attributed to want of *seasonable* registry.

The act of privilege not having been recorded on the day of its execution, the privilege itself was lost as to third persons, and Soye is a third person in this proceeding where the subjection of the two funds to the payment of the succession privileges turns upon the question of privilege *vel non*. Gayarré's mortgage was not lost. It was good from the day it was recorded, but it was junior to Soye's, and a senior mortgage can not be required to contribute to the payment of privileges of a succession until the junior mortgages are exhausted. Therefore

It is ordered, adjudged, and decreed that so much of our former decree as subjected the Soye-mortgage fund to the payment of the unpaid residue of the widow's portion, is set aside, and that after the sum derived from the sale of the movables is exhausted, the residue of the succession privileges be first charged against the junior mortgage fund of Charles Gayarré, and not until that is exhausted, can any portion of these privileges be charged against the more ancient mortgage fund of Soye, the costs of this appeal to be paid by the opponent, Gayarré.

* * * * * *

NOTES AND QUESTIONS

1. The court attempted to explain the effect of a "radical change" between the 1825 and 1870 Civil Codes. Under the 1825 Code, the vendor had six days within which to record his privilege. However, the 1870 Code, as originally adopted, required the vendor's privilege to be recorded on *the very day* of the contract creating it in order to be preferred to previously recorded mortgages. As mentioned above, the period was lengthened by an 1877 amendment to Article 3274. The period is 7 days if the property is located in the same parish where the act was passed; otherwise it is 15 days.

2. It is essential to an understanding of the case to remember that a vendor's privilege primes general privileges, but a mere mortgage does not. Under the facts of the case, the decedent's estate consisted of two immovables,

one of which was subject to a mortgage in favor of Soye and the other of which was subject to a later arising and untimely filed vendor's privilege in favor of Gayarre. Both immovables were sold, and the court was faced with the issue of which of the two creditors had to bear the privilege of the surviving spouse and the general privileges. On original hearing, the court held that the privilege of the surviving spouse had to be paid with the funds derived from the sale of the immovable subject to the Soye mortgage, since the privilege of the surviving spouse was inferior to the vendor's privilege. All general privileges were assessed against the fund derived from the sale of the Gayarre property, since that mortgage was the least ancient of the two. On rehearing, however, the court reassigned the privilege of the surviving spouse to the Gayarre fund in light of a "radical change" of two articles of the Civil Code. Thus, the court held that Gayarre had "no privilege whatever, as against third persons" since his vendor's privilege was not recorded on the day the sale was made. Gayarre's mortgage, however, was not lost, but since Gayarre's mortgage was the least ancient of the two, an application of the rule of "the least ancient" mortgage meant that the Gayarre fund had to contribute to the privilege of the surviving spouse before the Soye fund.

3. This case represents a classic application of Planiol's "degeneration" concept, which the court would later reject in the following case, *Wheelright v. St. Louis, N.O. & O. Canal Transportation Co.*, 17 So. 133 (La. 1895).

* * * * * *

WHEELRIGHT

v.

ST. LOUIS, N. O. & O. CANAL & TRANSP. CO.

47 La. Ann. 533 (1895)

General Statement.

On December 1, 1891, William D. Wheelright filed his bill in the circuit court of the United States for the Eastern district of Louisiana against the defendant company, a corporation of the state of New Jersey, for the purpose of foreclosing a mortgage upon the canal property belonging to said company, situated in the parish of St. Bernard. The defendant appeared, and, after litigation, a final decree was rendered in Wheelright's favor on the 15th June,

1893, for the sum of $310,720 in gold coin of the United States, with 6 per cent. per annum interest on $265,000 thereof from July 1, 1891, and with 5 per cent. per annum interest on the balance from various dates. The court further ordered a foreclosure of the mortgage, and a sale of the property in due form of law, according to equity proceedings. Wheelright was unable to execute this judgment, because the property of the defendant company was at that time in the possession of the Twenty-Second judicial district court for the parish of St. Bernard, under and by virtue of several writs of attachment in the cases of Cusachs, Guichard, and Henry Janin. The plaintiffs in those suits had prayed for personal judgments against the company, with recognition that payment of the amounts for which judgment was asked was secured by lien and privilege upon the company's property; the said property being the same as that which was covered by plaintiff's mortgage. They had recorded claims of privilege upon the property in the recorder's office of St. Bernard. . . . On September 8, 1892, Guichard obtained a judgment in his favor in the district court against the defendant company for $2,336, and recognizing that payment of the same was secured in his favor by lien and privilege on its property. Execution issued on the judgment, but no sale of the property was made for want of a sufficient bid. The property is still under seizure in that suit. On the 14th February, 1894, Wheelright filed his petition in the Twenty-Second judicial district court for St. Bernard, setting up the decree obtained by him in the circuit court for the foreclosure of his mortgage, setting up the possession of the property by the court under the various writs of attachment, setting up the claim of privilege of Cusachs, Guichard, Janin.

He then . . . prayed for judgment recognizing the decree in the circuit court of the United States, with first lien and privilege, and mortgage upon all of the property of the defendant company, and that the court might adjudge and decree that the lien of this mortgage was anterior to the claims of the other defendants, and that a sale under the judgment to be rendered by the court should wipe out and extinguish any and all pretended claims of the defendants, and that the defendants should not be entitled to have any part of the proceeds of the said sale until and unless the property should bring enough to pay the judgment of the plaintiff with interest and costs, and the claims of all other persons who hold mortgages concurrent with himself.

The court rendered judgment in favor of plaintiff against all the defendants, recognizing the plaintiff's claim as prayed for in his petition, with mortgage and privilege on the property, directing the property to be sold, and declaring and decreeing the claim of Guichard superior to that of the plaintiff.

NICHOLLS, C. J.

The first question which meets us is the correctness or incorrectness of the judgment of the district court recognizing that the amount of the indebtedness due by the defendant company to Guichard is secured by lien and privilege, and that by virtue thereof his claim primes the mortgage claim of the plaintiff. The latter admits the existence of the indebtedness to the amount declared on, but denies the existence, quoad himself, of a privilege as supporting it. He contends that even if, from the nature of Guichard's claim, the law created a privilege securing their payment, the same law made this privilege, in its effect, as such, upon pre-existing mortgages, dependent upon the registry of the claims, in the manner and at a time and place which has not been complied with. In support of this position, counsel refers us to article 3274 of the Civil Code as amended by Act No. 45 of the regular session of 1877, which article, as amended, provided that: "No privilege shall have effect as against third persons, unless recorded in the manner required by law, in the parish where the property to be affected is situated. It shall confer no preference on the creditor, who holds it over creditors, who have acquired a mortgage unless the act, or other evidence of the debt, is recorded within seven days from the date of the act or obligation of indebtedness when the registry is to be made in the parish where the act was passed, or the indebtedness originated, and within fifteen days if the registry is required to be made in any other parish of this state. It shall, however, have effect against all parties from date of registry." The registered act upon which Guichard relies was recorded on the 24th of December, 1891, long after the registry of plaintiff's mortgage.

Turning to the record of the case of Guichard against the defendant company, which has been copied into the transcript, we find, independently of any question whether the claims declared on in that case were really secured by privilege or not, that "the dates of the acts or obligations of indebtedness" preceded by over 7 or 15 days the date of the registry of Guichard's affidavit of indebtedness. The district judge was of opinion that that fact made no difference, for two reasons: First, for the reason that Guichard's right to a privilege had been recognized by a judgment of court; and, secondly, because the lawmaker had declared in the article cited that, although a privilege had been tardily registered, yet it should have effect against all parties from the date of its registry, and, inasmuch as a privilege, in its nature, and outside of the question of the date of its creation, outranks a mortgage, it necessarily follows that mortgage rights are subordinated to privileged rights, regardless of the dates of their respective registry.

Whether or not, in reaching his conclusion on the first point, the district judge adopted the view of the defendant that this litigation was a collateral attack upon Guichard's judgment, and that the issue attempted to be raised here could only be raised in a direct action of nullity, or whether he was of the opinion that the judgment obtained by him was conclusive of the question of privilege, as *res judicata*, he was equally wrong. Plaintiff was not a party to the judgment which declared the existence of the privilege. The privilege, if it existed, sprung neither from the convention of the parties, nor was it created by the judgment; it was the creation of the law. Its existence is outside of the judgment, and is to be determined, as to third parties, independently of it. This suit is not a collateral attack upon plaintiff's judgment; the attack is direct upon his right to a privilege, and upon his rank as a creditor.

The second position of the district judge is reached by a construction of the law which makes the lawmaker, in the latter part of an article, completely undo what he had otherwise provided for in its beginning. It is expressly declared in article 3274 that "no privilege shall confer a preference on the creditor, who holds it over creditors who have acquired a mortgage," unless the act or other evidence of the debt is recorded within a certain time. If this be the law, courts are bound to give it effect by placing on other portions of the article a construction which admits of this being done. The article in question presents no difficulty whatever. Article 3186 of the Civil Code, which declares that a privilege is a right which entitles the creditor holding it to be preferred over other creditors, even those who have mortgages, merely states the nature and effect generally of privileges, while article 3274 of the Code restrains and modifies this general effect in the special case provided for by it, when a privilege tardily recorded would come in competition with a pre-existing registered mortgage. For such a case it is provided that the tardily recorded privilege, though none the less a privilege because not promptly recorded, shall fall behind, and be subordinated to a prior mortgage; in other words, practically and substantially, that quoad prior existing mortgages, it should lose its peculiar character of a privilege, and be ranked and classed, as to it, as a junior mortgage. Such was, in express terms of the law, the effect of a tardily registered privilege under the articles of the Civil Code of 1825 as they stood originally. Article 3240, as it stood originally, declared that: "The privileges enumerated in the two preceding articles are valid against third persons, from the date of the act, if it has been duly recorded; that is to say, within six days of the date, if the act has been passed in the place where the registry of mortgages is kept or added one day more for every two leagues from the place where the act was passed to that where the register's office is kept." The following article (3241) was as follows: "When the act on which the privilege is founded, has not been recorded within the time required in the preceding article it shall have no effect as a privilege; that is to say, it shall confer no preference on the creditor who holds it over creditors who have acquired a mortgage in the meantime which they have recorded before it; it shall however still avail as a mortgage, and be good against third persons from the time of its being recorded." In the Revised Code of 1870, article 3273 was substituted for article 3240, and read as follows: "Privileges are valid against third persons from the date of the recording of the act or evidence of indebtedness as provided by law"; while article 3274, which replaced article 3241, was to the following effect: "No privilege shall have effect against third persons, unless recorded in the manner required by law in the parish where the property to be affected is situated. It shall confer no preference on the creditor who holds it over creditors who have acquired a mortgage, unless the act or other evidence of defendant, is recorded on the day that the contract was entered into." The amendment of 1877 has brought the law back, with some modifications, to what it was at first. Under the original articles, tardiness of inscription had the effect of reducing the privilege forever from a privilege to a mortgage. *Succession of O'Laughlin*, 18 La. Ann. 142; Paul Pont, under article 2095, Code Nap. p. 19. Under the present system its character is not changed at all, but its effect as a privilege, as to certain parties, is removed. As to parties other than those in whose favor this exemption is declared, the privilege retains its full effect. Independently of what we have just said, the defective character of the registered act on which Guichard depends is manifest. The object of registry is notice. When an instrument is recorded, whose registry is expected to affect the rights of third parties, the act registered should contain and show upon its own face, and not by reference to documents to be found elsewhere, or proceedings to be at some future time instituted, all the essential facts which go to create and fix the privilege. The act registered by Guichard utterly fails in this regard to carry out the requirements of the registry laws. We are of the opinion that, so far as the plaintiff is concerned, Guichard has no privilege, and that the judgment decreeing that he has such a privilege priming plaintiff's mortgage is incorrect.

* * * * * *

NOTES AND QUESTIONS

1. The case illustrates the interplay between Civil Code Article 3186, which declares that a privilege entitles the privileged creditor to be preferred over mortgagees, and Article 3274, which governs the effect of a tardily recorded privilege that is in competition with a previously recorded mortgage. As the court observes, the former article merely states the nature and general effect of privileges, while the latter article restrains and modifies this general effect when a privilege is not recorded within the time permitted by that article.

2. Articles 3273 and 3274 provide that a privilege on an immovable has effect against third persons from the time that it is recorded. Does the date that a privilege becomes effective against third persons necessarily govern its ranking? *See* 2 Marcel Planiol & Georges Ripert, *Traité Élémentaire de Droit Civil*, pt. 2 No. 3152 (La. State Law Inst. trans., 1959) (12th ed. 1939)(Fr.).

3. As it had in *Succession of Marc,* supra, the court attempted to explain significant differences between the 1825 and 1870 Civil Codes, but in doing so reached different conclusions than in the earlier case. Under the 1825 Code, tardiness of inscription reduced the privilege forever to a mere mortgage; as Planiol observes in the excerpt quoted above, the privilege has "degenerated" into a mere mortgage. In contrast, under the 1870 Code, the character of the tardily inscribed privilege is not changed; however, its effect as a privilege, as to *certain mortgagees* only, is done away with. As to other parties, the privilege retains its full effect.

4. To what extent does the court's rejection of the degeneration principle call into question the court's earlier decision in *Succession of Marc,* supra, which held that the vendor who failed to file his privilege in a timely manner enjoyed

"no privilege whatever, as against third persons"? The holdings of the two cases might be reconciled if Article 3274 is applied not just as a ranking rule when a privilege and mortgage exist on the same immovable but instead is given a more expansive effect to allow a mortgage holder to ignore *entirely* the status of a privilege as a privilege when it is not filed in a timely manner. In other words, even though the court's rejection of the degeneration principle would mean that the untimely filed vendor's privilege would still be treated as a privilege insofar as it competes with other privileges (such as the privilege of the surviving spouse in *Succession of Marc*), the untimely filed privilege would not be a privilege—for any purpose—insofar as a mortgagee holding a mortgage on another immovable is concerned. Thus, this other mortgagee could force the unpaid vendor to share in the payment of general privileges under Articles 3269 and 3270 as though the unpaid vendor held merely an ordinary mortgage rather than a privilege. This argument may stretch Article 3274 beyond its plain meaning: The article does not provide that an unseasonably filed privilege is wholly without effect as a privilege as regards all mortgagees, but rather provides simply that an unseasonably filed privilege "confers no preference" on the creditor who holds it against mortgagees.

5. There is another important difference between the 1825 and 1870 Civil Codes not mentioned in the court's opinion in *Wheelright*. Under Articles 3240 and 3241 of the 1825 Code, a privilege was valid against a third person from the date of the act if recorded within the required period of time. Under the 1870 Code, Article 3273 was substituted in place of Article 3240, providing that privileges are valid against third persons from the date of the recording of the act of evidence of the indebtedness. Article 3274, which replaced Article 3241, provides that no privilege affects third persons unless recorded in the manner required by law. Thus, the former rule that privileges are effective against third persons from the date they arise, provided that they are timely recorded, appears to have been replaced by a rule that privileges are effective against third persons from the time that they are recorded. Can you think of instances in which this difference might have a practical effect?

6. Was the entire discussion by the court in *Wheelright* on the ranking issue dicta, given that the filing made by the purported privileged creditor was defective and not just untimely?

D. Problem of the Vicious Circle

Much has been written, particularly by Professor Dainow, on the topic of vicious circles that exist in the ranking of the rights of privileged creditors holding interests in a debtor's property. Vicious circles exist when three or more competing creditors have rights in the debtor's property, and each can point to a provision of law giving him priority over some of the others, but none can demonstrate priority over all of the others. Generally speaking, the ultimate solution espoused by Professor Dainow in the face of irreconcilable statutory ranking rules is to apply the most recent legislative enactment, even if that results in a re-ordering of priorities of privileges not addressed directly by the enactment. This solution has been criticized on the ground that rarely, if ever, does the last enactment expressly purport to rank all of the competing privileges. *See* Michael H. Rubin, *Louisiana Law of Security Devices: A Précis* § 32.2 (2011).

* * * * * *

Vicious Circles in the Louisiana Law of Privileges
Joseph Dainow
25 Louisiana State Law Review 1 (1964)

Privileges or preferences among creditors constitute a kind of security device because the privileged or preferred creditors are not subjected to the general rule of proration but are paid in full before ordinary creditors get anything. When two or more privileged creditors are in competition, the Civil Code stipulates that there is also a ranking or priority among them; they do not rank concurrently except when the competing privileges are of the same nature or when concurrence is expressly provided. The subject matter of privileges is *stricti juris,* and therefore there must be a written text of law to support the creation and existence of each privilege, and there must also be an express text as authority for each ranking question as between privileges. Furthermore, by reason of the *stricti juris* nature of the subject, it is not appropriate in this discussion" to reopen any of the policy considerations which went into the creation of the privilege or into the rules of ranking among privileges.

However, for our frustration, the lawmakers have never tried to envisage the whole picture of rankings, so that there is an accumulation of piecemeal or partial sets of rules which do not constitute a coherent framework. Any effort to formulate a single, comprehensive order of ranking among existing privileges must fail because this is impossible. Furthermore, as a result of the separate, legal texts concerning the rankings among separate pairs or groups of privileges, there have developed the so-called "vicious circles," where privilege *A* primes privilege *B,* privilege *B* primes privilege *C,* and privilege *C* primes privilege *A.*

The general attitude in the legal profession has seemed to be that there is no way out of these vicious circles and that the important thing is to be able to identify such situations in order to know when to litigate and when to compromise (pro rata). Such a compromise does not resolve the legal issues involved, and it may be questioned whether this estimate of the situation is correct; there is reaction against the idea of a legal problem which defies solution. There is need for legislative clarification of rules and policies, but a realistic appraisal of such a possibility is not an optimistic one.

As to the general rules and principles, there is some guidance and a means of conflict-avoidance, in the Civil Code express ranking provisions for all the general privileges and in the rule that the general privileges which affect both movables and immovables should first be paid from available movables.

The Civil Code also contains some express provisions for resolving conflicts between special privileges. Another rule is that, unless the specific conflict is expressly provided for, special privileges come ahead of the general privileges.

There is also the rule of statutory construction *specialia generalibus derogant,* which reconciles a conflict by giving effect to the special law (regardless of enactment date) as an exception to the general law, and this also applies to the ranking of privileges.

In addition, a most helpful rule for the ranking of privileges is the settled rule of statutory construction that, in the event of irreconcilable conflict between two legislative texts, the later expression prevails over the earlier one.

* * * * * *

SUCCESSION OF COOLEY
26 La. Ann. 166 (1874).

TALIAFERRO, J.

The proceeds of the succession, after paying claims of a higher grade than that of the lessor, the vendor and the homestead claim, were reduced to the sum of $549.92. For this sum a contest arose between a vendor of a lot of furniture, claiming as due him by the estate $874.50; a lessor claiming $1,500 for lease of house and lot, and the tutor of the minor child of the decedent, left in necessitous circumstances, claiming a thousand dollars under the homestead law. Each of the contestants claimed superiority of privilege. In the court below judgment was rendered in favor of the minor's claim, and the opponent claiming the vendor's privilege, has appealed. In this court the contest is limited to the homestead claim, and the party asserting the vendor's privilege.

The conclusion arrived at by the judge *a quo*, seems to be founded upon these considerations: That as by article 3263 of the Civil Code, the privilege of the vendor on movables sold by him still in the possession of the vendee, is inferior to that of the owner of the house or farm which they serve to furnish or supply, for his rents; and, as it has been determined (*Succession of Bouvet*, 25 An. 431) that the homestead claim confers a higher privilege than that of the lessor, it must be deduced that the words "except those for the vendor's privilege," have reference alone to the privilege of the vendor of real estate; that this construction obviates all difficulty in construing the several articles of the Code bearing on the subject; that the homestead privilege was given the highest rank with one exception, that of the vendor; that as there are two privileges of the vendor, that on immovables, which enjoys the highest rank, and that on movables, which holds an inferior rank, the exception can not apply to both, but only to the one holding the first rank, that on immovables.

We concur with our learned brother of the court *a qua* in the conclusions he arrived at in this case, and adopt them as satisfactorily disposing of the otherwise awkward confliction that would exist between the several privileges contended for in this litigation.

It is therefore ordered that the judgment of the district court be affirmed, with costs.

* * * * * *

NOTES AND QUESTIONS

1. As the case recites, the original text of the 1852 statute creating the privilege of the surviving spouse and of Article 3252 of the 1870 Civil Code provided that the privilege was outranked by the vendor's privilege but was superior to all other debts. This led to the obvious possibility of a vicious circle in the ranking of privileges affecting movables, because the Civil Code ranks the vendor's privilege behind the lessor's privilege. Do you feel that the court's desire to avoid this vicious circle justified its interpretation of the "vendor's privilege" in Article 3252 to mean only the vendor's privilege on immovables?

2. The court's valiant attempt at avoiding a vicious circle was ultimately thwarted by Act 242 of 1918, which amended Article 3252 to provide specifically that the privilege of the surviving spouse is primed by vendor's privileges on *both* movable and immovable property. The 1918 act also amended the article to provide that the privilege of the surviving spouse is primed by all conventional mortgages. Thus, with apparent indifference to the consequences, the legislature not only resurrected the vicious circle that had been avoided in *Cooley* but created no fewer than three vicious circles on immovables: (i) the privilege of the surviving spouse primes general privileges, which prime conventional mortgages, which prime the surviving spouse; (ii) the privilege of the surviving spouse primes judicial mortgages, which prime a subsequently recorded conventional mortgage, which primes the surviving spouse; and (iii) the privilege of the surviving spouse primes general privileges, which prime judicial mortgages, which prime a subsequently arising conventional mortgage, which primes the surviving spouse.

3. By 1932, the Louisiana Supreme Court seemed to have lost its desire to interpret the law in order to avoid vicious circles. In *Morelock v. Morgan & Bird Gravel Co., Inc.*, 174 La. 658, 141 So. 368 (1932), the court was faced with the problem of ranking the vendor's privilege on movables against a privilege created under the corporate receiver statute in favor of those creditors lending money to the receiver. The receiver's certificates evidencing these loans were given a privilege over all other creditors of the corporation "save the vendor's lien and privilege." Citing *Cooley*, the court originally ruled that the vendor's privilege in question was limited to that on immovables. On rehearing, however,

the court held that this exception applied to the vendor's privilege on both movable and immovable property, notwithstanding arguments that the holding would create the possibility of a conflict among the holders of the receiver's certificates, the lessor and the vendor.

4. It is well known that there are myriad vicious circles in the ranking of privileges on movables. For a detailed analysis of a number of them, *see* Dainow, *Vicious Circles in the Louisiana Law of Privileges*, 25 La. L. Rev. 1 (1964), of which excerpts appear below. The classic example of a vicious circle involved competition among the vendor, the chattel mortgagee, and the lessor. Suppose that a debtor purchased movable property on credit, executed and recorded a chattel mortgage bearing upon this property, and then brought the property upon leased premises. Civil Code Article 3263 gives the lessor priority over the vendor. Under the former Chattel Mortgage Law, a chattel mortgage primed all privileges arising after the chattel mortgage was filed for public registry. Thus, under the facts assumed, the chattel mortgage would yield to the vendor's privilege but would have priority over the lessor's privilege. This vicious circle was eliminated by the adoption of Chapter 9 of the Uniform Commercial Code and La. R.S. 9:4770, which rank security interests ahead of privileges held by both the vendor and the lessor. Thus, the priority of a modern day security interest against these two privileges would be certain but different from the ranking that existed under the Chattel Mortgage Law: In first priority would be the security interest, which would prime the lessor's privilege, which would prime the vendor's privilege.

5. Numerous other vicious circles involving the vendor's privilege have arisen, chiefly because the legislature has often shown a propensity to protect the vendor when creating a competing privilege. A discussion of these can be found in L. David Cromwell, *Vendor's Privilege: Adheret Vicerbus Rei*, 75 La. L. Rev. 1165 (2015).

Chapter 7
The Private Works Act

A. In General

Under the regime of the Civil Code of 1870, a special privilege on an immovable was granted to "[a]rchitects, undertakers, bricklayers, painters, master builders, contractors, subcontractors, journeymen, laborers, cartmen and other workmen employed in constructing, rebuilding or repairing houses, buildings, or making other works," as well as to "[t]hose who have supplied the owner or other person employed by the owner, his agent or subcontractor, with materials of any kind for the construction or repair of an edifice or other work, when such materials have been used in the erection or repair of such houses or other works." La. Civ. Code art. 3249 (1870). *See also* La. Civ. Code art. 2772 (1870). Only the contractor, workers employed directly by the owner, and persons who supplied materials directly to the owner of an immovable were entitled to a privilege in their own right upon the immovable. Persons who supplied labor or material to the contractor were relegated to the right of subrogation to the contractor's privilege and to the right to sue the owner for any contract funds that might remain in his hands at the time they presented their claims. This regime found its genesis in the Digest of 1808, which provided a privilege only for workmen and laborers, in innovations made in the Civil Code of 1825, which extended privileges to suppliers for the first time, and in numerous statutory enactments that preceded the adoption of the Civil Code of 1870.

The construction privileges granted by the 1870 Code ranked concurrently and enjoyed a preference over all mortgages, provided that they were filed in a timely manner. *See* La. Civ. Code arts. 3272 and 3274 (1870). These privileges were not directly ranked against vendor's privileges, but instead the Civil Code provided for a separate appraisement procedure, with the vendor being paid the amount of the "appraisement on the land," and the other privileged creditors receiving "the appraisement of the building." La. Civ. Code art. 3268. In *City of Baltimore v. Parlange*, 23 La. Ann. 365 (1871), the Supreme Court observed that this separate appraisement procedure, protecting a contractor who subsequently performed work upon the immovable against the pre-existing privilege of the vendor, "exemplifies the intelligent sense of justice which distinguishes the civil law."

However intelligent and just this system may have appeared to the court, others apparently believed it to be insufficient. The Louisiana Constitution of 1879, in Article 175, mandated that the General Assembly "pass laws to protect laborers on buildings, streets, roads, railroads, canals and other similar works, against the failure of contractors and subcontractors to pay their current wages when due, and to make the corporation, company or individual for whose benefit the work is done responsible for their ultimate payment." Similar mandates were found in subsequent constitutions. The first attempt at fulfillment of this constitutional mandate appeared in Acts 1880, No. 134, which was followed by numerous other acts over the ensuing decades, including Act No. 139 of 1922, none of which purported to expressly repeal conflicting provisions of the 1870 Civil Code. Finally, in 1926, the Legislature enacted Act No. 298, which was not only comprehensive in its scope but also purported to repeal all conflicting laws, including inconsistent provisions of the Civil Code. On the basis of this repealing clause, it has been held that the 1926 statute was intended to cover the whole subject matter and thus repealed Civil Code Article 2772 and other provisions of the 1870 Code by implication. *See Robertshaw Controls Co. v. Pre-Engineered Products, Co., Inc.*, 669 F.2d 298 (5th Cir. 1982). The 1926 statute, with a few subsequent amendments, was the law in force at the time the Legislature, on the recommendation of the Louisiana State Law Institute, adopted in 1981 the present Private Works Act, which appears at La. R.S. 9:4801 *et seq.*

* * * * * *

Report to the Legislature in Response to in Response to SR No. 158 Of 2012 Louisiana Lien Laws (Private Works Act) (Feb. 15, 2013)

The current Private Works Act was drafted by the Law Institute and enacted by Acts 1981, No. 724. The 1981 enactment represented a comprehensive modernization of the predecessor statute that had been enacted almost sixty years earlier in 1922. The 1922 legislation was itself a comprehensive revision and consolidation of the laws regulating the rights and liabilities of persons who contract for the improvement or modification of an immovable. The Act serves as the framework for the implementation of two fundamental policies. The first is that persons who contribute to the improvement of an immovable are entitled to legal protection so that neither an owner nor his creditors appropriate the value of their efforts without compensating them. The second policy is that owners, who initiate and will benefit from the work, should take reasonable steps to see that their contractors and suppliers are paid and that contractors do not appropriate the price of the work and leave subcontractors, laborers, and suppliers unpaid. These basic policies devised by the Legislature have, for the most part, survived the test of time.

The basic means of accomplishing the policy objectives of the Act are quite simple. First, contractors, laborers, suppliers of materials, and others who deal directly with the owner of an immovable or who contribute to its improvement are granted a privilege on the immovable to secure the price of their work or materials. Secondly, owners who have work done on an immovable through a general contractor are expected to require the contractor to record a notice of his contract and to provide a surety bond protecting those persons who perform work or supply materials under the contract. The owner who fails to comply with these provisions is not only made personally liable for the claims that would otherwise be protected by the surety bond, but his property is subjected to a privilege to secure these personal claims against the owner. The Act also imposes personal liability upon a contractor for these claims, regardless of whether notice of contract is filed. In addition, a penalty is inflicted upon the general contractor who does not record notice of his contract. If the contract is over $25,000, he is denied a privilege on the immovable for the price of his work. The contractor's failure to record notice of his contract does not affect the personal liability of the owner or contractor, nor the privilege enjoyed by those who deal with the contractor.

The mechanisms of the Act work quite well if the owner requires the contractor to comply with the Act by filing a timely notice of contract with a proper bond attached. Upon completion of the work, a notice of termination is filed in the mortgage records by the owner. Anyone who worked on the project or supplied materials and was not paid may file a statement of his claim and send a copy of it to the owner. If no claims are filed within thirty days after the filing of the notice of termination, the owner obtains cancellation of the contract of all claims except that of the contractor, and thirty days later the owner may have the contract completely cancelled from the mortgage records.

If claims are filed, then the owner or any interested person can convoke a concursus against the contractor, the surety, and all of the claimants. If the owner demonstrates that a proper bond has been given by a solvent surety and that the owner has paid all he owed the contractor for the work, he may obtain an order directing the clerk to cancel the contract and all of the claims and privileges from the records. Thereafter, the owner has no further liability or concern in the matter, and the claimants litigate the validity of their claims with the contractor and the surety.

Often, however, for a variety of reasons, an owner fails to require the contractor to file notice of contract or to provide a surety bond. Work on immovables, particularly when involving individual residences, is often done on a small scale involving unsophisticated parties. In many, if not most, of those cases, the owner may be wholly unaware of the requirements of the Act and may not think it necessary to obtain legal advice. The employment of plumbers, painters, roofers, and similar workers seldom causes the owner to resort to the procedures necessary to protect himself—even though he may have some idea that such things as "mechanic's liens" or "construction liens," as they are popularly called, exist. Even when an owner is aware of the provisions of the Act and his potential liability for failing to require the contractor to provide a surety bond, it is often not financially feasible to obtain a surety bond. In many cases, the contractor might be unable to obtain a bond at any cost. In all of these cases, an owner is at risk if he pays his contractor before confirming that the contractor and his subcontractors have paid all workers and suppliers, even those whose identities are not known to the owner.

Under the Act, the owner's property is not only subject to a privilege for the amounts owed to unpaid claimants, but he is personally liable to them for these amounts. When notice of contract is not recorded and a bond is not given, a privilege by a subcontractor, laborer or supplier may be filed for up to sixty days after the work has been completed. If the owner is unaware of the risk, it is likely that he will have already paid his contractor the full price of the work, thus exposing the owner to the risk of having to pay twice and to then pursue his contractor, who, if he has not paid the suppliers and subcontractors, is not likely to be available to reimburse the owner.

Several arguments have been made to support the Act's imposition of personal liability on the owner to persons with whom there is no privity of contract, even after the owner has paid his contractor. First, and most importantly, the Act gives the owner a means to avoid personal liability by recording notice of contract and requiring a surety bond. Secondly, the presence of the bond permits, indirectly, the owner to agree to make his payments as the work progresses, or even after it is finished, and still permits the contractor to obtain credit for the cost of the work as it progresses. In the absence of some assurance of payment, subcontractors and suppliers are less likely to extend credit to the contractor, who would then need to have sufficient capital to complete the job. In a sense, the credit extended to the contractor is in effect credit extended to the owner, for in the absence of the contractor's ability to obtain services and supplies on credit, the contractor would demand that the owner fund costs in advance, rather than in periodic, after-the-fact progress payments. Moreover, it is obviously advantageous to the owner to defer paying until after the work or some definable part of it is finished, particularly since financial institutions are unlikely to lend even part of the funds without some assurances of completion and freedom from claims. The Act's balancing of interests among the contractors, those from whom they obtain services and supplies, the owner, and lenders, has proved to be essentially effective for more than a hundred years. This balancing of interests is ultimately founded in the policy judgment, which pervades many areas of Louisiana law, that one who receives an unmerited enhancement of his property should compensate those persons who cause that enhancement.

It should be borne in mind that claims arise under the Private Works Act not just when the general contractor fails to pay for work or materials but also when a subcontractor fails to do so. Under these circumstances, the general contractor may be just as free from fault as the owner, for he may have fully paid all persons who dealt directly with him. Like the owner, however, the general contractor is nonetheless made personally liable to the unpaid claimant and thus risks having to pay twice for the same work or supplies. Indeed, if the general contractor is solvent, he ultimately bears the entirety of the risk, because he is obligated by the Act to indemnify the owner against these claims.

In the thirty years since its last comprehensive revision, the Act has been amended, or proposed for amendment, in most sessions of the Legislature, and in some sessions by more than one act. Though those amendments have, for the most part, preserved the basic structure and policies of the Act, they have modified its details and procedures to deal with specific problems caused by the jurisprudence, changing economic conditions and business and financing practices, or the desire of certain classes of persons affected by the Act to correct what they perceived to be its deficiencies or unfairness as the Act applied to them in particular cases. However well-intentioned, these piecemeal changes to certain specific provisions of the Act have sometimes been made in a fashion that does not comport with the overall thrust of the Act. Some changes have introduced statutory language that is either imprecise or ambiguous or different from the words used to describe the identical concepts elsewhere in the Act. Some amendments have used the words "claim" and "privilege" almost interchangeably, even though these two concepts have entirely different meanings and consequences under the Act. Notice requirements have been added to the Act in a variety of places, rather than in a central location, with the unintended effect of creating traps for the unwary claimant. Some of these notice provisions appear to fail to achieve any real benefit, while others arguably allow a period of time for notice that is too long to allow the owner or general contractor to protect themselves. The Law Institute has also noted the existence of a number of changes to the Act that do not appear to state what was likely intended, leaving courts to struggle with the proper interpretation of the revision.

* * * * * *

GLEISSNER

v.

HUGHES

95 So. 529 (La. 1922)

DAWKINS, J.

Plaintiffs became the owners, by the last will and testament of Mrs. P. B. Barlow, deceased, of two mortgage notes, dated May 25 and June 18, 1920, respectively, each for the sum of $10,000, the first being secured by special mortgage upon lots 285 and 286, and the second secured similarly by lots 228 and 229, all situated in the Pinehurst subdivision of the city of Shreveport, La. Neither note was paid by the maker, P. E. Jones; they were duly foreclosed upon, and the property was bid in by plaintiffs at sheriff's sale who sought to have the amounts of their bids credited upon the notes. The sheriff declined to make title to the property, for the reason that it appeared by the mortgage certificate that there were a large number of claims, amounting to several thousand dollars, purporting to be for labor and materials performed and used in erecting certain improvements, recorded against the property.

Thereupon plaintiffs filed petitions for rules against the sheriff and all of the persons whose names appeared as claimants in the mortgage certificate, demanding that they show cause why said inscriptions should not be canceled and the property conveyed to petitioners free of incumbrance. Defendants (claimants) in rule responded, asserting liens and privileges alleged to be superior to plaintiffs' mortgages; and there were two separate judgments (the two causes having been consolidated below for purposes of trial) ordering plaintiffs to pay over in cash the amounts of their bids, and relegating all claimants to the proceeds. The judgments further ranked the claims, directing that they be paid in the order named, and that thereafter the mortgages, conventional and judicial, be paid according to the priority of their recordation. As between the Shreveport Long Leaf Lumber Company and the American National Bank it was ordered that the latter be paid the sum of $2,150, interest, and attorney's fees from the proceeds of the lien recognized in the former's favor. The decree further provided that the contractors, laborers, and materialmen be paid concurrently and pro rata as between themselves. The cases appear in this court in one transcript and under one number as the result of an appeal prosecuted by the plaintiffs.

The errors assigned by appellants are as follows:

"(1) The court erred in not holding that article 3274 of the Civil Code, and Act 229 of 1916, in so far as they attempt to give a preference to after-recorded liens over a prior mortgage, was violative of article 186 of the Constitution of 1898.

(2) In any event, the court erred in holding that the liens or privileges claimed by the lienholders could supersede and rank an existing mortgage when

the same were not recorded within seven days after the date of the contract for the same.

(3) The court further erred in holding that Act 229 of 1916 superseded or repealed article 3274 of the Civil Code of the state.

(4) The court erred in holding that under Act 229 of 1916 persons who furnished material or performed labor on a building are entitled to a lien superior to a prior mortgage recorded against the property.

(5) The court erred in holding that Act 229 of 1916, by its terms intended to give to lienholders a superior lien over an existing mortgage on the property."

Opinion.

1. Plaintiffs' first assignment is answered by the article of the Constitution (1913) itself (Article 186) upon which they rely. It reads:

> "No mortgage or privilege on immovable property shall affect third persons, *unless recorded or registered in the parish where the property is situated, in the manner and within the time as is now or may be prescribed by law*, except privileges for expenses of last illness and privileges for taxes, state, district, parish, ward or municipal; provided, such tax liens, mortgages, and privileges shall lapse in three years from the 31st day of December, in the year in which the taxes are levied, and whether now or hereafter recorded." (Italics ours).

There is no doubt but that liens and privileges such as those asserted in this case cannot affect third persons like the plaintiffs unless recorded (*McIlvaine v. Legare*, 34 La. Ann. 925; *Gay v. Bovard*, 27 La. Ann. 290; *Bank v. Fortier*, 27 La. Ann. 246; *Berwin v. Weis*, 28 La. Ann. 365; *Bank v. Ferry*, 32 La. Ann. 315; *Adams v. Adams*, 27 La. Ann. 275); but the article leaves it to the Legislature to determine "the manner and time" within which they shall be so recorded in order to bind such persons. Pursuant to similar provisions in the prior Constitutions, the Legislature had passed such laws, one of which was the Article 3274 of the Civil Code of 1870, in which it was provided that liens of the character now in question should "confer no preference on the creditor who holds it over creditors who have acquired a mortgage unless the act or other evidence of the debt is recorded within seven days from the date of the act or obligation of indebtedness. . . ." This article of the Code has been held to give such liens a preference over prior mortgages when seasonably recorded. *Jacob v.*

Preston, 31 La. Ann. 518; *Pedesclaux v. Legare*, 32 La. Ann. 385; *Johnston v. Weinstock*, 31 La. Ann. 698; *Gallaugher v. Congregation*, 35 La. Ann. 829; *Givanovitch v. Congregation*, 36 La. Ann. 274; *Brashear v. Alexandria Cooperage Co.*, 50 La. Ann. 587, 23 South. 540; *Brown v. Staples*, 138 La. 602, 70 South. 529.

The language of that article (3274) might have been construed differently, inasmuch as it does not expressly say that such liens shall prime pre-existing mortgages, the provision being:

> "It shall confer no preference on the creditor who holds it, over creditors who have acquired a mortgage," etc.

It might have been said, in view of the rule of strict construction applicable to privileges, that the lawmaker meant mortgages which creditors "have acquired" since the filing of the lien; but the jurisprudence of this court seems fairly well settled in favor of a construction which gives to such claims timely recorded, a preference over prior mortgages, and persons such as the claimants in this case are justified in relying upon that interpretation in performing labor and furnishing materials for improvements to be erected upon property previously mortgaged; and it is now too late to announce a different holding as against rights already acquired.

Of course, if the mortgage had been given before the law was passed, it might be said to come in conflict with constitutional provisions against divesting vested rights and impairing the obligations of contracts; but, where the rights of a mortgagee are acquired after the enactment of such a law, they pass subject to it, and the holder takes knowing that the mortgagee may create such superior rights against the property, and the constitutional provisions referred to have no application. And there is reason for subordinating prior mortgages to such claims, for the labor and material serve to create a greater value or security which would inure to the benefit of the mortgage, and such improvements should not be prevented or discouraged because of existing mortgages. However, the mortgage holder is not without remedy. In most, if not all, of such acts it is stipulated that the mortgagor shall not alienate or incumber the property to the prejudice of the mortgagee, and a vigilant creditor could doubtless protect himself against violation of such promise.

2. A determination of the second alleged error depends somewhat upon the question as to whether the Act No. 229 of 1916 has extended the period within which such liens must be recorded to affect third persons from 7 to 45 days. Section 1 declares that claimants of the class now before the court shall have

> "a privilege upon such building, erection or improvements and upon the land belonging to such owner or proprietor on which the same is situated, and upon the proceeds or balance of the contract price in the hands of the owner, due or to become due to the contractor, to secure the payment of such work or labor performed, or materials, machinery or fixtures furnished. *Such privilege shall be preferred to all other privileges or incumbrances which may attach to or upon the said building, erection or improvement* and upon the said land, or either of them, and upon the proceeds or balance of the contract price in the hands of the owner, due or to become due to the contractor." (Italics by the court.)

Section 2 requires that such claims shall be verified by affidavit, giving name of owner, contractor, claimant, description of the property, etc., and that:

> "Such statement must be filed [in the mortgage records] within forty-five (45) days after the *acceptance of the work* by the owner of the land on which work was done or his trustee or agent."

In view of the declared purpose of this statute (229 of 1916) as expressed in its title—"To provide for the creation, recognition and recordation of the liens and privileges of laborers, contractors, subcontractors, material men, mechanics and furnishers of machinery or fixtures, and to enforce the payment of said liens and privileges, and to repeal all laws in conflict herewith"—we think the intention and result was that it made such liens superior in rank to all other incumbrances upon the property, whether arising prior or subsequent thereto, provided the same were recorded within 45 days "after the acceptance of the work," meaning, in cases like the one now under consideration, the acceptance of the labor, material, machinery, etc., of each individual claimant, as distinguished from the completed job. In other words, as to a general contractor, his claim may be filed within 45 days from the date of the acceptance of the building or improvement undertaken to be constructed; as to a subcontractor,

45 days from the acceptance of such subcontract work by the owner or his agent.

This view of the matter appears to be further accentuated by section 8 of the act, which reads:

> "That all privileges under the provisions of this act are in full force and effect from and after the time the labor is performed, or material, machinery, or fixtures furnished."

We conclude that the Act 229 of 1916 had the effect of extending the period within which such liens may be filed from 7 to 45 days, and, instead of this delay beginning from "the date of the act or obligation of indebtedness," it was made to run from "the acceptance by the owner of the work," in the sense above indicated.

With regard to the language of section 1 of said act, and its purpose to make such liens prime prior mortgages, we think what we have said in regard to article 3274 of the Code is equally applicable, and that liens timely recorded, as required by section 2, acquire a preference over such mortgages.

3, 4, and 5. Assignments Nos. 3, 4, and 5 have been covered by what has been said with respect to No. 2.

It is [from the evidence] seen that none of the liens were filed within the 45 days from the date of furnishing materials and performing of the labor, except that of Shreveport Long Leaf Lumber Company, and hence, with this one exception, no lien was acquired which can prime the mortgage of plaintiffs.

For the reasons assigned, the judgments appealed from are amended by ranking the claims of plaintiff against the proceeds of the property as superior to those of all other claimants except that of Shreveport Long Leaf Lumber Company, and as thus amended, they are affirmed, at the costs of the appellees.

* * * * * *

NOTES AND QUESTIONS

1. Article 186 of the 1913 Louisiana Constitution was retained in the 1921 Constitution as Article XIX, Section 19 and still exists as statutory law today in the Constitution Ancillaries. It is reproduced and discussed in Chapter 5 above.

2. Act 229 of 1916, one of the precursors of the current Private Works Act, accorded privileges arising under the act preference over all other privileges or encumbrances upon an immovable. In rejecting a constitutional challenge to this ranking rule under Article 186 of the 1913 Constitution, the court in *Gleissner v. Hughes* cited Civil Code Article 3274 as another example of an exercise by the legislature of latitude allowed it under the constitutional provision to determine the manner and time in which privileges must be recorded.

3. The court observed that Civil Code Article 3274 merely *implies* that a timely filed privilege outranks a previously existing mortgage and that the reference to "creditors who have acquired a mortgage" in the article might be construed to refer only to creditors acquiring a mortgage *after* the privilege has been filed. As discussed in the preceding chapter, the court in *Homes Savings & Loan Association v. Tri-Parish Ventures*, 505 So. 2d 165 (La. App. 4th Cir. 1987), also appeared to suggest that Article 3274 is so limited. According to that court's opinion, Article 3274 gives "a grace period . . . to the privilege holder over *intervening* mortgages only, where the act importing privilege is recorded within a very limited period after the date of execution." 505 So. 2d at 167. Did the court overlook Civil Code Article 3186, which establishes the general rule that privileges by their nature outrank mortgages?

4. As will be discussed below, privileges arising under the present Private Works Act have retroactive effect against third persons to the earlier of the commencement of work or the filing of notice of contract; however, they no longer outrank all other encumbrances. Instead, Private Works Act privileges other than those in favor of laborers are subordinate to those mortgages and vendor's privileges that have previously become effective as to third persons. *See* La. R.S. 9:4820A and 4821. Laborer's privileges continue to outrank all mortgages and vendor's privileges.

5. In *Gleissner v. Hughes*, the court held that the period for filing a privilege under the 1916 statute commenced separately for each subcontractor on the date that the work under his subcontract was completed. As will be developed in the discussion below, this is not the rule under the present Private Works Act, which provides that the period for filing statements of claim or privilege generally runs for all claimants from the same events—either filing of notice of termination or substantial completion of the work—regardless of when the particular claimant's work was completed. *See* La. R.S. 9:4822.

B. Claims and Privileges Afforded

***See* La. Rev. Stat. 9:4801-4803.**

Private Works Act privileges arise under R.S. 9:4801 and R.S. 9:4802. There is a strict dichotomy between these two sections. The privileges established under R.S. 9:4801 are created in favor of persons who are in direct privity of contract with the owner, including contractors, laborers employed by the owner, suppliers who sell materials directly to the owner, lessors who lease equipment directly to the owner for use at the site, and professionals employed by the owner, such as surveyors, engineers, and architects and their professional subconsultants. R.S. 9:4801 provides all of these claimants with a privilege upon the owner's interest in the immovable for all amounts due to them within the scope of R.S. 9:4803.

In contrast, R.S. 9:4802 protects those who are not in direct privity of contract with the owner, such as subcontractors, laborers employed by a contractor or subcontractor, suppliers who sell materials to a contractor or subcontractor, lessors who lease equipment to a contractor or subcontractor for use at the site, and surveyors, engineers, and architects employed by a contractor or subcontractor, as well as their professional subconsultants. R.S. 9:4802 affords all of these persons two distinct rights. First, they are granted a personal claim against both the owner and the contractor for the amounts due to them within the scope of R.S. 9:4803. In addition, these claims against the owner are secured by a privilege upon that owner's interest in the immovable.

In order to preserve their claims and privileges, claimants under both R.S. 9:4801 and 4802 must file a statement of claim or privilege within the time provided by R.S. 9:4822, as discussed in a later section of this chapter.

* * * * * *

P.H.A.C. SERVICES, INC.

v.

SEAWAYS INTERNATIONAL, INC.

403 So. 2d 1199 (La. 1981)

DIXON, Chief Justice.

This is a suit instituted by two unpaid subcontractors who supplied labor and materials for the construction of an offshore drilling platform living quarters unit; defendants are the general contractor and the owner. The primary issue is what, if any, privileges are available to these plaintiffs.

The unit involved in this litigation is a three story steel structure which was built on blocks at a construction site in St. Mary Parish. It was then transported by the owner, Pennzoil Company and Pennzoil Producing Company, and attached to an offshore drilling platform located in the Gulf of Mexico off the coast of Texas.

Pennzoil contracted with Seaways International, Inc. for construction of the unit. This contract was not recorded and no bond was required of Seaways as contractor. Seaways contracted with P. H. A. C. Services, Inc. for installation of plumbing, heating and air conditioning in the unit, and with Acoustical Spray Insulators, Inc. for labor and acoustical materials for the unit.

It is uncontested that P. H. A. C. and Acoustical performed their work in accordance with their subcontracts with Seaways, and that they have not been paid. They have timely filed lien affidavits, and have instituted suit to enforce their privileges.

Three statutes are relied upon by plaintiffs: R.S. 9:4801 *et seq.* (Private Works Act); R.S. 9:4861 *et seq.* (dealing with privileges on oil, gas and water wells); and, in the alternative, R.S. 9:4502 (dealing with privileges on movables). The trial court ruled that the only privilege available to plaintiffs is that granted by R.S. 9:4861 *et seq.* The Court of Appeal disagreed, and held that only the Private Works Act, R.S. 9:4801 *et seq.* is applicable. *P.H.A.C. Services, Inc. v.*

Seaways International, Inc., 393 So. 2d 117 (La. App. 1st Cir. 1980). This court granted writs on application of all parties. 398 So. 2d 527 (La.1981).

R.S. 9:4861 *et seq*.

R.S. 9:4861 creates a privilege in favor of certain persons who perform work in connection with the exploration for oil, gas or water. . . . This statute confers a privilege to furnishers of labor or services whose work was done "in drilling or in connection with the drilling of any well," or "in the operation or in connection with the operation of any oil, gas or water well." The parties and the lower courts have focused on whether the work done by plaintiffs is the type of work intended to be protected by this statute. Specifically, the parties' concern has been on whether it is significant that the work done by plaintiffs was performed at a construction site miles away from the lease site.

The claim in this case does not appear to be covered by R.S. 9:4861. First, the lien is granted to "any person . . . who performs any labor or service . . . in connection with the operation" of any oil or gas well. The privilege, however, is on the production, the well, the lease, and "machinery, . . . equipment, buildings, tanks, and other structures thereto attached or located on the lease." The lien is further granted for transporting or furnishing "material or supplies . . . for or in connection with the operation" of any well; however, the privilege granted is on the production, the well, the lease and "buildings, tanks and other structures thereto attached for the . . . operation of the well."

It is clear that the building involved in this case was designed to be used "in connection with the operation" of oil or gas wells. It is not, however, clear that this statute was designed to govern the case where production equipment is constructed for use completely out of this state and on the high seas. The statute seems to contemplate that the lien be on the well, the lease, or property located on the lease. In this case, the building was ultimately located on a lease, but a lease which is completely outside the state. The statute does not purport to affect producing wells outside the State of Louisiana.

R.S. 9:4861 is therefore not applicable.

R.S. 9:4801 *et seq*.

The Private Works Act, R.S. 9:4801 *et seq.*, confers a privilege to certain persons who supply labor or materials "for the erection, construction, repair, or improvement of immovable property." R.S. 9:4801. The parties agree that the act applies if the living quarters unit is an immovable.

The Civil Code articles on the classification of thing were recently amended. 1978 La. Acts, No. 728, amending the Civil Code of 1870 articles 448-87. Because the revision became effective in 1979, and the operative facts leading to this litigation occurred in 1978, the rights of the parties are governed by the articles as they existed prior to the revision. Nonetheless, examination of the revision provides guidance and insight into a proper interpretation of the pre-amendment articles.

The Civil Code of 1870 divided immovables into three categories: immovables by nature, immovables by destination and immovables by the object to which they are applied. C.C. of 1870 art. 463. The Code attempted to define immovables by nature as things which "can not move themselves or be removed from one place to another." C.C. of 1870 art. 462. This definition was followed by a listing of those things considered to be immovables by nature.

This definition was deleted from the Code by the 1978 revision, because, as explained by the revision's redactors:

> "This analytical scheme definition and illustrations contradicts reality. Contemporary mechanical means make possible the relocation of immense quantities of earth, timber, buildings, and various kinds of constructions. It appears, therefore, that immovability by nature under present Louisiana law is a legal fiction based partly on practical considerations and partly on inherent characteristics of things. In the light of contemporary conceptions the only immovables by nature are tracts of land, i.e., portions of the surface of the earth individualized by boundaries." Expose des Motifs of Act 728, 1978 La. Acts, Vol. II, p. 1908.

Immovability is a legal concept and not merely an inherent quality of a thing. Whether a thing is classified as an immovable depends upon whether the legislature has accorded to that thing the preferred status of immovability.

Immovability "in fact" is not itself a prerequisite to immovability "in law," and things regarded as immovables by the law might be moved through the application of extraordinary mechanical means. To determine whether this living quarters unit is an immovable by nature, the Code articles listing the things which are immovables by nature should be considered.

The 1870 Code classified as immovables by nature buildings and other constructions. Although the Code did not define these terms, it did provide that buildings and other constructions are immovables regardless of "whether they have their foundations in the soil." C. C. of 1870 art. 464. Integration with the soil was not a prerequisite to immovability under former article 464, and the courts have properly classified as immovables things whose foundations rested upon blocks or posts. *See Prevot v. Courtney*, 241 La. 313, 129 So. 2d 1 (1961) (tractor shed and poultry house); *Lafleur v. Foret*, 213 So. 2d 141 (La. App. 3d Cir. 1968) (beagle and chicken brooders); *Vaughn v. Kemp*, 4 La. App. 682 (2d Cir. 1926) (small wooden frame garage).

The 1978 legislation made no changes in the classification of buildings. Under the revision, buildings which belong to the owner of the ground are considered component parts of a tract of land, C. C. 463, as amended by 1978 La. Acts, No. 728, and, when there is no unity of ownership, the building is considered a separate immovable. C. C. 464, as amended by 1978 La. Acts, No. 728. Thus, under the revision, as under the 1870 Code, buildings are always classified as immovables.

The trial court concluded that the living quarters unit was not a building because it "was not being used as a building; rather it was set upon wooden blocks while it was under construction." The Court of Appeal reversed, correctly noting that there is no codal requirement that a building have its foundation in the soil. Additionally, the trial court's reasoning would frustrate the purpose of the Private Works Act, which is to protect the claims of laborers and workmen. Many lien claimants perform work for the erection of new structures which naturally are not placed into use until completion. If classification must await actual use, then these lien claimants would find themselves unprotected by the act.

We agree with the conclusion of the Court of Appeal that this living quarters unit is a building. As the picture of the unit demonstrates, the facts speak eloquently for themselves. This is a three story high permanent steel structure with a helicopter landing pad constructed above it, built at a cost of over $400,000. It is designed to house offshore workers. Under prevailing notions, such a structure is a building and is therefore classified as an immovable.

Pennzoil maintains that the unit should not be classified as an immovable because the unit was intended to be moved offshore. The fact that the unit is capable of being moved by a powerful crane does not defeat classification of that thing as an immovable, for, as mentioned earlier, immovability is a legal concept and not an inherent quality of a thing.

The legislature has determined that a building is an immovable regardless of whether its foundation is integrated with the soil. This three story high permanent steel structure qualifies as a building and therefore is an immovable, and subject to the laws governing immovables. Consequently, the Private Works Act (including R.S. 9:4812) applies to this case.

For the foregoing reasons, the judgment of the Court of Appeal is affirmed, at the cost of defendants.

* * * * * *

NOTES AND QUESTIONS

1. The Private Works Act creates privileges upon immovables without purporting to define the term "immovable" for purposes of the act. As the case demonstrates, courts look to provisions of the Civil Code treating the division of things to determine what constitutes an immovable. *See* La. Civ. Code arts. 448 and 462 *et seq*.

2. Under the classification scheme of the Civil Code, buildings are always immovables, regardless of whether they are owned by the owner of the ground. *See* La. Civ. Code arts. 463 and 464. On the other hand, other constructions are classified as immovables only if they belong to the owner of the ground; when they are owned by someone else, other constructions are movables. *See* La. Civ.

Code art. 464, comment (d). Suppose that a servitude owner engages a contractor to erect a construction other than a building upon the land subject to the servitude. Does a privilege under the Private Works Act arise upon this construction? Does a privilege under the Private Works Act arise upon the servitude?

3. Suppose that the living quarters unit described in *P.H.A.C. Services* had been constructed in Louisiana with the intent that it be moved to a permanent location in another state. Would privileges upon the living quarters unit arise under the Private Works Act? Suppose that the identical living quarters unit had been constructed in another state and then permanently affixed to land in Louisiana. Would privileges under the Private Works Act arise in favor of those involved in the construction of the unit in the other state and, if so, would those privileges encumber the unit after it became affixed to the land in Louisiana? Would they encumber the land to which the unit became attached?

* * * * * *

CABLE & CONNECTOR WAREHOUSE, INC.

v.

OMNIMARK, INC.

700 So. 2d 1273 (La. App. 4th Cir. 1997)

ARMSTRONG, Judge.

This is a suit brought under the Private Works Act, La. R.S. 9:4801 *et seq.*, and other legal theories by an unpaid supplier of materials that were ultimately used in a construction project. The defendant prime contractor on the construction project, and its co-defendant surety, moved for summary judgment on the ground that the plaintiff was a supplier to a supplier, rather than a supplier to a contractor or subcontractor, and thus had no rights under the Private Works Act and on the ground that no other legal theory was applicable so as to allow the plaintiff recovery under the facts of this case. The trial court agreed with the defendants and granted the summary judgment. The plaintiff appeals. The judgment of the trial court is correct. In light of the facts which are uncontested or as to which there is no genuine issue, the plaintiff has no rights under the Private Works Act and the other legal theories urged by the plaintiff are without merit. Therefore, we affirm.

W.S. Bellows Construction Company contracted to act as general contractor to build out (i.e., complete the interior for tenant occupancy) a number of floors of the CNG Tower building in New Orleans. The space was to be occupied by McDermott and the project was variously described by the parties as the "CNG Tower job" and the "McDermott job."

Bellows subcontracted with the Sandoz Group, Inc. for installation of cabling for the computer system. Under that subcontract, Sandoz was to supply all the necessary cabling material.

Sandoz purchased the necessary cabling materials for the job from Omnimark, Inc. In turn, Omnimark had purchased the cabling materials from plaintiff Cable & Connector Warehouse, Inc. Sandoz and Omnimark were owned by the same person, Louis Sandoz, but were separate corporations.

Before beginning its on-site work, Sandoz invoiced Bellows for $112,066.23. The invoice states that $100,066.23 is for "pre-purchased materials" and $12,000 is for "professional fees for project design work-to-date." It is undisputed that the $100,066.23 was for all of the materials for the Sandoz subcontract with Bellows and that these were the materials which Sandoz purchased from Omnimark and which Omnimark purchased from Cable & Connector. Bellows first inspected the cabling materials, which were located at Cable & Connector's facility in Baton Rouge, and then paid the Sandoz invoice. However, while Sandoz was paid in full for the cabling materials by Bellows, Sandoz did not pay Omnimark and Omnimark did not pay Cable & Connector.

Cable & Connector shipped the cabling materials to the CNG Tower job site in several shipments over the course of several weeks. At or about the time of each shipment, Cable & Connector rendered an invoice for the materials shipped. Other than invoices which were solely for freight charges, there were nine Cable & Connector invoices. Each one of those nine invoices states that the materials are "sold to" "Omnimark, Inc./CNG Towers." Some of the invoices state "ship to" "The Sandoz Group/Omnimark," one states "ship to" Bellows and several state "ship to" "will call Bill Knock."

At some point in the project, Bellows terminated Sandoz as subcontractor because Sandoz' license was not in order. Bellows had Hi–Tech Electric, Inc., which was an electrical subcontractor already working on the CNG Tower project, complete the work that had been subcontracted to Sandoz. However, Sandoz continued in some sort of advisory capacity to assist Hi–Tech and Bellows to finish the job.

Cable & Connector was never paid for the cabling materials and recorded a Private Works Act lien against the CNG Tower Building. Bellows obtained a surety bond from Federal Insurance Company which was deposited with the Recorder of Mortgages so as to cancel Cable & Connector's lien. Cable & Connector sued Omnimark, Sandoz, Bellows, and Federal. The summary judgment appealed from dismissed Cable & Connector's suit only as against Bellows and Federal.

Because this case comes before us on an appeal from a summary judgment, we must determine whether there was any genuine issue of material fact and whether the mover was entitled to judgment as a matter of law. *See* La. Code Civ. Proc. art. 966(B); *see also* 1997 La. Acts 483 (amending Article 966); *Hayes v. Autin,* No. 96–287 (La. App. 3rd Cir. 12/26/96), 685 So. 2d 691, 694–95 (cited in Act 483), *writ denied,* No. 97–C–0281 (La. 3/14/97), 690 So. 2d 41.

A key legal point which impacts the issues and arguments in this case is that, while a supplier to a subcontractor or a contractor has certain rights under the Private Works Act, a supplier to a supplier does *not* have such rights under that statute. Put another way, in order to have rights under the Private Works Act, a supplier must sell directly to a subcontractor or a contractor. This arises from the statute's language granting rights to "Sellers, for the price of movables sold to a contractor or a subcontractor." La. R.S. 9:4802(A)(3). *See generally Leonard B. Hebert, Jr. & Co. v. Kinler,* 336 So. 2d 922, 924 (La. App. 4th Cir. 1976) in which the court stated: "Under the settled law of this State, a materialman who furnishes material to a materialman has no right to a lien." Because Cable & Connector sold cabling to another supplier (Omnimark), rather than to a subcontractor (Sandoz) or to a contractor (Bellows), Cable & Connector has no rights under the Private Works Act. Cable & Connector recognizes this legal rule but in an attempt to avoid its application advances a number of arguments, each of which will be discussed below.

Another legal rule that is of importance to some of the issues in this case is that, in a sale transaction, ownership of the things sold is transferred even if there has not yet been payment or delivery. A sale is perfected as soon as there is agreement between the buyer and seller as to the thing sold and the price. La. Civ. Code art. 2439. "Ownership is transferred between the parties as soon as there is agreement on the thing and the price is fixed, even though the thing sold is not yet delivered nor the price paid." La. Civ. Code art. 2456. In the present case, the purchase of the cabling materials from Cable & Connector was made by Omnimark using a purchase order on an Omnimark letterhead. Thus, the sale of the cabling materials by Cable & Connector to Omnimark, and the transfer of ownership of the cabling materials from Cable & Connector to Omnimark, was accomplished before the materials were shipped by Cable & Connector and before Cable & Connector rendered invoices for the cabling materials. This is of some importance because some of Cable & Connector's arguments are either explicitly or implicitly premised on the notion that the cabling materials were not sold until they were shipped and invoices were rendered by Cable & Connector.

Cable & Connector's first argument is that Bellows and Hi–Tech (the subcontractor who completed the cabling work after Sandoz was terminated) actually purchased most of the cabling material and, because that would constitute a sale to a contractor or subcontractor, Cable & Connector has rights under the Private Works Act as well as a contract claim against Bellows (Hi–Tech is not a party to this case). However, Cable & Connector's only factual basis for this argument is that part of the cabling material was delivered to the CNG Tower job site after Sandoz had been terminated as subcontractor by Bellows. Because of the termination of Sandoz, Cable & Connector assumes that the cabling materials delivered after that termination must have been "ordered" by Bellows and/or Hi–Tech. However, with respect to the question of who purchased the cabling material from Cable & Connector, it does not matter who "ordered" the delivery of the cabling material to the CNG Tower job site. Well prior to the termination of Sandoz' subcontract, the cabling material had been sold by Cable & Connector to Omnimark. Thus, when Cable & Connector delivered cabling material to the CNG Tower job site after Sandoz' termination, Cable & Connector did not own the cabling material and so could not be selling it to Bellows or Hi–Tech. Instead, at that time, the cabling material was owned by Omnimark or, if Omnimark had already re-sold it to Sandoz, it was owned by Sandoz.

As its next argument on appeal, Cable & Connector very briefly asserts that Bellows, "by ordering and authorizing the ordering and use of the Cable & Connector materials, engaged in acts that reasonably induced Cable & Connector to believe it would be paid for the materials." Thus, argues Cable & Connector, Bellows is liable for Cable & Connector's "detrimental reliance" upon Bellows. However, neither the excerpts of the depositions of Bellows' employees nor the other discovery materials filed by Cable & Connector in opposition to the motion for summary judgment show any such orders or authorization by Bellows. Also, the affidavit filed by Cable & Connector in opposition to the motion for summary judgment does not mention any reliance on Bellows or any facts from which such reliance might be inferred. Indeed, the record is devoid of any evidence that Cable & Connector was looking to or communicating with Bellows when it delivered the cabling materials. The mere fact that Bellows was the general contractor on the CNG Tower project, and that the cabling material was delivered to and used in the CNG Tower project, does not constitute an assurance by Bellows that Cable & Connector would be paid.

Cable & Connector's next argument on appeal is that Bellows is estopped from denying responsibility for the cabling because "Louisiana, under the doctrine of quantum meruit, recognizes that a person, such as Bellows Construction, may not escape the responsibility of paying for materials it uses by avoiding contractual formalities." In support of its argument, Cable & Connector quotes the following passage from *Royal Construction Co. v. Sias,* 496 So. 2d 1301 (La. App. 3rd Cir. 1986): "Quantum meruit is an equitable doctrine which is based on the concept that no one who benefits by the labor and materials of another, should be unjustly enriched thereby." But, in the present case, there was no "unjust enrichment" of Bellows. It is undisputed that Bellows paid Sandoz $100,066.23 for the cabling materials and there is no reason to doubt that $100,066.23 was a normal course of business price paid in an arms-length transaction. Furthermore, the issue is not merely one of an absence of contractual formalities. Indeed, Bellows contracted formally with Sandoz and Cable & Connector contracted formally with Omnimark. In contrast, there was no contract *at all* between Bellows and Cable & Connector.

Next, Cable & Connector argues that Omnimark's role in the transaction should be ignored for purposes of determining whether Cable & Connector has rights under the Private Works Act. In other words, Cable & Connector argues that it should be treated as if it sold the cabling materials directly to Sandoz rather than to Omnimark. Of course, as Sandoz was a subcontractor, rather than a supplier, such treatment would result in Cable & Connector having rights under the Private Works Act.

Cable & Connector asserts that Omnimark's role in the transaction should be ignored because Omnimark and Sandoz were not sufficiently separate—i.e., that we should disregard the separate corporate legal status of Omnimark and Sandoz for purposes of the Private Works Act. We believe this argument is unsound both factually and legally.

Factually, Omnimark and Sandoz were owned by the same person, Louis Sandoz, and Omnimark borrowed employees and office facilities from Sandoz (typically, with compensation to Sandoz although there is a dispute as to whether compensation was paid in the present case). However, Omnimark and Sandoz had separate bank accounts for their funds and kept separate accounting records. Also, the two corporations had different lines of business in that Sandoz provided services whereas Omnimark was a materials sourcing company. Sandoz bought materials from suppliers other than Omnimark and Omnimark sold materials to customers other than Sandoz. It is apparent that the two corporations functioned as distinct business entities.

Legally, Cable & Connector cites no legal authority for the proposition that the separate legal status of two corporations should be disregarded so that a supplier of a supplier will be given the Private Works Act rights of a supplier to a subcontractor. Further, the Private Works Act may not be applied expansively as Cable & Connector urges. To the contrary, lien statutes, because they are in derogation of common rights, must be strictly construed. *See e.g., Fruge v. Muffoletto,* 242 La. 569, 583, 137 So. 2d 336, 341 (1962); and *Hebert v. Kinler,* 336 So. 2d 922, 924 (La. App. 4th Cir. 1976). Cable & Connector's claim does not fit within the Private Works Act, and we may not stretch the statute to make it fit.

Lastly, Cable & Connector argues that Omnimark was merely an agent for Sandoz as to the purchase of the cabling material and that, thus, the cabling material was really sold to Sandoz. But, there is not a shred of evidence in the deposition excerpts, exhibits and the affidavit filed below that Omnimark was acting as an agent for Sandoz as to the purchase of the cabling material. To the contrary, the evidence is that Omnimark made its own purchase of the cabling material and then resold it to Sandoz. This is as Cable & Connector itself understood the transaction at the time as its invoices all state that the cabling material was sold to Omnimark.

For the foregoing reasons, the judgment of the trial court is affirmed.

AFFIRMED.

* * * * * *

NOTES AND QUESTIONS

1. Why could the plaintiff not claim a vendor's privilege upon the supplies it had furnished for the work?

2. Subcontractors of whatever tier, however remote they may be from the general contractor, are granted a claim and privilege by R.S. 9:4802, and suppliers to all of these subcontractors are similarly granted a claim and privilege. However, as the case demonstrates, suppliers to suppliers are granted no claim or privilege. What policy reasons justify denying a supplier to a supplier rights under the Private Works Act?

C. Definitions

1. "Owner"

The term "owner" as used in the Private Works Act has a much broader scope than its ordinary meaning. Under R.S. 9:4806(A), an owner can include a usufructuary, a naked owner, a holder of a predial servitude, a lessee, or even a mere possessor of an immovable. The claims that are granted against an owner by R.S. 9:4802 are limited to those owners who have contracted with the contractor and to any other owner who has agreed in writing to the price of the work and has specifically agreed to be liable for the claims granted by R.S.

9:4802. Notably, the privileges granted by both R.S. 9:4801 and 4802 affect only the interest in the immovable enjoyed by the owner whose obligation is secured by the privilege.

For these reasons, when a lessee contracts for work to improve the immovable subject to his lease, the lessor is not ordinarily responsible as an "owner" for claims of persons involved in the work, nor do the privileges granted by the Private Works Act encumber the lessor's ownership interest in the immovable; instead, they burden only the lessee's leasehold interest. Moreover, R.S. 9:4806 provides that the privileges upon the lessee's interest are inferior and subject to the right of the lessor to dissolve the lease for nonperformance of the lessee's obligations, as well as the lessor's right to execute upon the lessee's occupancy rights and sell them at a foreclosure sale free of Private Works Act privileges burdening the lessee's interest. Thus, if the lease terminates on account of the lessee's default, the Private Works Act privileges upon the lessee's interest are extinguished.

2. "Contractor," "General Contractor," and "Subcontractor"

R.S. 9:4807 defines a contractor to be a person who contracts with an owner to perform all or part of a work. Thus, it is apparent that there may be more than one contractor engaged on a single work. A *general contractor* is a contractor who contracts to perform all or substantially all of the work; this is the commonly understood meaning of the term. However, R.S. 9:4807 also provides that a contractor who would not otherwise qualify as a general contractor is nonetheless deemed to be a general contractor if timely notice of contract is filed with respect to the portion of the work that he agreed to perform. As will be seen below, this has significance not only for determining when privileges arising out of the portion of the work to be performed by that contractor are effective against third persons, but also when the deadline for filing statements of claim or privilege with respect to that portion of the work will arrive.

R.S. 9:4807 defines a subcontractor to be one who, by a contract made directly with a contractor or by a contract that is one of a series of contracts emanating from a contractor, is bound to perform all or part of the work contracted by that contractor. Thus, the Private Works Act protects not only those subcontractors who are hired directly by the contractor but also sub-subcontractors of whatever tier.

3. "Work"

R.S. 9:4808 defines a work to be a continuous project for the improvement, construction, erection, reconstruction, modification, repair, demolition, or other physical change of an immovable or its component parts. Consistent with the definition of "contractor," this single continuous work contemplated by R.S. 9:4808 may include elements of work contracted to be performed by several contractors who are in direct privity of contract with the owner. The existence of multiple contracts does not itself ordinarily cause a single continuous project to be divided into separate works.

Nevertheless, if a timely notice of contract is filed with respect to the work to be performed under a specific contract, then the work to be performed under that contract is deemed to be a work separate and distinct from other portions of the project undertaken by the owner. Moreover, as discussed above, the contractor under that contract is deemed to be a general contractor, even though he has not contracted to perform all or substantially all of the work. Because the portions of the project undertaken to be performed by such a contractor are deemed to be a separate work, privileges arising out of that portion of the work will be effective against third persons as of a date different from that of other privileges arising out of the work, and, in addition, the computation of the deadline for claimants to file statements of claim or privilege arising out of that portion of the work will begin to run at the conclusion of that portion of the work, rather than at the conclusion of the entire work.

It should be emphasized that the rules just stated apply to a *contractor* who files a notice of contract with respect to the portion of the overall work that he has contracted with the owner to perform; these rules do not apply to a *subcontractor* who has contracted with a contractor to perform part or even all of the work within the scope of that contractor's contract. The portion of a work to be performed by a subcontractor is never itself deemed to be a separate work.

Site preparation work of the nature described in R.S. 9:4808(C) is deemed to be a separate work to the extent that the site preparation work is not a part of the contractor's work. This rule has a number of consequences with respect to the dates that privileges arising out of the separate works become effective as to third persons and also with respect to the deadlines for filing statements of claims or privilege arising out of the separate works. These consequences will become apparent as the principles applicable to priority issues are developed in later sections of this chapter.

4. "Commencement," "Substantial Completion," and "Abandonment"

R.S. 9:4820(A)(2) defines what constitutes the beginning of work: the placement of materials in excess of $100 in value at the site or conducting other work at the site that would reasonably indicate from a simple inspection that work has begun. Notably, site preparation work is not considered in determining when work begins. The primary relevance of the date that work begins is that privileges arising out of the work are effective against third persons as of that date or, if earlier, the date of filing of notice of contract, as discussed more fully below.

Under a definition found in R.S. 9:4822(H), a work is substantially completed when (i) the last work is performed on, or materials are delivered to the site of the immovable, or (ii) the owner accepts the improvement, or possesses or occupies the immovable, although minor or inconsequential matters remain to be finished or minor defects or errors in the work are to be remedied. R.S. 9:4822(I) defines abandonment of a work to occur when the owner terminates the work and notifies persons engaged in its performance that he no longer desires to continue it or otherwise objectively and in good faith manifests the abandonment or discontinuance of the project. The date that a work is substantially completed or abandoned in many cases marks the beginning of the computation of the delay within which claimants must file statements of claim or privilege for sums due them.

The questions of when work begins, and whether there is a single work or separate works, are often of critical importance in determining the ranking of Private Works Act privileges against other interests, such as competing mortgages. *See, e.g., Keybank National Association v. Perkins Rowe Associates, LLC*, 823 F. Supp. 2d 399 (M.D. La. 2011), excerpts from which appear in the section below on priority of Private Works Act privileges.

* * * * * *

CAJUN CONSTRUCTORS, INC.

v.

ECOPRODUCT SOLUTIONS, LP

182 So. 3d 149 (La. App. 1st Cir. 2015)

DRAKE, J.

In this dispute concerning the scope and payment for work performed constructing a chemical processing plant, Cajun Constructors, Inc. (Cajun) appeals a motion for summary judgment granted in favor of Syngenta Crop Protection, Inc. (Syngenta), dismissing Cajun's claims against Syngenta, with prejudice. Cajun also seeks review of the trial court's interlocutory ruling denying its motion for partial summary judgment. For the reasons that follow, we affirm.

FACTS AND PROCEDURAL HISTORY

This case involves a state law contract dispute between two Louisiana companies and a lien filed pursuant to the Louisiana Private Works Act (LPWA). *See* La. R.S. 9:4801 *et seq.* Syngenta owns and operates a large industrial plant in St. Gabriel, Louisiana in Iberville Parish (Syngenta plant), that synthesizes and formulates certain compounds used in products for agricultural use. One of the byproducts of operations at the Syngenta plant is hydrochloric acid. Around 2003, Syngenta was approached by individuals from Texas who asserted they could convert the hydrochloric acid by-product Syngenta produced at its plant into marketable liquid calcium chloride ($CaCl_2$). These individuals eventually formed an entity called EcoProduct.

Subsequently, Syngenta and EcoProduct entered into a lengthy, detailed agreement dated September 29, 2004. The agreement granted to EcoProduct a lease of approximately five acres of immovable property within the Syngenta plant for the construction of a $CaCl_2$ conversion facility ($CaCl_2$ facility). The 2004 agreement between Syngenta and EcoProduct stated that the CaCL facility would be "engineered, designed, constructed[,] and owned by EcoProduct on Syngenta property leased to EcoProduct." During Phase I of the agreement, EcoProduct would construct the $CaCl_2$ facility; during Phase II, EcoProduct would complete the start-up of the $CaCl_2$ facility; and during Phase III, the $CaCl_2$ facility would be fully operational and commercial.

EcoProduct issued a request to Cajun to bid on the project to build the $CaCl_2$ facility. On June 30, 2005, EcoProduct issued three separate purchase orders to Cajun to perform the (i) site preparation work; (ii) fabrication and erection of structural steel; and (iii) mechanical construction services required for the construction of the $CaCl_2$ facility. The bid proposal and other documents pertinent to the construction of the facility identified EcoProduct as "owner" and Cajun as "contractor." EcoProduct is not a licensed contractor in the State of Louisiana.

Construction of the facility, Phase I, was completed by December 2005. Cajun submitted invoices for payment to EcoProduct, identifying EcoProduct as owner. Cajun was paid by EcoProduct for the work it had performed pursuant to the June 30, 2005, purchase orders, less a retainage amount for the mechanical construction services, which was disputed by EcoProduct.

Following the completion of construction of the $CaCl_2$ facility, EcoProduct asked Cajun to assist with the start-up of the facility, Phase II. EcoProduct agreed that Cajun would be paid on a time and material basis for the start-up work it performed. Cajun subsequently performed start-up related work on the $CaCl_2$ facility, but contended that EcoProduct failed to pay all of the invoices submitted for the start-up work. Specifically, Cajun contends EcoProduct failed to pay fourteen of twenty-eight invoices submitted for the start-up work. In total, Cajun claimed it was owed approximately $1.5 million for the June 30, 2005, purchase order retainage and for its performance of start-up work on the $CaCl_2$ facility.

On August 8, 2006, Cajun timely recorded a statement of claim and privilege against Syngenta's property for the sums allegedly owed to Cajun for work it performed on the $CaCl_2$ facility.

On October 13, 2006, Cajun filed a petition to enforce lien and for damages against EcoProduct, Syngenta, and numerous other parties in the Eighteenth Judicial District Court for the State of Louisiana. On November 22, 2006, Cajun filed an amended statement of claim and privilege, increasing its claim to $1,547,152.08. Cajun also sought damages for breach of contract, fraudulent inducement, negligent misrepresentation, unjust enrichment, as well as costs and attorneys' fees. EcoProduct removed the case to the United States District

Court for the Middle District of Louisiana on the basis of diversity jurisdiction; however, the case was remanded to state court in May 2007.

By written correspondence dated October 16, 2007, Syngenta terminated the September 29, 2004, agreement with EcoProduct for numerous breaches, including the fact that the $CaCl_2$ facility was not fully operational and commercial. Syngenta demanded that EcoProduct begin the process of removing the $CaCl_2$ facility from the Syngenta plant. When EcoProduct failed to remove its $CaCl_2$ facility, Syngenta noticed EcoProduct, via written correspondence dated April 3, 2008, that Syngenta was taking ownership of EcoProduct's $CaCl_2$ facility.

Syngenta filed a motion for summary judgment in February 2009, addressing all of Cajun's claims. The trial court denied Syngenta's motion without prejudice so as to afford the parties opportunity for further discovery.

Cajun filed its first supplemental, amended, and restated petition to enforce lien and for damages on July 23, 2009, adding claims for recovery based on intentional interference with contractual relations, single business entity doctrine, and a joint-venture theory. Cajun subsequently filed its second supplemental, amended, and restated petition to enforce lien and for damages on October 19, 2009, adding a claim for attorneys' fees and costs pursuant to the open account statute.

On October 10, 2013, Cajun filed a motion for partial summary judgment on its LPWA claim against Syngenta. Cajun also filed, on October 30, 2013, a revised motion for leave to file its third amended petition. Syngenta opposed both motions, which were set for hearing on December 5, 2013. . . . The trial court denied Cajun's motion for partial summary judgment (filed October 10, 2013), but granted its motion to file its third supplemental, amended, and restated petition to enforce lien and for damages, wherein Cajun asserted its LPWA claim against Syngenta. Following the hearing, the trial court rendered judgment on February 11, 2014.

Syngenta subsequently moved for summary judgment on February 13, 2014, on the basis that pursuant to the LWPA, specifically La. R.S. 9:4802 and 9:4806, Syngenta could not be liable to Cajun for the construction expenses that EcoProduct allegedly failed to pay. Cajun opposed the motion. Following a hearing on April 3, 2014, the trial court granted summary judgment in favor of Syngenta, dismissing all of Cajun's claims against Syngenta with prejudice. The trial court adopted the law and evidence presented by Syngenta in its motion for summary judgment, supporting memorandum, and reply to Cajun's opposition. The trial court held that La. R.S. 9:4806 was the controlling law and that Syngenta and EcoProduct entered into a lease; that EcoProduct owned the $CaCl_2$ facility; that EcoProduct contracted with Cajun for the construction of the $CaCl_2$ facility; and that the lack of recordation did not override controlling law, i.e., the LPWA. The trial court signed a judgment on April 17, 2014.

It is from the April 17, 2014, judgment that Cajun now appeals, seeking reversal of the summary judgment entered in Syngenta's favor. Cajun also asks this court to review the trial court's February 11, 2014 denial of its motion for partial summary judgment. Cajun asks that this court render summary judgment in its favor in the full amount of its amended lien claim, or in the alternative, render judgment establishing Syngenta's liability under the LPWA and remand the case to the trial court for further proceedings.

ASSIGNMENTS OF ERROR

Cajun assigns the following as errors on appeal:

1. The district court erred by misapplying language from La. R.S. 9:4806(B) concerning the work of a lessee that has no bearing on this case;

2. The district court erred by finding that EcoProduct was not a "contractor" as defined by La. R.S. 9:4807(A);

3. The district court erred by finding that Syngenta was not an "owner . . . who . . . contracted with the contractor" for purposes of La. R.S. 9:4806(B);

4. The district court erred by finding that an unrecorded agreement conferred ownership of a building or other construction to a person other than the owner of the ground from the perspective of Cajun, a third party to that agreement;

5. The district court erred by finding that an unrecorded alleged lease was effective toward Cajun, a third party to that alleged lease; and

6. The district court erred by finding that Syngenta and EcoProduct entered into a lease.

Cajun also requests costs and attorney fees pursuant to La. R.S. 9:4822(L)(2).

LAW AND DISCUSSION

The LPWA

The motion for summary judgment at issue here arose in the context of a suit under the LPWA, La. R.S. 9:4801 *et seq.,* which provides a method for contractors and other persons to recover the costs of labor and/or materials from a party with whom there is no contract. *Simms Hardin Co., L.L.C. v. 3901 Ridgelake Drive, L.L.C.,* 2012–469 (La. App. 5 Cir. 5/16/13), 119 So. 3d 58, 65, *writ denied,* 2013–1423 (La. 9/27/13), 123 So. 3d 726. A subcontractor has a claim against the owner of an immovable for the price of professional services rendered in connection with work that is undertaken by a contractor or subcontractor. La. R.S. 9:4802(A)(1). The claim against the owner shall be secured by a privilege on the immovable on which the work is performed. La. R.S. 9:4802(B). The claim against an owner under La. R.S. 9:4802 is limited to: (1) the owner(s) who have contracted with the contractor, or (2) to the owner(s) who have agreed in writing to the price and work of the contract of a lessee. La. R.S. 9:4806(B). The privilege granted by La. R.S. 9:4802 affects only the interest in or on the immovable enjoyed by the owner whose obligation is secured by the privilege. La. R.S. 9:4806(C).

For purposes of the LPWA, an owner is defined as "[a]n owner, co-owner, naked owner, owner of a predial servitude, possessor, lessee, or other person owning or having the right to the use or enjoyment of an immovable or having an interest therein." La. R.S. 9:4806(A).

In its first, second, and third assignments of error, Cajun avers that Syngenta is the sole, unified owner of the land as well as the $CaCl_2$ facility constructed by EcoProduct. Cajun avers that as owner of the St. Gabriel plant, Syngenta entered into a written contract to build the $CaCl_2$ facility with EcoProduct (the September 29, 2004 agreement); then EcoProduct, as general contractor, subcontracted work on the $CaCl_2$ facility to Cajun, making Syngenta an "owner who contracted with a contractor," pursuant to La. R.S. 9:4806(B). Under the LPWA, Cajun asserts it has the right to secure a privilege on the immovable, in the form of a lien against Syngenta's property, for Cajun's failure to be paid for work performed on the construction of the $CaCl_2$ facility pursuant to its contract with EcoProduct. Cajun argues that its claim for unpaid work against Syngenta, as owner, was properly secured by a privilege in the form of the lien filed on Syngenta's immovable property. *See* La. R.S. 9:4802(A)(1) and 9:4802(B).

Syngenta argues that the September 29, 2004, agreement is a valid lease agreement, wherein Syngenta granted a leasehold interest in immovable property to EcoProduct under the terms and conditions set forth in the agreement. Syngenta argues that the agreement was not a contract to build and that EcoProduct was not Syngenta's "contractor"—the agreement states that the facility will be "owned by EcoProduct on Syngenta property" leased by EcoProduct. Syngenta avers there was no contract to build, no sum, and no scope of the work included in the agreement, nor did Syngenta have a right to specific performance for construction of the facility. Neither Syngenta nor EcoProduct filed a notice of contract and bond because as Syngenta argues, the parties never entered into a contract to build. Syngenta argues that in fact it terminated the agreement and demanded EcoProduct remove its $CaCl_2$ facility from Syngenta's plant. Syngenta contends EcoProduct was its lessee, and pursuant to La. R.S. 9:4806(B), EcoProduct could be a lessee-owner of the $CaCl_2$ facility. Pursuant to La. R.S. 9:4806(B), Syngenta avers it was not an owner who contracted with a contractor, nor did Syngenta agree in writing to specifically be liable for any claims granted by the provisions of La. R.S. 9:4802. According to Syngenta, the LPWA does not impose personal liability on Syngenta, nor does any privilege attach to any of Syngenta's property.

Countering Syngenta's arguments, in its fourth, fifth, and sixth assignments of error, Cajun alleges that Syngenta has attempted to mischaracterize its September 29, 2004, agreement with EcoProduct as a lease to avoid liability under the LPWA. Furthermore, Cajun argues that even if the September 29, 2004 agreement could be interpreted as a valid lease agreement, neither Syngenta nor EcoProduct recorded the agreement in the Iberville Parish property records. Cajun avers that a section of the agreement expressly required recordation. Cajun also argues that recordation was required pursuant to the public records doctrine. Because the lease was not recorded, no evidence of EcoProduct's separate ownership of the $CaCl_2$ facility exists in the Iberville Parish property records, and furthermore, an unrecorded interest in immovable property cannot be asserted against third parties—in this case, Cajun.

Syngenta responds, arguing that the lack of recordation of the September 29, 2004, agreement does not create liability under the LPWA as to Syngenta for Cajun's claims. Syngenta argues that La. R.S. 9:4806 contains no recordation requirement and that as special legislation in derogation of general law, the LPWA is controlling over the public records doctrine. Furthermore, Syngenta argues that the section of the September 29, 2004, agreement that Cajun alleges requires recordation is not controlling. Syngenta avers that section required EcoProduct to perform certain acts, including recording the lease, upon completion of the start-phase of its $CaCl_2$ facility. Thus, the recordation requirement did not even come into play until after the $CaCl_2$ facility completed the start-up phase, i.e., after Cajun's work was completed.

We must therefore examine *de novo* the pleadings, depositions, answers to interrogatories, and admissions, together with any affidavits admitted for purposes of Syngenta's motion for summary judgment to determine whether Syngenta met its burden of proof that there is no genuine issue of material fact that Syngenta was not the owner of the EcoProduct $CaCl_2$ facility. *See* La. C.C.P. art. 966(B)(2) and (C)(2).

Syngenta acknowledged that it is engaged principally in the development, manufacture, and marketing of a wide variety of crop protection products including herbicides, fungicides, and insecticides. Syngenta also offers professional products utilized on grass and plants in parks, golf courses, and public lands. The Syngenta plant located in St. Gabriel manufactures and formulates certain crop protection products. The plant also manufactures raw materials utilized in the production of crop protection products.

The September 29, 2004, agreement between Syngenta and EcoProduct recites, in pertinent part:

> Whereas, Syngenta owns and operates a chemical manufacturing plant located at 3905 Hwy 75 in St. Gabriel, Louisiana . . . at which, as

a byproduct of Syngenta's manufacturing process, hydrochloric acid is produced.

Whereas, EcoProduct has the manufacturing and marketing expertise to neutralize the hydrochloric acid with lime and apply evaporation technology to produce 38% liquid calcium chloride for commercial use.

Whereas, manufacture of the marketable calcium chloride from the hydrochloric acid will be accomplished by EcoProduct at a calcium chloride plant to be located on the property of the Syngenta Plant. . . .

Whereas, the $CaCl_2$ Plant *will be engineered, designed, constructed[,] and owned by EcoProduct on Syngenta property leased by EcoProduct* and EcoProduct shall pay Syngenta for its contract services to operate and maintain the plant on behalf of EcoProduct. (Emphasis added.)

According to Section 7.0, the term of the agreement commenced on September 29, 2004, and would continue through the three phases of the agreement. During Phase I, EcoProduct would "complete the design, engineering, procurement, construction, installation[,] and commissioning of the EcoProduct Facilities." During Phase II, EcoProduct would complete the start-up of the $CaCl_2$ facility. During Phase III, the CaCE facility would be fully operational and commercial.

Section 2.2 of the agreement provides that "Syngenta shall grant to EcoProduct a leasehold interest in and to a parcel of real property measuring approximately five acres in area . . . being a portion of Block F–7 at the Syngenta Plant site." Section 2.2(b) provides that "[t]he term of the $CaCl_2$ Plant Site lease shall run concurrently with the term of [the] Agreement." Section 2.2(c) of the agreement states that "EcoProduct shall pay to Syngenta Annual lease rent and use fees totaling $10,000.00 for the use of Syngenta's property and facilities. . . ." Section 2.2(d) grants EcoProduct reasonable rights of use and ingress and egress to the $CaCl_2$ Plant Site, among other areas. Section 2.6 provides:

Upon completion of Phase II, a metes and bounds survey of all leasehold interest(s), easement(s)[,] and right(s) of way . . . shall be

> **prepared by EcoProduct,** at its expense, and **recordable memoranda of the leasehold interest,** all easements, all licenses and all rights of way, or the equivalent thereof . . . , shall be prepared, executed[,] and **recorded with the Parish of Iberville.** (Emphasis added.)

Pursuant to Section 3.2 of the agreement, EcoProduct was responsible for "all supervision, design, engineering and procedure services, consultations, construction and other required services, equipment and materials, labor, construction tools and supplies, temporary structures, and transportation. . . ." EcoProduct would also "be responsible for the safety related to, and during, the design, engineering[,] and construction of EcoProduct Facilities to protect workers, the public and all other people, Syngenta's other property[,] and the property of third parties." Furthermore, Section 3.2(e) of the agreement provides:

> EcoProduct shall cause its contractors, subcontractors[,] or vendors that provide services during Phase I to sign affidavits of payment and release and waivers of liens at the completion of services rendered in connection with the construction of the EcoProduct Facilities. EcoProduct shall defend and indemnify Syngenta against any loss or damage arising from any claims related to the enforcement of any such liens.

Section 5.2 states that "EcoProduct shall be responsible, at its expense, for all Capital Expenditures for the EcoProduct Facilities." EcoProduct was also responsible to pay "all sales, exoise [sic], *ad valorem,* property, franchise, occupational and disposal taxes, or other taxes associated with the ownership, operation, maintenance[,] or repair of the EcoProduct Facilities." Syngenta agreed to provide at its own expense "management, supervisory, technical[,] and labor personnel necessary for the operation and maintenance of EcoProduct Facilities." Syngenta would "operate, maintain[,] and/or monitor the EcoProduct Facilities on a 24–hour per day, seven-day per week schedule." However, Syngenta's services did not include "Capital Expenditures, utilities, extraordinary process control, parts, inventory[,] and [certain described] supplies."

Section 8.0 of the agreement states that neither Syngenta nor EcoProduct could terminate the agreement, except for cause upon a showing that the other party violated one or more of the terms of the agreement.

The Invitation to Bid for Contract, which EcoProduct sent to Cajun, states in Section 1.0 that "[f]or purposes of this Invitation to Bid and all other document associated therewith, the word "owner" shall be used interchangeably to describe EcoProduct Solutions and/or its Agent, ENGlobal Engineering, Inc. and the word "Contractor" or "Subcontractor" shall be used to describe the bidder." Cajun stated in its bid proposal that the company was "pleased to submit the attached proposal to perform contract construction services on the EcoProducts Calcium Chloride Plant Project at the Syngenta, St. Gabriel, LA site." The purchase orders issued by EcoProduct to Cajun, state that the purchase orders were issued for the "Contract Construction Services on the EcoProduct Solutions, LP Calcium Chloride Project at the Syngenta, St. Gabriel, LA manufacturing site." Additionally, a Cajun billing invoice dated January 4, 2006, lists EcoProduct as the owner.

In a sworn affidavit executed by Syngenta plant manager Ralph Caddell on January 5, 2009, Mr. Caddell stated that the 2004 agreement between Syngenta and EcoProduct was a lease and that EcoProduct was deemed the owner of the $CaCl_2$ facility at all times. Mr. Caddell further stated that while Syngenta did contract to operate and maintain the $CaC1_2$ facility, Syngenta did not share in any profits, losses, or risks associated with ownership of the $CaCl_2$ facility. Mr. Caddell indicated that the $CaCl_2$ facility was no longer operational and that Syngenta made demand upon EcoProduct to remove the $CaCl_2$ facility from the Syngenta plant premises. Mr. Caddell noted that various other creditors had reclaimed parts of the former $CaCl_2$ facility.

In its responses and objections to Syngenta's first requests for admissions and interrogatories, EcoProduct admitted that it never entered into a joint venture for the $CaCl_2$ facility. Furthermore, EcoProduct admitted that it never agreed to share any profits or losses with Syngenta from the $CaCl_2$ facility. EcoProduct also admitted that Syngenta did not control nor did Syngenta select contractors for the $CaCl_2$ facility. Furthermore, Michael T. Largey—the project manager for the construction of the $CaCl_2$ facility—testified in his deposition that since "EcoProducts' capital funds . . . were being expended" for the construction of the $CaCl_2$ facility, he "assum[ed] EcoProducts was represented as owner."

In his deposition, W. Yandell Rogers, III—the sole manager and member of EcoProduct Solutions GP, L.L.C. and manager during the construction of the $CaCl_2$ facility—responded affirmatively that EcoProduct was owner of the $CaCl_2$ facility. Mr. Rogers further stated that EcoProduct had control over the bid process, contractor selection, and supervision of the work site.

Cajun representative Thomas Hutchinson acknowledged in his deposition taken on October 10, 2008, that the EcoProduct $CaCl_2$ facility was located "on Syngenta property." Mr. Hutchinson admitted that he had "limited knowledge" of any profit-sharing measures between Syngenta and EcoProduct, but he testified that as to Syngenta's ownership of the EcoProduct $CaCl_2$ facility, it was his "understanding that EcoProduct would own it, but Syngenta would operate it." Mr. Hutchinson responded affirmatively that Cajun understood that the $CaCl_2$ facility was an EcoProduct project at the Syngenta plant site. However, in a sworn affidavit executed by Mr. Hutchinson on March 25, 2014 (six years after his deposition), Mr. Hutchinson stated he had no "direct or specific knowledge of any separate ownership arrangement between Syngenta and EcoProduct" regarding the $CaCl_2$ facility. He stated that "Cajun was subcontracted by EcoProduct . . . to perform certain portions of the work related to construction" of the $CaCl_2$ facility and that "Cajun was aware that EcoProduct had contracted with Syngenta to build" the $CaCl_2$ facility.

On July 3, 2007, Syngenta sent written correspondence to EcoProduct formally noticing material breaches in the September 29, 2004, agreement. Syngenta also demanded defense and indemnification from suits and liens filed against Syngenta property by Cajun and another contractor, MMR Constructors, Inc. and demanded reimbursement for defense costs. Syngenta followed up with a letter dated October 16, 2007, terminating the lease for EcoProduct's failure to cure material breaches of the agreement. Syngenta also formally demanded that EcoProduct remove the $CaCl_2$ facility from its premises. When EcoProduct failed to remove the $CaCl_2$ facility from the Syngenta plant, Syngenta formally noticed EcoProduct that it was assuming ownership of the $CaCl_2$ facility via written correspondence dated April 3, 2008.

The privilege granted to subcontractors against owners in La. R.S. 9:4802 is limited to: (1) the owner(s) who have contracted with the contractor, or (2) to the owner(s) who have agreed in writing to the price and work of the contract of a lessee and specifically agreed to be liable for any claims granted by La. R.S. 9:4802. La. R.S. 9:4806(B). Based on our *de novo* review of the evidence presented, it is clear that Syngenta did not contract with Cajun. Although Syngenta was a lessor, it did not agree in writing to the price and work of Cajun's contract with EcoProduct, nor did Syngenta specifically agree to be liable for any claims granted by the provisions of La. R.S. 9:4802. The evidence demonstrates that EcoProduct was the owner of the $CaCl_2$ facility, and Cajun contracted with EcoProduct.

We further hold that the fact that the September 24, 2009, agreement was not recorded in this instance does not override the provisions of the LPWA, in determining whether Cajun thus has a privilege against Syngenta. The public records doctrine does not alter the application of the statutory definitions of "owner" and "contractor" found in the LPWA. The fact that the agreement between Syngenta and EcoProduct was not filed in the public records does not make Syngenta liable to Cajun under the LPWA in this instance.

The Louisiana public records doctrine generally expresses a public policy that interest in real estate must be recorded in order to affect third persons. Simply put, an instrument in writing affecting immovable property which is not recorded is null and void except between the parties. *Cimarex Energy Co. v. Mauboules,* 2009–1170 (La. 4/9/10), 40 So. 3d 931, 943. The public records doctrine is generally set forth in La. C.C. art. 3338, which provides:

> The rights and obligations established or created by the following written instruments are **without effect as to a third person** unless the instrument is registered by recording it in the appropriate mortgage or conveyance records pursuant to the provisions of this Title:
>
> (1) An instrument that transfers an immovable or establishes a real right in or over an immovable.
>
> (2) The **lease of an immovable**.

(3) An option or right of first refusal, or a contract to buy, sell, or lease an immovable or to establish a real right in or over an immovable.

(4) An instrument that modifies, terminates, or transfers the rights created or evidenced by the instruments described in Subparagraphs (1) through (3) of this Article. (Emphasis added.)

In this case, Syngenta and EcoProduct executed a lease of five acres of immovable property located at the Syngenta plant. The September 29, 2004, agreement established the rights and obligations between Syngenta and EcoProduct. Because the agreement was not recorded, it is without effect as to third parties, i.e., Cajun. We note, however, that the agreement did not contemplate any rights or effect as to third parties. To hold Syngenta liable for EcoProduct's failure to perform its obligations under the agreement and its failure to pay its contractors would undermine the statutory provisions of the LPWA. Although Cajun's search of the Iberville Parish property records listed Syngenta as the record owner of the land upon which the EcoProduct $CaCl_2$ facility was built, there is simply no evidence that Syngenta "contracted with the contractor" as required by La. R.S. 9:4806(B).

Also, at the time the lease was executed, the $CaCl_2$ facility had not yet been built. Section 2.6 of the agreement required EcoProduct to record its leasehold interest *after* it prepared a metes and bounds survey of its leasehold interest(s), easement(s), and right(s) of way, *following the completion of Phase II* of the agreement, i.e., the start-up of the $CaCl_2$ facility. Although Syngenta acknowledged that the agreement did enter into Phase III, Syngenta ultimately terminated the agreement based on EcoProduct's material breaches of the agreement, including, but not limited to, EcoProduct's failure to meet its benchmarks pursuant to Phases I, II, and III of the agreement, and the fact that the $CaCl_2$ facility never became fully operational and commercial.

Cajun has failed to produce factual evidence sufficient to establish that it will be able to satisfy its evidentiary burden of proof at trial. *See* La. C.C.P. art. 966(C)(2). Thus, there is no genuine issue of material fact that Syngenta was not the owner of the EcoProduct $CaCl_2$ facility, and Syngenta is entitled to summary judgment as a matter of law. Cajun is not entitled to attorneys' fees pursuant to La. R.S. 9:4822(L)(2). We therefore affirm the April 17, 2014, judgment of the trial court, granting summary judgment in favor of Syngenta and dismissing the remaining claims of Cajun with prejudice. We likewise affirm the trial court's February 11, 2014, judgment, denying Cajun's motion for partial summary judgment on its LPWA claim against Syngenta.

DECREE

Based on the foregoing, the April 17, 2014, judgment of the trial court is hereby affirmed. The February 11, 2014, judgment of the trial court is also affirmed. All costs of this appeal are assessed to the plaintiff/appellant, Cajun Constructors, Inc.

AFFIRMED.

* * * * * *

NOTES AND QUESTIONS

1. The case demonstrates the rule, under R.S. 9:4806, that privileges arising out of a work contracted by a lessee burden only the lessee's interest in the immovable. The court held that this rule applies even when the lease is unrecorded and third persons may accordingly be unaware of its existence.

2. The court observed that the unrecorded lease was without effect as to third parties, specifically naming the plaintiff as one of those third parties; however, the court then stated that the lease agreement did not contemplate any rights *or effect* as to third parties. Do you find that statement to be convincing?

3. The plaintiff in the case was a contractor in direct privity of contract with the lessee, which, as the court observes, was the "owner" for purposes of the Private Works Act. Can the case be explained by the fact that the direct contractual relationship between the plaintiff and the lessee provided the plaintiff with an opportunity to inquire as to the lessee's relationship with the landowner? Would it have made a difference if the claimant were not a direct contractor but instead a more remote claimant, such as a supplier to a subcontractor? How could such a claimant be expected to know of an unrecorded lease?

4. As will be discussed in a later section of this chapter, R.S. 9:4822 requires a Private Works Act claimant to preserve his privilege by filing a statement of claim or privilege that describes the immovable upon which the work was performed and identifies "the owner thereof." When work is contracted to be performed by a lessee, which "owner" should the claimant identify in his statement of claim or privilege? What should the claimant do if the lease is unrecorded, and the claimant knows of neither its existence nor the identity of the lessee?

D. Filing Requirements

1. Notice of Contract

The Private Works Act envisions that, before work begins, a notice of contract, containing the information required in R.S. 9:4811(A), will be filed in the mortgage records and that a payment bond issued by a surety in the amount provided by R.S. 9:4812(B) will be attached to the filed notice of contract. When the owner complies with these requirements, R.S. 9:4802(C) provides that he is relieved of liability for claims and privileges under R.S. 9:4802. Nevertheless, his interest in the immovable continues to be subject to the privileges established by R.S. 9:4801 in favor of those persons who are in direct privity of contract with him. The reason for this is readily apparent: The surety bond protects those who directly or indirectly perform work or supply materials or leased equipment for the work to be performed by the contractor for whom the bond is given; it does not guarantee the owner's own performance.

The owner thus has a powerful incentive to file a notice of contract, with a proper payment bond attached, before work begins. The general contractor also has an incentive to see that timely notice of contract is filed. Under R.S. 9:4811(D), a general contractor under a contract exceeding the threshold amount specified in that section will enjoy the privilege granted to him by R.S. 9:4801 only if a timely notice of contract has been filed.

R.S. 9:4811(C) provides that the absence of a payment bond does not cause a notice of contract to be considered deficient. However, if no bond is filed with the notice of contract, the owner will not enjoy the benefit of being relieved of claims and privileges under R.S. 9:4802(C).

It is a common occurrence that, rather than filing the notice of contract contemplated by R.S. 9:4811(A), the parties will instead file the contract itself. This practice often creates problems for the owner and contractor, because the contract usually does not contain a sufficient description of the immovable and therefore does not satisfy the requirements of the act.

R.S. 9:4832 permits cancellation of a notice of contract upon written request of any person made after expiration of the applicable periods for filing statements of claim or privilege, provided that no uncancelled statement of claim or privilege was filed.

2. "No-work" Affidavit

As will be discussed below, a mortgage is inferior to Private Works Act privileges if the work out of which those privileges arose commenced, or a notice of contract with respect to that work was filed, before the mortgage became effective against third persons. R.S. 9:4820(C) allows a mortgagee or other person intending to acquire an interest in an immovable to guard against the possibility that work has already begun by timely filing an affidavit of an inspector to the effect that no work had begun at the time the inspector inspected the immovable. A discussion of this affidavit, and cases illustrating the application of this provision of the Private Works Act, appear in a later section of this chapter.

3. Notice of Termination or Abandonment of the Work

R.S. 9:4822 prescribes the required contents of a notice of termination or abandonment of the work: It must identify the immovable upon the work which was performed, must be signed by the owner, and must certify that the work has been substantially completed or abandoned or that the contractor is in default. Like most other filings under the act, the notice is filed in the mortgage records.

Often, rather than filing a notice of termination meeting the requirements of R.S. 9:4822, the parties will instead file an architect's certificate of substantial completion. Although this certificate may very well evidence the opinion of those signing or filing it that the work has reached substantial completion, which is sometimes relevant in determining whether the period allowed for filing statements of claim or privilege has begun to run, an architect's certificate of substantial completion usually does not qualify as a notice of termination because of the absence of a sufficient description of the immovable or other deficiencies, such as the lack of the owner's signature.

R.S. 9:4822(F) allows one or more notices of termination to be filed with respect to specified areas of an immovable. When such a notice of partial termination is filed, the time for filing statements of claim or privilege commences as to claims arising from the work done on the area of the immovable described in the notice. Thus, this provision serves to truncate the period during which those particular claimants must preserve their claims.

4. The Statement of Claim or Privilege

A person who is afforded a claim or privilege under the Private Works Act must preserve it by a filing in the mortgage records a timely statement of claim or privilege and by taking the other actions required by R.S. 9:4822. Generally, the statement of claim or privilege must be filed within 60 days after the filing of a notice of termination of the work or within 60 days after the substantial completion or abandonment of the work, if no notice of termination is filed. However, when a notice of contract has been properly and timely filed, claimants who are accorded a claim or privilege under R.S. 9:4802 must file their statements of claim or privilege within 30 days after the filing of notice of termination of the work and must deliver to the owner a copy of the statement of claim or privilege. Moreover, under those circumstances, the general contractor must file his statement of claim or privilege within 60 days after the filing of notice of termination. The key point is that, where a notice of contract has been filed, the period for filing statements of claim or privilege does not commence to run until a notice of termination is filed.

R.S. 9:4822 specifies the information that must be contained within a statement of claim or privilege.

It should be emphasized that the time periods contained within R.S. 9:4822 establish *deadlines* for filing statements of claim or privilege. Nothing in the act requires a claimant to await either substantial completion of the work or the filing of a notice of termination before filing his statement of claim or privilege for amounts due to him.

The Private Works Act contains many provisions requiring a claimant to give notice of his claim to the owner, the contractor, or both, often denying or limiting his claim and privilege when he fails to comply. An example of a notice requirement is found in R.S. 9:4822(A), which requires a claimant under R.S. 9:4802 not only to file his statement of claim or privilege in a timely manner but also to provide a copy of the statement to the owner if notice of contract has been timely filed.

R.S. 9:4823(B) provides that, even though a claimant may fail to file a statement of claim or privilege within the time required by R.S. 9:4822, his claims under R.S. 9:4802 against the contractor and the contractor's surety are preserved if a statement of the claim or privilege is delivered to the contractor within the period allowed for its filing under R.S. 9:4822. Mere delivery of the statement of claim or privilege to the contractor will not, however, be sufficient to preserve claims against the owner or the privilege upon the immovable.

5. Suit and Notice of Pendency of Action

A Private Works Act claimant must file suit against the owner within one year after filing his statement of claim or privilege. In addition, in order to preserve his privilege upon the immovable insofar as third persons are concerned, he must file a notice of pendency of action in the mortgage records within the same one-year period. These requirements are discussed in more detail in a later section of this chapter.

6. Release Bond

If a statement of claim or privilege or a notice of pendency of action is filed, R.S. 9:4835 provides a procedure by which any interested person may post a bond in order to have the statement or notice cancelled of record.

* * * * * *

NORMAN H. VOELKEL CONST., INC.
v.
RECORDER OF MORTGAGES FOR EAST BATON ROUGE PARISH
859 So. 2d 9 (La. App. 1st Cir. 2003)

McCLENDON, J.

By this appeal, a contractor contests the trial court's denial of a writ of mandamus to cancel a lien filed pursuant to the Private Works Act, LSA–R.S. 9:4801 *et seq*. For the following reasons, we reverse.

On February 25, 2000, Norman H. Voelkel Construction, Inc. entered into a construction contract with Albertson's, Inc. Under the terms of the contract, Voelkel agreed to act as the general contractor for the construction of Albertson's Store No. 2747 located at the corner of Airline Highway and Highland Road in Baton Rouge, Louisiana. Voelkel subcontracted a portion of the work to Cloy Construction, Inc. Cloy, then, contracted with Heck Industries, Inc. to supply concrete for a part of the project.

On April 27, 2000, Albertson's filed a notice of contract with the Recorder of Mortgages for East Baton Rouge Parish. It is undisputed that substantial completion of the project occurred on January 10, 2001, when Albertson's fully occupied the location and opened its doors for business to the general public. It is also undisputed that no termination of the work was filed in the mortgage records.

On July 18, 2001, Heck filed in the mortgage records a statement of claim or privilege against Voelkel, alleging that Heck carried an unpaid balance in the sum of $45,886.07 for concrete and/or labor furnished to Cloy for use in the construction of improvements on the Albertson's store. On September 24, 2001, after Heck refused to deliver written authorization to cancel the lien, Voelkel petitioned for writ of mandamus, seeking cancellation of subcontractor's lien.

After hearing the matter, the trial court rendered judgment, denying Voelkel's request for a writ of mandamus. Voelkel appeals, contending that the notice of contract and the statement of claim or privilege were improperly filed as neither contains a full and complete legal property description. Voelkel also asserts that Heck's statement of claim or privilege is untimely.

The Louisiana Private Works Act, LSA–R.S. 9:4801 *et seq.*, grants contractors, laborers, sellers and others a privilege on an immovable to secure the price of their work. LSA–R.S. 9:4801(1). The pertinent statutory provisions concerning perfection of this privilege provide as follows:

LSA–R.S. 9:4822 provides, in pertinent part:

A. If a notice of contract is properly and timely filed in the manner provided by R.S. 9:4811, the persons to whom a claim or privilege is granted by R.S. 9:4802 shall within thirty days after the filing of a notice of termination of the work:

(1) File a statement of their claims or privilege.

B. Those persons granted a claim and privilege by R.S. 9:4802 for work arising out of a general contract, notice of which is not filed, and other persons granted a privilege under R.S. 9:4801 or a claim and privilege under R.S. 9:4802 shall file a statement of their respective claims and privileges within sixty days after:

(1) The substantial completion or abandonment of the work, if a notice of termination is not filed.

LSA–R.S. 9:4811 provides, in pertinent part:

A. Written notice of a contract between a general contractor and an owner shall be filed as provided in R.S. 9:4831 before the contractor begins work, as defined by R.S. 9:4820, on the immovable. The notice:

(1) Shall be signed by the owner and contractor.

(2) Shall contain the legal property description of the immovable upon which the work is to be performed and the name of the project.

(3) hall identify the parties and give their mailing addresses.

B. A notice of contract is not improperly filed because of an error in or omission from the notice in the absence of a showing of actual prejudice by a claimant or other person acquiring rights in the

> immovable. An error or omission of the identity of the parties or their mailing addresses or the improper identification of the immovable shall be prima facie proof of actual prejudice.

LSA–R.S. 9:4831 of the Private Works Act further explains the requirements of a property description as follows:

> A. The filing of a notice of contract, notice of termination, statement of a claim or privilege, or notice of *lis pendens* required or permitted to be filed under the provisions of this Part is accomplished when it is filed for registry with the recorder of mortgages of the parish in which the work is to be performed. . . .
>
> C. Each filing made with the recorder of mortgages pursuant to this Part which contains a reference to immovable property shall contain a description of the property sufficient to clearly and permanently identify the property. A description which includes the lot and/or square and/or subdivision or township and range shall meet the requirements of this Subsection. Naming the street or mailing address without more shall not be sufficient to meet the requirements of this Subsection.

Under this legislation, both notices of contract and statements of claim or privilege must contain legal descriptions that "clearly and permanently" identify the immovable property at issue. *See Boes Iron Works, Inc. v. Spartan Bldg. Corp.,* 94–0519, p. 2 (La. App. 4 Cir. 12/15/94), 648 So. 2d 24, 26, *writ denied,* 95–0103 (La. 3/10/95), 650 So. 2d 1184.

Albertson's notice of contract contained the following property description: "Description of Property: Airline & Highland, particularly described on Exhibit A attached hereto and incorporated herein." Attached to the documents as "Exhibit A" was a copy of the AIA, Standard Form Contract in which the property was described as located at "SWC Airline Road & Highland Hwy, Baton Rouge, LA." The documents also incorporated by reference the sitework drawings that described the property at issue, but were not filed in the public record. Heck filed its statement of claim or privilege, describing the property solely as "Albertson's # 2747, Airline at Highland, East Baton Rouge Parish, Louisiana."

Under LSA–R.S. 9:4831C, a municipal address is insufficient to perfect a privilege. Heck avers that describing the property as located at the intersection of Highland Road and Airline Highway, along with the store number is sufficient to perfect a privilege. We disagree. Liens and privileges are to be strictly construed against claimants and liberally construed in favor of owners as they are in derogation of the common rights of owners. *Louisiana Nat'l Bank of Baton Rouge v. Triple R Contractors, Inc.,* 345 So .2d 7, 10 (La. 1977); *Circle H Bldg. Supply, Inc. v. Dickey,* 558 So. 2d 680, 682 (La. App. 1 Cir. 1990). Therefore, Heck must comply with all necessary requirements of the statute it claims establishes a lien or privilege. Herein, Heck advocates the acceptance of a description of lesser quality than a municipal address, a property description expressly deemed insufficient by the statute. We also reject Heck's contention that any deficiency in the property description is cured by the incorporation by reference of the sitework drawings into the notice of contract. The notice of contract and the statement of claim or privilege contain no lot, square, range or other information on which one can identify the specific property involved, without resorting to knowledge outside the public records. Therefore, we find the descriptions in both the notice of contract and the statement of claim or privilege are insufficient to perfect a claim of privilege. Heck cannot avail itself of the thirty-day time limitations for claims of privileges provided by LSA–R.S. 9:4811A.

Furthermore, Heck failed to timely file its claim of privilege. LSA–R.S. 9:4822C(2) provides:

> A. Those persons granted a claim and privilege by R.S. 9:4802 for work arising out of a general contract, notice of which is not filed, and other persons granted a privilege under R.S. 9:4801 or a claim and privilege under R.S. 9:4802 shall file a statement of their respective claims and privileges within sixty days after:
>
> (2) The substantial completion or abandonment of the work, if notice of termination is not filed.

Therefore, in the absence of a legal description and proper notice, Heck had only sixty days from the date of substantial completion of the construction project to file its claim. Substantial completion occurred on January 10, 2001, and Heck filed its lien on July 18, 2001, clearly exceeding the time limits for filing a lien. Therefore, Heck's claim or privilege, even if sufficient as far as a legal description, was not perfected because it was not timely filed.

On appeal, Voelkel also seeks attorney's fees under LSA–R.S. 9:4833B, which provides that a defendant contractor "who, without probable cause, fails to deliver written authorization to cancel a statement of claim or privilege . . . shall be liable for damages suffered by the owner or person requesting the authorization as a consequence of the failure and for reasonable attorney's fees incurred in causing the statement to be cancelled." Considering the complex issues presented in this case, we conclude that Heck had probable cause to refuse to voluntarily erase its lien. Therefore, an award of attorney's fees is not warranted in this case.

For the foregoing reasons, the judgment of the trial court is reversed. Judgment in rendered in favor of Norman H. Voelkel Construction, Inc., ordering the Clerk of Court of East Baton Rouge Parish as Recorder of Mortgages to erase and cancel the private works lien recorded by Heck Industries, Inc. at Original 67, Bundle 11250. Costs are assessed against Heck Industries, Inc.

JUDGMENT REVERSED AND ORDER ISSUED TO CLERK OF COURT.

* * * * * *

NOTES AND QUESTIONS

1. Would the outcome of the case have been different if the claimant had made specific reference in its statement of claim or privilege to the filed notice of contract?

2. When a notice of contract with a proper property description has been filed, is substantial completion sufficient to start the running of the period for filing statements of claim or privilege? *See* La. R.S. 9:4822(A).

3. In this case, a notice of contract was filed but without a proper legal description. The court followed the prior ruling of the Fourth Circuit in *Boes Iron Works, Inc. v. Spartan Bldg. Corp.*, 648 So. 2d 24 (La. App. 4th Cir. 1994), which had held not only that a municipal address in a statement of claim or privilege was insufficient but also that the effect of the same deficiency in the notice of contract was that the claimant was allowed 60 days, rather than 30 days, from

abandonment of the work within which to file his statement of claim or privilege. In other words, the deficient notice of contract was ignored, and it was as though no notice of contract had been filed. *Cf. Thompson Tree & Spraying Service, Inc. v. White-Spunner Construction, Inc.*, 68 So. 3d 1142 (La. App. 3d Cir. 2011), *writ denied*, 71 So. 3d 290 (La. 2011), which refused to follow *Norman H. Voelkel Construction* on this issue. In *Thompson Tree Service*, both the notice of contract and the purported notice of termination suffered from the same infirmity: the lack of a sufficient description of the property. The court held that, despite this defect, the notice of contract was nevertheless sufficient to bring the case within the scope of La. R.S. 9:4822(A) (thus requiring the filing of a notice of termination before the period for filing statements of claim or privilege would commence to run), but the notice of termination, suffering from the identical defect, was insufficient to start the running of the period for filing statements of claim or privilege.

* * * * * *

JEFFERSON DOOR COMPANY, INC.

v.

CRAGMAR CONSTRUCTION, L.L.C.

81 So. 3d 1001 (La. App. 4th Cir. 2012)

EDWIN A. LOMBARD, Judge.

This appeal is from the dismissal of the suit to enforce a subcontractor's lien filed by Jefferson Door Company, Inc. against Angela and Ryan Adams. After a review of the record in light of the applicable law, the trial court judgment granting the defendant's Exception of Prematurity is affirmed.

Relevant Facts and Procedural History

In 2009, the defendants, Angela and Ryans Adams hired Cragmar Construction, L.L.C. ("Cragmar") as the general contractor to construct their principal residence at 6223 General Diaz Street in Orleans Parish. The plaintiff, Jefferson Door Company, Inc., furnished materials for the project to Cragmar pursuant to a credit application with personal guaranty signed by Craig Martin, an authorized representative of Cragmar. The materials were used into the Adamses' residence but, although Cragmar was paid in accordance with the construction contract, Cragmar failed to pay the plaintiff the principal amount due of $37,623.98 and related charges.

Between July 2, 2009, and October 20, 2009, the Adamses paid Cragmar $344,592.92 to satisfy invoices for the construction of the Adamses' home. However, although the materials furnished by the plaintiff were used in the Adamses' residence, the plaintiff was not paid. Accordingly, the plaintiff sent a collection notice on December 2, 2009, to the Adamses demanding payment of $48,314.22, which included service and attorney fees per its agreement with Cragmar. On December 11, 2009, the Adamses terminated the contract with Cragmar on their home and recorded a notice of termination in the Orleans Parish mortgage records. On December 28, 2009, plaintiff filed a Lien Affidavit against the Adamses' property in the Orleans Parish mortgage records.

On December 23, 2010, the plaintiff filed its petition in the Civil District Court for the Parish of Orleans to enforce a statement of claim or privilege and breach of contract/open account naming as defendants, Cragmar and the Adamses, relying on its Lien Affidavit. Subsequently, the Adamses filed the "Defendants' Verified Dilatory Exception of Prematurity, Peremptory Exception of No Cause of Action, and Alternatively, Motion for Summary Judgment" at issue in this appeal.

After a hearing held on March 31, 2010, the trial court issued a written judgment signed on April 8, 2010, which stated that the "Defendants' Verified Dilatory Exception of Prematurity, Peremptory Exception of No Cause of Action, and Alternatively, Motion for Summary Judgment be granted." The judgment further ordered the dismissal of the Adamses from the case, and the cancellation and removal of Jefferson's invalid Lien Affidavit.

On appeal, the plaintiff assigns as error: (1) the trial court's determination that the Lien Affidavit filed by the plaintiff on December 28, 2009, was not a valid lien because it failed to reasonably itemize the elements comprising the obligation pursuant to La. R.S. 9:4822(G)(4) of the Private Works Act; and (2) the trial court's finding that the Lien Affidavit filed by the plaintiff on December 28, 2009 was not a valid lien because it attempted to secure amounts not owed.

Discussion

Although the judgment appears to grant the exception of prematurity, the exception of no cause of action, and alternatively, the motion for summary judgment, the first issue to be determined is whether the exception of prematurity was properly granted because if the action was prematurely filed, then all further actions are nullified. The Adamses' exception of prematurity asserted that the plaintiff had not preserved its privilege under the Private Works Act.

Louisiana Revised Statute 9:4822(G) of the Private Works Act states the following:

> G. A statement of a claim or privilege:
>
> (1) Shall be in writing
>
> (2) Shall be signed by the person asserting the same or his representative.
>
> (3) Shall reasonable identify the immovable with respect to which the work was performed. . . .
>
> (4) Shall set forth the amount and nature of the obligation giving rise to the claim or privilege and reasonably itemize the elements comprising it including the person for whom the contract was performed, material supplied or services rendered.

The Louisiana Private Works Act was enacted to facilitate construction of improvements on immovable property and does so by granting to subcontractors, among others, two rights to facilitate recovery of the costs of their work from the owner with whom they lack privity of contract." *Byron Montz, Inc. v. Conco Construction, Inc.*, 02–0195, p. 6 (La .App. 4 Cir. 7/24/02), 824 So. 2d 498, 502. The first of these rights is presented in Louisiana Revised Statute 9:4802(A)(1), which particularly provides that subcontractors have a claim against the owner and a claim against the contractor to secure payment of obligations arising out of the performance of work under the contract. Louisiana Revised Statute 9:4802(B) provides the second right, which states that, "[t]he claims against the owner shall be secured by a privilege on the immovable on which the work was performed." However, the claim and privilege that the Louisiana Private Works Act affords the subcontractor is limited by La. R.S. 9:4823(A), which provides, in pertinent part, that "a claim against the owner and the privilege securing it granted by R.S. 9:4802 is extinguished if: (1) the claimant or holder of the privilege does not preserve it as required by R.S. 9:4822."

In interpreting statutes granting liens and privileges for working materials furnished, courts have generally construed the statutes strictly against the claimant. *P.H.A.C. Services, Inc. v. Seaways International, Inc.*, 403 So. 2d 1199, 1202 (La. 1981). According to Comments 1981 to La. R.S. 9:4822(G), the purpose of filing a lien affidavit "is to give notice to the owner (and contractor) of the existence of the claim and to give notice to persons who may deal with the owner that a privilege is claimed on the property. . . . Technical defects in the notice should not defeat the claim as long as the notice is adequate to serve the purposes intended."

In this case, the trial court found that the Adamses were "correct in that the lien is deficient as to its failure to itemize the materials and that it seeks to secure payments that the Adamses do not owe as there is no privity of Contract between the Adamses and Jefferson." Accordingly, we must determine whether the lien requirements were correctly followed, and if they were not, whether the violation is purely a technical objection or a legitimate violation causing the lien to fail.

The Lien Affidavit at issue contains the following language:

> JEFFERSON DOOR COMPANY, INC., a Louisiana Corporation domiciled in the Parish of Jefferson, with mailing address of P.O. Box 220, Harvey, La. 70059 sold to CRAGMAR CONSTRUCTION, L.L.C., 3343 Metairie Rd., Suite 7, Metairie, LA 70001, certain materials consisting of but not limited to trim, millwork, etc., for the agreed remaining principal balance of \$37,623.98 and accrued service charges of \$879.36 from September 11, 2009 through December 7, 2009, for a total due of \$38,503.34, plus service charges at the rate of 18% per annum (\$18.55 per diem) from December 8, 2009, until paid in full, all expenses incurred in the collection of all monies due and reasonable attorneys' fees of not less than 25% of the entire sum due as will appear from the itemized statement of account attached hereto. . . .

That the said account represents materials sold and delivered to the aforesaid contractor and/or real property owners for use in and, which now forms a part of the construction of additions and renovations and/or improvements at the following described property, to-wit:

> All the buildings and improvements thereon and bearing a municipal street address of 6223 General Diaz, New Orleans, LA 70124, Lakeview, Second District, Square No. 268, Lot S, more particularly described in the legal description of said property which is attached hereto and marked for identification herewith as Exhibit "A."

The following document attached to the Lien Affidavit states as follows:

> *ITEMIZED STATEMENT OF ACCOUNT*
>
> Before me, the undersigned authority, duly qualified and commissioned in and for the Parish of Jefferson and therein residing, personally came and appeared:
>
> JOHN W. VAN DERVORT, an authorized representative of JEFFERSON DOOR COMPANY, INC., who, being first duly sworn by me, Notary, deposed:
>
> That he is an authorized representative of JEFFERSON DOOR COMPANY, INC. and as such is personally familiar with the accounts of CRAGMAR CONSTRUCTION, L.L.C., who is known by JEFFERSON DOOR COMPANY, INC. to be the general contractor(s) of the property situated at Municipal address 6223 General Diaz, New Orleans, LA 70124, and as more particularly described in the attached Lien Affidavit; based upon information and belief, THE PROPERTY OWNERS' NAMES ARE ANGELA JUNEAU ADAMS wife of/and RYAN D. ADAMS, with current mailing address of 209 Rose St., Metairie, LA 70005; and that various materials were delivered to the aforesaid real property for use and incorporation into the above mentioned property, as more particularly itemized on the attached invoices for the prices shown thereon representing a total principal balance of $37,623.98 and accrued service charges of $879.36 from September 11, 2009, through December 7, 2009, for a total due of $38,503.34, plus service

> charges at the rate of 18% per annum ($18.55 per diem) from December 8, 2009, until paid in full, all expenses incurred in the collection of all monies due and reasonable attorneys' fees of not less than 25% of the entire sum due all of which are made part hereof as though copied *in extenso.* [Emphasis in original.]

No invoices are in fact attached to the itemized statement although the statement says they are.

It is undisputed that Jefferson's statement of claim has satisfied the first three of the four requirements of La. Rev. Stat. 9:4822(G) and that the document was filed timely pursuant to La. Rev. Stat. 9:4822(E). Jefferson's statement of claim is in writing, signed by an authorized representative of the company, reasonably identifies the immovable with respect to which the materials were supplied, and was filed within thirty days from when the defendants filed the notice of termination. Accordingly, the only issue before us is whether the plaintiff met the last requirement of La. R.S. 9:4822(G)(4), to render the Lien Affidavit valid.

After review of the record in light of Comments 1981 to La. R.S. 9:4822(G), we do not find that the Lien Affidavit fulfills the requirements of the statute, specifically to "reasonably itemize the elements comprising it including . . . material supplied. . . ." Clearly, the reference in the Lien Affidavit to "*certain* materials consisting of but not limited to trim, millwork, etc." is not the requisite reasonable itemization of materials for purposes of the statutory requirements. (Emphasis added.) Moreover, although the attached Itemized Statement of Account states that the plaintiff provided "various materials" that would be "more particularly itemized on the attached invoices," the referenced invoices are not attached. In consequence, the Lien Affidavit did not meet the requisites listed in the statute.

Clearly, without the referenced invoices attached, the notice is inadequate to preserve the claim or privilege. Thus, the plaintiff's failure to fulfill the legal requirements is not a mere technical defect. Accordingly, because the lien is invalid, the exception of prematurity was properly granted in favor of the Adamses. Because no privity of contract exists between the plaintiff and the

Adamses, by the virtue of the granting of the exception of prematurity, the plaintiff has no cause of action against the Adamses.

Conclusion

Upon review of the record in light of the applicable law, we find that the trial court did not err in granting the Adamses' exception for prematurity and, accordingly, affirm that portion of the trial court's judgment. However, because the dismissal of a lawsuit on an exception of prematurity is necessarily without prejudice, the judgment is amended to dismiss the claims without prejudice. *See* La. Code Civ. Proc. art. 933; *see also Rausch v. Hanberry,* 377 So. 2d 901 (La. App. 4th Cir. 1979). (A suit subject to dismissal for premature filing must be dismissed without prejudice).

Finally, because the action was filed prematurely against the Adamses, to the extent that the trial court's judgment granted the exception of no cause of action and/or the motion for summary judgment; that portion of the judgment is vacated. Accordingly, the judgment is vacated in part, amended in part, and as amended, affirmed.

AFFIRMED AS AMENDED.

* * * * * *

NOTES AND QUESTIONS

1. With what degree of specificity must a Private Works Act claimant identify the elements of his claim? *See Hibernia National Bank v. Belleville Historic Development LLC*, 815 So. 2d 301 (La. App. 4th Cir. 2002), in which the court found to be valid a statement of claim or privilege reciting that the claimant was due sums under a contract "to furnish labor, material to construct 21 condominium units."

2. The court in *Jefferson Door* observed that "without the referenced invoices attached, the notice is inadequate to preserve the claim or privilege." Did the court mean that invoices must always be attached to a statement of claim or privilege, or rather that invoices were necessary under the facts of the case to cure a lack of specificity that existed in this particular claimant's statement of claim or privilege?

3. Apparently in response to the holding of *Jefferson Door*, the legislature added to R.S. 9:4822(G) a provision that "[t]his Paragraph shall not require a claimant to attach copies of unpaid invoices unless the statement of claim or privilege specifically states that the invoices are attached." What exactly does this provision mean? If this provision had been included in the Private Works Act at the time *Jefferson Door* was decided, would it have changed the result of the case? Was the claimant's mere failure to attach invoices that were referred to in its statement of claim or privilege the determining factor in *Jefferson Door*, or did the court implicitly find that, without supporting invoices, the claimant's statement of claim or privilege did not sufficiently itemize its claim? Does the provision added to the statute mean that, unless a claimant happens to refer to invoices in his statement of claim or privilege, invoices are never necessary, regardless of the lack of specificity that otherwise exists in a claimant's statement of claim or privilege?

E. Effectiveness Against Third Persons and Priority

R.S. 9:4820 specifies the date when privileges arising under the Private Works Act become effective against third persons: when notice of contract is filed or when the work is begun. Thus, Private Works Act privileges are given retroactive effect to the filing of notice of contract or the commencement of the work, even though a statement claiming the privilege is not filed until much later, perhaps after the completion of the work. There are, however, exceptions to this rule: Privileges in favor of surveyors, architects, and engineers do not become effective against third persons until their statements of claim or privilege are filed. Similarly, under R.S. 9:4808(C), a privilege arising out of site preparation work that constitutes a separate work under that paragraph does not become effective against third persons until a statement of claim or privilege is filed.

It is important to understand that the effective date given by R.S. 9:4820 is merely the date as of which Private Works Act privileges become effective against third persons, including buyers and others acquiring an interest in the immovable. This date does not necessarily determine the ranking of Private Works Act privileges, either among themselves or against mortgages and other privileges. As will be recalled from Chapter 6 above, privileges do not follow the general rule applicable to mortgages of ranking in accordance with the time of effectiveness against third persons. Rather, privileges have whatever ranking the law ascribes to them. The ranking of privileges arising under the Private Works Act is specified in R.S. 9:4821, whose substantive provisions are summarized as follows:

> Under R.S. 9:4821, all Private Works Act privileges are inferior to privileges for ad valorem taxes or local assessments.
>
> Privileges created by the act in favor of laborers, whether arising under R.S. 9:4801 or R.S. 9:4802, outrank all other privileges and mortgages, regardless of the order in which the competing privileges and mortgages become effective as to third persons.
>
> Other Private Works Act privileges are inferior to bona fide mortgages and vendor's privileges that have become effective as to third persons before the date that these Private Works Act privileges become effective as to third persons under R.S. 9:4820. These Private Works Act privileges outrank all other mortgages and all other privileges, except, of course, laborer's privileges arising under the act.
>
> Among themselves, Private Works Act privileges rank in the following order: (1) laborers' privileges rank first and concurrently with each other; (2) all other Private Works Act privileges, with the exception of those in favor of the contractor and surveyors, architects, and engineers, rank next and concurrently with each other; and (3) privileges in favor of the contractor and surveyors, architects, and engineers rank last and concurrently with each other. Notably, Private Works Act privileges of the same type rank concurrently, regardless of whether they arise from the same work or different works and regardless of the dates on which the privileges become effective as to third persons.

From these rules, it is obvious that a mortgagee desiring to outrank privileges that will arise under the Private Works Act should make a determination that notice of contract has not been filed and that work has not yet begun at the time his mortgage becomes effective against third persons. R.S. 9:4820(C) provides a means by which a mortgagee or other person intending to acquire an interest in the immovable can protect himself against the possibility that work has already begun. That provision allows such a person to rely upon an affidavit made by an inspector meeting certain prescribed qualifications to the effect that the inspector inspected the immovable at a specified time and that work had not already commenced. Provided that the affidavit is filed within the period provided by R.S. 9:4820(C), the person on whose behalf the affidavit is obtained may conclusively rely upon it, and the facts recited in the affidavit may not be controverted to affect the priority of the rights of that person unless actual fraud by that person is proved. This is the so called no-work affidavit that a construction lender routinely requires at the time of filing of a mortgage that will secure a construction loan.

* * * * * *

PRINGLE-ASSOCIATED MORTGAGE CORPORATION

v.

ERNEST R. EANES, JR., ET AL.

226 So. 2d 502 (La. 1969)

ON REHEARING

SANDERS, Justice.

Because of the importance of this case, we granted a rehearing to reconsider the following question: Is a subcontractor who pays wages to his employees as they become due for labor on a building project subrogated under Article 2161 of the Louisiana Civil Code to the superior privilege granted laborers by LSA-R.S. 9:4801 and LSA-R.S. 9:4812?

The facts are clearly and completely stated in our original opinion, and we condense them here: In 1965, Ernest R. Eanes, Jr. purchased a lot in East Baton Rouge Parish, for the purpose of subdividing the property and constructing apartment buildings. To secure funds for the construction, Eanes executed a promissory note for $335,000 in favor of plaintiff mortgage corporation, secured by a collateral mortgage affecting the land upon which the development project was to be erected. Eanes also entered into an agreement with Buddy Eanes Homebuilders, Incorporated, of which he was president, to construct apartments on the mortgaged property. Pursuant to this agreement, Buddy Eanes Homebuilders let various subcontracts to other firms to supply the labor and material necessary for construction. Although it did considerable work,

Buddy Eanes Homebuilders defaulted as prime contractor. At the time of the default, plaintiff had advanced Eanes $263,615.70 for the project.

On April 20, 1966, plaintiff sued Eanes in this proceeding on his promissory note and was awarded judgment for the amount then due. A writ of *fieri facias* issued under which the property subject to the collateral mortgage was seized and sold and, on June 8, 1966, plaintiff purchased the property at the sheriff's sale. This sale was made subject to certain previously recorded privileges.

Now competing with the mortgage holder, the claimants to these privileges are Livingston Roofing & Sheet Metal Company, Inc. for $2,961.74, representing wages paid by it for labor; J. R. McFarland, d/b/a United Masonry Company, for $5,606.86, representing wages paid to his employees ($3,214.24) and wages of $2,396.62 for labor personally performed by McFarland, as subcontractor of the masonry work involved; and Capitol Detective Agency, Inc. for $1,446.26, representing salaries paid two night watchmen who were assigned to protect the project during its construction.

The parties concede that no laborer, except McFarland, filed a lien or privilege, but the subcontractors timely filed a claim for the privilege of their laborers.

The Court of Appeal, rejecting the subcontractors' right of subrogation under Article 2161, LSA-C.C., held plaintiff's mortgage primed all liens filed by the subcontractors, except the lien for labor personally performed by J. R. McFarland for $2,396.62. On original hearing, we upheld the subcontractors' right of subrogation under our decision in *Tilly v. Bauman*, 174 La. 71, 139 So. 762 (1932), and reversed the holding of the Court of Appeal.

Subrogation is an ancient concept, having its origin in Roman law. It was more fully developed and refined in France and became part of the Code Napoleon of 1804. The Louisiana Civil Code Articles on this subject are almost identical to the corresponding articles of the French Civil Code. *See Comment,* 25 Tul. L. Rev. 358, 359.

As to legal subrogation, Article 2161 of the Louisiana Civil Code provides:

"Art. 2161. Subrogation takes place of right:

> 1. For the benefit of him who, being himself a creditor, pays another creditor, whose claim is preferable to his by reason of his privileges or mortgages. . . .
>
> 3. For the benefit of him who, being bound with others, or for others, for the payment of the debt, had an interest in discharging it."

The foregoing article enumerates exceptions to the general rule of Article 2134, that when a third person pays the debt of another, no subrogation takes place and the debt is extinguished. Under familiar principles of statutory construction, these exceptions should be strictly construed. *Succession of Andrews*, La. App., 153 So. 2d 470, *cert. denied* 244 La. 1005, 156 So. 2d 57; 50 Am. Jur., Statutes, § 431, pp. 451-452; 82 C.J.S. Statutes § 382, pp. 891-894.

Subparagraph 1 of Article 2161 declares that subrogation takes place "for the benefit of him who, being himself a creditor, pays another creditor, whose claim is preferable to his by reason of his privileges or mortgages."

The subcontractors in the present case, of course, are creditors of the prime contractor, Buddy Eanes Homebuilders, and we can assume they are creditors of the owner. For subrogation to occur, however, the laborers must also be creditors of the owner at the time their wages are paid.

When this litigation arose, LSA-R.S. 9:4812 provided:

> "The effect of the registry ceases, *even against the owner* of the property or the property itself, if the inscription has not been renewed within one year *from the date of the recordation*. Any person furnishing service or material or performing any labor on the said building or other work to or for a contractor or sub-contractor, when a contract, oral or written has been entered into, but no contract has been timely recorded, *shall have a personal right of action against the owner for the amount of his claim for a period of one year from the filing of his claim*, which right of action shall not prescribe within one year of the date of its recordation, or the reinscription thereof. This shall not interfere with the personal liability of the owner for material sold to or services or labor performed for him or his authorized agent. The said privilege shall be superior to all other claims against the land

> and improvements except taxes, local assessments for public improvements, a bona fide mortgage, or a bond fide vendor's privilege, whether arising from a sale or arising from a sale and resale to and from a regularly organized homestead or building and loan association, if the vendor's privilege or mortgage exists and has been duly recorded before the work or labor is begun or any material is furnished. *The wages of a laborer for work done by him in any building, shall, when properly presented and recorded by him in accordance with the provisions of this Sub-part, create in his favor a privilege on the land and improvements which will prime the right of mortgagees or vendors*." (Italics ours).

Since the laborers had no contractual relation with the owner, they can be the owner's creditors only if they are accorded that status by the foregoing statute. The statute provides, however, that a laborer shall have a personal right of action against the owner "from the filing of his claim." Until the laborer files this claim, he never achieves the status of creditor. At best, he has only an inchoate right to become a creditor of the owner. Concededly, the laborers in the present case never filed an affidavit under the statute; their employers, the subcontractors, paid their wages as they became due. Hence, the laborers cannot be considered creditors of the owner to fulfill the conditions of subrogation.

Another equally valid principle bars application of the first Subparagraph of Article 2161. No subrogation takes place under this provision when the creditor and potential subrogee acquits a debt for which he is primarily liable.

In *New Orleans Nat. Bank v. Eagle Cotton Warehouse & Compress Co.*, 43 La. Ann. 814, 9 So. 442, this Court recognized the principle: "It is the essence of the legal subrogation which is defined in the foregoing paragraph that the person making payment should be a third person in respect to the obligee of the debt he is seeking to prime by making the payment, and also that such payor should himself be a creditor of inferior rank of the common debtor whose debt he pays.

But Lallande was not only not a third person in respect to the obligee of the debt he sought to prime, but he was himself the original obligor, and more recently the plaintiff's pledgor."

The modern French authorities support this principle. *See* 2 Aubry and Rau, *Obligations*, § 321, pp. 187, 203 (English Translation by the Louisiana State Law Institute, 1965); 2 Planiol, *Civil Law Treatise*, No. 491, Footnote 27, p. 278 (English Translation by the Louisiana State Law Institute, 1959); 2 Baudry-Lacantinerie, *Obligations*, § 1560, pp. 670-671 (3d ed. 1907).

The basic theory of this type of subrogation is that payment must be made by another creditor for the benefit of the debtor. When such a payment is made, the debtor is not liberated. Instead, the credit paid is in effect transmitted to the paying creditor, who assumes the preferred status of the creditor who has been paid. A creditor who pays his own debt has done no more than he was obligated to do. He has given nothing for the benefit of the debtor. Hence, subrogation is normally disallowed.

To permit the subcontractors to invoke legal subrogation for the payment of their employees' wages would in effect award them a first ranking privilege for their own credit against the owner.

We conclude subrogation must be rejected under Subparagrah 1 of Article 2161.

The subcontractors maintain, however, they fulfill all requirements for subrogation under Subparagraph 3, declaring that subrogation takes place of right in favor of him, who "being bound with others" pays the debt that he had an interest in discharging.

Clearly this language presupposes the existence of a solidary obligation. If no solidary obligation exists, subrogation does not take place.

In denying subrogation under this clause, the Court of Appeal held:

> "(T)he subcontractors and owners were not and indeed could not have been solidarily liable to the laborers whose claims are herein asserted. Under the circumstances herein the owner was never liable to the laborers as no liens were filed by any party occupying such status. Under the lien law, no liability arises on the part of the owner until the lien is recorded. Since the owner was never liable to the

> laborers, it necessarily follows he was not liable for such wages, solidarily or otherwise, with those primarily obligated for the wages earned.
>
> In the instant case when the subcontractors herein involved paid the wages for which they now claim subrogation, said subcontractors were the sole debtors and prime obligors of the laborers concerned."

After reconsideration, we conclude the Court of Appeal correctly disposed of this issue. It is now apparent we erred in holding the owner became a debtor of the laborers "as soon as the services are performed." As we have demonstrated, the personal liability of the owner comes into existence only when laborers file their claim. Since the owner was no debtor, there can be no solidary obligation.

In holding the owner a debtor of the laborers on original hearing, we relied upon *Alfred Hiller Co. v. Hotel Grunewald Co.*, 138 La. 305, 70 So. 234, and *Rathborne Lumber & Supply Co. v. Falgout*, 218 La. 629, 50 So. 2d 295. A reexamination of these cases discloses a lien affidavit was filed in them as a basis for personal liability under the statute. Hence, they are inapposite.

We hold, as did the Court of Appeal, that subrogation is unavailable to the subcontractors for their wage payments.

Concededly, the 1932 decision of this Court in *Tilly v. Bauman* is in direct conflict with our present holding. That decision stands alone in the jurisprudence and has been criticized as a "strained" construction of the pertinent statutes. *See* Steeg and Meyer, *When Is a Security Not a Secured Right?* 39 Tul. L. Rev. 513, 516. The decision is unsound and must yield to the legislative will embodied in the statutes and code articles.

The clash of economic interests in this litigation has not escaped our attention. When asserted under the present circumstances, a laborers' privilege protects no laborers. They receive their wages in full as they accrue. On the other hand, the construction lender may be deprived of reasonable security for money already advanced.

Our present holding converges with a salutary policy: the optimum protection of recorded mortgages from the intrusion of later claims, unrecorded when the funds are disbursed. Our holding safeguards the security of the recorded mortgage—a catalytic force in the state's economy.

For the reasons assigned, the judgment of the Court of Appeal is affirmed. The right of the unsuccessful litigants to apply for a rehearing is reserved.

* * * * * *

NOTES AND QUESTIONS

1. The concept of subrogation by operation of law is now addressed in Civil Code Article 1829, subparagraphs (1) and (3) of which are analogous to the same numbered paragraphs that had been contained in Article 2161 of the Civil Code of 1870. Revision comment (d) to Article 1829 cites *Pringle-Associated Mortg. Corp.* for the proposition that a creditor who pays another creditor is not legally subrogated to the rights of the latter if the former was the principal obligor of the debt.

2. To the extent that the reasoning of the court in the case was that the subcontractor's laborers were never creditors of the owner because they had not filed statements of claim or privilege, would that reasoning be valid under the current Private Works Act?

3. If the owner had paid the subcontractor's employees, would the owner be legally subrogated to their wage claims against the subcontractor? *See* La. R.S. 9:4802, revision comment (b). If the mortgagee had paid the subcontractor's employees, would the mortgagee be legally subrogated to their wage claims against the subcontractor? Do the answers to those questions demonstrate the fallacy of the subcontractor's claim of subrogation against the owner?

4. In *Bayou Pierre Farms v. Bat Farms Partners, III*, 693 So. 2d 1158 (La. 1997), discussed in Chapter 5 above, the Supreme Court applied the rationale of *Pringle-Associated Mortg. Corp.* in a crop setting, holding that an agricultural contractor that had contracted to pick cotton was not entitled to claim legal

subrogation to the first-priority agricultural laborer's privilege accorded by law to the contractor's employees.

5. What would be the effects of allowing a contractor or subcontractor to claim subrogation to the wage claims of their own employees?

* * * * * *

AMERICAN BANK & TRUST COMPANY IN MONROE
v.
F & W CONSTRUCTION, INC.
357 So. 2d 1226 (La. App. 2d Cir. 1978)

PRICE, Judge.

This is an appeal by lienholders who contend the trial court improperly ranked their liens inferior to the collateral mortgage executed by the owner to secure advances from appellee, American Bank & Trust Co. in Monroe.

The trial court ruled that since the collateral mortgage foreclosed upon by American Bank was recorded prior to the date the first material was delivered to the job site, it is superior to the liens of appellants even though the note identified with the mortgage was not pledged until a later date.

This litigation arises from the following chronology of events: On July 7, 1976, F & W Construction, Inc., in anticipation of construction of a residence on Lot 16, Unit 3 of Pecan Bayou subdivision, Ouachita Parish, executed a collateral type mortgage to secure a note payable to any future holder. The mortgage was filed on July 15, 1976. On July 21, 1976, delivery of the first materials was made to the mortgaged lot. The following day, July 22, F & W Construction pledged the collateral mortgage note to secure construction advances under a written pledge agreement to American Bank. That same day the first advance was made and a hand note was given to the bank for the amount borrowed. F & W did not pay for the materials supplied on this job by appellants, and the subject liens were timely filed against the property. American Bank as pledgee of the collateral mortgage note petitioned for executory process to have the property sold to satisfy advances made by it to F & W during construction. Prior to the sheriff's sale, an intervention was filed in the executory proceeding to have the court determine the rank of the several liens in conjunction with the mortgage being foreclosed upon.

ISSUE OF RANKING

Since no written contract was executed or recorded in connection with the subject construction, the appropriate section of the Private Works Act to determine the ranking of the liens and mortgage in question is La. R.S. 9:4812. *See Courshon v. Til*, 344 So. 2d 719 (La. App. 2d Cir. 1977). This section of the statute provides in pertinent part:

> The said privilege shall be superior to all other claims against the land and improvements except . . . a bona fide mortgage . . . if the . . . mortgage exists and has been duly recorded before the work or labor is begun or any material is furnished.

Appellants contend the mortgage in question does not prime their liens under the above quoted language of the statute as it was not a bona fide and existing mortgage until the collateral mortgage note was pledged to the lender.

American Bank to the contrary contends this is not a correct interpretation of this section of the statute relying on *Courshon v. Mauroner-Craddock, Inc.*, 219 So. 2d 257 (La. App. 1st Cir. 1968). There is a crucial distinction in *Courshon* in that the mortgages in question were recorded and the notes delivered to the lender prior to delivery of any materials. There was no issue made in that decision as to whether the mortgage "existed" on the critical date for want of delivery of the note in pledge.

In the same *Courshon* decision the court defines a bona fide mortgage under s 4812 as one which "in legal terminology means valid in law." *Courshon*, supra, 266.

Although we are not aware of any appellate decisions which have resolved conflicting ranking of a materialman's lien and collateral mortgage under the Private Works Act, there are several cases concerning the ranking of other mortgages and liens with collateral mortgages. These decisions support appellants' argument that the rank of a collateral mortgage will be determined from the date the note is pledged and not from the date of recordation of the mortgage. *See Installment Plan Inc. v. Justice*, 209 So. 2d 68 (La. App. 4th Cir. 1968); *Wallace v. Fidelity National Bank*, 219 So. 2d 342 (La. App. 1st Cir. 1969); *Rex Finance Co. v. Cary*, 145 So. 2d 672 (La. App. 4th Cir. 1962).

The nature of a collateral mortgage includes elements of both mortgage and pledge. 41 TLR 785, 799. As to the pledge of a promissory note under the provisions of La. C.C. Art. 3158, delivery is essential to affect third persons. Nathan and Marshall in their comprehensive article, *The Collateral Mortgage*, 33 LLR 497, explain the distinction between the ranking of ordinary and collateral mortgages:

> . . . in the situation of the ordinary conventional mortgage, where the debt is either in existence or comes into existence at the same time as the execution of the mortgage, the mortgage is effective as to third persons from the time that the act of mortgage is filed for recordation, provided that it is thereafter promptly and actually recorded in the mortgage books. Since the general rule for ranking purposes is "first in time, first in rank," it is fairly easy to determine ranking priorities among ordinary conventional mortgages. The collateral mortgage departs from this ranking scheme and, . . . cannot be determined by examination of the public records. Except for the fact that filing and recordation are essential for the mortgage to be effective as to third persons at all, neither filing nor recordation time determines rank; it is the date of issuance (or reissuance) of the *"ne varietur"* note identified with the mortgage that determines the ranking of the collateral mortgage. (Page 512)
>
> The pledge of the *"ne varietur"* note to secure the hand note is commonly referred to as "issuance." The term "issuance" is important for, unlike the ordinary conventional mortgage that is effective upon filing in the mortgage office (if it is actually and promptly recorded thereafter), the act of collateral mortgage may be recorded and remain dormant for months, if not years, and only obtains ranking against third parties from the time of "issuance," i.e., when the *"ne varietur"* note is pledged to secure the debt. . . . (Page 504)

We therefore find that the term "bona fide" mortgage, as used in the Private Works Act in so far as the ranking of collateral mortgages is concerned, has reference to the date the collateral mortgage note is pledged to the lender.

For the foregoing reasons, the judgment is reversed in so far as it recognizes that the mortgage foreclosed upon by appellee, American Bank & Trust Company in Monroe, is superior to the materialmen's liens of appellants, and it is ordered and adjudged that there be judgment in favor of appellants and against appellee declaring that the mortgage executed by F & W Construction, Inc. on July 7, 1976, to any future holder, covering Lot 16, Unit 3 of Pecan Bayou Subdivision as per plat in Book 13, Page 144 of the records of Ouachita Parish, is inferior to the . . . liens recorded by appellants.

* * * * * *

NOTES AND QUESTIONS

1. At the time the case was decided, Section 4812 of the Private Works Act gave priority to a "bona fide mortgage . . . if the . . . mortgage exists and has been duly recorded . . . before work began or material is furnished to the site." Construing the former statute, the court held that a collateral mortgage, even though recorded prior to the commencement of work, was not a "bona fide" mortgage that would prime privileges arising out of work begun before the collateral mortgage note was pledged.

2. The holding of this case was taken into consideration in the 1981 revision of the Private Works Act. As revised, La. R.S. 9:4821 accords priority to "bona fide mortgages or vendor's privileges that are *effective as to third persons* before the privileges granted by this Part are effective." Recordation is not specifically mentioned.

3. The present ranking rule of R.S. 9:4821 applies to mortgages and vendor's privileges alike. If an act evidencing a vendor's privilege is properly recorded before work begins on the immovable, the vendor's privilege will certainly have priority over all Private Works Act privileges arising from the work other than those in favor of laborers. Suppose, however, that on a Friday afternoon a closing occurs in which a purchaser acquires an immovable under an act of credit sale that is not recorded until the following Monday morning,

well within the period permitted by Civil Code Article 3274 for its timely recordation. In the meantime, on Saturday, a contractor hired by the new owner begins work on the immovable. Which will have priority: Private Works Act privileges arising out of this work or the vendor's privilege? *See* L. David Cromwell, Vendor's Privilege: Adheret Visceribus Rei, 75 La. L. Rev. 1165, 1238-48 (2015).

4. The ranking rule applicable to collateral mortgages was codified at La. R.S. 9:5551 following the adoption of Chapter 9 of the Louisiana Uniform Commercial Code, which now applies to the granting of a security interest in the collateral mortgage note. *See* La. R.S. 10:9-102(a)(47) and (d)(2). Under La. R.S. 9:5551, a collateral mortgage takes effect against third persons only when the collateral mortgage has been recorded *and* a security interest in the collateral mortgage note has been perfected.

* * * * * *

THARPE AND BROOKS, INC.

v.

ARNOTT CORPORATION

406 So. 2d 1 (La. App. 1st Cir. 1981)

PONDER, Judge.

These appeals involve a ranking between plaintiff mortgagee and seven intervening lien claimants on a private construction project.

Defendant, Arnott Corporation, contracted with Bakerfield Electric, Inc., as prime contractor, to build a motel. Plaintiff, Tharpe and Brooks, Inc., agreed to supply defendant with interim financing. The note was executed on September 17, 1973. On December 18, 1973, plaintiff received an affidavit from a registered land surveyor attesting that no work had begun or materials delivered to the building site. That same day plaintiff filed in the mortgage records the site inspection affidavit, the mortgage and the building contract with an addendum.

In early 1974, Arnott severed relations with Bakerfield and thereafter itself endeavored to finish the project. When, in late 1974 and early 1975, Arnott defaulted on its obligations, claims against the project were recorded. Plaintiff filed executory proceedings to foreclose its mortgage. Several lien claimants intervened in the suit. Plaintiff then filed a rule to rank, which was dismissed on oral motion when plaintiff's then counsel failed to appear on the hearing date. The property passed by Sheriff's deed to plaintiff and was later sold by plaintiff to a third-party, Midland. Thereafter, plaintiff filed another rule to rank all the recorded claims and the mortgage. The court denied the intervenors' exceptions of res judicata, and no right and no cause of action and held that plaintiff's mortgage had priority over all liens except those for the labor of Doyle Dossman, George J. Neumiller d/b/a Delmar Plumbing and Leon Koury. Plaintiff appeals as do intervenors Washington, East, Eddie Knippers and Associates, Inc., and Lavergne.

We amend and affirm.

Tharpe could rely on the affidavit of no work, even though work had previously occurred and been "undone" prior to the inspection, in the absence of a showing of fraud on the part of Tharpe. The trial judge was not manifestly incorrect in finding Tharpe did not have knowledge that work had occurred on the site.

We therefore conclude, as did the trial court, that only laborer's liens took precedence over the mortgage to Tharpe.

Intervenors' final contention was that the trial court erred in not finding that each claimant was a laborer and thus primed Tharpe's mortgage. A subcontractor is not subrogated to the rights of a laborer for the wages he has paid his laborers, but, the fact that he has signed a contract does not prevent him from claiming a laborer's privilege if he meets the other qualifications. *Pringle Associated Mortgage Corporation v. Eanes*, 208 So. 2d 346 (1st Cir. 1968), *amended in part* 254 La. 705, 226 So. 2d 502.

Robert Washington entered into a contract to do electrical work for Arnott Corporation for $51,000.00, covering labor, materials, overhead and profits. While he may have performed some of the labor himself, he testified that over $6,000.00 of his lien was for wages paid to his employees and that approximately $2,000.00 of the lien was for materials. We do not believe the purpose of the laborers' lien priority covers this example. Furthermore, his conclusion that the remaining $4,200.00 should be given him as laborer's wages is not warranted; he was unable to substantiate his claim with specific information as to the hours he worked, the amount of his overhead or the measure of his profit.

Robert East, who contracted with Arnott Corporation to provide heating, air conditioning and ventilation work, filed a lien in the amount of $21,445.00. The trial court found that although East had a lien, it was not a laborer's lien that primed Tharpe's mortgage. East testified that 25% of the lien was for his own labor and supervisory work. He did not establish the type of work he performed nor the amount for labor alone. We find no error.

Eddie Knippers and Associates, Inc. contracted to furnish carpentry work. Although Knippers may have a right to a lien for wages paid to laborers under *City Bank and Trust Company v. Caneco Construction Inc.*, 341 So. 2d 1331 (3rd Cir. 1976), *writ denied* 345 So. 2d 52, it does not have the exceptional priority given to laborers' lien by LSA-R.S. 9:4812.

Huey Lavergne filed a lien on July 11, 1975, and an intervention on July 12, 1978, asserting his lien. The effect of recordation and the privilege perempts if notice of filing of suit is not filed within one year of recordation. The trial court held that Lavergne's lien had prescribed.

Intervenors contend that a notice of suit does not have to be filed if a sheriff's sale has previously occurred and alternatively that Tharpe should have raised prescription and peremption as an affirmative defense. The requirement of *lis pendens*, or notice of filing of suit, must be complied with unless a sheriff's sale occurs within the year of recordation and a fund is created for the benefit of lien claimants. *Federal National Bank and Trust Company v. Calsim, Inc.*, 340 So. 2d 611 (4th Cir. 1976), *writ denied* 342 So. 2d 1110, 1111. In the present case, the sheriff's sale occurred prior to the filing of the lien. Lavergne's lien was not cancelled by the sale and he was not relegated to a fund created for his benefit. Under the statute, Lavergne had to file an action and give notice of that action within the one year period.

A peremptive provision destroys the previously existing right, with the result that, upon expiration of the stated period, a cause of action or substantive right no longer exists to be enforced. *Ancor v. Belden Concrete Products, Inc.*, 260 La. 372, 256 So. 2d 122 (1971). Therefore, it was not necessary, that Tharpe file a special plea. *Succession of Pizzillo*, 223 La. 328, 65 So. 2d 783 (1953).

Tharpe appealed from the trial court's recognizing the priority of the laborer's liens of Dossman, Neumiller and Koury. Neumiller contracted with East to do plumbing. Tharpe contends that both of these men are either prime contractors or subcontractors and are not entitled to the special status of a laborer.

The trial court awarded Dossman priority for the personal labor performed by Dossman under an oral contract with Arnott to spray paint the sheetrock. The language of LSA-R.S. 9:4812 provides that "any person . . . performing any labor" may record his lien. It does not deny a lien to those contracting directly with the owner. *Executive House Building, Inc. v. Demarest*, 248 So. 2d 405 (4th Cir. 1971). This would be especially true when the contract was solely for labor that was understood to be performed by the contractor himself. *Pringle Associated Mortgage Corp. v. Eanes*, supra.

Tharpe further contends that since Dossman's contract was with the owner, it falls under LSA-R.S. 9:4802(A) and must be recorded in order for Dossman to perfect his lien. Although Dossman contracted directly with the owner he was not a general contractor under § 4802. *See Executive House Building, Inc. v. Demarest*, supra. In view of the provisions of LSA-R.S. 9:4812, giving protection even when the contract is not recorded, we find the contention without merit.

Part of Neumiller's claim was for guarding the project site from vandals; the rest was for wages not paid to him by East. Neumiller's contract with East was for wages of $400.00 per week for labor only. We agree that he should have priority for labor. While the calculations are quite confusing, we believe that the figure of $780.00 for materials bought for Arnott Corporation, $700.00 for truck rental and for $400.00 paid to Neumiller's son for repair work should not be awarded laborer's lien priority. We therefore amend the judgment so as to award him $9,412.00 instead of $10,112.00.

Tharpe contends that Koury, who was employed by Arnott, as a "job coordinator or construction manager" did not perform manual labor that would qualify him for a laborer's lien. The question is not without some doubt; the trial court held that Koury's lien was for labor. While Koury did not perform manual labor in the most common sense of the word, his work of coordinating the job for Arnott Corporation was labor. *Compare Devillier v. City of Opelousas*, 247 So. 2d 412 (3rd Cir. 1971). His lien primes Tharpe's mortgage.

Tharpe contends that Koury's lien is invalid since it was not filed until after the foreclosure sale and recordation of the sheriff's deed to Tharpe. However, Koury's lien was timely filed since work continued under the direction of Arnott to within sixty days of the filing.

Tharpe contends that Koury's timely recorded lien should be relegated to the proceeds of the sale. It should be noted that certain rules respecting a sale under a writ of fieri facias also apply to executory writs. Louisiana Code of Civil Procedure, Article 2724. This includes Louisiana Code of Civil Procedure, Article 2372 which provides that the property is sold subject to any real charge with which it is burdened superior to the right of the seizing creditor. Koury's lien followed the property into the hands of the purchaser and is superior to Tharpe's mortgage.

For these reasons the judgment is amended so as to decrease the amount awarded Neumiller to $9,412.00. As amended the judgment is affirmed.

Costs are assessed one-half to Tharpe and one-half to Robert Washington, Eddie Knippers and Associates, Inc., Robert East and Huey Lavergne.

AFFIRMED IN PART AND REVERSED IN PART.

* * * * * *

NOTES AND QUESTIONS

1. The court of appeal upheld a finding by the trial court that the mortgagee did not have knowledge that work had in fact occurred on the site but then had been "undone" prior to the inspection made for purposes of the

"no-work" affidavit. Would the result of the case have been different if the mortgagee had been aware of these facts?

2. The court applied the rule that laborers' privileges arising under the Private Works Act have priority over all mortgages, irrespective of the order in which those privileges or competing mortgages become effective against third persons. As the case illustrates, when an individual contracts with a contractor to provide work on a construction project, there is often an issue as to whether he is a subcontractor or a laborer. What factors did the court use in making this determination for the claimants involved in the case?

3. Unless notice of contract is timely filed, a general contractor does not enjoy a privilege under R.S. 9:4801 when his contract exceeds the threshold amount stated in R.S. 9:4811(D). As the case demonstrates, however, this rule applies only to *general contractors* and not to other contractors who contract directly with the owner.

4. Under the facts of the case, one of the laborers did not file his statement of claim or privilege until after the immovable had already been sold at a foreclosure sale held to enforce the mortgage. Why did this laborer's privilege survive the foreclosure sale? Was this privilege effective against the buyer at the foreclosure sale, even though it was not of record at the time of the sale?

* * * * * *

KEYBANK NATIONAL ASSOCIATION
v.
PERKINS ROWE ASSOCIATES, LLC
823 F. Supp. 2d 399 (M.D. La. 2011)

JAMES J. BRADY, District Judge.

[A recitation of the facts considered by the court in ruling on cross-motions for summary judgment filed by ThornCo, a subcontractor on a construction project, and by the mortgagee, Keybank, appears in the excerpts from the court's opinion contained in the chapter treating the law of mortgages, and those excerpts should be read again for a complete understanding of the portions of the court's opinion, reproduced below, addressing issues involving the Private Works Act. In the excerpts above, the court held that Keybank's mortgage ranked against third persons as of September 14, 2005].

To succeed in its summary judgment claim, ThornCo must prove that its lien claim predates and therefore outranks KeyBank's mortgage. To do so, ThornCo must establish that its lien was effective on or before September 14, 2005, the date KeyBank's mortgage ranks. . . . The only work alleged to have been performed prior to September 14, 2005, relates to the 1) site work on Tract A–5, and 2) construction of the medical office building ("MOB"), both performed by [the general contractor] Lemoine Company ("Lemoine").

1. Governing Law on Priority of Construction Liens and Mortgages

Under the Private Works Act ("PWA"), La. R.S. 9:4801 *et seq.*, subcontractors may secure their rights to payment against an owner and/or its general contractor for the price of their work by asserting a privilege in an immovable improved by their work. La. R.S. 9:4802(A)(1). The priority position for such a privilege is superior to a bona fide mortgage holder if the privilege arises and becomes effective prior to the mortgage. La. R.S. 9:4821(3)-(4); La. R.S. 9:4820(A).

The contractor's privilege becomes effective under the terms of La. R.S. 9:4820(A), which provides that work begins and the privilege attaches "by placing materials at the site of the immovable to be used in the work or conducting other work at the site of the immovable the effect of which is visible from a simple inspection and reasonably indicates that the work has begun." The section goes on to list certain actions that do not constitute the beginning of work for priority effectiveness purposes. Id. Section 4808(A) defines "work" generally as "a single continuous project. . . ."

Under the statutory framework, however, there are several instances where certain acts performed by a contractor or subcontractor must be considered separate "work" that does not comprise part of the overall, continuous "work" project. First, section 4808(C) defines certain preliminary, preparatory work which does not become part of the overall work. Similarly, section 4820(A)(2) defines the effective date for "work" which later-arriving third parties may seek to use to relate back the effective date of their privilege.

That provision clarifies that, for the parties who did not participate in the preliminary site work, their later-acquired privileges do not relate back to the beginning of the preliminary site work; their privileges relate back only to the beginning of actual construction work (i.e., work not defined as preliminary site work). La. R.S. 9:4820(A)(2). Thus, only the actual participants in the preparatory work may claim a privilege dating to that work. Preliminary site work performed by one contractor, which merely prepares the site for the actual construction of a building or other permanent structure to be performed by a different contractor, constitutes a separate work under the PWA. La. R.S. 9:4808(C). If the preliminary site work contractor also begins to erect the building or permanent structure, though, all the construction performed by the later contractor finishing the structure relates back all the way to the commencement of the preliminary site work. Id. The PWA thus contemplates a division of labor between contractors conducting initial, preparatory site work and contractors actually participating in the erection of a raised structure.

Second, an owner may by contract sever certain work from the overall work. If a written contract and proper bond are recorded before the general contractor begins work, then the work performed under that contract is conclusively deemed separate work from other portions of the overall project. La. R.S. 9:4808(B); *see also* La. R.S. 9:4807, comment (b); La. R.S. 9:4811 (requiring contract to be filed before work begins and to contain, *inter alia,* a legal description of property where work being done as well as a description of work to be done). This method also allows for delineation of multiple work sites within a single tract, even if only one general contractor is present. *See La. Nat'l Bank of Baton Rouge v. Triple R Contractors, Inc.,* 345 So. 2d 7, 9 (La. 1977).

KeyBank also argues another situation, embodied in § 4820(B), exists for separating work—a thirty-day suspension of work. However, ThornCo correctly points out that § 4820(B) on its own terms only applies to work "for the addition, modification, or repair of an existing building or other construction." It is uncontested that no work pertinent to this litigation was performed for the purposes of adding, modifying, or repairing an existing structure. Perkins Rowe was a ground-up development, and therefore this case does not implicate that part of the statute.

Finally, KeyBank contends a notice of termination pertaining to a specified piece of land or a specified contractor separates that terminated work from the overall project, citing La. R.S. 9:4822(F), which provides:

> A notice of termination or substantial completion may be filed from time to time with respect to a specified portion or area of work. . . . This notice shall identify the portion or area of the land and certify that the work performed on that portion of the land is substantially completed or has been abandoned. *Once the period for preserving claims and privileges has expired and no liens have been timely filed, the portion or area of work described in the notice of termination shall be free of the claims and privileges of those doing work on the area described in the notice of termination, as well as those doing work elsewhere on the immovable being improved.* (emphasis added).

ThornCo, though, relying on Comment (f) to this subsection, correctly points out that this provision merely speeds up the limitations period for filing liens. Section 4822(F) says nothing about creating separate "work," and therefore this provision has no affect [*sic*] on whether—instead of when—a contractor may use that work to relate back the effective date of its lien.

2. Can ThornCo Relate Back to Lemoine's Initial Site Work on Tract A–5?

ThornCo argues Lemoine's work under its April 1, 2004, site work contract began the overall "work" on Perkins Rowe, which ThornCo claims permits its liens to date from that time. ThornCo points to the affidavit of David Drummond, a KeyBank employee, to establish that Lemoine did road work which benefitted KeyBank collateral. (Doc. 402–8, p. 128, ¶ 12). ThornCo also cites the no work affidavit submitted in conjunction with the . . . mortgage, which states that "[e]xisting improvements designated as 'Grand Avenue' consisting of roadway paving, sanitary sewer and storm drainage collection system and associated utilities exist." (Doc. 402–1, Ex. 9). ThornCo thus asserts Lemoine conducted not only preliminary site work but also installed certain infrastructure improvements such as water mains, storm drains, curbs, and road paving, which it claims rise beyond the preparatory work defined as separate work under La. R.S. 9:4808(C).

KeyBank argues a) the facts of the no work affidavit cannot be controverted, and thus as a matter of law La. R.S. 9:4820(C) gives it priority by conclusively defeating ThornCo's attempt to relate back to Lemoine's work performed prior to the no work affidavit; and b) all of Lemoine's work was done under recorded contracts which created a separate work under § 4808(B).

Comment (c) to § 4820 makes clear that while a no work affidavit does not itself grant priority, "the facts recited in the affidavit as to the nonperformance of work at the time of the inspection are conclusive and may not be controverted. The effect of such facts will be determined under the other provisions of the act." The Court must accept the facts recited in the no work affidavit as true, but it may analyze whether the "roadway paving, sanitary sewer and storm drainage collection system and associated utilities" constitute actual construction work or mere preparatory site work.

The Court concludes that under § 4808(C), the work done by Lemoine was merely preparatory and must be considered a separate "work." Lemoine's work creating roads, drainage, and utilities differs in kind from the work that later contractors performed on the same site. Lemoine's work in this case was clearly a means to an end. Lemoine's work did not begin erecting the building or structure ultimately contemplated for the site. Instead, Lemoine—pardon the pun—paved the way for other contractors to raise the buildings which Perkins Rowe desired to be built on and around that job site. Lemoine's site work meets the statutory definition of preparatory work provided in § 4808(C), and therefore ThornCo cannot use that work as the basis for establishing the effective date of its liens.

3. Can ThornCo Relate Back to Lemoine's Contract for the Medical Office Building Construction?

Lemoine's work regarding the medical office building ("MOB") is even further insulated as a separate work. Lemoine recorded a contract for the construction of the medical office building on August 25, 2003, and recorded a notice of substantial completion on October 15, 2004. While it does argue that "Lemoine's work prior to the recordation of its [Tract A–5 site work] contract" renders the recordation of the site work contract invalid as a separate work under § 4808(B) because "Lemoine submitted an Application and Certificate for

Payment to the Owners" showing work conducted prior to the site work contract's recordation on April 1, 2004," that contention is simply beside the point for purposes of this contract. (ThornCo Memo. in Supp., Doc. 392–2, pp. 15–16). Payments made on the *site work contract* before the site work contract was recorded only affect the ability of the site work contract to constitute a separate "work" under § 4808(B) by virtue of the failure to record the contract before work began. *See* La. R.S. 9:4811 (requirements adopted in La. R.S. 9:4808(B)). It does not affect the ability of the medical office building construction contract to qualify as a separate work under § 4808(B). ThornCo has brought forward no evidence that any work had begun on the *medical office building* project prior to the date that contract was recorded, and thus the technical timing requirements imposed in § 4808(B) via its incorporation of § 4811 are not implicated. Section 4808(B) therefore operates to sever the work done under the medical office building contract from the rest of the overall Perkins Rowe development.

The medical office building construction contract and bond were recorded long before ThornCo alleges work under the site work contract (or any other contract) began, and the Court therefore has no evidence upon which to conclude the MOB contract was improperly recorded. The work performed under the medical office building contract thus qualifies as a separate "work" under § 4808(B). Since ThornCo performed no work on this separate medical office building project, § 4808(B) forbids ThornCo from availing itself of that work for ranking purposes.

No other work performed by any other contractor can operate to allow ThornCo to relate its lien back before the . . . mortgage. All of the work performed by the other relevant general contractors, EMJ Corporation and Echelon Construction Services, LLC, including all of their recorded contracts, post-date the . . . mortgage and thus provide no anchor to which ThornCo may attach its liens.

III. CONCLUSION; ORDER

The Court concludes KeyBank's mortgage has priority over ThornCo's liens.

Accordingly, the Court GRANTS KeyBank's motion for summary judgment (Doc. 394) and DENIES ThornCo's motion for summary judgment (Doc. 392).

* * * * * *

NOTES AND QUESTIONS

1. This case applies many of the rules developed in this chapter, including the concepts of separate works, the scope of site preparation work, the effect of a notice of partial termination of work, the effect of a "no-work" affidavit, and the ranking of Private Works Act privileges against mortgages. The numerous provisions of the Private Works Act bearing upon these issues should be reviewed in the study of this case.

2. Do you find textual support in R.S. 9:4808(C) for the court's holding that the installation of infrastructure improvements, including water mains, storm drains, curbs and paving, was mere site preparation work? Under the facts of the case, the consequence of this holding was that the subcontractor was unsuccessful in asserting that its privilege had effect against third persons as of the time this site preparation work commenced, long before the date that the competing mortgage became effective as to third persons. However, there are at least two other consequences that could flow from this finding, depending upon the circumstances. First, the period for filing statements of claim or privilege for site preparation work begins at the time that the site preparation work is substantially completed, rather than at the end of the entire project. Secondly, under R.S. 9:4808(C), privileges arising out of site preparation work are not effective against third persons until statements of claim or privilege are filed. As comment (c) to R.S. 9:4808 explains, once a statement of claim or privilege for the site preparation work is filed, then the privilege ranks equally with other Private Works Act privileges of the same nature but is inferior to mortgages that have become effective against third persons before the statement of claim or privilege is filed. Can you demonstrate how this rule could give rise to a vicious circle in ranking a construction mortgage, a subcontractor's privilege for site preparation work, and a subcontractor's privilege arising out of the later construction of a building upon the site?

3. As the court explains, the effect of a "no-work" affidavit is simply to cause the facts recited in it to be conclusively established in determining the rights of the person for whose benefit the affidavit was obtained. The affidavit does not, in and of itself, establish priority. Indeed, the facts recited in the affidavit may be irrelevant to the ranking determination. For example, if notice

of contract is filed before a mortgage, Private Works Act privileges arising out of the work will outrank the mortgage, even if a timely "no-work" affidavit is filed indicating that work had not yet commenced at the time the mortgage was filed.

F. Suit to Enforce Claims and Privileges

After filing a statement of claim or privilege to preserve his claim or privilege, a Private Works Act claimant must file a timely suit to enforce it. Under R.S. 9:4823, the claim or privilege is lost if the claimant does not institute an action against the owner for the enforcement of the claim or privilege within one year after filing the statement of claim or privilege. Moreover, under R.S. 9:4833(E), even if timely suit against the owner is commenced, the effect of the statement of claim or privilege and the privilege preserved by it shall cease as to third persons unless a notice of pendency of action is filed within one year after the date of filing of the statement of claim or privilege.

R.S. 9:4823(B) provides that a claimant's failure to file a timely action against the owner does not extinguish a claim against a contractor if an action for the enforcement of a claim is instituted against the contractor or his surety within one year after the expiration of the time allowed to the claimant for filing his statement of claim or privilege.

The extinguishment of a claim or privilege arising under the Private Works Act does not cause a loss of any other rights that the claimant or privilege holder may have against the owner, the contractor, or the surety, such as rights arising by contract. This rule is particularly important with respect to claimants who are granted a privilege by R.S. 9:4801: Since they are in direct privity of contract with the owner, their contractual claims against the owner will be subject to a much longer prescriptive period, often ten years, and their failure to file a timely statement of claim or privilege results only in a loss of the privilege that they would otherwise enjoy under R.S. 9:4801. The rule also has relevance for a subcontractor or supplier: His failure to preserve his claim and privilege will result in a loss of rights granted by R.S. 9:4802 against the owner, contractor, and surety, but will not impair any contractual rights he has against a contractor or other subcontractor with whom he is in privity of contract.

If statements of claim or privilege are filed, the owner is not relegated to awaiting suit by the claimants. R.S. 9:4841 provides that, after expiration of the period for filing statements of claim or privilege, the owner or any other interested person may commence a concursus proceeding against the contractor, the surety, and all of the claimants. In this proceeding, the owner may deposit into the registry of the court any remaining sums owed to the contractor. If the owner demonstrates that notice of contract was timely filed along with a payment bond issued by a solvent surety and that the owner has paid or deposited with the court all sums owed to the contractor, the court will issue an order directing the clerk of court to cancel the claims and privileges from the mortgage records and discharging the owner from further liability. Afterward, the claimants must litigate their claims against the contractor and his surety.

* * * * * *

METROPOLITAN ERECTION COMPANY, INC.

v.

LANDIS CONST. CO., INC.

627 So. 2d 144 (La. 1993)

LEMMON, Justice.

This is an action by a subcontractor against the general contractor and its surety to recover the balance due the subcontractor for work performed under a construction contract. The subcontractor did not file the action within the one-year period provided in La. Rev. Stat. 9:4813 for instituting an action asserting its claim against the surety. The issue is whether the general contractor's acknowledgment of the debt extended the period for the filing of the subcontractor's claim against the general contractor's surety.

Landis Construction Company, Inc. entered into a contract with MART-Perez, Inc. to construct an aerial transit crossing the Mississippi River for the 1984 World's Fair. United States Fidelity and Guaranty Company (USF & G) issued a payment bond as surety for the contract. The notice of the contract was duly recorded.

Landis subcontracted with Metropolitan Erection Co., Inc. (MECO) to erect the steel and pre-cast bracings for the aerial crossing. The Landis-MECO subcontract contained the provision that Landis would pay the final payment of the contract price to MECO when Landis received payment from MART-Perez.

MECO performed completely its obligations under the subcontract, and Landis completed the construction of the aerial crossing. Landis and MART-Perez filed a notice of termination of the work on June 20, 1984. The facility was used by MART-Perez during the World's Fair from May through November of 1984. However, MART-Perez failed to pay Landis over $800,000 under the general contract, and there was an unpaid balance of almost $88,000 due by Landis to MECO under the subcontract. According to the stipulation between the parties, Landis continually acknowledged its debt to MECO, but advised it would not pay until MART-Perez paid Landis.

MECO filed the present action against Landis and USF & G on September 13, 1985. Defendants answered and filed a third party demand against MART-Perez.

The trial court rendered judgment in favor of MECO in the amount due under the subcontract, reasoning that it was inequitable to allow Landis to file the certificate of termination of work without notice to MECO and thereby trigger the beginning date of MECO's period for filing suit, while Landis was claiming at the same time that MECO's claim would not mature until the owner paid Landis under the general contract.

The court of appeal affirmed. 613 So. 2d 1147. Citing Flowers v. United States Fidelity and Guaranty Co., 381 So. 2d 378 (La. 1980), the court held that Landis' repeated acknowledgments of the debt interrupted prescription and that the action was therefore timely.
We granted certiorari to review the decisions of the lower courts. 620 So. 2d 821.

Although MECO's claim against Landis is not presently before the court, we note that the MECO-Landis claim was based on a contract, subject to a ten-year prescriptive period. However, there was no contractual relationship between MECO and USF & G, and that claim was based on a special statute.

The Private Works Act, La. Rev. Stat. 9:4801-42, provides the method for contractors, laborers and suppliers of materials to secure and preserve a privilege, according to the circumstances, against the owner, the property and/or the general contractor's surety. As to the time for filing the claim, La. Rev. Stat. 9:4822A provides in part:

> A. If a notice of contract is properly and timely filed in the manner provided by R.S. 9:4811, the persons to whom a claim or privilege is granted by R.S. 9:4802 shall within thirty days after the filing of a notice of termination of the work:
>
> (1) File a statement of their claims or privilege.

La. Rev. Stat. 9:4813, providing for the liability of the surety, states in Subsection E:

> E. The surety's liability, except as to the owner, is extinguished as to all persons who fail to institute an action asserting their claims or rights against the owner, the contractor, or the surety within one year after the expiration of the time specified in R.S. 9:4822 for claimants to file their statement of claim or privilege.

In the present case, Landis and MART-Perez properly and timely filed the notice of the contract, but MECO did not file an action against the surety within one year of the expiration of the time for filing the statement of claim or privilege.

MECO first contends that the general contractor must notify the subcontractor of the filing of notice of termination of the work in order for Section 4822A's thirty-day period to commence. There is no such requirement in the Act. Moreover, there is no suggestion that the notice was filed prematurely or in bad faith. *See* La. Rev. Stat. 9:4822E(3)(a). Although a dispute existed between MECO and Landis whether payment on their contract was due at the time of filing, the filing of the notice was appropriate, and nothing prevented MECO from filing its claim and its suit to secure and preserve its privilege.

MECO further contends that Landis' continued acknowledgments of the debt interrupted prescription against both Landis and USF & G. MECO relies on La. Civ. Code art. 3504, as amended effective January 1, 1984, which provides that "[w]hen prescription is interrupted against the principal debtor, the interruption is effective against his surety." MECO cites Dinon Terrazzo & Tile Co. v. Tom Williams Constr. Co., 148 So. 2d 329 (La. App. 4th Cir. 1963), in which the court applied former La. Civ. Code art. 3553 in a Private Works Act case and held that a timely suit by a subcontractor against the general contractor interrupted prescription against the general contractor's surety who had not been sued until after the period for filing the action had expired. Accordingly, MECO argues in the present case that an interruption of prescription against the general contractor, based on the general contractor's stipulated acknowledgment of the debt, is also effective against the surety.

In response, USF & G argues that La. Civ. Code art. 3504 is not applicable because the time for filing suit under the Private Works Act is a peremptive period which is not susceptible of interruption.

A peremptive period is a period of time fixed by law for the existence of a right, and the right is extinguished unless timely exercised within the period. La. Civ. Code art. 3458. On the other hand, liberative prescription is a mode of barring actions to enforce a legal right as a result of inaction for a period of time. La. Civ. Code art. 3447. The right is not extinguished when the prescriptive period expires without the filing of an action; enforcement of the right is merely barred unless the obligee fails to object or unless prescription was interrupted or suspended. Peremption, by contrast, may not be interrupted or suspended. La. Civ. Code art. 3461.

The determination of whether a period of time fixed by law is prescriptive or peremptive turns on whether the Legislature intended to bar the action or to limit the duration of the right. St. Charles Parish Sch. Bd. v. GAF Corp., 512 So. 2d 1165 (La. 1987); Pounds v. Schori, 377 So. 2d 1195 (La. 1979). When the statute does not indicate in plain words that the period is one of peremption, the court must analyze the statute in its entirety and construe the statute with particular focus on whether the purpose sought to be achieved involves matters of public policy or other compelling reasons for absolutely extinguishing a right which is not promptly exercised. La. Civ. Code art. 3458, Revision Comment (c).

Peremption has been applied in actions of a public law nature, such as an action to contest a tax election where there is an obvious need for certainty as soon as possible. Guillory v. Avoyolles Ry. Co., 104 La. 11, 28 So. 899 (1900). The courts have also applied peremption where the public interest dictates against permitting suspension or acknowledgement, as in an action to disavow paternity. Pounds v. Schori, 377 So. 2d 1195 (La. 1979).

The Private Works Act does not expressly denominate the period for filing actions against the surety as a peremptive period. La. Rev. Stat. 9:4813E does provide, however, that the surety's liability is extinguished unless the claim is filed within one year.

In order to facilitate construction of improvements, the Private Works Act grants to contractors and others the right to recover the costs of labors and materials from a party with whom there is no contract. That right is in derogation of common rights and must be strictly construed against those to whom the right is accorded. Louisiana Nat'l Bank of Baton Rouge v. Triple R. Contractors, Inc., 345 So. 2d 7 (La.1977). Because the law grants a special right, there must be strict compliance with the provisions. City of Alexandria v. Shevnin, 240 La. 983, 126 So. 2d 336 (1961).

The surety bond required by the Private Works Act is furnished by the general contractor to provide a source for payment of claims that the general contractor fails to pay, as well as to protect the owner and the owner's property from unpaid claims. The Legislature, in adopting the Act, granted a special right in favor of specified claimants, but limited the time for enforcing that right in the manner prescribed in the Act, after which the right becomes extinguished and passes out of existence. The Legislature clearly intended to extinguish in short order the special rights of those claimants who did not file their privileges and their actions within the specified time limitations. The Act thus balances the private interest in asserting claims against the public interest in limiting special rights.

We accordingly hold that a right against a surety under La. Rev. Stat. 9:4813E involves a period of peremption and becomes extinguished if not asserted within the period of limitation, which cannot be suspended or interrupted. Therefore, the provisions of La. Civ. Code art. 3504 regarding interruption of prescription against the surety are not applicable in this case.

We conclude that the Private Works Act which provides the sole basis for MECO's claim against USF & G also provides the period within which the right must be exercised or become extinguished. Therefore, USF & G's liability to MECO became extinguished when the claim was not filed within the one-year peremptive period provided in La. Rev. Stat. 9:4813E.

For these reasons, the judgments of the lower courts are reversed, and the action by Metropolitan Erection Co., Inc. is dismissed as to United States Fidelity and Guaranty Company.

* * * * * *

NOTES AND QUESTIONS

1. What factors did the court cite in holding the one-year period for bringing suit against the surety to be peremptive rather than prescriptive? To what extent did the rule that privileges arising under the Private Works Act are *stricti juris* bear upon that determination?

2. Suppose that the subcontractor had, in fact, brought a suit against the surety within the one-year period and that the surety responded with an exception of prematurity, contending that payment was not yet due to the subcontractor because the owner had not paid the contractor. Should that exception be sustained?

3. Could the subcontractor still bring suit against the contractor? Could the subcontractor still bring suit against the owner?

4. This case illustrates a dilemma frequently encountered by Private Works Act subcontractors: As the deadline for filing their statements of claim or privilege or for bringing suit against the surety approaches, the general contractor may refuse to pay them because the owner has not made final payment to the general contractor. Sometimes, the general contractor is financially unable to make payment to his subcontractors in the absence of final payment from the owner. In other instances, the general contractor contends that, under the terms of his subcontracts, he has no legal obligation to pay his subcontractors until he receives payment from the owner. *Tymeless Flooring, Inc. v. Rotolo Consultants, Inc.*, 172 So. 3d 145 (La. App. 4th Cir. 2015), discusses

the difference between "pay-when-paid" and "pay-if-paid" clauses in construction subcontracts. The subcontract in that case provided that the subcontractor would be paid "subject to the conditions following, after payment by the Owner for Sub-contractor's work." When the subcontractor sued for amounts due, the contractor responded with an exception of prematurity on the ground that the owner had not yet paid the contractor the amounts due to the subcontractor. In reversing the trial court's ruling sustaining the exception, the court of appeal explained that a "pay-when-paid" clause governs the timing within which the general contractor must remit payments to its subcontractor, but under this type of provision the general contractor must make payment to the subcontractor within a reasonable time, even if the general contractor does not receive payment from the owner. Under the more restrictive "pay-if-paid" clause, the provision controls whether payment obligations exist at all. As the court explains, to create an enforceable "pay-if-paid" clause, the parties' intent to do so must be explicitly expressed in their agreement, by either expressly stating that payment to the contractor is a condition precedent to payment to the subcontractor, that the subcontractor is to bear the risk of the owner's non-payment, or that the subcontractor is to be paid exclusively out of a fund the sole source of which is the owner's payment to the subcontractor. Since the clause in the subcontract before the court did not satisfy these requirements, the court held that it constituted a "pay-when-paid" clause.